The British Post Office
A History

Princeton University Press
Princeton, New Jersey
1948

BY HOWARD ROBINSON

The British Post Office
A History

PREFACE

THE British Post Office has played a major role in the development of present-day postal practices now familiar the world over. Its beginnings, it is true, were by no means unique. The carriage of letters in the British Isles, as in other European countries, grew out of the use of royal messengers, and everywhere this evolved into a government monopoly rendering public service. But the British Post Office, under the impulse of an expanding culture and the stimulus of an unparalleled industrial and commercial activity, made more rapid and consistent growth than the post offices of neighboring countries. It pioneered in many methods for the speedy, cheap and safe carriage of mails.

Yet surprisingly little seems to be known of the remarkable postal advances made in Britain during the past three centuries, even though no other activity of government touches the lives of the people more closely. Social histories have been largely silent as to how people sent and received their mail. Histories of economic growth and accounts of the development of transportation and communication tell us little about this indispensable service. The present volume traces the growth of the Post Office in Great Britain not only as an institution but in its effect on social relations, and in its contribution to cultural and commercial advance.

The story is one of insistent demand for improvement. From the start government was obsessed by the desire to monopolize and control and even limit the communication of the people. It follows, therefore, that the record of expansion and improvement is not primarily an account of a government department easily meeting public needs. It is rather the record of a more or less constant demand for better and unfettered service. Here indeed lies the distinctiveness of British postal growth. Again and again, reformers labored to speed up a slowly evolving government department. The efforts of men like Witherings, Dockwra, Palmer of mail-coach fame, Wallace and Hill, the great postal reformers of a century ago, and of Henniker Heaton in the late nineteenth century usually voiced popular demand and gave a profoundly human character to the development.

Nor did British postal service progress only in the domestic field. An interest in oversea mails is found in Britain from the beginning. Packet boats became increasingly valuable as British leadership grew in commerce and industry. The packets at first served the nearby

Continent and Ireland, and later journeyed to the widely scattered colonies and many foreign lands. The Post Office of the United States originated as a colonial extension of the British Post Office, connected with the mother country by regular packet services. It grew naturally out of the colonial arrangements, for Benjamin Franklin, the first Postmaster-General, preceded his work for the independent states by a long appointment as a Postmaster General in the American colonies. And later when uniform penny postage and prepayment by stamps was freeing communication of so many inconveniences in Great Britain, the Post Office of the United States— like that of most other countries—found British pioneering practice worthy of imitation.

An adequate account of the British Post Office involves more than changes in the character of the department serving the public and the differing means of transmitting mail—whether by postboy or mail coach, railway or airplane. Modifications took place also in the actual character of the mail, and in the various postal markings that furnish a telltale record of the way letters fared on their journeys. The adhesive stamp also has its rightful place in the history of the Post Office.

Illustrations have been used liberally to make clear the changing vehicles for carrying mail matter, to show how letters evolved from the earlier single folded sheet to the form now familiar to everyone, to indicate the markings used by the Post Office, and to picture the various forms of the stamp by which the mail paid its way. In addition, actual letters of well-known literary and political figures are freely introduced to make earlier postal practices real. Maps prepared from official materials show the evolution of routes on land and overseas.

Up to the present there has been no comprehensive treatment of British postal development. Hemmeon's useful *History of the British Post Office* is largely confined to the economic aspects of the institution. Joyce's *History of the Post Office . . . to 1836* was published more than fifty years ago, and carries the story only to the agitation for penny postage. Marshall's so-called *History of the British Post Office*, a sumptuous volume, contains much valuable material for postal history from the philatelic side. It does not, however, pretend to be a history of the Post Office in the broader meaning of that word.

The staff of Oberlin College has given me assistance in many ways. As I spend my summers in the vicinity of Dartmouth College, I am indebted to that institution for many kindnesses: much of the manuscript was written in the Baker Library. The exceedingly valuable philatelic collection of books and magazines in the Collectors Club in New York furnished many rare sources for postal history. I am also indebted to the Social Science Research Council for a grant in aid that brought the work to a conclusion.

Acknowledgments of permission for the use of illustrative material are included in the list of illustrations on pages xiii-xvii.

HOWARD ROBINSON

Oberlin, Ohio
June 1947

CONTENTS

CONTENTS

ILLUSTRATIONS

TEXT FIGURES

MAPS

The British Post Office
A History

The Origins
of the English Post

MODERN postal service—carriage by the government of its own mail and that of the public—began only some three or four hundred years ago. But the transmission of letters and dispatches, especially for government purposes, goes back many centuries. A brief account of this earlier development will help to explain some of the character-istics of the English post. It had, naturally, a background of customs begun long before a definite postal service took shape under Henry VIII.

The first arrangements for sending letters were made by rulers who found some ordered form of communication necessary to an effective control of widespread territories. Herodotus informs us that Xerxes, after the Battle of Salamis (480 B.C.), used a well-established government messenger service to send back to Persia the news of his invasion of Greece. Men with horses were stationed at intervals of a day's journey on the main roads, the courier of the first station passing the message on to the second, he to the third, and so on: "So it is born from hand to hand along the whole line, like the light in a torch race." The rulers of the Roman Empire from the time of Octavius had similar arrangements for their far-flung domin-ions. The excellent system of Roman roads was used by messengers who requisitioned horses, carts and vessels along the way.

No service of ancient times, however, was open to the general public. Private letters were delivered by the slaves of the corre-spondents or by travelers who accommodated friends by carrying their letters. Communication, even by official messengers, was slow.

Seven days, for example, were required to deliver a letter sent from Sicily to the capital; a letter from Caesar, when he was campaigning in Britain, took more than a month on its journey to Rome.

Communication was badly disrupted following the break-up of the Roman Empire and the spread of barbarian settlements over western Europe. The feudal character of a primitive society did not make for extensive, safe or regular transmission of letters. Charlemagne established a system of royal couriers at the beginning of the ninth century, but it did not long survive his death and the subsequent division of his empire. A royal post organized on a permanent footing began in France when Louis XI, by a decree of 1464, formed a body of couriers for royal use. Private individuals could use the horses by special permission and the payment of a fixed sum.[1]

In central Europe, loosely governed by that sprawling organization known as the Holy Roman Empire, postal service was equally backward. The Emperor Maximilian—he ruled from 1493 to 1519 —badly needed some means of transmitting dispatches between territories that included such widespread holdings as Austria, northern Italy, Burgundy and the Low Countries. In 1491 he appointed the brothers Franz and Johann von Taxis as his chief postmasters. Maximilian's successor, Charles V, gave to Franz and his nephew Johann Baptista von Taxis the charge of an enlarged service that included Spain and southern Italy as well. After the death of Franz in 1519 Johann Baptista von Taxis became the "chief and master general of our posts." Thus began an imperial German post that remained for centuries under the hereditary control of the Von Taxis family. The imperial post gave efficient service for those days, since the couriers were horsed and their journeys regular and speedy. It was a "day-and-night post," as one of Maximilian's servants wrote in 1515 when promising his master the quickest information possible.[2]

---

[1] See Maxime du Camp, "L'administration et l'Hôtel des Postes" in *Revue des Deux Mondes*, XLVII (1867), 167 ff. An article on "Postes" in the famous *Encyclopédie* of the seventeenth century defines the word as "relays of horses established at various places for the use of couriers."

[2] Later on (1624) the family representative was granted an imperial title, the Count of Thurn and Taxis. Only in the nineteenth century was the family monopoly of the postal service seriously threatened. The various German states had slowly set up their own services, and they completely superseded the Taxis posts when Germany unified around Prussia in 1867. See below, pp. 159, 376, and p. 27 for the English connections with this post in the seventeenth century. A mounted courier of the imperial post was known in England at the time by an Italian name, variously spelled "staffeto," "staffette" and "estafette." In 1545, for example, an English official refers to the "ordinary staffette that goeth weekly to Antwerp." The Taxis family came originally from Ber-

The kings of England had the same desire as the Continental rulers for effective communication. This need became imperative during the time of the Hundred Years' War, fought as it was on the soil of France. But contact with distant lands was neither regular nor easy. One reads in the official records of the Privy Council of the use of friars and priests, of heralds and pursuivants. In 1430, for example, £10 was paid to two friars minor "who brought letters from the town of Paris and the King's Council there." Two years later a monk of Westminster and a pursuivant were rewarded for bringing letters. The Garter King at Arms received £20 in 1443 for carrying letters to the Duke of Bedford. The Snowdon Herald was paid 100s in 1451 for bringing letters from the King of Scotland. The only evidence of a planned arrangement during the Hundred Years' War is an entry of 1432: it was agreed that two heralds should go over to France to bring news, "the one remaining there while the other returns."[3]

Towards the end of the fifteenth century King Edward IV—a contemporary of Louis XI of France—set up a system of posts for relaying dispatches north towards Scotland when the two countries were at war. But this Edwardian post of 1481 was only temporary, and for official use only. No regular posting arrangement, even for the English kings, is found until the sixteenth century.

Before recounting the permanent establishment of the post under Henry VIII, something needs to be said of the nature of private correspondence before it was combined with the government service. On the Continent various private mail services began during the Middle Ages. The universities, which were often attended by "foreign" students, required messenger services of their own. As trade grew more and more rapidly in the late Middle Ages, the various leagues of merchant cities, such as that along the Rhine and the better-known Hanseatic League, had their own messengers. Famous commercial and banking houses—that of the Fugger family of Augsburg is an example—required information of conditions wherever they had their interests, in order that news letters of information could be transmitted as well as bills and advices. Continental merchants trading with England customarily used their own ships for

gamo near Milan. Were this a general account of European postal services, the messenger service of the Papacy and that of Venice would need attention.

[3] *Proc. & Ord. of P.C.*, IV, 8 June, 27 Nov. 1430; 10 May, 21 July 1432; V, 28 Nov. 1441, 21 July 1443; VI, 6 May, 5 July 1451.

this purpose. Early in the sixteenth century they had a regular system of communication with England that was known to Englishmen as the Strangers' Post. English merchants were not so forward, though they finally set up a messenger system of their own. The need for business communication was to have much to do with the expansion of the official Post Office in later centuries.

The letters of private persons were dispatched, as had been said, by retainers, by friends going the desired route, by chance travelers. Occasionally a messenger would go and wait for a reply. During the time of a fair, when population movement was somewhat greater, letters were sent with more ease.

As for the letters themselves, by the end of the Middle Ages a letter usually consisted of a sheet of paper only large enough to contain the message.[4] The needed paper was cut from a sheet that was originally about twelve inches wide by eighteen inches long. The paper used for a letter was then folded into an oblong packet about three inches by four, and an address was written on the face of the folded and sealed sheet. The letter was not enclosed in an envelope: this would have been a waste of valuable paper.[5]

The superscription frequently contained an exhortation in addition to the directions for delivery. The various forms of address used in the late fifteenth century can be illustrated from the Paston letters. "To Edmond Paston of Cliffordes Inn, in London, be this letter take." "To my ryte worchypful maystyr, Jon Paston, be this delyveryd in hast." "To my mastre, John Paston, en hast." "To John Paston, and to non othyr." "To John Paston or to hys brother Edmond Paston, at the George, at Powles Wharfe." "To Thomas Grene, goodman of the George, by Powles Wharffe, or to hys wyff, to send to Sir John Paston, whereso evere he be, at Caleys [Calais], London or other placys."[6]

The English post might conceivably have originated out of pri-

---

[4] In Roman times letters were not written on paper but on tablets (*tabellae*) of wood or ivory, in shape not unlike the old-fashioned slates, save that wax was used to fill the depressions within the frames. The message was traced by a stylus on the wax. Parchment did not come into general use until about the time of the break-up of the Roman Empire. Paper began to serve as a writing material in Europe by the twelfth century, but it was not in general use until the end of the Middle Ages.

[5] Envelopes were not generally used for letters until the great revolution in postal arrangements that came in 1840. See below, p. 299.

[6] The Paston letters were written between 1432 and 1509 by the members of a Norfolk family. See H. S. Bennett, *The Pastons* (1922), pp. 116, 127; *The Paston Letters*, ed. by James Gairdner (1872), I, 58, 115; II, 204, 380; III, 133, 177.

SIR BRIAN TUKE, MASTER OF THE POSTS, by Holbein

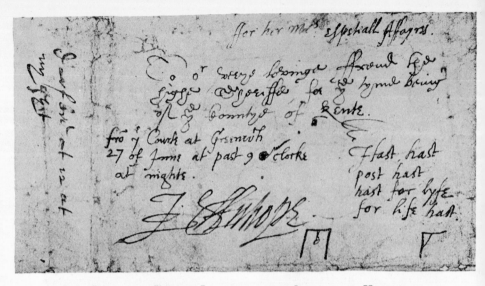

FACE OF A FOLDED LETTER TO THE SHERIFF OF KENT

Sent on her Majesty Queen Elizabeth's "espshall Affayres," from the court at Greenwich to "our verye lovinge frend ye highe sheriffe for ye tyme being of ye Countye of Kente." Stanhope's signature appears, as well as endorsements showing the time it left Greenwich and reached Dartford. The urgent demand for haste would seem imperative. The pictured gallows may indicate the purpose of the dispatch, or simply emphasize the desire for speed.

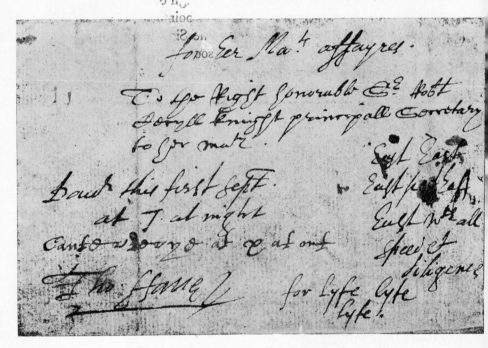

A LETTER ADDRESSED TO SIR ROBERT CECIL

An official dispatch sent at the end of the reign of Queen Elizabeth. The endorsement urging speed is unusually long: "Hast Hast Hast post Hast Hast with all speed & diligence for lyfe lyfe lyfe." It was sent to "Sr. Robt Cecyll knight principall Secretary to her Majesty." The postmasters at London and Canterbury indicated the time when each handled it.

vate or business correspondence organized by some private individual desirous of meeting the growing demand. Some attempts were made in the development of the Post Office in England to furnish facilities by nonofficial carriers, but political conditions in the sixteenth and seventeenth centuries—when the Post Office was taking form—prevented the success of any such private ventures. Autocrats like Henry VIII and Elizabeth and the Stuarts of the next century were unwilling to allow the private carriage of letters. Treasonable plots were only too easily hatched. If subjects must correspond, by all means keep such correspondence at a minimum, and see that it be supervised. The point of view was well put in an official report of many years later: "With regard to correspondence conveyed by other messengers than their own, our Monarchs viewed it with great suspicion. . . . The frequency of disputed successions to the Crown, and the constant jealousy entertained of the Court of Rome, will assist in explaining their desire to prevent such correspondence."[7]

Under such conditions, and with a long background that has been but briefly sketched, the organization of a government service in England took definite form. Early in the reign of Henry VIII, perhaps by 1516, a Master of the Posts was appointed. Brian Tuke, the first to bear this title, became Clerk of the Signet at the beginning of the reign, and Master of the Posts soon after. The term Postmaster-General, sometimes accorded to Tuke, was not yet in use.[8]

Just what sort of service was furnished in the early days of the Post Office when Sir Brian Tuke was responsible for the quick transmission of royal wishes by messenger or by letter? If a "post" was to be "laid" on a particular route, the Master of the Posts would divide the road into stages of ten to fifteen or more miles. Someone would be responsible for furnishing horses and postboys for each of these divisions or posts.[9] If a royal messenger was journeying in person by

[7] *Secret Com. on P.O.*, H.C. (1844), p. 4.

[8] See J. A. J. Housden, "Early Posts in England," *Eng. Hist. Rev.*, XVIII, 714. G. Walker, *Haste, Post, Haste!* has a full account of Tuke's career, but inclines to magnify unduly the role of the "first Postmaster-General." See also *Secret Com. on P.O.*, H.C. (1844), pp. 3, 21.

[9] The word "post" was used quite indiscriminately: it might refer to the system as a whole, or to the person in charge of a station, or to the person carrying packets, or to the material carried, and even to the horse used for the purpose. For example: "He shall tomorrowe take his jorney hitherwardes in post"; "order for his passage by post"; "as many of the said postes as will be content with twelve pence by the day shall remayne." *State Papers*, Henry VIII, I, 405; V, 481, 496; *Acts of P.C.*, IV, 151. Wyclif had used "curours" in his translation of 2 Chron. xxx, 6, but Coverdale's translation of 1535 reads, "The postes went with the letters."

these posts, that is, carrying his dispatches all the way, he would by going "thorough" or "through" post. At each station he hired a fresh horse to carry him to the next station. He was accompanied by a postboy, also on horseback, to show him the route and to lead back the horse when the messenger had traversed the stage. If, on the other hand, a packet was being sent through the stages to its destination but changing hands on the course, it went by what was called a "standing post." The postman or a deputy saw to its forward movement to the next station, and so on, until it reached its destination.

The method of going post was certainly a faster way for a packet or a man to be transported than if the same horse was used for the whole journey, with necessary periods of rest at the available inns. Hence arose the term "post haste." Shakespeare constantly used "post" to indicate speed, as in *King Lear* (II, iv, 30) "came there a reeking post, stewed in his haste, half breathless" or in *Richard III* (III, ii, 17) "take horse with him and with all speed post with him." By the middle of the sixteenth century the combination "post haste" is found. Its use was a misfit, at times, as a complaint was made to Protector Somerset in 1548 that a packet marked, "For life, for life," was nine days in going from London to Carlisle.[10] Statements that private letters as far back as the time of Edward II (the early fourteenth century) had "haste, post, haste" as part of the superscription, or even that such words were used on private letters at the end of the fifteenth century, are more than doubtful.[11]

Sir Brian Tuke did not establish a comprehensive system of post routes in the reign of Henry VIII. If a route was comparatively busy, such as the road northward to Scotland, or to the Continent by Dover, a post would be laid. Tuke wrote in 1535, for example: "There are always ordinary posts between London and Dover." In 1542 he was ordered to appoint to all the posts between London and Berwick two horses over and above the ordinary one horse. If the navy was at Portsmouth, a post might be laid to that place, although it was likely to be temporary. And, naturally, "wherever the King is, posts are laid from London to his Grace."[12]

A post laid by Sir Brian Tuke in 1536 is an example of a special

[10] Housden, *op. cit.*, p. 717.

[11] Such claims have been made in W. Lewins, *Her Majesty's Mail*, p. 5, and in the "Historical Summary" in the *First Report of the Postmaster-General* (1855), p. 8 (hereafter cited as *1st Rep. P.M.G.*). The earliest reference to "post haste" in the *Oxford English Dictionary* is 1538.

[12] *Acts of P.C.*, I, 20, 200; *Letters and Papers*, Henry VIII, IX, 27.

service. The rising known as the Pilgrimage of Grace occurred in Lincolnshire in that year, and proved to be so serious a revolt that Henry VIII took matters pretty much into his own hands, even though he had trusted representatives in the disaffected region. So important was the need for constant communication that Tuke ordered the mayors of Waltham Cross, Ware, Royston, Huntingdon, Stilton, Stamford, Sleaford and Lincoln "to provide able men well horsed to carry all such letters . . . from post to post with all diligence by night and day."[13]

Sir Brian Tuke, in his capacity as Master of the Posts, wrote an interesting letter to Sir Thomas Cromwell in 1533. Its phraseology, as well as its review of conditions, will make clearer the nature of the post in the early Tudor period. Tuke had been told there was "grete defaulte in conveyance of letters, and of special men ordeyned to be sent in post." He counters by declaring that the twelve pence a day paid the post provides for but one horse. He asserts that in the past the "postes northeward" have been the most diligent of all, but he has written them to obey "placardes and other writinges, sent for provision of post horses." The Master of the Posts insists that save for the "hakney horses betwene Gravesende and Dovour, there is no such usual conveyance, in post, for men in this realme, as is in the accustomed places of France." Horses cannot be kept in readiness unless someone bears the charges, "but when placardes be sent for suche cause, the constables [that is, the postmen] many tymes be fayn to take horses out of plowes and cartes, wherein can be no extreme diligence." As to posts between London and the Court, "there be nowe but 2, whereof the on [one] is a good robust felowe." If fault is to be found with either, Tuke is willing to make a replacement.

Tuke defends himself from the charge that the post is slow by writing that, in times past, some have dated their letters a day or two before they were written "and the conveyers have had the blame." He insists that he has also suggested to "my Lorde of Northumberlande to write on the back of his paquettes the houre and the day of the depeche . . . but it is seldom observed." He complains, also, that the northern post is overtaxed—"that many tymes happen 2 depeches in a day, on [one] way, and somtyme moo." In addition, there may be "countre postes, that is, that ride both northeward and southward; this is much for on horse or on man." Sometimes, North-

[13] *H.M.C. Rep.*, XIV, App. VIII, 35.

umberland "hath sent a post, my Lord Dacre an other in the neck of him; they of Berwick a 3rde, and somtyme Sir George Lawson aparte." It is clear that complaints against the postal service began early, even before the general public found criticism of the Post Office a congenial pastime. But Sir Brian continued to hold his office through dangerous times until his death in 1545.[14]

Some reference has already been made to the charges. When relations became important with Scotland in the forties, Sir Brian was ordered to have two horses over and above the ordinary one horse, the post to be allowed "for the said three horses two shillings by the day, which is twelve pence above the ordinary." Some years after his death, the allowance of two shillings seems to have been dropped, for there was a request for its revival. The "postes northward" complained that in this "busy tyme of the warres [1557] they were not hable to lyve of xiid [12d] by the daye, which in tyme of peace was their ordinary wages." Their complaint brought 16d, and this was raised to 20d later in the year.[15]

In addition to the allowance made the post for keeping horses and forwarding dispatches, mileage was charged for using the post. The customary payment for a post horse was a penny a mile, and a tip, of course, to the postboy who took the animal back. This regulation charge was even included in a statute of Edward VI. A typical "placarde" of the time reads: "For William Waan, Scottisheman, to be served from place to place between this and Bulloigne of oone hable poste horse, payeng after the rate of jd [1d] by the myle, being sent about the Kinges Majestes affaires."[16]

On the death of Sir Brian Tuke in 1545, the office of "Master of the Messengers, Runners, or Posts" was granted jointly to William Paget, one of the chief secretaries, and John Mason, the Secretary of the French Tongue. John Mason appears to have been the active member. Complaints were forthcoming in Mason's time as well of the "usual slackness of the posts layed northward in the conveyance of letters hyther and the opening of them by the way." When John Mason died in 1566, the reign of Queen Elizabeth had already begun.[17]

---

[14] *State Papers*, Henry VIII, I, 404-5. The letter has been reprinted in *Secret Com. on P.O.*, H.C. (1844), pp. 32-33. Walker, *op. cit.*, p. 44, uses parts of this letter as though they were the whole.

[15] *Acts of P.C.*, I, 20, 1542; VI, 136, 188.

[16] *Ibid.*, I, 164, 333, 465, 469; 2 & 3 Ed. VI, c.3 (1548).

[17] Mason's patent of Nov. 12, 1545, is reprinted in *Secret Com. on P.O.*, H.C. (1844), p. 21. The patent provided an annual fee to the holders of £66 13s 4d. See also *Acts of P.C.*, VI, 385.

Posting in the
Days of Elizabeth

THE reign of Elizabeth (1558-1603) was a time of changing manners and customs, with much penetration of Continental influences. Travel, of course, increased. Education was making some advance in this century as the grammar schools and the two universities grew more effective. Most noteworthy of all, the English Renaissance produced a great literature in prose and verse. Strangely enough, nevertheless, little progress was made in the transmission of letters. Though there may well have been a desire for better postal facilities, the government of Queen Elizabeth was inclined to stifle any such inclination rather than to give it encouragement.

John Mason, the second Master of the Posts, died in 1566. He was succeeded by Thomas Randolph. This great diplomat had been serving the Queen in Scotland during the early sixties. Shortly after his return from this particular field of foreign service, Randolph was put in charge of the post. This does not mean, of course, that he ceased to perform other duties. As head of the posting service, Randolph was known as "Master of the Posts," as "Master of the Queen's Posts and Couriers," and he is even called simply the "Post Master." On account of his frequent absences from England, he found it necessary to appoint a Robert Parmenter as "his deputy for executing said office." Thomas Randolph continued as the controlling Master of the Posts and as a valuable public servant in other ways until his death in 1590.[1]

[1] *Cal. S.P. Dom.*, 1547-80, 286, 310; *Acts of P.C.*, XI, 209; XIV, 328; XXIII, 128. Randolph's patent of May 4, 1567, entitled him to the annual income enjoyed by Mason

John Stanhope, first Baron Stanhope of Harrington, was the next holder, his patent granting him the "office of Master of the Posts and Courriers as well in England as in the parts beyond the seas, like as Sir John Mason and Thomas Randolph, lately defunct, had held the same." He was called by various titles, including "Postmaster of England" and "Controller-General of the Posts." John Stanhope died in 1621.[2]

The Merchant Strangers' Post, to which reference has already been made, continued side by side with the official posting arrangements of Mason and Randolph and Stanhope. The growing importance of commerce and of merchants, "whose number is so increased in these our daies," naturally gave this service greater value. Henry VIII had encouraged foreign merchants, and had given them considerable freedom in the matter of correspondence as well as in trade. English merchants, however, did not view this favoritism with pleasure, and complained of discrimination in favor of their foreign rivals. Yet out of necessity the English merchants used the Strangers' Post for sending and receiving packets to and from the Continent, for they lacked facilities of their own for any extensive communication.[3]

The Merchant Strangers had their own postmaster, who seems to have been selected by themselves. The conditions of the Merchant Strangers' Post were brought to the surface by the death of their postmaster, Christian Suffling, in 1568. Suffling's death led to a dispute as to his successor, two groups among the merchants proposing different candidates. Raphael van den Putte was the nominee of one group, and Godfrey Marshall, an Englishman but a Roman Catholic, was the candidate of the Italian faction. The matter came before the Privy Council for decision, where Van den Putte proved successful, and his appointment was confirmed by Randolph. It is not known how long Van den Putte held the office.

Later in the century, at least, the government looked with disfavor on the carriage of letters overseas by anyone not in the employ of the Master of the Posts. A proclamation of 1591 seems to have been intended to prevent unofficial services, and "redress the dis-

and to the same position. The patent is reprinted in *Secret Com. on P.O.*, H.C. (1844), p. 21.

  [2] *Cal. S.P. Dom.*, 1581-90, p. 672; *Acts of P.C.*, XXV, 358; XXIX, 192.

  [3] W. Harrison, *Elizabethan England*, ed. by Furnivall (1877), p. 131; J. A. J. Housden, "The Merchant Strangers' Post in the Sixteenth Century," *Eng. Hist. Rev.*, XXI, 739-42.

orders" that were so much a concern of the government at that time. The reader will recall that the execution of Mary Stuart and the defeat of the Spanish Armada had occurred but a few years before this proclamation. The activities of "divers disavowed persons . . . contrary to all good order" led to the proclamation that no one was to carry letters to and from the countries beyond the seas except such carriers as shall be named "either by our Master of the Posts or the Masters of the Postes General of those countreys reciproquel." The sheriffs and other officers were to make diligent search of "all males, bougets and other cariages of all such disavowed carriers."[4]

This action is in line with the desire to limit the available facilities for travel and communication, because of the numerous plots. After Mary Stuart's imprisonment in the sixties and the papal excommunication of Elizabeth in 1570, attempts on Elizabeth's life were ceaselessly watched. The Babington Plot immediately preceded Mary's execution in 1587.

Mary Stuart's efforts to correspond with her friends during her long imprisonment were varied. She kept up a regular correspondence with the Spanish ambassador. Alum was used to write on paper or cloth, books were used in which information was to be found on specified pages, letters were put in the heels of slippers or in the lining of trunks. Walsingham, Elizabeth's Secretary of State, was well aware of these devices, and read the letters while on their way. The dismissal of the Spanish ambassador in 1584 was one result. Later Mary's letters from abroad came in the French ambassador's official packet, and were then conveyed in the beer kegs of a nearby brewer into the moated house that served as her prison. This beer-keg post is surely one of the strangest ever devised. The letters were put in a waterproof container, and slipped into the bunghole of the filled kegs, and the answers came out the same way in the empty kegs. But even this clever plan was detected by Walsingham's agents. On the way, the letters were carefully opened, deciphered, resealed and sent on to their destination. Little wonder that the government at the time was not concerned with freer communication.[5]

The desire for wider use of the posting arrangements during these years is evident from the records of the Privy Council. The postmasters at the various stages, especially on the North Road to Ber-

---

[4] *Secret Com. on P.O.*, H.C. (1844), p. 36, where the proclamation is reprinted. A bouget (now "budget") was originally a pouch or wallet of leather.
[5] Conyers Read, *Mr. Secretary Walsingham* (1925), III, 6-22.

wick, complained of being overburdened. Their horses were evilly used, so they said, as the riding on that highway was excessive. The difficulties of the road were also given as a reason for slowness. The post at Belford claimed that the delay of a particular post to Berwick was caused by his postboy falling into the water.[6] Placards or "passeports" (permits for the use of the post horses) became so numerous that a curb was necessary. The Council ordered in 1566 there be "no passeport for any post horses except the same be for the Queen's Majesty's service." When the keeper of the post horses in London was required in the early seventies to have six horses in his stable, he was told to hire them only to "such as bring sufficient commissions with them.[7]

In the latter half of the century the slowness of the post led to much complaint. This may mean, of course, a growing sense of the need for haste in sending and receiving important dispatches, but there appears to have been no increase in the customary pace. The complaint to Mason of the "usual slackness" of the posts northward is echoed and re-echoed in the latter part of the century. Towards the end of the reign, for instance, the Governor of Berwick wrote to Cecil: "It were well that your Honour cause Sir John Stanhope to give the postmasters some check, that they have regard to their service; your last letter of the 11th [January 1601-2] although it was directed with all speed, did not reach me until the 20th, whereas letters can come in five or six days." A year later Cecil heard from York that the posts "ride slowly with the packets. Your Honour's last letters (though signed for life) were in running from the Court to York from eight in the morning of the 16th till four in the afternoon of the 18th. Packets signed with an ordinary pass are for the most part four days in running." The distance by road to York, it might be added, was just under two hundred miles. This would seem to show little advance during the reign of Elizabeth, for Cecil received a complaint back in 1569 that the posts between London and York "never come nor go under three days."[8]

In the later decades of the sixteenth century the various "Orders to be observed" imposed arrangements for the public service that

[6] Cal. S.P. Dom., 1580-1624, Addenda, p. 75.

[7] Acts of P.C., VII, 326; VIII, 181.

[8] H.M.C. Rep., Salisbury, XII, 27, 698; Cal. S.P. Dom., 1566-69, 109. Distances were not reckoned with accuracy at this time. The mile was somewhat longer than it proved to be when more carefully worked out by Ogilby a century later. The older British mile seems to have been over 2000 yards, instead of 1760 yards. See below, p. 62, and Gladys S. Thomson, "Roads in England and Wales in 1603," Eng. Hist. Rev., XXXIII, 234-43.

became more and more specific. Any man "having the place or name of an ordinary post" must reside in person and not execute his work by deputy. He was strictly enjoined to send official packets only by actual servants of his own. The supply of horses was specified: there were to be "three good and sufficient post horses" throughout the year for the service of the "packets for Her Majesty's affairs." In addition to saddles and "furniture" for the horses, he must have "three good strong leather bags lined with baize or cotton" and three horns to blow "by the way." Four additional horses and two horns were to be kept as well "for such as, either by Commission or otherwise, for better expedition, shall ride in Post." Both those riding on public or on private business must be "horsed by the standing Post of the place." Any innholder, hackneyman or anyone else was forbidden to hire out horses to be used in post, "if any Post there be appointed." And the guides were ordered to take a rider to the "dwelling place of the next Standing Post, that is also to furnish him of fresh horses."[9]

Directions for the journey were equally specific. Everyone riding post by commission was to pay "one penny halfpenny the mile" and if riding without commission twopence a mile.[10] No man was to ride without a guide and the horn was to be blown "as often as he meeteth company, or passeth through any town, or at least thrice every mile." The horn must accompany both the post, that is, the carrier of the packet, if he rode alone, and the guide who journeyed with those riding post. The guide was not to carry luggage exceeding forty pounds in weight. The rate of pay for the guide was fourpence the journey between stages, as we learn from directions given in 1589 to the mayor of Rye: "every man that rideth in post 2d the mile for eche horse that he rideth with, and 4d for the guyde."[11]

The packet was to pause at a post only a quarter of an hour and then to be carried forward with "all speed and diligence," the speed to be seven miles an hour in summer and in the winter "five miles an hour as the way shall fall out." If this rate of travel were maintained, the packet would go between London and Berwick in forty hours in summer and sixty in winter—a schedule that seems to have been altogether too optimistic.

A check was kept on the speed of travel by registering in "two fair paper Books, or one large and great one" the names, dates and the

[9] *Cal. S.P. Dom.*, 1580-1625, Addenda, pp. 75-76.   [10] *Ibid.*, p. 74.
[11] *H.M.C. Rep.*, XIII, App. IV, 88; *H.M.C. Rep.*, Exeter, p. 65.

number of horses used by such as "either with Commission or without shall run the Post." Packets for Her Majesty's affairs were to be entered in the second book, if there were two. Every postmaster must attach to the official packet "a label subscribed with his name and the day and hour it came into his hands," and the label must agree with the entry in the book. The posts were to report at the end of every month to the Master of the Posts on the amount of riding and on the packet service.[12]

By this time private letters were also included in the postboy's load. The "servant or boy riding with the Packet" must not deliver any "by-letters or private packets" before he had first delivered the official packet "into the hands of the next Standing Post." Those riding "with the Packet and having by-letters, or private packets" were warned by the threat of dismissal against opening public or private letters. Such were the regulations of the Post Office in the mid-eighties.

The routes first used in the developing postal system have some interest, since they remained much the same for centuries, even after the Post Office ceased to furnish the horses for rapid travel. Of equal interest are the rates of speed on the different routes in the sixteenth century. Fortunately, we are able to know something of such matters because the postmasters were required to sign the labels of the packets.

The North Road to Berwick and Edinburgh was much used. In 1589 the stages on the road south from Berwick were Berwick, Belford, Alnwick, Morpeth, Newcastle, Durham, Darlington, Northallerton, Boroughbridge, Wetherby, Ferrybridge, Doncaster, Scrooby, Tuxford, Newark, Grantham, Huntingdon, Caxton, Royston, Ware, Waltham and London. A branch of this route, in use during Elizabeth's reign, led west to Carlisle from Newcastle or Morpeth, and went by way of Hexham and Haltwhistle. We learn from contemporary accounts that it took seventeen hours at times to carry a packet from Berwick on the border of Scotland two stages toward London—to Alnwick. The stage from Newcastle to Durham of fourteen miles took sixteen hours! Farther south the stages must have been in better condition, as the seven miles from Scrooby to Tuxford took but two hours, and the thirty-eight miles between Grantham and Huntingdon seven hours.[13]

---

[12] *Cal. S.P. Dom.*, 1580-1625, Addenda, p. 75.
[13] Some of the itineraries broke up the 38-mile stretch between Grantham and Hunt-

I ELIZABETHAN POST ROADS

Post Stations

Sea Routes

Scale of Miles
0   20   40

Mention of Scrooby brings to mind a postmaster familiar to American readers. William Brewster—one of the founders of the Plymouth Colony—was brought to Scrooby by his parents in 1571. The father was appointed in 1588 the "post" for Scrooby, in addition to his duties as bailiff of the manor. When the father died in 1590 the son succeeded as postmaster, though young Brewster had some difficulty at the time, as the newly appointed Master of the Posts, John Stanhope, wished to put someone else in the place. Stanhope had listened to the request of a relative that he appoint another to succeed "old Brewster." The son, thereupon, wrote to a friend at court for help, and was granted the post. Brewster retained the postmastership of Scrooby until 1607, when he, as one of the Separatists, prepared to leave for Holland. As the post of Scrooby, Brewster received 20d a day.[14]

The Dover Road has been made famous by Chaucer, but in Elizabeth's day it did not go from London to Southwark and continue from the Tabard Inn. The customary route was by water to Dartford, or seven miles farther to Gravesend, if the tide was favorable. From Dartford by land it was fifty-six miles to Dover, with stages at Rochester, Sittingbourne and Canterbury. The length of the journey for official dispatches was about fifteen hours, or less than four miles an hour. A letter of 1593 to Cecil has the following endorsements: "For Her Majesty's affairs, hast, hast, post hast, hast. Delivered at Dover the 20th of May at nine of the clock in the evening. At Canterbury at almost one of the clock. Sittingbourne, past four in the morning. Rochester past syxe half anower, the 21st day in the forenoon. Dartford ten o'clock in the mornynge." Another from Essex to Cecil in 1597 reads: "For Her Majesty's especial affairs. Hast, Hast, Hast, Hast, Post Hast, Hast for Life. June 22 at Sandwich at seven of the clock in the afternoon. Canterbury past nine at night. Sittingbourne at past twelve at night. Rochester the 23 at one in the morning. Dartford the 23 four in the morning."[15]

<hr>

ingdon with stages at South Witham, Stamford and Stilton. *Ibid.*, p. 278. Lewins, *op. cit.*, p. 8, has a different list. See also Edward Arber, *Story of the Pilgrim Fathers* (1897), pp. 71-72. *Secret Com. P.O.*, H.C. (1844), p. 35, reprints an itinerary from the Exchequer records of 1572, showing the branch to Carlisle.

[14] Arber, *op. cit.*, pp. 79-84; *D.N.B.*, VI, 305; and *D.A.B.*, III, 29. Walker, *op. cit.*, has a chapter on "Mr Postmaster Brewster" that needs to be read with caution. Brewster could hardly have been born in the posthouse.

[15] *H.M.C. Rep.*, Salisbury, IV, 317-18, and also pp. 243 and 530; VII, 264, and also pp. 174, 231, 269, 287; VIII, 7, 36, 37. There are numerous others. See also *Shakespeare's England*, I (1916), 199.

An important route to the west connected the capital and the court with the south coast. One needs only to recall the course of the Spanish Armada, in the attempted invasion of 1588, to realize the importance of Plymouth and Exeter on that coast. The customary route at the end of the sixteenth century between Plymouth and London led through Ashburton, Exeter, Honiton, Crewkerne, Sherborne, Shaftesbury, Andover, Basingstoke, Hertford Bridge, Bagshot and Staines to London. The mails continued from Plymouth to Falmouth by way of Looe, St. Austell and Truro. Exeter was reckoned as 173 miles from London, and Plymouth as 217 miles away. The route was traversed at what would seem a very leisurely speed. A letter of 1597, sent "haste, haste for Her Majesty's service," left Exeter at 8 A.M. and reached Hertford Bridge at 10 A.M. of the second day. This schedule brought the dispatch to London about 6 P.M. —a rate of under three miles an hour. A letter from Essex to Cecil, sent from Plymouth in 1597 to tell Cecil that he was "planning to get the fleet out," left at midnight, reached Exeter at half past four the next afternoon and Basingstoke at the same hour on the second day. It would reach London early the next morning. Another from Plymouth, "haste, post haste," was over three days in reaching Hertford Bridge, and had thirty-five miles more to travel.[16]

The routes to Ireland were of growing importance on account of the plantation of Munster in the eighties and the expedition of the ill-fated Essex in the next decade. In 1596, for example, an open letter to the officers of the post towns on the Irish routes required more than the usual three horses in readiness: "so many post horses to be taken up as there shall be occasion" and the horses to be "fitt and hable." Stanhope wrote to Cecil in 1598-99 [February 17] of the "multitude of captains and others who daily ride post for the service of Ireland."[17]

Of the two routes to Ireland the more southern led by way of Bath and Bristol to Milford Haven at the southwest corner of Wales. The first part of the journey from London to Bristol had stages at Hounslow Heath, Maidenhead, Reading, Newbury, Marlborough, Chippenham, Marshfield and Bristol. The distance was slightly under 120 miles. The stages beyond Bristol to Milford Haven were Chepstow, Newport, Cardiff, Bridgend, Swansea, Carmarthen, Haverford West and Dale, "neere the Haven mouthe."

[16] *H.M.C. Rep.*, Salisbury, VII, 338, 350; IX, 152; XI, 254.
[17] *Acts of P.C.*, xxv, 358; *H.M.C. Rep.*, Salisbury, IX, 73.

In 1601 Lord Cobham was summoned post haste from Bath, the well-known watering place. He wrote Cecil: "I am in physic and should have gone tomorrow into the Bath. I leave all for obedience sake." The endorsement of this letter reads: "Hast hast post hast with all diligence," and the label indicates that the letter hastened toward Cecil at a speed of less than four miles an hour.[18]

The northern route to Ireland by way of Chester and Holyhead was much more important than the one to Milford Haven, since the route for dispatches to Dublin went to Holyhead. Milford served those parts of Ireland in the region of Waterford and Cork and to the west.[19] The northern route was used especially in the closing years of the century during the time of the revolts in northern Ireland and the efforts of Essex to put them down. An order of Sir John Stanhope, dated 1598, reads: "Ireland is now grown to that importance that former allowances are suspended. You take order for the speedy laying of the standing and ordinary posts again as was between the Courte and Hollyheade as by the way of Bristol toward Ireland." The post at Chester was to be allowed "two shillings by the daie," twice the grant of Henry VIII's time. In addition, he was to have five marks for every journey to the court with letters from Ireland and ten groats for every day of attendance after the first two days' stay for an answer. The stages to Holyhead were located at Barnet, St. Albans, Brickhill, Towcester, Daventry, Coventry, Coleshill, Lichfield, Stone, Nantwich, West Chester (that is, Chester), Rudland (Rhuddlan), Conway and Beaumaris. The distance to Chester was 180 miles, and to Holyhead 275 miles. A letter of 1598, endorsed "Haste, haste, post haste, haste," traveled from Chester to Barnet in thirty-six hours, or nearly five miles an hour.[20]

An important extension to the posts going west was the boat service to Ireland. The Holyhead service became so important towards the close of the century that two "barques" instead of one were put on this route, with a payment of £10 a month for the use of each.

[18] *Ibid.*, XI, 382; *Acts of P.C.*, XI, 209, 211; XXXI, 21. The endorsements that urged the postmen to greater speed are varied. One of 1597 has "Hast, Hast, Hast, Hast, Post, Hast," and another of 1598, "Haste post haste post haste." One of the letters sent by Essex to Cecil is even signed on the outside, "For life, for life, Essex." The admirals, Lord Thomas Howard, Raleigh and the others wrote an urgent letter with a very lengthy admonition on the outside: "Post post post hast hast post hast Howard." For other examples, see *H.M.C. Rep.*, Salisbury, VII, 287, 445; IX, 113, 336, 383.

[19] No reference is made to the Milford Haven route in a list of the routes and their stages for 1621. The four roads mentioned were to Berwick, Dover, Holyhead and Plymouth. *Secret Com. on P.O.*, H.C. (1844), p. 45.

[20] *Acts of P.C.*, XXIX, 192, 590; *H.M.C. Rep.*, Salisbury, IX, 97, 113.

The two were needed so that "there will always be one on either coast." The boats hired for these services were called "barques" or "postbarques," though the more common, indeed exclusive, term in later use was "packet boat."[21]

Port Patrick in Wigtonshire, Scotland, was early chosen as the place of departure for packet boats that plied between northern Ireland and northern Britain. It was the shortest crossing, the distance being only twenty-one miles from Port Patrick to Donaghadee on Belfast Lough. The drawback to this route was its remoteness from centers of population—it was 130 miles from Edinburgh—and its small and inconvenient harbor, a mere inlet between projecting ridges of rocks. It never attained the importance of the southern packet routes to Ireland, though its use was continued for centuries.[22]

More attention has been given to the last half of the sixteenth century than a history of the Post Office may deserve. By 1600 posting was, as yet, largely a service for the court, though some use was made of the facilities by persons on private business. The very hesitance of Elizabethan statesmen to extend the service shows the unwillingness of government as late as 1600 to undertake the carriage of letters for the public, though the orders of 1584 would seem to indicate that some letters of private persons were carried by the official post. The real beginnings of a public service only come in the next century.

Nor should it be forgotten that the postal service was necessarily a service on horseback. The use of coaches began in the days of Elizabeth, but they were of no value for rapid long-distance travel. Carts and wagons went across country, it is true, and sometimes in post, but too slowly to serve as carriers of mail. The most rapid conveyance of the time was the post horse. Richard III, according to Shakespeare, would have George "packed with post horse up to heaven" (I, i, 146). In *Richard II* (I, iv, 55), John of Gaunt sent "post haste to entreat your majesty" to visit him. And Cassio of an earlier day certainly uttered an anachronism when he told Othello that the Duke "requires your haste-post-haste appearance even on the instant" (I, ii, 37).

The speed of the post seems to have been usually less than the

[21] *Ibid.*, IX, 73, 377; *Acts of P.C.*, X, 418; XXX, 529-30.

[22] According to *Shakespeare's England*, I, 199, dispatches from London to Port Patrick went by way of the Great North Road and across the island, or by way of the Chester Road as far as Lichfield, where they turned north. I have found no early list of stages for the route from Lichfield north.

five-to-seven miles an hour required by the official directions. One exception is well known. When Elizabeth finally died in 1603, it was necessary to inform her successor, James VI of Scotland, as soon as possible. Sir Robert Carey, who carried the news, left London the morning of the 25th of March between nine and ten. He rode post. That same night he reached Doncaster, 162 miles away. The remaining 255 miles were made in the next two days, Carey reaching Edinburgh the night of the 27th after James had gone to bed. As would be said at the time, he rode "through post," and at a posthaste speed that was to be respectable, even memorable, for some time to come. Carey had traveled for three days and two nights at the rate of seven miles an hour.

The Beginnings
of the Post Office

THE first half of the seventeenth century saw the rise of a postal service for public use. This advance took place at a time of such great stress and strain in political matters that one wonders how anything was accomplished. James I was continually hampered by a people who regarded him not only as a foreigner but as out of line with the parliamentary efforts of the Puritans to obtain more power in government. His son, Charles I, found himself in even greater difficulty. Civil war ensued in the forties, to be ended by the defeat of the Cavaliers and the execution of the King in 1649. Despite the turbulence of this half-century, some significant steps were taken in making the Post Office more generally useful to the people, and foundations were laid for an organization that was to become permanent a decade after the death of Charles.

When James succeeded Elizabeth he caused regulations to be issued similar to those of the preceding reign. Her proclamation against the unauthorized conveyance of letters was reissued with little change. Those with special commissions, properly signed, now pay for the hire of each horse "twopence halfe-peny the mile besides the guide's groat." All others riding on their private "businesses" are to hire at the terms of the post. These directions, issued in 1603, were enlarged for the posts of the Dover Road in 1609, so that the packets, "being dated first by the sender or writer," were afterwards dated "by the Posts themselves as they come into their hands." By 1609 those riding "thorough post" were to pay at the rate of 3d a mile for each horse. Any horse taken for riding post was not to be "charged with any male or burden that exceeds the weight of 30 pound."[1]

The Stanhopes—John the father and Charles the son—were re-granted the control of the Post Office early in the reign of James I. The conditions were much the same, so they thought, as in the days of Elizabeth. When the older Stanhope died in 1621, his son, Charles, continued in control. This time the Stanhope patent was somewhat limited in its scope, though the perquisites of the Post-master still included a fee of 100 marks a year, £20 at the appointment of each deputy postmaster, and two shillings in the pound from the wages of the deputies. The posts complained in 1623 that these charges were exorbitant, and they were ordered to be reduced to "6d per pound for fees and 12d for each acquittance." In 1624 Charles Stanhope defended his receipt of comfortable perquisites on the ground that his deputies found their places so lucrative that they, in turn, appointed deputies. The office of a postmaster in charge of a station must have become more and more valuable as the years wore on, for we read that the postmaster of Stone on the West Road complained in 1637 that someone had tried to obtain his post by the payment of £40. The Stanhope patent is an excellent illustration of the monopolies to which there was increasing objection at this time.[2]

Stanhope's patent gave him control of the carriage of letters abroad as well as at home, save that the Merchant Adventurers had their own posts. For the official foreign service, a seemingly able person by the name of Mathew de Quester had been employed. This native of Bruges, though long a resident in England and a natural-ized citizen, took over the control of the foreign posts early in the reign of James I. By 1607 his "post servant," Henry Ballam, was going to and from Brussels where foreign mail was picked up and connections made with the Continental posts.[3]

In 1619 a new patent gave official recognition to Mathew de Quester's service for "many years in sending packets to foreign parts." It did more, for it recognized the father and his son as the "first and permanent Postmasters of England for Forraine Parts, being out of the kingdom." The patent states distinctly that Lord Stanhope's grant extended only to service "in our realm of England

[1] These proclamations were reprinted in *Secret Com. on P.O.*, H.C. (1844), pp. 38-43. A groat was 4d.
[2] *Acts of P.C.*, 1603-10, 366; *Cal. S.P. Dom.*, 1619-23, 572; 1623-25, 153; 1629-31, 266; 1636-37, 534; 1637, 527.
[3] *Ibid.*, 1635, 592; *H.M.C. Rep.*, Devonshire, II, 46, 110, 237, 443.

and other our Dominions." It was held, therefore, that "both grants might well stand together, being of distinct places." The patent to the De Questers was to extend so long as the survivor lived. The government clearly intended that the "said office should be forever a sole office of itselfe, and not a member, or part of, or belonging unto any other office or place of Postmaster whatsoever." Early in postal history a cleavage developed between the inland and foreign service, destined to make the two services fairly distinct for centuries, and to cause no end of confusion and overlapping as the Post Office became of more general use.[4]

The patent to the De Questers raised immediate difficulties. Stanhope, who declared that he was rightly "Master of the posts for England," held that this grant was an infringement of his patent. The result was a long squabble that we need not trace in detail. Stanhope appealed to the Council on the ground that the "foreign service had formerly been performed by those who had the same patent as he had." But he failed to sustain his position, for by 1626 the foreign posts were declared in the hands of the De Questers, and well settled there on account of the "labor and industry of the said De Quester."[5]

But the end was not yet. When De Quester endeavored to magnify his new patent to include the packets of the Merchant Adventurers, they appeared before the Council board to declare that "for above fifty years without interruption" they had sent their dispatches "by a post of their own election." The Council allowed this right to continue as far as Hamburg and Delft were concerned "where the staples of cloth are now settled." When Edward Quarles, who had long been the postmaster for the Merchant Adventurers, died in 1626, he was succeeded by Henry Billingsley, said Billingsley advertising that "Charles Stanhope had appointed him to convey letters between the City of London and foreign parts." The notice further specified the place where the letters would be received— "behind the Exchange at one widow Baynham's, at the sign of the George, a little beyond the Antwerp Tavern." A post was to leave for Flushing at midnight on Saturday "and so from time to time every Saturday."[6]

[4] *Secret Com. on P.O.*, H.C. (1844), pp. 45-47, where the patent is reprinted. See also J. W. Hyde, *The Early History of the Post in Grant and Farm*, pp. 6-7. This volume, by a Controller of the General Post Office in Edinburgh, seems based on documents, but it is innocent of bibliography or footnotes.

[5] *Cal. S.P. Dom.*, 1623-25, 131; *Acts of P.C.*, 1626, 112, 305, 361.

[6] The postal service of the Merchant Adventurers was similar to that of the earlier

During the absence from London in 1627 of Sir John Coke, the King's principal Secretary of State, Billingsley had been making progress in the work of taking over the postal service of the merchants, in defiance of the claims of De Quester. The Turkey and East India Companies and 210 other merchants of London appointed Billingsley in that year to receive and convey their letters. In reply to De Quester's objections, the merchants declared that "by order of the state we have liberty to choose our own Post for all places, and we have appointed Henry Billingsley to take up our letters here and to receive them from thence." But Coke set matters aright on his return, at least from the royal point of view, by putting an order through the Council in 1627, requiring the merchants to send their letters by De Quester. This was followed in the next year by a proclamation forbidding all persons to convey foreign letters "except such as shall be employed by Mathew de Quester, Postmaster of England for Foreign Parts."[7]

Sir John Coke was so incensed at the "insufferable carriage of this man Billingsley" that he wrote to his brother secretary, Conway, in the following fashion: "I confess it trobleth me to see the audacitie of men in theis times, & that Billingsley, a broker by trade, should dare to attempt thus often to question the King's service, and to derive [desire?] that power of foren letters unto merchants, which in al states, is a branch of regal authoritie; nether can anie place in Christendom bee named wher merchants are allowed to send their letters by other body or posts, then those only which are authorised by the state. . . . Indeed the merchants purse hath swayed verie mutch in other matters in former times, but I never heard that it incroached uppon the Kings prerogatives till now. Your Lordship best knoweth that accompt we shal bee hable to give in our places of that which passeth by letters in or out of the land, if everie man may convey letters under the covers of merchants to whom and what place hee pleaseth."[8]

Strangers' Post, in that its appointee had government sanction, but the Merchant Adventurers were Englishmen, not foreigners. *Ibid.*, 1626, 376; *Cal. S.P. Dom.*, 1603-10, 568; 1625-26, 220.

[7] *Ibid.*, 1627-28, 6, 405, 522; *H.M.C. Rep.*, XII, App. I, 295.

[8] *Cal. S.P. Dom.*, 1627-28, 106, 591; 1628-29, 177; *Secret Com. on P.O.*, H.C. (1844), pp. 50-51, where the letter is reprinted. Parts of it are also given in Dorothea Coke, *The Last Elizabethan, Sir John Coke*, pp. 220-21. This Coke is not to be confused with Sir Edward Coke, the well-known judge and the sharp critic of royal prerogative. Sir John Coke remained an important servant of the King until old age compelled his retirement in 1640. See also *D.N.B.*, XI, 244.

During the thirties the Post Office underwent some important changes and an attempted reform. Unfortunately, any achievement at this time was likely to be short-lived, as a result of the contest between King and Parliament. Yet the improvements in both the domestic and foreign postal arrangements during these years are worthy of attention as showing the way in which the Post Office would ultimately develop.

The carriage of letters overseas, which had been in charge of the De Questers, was granted to William Frizell and Thomas Witherings in 1632. The step was taken on the ground that Mathew de Quester, the son, was dead and that the elder De Quester was "aged and infirm." Witherings, a London mercer, was the ambitious and active member of the partnership, so active indeed that in the next year he ousted Frizell, and became the sole "Postmaster-General for Foreign Parts." Witherings was not a foreigner like De Quester, but came from a Staffordshire family. In addition to being a well-to-do merchant, he had an estate in Essex. His court position of Harbinger to Charles I's French Queen, Henrietta Maria, might well familiarize him with conditions across the Channel, since it was his duty to prepare for the Queen's lodging when she traveled.[9]

The appointment of Witherings was abundantly justified. He arranged for more rapid carriage on the Continent as well as for the crossing of the Channel. The carriers, it was alleged, usually required eight and sometimes fourteen days from London to Antwerp, under the administration of De Quester. Witherings provided for more mails per week and greater speed in the conveyance. Letters were carried between London and Antwerp, for example, in three days. The improvements resulted, apparently, from the use of what were called "staffeto" or packet posts, the sending of letters "from stage to stage, to go night and day, as had been continued in Germany and Italy."[10]

A letter written by Witherings to Secretary Coke gives some in-

[9] *Secret Com. on P.O.*, H.C. (1844), pp. 52-55, where the patent and the proclamations are reprinted. C. R. Clear, *The Birth of the Postal Service*, notes that Witherings was the Queen's Harbinger. Witherings died in 1651, and was buried at Hornchurch in Essex. A tablet there commends him as "Chiefe Postmaster of Greate Britaine and foreigne parts." *Cal. S.P. Dom.* for the years 1631-36 has much reference to the quarrel between Witherings and Frizell. At the Restoration, Frizell pleaded for consideration on the grounds of 17 years of banishment and his consequent poverty. *Ibid.*, 1660-61, 94. Hyde, *op. cit.*, pp. 17-21, 43, enlarges on these difficulties.

[10] *Cal. S.P. Dom.*, 1633-34, 39; 1631-33, 521. Day and night service had been used in England, but the better-regulated service on the Continent served as a stimulus. See above, p. 4, for the "staffette" of the Taxis family.

sight into the arrangements. Witherings wrote in April of 1633 from Calais that the secretary of the Countess Taxis had settled stages between Antwerp and Calais, and he requested that "we do the like." He declared that the Calais boatmen "who take their turns for Dover" were unwilling to depart immediately "upon the coming of the portmantle." Witherings announced to Coke that he had solved the difficulty by hiring a Dover boatman, who gave security for forty shillings that when the packet came from London "upon sight whereof he will depart, engaging himself to carry nothing but the said packet." In addition, he had agreed to stay in Calais until "the first packet shall come by staffeto from Antwerp."[11]

The regulations drawn up by Secretary Coke for Withering's packet post contain other interesting regulations. The posts between London and Dover were to run day and night without ceasing. Witherings was to have an office in London with clerks to keep a register of the writers and bringers of all letters, as well as the names of those to whom they were to be sent. The mail was to be put in a "bag or budget," and then locked up and sealed with the "postmaster's known seal." The bag was to reach Dover while sufficient daylight remained for it to be sent over sea. When the mail from the Continent reached London, letters for the King and his ministers were to be delivered immediately, "after which a roll or table of all other letters was to be set up in the office for every man to view and demand his letters." Here is definite evidence that the foreign postmaster was to serve private individuals. Thomas Witherings deserves much credit for endeavoring to meet the increased demand for a better service. Even the grumbling merchants were satisfied, for a time, with his arrangements.[12]

At the same time an important reform occurred in the domestic service: it became more expeditious, along the lines of the improved foreign post, and was extended to include the letters of private individuals, and to serve towns off the main post roads. Secretary Coke granted the superintendence of this new service to Witherings, as he had shown commendable zeal in the handling of foreign letters.

Some doubt exists as to who should have the credit for this great advance in the domestic postal service. In 1630 the posts of the western stages from London to Plymouth had agreed "among them-

[11] *H.M.C. Rep.*, XII, App., pt. 2, p. 6. "Portmantle" was the name for a commodious saddlebag.
[12] *Cal. S.P. Dom.*, 1631-33, 521; 1634-35, 389; Hyde, *op. cit.*, pp. 14-15.

selves" for the dispatch of all letters weekly from London to Plymouth and from Plymouth to London in three days. In addition, they would deliver all letters along the way within twenty miles of the road.[13]

Three years later, as we have found, Witherings set up a "staffeto" post via Dover and Calais, "in conformity with the practice of other nations." In that same year, 1633, appeared an interesting project "for a new arrangement of the business of the Post Office." The unnamed projector estimated that the thirty-two counties of England contained at least 512 market towns, and that each would account for an average of fifty letters per week. The average cost of these letters was reckoned at 4d or £426 a week. This would be ample to pay for the conveyance of these letters, and would cover as well the estimated £1500 per annum to be paid to the postmaster for "conveying His Majesty's packets." It was argued that the state would profit by the arrangement, as the cost at the time was more than twice as much. All letters on the "road to Scotland" would be charged 2d if single and 4d if a double letter, with 3d as the charge for letters to Yorkshire and Northumberland, and 8d for those that went to Scotland.[14] The postmasters in the country were not to take any money for letters, save a penny for carriage to the nearest market town. This very suggestive project included not only the road to Scotland but all the post roads of the kingdom.[15]

Two years later (1635) appeared another "Proposition for settling staffets or packet posts betwixt London and all parts of His Majesties dominions for the carrying and recarrying of His subjects letters." The main office was to be in London. If letters were sent to Edinburgh or to other places along that road, they were put in particular bags for the post towns, and all of these bags placed in the portmantle for Scotland. Thus, if a bag were directed to Cambridge, it would be left at the nearest station on the Great North Road to be taken to Cambridge. Letters in the Cambridge bag were then delivered, including letters to towns within ten miles of Cambridge. They were delivered by a footpost on market days, and the footpost was to take up letters from these towns. They, along with

---

[13] *Cal. S.P. Dom.*, 1629-31, 199-200.

[14] A single letter was a letter that took but one sheet of paper; a double letter had two sheets, or a sheet and an enclosure.

[15] *Ibid.*, 1633-34, p. 366. J. C. Hemmeon, *The History of the British Post Office*, p. 13, held that "probably" this plan was suggested by Witherings. Hyde, *op. cit.*, p. 52, is of the same opinion.

the Cambridge letters to London, were put in the portmantle on its return from Scotland. If a town was far off the main road—Hull was named as an example—the letters were to be carried there by horse post.

Other roads were to be used in a similar way, including the roads to Ireland by way of Holyhead and Milford Haven, to Oxford, "to Worcester and the marches of Wales, to Exeter and Plymouth, to Canterbury and Dover, to Chelmsford, Colchester and so to Harwich, and lastly to Newmarket, Bury, Norwich and so to Yarmouth." The plan proposed that the "further the letters go the post thereof is to be advanced, as to 3d, 4d and 6d, and to Scotland more." The portmantle was to go forward "day and night without stay," and the day and hour of the coming and going of the "said Portmantle to and from London to be always certain." It followed that all the posts would know when to expect the mail, and that the plan would greatly speed the carriage of letters. The proposer may have exaggerated the slowness of communication with Scotland; he declared that "letters being now carried by couriers or footposts 16 or 18 miles a day, it is full two months before any answer can be received from Scotland or Ireland to London." He certainly exaggerated the speed of the projected service: it was to travel at the rate of "120 miles at the least in one day and night." As a result, it was believed that "by this way of carrying and recarrying letters, His Majesty's subjects shall, once in six days, receive answer from Edinburgh in Scotland." This was certainly a wild calculation, for it forecast a rapidity of service not to be attained for two centuries.

The plan is of great interest because it was an elaborate arrangement for the general carriage of letters: "it will be a great furtherance to the correspondency betwixt London & Scotland & Ireland, and great help to Trades, & true affection of his Majesty's subjects betwixt theis kingdomes, which, for want of true correspondency of letters, is now destroyed, & a thing above all things observed by all other nations." Thus the news could come from the coast towns to London "sooner than thought," especially word of "anie fight at sea or anie wrong offered by anie other nation to anie of the coasts of England or anie of his Majesty's forts."

It might be alleged that this would infringe the rights of Lord Stanhope. In answer, the proposer declared that no one heretofore had had any "benefit of the carrying or recarrying of the subjects' letters." The plan claimed novelty for this extension of letter-carrying to the general public. It did not recommend substitution for Lord Stanhope's postmasters, but their better payment as a result of increased service.[16]

The plan for a bypost, that is, a postal service to a town not on the main road, had been suggested, as we have found, for the Plymouth road in 1630. A record has also been preserved of an actual bypost service in use in the year 1633. It ran between Exeter, on the main road, and Barnstaple. A footpost left the latter town every Tuesday at 7 A.M. for Exeter. He was to be at the postmaster's house in Exeter on Wednesday morning, in time for the post leaving for London. The footpost was to stay in Exeter until the mail for that week had come down from London. By this "speedie" arrangement, men in Barnstaple could write to London and receive answers from "their friends and factors" in eleven days. And this would give their London correspondents three days in which to make a reply. The charge between London and Exeter was 6d for a single letter and 8d for a double letter.[17]

These suggestions are very interesting to the student of postal history because they propose postal arrangements that come up again and again. The 2d charge for a single letter was to remain the basic rate for two centuries. The increasing cost, according to the distance a letter traveled, was also to be a long-lived device of the Post Office. The use of the footpost was to remain an important part of the system both in town and country. Postal service away from the few main lines of travel was to be extended by the establishment of byposts such as the one just described for the use of Barnstaple. Later on the byposts were to become cross posts, that is, they were to connect main post roads. Only in the course of a century, however, was the postal service to spread a network over the whole of the country. If the courageous efforts of the thirties, now being described, had not been interrupted by the Civil War, the network might have been spread much earlier.

The culmination of these projects came on July 31, 1635, with a "Proclamation for the Settling of the Letter-Office of England and Scotland." The suggestions of the "Proposition" of June 1635 are repeated. Thomas Witherings, the Postmaster of England for for-

---

[16] *Cal. S.P. Dom.*, 1635; 166; *Secret Com. on P.O.*, H.C. (1844), pp. 55-56, where this interesting project is printed; Hyde, *op. cit.*, pp. 71-74.

[17] *H.M.C. Rep.*, IX, pt. 1, App. 214. As the two towns were over forty miles apart, the footpost had a good journey for one day and night.

eign parts, was given the task of setting up the new Letter-Office. The charges were made somewhat more specific—2d for a single letter traveling under eighty miles, 4d for a single letter going between eighty and 140 miles, and "if above 140 miles, then 6d, and upon the borders of Scotland and in Scotland, 8d." If there were "two, three, four or five letters in one packet, or more, then to pay according to the bigness of the said packet after the rate as before." Witherings agreed to extend this service as rapidly as possible to the Chester and Holyhead road, as well as to that between London and Plymouth. Later he was to improve the roads to Oxford and Bristol, Colchester and Norwich. The cost of a post horse was put at 2½d a mile. Strict orders were given that no one but the messengers of Witherings were to carry letters.[18]

The authorship of the improvements put in force by the proclamation of 1635 is in doubt. Witherings may have been chiefly responsible for the suggestion of a service that is strikingly like the one he knew on the Continent. On the other hand, reforms somewhat like those ordered in 1635 had already begun on one of the roads several years before. If Thomas Witherings did originate the suggestion, he deserves much credit, even though his name is hardly the "most distinguished in the annals of the British Post Office."[19]

Sir John Coke, the Secretary of State, appears to have had some share in the reform of 1635. Coke had a lively interest in the sphere that would now be within that of the Home Office. That he was greatly interested in the reform is certain, and that he selected Witherings as most capable of carrying out the project can also be affirmed. Then too, among the *State Papers, Domestic,* for 1635 there is a draft in the handwriting of Secretary Coke—it runs to nine and one-half pages—of "Orders for a letter office for missives within the land."[20] Coke's plans are strikingly parallel to those that found form in the actual arrangements. His list of the roads is somewhat more specific, and his plans called for a common letter carrier to every "shiretown and eminent place" from the "nearest stage in the com-

---

[18] *Cal. S.P. Dom.,* 1635, 299. The regulation that no one but the messengers of Witherings were to carry letters led to some difficulty with the Norwich merchants. They had been accustomed to transporting letters weekly by their own carriers. After some delay, the government allowed the common carriers to take the letters of merchants and others, "but not above eight hours before the carts, waggons, or pack horses." *Ibid.,* 1637-38, 177, 183. The Proclamation is conveniently reprinted in *Penny Postage Centenary,* pp. 27-30.

[19] Hemmeon, *op. cit.,* p. 14, accords him this praise.

[20] *Cal. S.P. Dom.,* 1635-36, 32.

mon road," and a footpost for every market town. The rates of postage in his "orders" are a duplicate of those in the proclamation of
1635. John Bruce, the editor of the *Calendars of State Papers, Domestic,* for those years, believed Coke to be the responsible person.
In the preface to the volume for 1635, he wrote of "the development of Secretary Coke's great reform of the system of transmitting
letters, which was the foundation of our old mode of forwarding letter bags. . . . Coke's labours in this respect entitle him to rank among
unquestionable public benefactors."[21]

The outlook for the beginning of a real postal service appeared
excellent, a service that would be more rapid and that would, for the
first time, attempt a systematic carriage of the letters of the people.
But the unsettlement of the times prevented any real trial of the
arrangements of 1635. By 1637, the differences between Charles and
his subjects of Scotland and England were growing more acute, cul-
minating in civil war five years later. It seemed unwise, with such
conditions obviously impending, to attempt postal reforms under the
leadership of a person unconnected with government, an "unsworn
person" like Witherings. The Secretaries professed to believe as well
that persons of quality would not deign to correspond with a man
of Witherings' "mean condition." This objection must not be taken
too seriously, nor Frizell's accusation that Witherings was but a
"homebred shopkeeper without languages."[22] At any rate, Thomas
Witherings was deprived of his place of postmaster in June 1637,
and the Post Office was put directly under Coke and Windebank, the
Secretaries of State. This meant only that Witherings lost control of
the inland post, for he seems to have acted for a time as the deputy
of the Postmasters-General, and to have continued in charge of the
foreign service. But in 1640 the foreign office was sequestered as
well, on the alleged ground that letters were being opened, greater
rates than usual were being taken and prohibited commodities transported. Again, the accusations need not be taken too seriously. Witherings was the victim of intrigue and cupidity, and, in particular, of
the national crisis that was becoming increasingly grave.[23]

The royal orders of July 1637 limited the postal service to letters
on His Majesty's business and to those subscribed by persons con-

<hr>

[21] *Ibid.,* 1635, p. lii, and 418; Coke, *op. cit.,* 217-19.
[22] *Cal. S.P. Dom.,* 1637, 255; 1637-38, 51.
[23] *Ibid.,* 1660-61, 93, where the petition of his nephew, William Witherings, is given.
For the accusations, see *H.M.C. Rep.,* V, 47, 62; *Secret Com. on P.O.,* H.C. (1844), 59.

nected with the government. Disappointing as this order must have been to the public who wished to use the Post Office, the regulations entered with care into the conditions for riding post. The Post Office seemed to need, more than ever, careful direction and control. Several regulations with which the reader is already familiar were repeated and specific directions were added to check letters and their senders. Each postmaster was to keep a "fair ledger book" to enter the packets, with the name of the bringer, the exact time each was received, and the name of the sender and the one to whom each was being sent. A label was to be fastened to every one of "our packets," and on it each postmaster was to write the time of its receipt, "and not on the packet or letter as hath been disorderly used." The mail was to be weekly. "Every Poste in his severall Stage is commanded, and hereby required to carry out and in once a week, the Maile of Letters that shall come from, and goe to the Letter Office of London, free without charge." Every post was required to deliver all the letters in the country, "either at or neere his Stage, as shall be sent to him from the Master of the Letter Office, and to receive port according to the taxe set upon every letter. . . . And in case Post Paid be written upon any letter that shall come from London, they are not to take port for it in the country againe."[24]

Much more is known of the postmasters in the first half of the seventeenth century than those of Elizabeth's time. They were often proprietors of inns for the housing of travelers. The mayor and others of Coventry recommend an innholder for the post in their town, declaring that the present postmaster, a John Fletcher, is poor and by reason of lameness employs a John Scott, "another poor aged man," and that neither John has "so much as one horse, mare, or nag." Another petition from an innkeeper at Stilton, who wanted this post "in the high north road," declared that the present holder "lives twelve miles away and has as his deputy an alehouse keeper and who is unable to receive gentlemen and travelers, much less noblemen." A complaint against the innkeeping post at Royston accuses him of hindering poor men coming to market by taking horses for post when there is no cause, and of double-posting the horses. Anthony Spittle, the postmaster at Basingstoke, was ordered punished for taking up horses for private gain. The Lord Deputy of Ireland complained that a packet arrived from the Secretaries with the seals broken. On inquiry, it was found that the boy taking it from

[24] *Cal. S.P. Dom.*, 1637, 338; Hyde, *op. cit.*, pp. 108-19.

St. Albans could find no box of his master large enough for it, and so had tied it with his master's girdle, "and the seals were broken thereby."[25]

The postmasters complained bitterly of their lot. The Canterbury post, who found it necessary to keep twelve or more horses, objected to unfair competition. The post at Dartford, who had to keep sixteen horses, sought arrears in pay from the Postmaster-General. The post at Daventry declared that a pursuivant, to whom he furnished two able post horses, did not pay for them and was "violent and abusive."[26] In 1629 the deputy postmaster of the court, John Wytton or Wotton, was asking for nearly £900—six years of arrears. The post for Hertford Bridge was asking for seven years of back pay about the same time. In 1628 there was a collective petition of all the postmasters of England, "being in number 99 poore men," some of whom "lye now in prison, and many of the rest daily threatened to bee arrested by reason of their great debts." They claimed to have been unpaid since 1621, the total sum due them being over £22,000. Two years later, the arrears had amounted to £25,535. A petition of the survivors some years later would indicate that they, "for the most part poor innkeepers," undertook the carriage of private letters in 1637 as a supplement to their service for the government, in the hope that they might offset somewhat the payment from the government so long in arrears. They reported in 1637 upwards of £60,000 due them on their wages, "whereof they have never received a penny."[27]

The complaints of the posts against Stanhope and his paymasters were made frequently through a certain Thomas Hutchins, postmaster at Lichfield. He seems to have begun his pestiferous complaints as early as 1617 "in behalf of the postmasters of England." In the next year they were promised pay from the customs. An effort was made to quiet Hutchins, as he received £30 from Stanhope in satisfaction of past grievances, and pledged himself to refrain from all clamor in the future. But the "turbulent Hutchins" was not stilled, for in 1623 he was imprisoned and later released on the understanding that "he no more trouble this board with any more petitions about this business." The gigantic arrears at the end of the

---

[25] *Cal. S.P. Dom.*, 1623-25, 510; 1635, 18; 1637-38, 52, 390; 1638-39, 83, 199.

[26] *Ibid.*, 1631-33, 298; 1611-18, 126; 1635-36, 31.

[27] *Ibid.*, 1627-28, 307; 1628-29, 184, 482; 1631-33, 421; 1629-30, 379; *H.M.C. Rep.*, VII, 140; *Secret Com. on P.O.*, H.C. (1844), p. 52.

twenties, which have been referred to in a previous paragraph, again brought the meddlesome Hutchins to the fore. The paymaster of the posts, Ranulph Church, succeeded in having Hutchins imprisoned in the Marshalsea at the time.[28]

The Hutchins family contained several unsung "village Hampdens," for two sons of Thomas are heading a petition in 1633 against Stanhope and his paymaster for raising the valuation of the post places on the Western Road from £20, anciently given, to £100, and for assuming all the benefit of the merchants' letters. The two sons pray that for £20 they may have the post their father and grandfather held for seventy years. And on the restoration of Charles II in 1660, an Edward Hutchins and a John Castleton head a petition "for all their fellows, the postmasters of England."[29]

The postal history of the first half of the seventeenth century is a confusing record, with the financial difficulties of the first two Stuarts playing a major part in the confusion. An attempt was made to set up a postal service for the people as a whole. The remarkable suggestions of Thomas Witherings and others and the interest in a better service by Sir John Coke forecast a more useful Post Office. The approach of the Civil War, however, put a stop to any large-minded advance, and brought disorder into the existing peace-time regulations. Government naturally reverted to Tudor concepts of a carefully supervised service that was intended primarily for government use.

[28] *Cal. S.P. Dom.*, 1611-18, 478, 562; 1619-23, 567; 1623-25, 117, 153; 1629-31, 440; *Acts of P.C.*, VI, 510.
[29] *Cal. S.P. Dom.*, 1633-34, 101; *H.M.C. Rep.*, V, 62.

The Cromwellian
Post Office

THE twenty years from the summoning of the Long Parliament in 1640 to the restoration of the Stuarts in 1660 were decades of confusion. The Post Office that had started so hopefully as a General Letter Office under Witherings in the late thirties was bandied about after 1640. It was badly disorganized by the Civil War, and remained in an unsettled state after the death of Charles I in 1649. Not only did covetous Roundheads seek it as a monopoly under government supervision, but independent carriers made determined efforts to give postal service free from government control. Careful state supervision was finally established by a Cromwellian statute of 1657, the first legislative act in the history of the British Post Office. This statute was to be the model for the so-called Charter of 1660.

Thomas Witherings, as we have found, lost his control of the Inland Office in 1637 and of the Foreign Letter Office three years later. In 1640 the King turned over both services to a London merchant named Burlamachi, a naturalized foreigner who had been of much assistance to the King. Burlamachi's control was similar to that of Witherings: the service was to be conducted "in the same course in which it was formerly," under the supervision of the Secretaries of State. Secretary Falkland, in particular, bore the title Controller-General of the Post Office.[1]

The Post Office did not, however, continue in the same course as formerly. King and Parliament were at loggerheads. Although the

[1] H. Joyce, *The History of the Post Office*, p. 21; *Secret Com. on P.O.*, H.C. (1844), p. 59.

Lords and Commons were more or less agreed in snatching authority from the King, they were not at one as to where the control of the Post Office should ultimately rest. A spirited contest ensued among the various claimants, who declared that the Post Office belonged to this or that patentee, or his heir or legal successor by assignment. The situation was further complicated by the support given these claimants by the Lords and the Commons. Only the general outlines of this rather unseemly rivalry need be given. The very vigor with which the Post Office was sought only emphasizes the new value it seemed to possess after the postal service had been reorganized during the administration of Secretary Coke.

Both Houses were opposed, naturally enough, to Burlamachi because he was a royal appointee. Witherings so much obtained the sympathy of the House of Lords in 1642 that Burlamachi was ordered to show cause why the sequestration to him, "Which is voted by both Houses to be illegal," should not end. The Earl of Warwick, to whom Witherings had made an assignment of the Office, became a claimant as well. Charles Stanhope, who had succeeded his father in 1621, thought this a good time to reassert his right to both the inland and foreign offices. In a later petition—of 1660—Stanhope declared that he had held the position "quietly" until 1637, a statement that we have found to be untrue. Stanhope later asserted as well that "by the contrivance of Witherings and some great persons" he was brought before the Council in 1637 and forced to surrender his patent. Two years earlier, apparently, Stanhope had conveyed his rights under the patent to Endymion and Charles Porter, and they had transferred their rights to the Stanhope patent at the beginning of March 1641-42 to a Henry Robinson. The office was obviously a desirable perquisite.[2]

The strife became bitter by 1642. The Lords ordered in November that the "possession of the said Letter Office be delivered unto the Earl of Warwick," arguing that the Letter Office had long "depended in the Peers, and that it concerned a person of Honour." Burlamachi, however, was so tenacious that he refused to recognize this decision of the House of Lords. The upper house found that "notwithstanding the said order, the mail of letters for the western road was delivered at Mr. Burlamachi's house . . . and were there dis-

[2] For these various claims, see *ibid.*, p. 61; *H.M.C. Rep.*, V, 62; XII, 82; *Cal. S.P. Dom.*, 1636-37, 530; 1641-43, 40; 1651-52, 15; 1654, 21-22; *Journal H.C.*, VII, 192; VIII, 588.

tributed by Job Alibond and James Hickes; and the letters of the other roads were delivered in by them at the said Burlamachi's house; and the said Alibond and Hickes do execute the said office in Burlamachi's house, in the same manner as they and others had formerly done."[3] When Burlamachi finally appeared before the House of Lords to give reasons for the disobedience he had shown to their orders, his reply revealed a further complication in the postal control. The office, so he declared, was no longer in his possession even though it was kept at his house. The office was really in charge of Edmond Prideaux, a member of the House of Commons. Prideaux, said Burlamachi, had hired his house and his servants and "disposes of the letters."[4]

The result of this extraordinary situation was a spirited contest between the Earl of Warwick and Edmond Prideaux for the possession of the Post Office, one supported by the House of Lords, and the other by the House of Commons. In mid-December representatives of the Earl of Warwick attempted to seize the "West Chester letters" when they reached Barnet in order to bring them to "his Lordship's office near the Exchange." They found them in the possession of James Hickes, who had them "behind him in a cloak bag." When Warwick's men and Hickes reached Highgate, they were met by five persons "on great horses, with pistols, habited like troopers," who took Hickes under their protection. The letters were finally taken away by the troopers, who admitted they were Prideaux's men. The Lords then imprisoned Hickes by warrant, but he was released by order of the House of Commons, because he was a servant of a member of that House.[5]

The House of Commons and Prideaux won out, for he continued "the management of the Inland Post Office for carrying the weekly letters." Prideaux had been busy for several years before his formal appointment in "erecting and settling post-stages for the State," especially between Parliament and the military forces. By the end of the Civil War, he had succeeded in re-establishing weekly services throughout England. So ably did he care for the matter that rumor had it that his income as holder of the office was £15,000 a year.[6]

[3] *H.M.C. Rep.*, v, 47; *Journal H.L.*, v, 459, 470; *Journal H.C.*, II, 722, 881.

[4] *Journal H.L.*, v, 471. Edmond Prideaux, who was administering the Post Office through the channels formerly used by Burlamachi, was a lawyer and a "very fierce republican"; he represented a Norfolk constituency in the Long Parliament. He became Attorney-General after the death of Charles I. Prideaux died in 1659.

[5] *Journal H.L.*, v, 508, 514.

[6] *Journal H.C.*, III, 621; *H.M.C. Rep.*, App. I, 74; *Cal. S.P. Dom.*, 1649-50, 147;

Sir Edmond Prideaux was continued in charge of postal matters after the execution of Charles. In 1650 the whole matter was again under discussion as the result of an attempt of the Common Council of London "to settle postages by their own authority on the several roads." According to Prideaux, they "appointed a natural Scott unto the north, who is gone into Scotland and hath settled postmasters on all that road." As a result, the Irish and Scottish committee to which the matter was referred reported in favor of a contract for the postal service. Parliament, thereupon, announced its willingness to receive suggestions from anyone for improving the office "for the best service of the state and ease of the people."[7]

Various suggestions seem to have been made, including possible lowering of rates, free carriage of letters sent by members of Parliament, and grant of the postal service to a "farmer." The government finally decided to let out the post under contract, with certain conditions to be met by the person who took charge of the service. It was felt that a weekly service should be maintained between Milford Haven and Waterford, Chester and Dublin, and that additional post services should connect Lancaster and Carlisle in the west of England. As to letter rates, they were not to exceed for single letters 2d within eighty miles of London, 3d to remote parts of England and Wales, 4d to Scotland and 6d to Ireland. As to the carrying of official mail fee—franking, as it came to be known—the conditions were set down as follows: "Letters of all members of the legislative power are to be carried free from postage, an endorsement indicating that they are for 'the service of the Commonwealth.'" The free letters were to be signed on the outside by the senders themselves or their clerks.[8]

Bids for a postal contract, based on these general provisions, were then sought, the successful "undertaker" to be a man of known integrity. Offers ranged from £7000 to over £10,000. Henry Robinson sought the farm at £8041, John Manley for £8259, Ben Andrews for £9100, and an offer by Ralph Kendall reached £10,103. The names of the other bidders were John Goldsmith, Richard Hicks

1650, 38, 73. See also *E.B.* (9th ed., 1885), XIX, 564. In 1646, the House of Lords reported that the Earl of Warwick's claim was valid, but the claim did not affect Prideaux's control.

[7] Firth & Rait, *Acts and Ordinances of the Interregnum*, II, 248, 251, 1007; *Cal. S.P. Dom.*, 1649-50, 38; 1651, 467; 1651-52, 444; *Journal H.C.*, VI, 385; *D.N.B.*, XLVI, 351-52.

[8] *Cal. S.P. Dom.*, 1651-52, 507.

and Richard Hill. The successful bidder proved to be John Manley, though several had made higher original bids. A disappointed applicant later accused Manley of taking advantage of a knowledge of the Kendall offer and making a private agreement with the Council for £10,000.[9]

One of the unsuccessful bidders was Henry Robinson, the same man who had claimed the Post Office in the early forties on the basis of an assignment by Stanhope to the Porters, who had, in turn, assigned their rights to Henry Robinson. He again revived his claim when the government decided to farm out the office, but it was declared invalid. Robinson then made the best of the situation by bidding for the farm, but his offer was too low. If Henry Robinson had been successful, the Post Office would have been in good hands. He was a substantial London merchant, Oxford trained, and a prolific as well as thoughtful writer on government, politics and religion. He had become very desirous of controlling the postal service in the forties, as a financial activity of growing value. Just how much Henry Robinson had to do with the Post Office after Thomas Witherings had been deprived of it is not clear. Robinson's son claimed in a petition to Charles II in 1665 that his father had increased the postal revenues from £3000 a year to £30,000 a year (presumably in the early forties), that he had established a cheap domestic service from London thrice weekly at 3d a single letter, and that he had been active in soliciting business in various English towns and even on the Continent. The petition stated further that Prideaux's service had been once a week only and was twice as expensive as that of Henry Robinson.[10] The claims in the petition appear to have been very much exaggerated. Whatever Robinson's part in postal affairs during the early forties, his efforts to obtain the Post Office show how important it seemed to a man of wealth, who thought and wrote much on the advance of trade and navigation. His desire to develop the posts was part of a general plan for expanding industry, establishing new ports, cultivating international trade on a relatively tariff-free basis, improving roads and constructing canals—in short, the general betterment of communications.[11]

[9] *Ibid.*, 1654, 23; 1652-53, 109, 312, 448-55; Firth & Rait, *op. cit.*, II, 1008.

[10] *Cal. S.P. Dom.*, 1665-66, 161. See also W. K. Jordan, *Men of Substance, A Study of the Thought of . . . Henry Parker and Henry Robinson*, pp. 55-62 and 62n. The volume declares that the "modern post, as a monopoly administered by or under government supervision, had developed in England during Robinson's lifetime," that is, from Stanhope's patent of 1590. But see above, p. 7.

[11] Jordan, *op. cit.*, pp. 248, 258.

John Manley, the new farmer, entered on his duties June 30, 1653, with power to handle all posts, both inland and foreign, and to stop all mails carried by unauthorized persons. The right to stop all other carriers of mails was more than a rhetorical flourish. When the Council gave the farm to Manley, he was permitted to enter on his new office "tonight." And there was immediate trouble for those who believed that the carriage of the public's letters should not be a monopoly. Those who opposed the monopoly were prepared to do the work for much less than was customary. This explains why the Council had required that the postal rates be more reasonable than they had been. The Act of 1654, which gave Manley's contract additional validity, included in the preamble the provision "that prices for the postage of letters may be reduced to a lower rate . . . for the ease and advantage of the people."[12]

Of the persons who continued of the opinion that the carriage of letters should be based on competitive service, none were more stubborn than Clement Oxenbridge and Francis Thomson. In a petition of January 1654, these co-workers claimed to be the "first undertakers for reducing the postage of inland letters to half the former rates." They were satisfied of the "freeness in law of the postage of letters to any who would undertake the same." During Prideaux's regime they offered a service that carried letters for 2d when, so they claimed, Prideaux was charging 6d. As their petition put it: "The undertakers, observing this extortive rate to be held up, as well in Withering's lifetime as after his death—when the pretence of that illegal grant was ended in point of limitation—and observing that the whole benefit went into one private hand, . . they conceived it would be a work both acceptable to the State and beneficial to the people, to contrive the abatement of these excessive rates; and therefore, maugre all oppositions and abuses of the monopolizer and his interest, they at first dash ventured on postage at the rate of 3d a letter beyond eighty miles, and 2d a letter within or to eighty miles; and to make return three times weekly."

Prideaux tried to prevent this successful competition by various methods. Prideaux's men murdered one of the carriers of his rivals and threw his body into the river. Another was assaulted with a drawn sword. According to the petition of Oxenbridge and Thomson, "Libels also were posted up and down the city by him or his agents, signifying that our mails should be stopped, but his go free.

[12] Firth & Rait, *op. cit.*, II, 1008.

This project failing, Mr. Prideaux, out of a hypocritical pretence of keeping the Sabbath day, by his own warrant commanded his post-masters to require the justices of the peace in the several counties to stop our mails on the Sabbath, whereas his own went free."[13]

They declared further that they were the only persons performing the "state's service in conveying their letters" when Parliament dissolved on April 20, 1653. This was two months before Manley obtained the farm. After Manley had been awarded his contract, Oxenbridge and Thomson complained that they had been turned out of their employment "at less than an hour's warning." Hence their petition, praying restitution of "freedom to carry letters as formerly, doing the state service and accommodating private persons at more reasonable rates, there being a multitude of complaints against the exactions and miscarriages of the present farmer."[14]

Another believer in free competition was an attorney of York, John Hill. His name has been preserved because of a pamphlet he published in 1659, with the felicitous title, *A Penny Post*.[15] Hill had post horses on the road between London and York towards the end of 1652. They were used to carry "Letters & small commodities, at the half rates, and less, then [sic] the same had at any time been carryed at."[16] His service was soon enlarged so that it included most of the northern roads. In March 1653 he came to London with the intention of proceeding "in settling the rest of the roads." His rates for letters were to be a penny for England, 2d for Scotland and 4d for Ireland, with small commodities carried for 3d an ounce. He, like Oxenbridge and Thomson, petitioned the Council on the matter, his petition of April 1655 bearing the title, "How the whole business of the postage of letters may be best managed." His brief pamphlet appeared in print four years later, and served to perpetuate an interesting incident in postal history. As late as 1659 he still had hopes of convincing all "unbiassed persons of the unreasonableness of the farming of the carriage of letters," and hoped to move

[13] Hyde, *op. cit.*, pp. 226-29.
[14] *Cal. S.P. Dom.*, 1653-54, 372; 1654, 23; 1690-91, 10.
[15] The subtitle reads: "or a Vindication of the Liberty and Birthright of Every *Englishman* in Carrying Merchants & other men's *Letters* against restraint of Farmers of such Employments. By John Hill, London, 1659." It is a much-overrated pamphlet, poorly composed, and with but seven pages of text. There is a copy in the British Museum. See H. B. Wheatley, "Post-Office Reform" in the (London) *Academy*, XVI, 463-65. This article, and the title of the pamphlet, may account for John Hill's undeserved place in postal history.
[16] *A Penny Post*, p. 3.

the public in this matter "before a full and free parliament convene."[17] The coincidence of the name of this advocate of a penny post with the nineteenth century penny postage reformer, Rowland Hill, has led to undue emphasis on John Hill. Rowland Hill was not a descendant of the seventeenth century "undertaker," nor did he know of the pamphlet called *A Penny Post* until after his own plan was in operation. He would have obtained no help from the pamphlet had he read it.[18]

It was such competition that led to an ordinance of September 2, 1654, by which the "Lord Protector by and with the consent of His Council" confirmed to John Manley "the said office of the Postage of Letters both Inland and Foreign." The terms of the ordinance are already familiar to readers of this account. Franking was allowed for letters or packets in the service of the state. The postage of other letters was limited to the original proposals that prompted the bids, the cheapest rate being 2d for single letters within eighty miles of London. Double letters were to be charged double and "treble or greater Packets of Letters proportionably [sic]." There was to be a weekly packet service with Ireland, as well as a weekly service "for the Foreign Posts, as hath been formerly used and accustomed."[19]

The speed of carriers was to be the familiar seven miles an hour in summer and five in winter. Horses were to be in readiness at the stages so that the delay of not more than a "quarter of an hour at most" should occur. Speed was to be assured by an order that no other person should ride with the "Post that carrieth the Male." Persons could use the post for riding only if particularly authorized. They were to be charged no more than 3d a mile, and were not to ride a horse more than one stage without the consent of the postmaster. The monopolistic nature of the contract was emphasized in the ordinance: no other persons "shall be allowed or suffered to set up any Post, or keep Horses, or any Packet-Boat or Boats for the carrying, or sending of Letters Inland or Foreign."

Men like Oxenbridge, Thomson and Hill were unsuccessful largely because the Protector and his Council found eternal vigilance the price they had to pay for continuance in power. The mails and the use of post horses were supervised with an effectiveness that was regally autocratic. The private instructions issued to the postmasters at the end of 1653 are very revealing. The deputies were to be dis-

[17] *Ibid.*, p. 7. [18] G. B. Hill, *The Life of Sir Rowland Hill*, II, 29.
[19] Firth & Rait, *op. cit.*, II, 1007-13.

creet men, and they were not to receive private packets of letters, but "if any such were given them to send them up to me." Every letter received and sent was to be certified "up to London." Even if no one was to ride post without warrant, nevertheless the names and qualities of all who rode post were to be kept. The postmasters were to be vigilant to discover any designs against His Highness or the state. "Have an eye upon the disaffected who live near you: observe their meetings and conversations." The postmasters were cautioned not to communicate these instructions to anyone. No wonder Oxenbridge had trouble. The Post Office had taken on functions quite foreign to the "free carriage" of letters.[20]

Suspected letters were constantly opened. John Thurloe, the Secretary of State, had in his employ an expert letter-opener in the person of Isaac Dorislaus, the younger. He worked in a secret room "adjoyning to the forreign office, and every post night about eleven o'clock he went into that room privately." The large collection of Thurloe's state papers shows that this was being done even before the end of Manley's contract. In June 1653, for example, Dorislaus wrote to Thurloe: "I have been up all night. The enclosed are my last nights worke. . . . I am very sleepy, and will tell you more of my mind at Whitehall." From June through October of 1653 some eighty-five "intercepted" letters are recorded in Thurloe's state papers.[21]

Manley's contract continued for slightly more than two years, to the end of July 1655. The Post Office was then put directly under the control of Secretary Thurloe, at the same price, £10,000 a year, that Manley had paid for the farm. This step is strikingly similar to that taken by Charles and Secretary Coke in the late thirties when they, too, found their difficulties increasing. The Cromwellian orders of August 1655 restate the conditions for the service much as we have already found them. Letters were to be delivered by each postmaster in the nearby country, and he was to be paid "according to the tax on the letters, except such as are marked postpaid." The time of receipt was to be indicated on the packets by a "label fastened to the packet, and not on the packet or letter as before." The orders of the Protector indicate as well that "our chief secretary of state" is to have charge of both foreign and inland service "to insure security

[20] *Cal. S.P. Dom.*, 1653-54, 328.
[21] C. H. Firth, "Thurloe and the Post Office," *Eng. Hist. Rev.*, XIII, 527-33; *D.N.B.*, XV, 244. *A Collection*, etc., II, 303, and VI, 85, where detailed private instructions to the postmaster of Leeds are given.

and expedition." One suspects that expedition was less important than security.[22]

This completes the record of the Post Office during two tempestuous decades, save to note that the second Parliament of the Protector passed an act in 1657 "for settling the Postage of England, Scotland and Ireland." This is the first regulation by an act of Parliament of a Post Office for the British Isles as a whole. The precautionary attitude of Cromwell and Thurloe is justified by the erection of "one general Post Office" that will not only benefit the "People of these Nations," but will "discover and prevent many dangerous and wicked designs, which have been, and are daily contrived against the Peace and Welfare of this Commonwealth, the intelligence whereof cannot well be Communicated but by letter." The only exception to the monopoly was the carriage of letters by the "common known" carriers of goods "along with their Carts, Wagons, and Pack-Horses, and Letters of Advice of Merchants." Persons were allowed, of course, to send letters within the "said Nations" by messengers "on purpose for their own Affairs."[23]

The rates charged under the Act are worth noting: they serve as the basis for later practice. The cost for letters not going more than eighty miles from London was 2d, 4d and 6d, depending on whether the letter was single, double or triple. If the packet was of greater bulk, it was charged at the rate of 8d the ounce. Rates within Ireland appeared for the first time, 2d within forty miles of Dublin, and 4d for single letters beyond that radius. Scottish rates were not given, save that letters between London and Scotland were 4d, single. Persons riding through post or in post paid 2½d the mile, besides the guide's groat for every stage.[24]

The Act also gives rates for letters that were sent abroad. The charge was 1s for single letters and 3s 9d the ounce for letters to Leghorn, Genoa, Florence, Lyons, Marseilles, Smyrna, Aleppo and Constantinople. Ninepence single and 2s the ounce was the charge to Bordeaux, La Rochelle, Nantes, Bayonne, Cadiz and Madrid. A single letter cost 8d to "Hamborough, Frankfort and Collogne,"

---

[22] *Cal. S.P. Dom.*, 1655, 138, 285-86; *Secret Com. on P.O.*, H.C. (1844), pp. 71-72.

[23] Firth & Rait, *op. cit.*, II, 1110-13; *Journal H.C.*, VII, 541, 549, 551-53.

[24] The mile still varied in length in different parts of the British Isles. It was not to be standardized until Ogilby's survey in 1675. See above, p. 14n, and below p. 62. The high rates for Ireland are partly explained by the length of the Irish mile: it was more than 2200 yards in length.

and is to "Danzicke, Lipswiche, Lubecke, Stockholme, Copenhaven, Elsnore and Queensborough."

The Restoration was at hand. With the coming of Charles II the Post Office was to be re-established on something like a permanent foundation after more than two decades of unsettlement and confusion.

The Post Office
of the Restoration

WHEN Charles II returned to England in 1660 he took the position that the years since his father's death in 1649 were the first eleven years of his own reign, and that the government of England by Commonwealth and Protectorate during his absence was illegal. The "pretended" Post Office Act of 1657 was not recognized, in consequence, even if the basic principles contained in its provisions might have proved of value. As a result, the Convention Parliament of 1660—it had been convened to recall the King—passed an act "for erecting and establishing a Post Office." The measure became law just at the close of the year, one of the last passed by this Parliament. The Act of 1660, which "legally settled" the Post Office, became the first of a long series of laws for the regulation of postal matters. It is so fundamental that it became known as the Post Office Charter.[1]

It provided for a well-ordered establishment to furnish "speedy and safe dispatches" and to prevent the "many inconveniences happening by private posts." One general Post Office was erected under a Postmaster-General to be appointed by the King for life or a term of ten years, who was to pay a yearly rental such as the King may "think fit for the best advantage and benefit of the kingdom." The Postmaster-General was granted the exclusive right of providing horses for those riding through post or in post with or without commission. If the postmaster at a station did not furnish the needed horses within half an hour, the person riding in post was at liberty

---

[1] 12 Car. II., c.35 (1660); *1st Rep. P.M.G.* (1855), p. 8; *Parl. Hist.*, IV, 166.

to obtain horses where he could. Posting rates were 3d the mile and 4d for the guide for every stage.[2]

The rates were similar to those in the Cromwellian Act. A one-sheet letter was to be carried eighty miles for 2d, and beyond that distance for 3d. This was for England. Beyond Berwick on the Border the rates were 2d for the first forty miles and 4d for greater distances. The rate to Dublin for single letters was 6d, and in Ireland the charge was 2d for the first forty miles from Dublin, and 4d beyond. For all distances, two sheets were charged double, and so on, save that packets of "writs, deeds and other things" went at the quadruple rate for every ounce.

The foreign rates did not differ greatly from those of the previous Act. Single letters from Rouen and nearby places, if postpaid to Rouen, cost 6d. From Calais, Dieppe and Boulogne the charge was 4d, from Paris 9d, and from central France, if postpaid to Paris, 1s. Single letters from Germany, with postage paid to Antwerp, cost 8d, from Italy by way of Venice 9d, and by way of Lyons 1s, if postpaid to Lyons. Single letters to and from Flanders and Holland were charged 8d. An interesting provision applied to letters that were to go to Turkey from Marseilles, Venice or Leghorn: they were allowed to have "covers" free of the charge for an extra sheet of paper, provided the enveloping paper did not exceed the fourth part of a sheet.

The Postmaster-General was to continue "constant posts for the carriage of letters to all places, though they lie out of the post roads, as hath been used for the space of three years last past." Special mention was made of Kendal, Penrith, Lincoln and Grimsby as entitled to a weekly post, and of some Cornish towns, including Truro and Penryn, that were to be served twice a week. Inland letters were to be paid for at the place last delivered, though they could be prepaid if the sender so desired.

The appointment of the Postmaster-General had been made before the passing of the Act when John Thurloe was succeeded in the summer by Col. Henry Bishop of Henfield, Sussex. The Post Office was farmed out much as before, save that the amount due for the farm was greatly increased. By 1660 the proceeds of the farm were so much in excess of the £10,000 paid by Thurloe that Henry Bish-

---

[2] This was no change from the former payment to the guide of a groat. The groat, a fourpenny piece, was not issued after 1662.

op's contract called for a rental of £21,500 annually—clear evidence of the rapid growth in communication.[3]

No provision was made for the free carriage of letters, a privilege that had been granted by the Council of State in 1652 and was confirmed in the ordinance of 1654.[4] Debate on the Post Office Bill of 1660 in the House of Commons included franking. When a proviso for the letters of members of Parliament to go free was proposed, some of the members were greatly ashamed of the idea, one asserting that it was below "the honour of this house." The Speaker, Sir Harbottle Grimston, was so opposed that he was unwilling at first even to put it to a vote. It carried, nevertheless, and became a part of the bill, only to be thrown out by the House of Lords. The clause to which the Lords objected was worded: "that all the letters, which at any time hereafter, be sent by or unto any of the knights, citizens, and burgesses chosen and continuing to be members of the parliament, . . shall be freely, and without any charge to them, safely carried and conveyed by all and every letter-post established by this act."[5]

Franking continued, however, despite the disgruntled House of Lords. Bishop's indenture required him to carry "the single Inland Letters only of the members of the present Parliament during the continuance of this Session of this Parliament," as well as the mail of some of the principal officers of state. A warrant of February 1661 granted the farmer over £500 on his quarter's rent for carrying "over and above all their single letters" the packets and parcels of the members of the "late Parliament." The members, it would seem, refused to pay any postage, and the farmer was unable to collect it "by reason of the privilege of Parliament." A royal warrant of May 14, 1661, continued this concession. It declared: "The King being informed by the principal Secretaries of State that the members of Parliament seem unwilling to pay for the postage of their letters during the sitting of Parliament, his Majesty was thereupon graciously pleased to give direction to the farmers of his Post Office, that all single letters, but not packets, sent by the Post Office, to or

---

[3] Bishop's term began June 25, and was to run for seven years, not ten. For the contract, see *Secret Com. on P.O.*, H.C. (1844), pp. 76-78; *H.M.C. Rep.* IV, 329; VII, 140; *Cal. Tr.B.*, I, 210; *Cal. S.P. Dom.*, 1660-61, 209, 252.

[4] See above, pp. 40, 44.

[5] *Parl. Hist.*, IV, 163; IX, 843. The latter reference is for the year 1735, when the whole matter of franking came up for review. See below, p. 113.

from any member of either House of Parliament, go free, without payment of anything for the port thereof."[6]

The years of transition must have been tempestuous. The spoils went to the victors in no uncertain way. Many of the postmasters were turned out on grounds of loyalty to the previous regime. Those who had suffered under the Cromwellian rule or had been displaced in their jobs as postmasters sought their places again. Robert Hutchins asked for the post office of Crewkerne, long held by his ancestors. Joseph Strubie of Ware desired to oust the holder of that post office on the ground that the latter was "disaffected to government." George Cooling asked the post at Doncaster "in place of Thomas Bradford put in by the late pretended Protector." Richard Rosser, in asking for the post at Exeter, asserted that he had been a "constant sufferer from the tyranny of His Majesty's enemies." He would have hesitated to mention his sufferings "in the joy of the Restoration" were it not for his "wife and children, those patient partakers of all his troubles." John Slocombe wanted the office at Staines, the present holder being a dangerous man, "put in by the tyrant Oliver." Thomas Taylor asked for the post at Tadcaster, "in which his ancestors have served since Queen Elizabeth's time, and where his father was murdered by Lord Fairfax for carrying an express to Prince Rupert." Many other requests of like purport could be called to witness the thoroughness of the reshuffle that took place in 1660.[7]

With some of the petitioners we are already familiar. William Witherings petitioned for the restoration of the Foreign Letter Office, which his uncle Thomas had held. William claimed to have held it after his uncle's death until 1653, when he was ousted and never got it back. Frizell sought the superintendence after seventeen years of banishment. James Hickes asked to retain the office of clerk at the Post Office, which he had held for nine years, on the ground that his aged father was killed at Edgehill, and because he, the petitioner, had settled the Bristol and York posts. George Porter, as the deputy of the "very aged and infirm Stanhope," asked for the Post Office, and Stanhope petitioned for the recognition of his patent on his own account. Henry Robinson's son also petitioned on the basis of the claim that stemmed from the original Stanhope patent.[8]

[6] *Parl. Hist.*, IX, 844; *Secret Com. on P.O.*, H.C. (1844), pp. 77, 83; *Cal. S.P. Dom.*, 1660-61, 252, 277-78; *Cal. Tr.B.*, I, 210.

[7] *Cal. S.P. Dom.*, 1660-61, 83, 93-100.

[8] *Ibid.*, 1660-61, 93, 94, 445; 1665-66, 161; *H.M.C. Rep.*, VII, 82, 109, 154.

Henry Bishop was recognized, however, as having a valid claim, even though the grant had been made previous to act of Parliament. Both Stanhope and Witherings were bought off, and Frizell and Hickes found service in the Post Office.[9] Any "intruders" were to be severely punished. The penalty was £5 for every offense, and £100 for each week that any offender should maintain any "foot post, horse post, coach post or pacquet boat." But the new Postmaster-General did not prosper. He embittered the postmasters of the stages by lowering their wages, requiring them to purchase their places and "to give unheard of security by bond not to disclose the conditions they make with him."[10] This curious requirement, however, does not seem to have been the real cause for his resignation of the farm. The accusation of continuing "disaffected" persons in the Post Office service was the charge, real or fancied, that led to the ousting of Bishop. Nor is it surprising, since there was growing rigor against former Cromwellians and sectaries. The Cavalier Parliament—the one that succeeded the Parliament that had set up the "restored" Post Office—dealt much more harshly with the sectaries by its Clarendon Code, and with all who might be suspected of qualified loyalty.

Henry Bishop was replaced in 1663 by Daniel O'Neale. This prominent royalist, who had fought for Charles in the Civil War, must have wanted this profitable farm very badly, as he offered Bishop £8000 for resigning his grant, and gave the Secretary of State, Henry Bennet—made Lord Arlington in that same year—£2000, in addition to £1000 annually during the time that the Bishop lease had to run. On O'Neale's death in the next year, his widow, Katherine Stanhope, the dowager Countess of Chesterfield, carried on until her death in 1667.[11]

The farming system continued after the death of the Countess of Chesterfield. Indeed, the lease of the Post Office was already allocated by 1666. The next Postmaster-General was to be two persons, Lord Arlington and John Berkeley, the first Baron. They succeeded

---

[9] *Cal. S.P. Dom.*, 1664-65, 489; *Cal. Tr.B.*, I, 81, 111, 223.

[10] *H.M.C. Rep.*, VII, 140.

[11] For O'Neale, see *D.N.B.*, XLII, 181-84, where his name is spelled O'Neill. For his wife, see *Cal. S.P. Dom.*, 1663-64, 122, 156, 497; 1664-65, 194. Her first husband, Henry, Lord Stanhope, died in 1634. Daniel O'Neale was her third husband. The Countess of Chesterfield was close to the royal family, and not unfitted to enjoy this rich reward for constancy. For O'Neale's lease, see *Secret Com. on P.O.*, H.C. (1844), pp. 86-88.

in the midsummer of 1667, with the grant to run for ten years. Lord Arlington is usually referred to as the Postmaster-General.[12]

In the meantime, the Duke of York, Charles' brother and later to become his successor as James II, had been granted the profits of the Post Office by an act of Parliament.[13] The sum of £5382 10s was reserved annually for the King's disposal. Out of this goodly sum came the wages for the court post, or carrier of the royal letters between the court and the nearest post office. The court post received 10s a day, or £182 10s a year. The remaining £5200 went as pensions to two women, the Duchess of Cleveland and Lady Green. It was not equally divided, however, between these "ladies": the Duchess of Cleveland, the well-known mistress of Charles II, received £4700, and Lady Green a paltry £500 as her annual reward. These untoward additions to the pension roll are early examples of what was to remain for long a heavy burden on the postal services, and to hamper any adequate effort to serve the public.[14]

The government clearly had no particular desire to serve the public through the Post Office, even though the increasing use of its facilities might well have counseled such a viewpoint. Growing postal profits were a royal monopoly, and the receipts were used for almost every purpose except the improvement of the service. In 1684 James II agreed in the articles of marriage for his daughter Anne— later the Queen—to settle £5000 annually on the newly married couple out of the profits of the Post Office. The postal income was also used for secret-service money, £3700 being so expended annually for a time in the sixties.[15]

Lord Arlington as Postmaster-General could not, of course, oversee the actual working of the Post Office. The real head during the first part of his overlordship was his brother, Sir John Bennet. Sir John, known as the Deputy Postmaster, incurred the ill will of the permanent staff by severe regulations as to the sending of letters and newsbooks free, and by reducing the postmasters' salaries from £40 to £20 a year. That veteran of the service, James Hickes, complained

[12] *Cal. S.P. Dom.*, 1664-65, 485; 1677-78, 123; *Cal. Tr.B.*, II, 159, 466; III, 271, 469, 523. Arlington was a Catholic and a member of the notorious Cabal.

[13] *Journal H.C.*, VIII, 491; 15 Car. II, c.14 (1663).

[14] *Cal. Tr.B.*, VIII, 226. £4700 was but a part of the munificence that Charles showered on the Duchess of Cleveland. See *D.N.B.*, LVIII, 314, where it is wrongly stated that this pension began in 1669. Violet Barbour, *Henry Bennet, Earl of Arlington* (1914), p. 101n, has £5382 10s paid by Arlington to the Duke of York for the farm!

[15] *Cal. Tr.B.*, VII, 1123; *H.M.C. Rep.*, Laing, 434.

for his fellows against restrictions that would lead him, for one, to withdraw and live on salt and water![16]

Sir John Bennet was succeeded in 1672 by John Ellis, and on the latter's death in the same year, Col. Roger Whitley became the deputy of the Postmaster-General. He held the position until 1677, when he was replaced by Sir Philip Frowde. Sir Philip, long connected with the service, proved a practical and successful superintendent: he continued until the end of Charles II's reign as the "Governor of the Post Office." When the Duke of York succeeded in 1685 as James II, the Post Office was continued under the direction of Sir Philip Frowde, though the nominal Postmaster-General was Laurence Hyde, the Earl of Rochester. Just at the end of the period another sizable pension was attached to the postal service: the Earl of Rochester obtained an annual grant of £4000 out of the Post Office receipts, "to run for two lives."[17]

During the Restoration the strict royal control of the Post Office led to abuses. As might be expected, the opening of letters by government officers continued during a time when plots were rife, and Charles was determined not to go on his travels again. When the Great Fire of 1666 burned down the General Letter Office, it destroyed a device for the expert opening and resealing of letters. This elaborate apparatus, so it seemed, could open letters whether they were fixed by seal or wafer, and do it so that no one could detect the tampering, and it was capable of reproducing handwriting in facsimile so exactly that the writer himself could not distinguish the original letter. The inventor, Samuel Morland, also declared that copies of letters of eight or ten pages could be made in as many minutes. The secret of the machine will never be known, for it died with the inventor. Charles II knew of the process and was so interested that he spent midnight hours testing its effectiveness.[18]

The idea of a device for opening letters survived the Fire, however, for the Dutch deputies were complaining in 1672—on the eve

[16] *Cal. S.P. Dom.*, 1667, 7, 248, 260.

[17] *Ibid.*, 1672, 282, 449; 1672-73, 8; 1678, 351; 1670-80, 15; *Cal. Tr.B.*, VI, 68; VIII, 461; IX, 279; *D.N.B.*, XXVIII, 397.

[18] A. Bryant, *King Charles II* (1931), p. 164; W. G. Bell, *The Great Fire of London* (1920), pp. 52-53, and the same writer's *Unknown London*. Morland had been in communication with the exiled Charles II at the time that he (Morland) was supposed to be serving Cromwell and Thurloe. In 1660 a part of Morland's pension of £500 was paid out of the profits of the Post Office, and as late as 1689 half of it was still coming from the same source. When William became King in 1689, Morland was desirous of reviving the device, but the King refused his consent. *Cal. Tr.B.*, I, 360; IX, p. cclxv.

of the war between Holland and England—of the opening of their letters at the General Post Office, "where by art they were resealed." Ten years later suspected letters were sent to the Secretary of State's office for inspection. In order to avoid this well-known inquisition, letters were commonly addressed to someone else than the real correspondent. The letters were then delivered personally to the one for whom they were intended. As the public came to use the facilities of the Post Office more freely, it was to grow much more concerned over this violation of the secrecy of correspondence.[19]

The General Letter Office in London was staffed by what would seem a small personnel. At the opening of the Restoration forty-three persons served the Inland Office, including officers, clerks and various assistants. Four more sufficed for the work of the Foreign Office. Although the two divisions were sharply separated, they were housed in the same building. In 1678 the two offices were removed from Bishopsgate Street to Lombard Street. They were kept as distinct establishments, partly because of the separate origin of the Foreign Office in the early years of the century, and partly because it was felt that the effectiveness of the foreign service was hampered if foreign letters were mixed with those that came into the Inland Office.[20]

By the end of the reign of Charles II the personnel was somewhat larger. It was headed by the Governor of the Post Office, Sir Philip Frowde, who was in charge of both branches. In the Inland Office there was a Comptroller, an Accomptant and two cashiers, besides a clerk for each of the six roads—the Chester Road, the North Road, the West Road to Exeter and Plymouth, the Bristol Road, the Yarmouth Road and the Kentish Road. The most important was the Chester Road; its clerk not only received the largest salary, but had an assistant. An alphabet man recorded the letters arriving for merchants, three window men received mail and the pay for its carriage, and a clerk checked undertaxed letters. Four sorters and another sorter for the paid letters—the paid and the unpaid letters were handled separately—a bye-night window man and several letter carriers, besides letter receivers and letter bringers, were also included.[21]

---

[19] See below, pp. 119 ff., 337 ff.; Cal. S.P. Dom., 1672, 403; 1676-77, 452, for the Dutch objections, and the sending of letters to the Secretary's office.

[20] Cal. S.P. Dom., 1667-78, 67; 1689-90, 59. R. C. Alcock and F. C. Holland, The Postmarks of Great Britain and Ireland, p. 18; J. G. Hendy, The History of the Early Postmarks of the British Isles, p. 52.

[21] The term "bye-night window man" or "clerk of the bye-nights" (see below, p. 110)

The Foreign Office division had its Comptroller, two sorters, an alphabet man, a rebate man, as well as letter receivers and letter carriers of its own. When foreign mails arrived letters for the court and for the great officers of state were delivered "to such messengers as are waiting" before any other persons received their letters. No others were to be given out "till the window of the office is open for general delivery."[22] In Col. Whitley's time, he "appeared at the office every post night and never goes to bed until the King's letters are come down," that is, are ready for the messengers. And Hickes, who was the clerk of the Chester Road, added: "Every person concerned here is positively forbidden to deliver any letter till the King's letters may be at court."

London had receiving stations where letters could be left and thence taken by the members of the staff to the General Office. It is not known just when these receiving offices were first put to use. In 1677 there seem to have been eight in the region from Pall Mall and Westminster to Gray's Inn Lane.[23] However, the main office was the only real post office for London. The duties there required much night work, by candlelight, of course. The staff lived for the most part in or near the office, because of the hours of their work. Most of the mails from the post roads arrived early in the morning, and the dispatch of the mails for the country took place shortly after midnight. Of ninety-five post labels preserved for the year 1666, four show departures at 3 A.M. and the remainder at 2 A.M. James Hickes, who had taken a house at London Stone, "which is not far from my business," complained that, at times, he was in the office until half past three in the morning, "though two is the time for going to bed." He wrote in 1678 to Williamson in the Secretary of State's office: "Yours came to hand at past three this morning, all our mails being gone, but were sent away express at past five. We were all gone to bed and they could not be dispatched until the Comptroller was up

---

has long been out of use. At this time mail for the main post roads left the London office only three nights a week (Tuesdays, Thursdays and Saturdays); on the other nights, the bye-nights, it departed for Kent only, and the Downs. Hence the phrase, "Clerk of the Kent Road bye-nights" in *Cal. Tr.B.*, VIII, 1283. Mails for the main post roads were not sent out every week day until the mid-eighteenth century. The *O.E.D.* defines the noun "by-night" as a "letter dispatched by the night post," and cites a use of 1766 for this doubtful definition. But all mails left London by night in the days of the horse post and the mail coach: only after 1830, with the advent of the railway, were day posts dispatched from London.

[22] *H.M.C. Rep.*, XV, pt. 1, pp. 19-20; *Cal. Tr.B.*, VIII, 1512; *Cal. S.P. Dom.*, 1661-62, 239; 1667, 260.

[23] Hendy, *op. cit.*, p. 50.

to sign the labels in Mr. Frowde's name, which he did immediately he arose."[24]

With the heart of the postal system centered in London, one can well imagine the dislocation caused by the disastrous plague of 1665 and the devastating fire of the following year. On account of the plague, the post was changed in August 1665 to avoid the transmission of letters through London. At the General Letter Office in London the mail was "aired over vinegar" in the hope of preventing the spread of the plague by correspondence. James Hickes reported at the time that the "Post Office is so fumed morning and night that they can hardly see each other." He added: "Had the contagion been catching by letters they had been dead long ago." Hickes proved faithful in trying times: he claimed to be the only member of the staff "who did not withdraw from the office during the sickness, when between twenty and thirty of them died."

When the Great Fire of 1666 began to eat its way towards the Post Office, James Hickes saved such packets as he could hastily remove, and settled the Post Office temporarily at the Sign of the Golden Lion in Red Cross Street outside Cripplegate. This was the night of Monday, September 3, the Fire having started its devastating course early Sunday morning. Thence he forwarded to Lord Arlington's secretary the state letters that had come by the Chester Road, with the comment: "How we shall dispose of our business, only the wise God knows." By Tuesday, September 4, Hickes and his family were at Barnet, whence he addressed the postmasters of the Chester Road: "I am commanded to tell you that letters for ministers of state are to be sent hither to me, that I may convey them to the Court. When the violence of the Fire is over, some place will be fixed upon for the general correspondence."[25]

When Hickes fled on the night of Monday, the Post Office was probably located in Dowgate not far from the river. It could not have been in Bishopsgate Street, as has been stated by various histories of the Post Office. The Fire never reached that part of London, and could not have burned down the Post Office on Tuesday or at a later date. For a time after the Fire Gresham College was used as an Exchange and Post Office. Sometime before 1678 the Post Office was located in Bishopsgate Street, and in that year it was re-

[24] *Cal. S. P. Dom.*, 1666-67, 388-89, 481; 1677-78, 654; 1678, 351. James Hickes' voluminous correspondence, as given in the *Cal. S.P. Dom.*, ended in 1678.

[25] *Ibid.*, 1666-67, 95; W. G. Bell, *The Great Fire of London*, pp. 52-53.

moved to Lombard Street where it was to remain for a century and a half. Before the Fire, a separate office for the Kentish and Sussex service had been located at the Round House in Love Lane near Billingsgate.[26]

Vigorous efforts were made to increase the speed of communication. One device was the stamping of letters. The so-called Bishop marks were described as follows: "A stamp is invented that is putt upon every letter shewing the day of the moneth that every letter comes to the office, so that no Letter Carryer may dare to detayne a letter from post to post, which before was usual."[27] These first postmarks for letters were confined, in London, to the Inland Office.

The first British postmarks—the Bishop marks.

The earliest type consisted of a simple circle divided horizontally, the two semicircles indicating the day and the month respectively. Postmarks of the early seventies have been found that may have been used at receiving houses, the number on the postmark indicating the number of the branch office. Stamps also exist with one or two initials representing the name of the person in charge of the receiving office.[28]

Another plan for speeding the carriage of letters was a suggestion made by Arlington to Frowde that a postal map be prepared that would give the names of the stage towns and the mileage between them, so that one might calculate easily how many hours any letter ought to take by the "ordinary" or by an "express" dispatch. A table of stages printed in 1669 was the "first essay in this matter." The

[26] *Cal. S.P. Dom.*, 1664-65, 517; 1670, 577, 713; *H.M.C. Rep.*, XII, App. VII, 41. Alcock and Holland, *op. cit.*, p. 18, has the Post Office in Bishopsgate Street from 1600 to 1678. Hyde, *op. cit.*, pp. 283-84, locates it in Bishopsgate at the time of the Fire. See Bell, *op. cit.*, p. 52n. Alcock & Holland, *op. cit.*, p. 18, pictures a fine oval stamp of the Round House office.

[27] *Ibid.*, p. 17; Hendy, *op. cit.*, pp. 3-4; *Cal. S.P. Dom.*, 1661-62, 57; 1664-65, 183.

[28] Alcock & Holland, *op. cit.*, pp. 17-18; T. Todd, *A History of British Postage Stamps*, pp. 17-18; C. L. Ewen, *The Earliest Postal Stamps, Introducing Some Recent Discoveries, passim.* Bishop marks are also known for the offices in Dublin and Edinburgh. C. L. Ewen has discovered that, for a short time in the sixties, a rectangular hand stamp was used in London to indicate postage due on letters from Scotland.

posts had difficulty, nevertheless, in keeping to a careful schedule on account of the "bad weather and the ill ways."

The most successful plan for increasing speed was the continued use of the post label. This device had long been customary with particular dispatches. The post label was valuable since it could check the carelessness of any particular postmaster on the road. An order of 1666 required the labels that were sent with the letters "to be signed by the postmasters stating the hour of arrival and dispatch of each mail." A complaint, for example, was received against the postmasters of the Derby Road: weekly mails had been coming in a day late. Thomas Palmer of Harborough was found to be the most guilty, for he did not date the labels. The postmaster at Ipswich, when blamed for keeping express letters and packets too long, replied that he kept them only to get the boy ready and to feed and saddle the horse. He insisted that he kept "as good horses and as pretty boys to perform the business as any postmaster in England." Printed directions as to speed were attached to the mail bags in 1667, with spaces left to be filled in by the postmasters at each stage, showing the times of arrival and dispatch.[29]

Despite all this care, the rates of travel do not show much improvement. Hickes wrote in 1665 that the postmaster at Reading and others should be punished, for they had been pressed in vain to show more activity, "or men will walk on foot faster than the postmaster rides." In May of the next year he complained of the slowness of the riding on the West Road: the posts from Plymouth on three successive days took "56, 55, and 57 hours, or between three and four miles an hour." On the Gloucester and Yarmouth roads the riding was at the rate of three and one half miles an hour, on the Bristol, Chester and York roads four miles. Labels for the North Road made clear that the "post is riding only three miles an hour and in some places less than two miles." A mail from Edinburgh left on November 18, 1666, at 3 A.M., and reached London on the 23rd at noon. This was considered a slow journey, as the ordinary run between the two capitals took less than five days. London was usually reached from Chester in a few hours over two full days, and from Plymouth in about the same time.[30]

---

[29] *Cal. S.P. Dom.*, 1667-68, 116-18, 384, 388-89, 510; 1665-66, 260; 1675-76, 179.

[30] *Ibid.*, 1665-66, 8, 403; 1666-67, 282, 388; 1667-68, 116-18; Hyde, *op. cit.*, p. 291. Other examples on the Great North Road: London, Nov. 7, 3 A.M., arriving in Edinburgh, Nov. 11, 9 A.M.; London, Dec. 2, 2 A.M., in Edinburgh, Dec. 6, 2 A.M.; London, Jan. 4, 2 A.M., Edinburgh, Jan. 8, at noon.

The journey from London to Bristol ordinarily took about thirty hours, if the postmasters were diligent. A condition that too often existed is illustrated by a reprimand of a postmaster on that road. "To Mr. Sadler, postmaster of Marlborough. I can no longer endure your shameful neglect of the mails. I have grievous complaints from Bristol of the prejudice they receive thereby; and find that it is 7, 8, 9 or 10 hours commonly betwixt you and Chippenham, which is but 15 miles, and ought to be performed in 3 hours. This is a most abominable shame and scandal to the office and I tell you, Mr. Sadler, in a few words (for I will not any more trouble to write you on the subject) that if this be not speedily amended, but the like abuse committed again, you may expect a messenger. . . . Be advised to look better about your business, or you will suffer for it." Another warning, this time to the postmaster at Monmouth: "I am tormented with complaints from the gentlemen of Glamorgan and Monmouthshire, of the neglect and slow coming of the mails. I observe the labels after they have passed Gloucester, commonly omitted to be dated. . . . I have writ so often on this subject that I am weary of it. . . . I pray let this neglect be amended or it will make a breach; consider well of it."[31]

The going and coming of a reply was, naturally, of great importance to the merchants. A letter leaving London at 2 A.M. of the first day would reach Bristol in the early morning of the second day, enabling the receiver to reply by the mail that left Bristol at 1 A.M. of the third day; the reply would reach London by daylight of the fourth day. Five days were necessary for a reply from Manchester, just over five days for one from Plymouth, just under five days from Chester. The return from Dublin depended so much on wind and weather that an estimate is of little value. Postally speaking, Dublin was farther than Edinburgh from London, as the journey usually took five or six days one way.

Speed might have been increased had serious efforts been made to improve the roads used by the postboys, for the older system of road repair by neighborhood men had broken down under the increasing strain put on the roads. Heavy stage wagons and coaches, as well as pack horses, were too much for the primitive system of road upkeep; seventeenth century roadmenders felt they were doing their duty by throwing stones of any size into ruts, in the hope that the traffic would crush them into shape. Roadmaking as a profession

---

[31] Letters of Roger Whitley in the next decade, as given in Hyde, *op. cit.*, pp. 308-10.

II PRINCIPAL ENGLISH AND WELSH
ROADS IN 1675
(According to John Ogilby)

Direct Roads
——— Independent
- - - - Dependent

0   20   40   60
Scale of miles

was not to develop until men like Metcalf, Telford and McAdam were to introduce more intelligent methods.

The need for better highways was recognized early in the reign of Charles II when the first of a long series of turnpike acts was passed in 1663. This Act provided for keeping in repair sections of the Great North Road near the London terminus, in Hertford, Cambridge and Huntingdon. The preamble of the bill declared that this "ancient highway and post-road" had become "very ruinous and almost impassable, insomuch that it is become very dangerous to His Majesty's liege people that pass that way." A provision in the Act exempted posts from tolls. This method of keeping up a road was not applied extensively for some time. A quarter-century elapsed before another turnpike act was sought.[32]

The increased interest in travel is well illustrated by an elaborate survey of the roads of England and Wales during this time. John Ogilby "actually admeasured and delineated" the roads at this time by a survey that displaced the older reckonings of distance that had been in use for centuries. The statute mile of 1760 yards became the standard after Ogilby's survey, though local custom still continued the older reckonings in many regions.[33] Ogilby became Royal Cosmographer about 1671, the warrant providing for any needed help "in affixing of sufficient Marks for the better direction of Travellers and Ascertaining the Distances from Stage to Stage in Our said Kingdom." Two printed results of his surveys appeared in 1675: both contained elaborate maps on "imaginary scrolls" that were so arranged as to form a continuous itinerary for any given road. Mileage was indicated along with the various identifying natural features, such as hills, streams, bridges, arable and hedges.[34] The distances

[32] See below, p. 127. For further information, see E. A. Pratt, *A History of Inland Transport and Communication in England*, chap. IX; Joan Parkes, *Travel in England in the Seventeenth Century*, pp. 25-27. For the acts relating to roads, see 15 Car. II, c.1; 7 & 8 Wm. III, cc.9, 26; 8 & 9 Wm. III, c.16; 9 & 10 Wm. III, c.18.

[33] See above, pp. 14n, 46n.

[34] The titles of the two works are *Britannia . . . a Geographical and Historical Description of the Principal Roads thereof, etc.* and *Itinerarium Angliae: or a Book of the Roads, Wherein are Contained the Principal Road-Ways of His Majesty's Kingdom of England and Dominion of Wales*. The maps in the two forms are the same, but some additional written material appeared in the *Britannia* on the "Post Roads of England." A second edition of the *Britannia* appeared in 1698. After Ogilby's death in 1676, his collaborator, William Morgan, succeeded as Royal Cosmographer. In that same year appeared the first edition of the *Pocket-Book of the Roads of England and Wales*, to be followed by numerous editions, the 24th and last coming out in 1794. Through them, Ogilby dominated for more than a century the road-book literature of England. See "John Ogilby (1600-1675). His *Britannia* and the British Itineraries of the 18th Century" by Sir George Herbert Fordham in *The Library*, 4th series, vol. 6. no. 2 (1925).

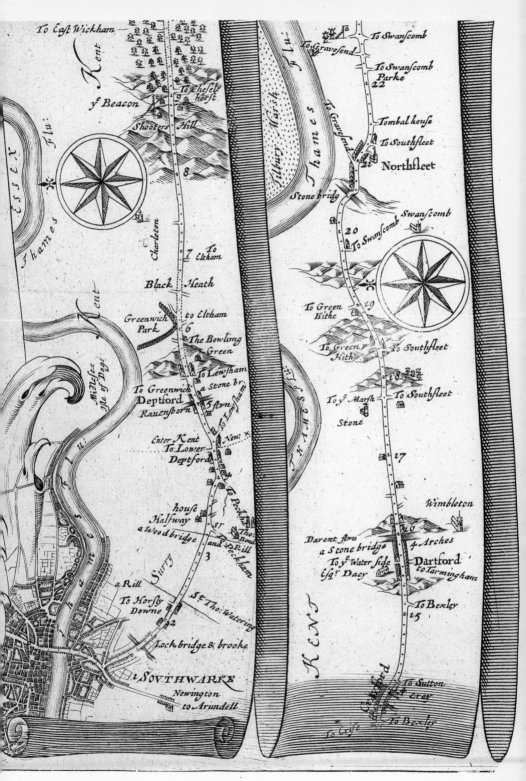

III. OGILBY'S MAP OF THE LONDON END OF THE DOVER ROAD, 1675

Note the mileage marks. Only parts of the first stretches of the road are shown.

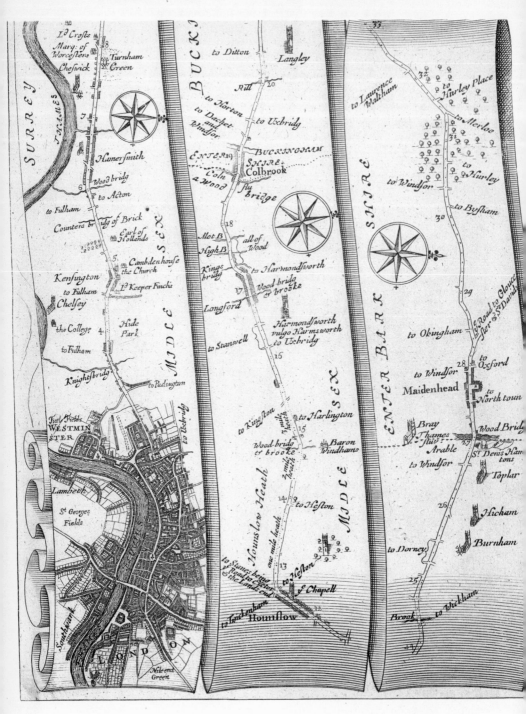

IV. OGILBY'S MAP OF THE LONDON END OF THE BRISTOL ROAD, 1675

between London and some of the principal towns were reckoned by Ogilby as follows: to York 192 miles, to Berwick 339, to Bristol 115, to Chester 182, to Haverford West 254, to Holyhead 269, to Exeter 172, to Plymouth 216, to Dover 71, to Harwich 70, to Portsmouth 73 miles.[35]

In various ways the foundations were being laid for a better postal service.

[35] Reference to a modern guide shows that the length of the main roads has changed but slightly since Ogilby's day. Muirhead's *England* has the motor road to Bristol as 118 miles, to Exeter via Salisbury 172 miles, to Portsmouth 72 miles.

The Rise of Byposts
and the London Penny Post

THE Charter of 1660 required the Postmaster-General to continue "constant posts for the carriage of letters to all places, though they lie out of the post roads, as hath been used for the space of three years last past." The post roads consisted, even as late as 1660, of some half-dozen main routes. They were like the spokes of a great wheel, the hub being London with the six spokes of uneven length radiating from this center. These main post roads had been set up originally for royal convenience, the objective usually being the end of the route. The road to Dover was important because it made connections with the Continent and not because it served Canterbury and Dover, that to Berwick served as the route to Scotland, the one that led to Chester and Holyhead was of importance because it was the road to Dublin.

In the course of time, however, important centers of town life and of developing trade grew into numerous urban centers in England, many of them not located, originally, on one of the main post roads. The growth of such towns as York, Hull, Norwich, Lincoln, Derby, Sheffield and Leeds, to mention a few examples, required postal communication. It was not provided by the older arrangements.

Another inconvenience that needed correction was the absence of direct and shorter routes between towns that were on different post roads. Chester on the West Road, for example, might want to communicate with Bristol, or Bristol with Exeter. The earlier arrangement had been very roundabout. A letter from Chester to Bristol would have to go by way of the General Letter Office in London, first coming up to London via the West Road, and then going to Bristol on the post road that led that way. This was not only slow but expensive, for the mileage charged for a letter was the distance it actually traveled, not the shortest distance across country between the two towns.

The need for laying out branches for the main post roads was being felt before 1660, and was met to some degree. One recalls, in that connection, the ambitious plans made during the regime of Secretary Coke three decades earlier. The Restoration saw the introduction of additional branch roads and of cross-road connections as well. These additions were tending to make the ill-shaped wheel of the main post roads into a web of routes that would in time gossamer the whole land.

A word about terminology before extensions of this sort are considered. The word "bypost" appears at first to refer to any service of less importance than that of the main roads, and a by-letter would be one carried on a subsidiary route. Thus Ralph Allen, whose work we shall examine in a later chapter, received in 1720 the "farm of all the Bye Way and Cross-post Letters." A cross post was definitely a service settled between post towns on different main roads, such as the later cross post between Bristol and Chester, two towns that have already been used as examples of the need for a more direct postal service. The word "by-letter" might also mean a letter that did not touch the General Letter Office in London as it made its journey from writer to receiver. A cross post could carry a by-letter from Bristol to Chester, but if the letter went from Bristol to Chester via London it was not a by-letter. The word "by-letter" also applied to letters that traveled the same post road but stopped short of London. Thus, letters from Doncaster to Alnwick, Canterbury to Rochester, Chester to Lichfield would be by-letters. The postal Act of 1711— the next important one after that of 1660—required the postmasters to charge according to distance for letters carried in "cross stages, as for all by or way letters and packets."

The carriage of letters to places that "lie out of the post roads" had begun before the Restoration. The Act of 1660 made special provision for a weekly post to Kendal by way of Lancaster, to Penrith in Cumberland by way of Newcastle and Carlisle, to the city of Lincoln, as well as a post twice a week in Cornwall by way of Truro and Penryn.[1] A post had been established before 1660 between Lon-

[1] See above, p. 49.

don and the towns of Yarmouth and Norwich. According to a petition of James Grover in that year, he claimed to be the first to establish this post, which was "now going three times a week instead of
twice." Grover had been the postmaster at Ipswich for forty years.
James Hickes, by now a familiar postal employee to the reader,
stated in the same year, 1660, that he had "settled" the Bristol and
York posts, that is, had laid them out. Hickes asserted also that he
sent the first letter from Nantwich to London by post in 1637. A
strange claim, indeed, since Nantwich had been a stage on the main
post road from London to Chester back in the days of Elizabeth.[2]

A number of important branch roads, also, had been settled before
1660. Thomas Challenor of Stone asked for the post of that town—
it was the next stage east of Nantwich on the Chester Road—on the
ground that he had formed the branches on the Chester Road,
"which had been an example to others." He complained in 1660
that he had been deprived of his just profits back in 1648. Another
petition of 1660 asked for the right "to carry the Post Letters, as a
bye-post between Leeds and Ferrybridge," this serving as the branch
that connected Leeds with the nearest station on the Great North
Road.[3] In 1660 the important town of Derby was first connected
with the Chester Road by a branch that came into this road at Towcester. We have already noticed a criticism of one of the postmasters
on this branch, Thomas Palmer of Harborough, for his delay of the
mails.[4] By the Restoration, Sheffield was of sufficient importance
that Postmaster-General O'Neale erected a post in 1663 to travel
between London and Sheffield with arrangements so made that "letters can be dispatched from adjacent towns to meet the post."
Clearly, this sort of extension of the postal service had become a
settled policy early in the reign of Charles II. A proclamation of
1669 for preventing common carriers from infringing on the Duke
of York's profits declared that posts were to be established on the
byroads "by 29 September next." At this time, the leading roads
were considered to be the Great North Road, and those to Chester
and on to Holyhead, to Bristol and on to south Wales, to Dover and
Rye, to Bristol and on to Plymouth, to Norwich, to Derby, to Yarmouth and to Portsmouth.[5]

[2] See above, p. 20. *Cal. S.P. Dom.*, 1660-61, 94, 97; 1670, 578; *H.M.C. Rep.*, Salisbury, IX, 97, 113, 152.
[3] *Cal. S.P. Dom.*, 1660-61, 94, 100.
[4] See above, p. 59, and Parkes, *op. cit.*, p. 53n.
[5] *Cal. S.P. Dom.*, 1663-64, 409; 1667, 499; 1668-69, 376.

If the government really intended to carry out the extension of the byroad posts in 1669, it did little if anything about it. Fourteen years later, another proclamation declared that "after 14 September next all considerable market towns will be connected with the next post office stage," and the promise was explicit that posts were "to be set up on the bye roads."[6] Sir Philip Frowde, the Governor of the Post Office, was instructed in 1685 to see that a riding surveyor view the roads and establish posts "where there are none," an order that seems to have been prompted by the needs of Buckingham and Aylesbury, for these towns are specifically mentioned in the order. An additional indication of the need for expansion was Frowde's recommendation of salary increases for the clerks in the London office. He justified the request by the statement: "The number of letters in the post office is very much of late increased."[7]

One of the best proofs that the authorities did not extend the regular services rapidly enough to meet the growing demand was the widespread use of illegal means of sending letters. The official records of these years contain many references to efforts at curbing the "secret conveyance" of letters and packets. The infringers were of various kinds, and used diverse conveyances. Carriers, it would seem, transported letters that did not concern their goods; it was declared in 1669 that the Act of 1660 "is daily infringed upon by the common carriers of goods." Stage wagons were also used. These long, covered four-wheeled vehicles—not unlike a "prairie schooner" in appearance—were for the use of passengers, and had been making their journeys between English towns for much of the seventeenth century. But they were very slow, as the horses were not changed at stages, even though the names for these vehicles would seem to imply this. They were not supposed to be used for carrying letters, although there was no prohibition of the carriage of letters by passengers in these stage wagons, provided it was not done as a regular practice.

The stage wagons were used only by the lower classes. They became even less attractive as the coaches extended the area of their activities farther and farther from London. Hackney coaches had been in considerable use in London before the Restoration. At first, they were so uncomfortable that one wonders why the stigma of effeminacy should have been leveled at their users. But the appear-

6 *Ibid.*, 1683, 328; Parkes, *op. cit.*, p. 56.
7 *Cal. Tr.B.*, VIII, 264, 1848.

ance and comfort of the coach gradually improved; even glass windows began to appear during the Restoration. By 1662 hackney coaches were so numerous that a law of that year—13 & 14 Car. II, c.2—required that they have a license and limited their number in London to four hundred. As a result, many of them scattered to the small towns within easy reach of London, and set up as stages. This proved very unpopular with the postmasters, not only because it led to less business in the hiring of post horses, but to the carriage of letters by the coaches. Among the reasons that John Cresset presented to the government in 1672 for suppressing all hackney coaches was their carriage of "multitudes of letters." He declared, too, that there were large numbers of coaches "in all parts of the kingdom."[8]

The stage coach grew in popularity after 1660. Indeed, their number so increased in the reign of Charles II as to produce something like a revolution in travel. The first important long-distance service was on the Chester Road. An advertisement of 1675 announced that a stage coach would leave every Monday, Wednesday and Friday from London for Westchester, and on the same days from Westchester for London. The advertised time was four days for the journey. But the proprietors seem to have been overconfident, for two years later they are announcing the length of the trip as five days; ten years later they are satisfied with promising to do the journey in six days. An interesting feature of this coach trip was the change of horses once a day. The more common procedure in the seventeenth century was the completion of the whole trip without recourse to fresh horses. About the same time, stage coaches for Exeter and also for York were advertised as consuming four days for each of these journeys. In 1667 a London and Oxford coach undertook to perform that journey of some fifty miles in two days. The first of the coaches to use the famed Bath Road also began in that year. It was known as a "Flying Machine," said "machine" undertaking to "perform the Whole Journey in Three Days, if God permit."[9]

The state of the roads, however, was such that these advertised times were more often honored in the breach than in the observance. Nor must it be assumed that the service was a year-round offering in the early days of long stage-coach trips: customarily the coaches resumed running in the spring. Yet by the end of Charles II's reign

[8] *Cal. S.P. Dom.*, 1672-73, 64; Parkes, *op. cit.*, pp. 84, 92-94.
[9] C. G. Harper, *Stage-Coach and Mail in Days of Yore*, I, 60-70.

there were some seventy coaches doing long distances, five serving Bath and Bristol, and four traveling to Exeter. Chamberlayne in the 1684 edition of his *Angliae Notitia, or the Present State of England* extols this new method of travel: "There is of late such an admirable commodiousness for both men and women to travel from London to the principal towns in the country, that the like hath not been known in the world." Chamberlayne was overly enthusiastic, for the accommodation offered in the seventeenth century was one that carried passengers at some four miles an hour, under conditions that Englishmen would have scorned a century later. A service of which to be proud had to await better roads and greater concentrations of population, and only in time would the stage coach be so improved in comfort and in speed that it would serve as the precursor of the mail coach.[10]

The rise of stage coaches for long journeys worried the Post Office. It complained in 1678 that a royal speech was not given the Post Office to send by post. As a result, declared its officials, the "sneaking booksellers will send them by their carriers and stage coaches." A few years later, in 1683, a proclamation was issued for the protection of the Duke of York's postal profits. None but the postmasters were to collect or deliver letters, nor could anyone set up "post coaches or packets or carriers" to carry letters except such as relate to their goods, nor could the stage-coach drivers convey letters. The same proclamation promised the setting-up of posts on the byroads. As usual, the government was far behind the growing postal necessities and public wishes in the matter of communication. An obvious way of meeting the illicit conveyance of letters would have been to furnish adequate services of a legal sort. But that was asking too much of a Post Office that was in the Duke of York's possession.[11]

An even more interesting illustration of governmental backwardness was the effort, at this time, to furnish London with a better local service. During these years a private penny post arose in London, although a more inopportune time, it would seem, could hardly have been chosen for starting such a venture. Two years before Dockwra set up his Penny Post in 1680, Titus Oates had made rev-

[10] See Parkes, *op. cit.*, p. 86; W. T. Jackman, *The Development of Transportation in Modern England*, pp. 109 ff., 134-38; Harper, *op. cit.*, pp. 77-79.
[11] *Cal. S.P. Dom.*, 1678, 478; 1683, 328.

elations with regard to a popish plot. And in 1680 the fear of such plots was still at fever point. The cry for the exclusion of the Duke of York from the succession to the throne, and such slogans as "No Popery, No Slavery," kept London in a constant dither. It was in such an atmosphere that a merchant, William Dockwra, who had been a subsearcher in the Customs House, set up a penny postal service for London and Westminster.

Such a service was badly needed. The Post Office had made even less adequate provision for London than for the smaller urban communities elsewhere in England. There was but one General Letter Office in London, though receiving houses for London letters were already in use, that is, for London letters that were going out of town. A Londoner could send a letter to Edinburgh or Exeter or even suburban Barnet with little trouble, but the Post Office offered no provision for sending a letter from Westminster to Blackwall in the eastern part of London, or from Hackney in the north to Lambeth or Southwark on the south side of the Thames. The disregard of this obvious use of the Post Office is astonishing if we realize that at least one in ten of the total population of England lived in the sprawling metropolis: London had at the time about half a million people in its various parishes. When Dockwra later justified his setting up of the London Penny Post, he declared that the chief cause was the rapid growth of London "with vast additions of buildings and great increase of inhabitants." He gave as another reason the great expense of using servants for this purpose, an excessive burden for those wishing to send letters and parcels within London.[12] What is more, letters that came from outside the metropolis were not delivered by the Post Office to the various houses, nor even sent to districts. They had to be called for at the General Letter Office by the persons for whom they were intended, or by their servants, or by messengers who were regularly hired for the purpose.

The new service furnished by William Dockwra and his associates began on April 1, 1680. The broadside that announced the unheard-of facilities reads as follows: "A Penny Well Bestowed, or a Brief Account of the New Design contrived for the great Increase of Trade, and Ease of Correspondence, to the great Advantage of the Inhabitants of all sorts, by Conveying of Letters or Pacquets under a Pound Weight, to and from all parts within the Cities of London

[12] *Ibid.*, 1700-2, 541.

and Westminster; and the Out Parishes within the weekly Bills of Mortality, for One Penny."[13]

The "undertakers" had worked out a surprisingly capable system. The urban areas were divided into districts, with subordinate offices for the districts, and with the principal office at Dockwra's house in Lyme Street. The district offices comprised a St. Paul's office in Queen's Head Alley, Newgate Street, one for the Temple region in Chancery Lane, a Westminster office in St. Martin's Lane, one for Southwark near the Church of St. Mary Overy, and the Hermitage office in Smithfield. These were sorting stations. In addition, hundreds of receiving houses were open throughout the region served by Dockwra's post. Large placards were hung up at these receiving houses—they were in all the principal streets—reading, "Penny post letters taken in here."[14] Messengers collected letters and parcels at the receiving houses every hour, and brought them to the regional sorting offices. Deliveries were made from the sorting offices to the houses and business establishments in the district at frequent intervals, even ten to twelve times a day in the business districts, and four to eight times a day in other parts of the urban area. This comprised, as indicated in the broadside quoted above, all the region within the weekly bills of mortality. The four towns of Hackney, Islington, South Newington Butts and Lambeth were included, in addition to the densely populated district from Westminster to Poplar and Blackwall. According to Dockwra's own statement, the latter region was "seven miles in length from east to west."

In defending his "invention," William Dockwra pointed out that his arrangements did not conflict with the postal services of the Inland Office, since the neighboring towns and villages which were served by the Penny Post were all "within less distance than the nearest post stages, . . . where the General Post Office had never settled any accommodation."[15]

The penny rate was uniform for all letters and parcels up to a pound in weight. Dockwra thus avoided the troublesome charge made according to the number of sheets of paper used in a letter. It made, of course, for a speedy delivery, since the penny charge was

[13] *H.M.C. Rep.*, xv, App. 1, 325. *Angliae Metropolis, or the Present State of London* (1690), p. 348, gives credit for this "useful undertaking" to the "most ingenious Mr. Murray, and Mr. Dockwra, Merchant." "Within the weekly Bills of Mortality" denoted the parishes in and about London whence returns of deaths were made periodically.
[14] Lewins, *op. cit.*, p. 32.
[15] *Cal. S.P. Dom.*, 1700-2, 541.

prepaid. Not less surprising was the insurance of the safe delivery of a letter or packet through the Penny Post by the payment of the original penny only. This insurance provision included articles in parcels that were valued up to £10. It should be added that, after a year's experience, Dockwra discontinued the insurance of safe delivery except for packets tightly sealed and with the contents and value clearly indicated on the outside.[16]

The area of the Penny Post included remote and thinly inhabited districts in the outskirts of London. In such areas, the letters were received for a penny prepaid, and were delivered in the main area without extra charge. Delivery in the country districts, however, cost an extra penny. This seemed a reasonable provision, since delivery in a thinly populated area required much more effort per letter or packet.[17]

A considerable source of revenue for Dockwra's post was the collection of letters for the General Post, that is, letters that were to go out of London. The Penny Post seems, also, to have collected letters and parcels for delivery to carriers and coachmen. This service, which was openly advertised, may have been one of the causes for official interference, and for the proclamation—already noted—against the unauthorized carriage of letters.[18]

Dockwra used postmarks to insure the safe and prompt delivery of letters and parcels. Although postmarks had already been adopted in the London office of the General Post, those used by Dockwra were more elaborate and efficient. Each letter or packet when it came to a sorting office was stamped with a distinguishing mark showing where it was originally received. These postmarks or "stamps" had the words "Penny Post Paid" on the three sides of a triangularly shaped postmark; in the central part of the triangle was a capital letter indicating the office—"W" for Westminster, "L" for Lyme, "T " for Temple, etc. An additional stamp, heart-shaped, indicated the hour when the letter was marked for delivery. "Af" with a "3" below it, for example, meant that the letter was delivered at three in the afternoon, a "Mor" and "8" that it went out at eight o'clock in the morning. This additional time stamp was invented and added by Dockwra, after the sorting-office postmark was already in use. The

[16] George Brumell, *The Local Posts of London, 1680-1840*, pp. 9-10.

[17] This distinction between the urban and country districts of the London Penny Post remained until the local post of London was absorbed in the General Post Office 160 years later.

[18] Brumell, *op. cit.*, p. 9.

time stamp has long since been accepted all over the world as an indispensable device. Dockwra found it valuable, not only in preventing critics of the scheme from claiming delays in the delivery of letters, but also useful as an incentive to his employees.[19]

In 1681 an instruction regarding the stamps was issued for the purpose of quieting criticism of the supposed delays in delivery. It was entitled, "The Practical Method of the Penny-Post, being a Sheet very necessary for all Persons to have by them for their Information in the Regular use of a Design so well Approved of for quickening Correspondence, Promoting Trade and Publick Good. With an Explanation of the following Stamps, for the Marking of all Letters." The use of the stamps was made clear, as well as the time when the deliveries might be expected. "The Undertakers have provided the Stamps aforesaid to Mark the Hour of the Day on all

The Dockwra stamps indicating prepayment, and the time mark used in addition.

Letters when sent out, . . . and all Persons are to expect their Letters within one Hour. . . . Each Office having its proper Letter, with an acknowledgement that the *Penny-Post* is paid, to prevent the giving of anything at the Delivery. . . . Letters coming too late at night, shall be by Seven next morning sent out, and Deliver'd by Eight and sometimes sooner. . . . But all Letters to the four Towns of Hackney, Islington, South-Newington and Lambeth, and to the Remote Parts, must be left much earlyer, or they will not be Delivered till next Morning."[20]

The Penny Post was sharply criticized. The porters were loud in their objections, as one might expect; they even assaulted Dockwra's messengers and tore down the placards that advertised the service. Others denounced it as a "popish contrivance," Titus Oates hinting in his customary way that Jesuits were at the bottom of the scheme. The authorities in the Post Office were also against it, partly because

[19] Brumell, *op. cit.*, p. 38; Alcock & Holland, *op. cit.*, p. 36.
[20] This sheet is reproduced in *Penny Postage Centenary*, pp. 133-36. Robson Lowe, *Handstruck Postage Stamps of the Empire*, has an illustration of a Dockwra cover.

of the connection made between the Penny Post service and the carriers, and partly because of the very success of the scheme. Postal profits might suffer and the shortcomings of the General Post Office appear more glaring, if this unauthorized post were allowed to go on its course unhampered. It certainly served as an unpleasant reminder of what the government monopoly might have done, and pointed the way to possible extensions of this service to other urban communities.

Dockwra's undertaking was attacked, consequently, after it had been running for about two years. In 1682 the Duke caused twenty actions to be brought against the "undertaker" at one time and two more at another time, according to Dockwra's own statement. The latter were for £10,000 damages, on the ground that the Penny Post affected adversely the General Post. Dockwra retorted that it helped the General Post. His legal defense was based on the right of an inventor, under the Statute of Monopolies of James I, to have the benefit for fourteen years of any new contrivance for the public good.[21] The Penny Post, he held, was a true invention, since it was "essentially different from the General Post, being carried on by methods not practiced nor practicable for the General Post." He asserted that the entire lack of accommodation for the districts served, which were nearer the London office of the General Post than the first post stages, made his continuance of the Penny Post no infringement. Dockwra had difficulty meeting the obvious retort that the Charter of 1660 had created a monopoly.

A private individual had no chance against the brother of the King. In one of the two actions against Dockwra in 1682 he was cast for £100 damages before the King's Bench. The money, apparently, was not demanded of him, since the Duke was more concerned in stopping the Penny Post as an infringement of his monopoly. As a result of the judgment given on November 23, 1682, the Penny Post ceased as a private undertaking. Dockwra might have had more success in his appeal to an earlier parliamentary act had parliament been a going concern in 1682. But these were the years when Charles was ruling without parliament.[22]

The Duke of York clearly intended to take over the profitable Penny Post. Four days after the judgment against Dockwra, the *London Gazette* announced that the Penny Post would shortly be

[21] The Act he had in mind appears to have been 21 Jas. I, c.3 (1623).
[22] For the lawsuit, see *Cal. S.P. Dom.*, 1697, 544; 1700-2, 541-43; Brumell, *op. cit.*, p. 10. Dockwra declared some years later that the undertaking cost him £4000. It is significant that Dockwra appealed to Parliament for redress after the fall of James II.

reopened: it was in operation before the end of the year, as a part of the government service. In the action against Dockwra, the Duke of York had claimed that "the penny post and the general post have identical methods." But this was so far from true that the government Penny Post was run as a distinct and separate organization from 1682 until the middle of the nineteenth century!

The official Penny Post, or London District Post as it came to be known, continued Dockwra's system of postmarks with but slight changes. Both used triangular postmarks for the sorting offices with the three words, "Penny Post Paid." Collectors of stampless covers can easily distinguish them, as the three words all faced inwards on the London District Post markings, and were spelled "Peny Post Payd." The triangular forms for these postmarks remained in use until 1794.[23] Within the small triangle were placed the initials for

The government Penny Post replaced the heart-shaped form used by Dockwra with a circular time mark. The dotted heart-shaped mark indicated transfer of a letter from the General Post to the Penny Post. "M" and "W" indicate days of the week.

the office and for the day of the week. The Dockwra hour stamp was used as well, but here a greater change was made; the heart-shaped date stamp was replaced, in general, by the circular form similar to that of the General Post Office. The main office of the District Post was transferred to Crosby House, Bishopsgate, and later to Threadneedle Street. The branch sorting offices were those for Westminster, the Temple, Southwark, St. Paul's and the Hermitage on Little Tower Hill, but the number was soon increased. A list of 1704 includes the Exchanging House as an additional office.

The staff of the Penny Post shortly after it was taken over by the

[23] See below, p. 199, for the reorganization of the London District Post made in that year. I might hasten to add, for the information of would-be collectors of these stampless covers, that the letters with the Dockwra postmarks and the early government Penny Post markings are exceedingly rare. For further illustrations of the postmarks, see Brumell, *op. cit.*, pp. 41, 43, and Alcock & Holland, *op. cit.*, pp. 37-38.

government consisted of a Comptroller, an Accountant, a Collector, sorters, subsorters and messengers. In 1686, for example, there were six sorters, eight subsorters, fifty-three messengers for the town service and four country messengers. The town messengers received 1s 4d a day each. The country messengers got only 5d, but they kept the extra pennies for the letters they delivered in the outer or twopenny area.[24]

The very useful Penny Post, founded by Dockwra, is an excellent example of private initiative meeting the need for cheap carriage of letters and parcels in London. The loss of this private enterprise to the Duke of York marks the end of any conspicuous attempt to set up nonofficial arrangements, though one more fleeting effort for a cheap London post was attempted early in the next century.[25] The government, for better or for worse, assumed the responsibility for improving the means of communication, though its arrangements usually lagged far behind the public demand. The Post Office continued to be used, all too frequently, to support projects alien to its true purpose.

[24] *Cal. Tr.B.*, VIII, 1512; XIX, p. ccxvii.
[25] See below, p. 87.

The Post Office
Following the Revolution

THE Revolution of 1688 was certain to affect the postal services. For one thing, King James on his "abdication" necessarily left in other hands the postal monopoly that had been under his control for more than a quarter of a century. When James II became King in 1685, he ceased, technically, to have the profits, for the revenue reverted to the Crown. From 1685 to 1760, the income of the Post Office was a part of the hereditary revenues.[1]

The Revolution resulted in a much greater use of the Post Office. The many limitations on freedom exercised by Charles II and James II are well known: they had become so burdensome in the short reign of James that a widespread revolt proved bloodless, and the solution glorious. Among the restraints removed, none was welcomed more gladly than the relaxations of the restrictions on speech. Freedom of communication, not only of ideas but of letters, greatly increased. The well-known Act of Toleration is an example of the greater liberty that followed the Revolution. Another was the discontinuance of the Licensing Act. The immediate effect of these somewhat timid measures can be exaggerated, for the restrictions on freedom of expression were still rather burdensome for some time to come. But there was a growing "itch for news," with a rapid growth of the intellectual class,

[1] The change in 1760, on the accession of George III, was the result of surrendering a part of the hereditary revenues, and their replacement by a Civil List. The Post Office income was carried to the Aggregate, later the Consolidated, Fund. See Sir Thomas Erskine May, *The Constitutional History of England since the Accession of George III*, chap. IV, and *The Post Office, an Historical Summary* (hereafter cited as *Hist. Sum.*), p. 121.

and an appeal to this enlarging group by such publications as *The Spectator*. The result was increased business for the Post Office. In 1694 the Postmaster-General asked for an additional secretary because "the business of the Post Office is of late very much increased."[2]

A change in the personnel of the Post Office was inevitable—a change not unlike that of 1660, if not so drastic. Sir Philip Frowde, the Governor of the Post Office before the Revolution, was replaced by Major John Wildman. The latter had been a Cromwellian soldier, was a prisoner in the early days of the Restoration for his alleged republican leanings, and an exile at the time of the Revolution. Wildman returned in the army of William, with the Post Office as the reward for his services. His salary was the same as formerly paid to Frowde, £1500 a year. His tenure was brief, for in less than two years—February 1691—Wildman was replaced by Sir Robert Cotton and Thomas Frankland.[3]

The choice of two Postmasters-General was an innovation. It may have been done to satisfy the two groups that had combined to bring about the Revolution. One man was a Whig, the other a Tory, according to some, but both were considered moderates. If the arrangement seemed strange in 1691 and appears unnecessary to the modern reader as he looks back at the modest Post Office of those days, it soon became an accepted plan for the headship of the Post Office. Two Postmasters-General instead of one were henceforth to be in charge —until 1823 when the uselessness of a plural executive for the Post Office caused so much objection that the two were replaced by one Postmaster-General.[4]

Another important change was the more direct subordination of the Post Office to the Lords of the Treasury. Indeed, this seems to have occurred when James II became King, as the Lord Treasurer, the Earl of Rochester, was also made Postmaster-General. A Post Office directly responsible to the Treasury seemed a convenient arrangement, since the service was viewed by the government primarily from the financial angle. Though Wildman, and after him Cotton and Frankland, are called Postmasters-General, their relation to the

[2] *Cal. Tr.B.*, x, 661.
[3] *Cal. S.P. Dom.*, 1689-90, 59; 1690-91, 40, 283; *Cal. Tr.B.*, IX, 1037. Joyce (p. 430) seems to be in error in making Wildman's regime end in March 1690. The cause for Wildman's loss of the Post Office could not have been very serious, even if it was the "talk of the town." He was knighted by William in 1692, and died in the following year.
[4] The usual official designation of the two heads was in the singular, "our Postmaster-General" meaning not one or the other but the two combined.

Treasury is much the same as that of Frowde before 1689 when he was Governor under the Earl of Rochester. Cotton and Frankland are also designated occasionally as the Commissioners of the Post Office.[5]

Cotton and Frankland were empowered to regulate and settle posts in any of the King's dominions. This included the Inland and Foreign Office, the Penny Post of London, and, as well, the control of any posts established in the oversea plantations. Their powers included, of course, the furnishing of horses for those riding in post. The Crown, that is, the Treasury, was to receive all moneys paid over to the Postmaster-General. The salary remained as before the Revolution, £1500 serving as the salary for the two incumbents. It was not long, however, before the joint Postmasters-General obtained an advance to £1000 each. The two holders in 1711—one was still Frankland—complained to the Lord High Treasurer: they thought that their salaries should be £1500 each as in the cases of Frowde and Wildman.[6]

During these years the pension roll based on Post Office funds grew larger and larger. Lady Frances Green was not forgotten, and the Duchess of Cleveland continued to receive her enormous pension of £4700 a year. The pension of the Duchess was paid with some reluctance, according to the Treasury minutes on the matter, but the obligation was met sooner or later, even though there was occasional delay in satisfying the warrants of the grasping Duchess. She passed to her eternal reward in 1709, but her earthly pension went on and on. It descended to the Dukes of Grafton, as the first Duke had the Duchess for a mother and Charles II for a father. These scions of royalty continued to collect the pension until 1856, when it was commuted for the magnificent sum of £91,000![7]

Of the other pensions charged against the postal funds, that of the Earl of Rochester has already been noticed. By the end of the century, the pension roll of the Post Office—mostly for persons who had done nothing whatever for the postal service—included, in addition to those already mentioned, Lord Somers for £1500, the Earl of Rochford for £1000, the Duke of Leeds for £2625, and the Duke of

---

[5] *Cal. Tr.P.*, 1557-1696, 127, 200, 202, 307; *Cal. Tr.B.*, VIII, 220, 227, 264; IX, 52, etc. The material in the Treasury Books regarding the Post Office is abundant after 1685.

[6] *Cal. Tr.B.*, IX, 1037; *Cal. Tr.P.*, IV, 330.

[7] *Cal. Tr.B.*, IX, 1198; XII, 73 and elsewhere. For the end of the matter, see *Hist. Sum.*, p. 122. This account declares erroneously that the pension was granted in 1686. See above, p. 53.

Schomberg for £2000. The last-named pensioner was the son of the well-known general who had been of so much assistance to King William at the time of the Revolution. In 1697 Isaac Manley was accorded £200 annually during the life of his father, John Manley. A rather surprising drain on the funds of the Post Office was a grant made in August of 1698 to Dr. Titus Oates. This was stated as for ninety-nine years, but was terminable with the lives of Titus and of Rebeckah, his wife. It has been estimated that the pensions drawn from the Post Office revenues at this time totaled about a third of the postal receipts.[8]

Queen Anne's reign only added to the burden. In 1702 the Duke of Marlborough received £5000 from the Post Office towards his princely annuity. One hundred and thirty years later, at the time of the Great Reform Bill, his descendant, the current Duke, was still receiving that amount, surely a large price to pay for the glorious victories of the War of the Spanish Succession. After Anne's accession, her worthless husband, Prince George of Denmark, received £8250 annually from the Post Office. Indeed, in the year 1703-4, this Prince—regarded even at the time as a useless appendage—had £29,250 out of the postal receipts. An annuity of £1000 was granted in 1708 to Barbara, Viscountess Fitzhardinge, during the joint lives of herself and the Queen: it, too, was charged upon the Post Office. It is a wonder that there was any postal progress to record for these years, with income being allocated to every end but the improvement of the service.[9]

Yet advance there was, nevertheless. The farm had been raised in 1660 from £10,000 per annum to £21,500. When the Revolution occurred, the receipts from the Post Office were just under £90,000. When the additional secretary was sought in 1694, the postal income was about £100,000. Shortly after Queen Anne succeeded William in 1702, the Receiver-General and the Accountant-General of the Post Office asked for increases in salary on the ground that the income of the department had doubled during their time of service. The declared accounts for these years justify their contention. The net income, which had been about £90,000 at the time of the Revolution,

[8] For Titus Oates, see *Cal. Tr.B.*, XIII, 409. *Hist. Sum.*, p. 122, made the above estimate, but it is an exaggeration, for they amounted only to about a fifth of the total revenue.

[9] For Marlborough, see *Cal. Tr.B.*, XVIII, 232, and [John Wade] *The Extraordinary Black Book* (1832), p. 554. For other pensions, *Cal. Tr.B.*, Introd. to vols. XI-XVII, p. dxxxvii; XVIII, p. clxix; *H.M.C. Rep.*, XIV, App. IV, 160-61; XVI, App. II, 205.

had advanced to £108,000 by 1693-94. Following the Peace of Ryswick the increase was amazing, from about £116,000 in 1697-98 to nearly £148,000 in 1699-1700. By the year 1703-4, despite, or because of, the Spanish Succession War, the income was over £156,000.[10]

If the total income is broken down, the foreign service for these years is found to account for a quarter to a fifth of the business. The Irish Post Office and the Penny Post Office accounted for another 10 per cent. The remainder, about two-thirds of the whole, was the profit from the workings of the Inland Office. Clearly, the marked increase of the revenues for these years came largely as a result of the growth of the correspondence within the country—from the expansion of the Inland Office.

One cause for the enlarged activity of the Inland or General Post Office was the settling of additional cross posts and the greater use of byposts. Some examples of such extensions will show the way in which the Post Office was serving an ever-enlarging clientele. Warwick, Stratford and several adjacent places petitioned in January 1697 for a more efficient service. They were being served from Coventry, but desired a post from Banbury, because it was nearer London and would result in making single letters to and from London cost 2d instead of 3d. About the same time, 1696, an important cross post was erected between Exeter and Bristol, to go twice a week, and to take twenty-four hours each way. Formerly, the letters between Exeter and Bristol had to go via London, with the consequent charge 6d—3d up to London and the same amount for the second half of the journey. As the cross-country route between the two towns was only 76 miles long, the charge for a single letter became 2d.[11]

Two years later this service was continued to Wotton-under-Edge "for the convenience of the clothing trade." In 1699 Shrewsbury petitioned that the post stage from Bristol "may continue to their town." In the next year, a cross post was laid between Bristol and Chester. We know that this soon began to prove worth while, for the declared accounts for the year 1701-2 included over £1200, being "the deputy

---

[10] *Cal. Tr.B.*, XVIII, 292. The Treasury Books furnish the figures year by year. The reckoning was from Lady Day to Lady Day (March 25), the date used for the beginning of the calendar year at the time. The arrears due from the postmasters were always large at the end of the year. This shortage has been deducted to make the amounts given, the actual income. See *Cal. Tr.B.*, IX, pp. cclxv-cclxix; Introd. to vols. XI-XVII; XVIII, p. clxix; XIX, p. ccxv.

[11] Joyce, *op. cit.*, p. 58; *Cal. Tr.B.*, XI, 303. The connecting stages were Tiverton, Wellington, Taunton, Bridgwater and Wells.

postmaster's charge for letters sent into the cross roads between Exeter, Bristol, and Chester." In 1703 a new post was set up from Exeter to Truro to serve the inland towns in Cornwall, since the main post road followed the coast.[12]

An early example of the farming of byposts was that made to Stephen and Richard Bigg in 1687 for branches set up in Herts, Bucks and Warwickshire. Their rent by the end of the century was £950 a year, and they had to account to the Post Office for the "port" of all letters coming from beyond sea or from Scotland. The Biggs seem to have been careful and industrious in their management, "to the great satisfaction of the country." Stephen Bigg was carrying on this service in a large way, since he received a contract in 1700 for extending the post to places in Lancashire and Westmoreland at a rent of £2500 a year. The profits from this extension were to be his for the first year "in view of his charge of settling several new stages, but in the second and third years he was to account for a third of any excess." Bigg was granted this farm on the ground that he "has been concerned for some years as farmer and manager of the Buckingham branch which extends as far as Norwich." The Treasury found such arrangements an advantage to the revenue.[13]

This sort of extension was growing very general by the end of the seventeenth century. The declared accounts of the Receiver-General of the Post Office included receipts from several farms, in addition to that of Stephen Bigg. By the end of the century, the receipts from these farms were over £7000 a year, totaling about 5 per cent of the income of the Post Office.[14] To the author of the *Angliae Notitia, or the Present State of England*, this expansion of the Post Office beyond the older post roads seemed the climax of its development. He wrote: "And as the Master-piece of all those good Regulations established by the Post-Master-General, . . he hath annex'd and appropriated the Market-Towns of England, so well to the respective Postages, that there is no considerable Market-Town, but hath an easie and certain Conveyance for the Letters thereof, to and from the said grand Office, in the due Course of the Mails every Post."[15]

[12] *Cal. Tr.B.*, XIV, 278, 388; XV, 407; XVIII, 43; Introd. to vols. XI–XVII, p. dxlvi; *Cal. Tr.P.*, II, 440; III, 205.

[13] Bigg objected to the terms of the farm in 1700 because of the recent establishment of the Exeter-Chester cross post, already described. See *Cal. Tr.B.*, XVI, 246; XVIII, 112; XIV, 241–42; XV, 396.

[14] *Ibid.*, Introd. to vols. XI–XVII, p. dxxxvii.

[15] *Angliae Metropolis, or the Present State of London* (1690), p. 344; Edward Chamberlayne, *Angliae Notitia* (19th ed., 1700), p. 426. The quotation is to be found in both volumes.

Although the Penny Post did not contribute heavily to the exchequer, its development after the Revolution is of great interest and importance. The departure of James II gave Dockwra his opportunity. He made application to Parliament in 1689 for redress of the oppression under which he and his family—a wife and eight children—had been suffering for "above seven years." The appeal was made to Parliament on the ground that the action of the law courts in 1682 made it necessary for him to ask Parliament to be the judge of its own statutes. By that he meant that the claim for the profits of his "invention" under the Act of James I concerning monopolies could be judged best by Parliament. He contended that the Penny Post was a real invention, because it was based on his new application of the methods used, "for there is nothing new under the sun but application," according to this inventor.[16]

The times were favorable, naturally, to appeal for redress from an action taken by James II. Dockwra asked for the undertaking "to be restored to him or that he have a competent annual pension." In May 1690, nearly a year after the petition was presented, the House resolved to recommend Dockwra to His Majesty. As a result, he was granted an annuity of £500 a year for seven years, to begin on June 24, 1689. It was to come out of the revenue of the Penny Post, "in consideration of his good service in inventing and settling the business of the Penny Post Office." Even if he did not have the Post again under his supervision, his work of establishing the new service was recognized at last.[17]

A few years later, Dockwra's good fortune reached its peak. The Comptroller of the Penny Post, Nathaniel Castleton, was removed in 1696 on the charge of disaffection and various abuses. Dockwra was then appointed in his stead, with a salary of £200 a year in addition to the pension that he was already receiving. But this stroke of good luck was short-lived. Reports came to the Postmaster-General that Dockwra was unfitted to carry on the work of Comptroller. He was accused of mistreating subordinates and of inadequately serving the public. Some of the officers and messengers belonging to the Penny Post asked for his removal, "as he was irregular, vexatious and troublesome, and not fit to be any longer borne with." They even

---

[16] *Cal. S.P. Dom.*, 1700-2, 541-43.
[17] *Journal H.C.*, x, 226, 384, 417; *Cal. Tr.B.*, ix, 844, 939.

alleged that he was trying to reduce the revenues to as low a level as possible in order to ask for the farm of it for himself at an advantageous figure. They complained in addition that Dockwra forbade the taking-in of any "bandboxes (except very small), and all parcels above a pound, which, when they were taken, did bring in considerable advantage to the office, they being now at great charge sent by porters in the citty, and coaches and watermen into the country." He was also accused of opening and detaining letters.[18]

We need not take these accusations too seriously. Dockwra replied by declaring that he had improved the revenue, a claim that was true. But he was removed, nevertheless, after a hearing before the Treasury Lords, as "not fit to have the office any longer." Nathaniel Castleton—doubtless a major worker in the effort to demote Dockwra—returned as Comptroller. Dockwra lost both his office and his pension in the same year—1700.[19]

When Queen Anne came to the throne in 1702, Dockwra made still another appeal for some settled provision. But this effort was unsuccessful, and it was his last. Little more is known of the man who had invented the Penny Post over twenty years before.[20] Dockwra had certainly suffered much change of circumstance. This may have been the result partly of his inability to work with others, and partly of the jealousy aroused by the financial success of the Penny Post. Whatever qualifications one may make regarding the man, he deserves a high place among Post Office reformers for his distinctive and unique contribution to the postal services.[21]

The remarkable usefulness of the Penny Post can be realized by a glance at its progress during these years. In 1688-89, the annual receipts were slightly over £3360 for the year. In the year 1696-97—before Dockwra's return as Comptroller—the income of the Penny Post was about £3500. Whether Dockwra was responsible or not, the business of the office began to increase rapidly: in the last year of his headship the revenue had grown to nearly £3900. This would seem to disprove clearly the accusation made against him in 1700, that he

---

[18] *Cal. Tr.P.*, II, 368, 377, 398; *Br. Almanac* (1838), Companion, pp. 115-16.

[19] *Cal. Tr.B.*, XV, 90, 92, 97.

[20] Dockwra seems to have had something to do with stimulating postal developments on the continent of North America. He was an East Jersey proprietor. See below, p. 167. Dockwra died in 1716.

[21] *Cal. Tr.P.*, III, 26. Brumell, *op. cit.*, p. 12, has 1700 as the date of his application for relief.

was trying to lower the income. And the advance continued, for by Anne's accession (1702) the revenue was well over £4000.[22]

The value of the Penny Post can be shown in another way—by the number of letters that were circulated. Because of the uniform charge made for letters and packets, we know the actual number of pieces of mail that were carried by the post annually. In 1697-98, for example, there were 77,530 letters and packets that paid the second penny, that is, that were directed to the country. The penny letters and packets totaled for that year 792,080. For 1701-2, the Penny Post took in and delivered 886,583 penny letters and packets and 86,719 that paid the second penny. In the next year, the total number of pieces of mail that passed through the Penny Post included 95,694 two-penny letters, and 951,090 penny letters. A cheap service had proved abundantly that it was meeting a growing need.

This "very commodious" Penny Post provided numerous conveniences—gentlemen could give notice at small cost of their arrival in London, shopkeepers and tradesmen could send to their workmen for what they wanted, bills and publications could be dispersed, "summons or tickets conveyed to all parts, appointments made by men of business, much time saved in solicitation for money, lawyers and clients mutually correspond, patients may send to doctors, apothecaries and chirurgeons for what they shall want, besides many other advantages."[23]

Writing some twenty years later, Daniel Defoe declared: "The Penny Post, a modern Contrivance of a private Person, one Mr. William Dockraw [sic], is now made a Branch of the general Revenue of the Post Office; and though for a time it was subject to Miscarriages and Mistakes, yet now it is come also into so exquisite a Management, that nothing can be more exact, and 'tis with the utmost Safety and Dispatch, that Letters are delivered at the remotest Corners of the Town, almost as soon as they can be sent by a Messenger,

---

[22] The figures are worth recording. They have been gathered from the *Cal. Tr.B.*, vol. IX, and Introd. to vols. XI-XVII, XVIII, XIX.

For 1688-89	£3362	12s	5d	1696-97	3497	8	11
1689-90	3273	10	5	1697-98	3623	7	6
1690-91	3190	7	3	1698-99	3629	9	3
1691-92	3369	5	5	1699-1700	3884	15	7
1692-93	3448	17	3	1700-1	4007	16	9
1693-94	3427	19	3	1701-2	4055	8	6
1694-95	3446	7	1	1702-3	4174	7	8
1695-96	3358	11	10	1703-4	4437	17	11

[23] Chamberlayne, *op. cit.*, p. 428.

and that Four, Five, Six to Eight Times a Day, according as the Distance of the Place makes it practicable. . . . Nor are you tied up to a single Piece of Paper, as in the General Post-Office, but any Packet under a Pound weight goes at the same Price." And he added: "I mention this the more particularly, because it is so manifest a Testimony of the Greatness of this City, and to the great Extent of Business and Commerce in it, that this Penny Conveyance should raise so many Thousand Pounds in a year, and employ so many poor People in the Diligence of it, as this Office employs. We see nothing of this at Paris, at Amsterdam, at Hamburgh or any other City, that ever I have seen or heard of."[24]

A few years later a foreign visitor was equally impressed. "The Penny Post is also here a useful institution, which consists in this, that if one has a letter or anything else which does not exceed a pound in weight, to send to any one in London or the places situated close by, it is sent by the penny post, which is established at several places in London, and one pays for it one penny, when it quickly and safely reaches its destination."[25]

There were several attempts to apply the idea of the Penny Post to local letters elsewhere than in London, the success of Dockwra's undertaking serving as a stimulus. In 1690 one Blackburne proposed to the Treasury the "usefulness and necessity of setting up a penny post in the country as well as in and about London." Another proposal was made in 1691. A third plan was presented in 1699 for letting a Penny Post arrangement out to farm. The authors of the idea "would deliver letters from the General Post in towns and places where the General Post came not." This, it was argued, would correct the excessive charge by special messengers, who often took as much as a shilling above the regular postage. But the authorities were opposed to farming such extensions.[26]

Several suggestions were made for Penny Posts in Ireland. In 1692 Christopher Perkins and William Waller, who had lived in Limerick and Tipperary for thirty years, presented a petition in which they claimed to have projected and erected a Penny Post in Ireland, "which in time may be as useful as that in England." They asked the right to carry on their project for twenty-one years. It was referred

---

[24] *A Tour Thro' the Whole Island of Great Britain* (1727, reprinted 1927), I, 343-44.

[25] *Kalm's Account of His Visit to England on His Way to America*, tr. by Joseph Lucas (1892), p. 63.

[26] *Cal. Tr.B.*, IX, 912, 1210; *Cal. Tr.P.*, II, 337.

to the authorities in 1694 and considered again in the next year, but nothing came of their request.[27]

Another interesting Irish proposal was that of Elizabeth, Dowager Countess of Thanet: she wanted to start a Penny Post in Dublin, a post that would have been strictly subordinate to the General Post, with no receiving house of the Penny Post within two miles of any of the stages of the General Post Office. She wished a lease to run for fourteen years at a nominal rent. The Duchess agreed to collect and deliver free the letters called "country letters" that came to the General Letter Office. The motives behind her proposal, made in March 1704, seems to have been two, the slender resources of the Dowager Countess—her jointure was proving insufficient—and the rapid growth of Dublin. But the postal heads were not sufficiently gallant, and Dublin as well as the Dowager had to get along with the existing facilities. The first local post outside London was to be established in Dublin, but not until 1773. In fact, Penny Posts apart from that in London were not legalized until 1765.[28]

Before we conclude this matter of town posts in the early eighteenth century one other suggestion needs notice. Charles Povey not only proposed but actually set up a footpost in London in 1709 under the name of the Half-Penny Carriage, "To the End that Her Majesty's Revenues arising by Posts may be encreased, and the Inhabitants within the main Pile of Buildings of the Cities and Suburbs of London and Westminster, and Burrough of Southwark, may save 14000 l. per Ann." Povey had receiving houses in London, Westminster and Southwark, and his collectors used the novel device of announcing their approach by the ringing of a bell. The plan seemed a direct infringement of the service already in use, though there were differences in charges and in the area served.

The Post Office warned Povey that he would be prosecuted if he did not stop his "illegal" halfpenny carriage. The following warning appeared in the *Gazette* in December 1709: "Whereas Charles Povey and divers Traders and Shop Keepers in and about the Cities of London and Westminster, Borough of Southwark and parts adjacent, and several Persons ringing Bells about the Streets of the said Cities and Borough, have set up, imploy'd and for some time continued a Foot Post for Collecting and Delivering Letters within the

---

[27] *Cal. S.P. Dom.*, 1691-92, 449; 1694-95, 9, 416.
[28] *Cal. Tr.B.*, XIX, 180; Joyce, *op. cit.*, p. 70; Hendy, *op. cit.*, pp. 118, 153. See below, pp. 111-12, 208 ff.

said Cities and Borough, and Parts adjoining, for Hire under the Name of the Halfpenny Carriage . . . Her Majesty's Postmaster General has Therefore directed Informations in her Majesty's Court of Exchequer to be exhibited against the said Charles Povey, and several Shop Keepers and Ringers of Bells, for Recovery against every one of them £100 for such setting up, and for every week's continuance thereof; and also £5 for every Offence in Collecting and Delivering of Letters for Hire as aforesaid, contrary to the Statute for erecting and establishing a Post Office."[29]

Charles Povey seems to have been a man of spirit. He welcomed prosecution, declaring that he lived under a different "constitution" from the one that mistreated Dockwra. In those days, he asserted, government was arbitrary and judges could be bribed. The Post Office was not intimidated by Povey's bravado and insinuations. The prosecution was carried forward, if with some difficulty. The conductor of the halfpenny carriage switched his bellmen about, and had them assume fictitious names. There was so much delay that Povey's post carried on for some months, pending judgment. But the prosecution came to a successful conclusion in the Easter Term of 1710, when Povey was fined £100. His venture had lasted for seven months.[30]

Povey's plan had one interesting effect: the Post Office adopted his use of bell ringers for collecting letters. The practice seemed so useful that it was extended to the provincial towns as well. It persisted, in fact, until the middle of the nineteenth century. Even in London the bellmen were used until 1846, several years after the general reform of the Post Office brought about by Robert Wallace and Rowland Hill. In 1712 the well-known letter writer, Lady Mary Wortley Montagu, concluded a letter from London to a friend in this abrupt manner: "The post-bell rings; my next shall be longer, with

[29] John Ashton, *Social Life in the Reign of Queen Anne* (1883), p. 102.
[30] For Povey, see *Cal. Tr.P.*, IV, 165; Joyce, *op. cit.*, 121-22; Hendy, *op. cit.*, pp. 61-62; *D.N.B.*, XLVI, 233-35. In *Complaint and Reform in England*, ed. Wm. H. Dunham and Stanley Pargellis (1938), pp. 875 ff., one of Povey's pamphlets is reprinted. The biographical notice accompanying it erroneously calls Povey's halfpenny carriage a "successful penny post." Povey was mixed up in many other things besides the halfpenny carriage. He was a prolific writer in religious, political and economic fields, publishing at least five books and scores of pamphlets. His fertile mind produced numerous schemes for the public, and his private, benefit, including an invention for clearing coal ships, and the flotation of fire and life insurance companies. He had a plan as well for a Parcel Post in the country. Povey was vain and quarrelsome, as his experience with the Post Office makes clear. There is an article on Povey by Samuel Graveson in *The Philatelist* for August 1938.

some account of your fair family." An amusing reference of 1718 to the bellmen is found in the attempt of a wife to explain why her husband did not receive an expected letter. A Mrs. Ogilvie wrote thus to a Capt. John Ogilvie: "As to answering your letter... I wrote to you in the afternoon before stirring out, and was sot enough to keep the letter in my pocket till near twelve at the night, waiting until the bell should come about for letters, without considering that it comes only on Tuesdays and Thursdays, and when I found it too late to send to the post office, I burnt my letter in a rage."[31]

[31] *Letters from Mary Wortley Montagu*, ed. R. B. Johnson (1906), p. 10; *H.M.C. Rep.*, Stuart, v, 606; Lewins, *op. cit.*, p. 123.

A Unified Post Office for the British Isles

THE postal services of England and Wales have, thus far, taken the most attention. The Cromwellian Act of 1657, it is true, included the whole of the British Isles, though neither that measure nor the Charter of 1660 paid much attention to Scotland and Ireland. Both were backward, postally speaking. Previous to the union of the Scottish and English Parliaments in 1707, Scotland was little affected by the changes in communication taking place south of the Border. Ireland was even more backward than Scotland, since Irish postal services were regarded as merely extensions of those centered in London, and as a convenience for English rulers and landlords in and about Dublin. A review of earlier postal developments in both Ireland and Scotland will bring out the full importance of the Act of 1711 in creating a unified Post Office for the British Isles.

A public service for Ireland appears to have begun in the reign of Charles I, at the time that Thomas Witherings was active in England. But this service was temporary, as the Irish Rebellion in 1641 and the Civil War that followed shortly brought an end to orderly arrangements in both islands. During the Commonwealth the Irish posting arrangements were renewed under the able care of an Evan Vaughan: he incurred the enmity of Secretary Thurloe when Vaughan's activity seemed to infringe on the Secretary's monopoly.[1]

After 1660 the Deputy Postmaster in Dublin was chiefly concerned with the packet service to England. This service, as we have found, grew in importance whenever Irish affairs were in tension and

---

[1] *Ireland under the Commonwealth* (1913), ed. by Robert Dunlop, p. 559.

government officials needed certain and rapid touch with Ireland.[2] Packet services by the two northern routes—between Port Patrick and Donaghadee and between Holyhead and Dublin—had been used more or less continuously, though the Scottish route was comparatively unimportant. The southern service, from Milford Haven to Waterford, does not appear to have been active in the reign of James I, but was revived during the time of the Commonwealth following a complaint to the Committee for Irish Affairs. The Committee was told by a Board of Commissioners sent to Ireland that trade was discouraged and the exchange of letters much obstructed because there was no provision for packet service "but by way of Dublin." As a result, two packet boats were to ply in the future "between Milford and Waterford."[3]

About a dozen persons sufficed for the needs of the Dublin office by the end of the seventeenth century. The Deputy Postmaster, at the head of this establishment, received £600 a year by 1703, as we learn when Isaac Manley was appointed to succeed a Mr. Warburton, who had absconded. The revenue of this service, though small, was increasing, for the receipts at the opening of Anne's reign (1702) were £16,000 annually, a considerable advance over the figure for 1689. About that time the services out of Dublin to other parts of Ireland were increased from two to three a week. It was not until 1768, however, that the posts out of Dublin went every weekday.[4]

Scotland, to which we turn next, also lacked an adequate service before the eighteenth century, but it was more sharply separated from the English Post Office than that of Ireland. This was partly the result of the possession of its own Parliament until 1707, along with a strong feeling of nationalism in Scotland. Even so, the chief post road was the one that connected Edinburgh with England. The Great North Road, which we have already traced from London to Berwick on the Border, led on, of course, to Edinburgh. It was an important artery from the beginning, and some attention has been paid to it.[5] The Scottish extension of the Great North Road was run as a horse post, and by stages, being the only horse post in all of Scotland until well into the eighteenth century. The stages from Berwick to Edinburgh were settled at Cockburnspath, Haddington and at the foot of

---

[2] See above, pp. 19 ff.

[3] *Ibid.*, p. 289. The complaint was made in 1652.

[4] *Cal. Tr.B.*, XVIII, 178, 394. Manley was still in office in 1710, at the same salary, according to *Cal. Tr.P.*, IV, 175. See also Hendy, *op. cit.*, p. 153.

[5] See above, pp. 16, 29, and Map, p. 17.

the Canongate near Holyrood Palace. The postmasters received £600 Scots annually, to be paid by the Scottish Treasurer: in addition, they had the usual privilege of hiring horses for posting. The growing towns near the Great North Road in Scotland were disregarded in much the same way as the towns off this road in England. As late as 1732 the inhabitants of Dunbar asked that the road be altered so as to go through their town, because of the "great increase of trade in Dunbar" and the "frequent miscarriage" of the letters that were left at an alehouse.[6]

The Edinburgh office was being farmed in the late seventeenth century. On the death in 1689 of the General Postmaster, John Grahame, it was obtained by an Edinburgh apothecary, John Blair, who was to have the office for seven years. Blair, in addition to keeping a general letter office in Edinburgh, was required to furnish services to the other Scottish towns, including Port Patrick. His grant, however, was not to affect the postmasters between Edinburgh and Berwick, as they had been established before his time. Sir Robert Sinclair of Stevenson obtained the farm in 1698, but soon gave it up as unprofitable. Alexander Smith, who held the office at the turn of the century, was no better off, for he owed the Treasurer of Scotland over £1776 in 1703. On Smith's death in that year his sureties were allowed to compound the debt for £500. The London officers of the Post Office seemed grateful even for that amount, since the laws of Scotland were "very favorable to cautioners." The Treasury had much difficulty also with the Scottish post-renters, that is, the deputy postmasters of the roads. It complained in 1701, for example, that the "post-renters in Scotland use all endeavor to avoid paying," and two years later the Treasury summed up its experiences by declaring that "money is so difficult to be got out of Scotland." In 1704 George Main, a jeweler of Edinburgh, accepted the lease at a yearly revenue of £1194 sterling. At that time the Edinburgh office employed seven persons—the Postmaster, an Accountant, a clerk and his assistant and three letter carriers.[7]

Edinburgh held the same place in Scotland as London in England, in that the post roads radiated from the capital. One service con-

[6] *Cal. S.P. Dom.*, 1703-4, 410-11; *Cal. Tr.P.*, 1731-34, 363; 2nd *Rep. P.M.G.* (1856), p. 78, an account based on T. B. Lang's *Historical Summary of the Post Office in Scotland*, published at Edinburgh in the same year. For the Dunbar by-pass, see Map, p. 62.
[7] *Cal. Tr.B.*, XVI, 395; XVIII, 224; *E.B.* (8th ed., 1859), XVIII, 406; *Bulletin*, Postal History Society, No. 15 (1940). Compare below, p. 111.

nected Edinburgh with Glasgow. This wholly Scottish service—the most important in the country apart from the road to Berwick—was but a foot post at the opening of the eighteenth century. Back in 1663 the carrier on this route, John Ferguson by name, had wages of £3 Scots 5s in addition to a penny sterling "for ilk letter he receaves and als much for ilk letter hamewards." Lord Broghill had written Thurloe shortly before that a horse post anywhere else than on the Edinburgh-Berwick road was not necessary and would not "counterbalance" the charge.[8]

Glasgow appealed in 1710 for a horse post to Edinburgh, on the ground that there was not sufficient time for answering letters between the coming and the departure of the foot post. The Treasury was unwilling, however, to pay the £20 a year needed for the greater convenience that a horse post would furnish. At the time, the foot post was paid £40 a year, for a twice weekly service: he left Edinburgh on Tuesdays and Thursdays at midnight, and reached Glasgow —fifty miles away—in the evening of the next day. A horse post was finally granted for this service by 1717, and so improved the connection between the two principal towns in Scotland that mail leaving Edinburgh at eight in the evening was in Glasgow the next morning.[9] The good people of Glasgow—the population was 12,000 at the time —must have been thrifty in postal matters, for by the mid-century the staff of its post office numbered only five, of whom two were letter carriers.[10]

The only other important postal route in Scotland went up the east coast to Aberdeen, via Perth and Dundee. As late as 1740 the route between Edinburgh and Aberdeen, sixty-eight miles long, was served on foot. In the early part of the century the service was carried on by three foot posts, each traveling the whole distance; the mails went twice a week. By 1740 the inhabitants of the towns served were loud in their complaints, for the service was not on schedule: often letters were three or four days on their way to Aberdeen. This slowness had an adverse effect on business, so they declared, owing to the lack of a knowledge of the changes in prices. To make matters worse, the post often "sets out one whole day and frequently two days after the English mail arrives in Edinburgh." These towns de-

[8] *Acts of the Parl. of Scotland*, VI, 894; Andrew Macgeorge, *Old Glasgow* (1888), p. 275.
[9] *Cal. Tr.P.*, IV, 224; Henry Grey Graham, *The Social Life of Scotland in the Eighteenth Century* (1928), p. 47.
[10] Macgeorge, *op. cit.*, p. 275.

clared in 1740 that they should not be "on a worse footing than Glasgow." A horse post was sought with stages at Queensferry, Perth, Dundee, Arbroath, Montrose, Bervie, Stonehaven and Aberdeen.[11]

Elsewhere in Scotland, the postal facilities were slight. Edinburgh had postal connection with Port Patrick and the packet that crossed to Donaghadee in Ireland. In the seventeenth century the route was by way of Glasgow, Kilmarnock, Dumboag, Ballantrae and Port Patrick. Reference is also found to a "laggard post" that went north from Carlisle through Dumfries. The western Highlands were without any service as late as the mid-century. When Dr. Johnson and the inseparable Boswell made their well-known visit to the Highlands in the seventies, they were completely cut off from home. As Boswell puts it: "On our arrival at the Saracen's Head Inn at Glasgow, I was made happy by good accounts from home; and Dr. Johnson, who had not received a single letter since we left Aberdeen, found a great many here, the perusal of which entertained him much."[12]

The relations of the Scottish and English branches of the Post Office had not been happy in the later years of the seventeenth century. Scotland, in general, had a difficult time after the Revolution, what with vestiges of Stuart loyalty, the differences with England over religion, and the Scottish desire for better trading conditions. The Scots felt that they were losing their liberties under the rule of King William. One result of this growing ill-feeling was the passage by the Scottish Parliament of the first and only legislative act for the creation of a national Post Office. The measure, enacted in 1695, did not have a long life, for the union of the two countries in 1707 led to a postal act four years later for the whole of the British Isles. But the short-lived Scots Act of 1695 illustrates the conditions north of the Border in the seventeenth century.

The master of the General Letter Office "to be keeped within the City of Edinburgh" was to be appointed by His Majesty, and to be called his Postmaster-General. The office could be "set in tack" as should be thought most expedient. The master of the office, or Tacksman, and his deputies and their servants had a monopoly of the carriage of letters, save for the exceptions familiar in the English Act of 1660. They also controlled the furnishing of horses for riding

[11] *Cal. Tr.B. & P.,* 1739-41, 240.
[12] Boswell, *Journal of a Tour to the Hebrides* (N.Y., 1936), p. 364. *E.B.* (8th ed., 1859), XVIII, 406; Graham, *op. cit.,* p. 45. For a postal map of Scotland of a later date, see below, p. 228.

post. The rates of postage were 2s for a single letter and proportionally for double letters between Edinburgh and Berwick or fifty miles from Edinburgh.[13] For distances over fifty miles from Edinburgh and not more than one hundred miles, the charge was 3s Scots, and above one hundred miles to any place in Scotland, 4s for a single letter. Bills of lading or exchange could be enclosed and the letter would still be reckoned as a "single." The post-horse charges were 3s Scots "for ilk horses hyre for postage for every scots mile," evidence that national feeling was running high at the time.

The Act provided for weekly posts to Ireland by packet boat. Care was to be taken by the "General Post Master or Tacksman" that posts be established over all the kingdom at places most convenient. Such was the one act of a Scottish Parliament regarding a national Post Office.[14]

The reordering of postal matters by the British Act of 1711 was badly needed. The Scottish Act of 1695 had set 2s Scots, that is 2d in England, as the charge for a single letter going not more than fifty miles. The English Act of 1660 had set the charge at 2d for forty miles beyond Berwick in Scotland, a distance that did not include Edinburgh. Confusion developed also in the relation of the two Post Offices, as the mile differed in the two countries. The Union of 1707 made a new measure even more necessary.

In England, as well, postal regulations were out of date; the Act of 1660 had become ambiguous with the lapse of time. Added to this was the matter of the London Penny Post. The Act of 1660 provided for no lower postage than 2d. Then, too, continuous trouble arose about possible extensions of the Penny Post. Promoters sought the right to set up such a service elsewhere than in London. And in London there seemed no end to the confusion, for Charles Povey had launched his "halfpenny carriage" as late as 1709. Indeed, one of the major causes for the Act of 1711 was Povey's attempted infringement of the government's Penny Post. Another reason for a new act at this time was the rise of postal services in the colonies.[15]

The chief reason, possibly, for the new act was the desire of the government to make the Post Office pay more liberally toward the pressing needs of the state. England had been at war since 1689,

---

[13] The shilling Scots had suffered so much debasement that it was worth an English penny at this time. The Scots mile also differed from the English mile. It was somewhat longer, though not so long as the Irish mile.

[14] *Acts of the Parl. of Scotland*, IX, 417-19.

[15] See below, Chap. 13.

save for a brief recess at the close of William's reign: the War of the Spanish Succession had begun in 1702. The financial burden, as a consequence, was becoming very heavy. In the Queen's speech opening the session that passed the Post Office Act, Anne was made to say: "I cannot without great concern mention to you that the Navy and other Offices are burdened with heavy Debts, which so far affect the public service that I must earnestly desire you to find some way to answer these demands."[16] Why not extract some of the needed funds from an expanding Post Office?

The Act of 1711 definitely repealed the Act of 1660 and the Scottish Act "anent the Post Office." In their place a "general post office" was erected throughout Her Majesty's dominions centering in London and under one Postmaster-General.[17] The purpose of increasing the revenue was clearly stated in the preamble: "Whereas the several rates of postage may in many parts, with little burthen to the subject, be encreased, and other new rates granted, which additional and new rates may, in some measure, enable your Majesty to carry on and finish the present war, etc." Precise arrangements were made as to the use of these increased funds for war purposes. The Postmaster-General was enjoined to pay £700 weekly—"upon Tuesday in every week"—into the exchequer. This was to go on for the next thirty-two years. The sum, totaling £36,400 annually, was the additional income that the higher postal rates were supposed to produce.[18] Thus the postal revenues were being used once again for purposes other than the improvement of the service. It might be added that the estimated increase from the additional rates never reached expectations. For a time at least, the charge was a heavy tax on postal resources.[19]

The rates were as follows. In England and Wales a single letter was carried eighty miles for 3d, instead of the 2d previously charged, and beyond eighty miles for 4d instead of the former 3d. Double

[16] *Parl. Hist.*, VI, 928.

[17] 9 Anne, c.10. There were two at this time, as we have already found, but the authority was centralized in them as "our Postmaster-General."

[18] It might be added that the end of thirty-two years saw no reversion to the older rates, as promised in the Act (sect. 39). On the contrary, the new rates had been made perpetual in 1716 by 3 Geo. I, c.7, and were to be subject to further increases as time went on. See below, p. 137. It has always been difficult, almost impossible, to obtain a relinquishment by the central authority of funds that it has once been empowered to collect. The history of the income tax in the nineteenth century—also a "temporary" expedient—is another example.

[19] *Cal. Tr.P.*, V, 287, where the judgment of the Postmaster-General is given, in the year 1717.

letters, that is, letters of two sheets of paper, were levied "double postage." "Packets of writs, deeds, and other things" were charged at four times the single rate for each ounce. The rate for a single letter between London and Edinburgh was raised from 5d to 6d. Within Scotland the first fifty miles for a single letter cost 2d; between fifty and eighty miles, 3d; above eighty miles, 4d. The reckoning was changed from the basis used in the Scottish Act "anent the Post Office": it was in English miles and in British money after 1711. The rate between London and Dublin remained unchanged, 6d for a single letter. Within Ireland, the rates were 2d for a single letter for the first forty miles and 4d for greater distances.

Foreign and colonial rates were fully treated in the Act, with increases all along the line. Though they do not concern us primarily at this point, sample rates will give an idea of oversea postage. All single letters between any part of France and London cost 10d, whereas the Act of 1660 had charged only 4d for letters to Calais, Dieppe or Boulogne. Single letters through France to any part of Spain and Portugal cost 1s 6d after 1711, through France to Italy or Turkey, 1s 3d. The rate to the Spanish Netherlands was 10d; in 1660, Antwerp had obtained its letters for 8d. Letters through the Spanish Netherlands to northern Europe cost one shilling. The rates to and through the United Provinces were the same as for the Spanish Netherlands.

West Indian correspondence was 1s 6d for a single letter. A single to New York cost one shilling. Rates within the American colonies were based on a 4d charge for single letters that traveled less than sixty miles, and 6d between sixty and one hundred miles. If the distance was greater than one hundred miles, the rate would be stated from New York to an important place, and the 4d and 6d rates would be reckoned from the latter place as an addition. From New York to New London, "the chief town in Connecticut," or to Philadelphia, the charge was 9d for a single letter. Beyond New London or Philadelphia, the rate was 4d for the first sixty miles, etc. Letters from New York to Boston, Portsmouth, N.H., or Annapolis, Md., paid a shilling. It cost 1s 6d for a single letter to Charleston, S.C.

The nature of single and double letters is already so familiar to the reader that it needs no further explanation. But the rise in postage by the Act of 1711 led to sharp practice, in the hope of avoiding the heavy charges. The London merchants combined their letters to a particular place by using, so far as possible, the same sheet of paper

—in the hope that it would go as a single letter. After some delay, an Act of 1719 prevented this attempted evasion as well as other frauds.[20]

Other sections of this Act of 1711—it remained the basic Act for over a century—dealt with the clandestine carriage of letters. Carriers were not to transport letters that did not concern their goods, and stage coaches as well as higglers and watermen were forbidden to carry mail. The private collection of letters such as Dockwra and Povey had attempted was forbidden. Other sections of the measure dealt with the riding by post, with rates set at 3d per mile for a horse, and 4d for the guide. In order to discourage private ventures in the country, the Postmaster-General could set up cross stages at the same rates as already charged on the post roads. Ship letters, that is, letters brought overseas in vessels other than packets, were to be turned into the nearest post office by the captain immediately on landing, the captain to receive a penny for every letter and packet that he delivered. Ship letters were then charged, in addition, at the regular rates.

The London Penny Post was given parliamentary sanction for the first time by the Act of 1711. The only change made in the Penny Post was to limit the area it served to a radius of ten miles from the General Letter Office in London. A second penny, as we have found, had been collected by the carrier in the outer region of the Penny Post. So long as a letter was carried eighty miles for 2d by the General Post, it made no difference as to the area of the Penny Post, but when the general rate for the inland service was made 3d, a limit had to be set to the twopenny service of the London District Post. Unfortunately, the ten-mile limit excluded from the Penny Post service some neighboring towns that had enjoyed this accommodation previously.

Such were the principal features of the Act of 1711. It was so comprehensive as to succeed the earlier basic Act of 1660, and to become a sort of second charter for the Post Office. It was to remain fundamental law for this department of government for over a century—until the great reform in the Post Office that took place just as young Victoria became Queen in 1837. By that time the Act of 1711 had been modified again and again until the postal regulations were in a mad jumble. When a comprehensive measure was passed in 1837, no less than 140 acts were thrown into the wastebasket together with the long-outdated Act of 1711.

[20] 6 Geo. I, c.21, secs. 51, 52.

The Post Office during
Ralph Allen's Time

THE war for which the Act of 1711 made provision was as good as finished in that year: the peace-loving Tories had come into power. Their victory was not for long, however, as Queen Anne died in 1714 and the Whig advocates of the Hanoverians took over the government. The political reshuffling that followed naturally affected the Post Office. Sir Thomas Frankland and Sir John Evelyn, the Postmasters-General, were replaced by Charles, the fourth Lord Cornwallis, and James Craggs. One reason for the appointment of Craggs was the belief that he was a man of great financial ability.[1]

One of the frauds that the new officers attempted to check was the loss of postal revenue through the careless checking of by-letters. The Act of 1711 had indicated much leakage in this way, for it declared that "divers deputy postmasters do not collect great quantities of post letters called by or way letters, and by clandestine and private agreements among themselves do convey the same post . . . without accounting for the same on their bills." Deputy postmasters were warned by the Act of severe penalties if they did not report the cost of these letters to the Receiver-General.[2]

One device for the preventing of this waste was the use of surveyors—men who traveled up and down the roads in order to detect this and other frauds. By their unexpected examination of mail bags and letter bills the surveyors were believed to be an effective check

[1] Frankland had held the office since 1690; Sir John Evelyn had replaced Sir Robert Cotton in 1708. Craggs had sufficient financial ability to accumulate a considerable personal fortune by his death in 1721. He seems to have been a man of few scruples.
[2] 9 Anne, c.10, secs. 18, 33.

on the postmasters. Three were tried out as early as 1715, the experiment proving such a success that they came to stay. They were soon traveling the six main roads, and were before long to be used on the cross roads, as we shall find. The former farmers of the branches, that is, the by and cross road services, also ceased to be used after 1711, being replaced by managers who were more directly under Post Office control. They were paid 10 per cent of the produce of the letters, in the hope that the change would aid the revenue.

Much more responsible than the surveyors and the new managers for whatever advance came in these years was the appearance at this time of a competent supervisor of all the business of the by and cross road letters. In 1720 the Post Office again resorted to farming, this time to one man, Ralph Allen of Bath. The change proved to be of great advantage to the revenue and to the postal system in general. Allen was an exceedingly able person, deserving more than a mere niche in the Post Office hall of fame. The Postmasters-General for the years 1720 to 1764 can be passed over without any serious omission in the narrative of postal history. To disregard Allen would be an unpardonable loss in the record.[3]

Ralph Allen, whose father was a Cornish innkeeper, was sent at the age of eleven to live with his grandmother at St. Columb, where he assisted her in the work of conducting the local post office.[4] His ability as well as the care with which he kept accounts led to Allen's employment in the important post office at Bath, where he later became the postmaster. Shortly before 1720 he proposed to the Post Office that he be given the farm of all the by and cross road letters. This was granted in 1720 by a contract that ran for seven years, and it was regularly renewed thereafter until death removed Allen nearly a half century later. This long control by one man of the by and cross road letters came at a very important time. The need for improved communications was growing with the expansion of industry and commerce in the first half of the eighteenth century. Ralph Allen expanded the services of the Post Office at an opportune time.[5]

Allen was a distinguished man. He was mayor of Bath in 1742,

---

[3] Between 1715 and 1765 there were nine pairs of Postmasters-General. The Post Office was already something of a political football, but as yet a football of minor political importance.

[4] The office at St. Columb had been newly established in 1703, as the result of setting up a post road that would serve the inland towns. See above, p. 82.

[5] *D.N.B.*, I, 311-12; Joyce, *op. cit.*, 146 ff.; W. L. Cross, *The History of Henry Fielding* (1918), I, 376-77.

and had considerable wealth, owing not only to his fortunate postal contracts but to the produce of large quarries. At his magnificent home just outside the city, Allen entertained lavishly. Among his guests were members of the royal family, leading politicians and the literary figures of his day. He was an intimate friend of Pitt, Warburton, Swift, Pope and Fielding. Pope's couplet regarding him has often been quoted:

> Let humble Allen, with an awkward shame,
> Do good by stealth and blush to find it fame.

Fielding's relations with Allen were so intimate and their mutual regard so deep that Fielding has perpetuated the memory of the postal reformer in several works. In *Tom Jones*, the character of Squire Allworthy was an accepted portrait of Allen, whose kindliness, generous spirit and hospitality are well portrayed in the benevolent Squire. Fielding dedicated *Amelia* to Allen, and in *Joseph Andrews* the novelist refers to Allen as a "commoner raised higher above the multitude by superior talents than is the power of the prince to exalt him; whose behavior to those that he obliged is more amiable than the obligation itself."[6]

Just what was Allen's exact sphere of activity as a postal reformer and organizer? A by-letter has already been defined as one that did not enter the London Post Office in the course of its journey: it might travel a portion of a main post road, one stage or several, but stopped short of London. A cross-post letter journeyed by one of the posts that joined the main roads at some distance from London. Already by 1720 a number of cross posts were serving towns near the main post roads. The very important one between Exeter and Bristol was laid in 1696 and extended to Chester just at the turn of the century.[7]

The Post Office had found it very difficult to keep a sufficient

---

[6] See Cross, *op. cit.*, I, 376-77; II, 162, 304. *Joseph Andrews* appeared at the time that Allen was the Mayor of Bath. Fielding named one of his sons Allen, and made Ralph Allen the sole executor of the Fielding will.

[7] Some earlier accounts of the British Post Office need correction at this point. Lewins, *op. cit.*, p. 53, makes Allen set up the Exeter-Bristol-Chester road. The service between Exeter and Bristol was proposed when Allen was two years old, and the extension to Chester was added while he was still a humble assistant to his grandmother at St. Columb. An article in *Fraser's Magazine* for September 1862—a review of the history of the Post Office by M. D. Hill, the brother of the reformer, Rowland Hill—makes the same claims for Allen, and may be the source of Lewins' error. The 9th edition of the *Encyclopaedia Britannica* even makes Allen the "inventor of the cross roads postal system."

check on letters that did not go through London. Many letters went by illegal conveyance, for the postboys were notoriously slow. Other than postal channels were also used for letters because the charges, in addition to the legal rates, were often exorbitant. Perquisites, it would appear, were not infrequently levied to an amount equaling the regular postage. The postboys were also accustomed to deliver letters that never found their way into the official postbag. One surveyor even discovered the house in Plymouth where the postboys met and exchanged letters—a veritable postal system *sub rosa*.[8]

Another grievance was the loss or miscarriage of by-letters. As Allen himself put it: "The by and way letters are thrown promiscuously together into one large bag, which was to be opened at every stage by the deputy or any inferior servant of the house, to pick out of the whole heap whatever might belong to his own delivery, and the rest put back again into this large bag, with such by letters as he should have to send to distant places from his own stage."[9]

Allen's proposal of 1719 for the farm of the by and cross post letters was based on the annual income of these letters—about £4000 a year. Allen offered to farm this branch of the postal service for £6000, the farmer to keep any excess that he might be able to collect. The contract required him to maintain services three times a week at a speed of not less than five miles an hour. This referred to the branches, formerly farmed as well, that were off the main post roads. Allen also agreed to pay the surveyors, since they would be working not only for the Post Office but for him as well. The surveyors, nevertheless, were regarded as under the direct supervision of the Postmaster-General.

The first seven years of Allen's farm were not profitable, but he had matters so well in hand by the end of the contract that he believed it worth while to renew the agreement. The Postmasters-General were agreeable, of course, because they saw that Allen's development of the cross posts was having a good effect on the number of "country letters," that is, the letters that went to or through London from the provinces. The country letters, which averaged £15,434 a year for seven years before the first contract, increased to £16,553 between 1720 and 1727, and brought in £17,464 annually from 1727 to 1734.[10] On the renewal of Allen's contract in 1734, he

---

[8] Joyce, *op. cit.*, p. 164.

[9] *Cal. S.P. Home*, 1760-65, 85. The date given in the calendar for Allen's suggestions is 1710, a probable error for 1719. See *Cal. Tr.B. & P.*, 1739-41, 445.

[10] *Cal. S.P. Home*, *loc. cit.*; *Cal. Tr.P.*, 1731-34, 539.

guaranteed a further increase in the income from the country letters. The next contract, of 1741, included the requirement that he increase the service from three days a week to six days a week from London to Bath, Bristol, Gloucester and the intermediate towns. The increased service arranged for at that time was largely stimulated by the citizens of Bristol: they asked for improved communications with London, on account of the increase in Bristol's population and trade.[11]

The later renewals of Allen's contract required him to supervise and extend this daily service to numerous other roads. In 1748, for example, a daily schedule was extended to the Midlands, including the growing manufacturing town of Birmingham.

The contract for 1755 included further extensions. Already a mail left every post night—except Sunday—from London over a thickening web of routes. The accompanying map, based on the postal services in 1756, will give some idea of the postal routes to which Allen was giving so much attention. Daily services—save Sunday—went out the main roads to the west leading to Exeter and Plymouth, and by way of Exeter to Truro, passing through Allen's early home of St. Columb. Another daily service led to Bristol, and a third by way of Gloucester gave daily service as far as Swansea in south Wales, and by way of Hereford to Carmarthen and Pembroke. Neither Falmouth nor Milford were important at this time, though the war about to open—the Seven Years' War—was to bring Falmouth into the limelight postally, owing to the increasing value of the packet services. The Holyhead road had a daily service with a branch that gave the same advantages to Shrewsbury. In the west of England, the daily mail went north through Warrington as far as Lancaster. The Great North Road had service every weekday, and Carlisle was served by daily mails that left the Edinburgh road at Boroughbridge. Central England had a number of such services— to Sheffield via Nottingham and to Derby through Northampton. Several went south and southeast from London to the nearby coast.[12]

A number of new mail roads received daily service in 1755. The additions included routes to Portsmouth, Yarmouth, Norwich, Southampton, and the already mentioned cross road from Exeter to Chester through western England. The Exeter-Chester road was

[11] *Cal. Tr.B. & P.*, 1739-41, 450; W. T. Jackman, *op. cit.*, 323.
[12] The map has been constructed from data furnished by *A New and Accurate Description of the Present Great Roads of England and Wales* (London, Dodsley), 1756.

THE GREAT ROADS AND PRINCIPAL
CROSS ROADS IN 1756

———— Roads having daily Postal service
(save Sunday) from London
------ Extensions not served six days
a week

0   20   40
Scale of miles

NORTH

SEA

Irish Sea

English Channel

LONDON

now extended to include Manchester and Liverpool at the northern end. At this time there were some thirty important cross roads and ten additional "accidental cross roads." Examples of "accidental" cross roads were those leading from York to Whitby and Scarborough, from Exeter to Dorchester, from Plymouth to Dartmouth and from Carmarthen to Aberystwyth.

The contract to which Allen agreed in 1761 was the last that he made. The yearly rent was still to be £6000. If receipts from country letters fell short of £20,000 annually, Allen was to reimburse the Post Office for the shortage. This amount in the contract was based on the "considerable increase" of country letters "during the last contract." The agreement further provided that all of Allen's servants should have salaries set by the Post Office, the three surveyors, for instance, each receiving £300 a year. The contract went at length into the branches to be established by Allen at his expense, the number of posts they were to have per week, the rate of speed and the towns to be served. Several new stages and cross branches were added, including services between Manchester and Chesterfield, Newcastle and Whitehaven (a service from coast to coast), Wakefield and Leeds, Halifax and Manchester. It is clear from the names of the towns included in this contract that the expanding manufacturing districts of the Midlands were receiving special consideration.[13]

Ralph Allen was the grand go-between of the Post Office for all the services "distinct and apart from the grand Post Roads," that is, the six roads leading out of London, and for all letters that did not go through or by way of London, that is, the so-called "country letters." His grant of the carriage of the "Bye or Way Letters" included all such collected or delivered at any "Post Road or Town within England or Wales." This meant, therefore, that his contract included supervision, through his surveyors, of the services on the main post roads as well. He was much more than a mere farmer of the by and cross post letters. Allen was the medium through which the Post Office increased the services as the needs arose during the first half of the eighteenth century.

[13] The contract for 1761 is contained in the Report from the "Committee who were appointed to consider the agreement made with Mr. Palmer, etc." (1797). This Report is cited hereafter as *Rep. Com. on Palmer's Agreement*. The correspondence of Samuel Johnson contains a reference to the bypost. He wrote Mrs. Thrale from Lichfield in 1777: "I forgot that the post went out yesternight, and so omitted to write: I therefore put this in the bypost and hope it will come." *Letters of Samuel Johnson*, ed. G. B. Hill (N.Y., 1892), I, 359.

The result was a remarkable expansion just at the time that it was sorely needed, for his work not only augmented the revenue of the country letters, but it "quickened and improved the life of trade." Nor did Allen himself suffer financially, for the chief source of profit from the by and cross post letters arose, as he realized, "from correspondence between trading towns in distant parts of the kingdom."[14] It is a curious situation. Ralph Allen had no official position in the Inland Office. Yet under the guise of a contractor of the by and cross post letters, he was the prime mover in extending the postal service to all parts of the country, setting up numerous new branches, and effecting nation-wide increases in the number of posts per week.

The methods Allen used for checking frauds and increasing his own profits throw much light on the postal arrangements of the time. He used a system of post bills or vouchers for the accurate checking of the number of letters. Postmasters were required to send a post bill that would show the amount to be collected. This was intended for the by-letters. The country letters—to or through London—had long been checked by means of a waybill or label, giving the time of the arrival and dispatch of the letters, as well as their number and value.[15] The voucher introduced by Allen served as an acknowledgment of the amount the postmaster was to collect for by and cross post letters that he received. The post bills were to be sent in to Allen every quarter, and were carefully gone over in Bath. Through his own full knowledge of conditions and the work of his surveyors, Allen could detect by this double check any discrepancies in the number of letters from and to the various offices. He carefully examined these reports, as the contractor lost revenue if the postmasters connived in fraud by falsifying the post bills. To lessen this possibility of fraud, he required the postmasters to verify their claims for allowances by an oath.

Stamping of all the by and cross post letters was an additional safeguard, for it furnished a check on the number of letters that had passed officially from one postmaster to another, and also gave a basis for the allowance to the receiving postmaster when the postage due was uncollectable, that is, if the letter was missent or proved a dead letter. Its use in checking allowances to postmasters who turned them in to Allen was an effective argument with the deputy postmasters. They needed prodding at times to furnish the necessary

[14] *Cal. Tr.B. & P.*, 1739-41, 445.   [15] See above, p. 59.

identification, as one amusing instance illustrates. An old postmistress had asked allowance for a number of unstamped letters. As the letters showed no indication of the place whence they came, they were returned with the statement that no allowance would be granted on unstamped letters. The postmistress was equal to the occasion. The letters were soon returned to Allen, each carrying on the outside the place of its origin. Allen, to his surprise and dismay, found that she had obtained the information by opening each letter.[16]

Allen's plan of stamping by and cross post letters when they were sent was intended to check the genuineness of the letters submitted for credit, since some of the postmasters had circulated bogus dead letters. The idea of the stamp was not new, though Allen put it to new uses. The Bishop postmarks used in the London office have already been noticed.[17] Even their use by provincial postmasters is

ASHBY
Z

AB·N·DON

known to have occurred before 1720, though their use in the country was rare before that time. One writer asserts that orders were issued to provincial postmasters in the year 1715 for each post town to make use of a stamp "so that a check may be kept on letters passing from one stage to another."[18] In any case, the stamping of letters was greatly extended under Allen's supervision after 1720. Henceforth, it is to be a permanent feature of postal practice.

The provincial stamp of those days consisted only of the name of the sending office. It was impressed in black or red on the outside of the folded letter. At first, only the name was used without an encircling line, nor was there a date affixed. The Bishop stamps were date stamps, and the Penny Post stamps were date stamps and also a receipt for payment. The unpaid postmarks of the provincial post

[16] Joyce, *op. cit.*, p. 159.   [17] See above, p. 58.
[18] Hendy, *op. cit.*, p. 83. The source of his information is not given, and Alcock & Holland, in referring to "Hendy" at this point, seem to do so with some reservation.

offices appeared in many forms. Ashby de la Zouche and Abingdon are examples of simple arrangements. The name might also appear in two straight lines. More fanciful forms were also found for such places as Bristol and Chester. As we have already said, these stamps were not to indicate payment, but simply posting, nor are they cancellations, since there was, as yet, no adhesive stamp to cancel. They simply record the source of the letter, and are for the most part very crude. The date of posting, in addition to the name of the office, was not in general use until the end of the eighteenth century.[19]

What we call "dead letters" must have been numerous in Allen's day, for the widening of the postal service made it a novelty to many users. Dead letters in the by and cross posts were sent to him. Dead letters in the General Post were sent to London presumably, for the staff in London included two men receiving good salaries "to inspect dead and missent letters."[20] No effort, so far as is known, was made to return them to the senders. A Dead Letter Office was not set up until late in the century, and even then the nondeliverable letters were not returned. Indeed, all dead letters were destroyed by the Post Office both in Great Britain and in the United States well into the nineteenth century.[21]

Another device used by Allen for improving the revenue was the checking of franked letters. As the postmasters did not have to pay for such letters sent or received, great temptation developed to use this means for general correspondence. Letters to local people might be received by the postmaster under his name and distributed outside the ordinary postal arrangements. In order to prevent the loss of postage in this way, Allen ruled that franked letters to postmasters must be single letters. An interesting case of fraud came to Allen's attention when an advertiser sent notices of a publication about the treatment of horses to all postmasters, with instructions to reply to the postmistress at Lancaster, and save the advertiser the postage. Unfortunately for the advertiser, Allen, as the postmaster of Bath, received one of the advertisements, and its advice for saving postage.[22]

Allen was allowed a large amount of freedom in handling the services, for the postal officials were contented to give him the opportunity to use his own initiative. The chief requirements made of

[19] Alcock & Holland, *op. cit.*, pp. 57 ff; Hendy, *op. cit.*, pp. 83 ff.
[20] Chamberlayne, *Magnae Britanniae Notitia* (1755), General lists, p. 69.
[21] Alcock & Holland, *op. cit.*, p. 435.   [22] Joyce, *op. cit.*, p. 161.

Allen were a rental paid to the Post Office of £6000 annually, and a guaranteed postal income from the country letters. He seems to have found the arrangement to his great personal advantage. When John Palmer—also a man of Bath—sought a financial agreement with the Post Office later in the century, Palmer asserted that Allen's profits were "very large," amounting to £12,000 a year. If so, one can see why Allen would have given so much attention to the improvement of the services of the by and cross post letters.[23]

Postal revenues increased considerably in these years. Back in 1688 the income of the Post Office was nearly £90,000. Ten years later it was more than £116,000, and by 1715 had increased to about £150,000. The gross income had reached £175,000 by 1725, £182,-000 by 1735, £194,000 by 1745, £210,000 by 1755, and at the time of Allen's death (1764) the total was more than £225,000. Such a forward movement cannot be laid, of course, to any one cause, such as the work of Ralph Allen. Yet his part in the advance cannot be denied, even if his activity came at a time when advance was likely. Interestingly enough, the War of the Austrian Succession and the Seven Years' War—they took up most of the twenty-five years before 1763—did not lessen the income of the Post Office.[24]

Despite this marked advance in revenue, the establishment itself does not prove to have been imposing or to have grown to any extent during the years between 1711 and 1763. This statement applies to the official Post Office, and not to the work of Ralph Allen. We may well conclude our study of the Post Office during these years by a look at the actual postal arrangements of the time.

[23] *Rep. Com. on Palmer's Agreement* (1797), pp. 55, 58, and see below, Chap. 12.
[24] *Ibid.*, p. 151. George Chalmers, *An Historical View of the Domestic Economy of Great Britain and Ireland,* paid considerable attention to the postal revenue. Chalmers gives £280,000 as the receipts for 1764. This is high, as the "Gross Produce" of the Post Office, exclusive of franks, was under £266,000 at the end of the fiscal year, 1765-66. The tabulation for the years after 1724 is given in *Rep. Com. on Palmer's Agreement* (1797), pp. 60-61, 80. The figures for every five years are as follows:

for the year ending March 25, 1726............£178,065	6s	11d
1731......................... 171,412	0	5
1736......................... 188,210	11	4
1741......................... 191,408	17	10
1746......................... 201,460	14	4
1751......................... 203,748	6	10
for the year ending April 5, 1756......................... 238,455	17	9
1761......................... 240,497	16	0
1766......................... 265,427	17	8

There was great fluctuation at the end of the Seven Years' War. In 1764 the gross income had been £225,000; in the next year it was £262,000, and in 1765 over £265,000. See below, p. 146n, for a continuance of these figures.

The central or General Post Office in London was housed in what a contemporary writer called a "handsome and commodious building" in Lombard Street, adjoining the parish church of St. Mary Woolnoth.[25] The staff of the General Post Office seems small compared with the size of its business and the ramifications of the postal services. Some seventy or eighty people served the establishment in London. At the head were the two Postmasters-General, receiving £2000 a year. Next in importance, were the Receiver-General, the Accomptant-General and the Resident Surveyor, each in receipt of £300 a year. The Secretary of the Post Office had £200, as well as the Comptroller of the Inland Office and the Solicitor. By the mid-century, each of these main offices had deputies, the Secretary having three clerks. One of these was a young man named Anthony Todd, whose salary was but £50 a year. We shall hear more of him presently.

In the Post Office of the mid-century, the members of the staff who were next in importance to these general officers were the clerks of the six roads, of which there were two for each road, all receiving £60 a year, save the chief clerk of the Chester Road, whose salary was £100.[26] These "trifling salaries" were supplemented by perquisites that made the clerkships of the roads of considerable importance. The rest of the staff at the General Post Office included a clerk of the Bye-Nights, one window man and alphabet keeper, two men to "overlook the franks and missent letters," a court post and two mail makers. There were some sixteen sorters of letters, as well as one "facer of letters." The outdoor service of the Inland Office in London accounted for most of the staff, for there were sixty-seven inland letter carriers: they received 11s a week each.

The Foreign Letter Office, which cared for mail coming from or going to the Continent, had a separate staff. It included a Comptroller, an alphabet keeper, a secretary, six clerks and eight carriers to distribute the foreign letters.[27]

The chief office of the Penny Post was in St. Christopher's Alley in Threadneedle Street "near the Stocks-Market." The other offices

[25] John Entick and others, *The Present State of the British Empire*, 4 vols. See vol. III, 21.

[26] The roads were the Chester Road, the West Road, that is, to Exeter and Falmouth, the North Road, and those to Bristol and beyond, to Yarmouth, and the road into Kent usually known as the Dover Road. See Chamberlayne, *op. cit.* (1755), p. 68 of the English lists, and Entick, *op. cit.*, III, 21. For "bye-night," see p. 55n.

[27] Chamberlayne, *op. cit.* (1755), p. 69 of the English lists; Entick, *op. cit.*, III, 22.

were five in number, and were located "within the Bills of Mortality."[28] The Penny Post, as we have found, was "kept in a separate state," with its own Comptroller, collector and accomptant. Each office had two or three sorters. A company of some eighty messengers or runners did the outdoor work of the Penny Post. In the more densely populated areas, Penny Post letters were collected and delivered three times a day.

Surely these three offices combined would not have made a large establishment for a great urban center like London, with its population of over half a million, and the capital of a country that probably numbered seven million people by the middle of the eighteenth century.[29]

The next offices in size were those of Dublin and Edinburgh. Dublin required a staff of eighteen persons, including the letter carriers. Edinburgh's post-office service was even more meager. There was a Postmaster-General, an accomptant, a secretary, five clerks and three letter carriers. There were 182 other post offices in Great Britain and 45 in Ireland, in addition to the main office in Dublin.[30]

Such was the state of the Post Office in Great Britain and Ireland as we come to the end of the period dominated by the activity of Ralph Allen. There was but little growth during this time in the Post Office staff, and little expansion apart from the work of Allen. But a new period was at hand. Following the conclusion of peace in 1763, a postal act was passed to meet the new conditions. New rates had to be set up for the enlarging oversea dominions.[31] The Act of 1765 slightly altered the charge for letters in the British Isles. The rate for longer distances remained the same, but letters going but one stage cost but a penny, and if going but two post stages the charge was 2d. This change amounted, in a way, to the extension of the Penny Post to places outside London. The Act also permitted the authorities to establish a "Penny Post office, in any city or town, and the suburbs thereof and places adjacent . . . where such post

---

[28] The St. Paul's Office was in Queen's Head Alley in Paternoster Row, the Temple Office in Chancery Lane, that for Westminster near Charing Cross, the one for Southwark in Green Dragon Court near St. Mary Overy's Church (the present Southwark Cathedral) and the Hermitage Office was on Little Tower Hill. Chamberlayne, *op. cit.* (1755), pp. 70-75 of the English lists.

[29] The first census, taken in 1801, showed that England and Wales then contained over nine million inhabitants.

[30] Chamberlayne, *op. cit.* (1755), p. 44 of the Scottish lists; Entick, *op. cit.*, IV, 71-72. Cf. above, pp. 91-92.

[31] For the posts in the colonies and the rates arranged by the Act of 1765, see below, Chap. 13.

shall, by the postmaster-general, be adjudged necessary and convenient." Dublin at last received the privilege that had been sought for it by the Countess of Thanet at the beginning of the century. A Penny Post was set up in Dublin in 1773 and in Edinburgh not long after. As time went on, numerous Penny Posts were to be arranged for the growing industrial areas, radiating from those centers in much the same way that London's Penny Post reached out into the environs. It was to prove a natural extension, and will be treated as a unit in a later chapter.[32]

[32] Chap. 16.

Abuses in
the Post Office

THE habit of grumbling about the public services has become almost instinctive with English-speaking peoples. Among these services, the postal arrangements have suffered more criticism, probably, than any other government department. This may result from its being in touch with the public more constantly than the war or naval services, or even the customs.

The modern post office, however, would come off with a relatively clean bill of health as compared with that of the eighteenth century. Ralph Allen may have been adding greatly to the usefulness of the postal services, but the department, as a whole, was burdened with obsolete practices and bureaucratic management. The eighteenth century was a time of much corruption in the high places of government, with no adequate public opinion capable of focusing popular disapproval on a dilatory service or actual malpractices. The unreformed Post Office was probably at its worst in the eighteenth century. Hence the reason for giving some attention to the more obvious abuses in the service before moving on to the beginning of reform. The two faults most criticized at the time, apart from the use of postal money for pensions, were the extreme use made by the government of the privilege of opening mail and the extraordinary growth of the franking system.

Franking had begun much earlier than 1711, but its great extension came after that time. It had started in the Cromwellian period: letters that were "for the service of the Commonwealth" were to pass free. The Restoration continued the practice, but without specific reference regarding franking in the Charter of 1660. Since the Post Office was in control of the Crown, royal warrants were used to extend or regulate the privilege.[1] Before the Revolution of 1688, the Postmaster-General was regularly granted an allowance for the number of franked letters circulated by the Post Office. In 1670 the amount was £4000, four years later it was £6000, and by 1677 the annual allowance had reached £7200.[2] In William's reign, the members of Parliament were allowed free postage for their franked single inland letters during the sessions and for forty days before and after.[3] There was some effort to restrict the privilege in 1693, by limiting it, so far as government officials were concerned, to the two principal Secretaries of State in England, the Secretary for Scotland, the Secretary in Holland, and the Earl of Portland. These five were not to permit anyone to send letters under cover to them, that is, letters addressed to their care for someone else, nor were they to "cover any man's letters whatsoever but their own."[4]

The Act of 1711 made no more reference to franking than the Charter of 1660, despite the increasing abuse of the privilege by that time. In the very year of the Act, the Treasury learned that booksellers endorsed their letters and newspapers with the names of members of Parliament. After 1711, franking grew apace. The total amount of franked material by the end of Queen Anne's reign (1714) had risen to the amazing figure of £25,000.[5]

By the opening of the reign of George II (1727), the royal warrant allowing franking included "our principal secretaries of state for the time being, the commissioners of our Treasury, now being, .. the Secretary at War, the Secretary of our Admiralty, our lieutenant-general or other chief Governor or governors of our kingdom of Ireland for the time being, and his or their secretary; excepting also the members of both our Houses of Parliament, during every session of Parliament, and for forty days before and forty days after every session." But members' letters or packets were not to exceed

---

[1] See above, p. 50.

[2] Cal. Tr.B., III, 523, 602, 673, 888, 1203; IV, 821, 826; V, 1283.

[3] Ibid., X, 82.

[4] Ibid., X, 79. The Earl of Portland, William Bentinck, was the well-known Dutch general, and the closest of King William's advisers. He served the King on diplomatic missions, being a sort of Secretary of State for Foreign Affairs. Dutch William did not trust his English advisers in such matters.

[5] Cal. Tr.P., 1708-14, 332; 1714-19, 287. In 1715, the "State's franks" amounted to £8270 per annum and the members' letters to £17,470 a year. In addition, the clerks of the Inland and Foreign Offices "have always been allowed the privilege of franking some news letters to their correspondents."

two ounces in weight. The warrant stated that the abuses of franking "as we have been informed, have been frequently practiced by
divers persons." Among the misuses that were recognized was the
counterfeiting of members' names on letters, the directing of letters
to members when they were intended for someone else, and the
sending by members of letters that did not "concern themselves."[6]
About the same time, the postmaster at Dublin complained of excessive franking in Ireland. The "extravagant freedom" used there
was defended by some on the ground that franking prevented
money from going out of the country. To the self-conscious Irish,
franking seemed a "public good and a virtuous action."[7]

The whole matter came up for review in the thirties. The Post
Office examined the matter in 1734, the result being "An Account
of the diminution of the revenue by franking of letters, from the
year 1715 to the year 1734." This examination, along with the irri-
tation of members of Parliament by the effort of the Post Office to
detect false franks, led to an airing of the whole matter in the House
of Commons in 1735. A committee of the House examined this matter and reported its findings.[8] The most interesting evidence presented to the House came from examining the supervisor of franks,
Edward Cave. He had been checking the franks since 1721, and had
noticed that "franks increase with every parliament." In his efforts
to "control" franks, Cave charged all letters not wholly superscribed
by the member, and all that were not about the member's business.
When asked how he would know that a letter was chargeable, he
explained his methods. "A letter coming from a place where he
knew the member signing was not, was a reason to him to think it
was not about the member's business, . . that he could frequently
see by the help of a candle, through a cover directed to a member,
an inclosed letter directed to another person; in which case, his way
was to charge it, and to notify its not being about a member's business, or to stamp H.J. upon it, which were the initials of Henry
Jaques, his predecessor in the office, under whom he had learned the
art of finding out false franks."

Another evidence of a false frank, according to Cave, was the
absence of black sealing wax on the supposed letter of a member
whom he knew to be in mourning. Cave also noticed that members
of Parliament, not re-elected, "do not willingly part with the privi-

[6] *Parl. Hist.*, IX, 839-42.   [7] *Cal. Tr.P.*, VI, 77.   [8] *Parl. Hist.*, IX, 842-48.

lege of franking." They got blank franks from their friends in the existing Parliament. But if he apprehended such a use he struck off the frank. Edward Cave declared that it was better to err in refusing the use of the frank, even if genuine, since it was "the postmaster-general's maxim, 'we can give redress at any time, but can never recover what is slipt.' "[9] It is little wonder that Ralph Allen objected to the excessive franking when he sought the renewal of his contract with the Post Office in 1741.[10]

The actual amount of franking during these years is difficult to check, though the tendency to a rapid increase in the number of franked letters is undeniable, and was certainly a common belief at the time. As we have already found, the total value of franked mail in Great Britain by 1715, if charged at its proper weight, was about £25,000 annually. In Ireland, the amount of franks used was enormous. By 1718 the unfranked mail was believed to be five times greater than the letters that paid postage.[11] According to Allen, the total for England exceeded £50,000 in 1741. By the time of his death in 1764 the value of the franked letters had reached the enormous total of £170,000. This would certainly argue an amazing increase in parliamentary and bureaucratic activity, or tremendous venality. It was estimated that the amount of franked mail, if computed by weight, was about half the amount of the mail that paid postage.[12]

As a result, an act was finally passed in 1764 "for preventing frauds and abuses in relation to the sending and receiving of letters and packets free from the duty of postage."[13] In order to stop "great and notorious frauds," elaborate regulations were put into statutory form for the first time. Letters to and from the King went free, as well as letters of members of Parliament during a sitting and for forty days before and for forty days after the session. The parliamentary frank had to be signed in full by the member, and any letter received free by him must be at his usual place of residence, or where he actually was to be found at the time. Public officials who were allowed to frank letters and receive letters free were listed in the Act. The list, somewhat longer than that of 1727, included the

[9] *Ibid.*, IX, 845-46. [10] *Cal. Tr. B. & P.*, 1739-41, 450.
[11] Joyce, *op. cit.*, p. 142.
[12] *Cal. Tr. B. & P.*, 1739-41, 450; *The Athenaeum* (London), Dec. 4, 1852, p. 1329.
[13] 4 Geo. III, c.24. An additional reason for the act was the change of control of the postal revenues. In 1760, they were carried to the Aggregate, later the Consolidated, Fund. See above, p. 77.

Lord High Treasurer, the Secretaries of the Treasury, the high officers of the Admiralty, the Secretaries of State and their under-secretaries, the Secretary of War and his secretary, similar officers for Ireland and the colonies, the Postmaster-General, the Secretary of the Post Office, the farmer of the by and cross road letters, the surveyors of the Post Office, and the Deputy Postmasters for Scotland, Ireland and America. Particular lists of those who were to endorse letters in the government offices had to be sent to the Post Office. Printed proceedings of Parliament were to go free, likewise newspapers, "being sent without covers, or in covers open at the sides, which shall be signed, on the outside thereof, by the hand of any member of parliament."

The Act of 1764—the first to recognize the existence of franking —concluded with a severe penalty for anyone counterfeiting handwriting in order to send mail free of postage. Such a person was adjudged guilty of felony and was to be transported for seven years.

The widespread use of illegal franks can be illustrated from the correspondence of the time. When Horace Walpole was elected to Parliament in the late forties, his frank was used to cover his friends' letters. George Montague regularly used this means to avoid the payment of postage. He wrote to Walpole in 1761, for example: "Pray put your name to my sister's letter." At another time: "Pray frank the good tidings that I have sent to my sister." Again: "Be so good as to frank my brother's letter." In 1762 Montague asked Walpole to put his name to a letter of the Bishop of Ferns, whose right to frank did not extend beyond Ireland. When Walpole was no longer able to frank—in 1768—Montague directed a letter to him by way of one who had the privilege: "I have directed this packet to my cousin, F. Montague; 'tis not just you should pay for my stuff."[14]

Another of Horace Walpole's correspondents, the Rev. Wm. Cole, saw no more wrong in using his friend's frank than did the Irish Bishop of Ferns. "May I presume to beg the favour of you to frank the enclosed two letters, which may go to the post office whenever your servant carries your own." On another occasion, he wrote: "I am sending my servant to Lord Montfort's, and will get him to

[14] *Horace Walpole's Correspondence with George Montague*, ed. W. S. Lewis and A. Dayle Wallace (1941), I, 51, 396, 402, 405; II, 27, 261.

frank this." And Walpole wrote him on one occasion: "I will return you Mr. Gough's letter when I get a frank, Adieu."[15]

Samuel Johnson was another who did not disdain the use of another's frank. In his intimate correspondence with Mrs. Thrale, Johnson often addressed his letters to the husband, since Thrale's parliamentary membership allowed him to receive letters free. Johnson wrote Mrs. Thrale in 1770 from Lichfield: "I have taken the liberty to enclose a letter; for though you do not know it three groats make a shilling." A groat, that is, fourpence, was the cost of a single letter from Lichfield to London. Again writing a letter to Mrs. Thrale, but addressing it in her husband's name, he declared: "If such letters as this were to cost you anything, I should hardly write them." The limit of a frank to two ounces explains the language of another letter to the same correspondent: "Can it [some medicine] be franked? If it cannot, the best way will be to unite it with something of greater bulk." And there is good reason to believe that Mrs. Thrale, in writing to Johnson, franked her letters by counterfeiting her husband's signature on the outside for purposes of sending her messages free.[16]

Sir Walter Scott makes reference to the practice in *Redgauntlet*, a tale of the eighteenth century. At the end of the first letter written by Latimer to Fairford, the latter is spoken of as having a frank "which you had from an old peer," which being handled gently and opened with precaution may be returned again and again "and serve to make us free of his Majesty's post-office during the whole time of my proposed tour." In a note explaining these references, Scott mentions "one noble lord" who showed his regard for a particular regiment by franking a letter for every rank and file. He added: "It was customary, also, to save the covers and return them, in order that the correspondence might be carried on as long as the envelope could hold together."[17]

Franking, a growing burden in the eighteenth century, was to become heavier and heavier until the evil reached such intolerable proportions that parliamentary franking was to cease in 1840, and official franking to be severely restricted. Once such a privilege as

---

[15] *Horace Walpole's Correspondence with the Rev. Wm. Cole*, ed. by W. S. Lewis and A. Dayle Wallace (1937), I, 59, 194, 296, 385. The references to franking are scattered throughout these carefully edited and fully indexed volumes.

[16] *Letters of Samuel Johnson*, ed. by G. B. Hill (N.Y., 1892), I, 161; II, 19, 94, 123.

[17] By "envelope," in this use, is meant the enveloping sheet of paper on which the frank was written.

franking was granted, the Post Office and the Treasury found it exceedingly difficult to curtail the practice. Numerous additions were to be made after 1764 to the list of persons in government offices who were allowed to frank mail. The Post Office here, as well as in regard to pensions, and, we might add, with regard to war expenses such as those of 1711, was shouldering burdens it should not have been required to carry. The postal service might more wisely have been developed to make easier communications between private individuals and also between the industrial and commercial sides of eighteenth century life, in addition to its legitimate use by government. Instead, it became a vested interest and a medium of taxation.

Another practice of the Post Office to which there was strong objection was the opening by officials of private correspondence, in order to obtain information of value to the government. This abuse differed from franking in that the very persons who enjoyed the free use of the mails were most vigorous in their clamor against the violation of the secrecy of correspondence. As this malpractice was prevalent in the period we are reviewing, we may well consider it before moving on to examine the postal changes of the late eighteenth century.

The opening of private letters was not new in the days of Robert Walpole, but it received its first severe criticism at the time when he was the head of the ministry in the reign of George II. Under the Tudors, the postal service was carefully supervised and intended largely for the use of official personages. Even when the Post Office expanded in the early seventeenth century, the strict supervision of the service implied that no great freedom would be allowed for private correspondence. Efficient control was the order in Cromwell's day, with the opening of private letters a regular practice of specially appointed experts in unsealing and resealing letters.[18]

Although the Act of 1660 was silent on the matter of opening letters, this device for detecting plots and treasonable ideas was a regular practice of the Stuart kings following the Restoration. When the Popish Plot was at its feverish height in the seventies, the London officers had directions to send to the authorities letters of suspected persons. When the government, for example, obtained the correspondence of Coleman, the secretary of the Duke of York, it was considered sufficient ground for his conviction. The farmers in the Restoration period were required to turn over to the Secretaries

---

[18] See above, p. 45.

of State for inspection all letters that the government wished to examine.[19]

This practice increased, if anything, after the Revolution of 1688. Viscount Sydney, for example, wrote the Postmaster-General in 1692: "Whenever any letters shall come into your office directed to 'Mr. Brett, at Mr. Hugh's, a stationer at the Unicorne in Paternoster Row, London' or with this direction 'To Mr. Brett, at Dr. Harborough's over against the back gate of Doctor's Commons,' I desire that you will take care to have them stopped and transmitted to me."[20] During King William's reign—mostly occupied by war—there was a "secret man" at the Post Office performing functions similar to those of Dr. Dorislaus forty years before. The "secret man" was to keep letters no longer than the next morning, so that the correspondents, who were being watched, might not suspect the examination, and change the course of their letters.[21] In 1701 Sir John Trumbull wrote to St. John, the well-known Tory: "Letters by the post are subject to casualties." And St. John replied: "You may venture to speak freely, for I have given orders at London to have your letters sent me by a private conveyance."[22]

The Post Office was given specific directions in the Act of 1711 as to the opening of letters. A carefully drawn oath had to be taken by every Postmaster-General on this matter when he assumed office: "I will not wittingly, willingly, or knowingly open, detain, or delay . . . any letter or letters, packet or packets which shall come into my hand . . . except by the consent of the person or persons to whom the same shall be directed or by an express warrant in writing under the hand of one of the principal secretaries of state for that purpose." The only letters that could be opened without express warrant were those on which payment of postage had been refused by the addressee, those where the lack of a sufficient address made the delivery impossible, and letters to persons who could not be found. The right of examining letters by warrant was a legalized practice henceforth. The Jacobite troubles of the first half of the eighteenth century gave

---

[19] *Cal. S.P. Dom.*, 1676-77, 452; Edward R. Turner, "The Secrecy of the Post," *Eng. Hist. Rev.*, XXXIII, 321.

[20] *Cal. S.P. Dom.*, 1691-92, 132; 1700-2, 181.

[21] In order to avoid this examination, it was not uncommon for persons who felt that their correspondence was suspect to deliver their letters, especially those for the Continent, to the postboys outward bound on the outskirts of London. The postboy was given 2d for each letter, as if they were sent from some neighboring gentleman. The letters were put in the mailbag at the next stage. *H.M.C. Rep.*, Downshire, I, 487.

[22] *Ibid.*, I, 805, 807.

much excuse for tampering with the mails. In 1718, Mar was told: "There is no trusting the common post. . . . They begin anew to open all letters going to or coming from the north." In the trial of Bishop Atterbury for Jacobitism in 1722-23, the chief evidence was obtained from letters that were legally opened.[23]

During the "reign" of Sir Robert Walpole, a good deal of openly expressed suspicion was directed against the supposed misuse of this right by the government. The House of Commons became so exercised over the matter in 1735 that the "abuses of the Post Office" were aired at the same time that franking came up for discussion. Walpole defended the discretionary power of the government "of ordering letters to be opened at the post-house in times of public danger." Else how discover "any bad practices against the government"? And he referred to the trial of Bishop Atterbury as proof. Members in opposition did not hesitate to talk of the use of "blank warrants," of the desire of government to learn of the private dealings and circumstances of merchants and of other perversions of the right to examine private correspondence. In 1730 Newcastle sent to the Post Office a list of 112 persons whose letters were to be opened and copied. The right was also used to detect the violations of customs regulations, to trace robberies and to find the actual condition of bankrupts. A warrant was issued in 1735 to open all letters to and from the Portuguese envoy, and also any merchant's letters by which it was suspected that the envoy might have shielded his correspondence.[24] The members also objected to having their letters "broke open and perused" by the "little clerks" about the Post Office, prying into the affairs of every merchant and gentleman.

The House appointed a committee to report on the matter, along with franking. The resolutions that were passed included a strongly worded statement about opening letters of members: "It is an high infringement of the privilege" of the members of the House of Commons "for the postmaster, his deputies or agents in Great Britain or Ireland, to open or *look into* by any means whatsoever, any letter directed to or signed by the proper hand of any member without an express warrant in writing . . . for every such opening or looking into."[25]

Just how many letters were opened officially, and to what extent

[23] *H.M.C. Rep.*, Stuart, V, 395; VI, 161; E. R. Turner, *op. cit.*, p. 321; *Parl. Hist.*, IX, 839.
[24] Turner, *op. cit.*, p. 323.　　　　[25] *Parl. Hist.*, IX, 848.

was snooping practiced by underlings in the Post Office? When the same matter came up for severe criticism a century later (1844), each House appointed a "Secret Committee on the Post Office" to find the extent to which letters were opened by warrant at that time and in the past. According to the report made by the Committee of the House of Commons, ninety warrants for opening letters were issued between 1712 and 1778. That does not mean that the letters of ninety persons only were examined by the government. A warrant like that of 1730, just noticed, included 112 persons. Some of the eighteenth century warrants would seem justified, such as that of 1783 for opening all letters of Lord George Gordon of "Riot" fame. But there was a warrant in 1735—it would seem to have merited the disapproval of Parliament—arising out of a political libel. An even less justifiable violation of private correspondence occurred in 1741: a warrant was granted at the request of a father, permitting his eldest son to examine the letters of a younger brother addressed to two women. It seems that the younger son had married one of the women contrary to his father's wish.[26]

In general, however, the warrants were used to detect treason and sedition, to ferret out murders, thefts and frauds, and to watch over dangerous foreign correspondence. A number were granted at the request of the Bank of England. Warrants were issued in 1763, at the request of the Commissioners of Customs, to detain and open letters of tobacco merchants "lately failed." The Commissioners had been informed "that other tobaccos are daily expected from Virginia."[27]

The committees of 1844 found that the practice from 1712 on had been to detain letters just long enough to ascertain their contents, and then to close and reseal them and send them on to their destination "with no indication that they have been detained and opened." The practice was easily subject to abuse, but it is impossible to determine how much misuse of the privilege took place. In 1844 the Committee of the House of Commons found that there were three times as many warrants issued between 1799 and 1844 as were granted from 1712 to 1799. The evil may have been increasing in the nineteenth century, or there may have been more care in obtaining warrants.[28]

[26] *Secret Com. on P.O.*, H.C. (1844), pp. 9, 12.
[27] *Cal. S.P. Home*, 1760-65, 1031, 1061. Cf. also pp. 1035, 1966, in the same volume.
[28] *Secret Com. on P.O.*, H.C. (1844), pp. 11, 16.

Whether or not the official warrants were few or many, the letter writers of the eighteenth century were sure there was too much examination of private correspondence. Some illustrations will show the extent of the suspicion and the practice. Jonathan Swift sent a letter to a friend with an enclosed letter addressed: "Direct the enclosed and deliver it to the greatest person in your neighborhood." In writing from Ireland on the sacramental test, Swift felt it necessary to use the name of a member of the House of Commons in Ireland and the name of a member in England. In 1726 John Gay wrote to Swift: "The letter you wrote was not received till eleven or twelve days after date, and the Post Office, we suppose, have very diligent officers, for they had taken care to charge for a double letter." In 1731 Bolingbroke admonished Swift: "If you answer by the post, remember while you are writing that you are writing by the post." In the next year, Gay wrote to Swift: "If I do not write intelligibly to you, it is because I would not have the clerks of the post office know everything that I am doing."

The most amusing letter of this sort in the correspondence of Dean Swift was a letter of 1737 from William King to a Mrs. Whiteway. The postscript reads: "To the gentleman of the Post Office, who intercepted my last letter addressed to Mrs. Whiteway at her house in Abbey Street, together with a letter enclosed and addressed to the Dean of St. Patrick's [Swift]. When you have sufficiently perused this letter, I beg the favour of you to send it to the lady to whom it is directed. I shall not take it ill though you should not give yourself the trouble to seal it. . . . I shall think myself obliged to you if, at the same time, you will be pleased to send Mrs. Whiteway those letters which are now in your hands, with such alterations and amendments as you will think proper, but I cannot believe that your order will justify you in detaining letters of business, as . . . I conceive you have not a license to rob on the highway."[29]

Horace Walpole's correspondence frequently repeats the belief that letters were opened, though the reason is not so clear in his case as in that of Swift. In Walpole's correspondence with Madame du Deffand in Paris, both writers refer frequently to the reading of their letters in the Post Office. The custom seems to have been practiced freely in France as well as in England. "C'est une chose assez

[29] *The Correspondence of Jonathan Swift*, ed. F. E. Ball (1910), I, 85, 130; III, 351; IV, 256, 340, 395; VI, 26.

fâcheuse que toutes les lettres soient ouvertes." "Il m'est trop désagréable l'ouverture de mes lettres." She wrote more freely when private channels were used: "Cette lettre vous sera rendue par l'ambassadeur, et que je ne parlerais pas si librement si elle était confiée à la poste."[30] Walpole wrote to Montague in 1758: "Remember nobody is to see this letter but yourself and the clerks of the post office." And in the next year: "Don't send for it, for there are private histories in it, that should not travel by post."[31]

Benjamin Franklin, who resided in London for some years prior to the American Revolution as the colonial agent of several of the colonies, knew his letters to have been opened on occasion. This is surprising, since Franklin was one of the Deputy Postmasters-General for America at the time. But it must also be remembered that, as the agent for American demands, he was regarded with suspicion. He wrote in 1771 to Thomas Cushing in America: "The letters I have received from my friends in Boston have lately come to hand, badly sealed, with no distinct Impression, appearing as if they had been opened." And in the next year, writing to his son William, he declared: "I am persuaded that your Packets were not open'd at the Office: for tho' a Secretary of State has the power of ordering Letters to be opened, I think it is seldom used but in times of War, Rebellion, or on some great public Occasion, and I have heard they have means of copying the Seal so exactly, as that it cannot be discovered that the Letters have been look'd into."[32]

Illustrations are legion, but one more will have to suffice: it indicates the practice at the time of the American Revolution. Richard Champion, a Bristol merchant in the American trade, wrote in September 1775: "It will soon be very difficult to keep up a Correspondence, and if these violent measures encrease, rather dangerous, as the Letters in the post office are now opened. A Gentleman lately had a bill for £1500 [which was sent him from America] sent to him from the Post Office with this message, that the Letter was not fit to be seen, and the Bill had been therefore taken out. It will be imprudent therefore to write by the pacquet, or any Conveyance

---

[30] *Walpole's Correspondence with Madame du Deffand and Wiart* (1939), II, 73; III, 3-4, 247; IV, 169, 266, etc.

[31] *Walpole's Correspondence with George Montague*, I, 229, 234.

[32] *The Writings of Benjamin Franklin*, ed. A. H. Smyth (1907), V, 326, 461-62; Ruth L. Butler, *Doctor Franklin, Postmaster General*, pp. 150-51. And see below, pp. 170 ff.

[through the] Post office, particularly London. . . . I must leave the Conveyance to you."[33]

All of the letter-opening cannot be attributed to specific warrants. Some of it grew out of the practice of checking for false franks, of "candling" for detecting double letters and more numerous enclosures, and some, doubtless, from the prying of little minds into other persons' affairs. The need of opening and of candling letters was the result of the system of charging postage according to the number of sheets. This unfortunate practice was not to be superseded until postage was charged by weight in 1840. The opening of letters by warrant continued with full legal sanction, nor is there any reason to believe that government was much restrained by the debate of 1735. The prevalence of war in the eighteenth and early nineteenth centuries naturally made the government wary. Irish complications in the late eighteenth century added to the general distrust, and Jacobinism was magnified into a serpent that needed every effort to detect its sly and penetrating course. In 1799 the letters of seventeen persons in Manchester were ordered opened, and those of eighteen persons in Manchester and Liverpool were opened by warrant in 1809. A warrant was issued at the time, also, for opening the letters of the Radical, Orator Hunt.[34]

Such were some of the abuses in the Post Office. But worse than such evils as the extension of franking, the cost of pensions and the opening of private letters was the general backwardness of the postal service at a time when it should have kept pace with the advances made elsewhere in British life.

The improvement of the carriage of mails on the roads was badly needed. From the beginning postboys or riders had been used, and they were still being used in 1765. Postal officials had no interest in using the coach for their business, though coaches had developed remarkably by the mid-century. But it was reserved to John Palmer—an innovator no less distinguished than Ralph Allen—to force on a reluctant Post Office the use of the mail coach. It is the most important advance in the postal service during the latter part of the century. To it, we next turn.

[33] *The American Correspondence of a Bristol Merchant, 1766-1776*, ed. G. H. Guttridge (Berkeley, Cal., 1934), p. 62.
[34] *Secret Com. on P.O.*, H.C. (1844), p. 13.

The Introduction
of the Mail Coach

WHEN an outsider by the name of John Palmer forced on a reluctant Post Office the use of the mail coach, he brought about the greatest change in postal transportation since the days of Sir Brian Tuke and Robert Carey. The change to the mail coach in 1784 marked a new era in postal facilities; it became the "last word" in travel and in the carriage of mail until the railway, in its turn, displaced the horsed coach half a century later.

Ralph Allen, great innovator that he was, had not attempted to employ the mail coach. Stage coaches had long been in use when Allen began his series of contracts for carrying the by and cross road letters and for extending the daily services to the rising towns off the main roads. But Allen's interest was largely centered on the minor roads rather than on the "grand" post roads radiating from London. Conditions were such that the coach was not as yet a practicable postal conveyance.

Before the mid-century the roads were so bad that the general use of coaches was impossible. The attention given to the upkeep of roads before 1760 was haphazard and ineffective. Although turnpike legislation had begun in the reign of Charles II, the early acts were few and usually applied to but short stretches of road. At each end was a tollgate and a collector to charge for the use of a section of the highway that, in many cases, seems to have been no better than the adjoining stretches of the road. Each turnpike took a special act of Parliament, only four such measures having become law before the opening of the eighteenth century. After 1700 the number of turnpike acts greatly increased. Parliament passed over four hundred turnpike and other road acts before 1750; during the next two decades the number of acts was twice as large as for the first fifty years of the century. In 1773 a General Turnpike Act facilitated the passage of these measures by incorporating into one law the provisions for all such legislation.[1]

This method of road improvement was being widely used by 1784, and with considerable results. The turnpikes, however, were not always a success even in the later stages of this legislation. Daniel Paterson, author of the well-known roadbooks for travelers, warned his readers against thinking that all turnpike roads were uniformly satisfactory: "It is recommended to all travellers to make previous inquiry into the state of them, as many of the cross turnpike roads are, in winter, and often after wet weather, rendered almost impassible." This advice appeared in the edition of 1808![2]

Road repair was primitive indeed in the days of Ralph Allen. Although various acts required surveyors to see that ruts were filled in, this simple method of road repair was not used intelligently. Stones, large and small, were dumped on the road, and they varied in size from that of an egg to a man's head. Arthur Young spoke of the roads of Oxfordshire in 1760 as "formidable to the bones of all who travelled on wheels. . . . They were repaired in some places with stones as large as could be brought from the quarry." He asserted that the so-called turnpikes west of Chepstow were "mere rocky lanes, full of hugeous stones as big as one's horse, and abominable holes." His epithet for the road between Preston and Wigan in Lancashire was "infernal," and his readers were advised to avoid it "as they would the devil: they will meet with ruts which actually measured four feet deep." Shapleigh, writing on *Highways* in 1749, declared that "there has always been, and now is, great reason to complain of the neglect of the repair of most roads within this kingdom." Ralph Allen's friend, Fielding, thought so too. Although Squire Western is made to provide a coach and four for his good

[1] See above, p. 62, and W. T. Jackman, *The Development of Transportation in Modern England*, pp. 68, 223; Sidney and Beatrice Webb, *The Story of the King's Highway*, chap. VII.

[2] Local people much objected to the turnpikes as interfering with their use of the highway. Turnpike riots were not infrequent between 1735 and 1750, and they continued after the mid-century. Various other devices were used for the upkeep of roads, including acts limiting the weight of stage wagons, restricting the number of horses attached to each wagon, prescribing the width of wagon and coach wheels, etc. An Act of 1735, e.g., required wagons of certain sorts to have tires that were nine inches broad.

wife, "unhappily the badness of the neighborhood and of the roads made this of little use, for none who had set much value on their necks would have passed through the one, or who had set any value on their hours would have visited the other."[3]

Coach travel, in consequence, was not rapid nor of uniform speed in the early eighteenth century. Winter traveling by coach usually took twice as long as in the summer on account of the conditions of the road. At the beginning of the century, York was a four-day journey from London by coach. At least that was the advertised time between the two cities in 1706. Coaches left from both places every Monday, Wednesday and Friday at five in the morning, with Stamford the mid-point of the journey. The same broadside announced a coach twice a week from York to Newcastle. The Fly Coach, which connected London and Exeter, was making the journey at the beginning of the eighteenth century in five to six days—a rate of about thirty miles a day. Progress was so deliberate that a woman "shaved the coach" at Axminster, preparatory to the appearance of the travel-worn occupants in Exeter. A Birmingham-London service advertised in 1731 to make the journey between the two places in two and a half days. The coach left Birmingham at six in the morning on Monday: traveling by way of Warwick, Banbury and Aylesbury, it set the passengers down at the Red Lion in Aldersgate Street about Thursday noon, "if God permit." Ordinarily the coach journey between London and Oxford was a two-day affair: this was the summer schedule as late as 1750. The longer journeys by stage coach were so deliberate that it was not uncommon to appoint a chairman at the beginning, and for the passengers to vote on the inns they favored and the amount of time for the stops.[4]

Although a history of the Post Office need not give much space to the rise of the stage coach, yet it is well to know something of the conditions of coach travel in the eighteenth century when the coach was becoming sufficiently useful to suggest to John Palmer the idea of its carrying mail. These vehicles were not fast, nor comfortable. The use of leather straps for hanging the body of the coach on the "chassis" caused so much swaying as to give travelers an experience

---

[3] *The History of Tom Jones*, Bk. VII, chap. IV; Jackman, *op. cit.*, pp. 214, 254, 673; Arthur Young, *Six Weeks' Tour through the Southern Counties* (1769), pp. 88, 153-55, and his *A Six Weeks' Tour through the North of England* (1770), IV, 31.

[4] Jackman, *op. cit.*, pp. 122, 135; G. R. Porter, *The Progress of the Nation* (1838), II, 17; Samuel Smiles, *The Life of Thomas Telford*, pp. 23-24; Harper, *op. cit.*, I, 75, 80-81.

akin to seasickness. Springs of a rudimentary sort were only introduced in the latter part of the century. The stage coaches carried no
outside passengers until well after 1750: the journey would have
been too hazardous. As it was, a German traveler of 1782 was nearly
jolted to death by riding on the outside of a stage coach. He wrote
of the practice as follows: "I observe that they have a curious way
of riding, not in, but upon, a stage coach. Persons to whom it is not
convenient to pay a full price, instead of the inside, sit on the top of
the coach, without any seats or even a rail.[5] It should also be remembered that eighteenth century stage coaches invariably put up for the
night, convenient hostelries being used "to inn" the coach. The roads
were such that coaches during the eighteenth century were drawn by
six horses, one of the leading pair being ridden by a postilion. Six
horses were still used on coaches when John Palmer decided to have
light mail coaches drawn only by a four-in-hand. As time went on,
it became the practice to use changes of horses. A nine-day coach
between London and Newcastle, running in 1734, explained the
speed of the journey—"three days faster than any other coach that
travels the road"—by the use of "eight stout horses stationed at
proper distances."[6]

Coach travel improved after 1750, as through services worked on
shorter schedules, and as regular connections were added for the
important industrial towns at some distance from London. A coaching advertisement in the Edinburgh *Courant* of 1754 announced a
"new genteel Two-end Glass Machine, hung on steel springs, exceeding light and easy, to go in ten days in summer and twelve in
winter." Coaches started from Edinburgh and London simulta-
neously on Tuesdays in summer and met at Boroughbridge on Saturday night, whence they departed on Monday morning so as to reach
the destination on the following Friday. The winter schedules called
for departures on Monday, and the arrival in Edinburgh or London
a week from the following Saturday.[7] Glasgow obtained its first stage
connection with Edinburgh in 1749 by means of the "Glasgow and
Edinburgh Caravan," which made the journey of less than fifty
miles in two days. When the "Caravan" was succeeded by the "Fly"
ten years later, the trip was shortened to a day and a half. In 1754
a flying coach connected the rising town of Manchester with London:

[5] Karl Philip Moritz as quoted in Harper, *op. cit.*, I, 99.
[6] Harper, *op. cit.*, I, 82-83, 88-89, 99.
[7] Harper, *op. cit.*, I, 89.

the journey of 180 miles took four days and a half. Shrewsbury had a four-day coach to London by that time. A summer coach between Bristol and Gloucester, a distance of forty miles, took a day for the journey. These schedules were being improved as the third quarter of the century wore on. The ride by coach between London and York took four days in 1750, but when Palmer introduced his mail coaches thirty years later the two cities were less than three days apart. The journey from London to Sheffield, done in four days as late as 1760, was taking but twenty-six hours by 1780.[8]

One of the very best roads was the western road connecting London with Bath and Bristol, and one of the most used as well, for all the world went to Bath. As late as 1750 a flying coach made the whole distance between London and Bristol, 120 miles, in two days under favorable summer conditions. When John Palmer projected his mail diligences some thirty years later, this stagecoach journey could be done in sixteen or seventeen hours. No wonder that John Palmer of Bath, often traveling this comparatively "fast" road, should have thought of the coach as a possibility for the carriage of mails. Palmer declared in defense of his plan that "diligences now go regularly in sixteen hours from Bath to London, which is nearly seven miles an hour."[9]

A great change had taken place in the third quarter of the century. A writer who could speak in 1753 of the "almost impassible state of the roads" declared fourteen years later that "there never was a more astonishing revolution in the internal system of any country. . . . Everything wears the face of dispatch." He may have been exaggerating, but improvement was the order of the day. And this because several famous road builders were beginning to make hard-surfaced highways. John Metcalfe, the first of a triumvirate that included Telford and McAdam, began laying down solidly built and enduring roads as early as 1765. They made feasible the assertion of Palmer that mail coaches could be used, not only for the London-Bath service, but throughout the land as a whole. "Where new roads are now continually making," he declared, "and villages growing into great manufacturing towns, the Post of such a country must be open to continual variation and improvement."[10]

[8] Smiles, *op. cit.*, pp. 55, 60; Jackman, *op. cit.*, pp. 96, 137, 285-86; S. & B. Webb, *op. cit.*, p. 72, and throughout chapters V and VII. Numerous additional examples could be given were this a volume on transportation and not on the Post Office.

[9] Jackman, *op. cit.*, pp. 136, 293; *Rep. Com. on Palmer's Agreement*, pp. 102, 106.

[10] Jackman, *op. cit.*, p. 268; Smiles, *op. cit.*, chap. VI; *Rep. Com. on Palmer's Agree-*

John Palmer was born in 1742 at Bath, where his father was a prosperous brewer and the proprietor of two theaters. The son, who took over the management of the theaters and traveled considerably in connection with his business, could hardly help noticing the difference in travel between the coaches and the postboys, especially on the London-Bath road. Nor must we forget that he grew up in a town where Ralph Allen had lived and prospered as a result of his Post Office contracts. Palmer's experience and observation led him to suggest another postal reform of the "tedious and insecure methods of conveying the mails."

What were his proposals? Palmer began with the assumption that "the Post at present instead of being the swiftest, is almost the slowest conveyance in the country; and though, from the great improvement of our roads, other carriages have proportionately mended their speed, the Post is as slow as ever." He used as an example the time taken by the diligence and the post in going from Bath to London.[11] The horse post left Bath at ten or eleven P.M. on a Monday, for example, and did not deliver a letter in London until two or three Wednesday afternoon. The diligence left Bath at four or five Monday afternoon, and was able to deliver a letter that it carried illegally about ten the next morning. It is no wonder that much mail was sent by coaches in boxes and parcels, despite the greater cost. Palmer believed that the postal use of coaches would prevent this loss to the revenue. It was a hardship, he felt, to penalize letters sent by diligences when they were so much faster than the postboys. If the post were as fast or faster than any other conveyance, "that will secure the business better than any penalties."

His reform also included greater safety for the mails. At present, he declared, the mail was entrusted to "some idle boy without character, mounted on a worn-out hack, who so far from being able to defend himself or escape from a robber, is more likely to be in league with him."[12] This is not the first time that the postboy had come in for criticism. The Act of 1765 had insisted that he must not loiter on the road, nor "willfully misspend" his time, but travel at the rate of six miles an hour at the least. Palmer believed that, since

---

ment, pp. 102, 104. Telford and McAdam did their road-building after the introduction of the mail coach.

[11] Ibid., p. 101. A "diligence" was a fast coach. A coach was also called a "machine," and its driver was sometimes referred to as a "machine driver." The term "mail coach" came into use shortly after 1784: the first recorded use in the O.E.D. is in 1787.

[12] Ibid., pp. 25, 101-3.

the postboy was unarmed and did not wish to be murdered by offering resistance to attack, the robbery of mails was almost invited.

Several devices were in use for the protection of valuable mail matter. One was to send mail in parcels by the stage coaches. The only solution the Post Office had to offer was a suggestion made in the same year that Palmer set forth his plan: when sending bank notes by post they should be cut in half and the two parts sent in separate letters by different posts. Lord Brougham when referring some years later to this proposal of 1782 said of it: "People must send one half, and wait until informed of its safe arrival before they send the other." It may have prevented a robber from cashing the note, but it greatly hindered the speed of money transactions by mail. Such a practice caused much annoyance, even if the two halves finally reached their destination.[13]

Palmer's solution was the use of soldiers for guarding the mails, since they were accustomed to firearms and "to watch and fatigue in late hours." He would distribute them over the kingdom in such numbers that a soldier would always be available for this service. The soldier was to be seated on the top of the coach just in front of the mail and, since Palmer planned for no outside passengers on the mail coaches, the soldier would be in a position to give the needed protection. Since coach schedules were likely to be more punctually observed than those of the postboys, any delay would cause immediate investigation and thus lessen the likelihood of successful looting of the mails. Palmer's idea of using soldiers did not prove feasible, but the guards which were used on the coaches served the same purpose. With the coming of the mail coach, highway robbery of the mails practically ceased.[14]

To add to the speed of the coaches, Palmer proposed that they be free from the turnpike tolls, since the mails then going by horse post paid no tolls. The gatemen, according to Palmer's suggestions, were to have the toll bars open on the approach of the mail coach, notice being given by blasts on the coach horn. The horn would also

---

[13] It might be added that this device was also a protection against the robbery of mail by postal clerks, who candled letters to see if they were double, that is, had an enclosure. This may help to explain the continuance of the practice of halving notes long after the mail coach came in, and robbery on the highways was largely a thing of the past. The practice of halving notes was still in use a hundred years ago. The writer has in his possession a letter of Jan. 4, 1831, that reads as follows: "Enclosed you will receive half Notes, amount when complete Forty Pounds, being half year's rent for . . . You will please advise me of the receipt of the same."

[14] *Ibid.*, pp. 36, 102.

be used to obtain the freedom of the road when overtaking or meeting traffic. The deputy postmasters in the towns were to know of the exact coming of the mail and be ready, while the horses were being changed, to put his packet of letters into the general bag. The speed to be maintained by the coaches was eight or nine miles an hour. Better time would also be insured if the mails going out of London left promptly at the time set. He also suggested that the time of departure be eight in the evening rather than some time after midnight, which had been the custom since time immemorial. Some might be incommoded by this earlier departure, Palmer admitted, but "as the Post on this plan will be so much more expeditious, the indulgence may certainly be dispensed with," especially by the different offices of government where the delays too often found their origin.[15]

Two other parts of his plan merit attention. The use of franks had grown to such a burden that Palmer proposed more adequate checks. He would have the members who had the privilege of franking write on the letter the exact date that it was sent, so that if it was not sent on the day indicated, the letter could be charged. Inasmuch as he was making an appeal to the Chancellor of the Exchequer for the adoption of his plan, Palmer also suggested that the postage might well be increased. The public, he held, would not seriously object, since it would still be much cheaper than, and as fast as, any other conveyance. In raising the rates, the charge on double and treble letters might be advanced, he thought, in a smaller degree than the charges for single letters, so as to encourage the use of the mail coach for small packets. He proposed that letters go thirty miles for 2d, instead of a stage for a penny and two stages for 2d, forty miles for 3d, sixty miles for 4d, etc.

Palmer seems inconsistent in advocating a rise in the rates of postage, since he also asserted that "postage is really no tax, but a fair and reasonable price for so much labour which Government, by its monopoly, is enabled to do cheaper than any individual, and should do quicker and safer." It is a pity that Palmer's proposals had this inconsistency of increasing the tax and at the same time declaring that postage was no tax. He had, of course, a desire to make his proposal so appeal to the Treasury that he would obtain a contract that

---

[15] *Ibid.*, pp. 102-3. See above, p. 56, for an example of delay.

might be as lucrative as that of Ralph Allen. No attempt was made at the time to check the actual cost of carrying the mail.[16]

The plan was first presented to William Pitt in 1782, but its acceptance was postponed owing to a change of administration in the next year. In the meantime, Palmer's suggestions were examined by the postal officials.

Their observations would be amusing if they did not reveal so much bureaucratic smugness. The Postmaster-General turned the suggestions over to the district surveyors. One of them, named Allen curiously enough, was sure that the post "cannot travel with the same expedition as many other conveyances do." He took the London-Bath road as an example. Even on this road, one of the best in the country, "the post is frequently obliged to quit the direct road for others, to supply many towns with their letters." If coaches, therefore, took the direct routes, many towns upon the cross roads would be deprived of their present communications. Allen was sure "irreparable confusion would result from trying to convey mails by machines." "If the mails were speeded up on the direct roads, the same attention must be paid to accelerate the mails upon the branches." The more Allen thought of the plan the more foolhardy it seemed. He deluged himself and Mr. Palmer with details that would need attention. He felt that the Post Office after all was the best judge. "Upon the whole, the more Mr. Palmer's plan is considered the greater number of difficulties start to its ever being carried completely into execution." He concluded by condemning the scheme "in toto." Palmer rather sharply replied that Allen's observations summed up to this: "Don't try it at all, lest it should succeed."[17]

A surveyor named Draper was sure that "no Diligence in the Kingdom travels at the rate of eight or nine miles an hour." The post necessarily had different hours from the diligences, and the post must "unavoidably set out from London from one to three in the morning." Nor could one expect much shortening of the stops at the post offices en route. It is not sufficient for the postmaster to have his bag ready: "He must open the bag or bags he receives, and take out such letters as are for towns and places in the road between his and the next stage, to be dropped by the rider at some places."

[16] *Ibid.*, p. 105. Palmer differs fundamentally at this point from the reformer, Rowland Hill. See below, pp. 266 ff.

[17] *Rep. Com. on Palmer's Agreement*, pp. 105-7, 110-12.

JOHN PALMER, by Gainsborough

A STAGE COACH WHEN MAIL COACHES WERE INTRODUCED, by Rowlandson

A Four-Horse Coach, or the Worcester Mail in 1804, by Atkinson

"Small bags," he added, "are to be made up with letters for the towns and villages and gentlemen's houses in the neighboorhood; at others, bags which are to turn into cross-road branches and join others at a certain point." If all this were altered, the "circulation of letters would be interrupted over the whole kingdom."[18]

His observations on the robbery of the mails are amusing. "Experience has shown that no invention can prevent desperate fellows" from robbery. "It was lately the case upon the North Road, where an iron cart, as strong as an iron chest, was stopt, taken out of the road and broke open. . . . When desperate fellows had once determined upon a mail robbery, the consequence would be murder in case of resistance." In short, the present arrangement had been found from long experience to be the best. Any alteration should not be adopted until it was "perfectly ascertained to be as feasible in practice as it is specious in theory." Strange reasoning, to say the least.[19]

A third surveyor, Hodgson by name, was frankly contemptuous: "I do not see why the Post should be the swiftest conveyance in England." Indeed, the "generality of stages do not travel more than five miles an hour whilst travelling." The speed of diligences on the Bath Road resulted, so he believed, from an exceedingly high spirit of competition: "in consequence, the passengers are hardly allowed time to stretch their legs, much less for rest or diet, and so with light weights or empty carriages away they wheel." To get the Bath mail to London in sixteen or eighteen hours was, to his mind, an "impossibility." He was sure the rate of six miles an hour was pretty well kept by the posts, though Hodgson admits that on some stages the stops between the post offices were numerous. "In some, they exceed twenty, in few are less than eight or ten." He felt that no gentlemen, merchants or outriders, that is, traveling men, could instruct Post Office Officers: "It is particularly to be hoped, if not presumed, that the Surveyors need no such information." The post as now managed, Hodgson held, "is admirably connected in all its parts, well regulated, carefully attended to, and not to be improved by any person not acquainted with the whole." Palmer should leave well enough alone: "It is a pity that the author of the plan should not first have been informed of the nature of the business in question." This confident critic of Palmer declared, finally, "that the constant eye that has been long kept toward their improvement, in all situ-

18 *Ibid.*, pp. 117-18.　　　　19 *Ibid.*, pp. 116, 120-21.

ations and under all circumstances, has made them [the post and the Post Office] now almost as perfect as can be."[20]

Palmer answered fully the objections made against the plan, and journeyed widely to improve the details of his project. Pitt returned to office in December 1783 as head of the ministry and Chancellor of the Exchequer, beginning a long leadership in government that was to last almost continuously until his death over twenty years later. Again he gave consideration to Palmer's proposals. A conference at the Treasury in June 1784 resulted in a favorable decision.

Pitt's willingness to try out Palmer's suggestions came in part at least from his difficulties as Chancellor of the Exchequer. The public debt was at a very high point, the civil list was in arrears. In consequence, revenue was sought in every way possible. Pitt even proposed a tax on coal, but it proved so unpopular that he looked for other ways of obtaining the needed funds. Palmer's proposals, as we have found, included an increase in postage on the ground that letters, if delivered in half the time, would be paid for on an additional basis "with less ill humour." That this was an important factor in Pitt's mind is made clear by Palmer's statements: "Some time afterward, Mr. Pitt finding an intended tax on Coals would be unpopular, sent to your Memorialist [that is, Palmer] to converse further respecting his plan, and the probable increase of revenue to accrue from it; when he was so well satisfied of its productiveness as to make the latter a substitute."[21] It certainly accords ill with Palmer's later statement that "postage is really no tax," and it detracts from the quality and disinterestedness of the reform.

The result was a new act for granting additional rates of postage "for the conveyance of letters."[22] The rates were as follows. Single

[20] *Ibid.*, pp. 120, 122-23, 128-29, 131-32. Lord Brougham made very effective use of these objections to Palmer's plan when Rowland Hill suggested further reform in 1837. He regaled his hearers in the House of Lords with these "specimens of the wisdom of their ancestors." *Parl. Deb.* 3rd s., XXXIX, 1206. Rowland Hill himself used this same data in the preface to the third edition of his *Post Office Reform*, pp. v-xi.

[21] *Rep. Com. on Palmer's Agreement*, pp. 53, 104.

[22] 24 Geo. III, 2nd session, c.37 (1784). This was the first important postal act since the one that slightly lessened the rates in 1765. See above, p. 111. There were some other legislative steps taken at this time. In the next year members of Parliament were allowed to frank newspapers by 7 Geo. III, c.50 (1766). In 1783, the Irish Post Office was separated from that of Great Britain, one of the results of the demand for home rule in Ireland, 24 Geo. III, c.6 (1783), and 24 Geo. III, c.8 (1784). Not long before, the Post Office had lost its monopoly of letting post horses out for hire—a right that had been held, without interruption, for two centuries. The privilege was given up as a result of comprehensive licensing bills for the use of horses and carriages, 19 Geo. III, c.51, and 20 Geo. III, c.51. See also Joyce, *op. cit.*, p. 205.

letters going one stage had cost a penny, 2d for a double, etc. They were now to pay 2d for a single letter, 4d for a double, and so on. The same addition was made to the charge for two stages, making a single cost 3d instead of 2d, a double 6d, a treble letter 9d and an ounce letter a shilling. Beyond two stages and up to eighty miles, the charge for a single was 4d instead of 3d, between eighty and 150 miles 5d for a single, and beyond 150 miles a single letter cost 6d instead of the former 4d. Letters between Edinburgh and London now cost 7d instead of 6d for a single. Within Scotland the rates were raised on much the same basis as in England, save that in place of a second stage as the second taxing distance, the basis was fifty miles. Beyond one stage and up to fifty miles, the postage of a single letter cost 3d instead of 2d, from 50 to 80 miles 4d instead of 3d, and for greater distances as in the English rates. Palmer's idea of lesser charges, in proportion, for double, treble and ounce letters was not adopted by the Exchequer.

The Act of 1711 had directed that £700 per week go to the Exchequer "in order to raise a present supply of money to carry on the war." The weekly payment had continued during war and during peace for some seventy-five years. It was now steeply increased, and with no war to justify it: the weekly payment directly to the Treasury was raised to £2300.

The Act included additional rules regarding franking, and again Palmer made the suggestion that a person who franked must write "the whole superscription upon every letter or packet." This included his own endorsement, the post town whence sent, "and the day, month and year when the same shall be put into the post office, the whole to be in the handwriting of the member." Unless sent on the day it was dated, the letter was to pay postage. His suggestions were intended to check the wholesale use of franks, such as the reported payment to a member of Parliament of £300 a year to frank the correspondence of a large firm. Palmer's suggestions did not prove effective, since franks could be dated for the times when they were to be used. Another of Palmer's proposals became law at this time: mail coaches were freed from tolls in 1785.[23]

As to the actual introduction of the mail coaches, Pitt had declared that a trial be made on the Bath Road. The first coach, accordingly,

[23] J. Holland Rose, *William Pitt and the National Revival* (1911), p. 186. 25 Geo. III, c.57 (1785). The preamble declared it was to the "advantage of the publick" that mail should be carried "by carriages or public diligences."

made the trip on August 2, 1784, starting from Bristol where Palmer saw it off. The advertisement in the *Bristol Journal* will give some idea of the character of the journey. The proprietors of the "Mail Diligence" agreed to convey the mail between London and Bristol "in sixteen hours, with a Guard for its Protection." They respectfully informed the public that the "Diligence" was constructed "so as to accommodate four inside Passengers in the most convenient Manner,—that it will set off every Night at Eight o'Clock from the Swan with Two Necks, Ladlane, London, and arrive at the Three Tuns Inn, Bath, before ten the next morning, and at the Rummer-Tavern, near the Exchange, Bristol, at Twelve." The mail coach was to depart "from the said Tavern at Bristol, at four o'Clock every Afternoon, and arrive in London at Eight o'Clock the next morning." The price to a passenger for the journey was £1 8s. No outside passengers were to be allowed. The advertisement concluded: "Both the Guards and Coachmen (who will likewise be armed) have given ample Security for their Conduct to the Proprietors, so that those Ladies and Gentlemen who may please to honour them with their Encouragement may depend on every Respect and Attention."[24]

The experiment proved so successful that Pitt authorized extensions. Mail coaches were established on the Norfolk and Suffolk roads in March 1785. Two months later the cross post between Bristol and Portsmouth was running as a mail diligence. "They will now," wrote Palmer to Pitt, "have a direct and expeditious post guarded, six times a week, instead of a slow and circuitous one unguarded, only three times a week."[25] Palmer's chief assistant, Francis Freeling, superintended the beginning of this service, and traveled by the coach on its first journey. Freeling was later to be a very important postal official.[26]

Mail coach service was extended to Leeds, Manchester and Liverpool in the summer of 1785, and before October of that year they were running to Gloucester and Swansea, Carmarthen and Milford Haven, Worcester, Birmingham and Shrewsbury, Oxford, Chester

---

[24] Jackman, *op. cit.*, pp. 324-25. The Swan with the Two Necks was one of the best-known inns of the coaching era. Lad Lane, where it was located, is no longer to be found on London maps: it was near the present Gresham Street, not far east of St. Martin's le Grand. The odd name is usually explained as a corruption of the "swan with the two nicks." The ownership of swans was indicated by nicks on the bill, the Vintner's Company using two nicks. This famous inn was in existence before the Civil War, and "nick" had already become "neck."

[25] *Rep. Com. on Palmer's Agreement*, p. 45.

[26] F. E. Baines, *On the Track of the Mail Coach*, p. 27.

and Holyhead, Carlisle, Dover and Exeter. The Great North Road was the last of the principal highways to receive the improvement —in the summer of 1786. The journey of some four hundred miles to Edinburgh was performed in sixty hours. Before 1750 the mail on this road took eighty-five hours going north, and one hundred and thirty-one hours traveling south from Edinburgh! This horse post was further improved in 1757 when the time was shortened to eighty-two hours going north and eighty-five hours coming south. By the extension of Palmer's plan to the Great North Road, the time "has been still further shortened to about sixty hours in each case."[27]

The change must have seemed revolutionary to the people of the time. Before 1784, London letters sent to Bath, Bristol, Norwich and many other places on a Monday could not receive an answer until Friday. Henceforth, the answer could be received on Wednesday. After this change, letters from Dublin were due on the third instead of the fifth day. The earlier system of expresses—a cause of much expense and inconvenience—ceased to be necessary. Letters by stage coach were no longer necessary, as the mail coach, in the words of Palmer, "outruns every conveyance."[28]

To some, the mail coach seemed to "outrun" reason. The stage coach proprietors started rumors that the overly rapid mail coaches encouraged accidents and ruined horses. In order to silence such statements, Palmer published a letter stating that the mail coaches did not travel faster than the post chaises, and that their contracts required them to go only eight miles an hour, counting stops.[29]

The change can be well illustrated by the use of the Great North Road. Communication between London and Edinburgh seemed slight and unimportant in the mid-eighteenth century, as Scott records it in his novel, *Redgauntlet*. On dinner being postponed in Edinburgh until three in order to give time for answering London correspondents, Mr. Maxwell remarked, "London correspondents, and pray what the devil have the people of Auld Reekie [Edinburgh] to do with London correspondents?" A footnote by Scott

[27] *Rep. Com. on Palmer's Agreement*, pp. 37, 137, 139; *E.B.* (3rd ed., Philadelphia, 1798), XV, 426.
[28] *Ibid.*, p. 36; Baines, *op. cit.*, p. 98; E. Watson, *The Royal Mail to Ireland*, p. 84. A medal was struck at the time in honor of "J. Palmer Esqre . . . as a token of gratitude for benefits received from the establishment of mail coaches." On the obverse, the designer pictured a coach and four horses, with the significant words: "To Trade—Expedition. To Property—Protection." Palmer was to receive much more substantial rewards. See below, p. 158.
[29] Jackman, *op. cit.*, p. 327.

explanatory of this remark declares that "within my recollection the London post was brought north in a small mail cart. And men are yet alive who recollect when it came down with only one single letter for Edinburgh, addressed to the manager of the British Linen Company."[30]

Niebuhr, the well-known German historian, spent over a year in Great Britain just at the close of the century. In writing to his wife of the journey from London to Edinburgh, he complained of the rapid motion with the coaches going over seven miles an hour. It was altogether unnatural: "You can only get a very piecemeal view of the country from the windows, and on account of the tremendous speed, you have no object long in view." Niebuhr took his time for the journey. He started from London on Monday, stopped off at Newcastle after "three weary days of traveling," and reached Edinburgh late Saturday night.[31]

Lord Campbell, the Chief Justice, was more venturesome. Writing of his initial journey to London from Edinburgh in 1798, he said: "A journey to London in those days was considered a very formidable undertaking. I was to perform it by a mailcoach, which had been recently established and was supposed to travel with marvelous celerity, taking only three days and two nights for the whole distance. But this speed was thought to be highly dangerous to the head, independently of the perils of an overturn, and stories were told of men and women who, having reached London with such celerity, died suddenly of an affection of the brain. My family and friends were seriously alarmed for me, and advised me at all events to stay a day in York to recruit myself . . . [but] I boldly took my place all the way through to London."[32]

Speed, of course, is a relative matter. But fear or no fear at the speed of these "machines," the mail coach had come to stay—until the railway in its turn furnished a quicker conveyance for the all-important mails.

---

[30] Chapter XII. *Redgauntlet* was first published in 1824. The British Linen Company was a Scottish bank.

[31] Chevalier Bunsen, *The Life and Letters of Barthold George Niebuhr* (N.Y., 1852), pp. 102-3, and *Lebensnachrichten über Barthold Georg Niebuhr* (Hamburg, 1838), I, 198.

[32] *Life of Lord Campbell*, ed. his daughter (2nd ed., London, 1881), I, 29.

The Post Office during
Peace and War—1784-1815

THE changes made in 1785 came at a very fateful time in British history. The eighties under the lead of the younger Pitt were years of a "national revival" that seemed to forecast indefinite advance. But in 1789 Europe was shocked by the French Revolution, and so antagonized by republican fervor that the Revolution ceased to be a domestic matter: by 1793 Great Britain was involved in a continent-wide war. Henceforth war was to be continuous—save for a few months of truce in 1802-1803—until general peace was re-established in 1815. The Post Office in Britain was deeply affected by the vicissitudes and the strain of these years.

Let us turn first to Palmer's relation with the Post Office. When he suggested his plan to William Pitt, Palmer had in mind a thorough reform under his own guidance and a substantial profit out of the changes. Despite the objection of the Post Office, Pitt saw to Palmer's appointment as Surveyor and Comptroller General of the Mails in October 1786, an appointment that was made permanent by Treasury warrant in September 1789. His salary was set at £1500 per year, and in addition he was to receive 2.5 per cent, or one-fortieth, of any increase in the net revenue above £240,000 a year, the idea of a percentage serving—so thought Pitt—"as an incentive to Mr. Palmer." He was to work independently of the Postmaster-General, and directly under the Treasury: as Palmer put it, "an appointment for life, as placed me in independence of the controul and interruption of the Postmaster-General."[1]

[1] *Rep. Com. on Palmer's Agreement*, pp. 26, 31, 49-54, 74.

Palmer, obviously, was in a difficult situation, for he was technically under the Postmaster-General, but was to be free to carry on his reform. Actually, Palmer acted as though he were independent of any control by the Post Office authorities. He believed himself, in fact, to be another Ralph Allen. Like his fellow townsman, Palmer thought of his reform and his work as largely separate from the regular Post Office regime. Palmer referred time and again to Allen's experience as an example of the privileges that he should have received but did not. In truth, he misread the facts with regard to Allen's relation to the Post Office, and belittled Allen's accomplishments in order to magnify his own—in the hope of obtaining better terms. He even sent to Pitt a narrative of "Allen's transactions in 1720, respecting the Cross Posts, in order to point out the powers requisite to such an undertaking." Palmer held that Allen had "full liberty to make all kinds of improvements . . . without any restraint or impediment from the authority of the Post Office Board."[2] Again, he declared that Allen met with none of the difficulties that he was experiencing. He forgot or did not choose to know that Allen was not free of supervision and that his limitations in the matter of appointments were very real.[3]

Palmer's depreciation of Allen's work was not very gracious. The former wrote to Pitt in 1788: "I hope, sir, that it may not be imputed to vanity in me to mention, that though Mr. Allen derived upward of £12,000 per year from his very partial improvements of the Cross Posts only, the regulations I have introduced, . . have increased that particular branch of the Revenue more in the course of two years than he did during the whole forty years he farmed the same." Elsewhere, Palmer stated that Allen improved the cross posts "sparingly at intervals of several years, under his own exclusive management, and through the means of his own surveyors, but without disclosing his plans."[4] One cannot help but rise from reading Palmer's statements with the feeling that Allen was belittled deliberately and for a purpose, and that the snug fortune he had made was chiefly in Palmer's mind as he sought an independent position.

John Palmer did not get on with the Post Office. Whereas Allen worked easily with others, Palmer found himself constantly hampered, partly through a lack of tact on his part. He even wrote,

[2] *Ibid.*, pp. 53, 55.   [3] See above, pp. 102, 105.
[4] *Rep. Com. on Palmer's Agreement*, pp. 44-45, 58, 76.

chiding the Postmaster-General, of "this wanton interference, threatening me, and insulting and degrading valuable officers who are known to be attached to me. . . . Indeed, my Lords, if you persist in such treatment of them, I shall not have an officer of any value remain with me." He wrote to Pitt, asking him to put a stop to the "rascality of that office," and declared that he had suffered "every possible opposition," that "certain Officers at the General Post Office, practiced every art, and excited every opposition" against him.[5] Palmer would have liked to control the internal arrangements of the Post Office as well as the mail coach regulations. In the "internal arrangements of the Post Office business," he declared, "mistakes are innumerable. . . . It is scarcely possible for greater abuses and neglect to prevail." He even promised, if allowed, "to regulate it in a fortnight to your's and the Public's satisfaction. . . . Indeed, the plan cannot be further extended, till I am suffered to establish regulations within the Office to fit the new ones without, as the new and the old plan now act against each other."[6]

Palmer was not without ground for his grievances. A surveyor tried to defeat his plan on the Bath Road. Palmer had difficulty in obtaining cooperation from the deputy postmasters on the roads, despite open orders that he suspected were counterbalanced by secret instructions. He was opposed in starting the earlier eight o'clock departure of the mail coaches from London, and believed that departures were often held up intentionally, even after the new time schedule was in use. Delayed decisions of the officers of the General Post on various matters were suspected of being intentional.

Friction was probably inevitable, but was made even more certain by the character of the Postmasters-General at the time. When the reform was introduced they were the Earl of Tankerville and Lord Carteret. Though these men disliked Palmer's innovations, they did not actively oppose the mail coach. Tankerville ceased to be a postal official in 1786, Carteret continuing as a Postmaster-General until the autumn of 1789, when he was joined by Thomas, Lord Walsingham.[7] And after Carteret's retirement in 1789, Walsingham became the leader of the joint Postmasters-General until 1794. Palmer had the most trouble with Walsingham, for he was as vigorous and determined as Palmer, a leader, vigilant, industrious, a lover of detail and firmly determined to run the Post Office. It was trouble be-

[5] *Ibid.*, pp. 46, 76, 140.   [6] *Ibid.*, p. 46.
[7] See below, p. 151, for friction between Carteret and Tankerville.

tween them that led to Palmer's dismissal. Palmer had set up a Newspaper Office without consulting his "superiors." He also declined to attend Board meetings, to answer inquiries, and in other ways seemed bent on defiance. At last, when some irregularities were found in the payment of mail guards, Walsingham demanded information. The result was an appeal to Pitt on this and other differences between the two, the suspension of Palmer in March of 1792, and his subsequent dismissal. Thus, instead of some forty years and more of service with the Post Office, such as had been Allen's lot, Palmer was through after a connection of less than eight years.[8]

Palmer's later activity needs but brief notice. He was granted an annual pension of £3000 in 1793, but held out for the original percentage that he had been allowed. An investigation of 1797 reported in his favor, but Pitt's government was unwilling to do more than continue the pension. During the first decade of the nineteenth century he was a member of Parliament for Bath, and was succeeded by his son in that representation in 1808. Palmer renewed his application in 1807, after Pitt's death, hoping to obtain what he felt was the full reward for his work. In the debate in the House of Lords at the time, the former Postmaster-General, Lord Walsingham, declared that Palmer had been dismissed for "contumely and insubordination," and that the pension was "fully adequate." The matter came up for discussion again in 1813, and this time Palmer won out; a bill, the fourth one that had been introduced, finally passed. By it Palmer received £50,000 on his claim for a percentage in the increase of the Post Office revenue. This was in addition to the pension.[9]

To what extent was Palmer's plan a success? Possibly one of the

[8] The trouble had been hastened by a quarrel between Palmer and one of his deputies, a man named Bonnor. When Palmer dismissed Bonnor, the latter delivered some compromising letters by Palmer to the Postmaster-General. They did not involve Palmer's integrity, which seems never to have been questioned, but the propriety of his language and attitude. In one of the letters revealed by Bonnor, Palmer wrote of "two coxcombly Lords," and of his desire to have a "downright quarrel with them, and a thorough exposure." He declared it was too bad there were not "men of sense at the head of the department." See *Rep. Com. on Palmer's Agreement*, p. 68, and Joyce, *op. cit.*, pp. 243 ff., where the matter is revealed fully. The *Report*, to which reference frequently has been made, contains the documents. A full treatment of the incident will be found in the *Br. Almanac* (1840) Companion, pp. 68-74, where the "History of the Post Office" is given. At that time, 1840, the relations of Rowland Hill with the Post Office seemed strikingly like the situation Palmer had occupied. Bonnor, it might be added, has a niche in the *D.N.B.*, V, 361-62. He was rewarded for helping to oust Palmer by the grant of the Inland Office, but was let out in 1795 on a pension.

[9] See Cobbett, *Parl. Deb.*, XI and XXVI, for the extensive debates. The act is 53 Geo. IV, c.157. Palmer lived to 1818 in the enjoyment of his reward.

best proofs was the magnificent financial reward that came to him in 1813. It must be admitted that Palmer, entirely apart from his unpleasant personality and tactlessness and obvious desire to feather his own nest, had brought about a great change in the postal services. The mail coach came to stay, for there was no question of its disuse when its "inventor" was dismissed. Even before his departure from the Post Office, Palmer had considerably improved the coach as a vehicle, following a series of accidents that had shown up faults of construction. The coach, too, did much to end the robbery of the mails: no mail coach was robbed for some years after their introduction.

Palmer also improved the organization by enlarging the postal districts to six, with a surveyor over each, and an additional surveyor for special needs, a sort of continuance of the old resident surveyor. He chose excellent men, on the whole, for these and other tasks subordinate to his part of the postal work. A very valuable appointment was the selection of Francis Freeling as a surveyor. Appointed in 1785, he was to become Secretary of the Post Office at the close of the century, and to remain as the active head of the organization until 1836, on the eve of another reform.[10]

The strict regulations set up by Palmer for speeding the mails proved effective. The departure of the coaches from London at eight in the evening instead of after midnight was continued without question after his dismissal. His severe regulations for speed on the routes began a practice that was improved as time went on. It was said that at places on the Great North Road not more than a minute's delay was needed for the change of horses and the exchange of mail.[11] All this was gratifying to the merchants and manufacturers. The growing centers of commerce rewarded Palmer with their commendation. The Glasgow Chamber of Commerce presented him with a silver cup, and he received the freedom of such places as Liverpool, York, Hull, Edinburgh, Glasgow, Aberdeen and Chester.[12]

Did the revenue increase? The reader will recall that at the end of Allen's regime the gross revenue of the Post Office was some £225,000. Although the gross revenue had doubled during the time of Allen's activity, the net revenue—the income exclusive of expense

---

[10] See below, p. 152.   [11] Jackman, *op. cit.*, p. 327.
[12] *D.N.B.*, XLIII, 142. Palmer was mayor of Bath in 1796 and again in 1809.

—had remained about the same, some £100,000. The Post Office was spending nearly 60 per cent of the intake for operation.[13]

During the next decade—1765 to 1774—the gross revenue grew from £262,000 to £313,000, and the net proceeds remained almost stationary, £161,000 in 1765 and £164,000 in 1774. From 1775 to 1783, that is, before Palmer's reform and the new postal Act raising the rates, the gross ranged from £322,000 to £398,000, and the net from £173,000 to £159,000. In other words, there was an actual decrease in the net produce of the office.

The nine years, 1784 to 1793, that follow Palmer's entrance into the Post Office saw a remarkable change. The gross revenue rose from £420,000 to £627,000, and the net from £196,000 to £391,-000. The gross revenue increased 50 per cent and the net produce of the office almost exactly doubled. Palmer held that these figures justified his claims that the changes he had wrought made the difference.[14] When the mail coaches came in, the net revenue was about £150,000. The income from the additional rates on letters by the Act of 1784 was reckoned at some £90,000, so that the total of £240,000 was held the proper basis for estimating Palmer's percentage.

Walsingham demurred, insisting that it was impossible to say whether the increase of the revenue was owing to the plan, and what part resulted from the additional rates of the Act of 1784. He held that a net increase of £60,000 in the eight months when Palmer had but one mail coach running could hardly be a result of the plan. Before the Committee of 1797 Walsingham admitted that "there was a progressive and latterly a very considerable increase." But, he added, "I do not know how anybody can prove, whether that was owing to the mail coach plan, or to the Act, or to the general increase of the revenue of the nation in all its branches." Certainly Palmer's

---

[13] Palmer argued that there was an actual decrease in the net revenue in these years, but he chose a bad year, 1762, for making his calculations. *Rep. Com. on Palmer's Agreement*, pp. 36, 57.

[14]

	GROSS REVENUE			NET PRODUCE		
1766	£265,427	17s	8d	£161,940	0s	10d
1771	292,782	7	3	155,543	0	1
1776	318,418	7	4	167,482	4	2
1781	417,634	12	9	154,157	2	7
1786	471,176	8	1	285,975	15	11
1791	575,079	3	10	355,999	6	6
1796	657,541	10	8	466,457	15	4

These figures continue the figures as given on a previous page (109), save that the net produce is added. See *Rep. Com. on Palmer's Agreement*, p. 61.

mail coaches began running at a fortunate time. It is the old riddle of the chicken and the egg. The notable increase in postal business that came in these years was the result only in part of Palmer's mail coaches.[15]

Another innovation of this time, established during Palmer's short regime, was a Newspaper Office. The importance of, and the reasons for, this Office will be clearer if we summarize briefly the growth of the newspaper as a part, and a heavy part, of the post-master's burden. The newspaper goes back, in its origins, to an earlier century: the well-known *London Gazette*, started in 1665, was partly the responsibility of Joseph Williamson, the Under Secretary of State.[16] When the licensing acts were discontinued after the Revolution, periodicals and newspapers multiplied, some bearing such suggestive titles as the *Post*, the *Postman*, the *Flying Post*, the *Postboy*, and its rival, the *Protestant Postboy*. As soon as the periodicals began to increase in number, they became subject to tax. An Act of 1711, like the Post Office Act of the same year, was an effort to provide "supplies of money to carry on the present war."[17] A halfpenny tax was put on newspapers of half a sheet or less, and a penny was charged for each sheet of larger papers. An additional halfpenny was added in 1756, and the tax was again raised by a half-penny in 1789, making 2d the charge for a single sheet. A stamp impressed in red ink on each sheet indicated that the tax had been paid.

Newspapers increased greatly in numbers and in frequency of appearance after the mid-century. Nearly ten million copies were appearing annually by 1760. By the time that Palmer came to the Post Office in the eighties over fifty newspapers were being published in London. The *Public Advertiser* was probably the most important, although the *Morning Chronicle* and the *Morning Post* had already started. The *Times* began its eventful history the year after the introduction of the mail coach.

It had been the custom to allow newspapers free passage in the mails, the clerks of the roads receiving 2d for each paper from the local postmasters. They, in turn, circulated the papers to their own benefit. The Post Office thus became a sort of news agent on a grand

---

[15] *Ibid.*, pp. 8, 23, 36, 57-58.

[16] See above, p. 56, and Hyde, *op. cit.*, p. 289.

[17] 10 Anne, c.19, sect. 101. See C. D. Collet, *History of the Taxes on Knowledge* (1899), I, 8-17. A tax on advertisements also came in at this time.

scale.[18] This was changed materially in 1764 when the franking act allowed members of Parliament, as well, to send free printed newspapers, without covers or in covers open at the sides, "which shall be signed on the outside by the hand of any member of parliament."[19] The privilege was soon used without any moderation. Customers' addresses were certified wholesale by certain members of Parliament.

For several reasons, this abuse had become very noticeable by Palmer's time. The great increase in newspapers added an enormous burden to the work of the Post Office, and the cost of their carriage did not appear as an asset in the postal revenues. By 1784 over three million newspapers were going out of London each year, or nearly ten thousand a day: within a decade the number doubled.[20] The appearance of evening papers made the load heavier, literally speaking, for the papers were brought to the Post Office as late as possible, still wet from the presses. One of Palmer's critics in the Post Office objected to his proposal for lowering the cost of packets of more than an ounce on the ground that it would increase the mails "already too much loaded and encumbered by wet newspapers."[21] Late delivery of the newspapers naturally retarded the departure of the coaches, and their dampness tended to injure addresses on mail with which they came in contact. There was also insufficient time to examine carefully the bundles of papers. When the Post Office became convinced that "many letters have been put up with newspapers to avoid postage," it was time something should be done.

Palmer, so much concerned over his percentage, attacked the evil by establishing a Newspaper Office. It had been proposed as early as 1782, but nothing was done about it until Palmer took the step in 1787. Thereafter the newspapers were received, examined and

---

[18] The money obtained by the clerks was used partly to supplement salaries, including their own, and partly as a benevolent fund for Post Office employees. Joyce, *op. cit.*, pp. 50, 191. He believed that the result of the privilege was an income of £8000 a year by 1764.

[19] 4 Geo. III, c.24.

[20] *Rep. Com. on Palmer's Agreement*, p. 95, has a listing of papers in and out of London annually. The figures for

		in	and	out
1784	are	70,526	in and	3,090,948 out
1787		78,660		3,210,463
1790		123,789		4,653,904
1793		204,902		6,473,065
1796		199,537		8,622,128

The jump in circulation after the opening of the war may be accounted for, in part, by the desire for news, military and naval.

[21] *Ibid.*, p. 131.

sorted by a staff of some eighteen persons. The papers were kept in bundles distinct from the letters for reasons already given. The one fly in the ointment, as we have found, was the way it was done. Palmer went ahead on his own without consulting Walsingham. The Comptroller even fixed the wages of his appointees. Although the step angered Lord Walsingham, the Postmaster-General authorized the Palmer establishment, and continued a service, after Palmer's dismissal, that was growing more necessary with the rapid increase of newspapers.

Another elaboration of the postal service that occurred at this time was the creation of a Money Order Office—now so familiar a part of the postal service of our day. The reader will recall that the postal officers had suggested the cutting of bank notes in half, if they were to be sent through the mail, and that the halves be sent for the sake of security at different times. To send coin through the mails simply courted loss. The government also seemed desirous of finding some convenient way by which sailors and soldiers could send home in safety such sums as were saved from their small wages.

The proposal of a Money Order Office was made by an accountant named Gosnell. But when he suggested that the Post Office take over the business, the legal adviser of the Post Office doubted its legality.[22] The result was a money order office run as a private venture, though closely attached to the Post Office. The clerks of the road, who had long conducted a large newspaper business for their own advantage, presumably used in this office money that had been obtained through the carriage and sale of newspapers. The Money Order Office began in this curious way in 1792. The limit for an order was five guineas, that is, £5 5s, the cost of the order being 6d per pound. At first, half of the charge was to be paid by the receiver of the money, but when the cost of an order to or from London was reduced a year later to 4d, the remitter was to pay the whole cost. A stamp duty was added if the amount exceeded two pounds, and, of course, the letter in which the money order was sent required double postage.[23]

The Money Order Office did not prosper under the clerks of the road, and was made a private venture in 1798 under three partners.

[22] 42nd Rep. P.M.G. (1896), pp. 26 ff. Hist. Sum., p. 101; Lewins, op. cit., p. 94.

[23] To prevent the charge for double postage, the money order was later printed on a sheet of paper large enough to allow for a brief letter. But this development occurred first in Ireland only as early as 1827, and in Great Britain ten years later. Hist. Sum., p. 102.

The most important was Daniel Stow, Superintending President of the Inland Office. Nor was the business of the Office large under Stow and his partners and their successors. In the last decade of the eighteenth century the number of orders averaged less than twelve thousand a year. Despite its slow development, the rise of an office of this sort as early as 1792 is surprising.[24]

The public insisted on sending coins and jewelry and rings through the mail. Provision was made for this type of mail in the same year that saw the beginnings of the Money Order Office. Such letters, called "money letters," were handled in a special manner, with much the same care as is now given to registered letters, or perhaps they can be likened more fittingly to the kind of service known today as "special handling." The public of 1792 was advised as follows: "That all persons sending money in letters to deliver their packets to the clerk at the window, or the postmaster in the country, by way of giving additional security to its conveyance."[25] The postmaster wrote "money letter" in red ink on the folded letter. The packet was then entered on the bill as a money letter, and wrapped in the bill. On its delivery, the postmaster received a receipt, though it was not returned to the sender. No charge was made for this special handling, save the double postage required for a letter with an enclosure. The greater care such letters received sometimes led correspondents to enclose a farthing in an ordinary letter so that it would become a money letter. Letters containing money orders or halved bank notes were not, of course, regarded as money letters.

Earnest attempts were made during this time to check the corruption and wastefulness of the establishment. We have already found much corruption in the Post Office in the earlier part of the century. The general attack in the eighties on the extravagance of government expenditure—"economical reform" was the phrase in use— included the misuse of Post Office funds. The most thoroughgoing examination of the government departments was made by a body of Commissioners appointed "to enquire into the Fees, Gratuities, Perquisites and Emoluments." The Tenth Report of the Commissioners treated the Post Office. Though the postal inquiry was not prompted solely by Lord Tankerville, the Commissioners solved the matter of some mysterious leakages in the postal revenue over which Lord

[24] It became a department of the Post Office in 1838. See below, pp. 254, 328.
[25] Hendy, *op. cit.*, p. 9.

THE NEW POST OFFICE AT ST. MARTIN'S LE GRAND, 1830

THE YARMOUTH MAIL CHANGING HORSES AT THE COACH AND HORSES, ILFORD,
by Pollard

THE *Quicksilver* ROYAL MAIL ARRIVING AT TEMPLE BAR, 1834, by Newhouse

Tankerville had been concerned. When John Lees had been appointed as Secretary of the Irish Post Office in 1781, he had agreed to pay his predecessor an annuity—and an additional payment of £350 to a person known as A. B. Lord Tankerville, try as he would, could not find out who A. B. was, even though Lord Carteret knew of A. B.'s identity. When Carteret refused the information, his colleague demanded an inquiry. The parliamentary inquiry of 1787 revealed that A. B. was a man with the odd name of Peregrine Treves, who was not only a foreigner but a friend of Carteret. When A. B. was asked by the Commissioners for what services he received £350 annually from the Secretary of the Irish Post Office, Treves replied that the money was given "from friendship entirely."

The Commissioners found other scandalous conditions. The Receiver-General gave attendance but three days a week. The court post, by now a sinecure with a salary of £730, had his work done by a deputy for £58. The Commissioners also found what they regarded as an immense expenditure on the packet services, and advised that £68,000 of the annual packet expense "might and ought to have been saved." The income of Anthony Todd, the Secretary of the Post Office, received particular attention. Todd, who had occupied this lucrative post since 1762, was receiving by 1787 all sorts of supplements to his salary of £200. He obtained £75 a year from the Bye-Letter Office, £100 a year for coach hire, fees on commissions, a gratuity of £100 a year from Lloyd's Coffee House, and a commission of 2.5 per cent on the whole expenditure for packet boats on the Dover, Harwich and Falmouth stations. His receipts totaled £1738 a year. To this should be added a house, twenty chaldrons of coals, sixty-four dozen pounds of tallow candles, twenty dozen pounds of wax candles and eight pounds of tea from the East India Company. Todd was also part-owner of several packet boats. In fact, the packet establishment was so shot through with corruption that the Commissioners recommended that no one in the Post Office have any connection, directly or indirectly, with the packets.[26]

At the time of Palmer's dismissal, the most promising young official was Francis Freeling, then the Resident Surveyor in London. He was one of Palmer's selections, and his agent in the country for setting up the mail coach services. As Todd grew older and less easy

[26] *Tenth Report on the Post Office by Commissioners, etc.* (1788), pp. 4-5, 19, 25-28, 33-36. The three commissioners were John Dick, Wm. Molleson and F. Baring. Joyce, *op. cit.*, pp. 227, 232, makes some reference to this Report.

to work with, Freeling was intended as his successor: in 1797 Freeling was made Joint Secretary to do the work of the office, while Todd continued to draw the rich financial rewards. It so happened that a further inquiry was made in that year as to the effect of the Report of nine years earlier. The Select Committee on Finance, which made the investigation, was particularly harsh on the Todd-Freeling secretaryship. It pointed out that Todd, instead of retiring from his post "upon becoming unable to perform that office," had retained his income. They found that the duties were performed by the principal Resident Surveyor (Freeling) "who is within these five months appointed joint secretary with him." The Committee also found that Freeling retained the emoluments of his former office, though it had been abolished: "He is to become sole Secretary, with the £700 he now receives retained, and £500 a year in addition." In the next year Todd died. Henceforth Francis Freeling was to be the sole Secretary, an office he held for nearly forty years.[27]

It should be added that the Commissioners of 1788 examined fully Mr. Palmer's introduction of mail coaches in order to see if the "oldest and ablest officers in the service" were right in claiming that the plan was "impracticable and dangerous to commerce." The Commissioners reported favorably on Palmer's innovation. They found that it had exceeded expectations, that the revenue was increased, that answers to letters were received in less than half the time formerly required, and "with a degree of punctuality never experienced before." They also found that the mail coaches, traveling eight miles an hour, had outmoded the former expresses, which had traveled but six miles an hour.

One of the greatest abuses of the mid-eighteenth century, as we have found, was the excessive use of franking. Instead of decreasing, franking seemed actually on the increase as the century wore on. The war that began in 1793 only added to the temptation and the opportunity for illicit franking. The Act of 1784 was an attempt to restrict franks, for by that time their number had reached the enormous annual total of 800,000. The Act succeeded in lessening the number temporarily, but by the time of Palmer's dismissal in 1792 the number exceeded 900,000 annually.[28]

---

[27] See *7th Rep. Sel. Com. on Finance* (1797), p. 179. The Committee recommended a Board of Commissioners to control the Post Office, "the plan upon which other departments are conducted." See also *18th Rep. Commrs. of Rev.*, pp. 109, 110, 342, for Todd's income. When Freeling retired in 1836, his perquisites proved to be considerable, and were also the subject of criticism. See below, pp. 249, 255.

[28] *Rep. Com. on Palmer's Agreement*, p. 95.

At least half a dozen franking acts were passed by Parliament between 1784 and 1815. By an Act of 1795, for example, parliamentary franking was limited to letters and packets not exceeding an ounce in weight. An endorsed letter to be valid for free transit had to be mailed within twenty miles of where the one endorsing actually was on the day or the day before mailing. As a further precaution, a member of Parliament was restricted to sending ten a day free, and receiving fifteen; any excess paid the regular postage.[29] This strict limitation grew out of the stupendous misuse of the privilege. By 1794 members of Parliament, who sat in the banking interest, franked over a hundred thousand letters in three months! The merchant members were a bad second with only 27,000 franks to their credit.[30]

The same Act allowed cheaper postage to noncommissioned officers, seamen or privates in the navy, army, militia and reserves. They were allowed to send single letters for one penny, the cost of postage being paid in advance. Every such letter had to be from a person actually in service, and was to be countersigned on the outside by his commanding officer, with the name of the ship or regiment to which the sender belonged. Letters were received, also, for a penny prepaid. The privilege was misused by officers, it would appear, for in 1806 it had to be stated specifically that this right did not apply to commissioned officers, that no one could endorse such a letter who did not have command, and that letters addressed to noncommissioned officers and privates but intended for someone else were not to enjoy the low rate. A penalty of £5 was set for violation of these conditions, or for using the low rate for any letter not on "private concerns." This is just one more illustration of the difficulties in enforcing a system of franking or the right to use a lower rate.[31]

Illegal sending of letters became more and more general during the war years, largely because of conditions created by a war-time government. Pitt, as Chancellor of the Exchequer, was not averse to additional rates of postage in peace time, especially if the mail coach could be used to stimulate the use of the Post Office. War finance, which caused much greater demands on the Treasury, can explain, if not condone, an unfortunate demand for higher charges on correspondence. Pitt's attitude in this matter is open even to more

[29] 35 Geo. III, c.53.   [30] Joyce, *op. cit.*, p. 315.
[31] The same regulations were extended to Ireland in 1803 after the union of the parliaments. See 43 Geo. IV, c.28. Hendy, *op. cit.*, pp. 123-25; Alcock & Holland, *op. cit.*, pp. 204-5, 511.

criticism, since he professed to be a follower of Adam Smith in free-ing business from galling restrictions. He held that "manufactures in general ought to be free from taxes, lest otherwise they should be so depressed as either to endanger their exportation, or diminish their home consumption." He tried in many ways to avoid stifling taxes for industry—by a Loyalty Loan, a Patriotic Contribution, the sale of annuities, and finally by additions to taxes on income.[32]

Freedom of correspondence would appear to be closely related to the freedom that Pitt desired for manufactures and the world of business. The record is otherwise. Letters, he felt, should pay as much as could be collected without stifling correspondence. As a re-sult, the war years saw rates of postage rise to heights never before attained in the whole history of the Post Office. It was a very ques-tionable treatment, not only of the industrial world, but of the non-manufacturing public as well.

Pitt was hard put to it in 1796, as the government was making liberal advances in funds to Britain's Continental allies, in addition to its own heavy war expenditure. The budget Act of that session included increases in duties on a very diverse list, such as drinks, tobacco, bricks, game licenses, glass, snuff, auction sales, bar iron, servants, newspapers, stage coaches and letters.[33] The postage rates that went into effect in 1797 were no longer reckoned in stages for the shorter distances. A single letter going less than fifteen miles cost 3d with corresponding rates for double, treble and ounce letters. Between fifteen and thirty miles, the cost of a "single" was 4d; be-tween thirty and sixty miles, 5d; between sixty and one hundred miles, 6d; between one hundred and one hundred and fifty miles, 7d; and to and from Edinburgh, 8d.[34] It was, in general, an advance of a penny for single letters all along the roads. The tax on news-papers was raised from 2d the single sheet, imposed in 1789, to 2½d. What makes this heavier charge on letters and newspapers even more objectionable was its acceptance by Post Office officials. Francis Freeling was as obsessed as Pitt with the desire for high rates of postage.

William Pitt resigned office in March 1801 over the matter of the union with Ireland. Addington, who succeeded him as Prime Min-ister and Chancellor of the Exchequer, proceeded to raise the rates

---

[32] J. H. Rose, *A Short Life of Pitt* (1925), p. 37, and the same author's *William Pitt and the Great War* (1911), pp. 305, 307, 329-30.

[33] The stage coach duty was made a penny more per mile. 37 Geo. III, c.16.

[34] 37 Geo. III, c.18.

of postage still further on a basis proposed by Francis Freeling. By the Act of 1801, the lowest distances—up to fifteen miles and from fifteen to thirty miles—were unaffected. But the longer distances were subdivided still further in the effort to add to the revenue. A letter could travel before the Act of 1801 as far as one hundred and fifty miles for 7d: after 1801 it could travel only one hundred and

NOTTINGHAM 127

YORK o o 196

81 THETFORD

BROAD WAY 93

GLASGOW
1 OCT 1816
405 → G

twenty miles for the same charge. A letter from London to Edinburgh no longer cost 8d but one shilling, and a letter from London to Bristol now cost as much as a letter to Edinburgh before the change in rates.[35]

An interesting postmark came into use in the latter part of the eighteenth century, as a result of the changing rates of postage. After the Act of 1765, the emphasis on exact mileage became greater, and this was increased as succeeding postage acts varied the rates and made further subdivisions. As a result, the so-called mileage marks came to be used by the provincial offices. These indicated the distance of the post office from London if in England, Scotland or Wales. The mileage marks began at the time of the introduction of the mail coach in 1784. They were discontinued in 1797, pending a more accurate measurement. They were reintroduced in 1801, when an act of that year further subdivided the rates for letters, and made accurate measurements of the distances even more important. The mile-

---

[35] 41 Geo. III, c.7.

age marks were usually stamped on the back of the folded letter by the sending office. They were of value for letters that went to London or to some other post office via London, as the distance would aid in reckoning rapidly the charge on unpaid letters. But their value for letters not going to London would certainly seem slight. The eighteenth century mileage marks are in straight lines and are both framed and unframed. In the nineteenth century, circular mileage marks were added. They grew less frequent, however, in the decade before the adoption of penny postage. After 1840 a mileage mark was needless, as the penny carried the stamp any distance.

Examples of some British mileage marks are shown above. The system, first used in England and Wales, began to be employed by Scottish and Irish offices in the early nineteenth century. In Ireland, the distance was reckoned from the provincial office to Dublin. The later mileage marks sometimes included the date as well.[36]

In 1805—Pitt was once more in office—the charges rose again. A penny was added to the cost of single letters, 2d for double letters, etc. This made the "single" to Edinburgh from London 1s 1d, and a "double" 2s 2d. A letter had to be important to go such a distance at such a charge.[37]

The correspondence of the poet Shelley illustrates the efforts at

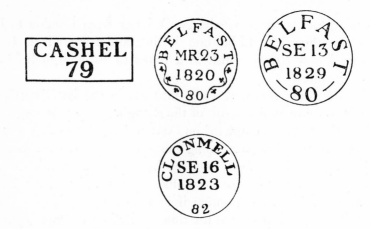

evasion so common at the time. When in Dublin during the spring of 1812, he sent both letters and pamphlets under newspaper covers

---

[36] For a full treatment of these interesting postmarks, see Alcock & Holland, *op. cit.*, pp. 62-68, 110-14, 143-45.
[37] 45 Geo. III, c.11.

to his English friends. A pamphlet so sent to Godwin was discovered by the postal authorities, and Godwin was compelled, in consequence, to pay £1 1s 8d for its carriage. He remonstrated with Shelley in these words: "You say that you send it in this way to save expense. The post always charges parcels that exceed a sheet or two by weight, and they should therefore always be forwarded by some other conveyance." Between Dublin and London letter postage at that time was 1s 1d for a single sheet. Shelley wrote not long after to another friend in England: "In a day or two I shall make up a parcel to you which will come per coach."[38]

A well-known contemporary of Shelley, Samuel Taylor Coleridge, regularly imposed on the good nature of a friend in order that his letters might enjoy free passage through the mails. The friend was John Rickman, secretary to the Speaker of the House of Commons. On the eve of his departure for Sicily in 1804, Coleridge learned that a transcription of all of Wordsworth's manuscript poems was being prepared for him. He wrote to the Wordsworths at the time that the manuscript should be sent "lettered up in parcels not exceeding two ounces and a quarter each, including the seal." Each parcel was to be enclosed within three "envelopes," the outer one to the Speaker, the next addressed to John Rickman, and "under that one to *me*."[39]

Postal charges were raised again towards the close of the seemingly endless war with Napoleon. A hard-up Chancellor of the Exchecquer, Vansittart, added another penny to single letters, 2d to double letters, etc., this applying to all letters that traveled beyond a distance of twenty miles. Thus by 1812 a single letter from London to Edinburgh—the cost in 1765 had been but 6d—had increased to 1s 2d. War had made the Post Office an instrument of taxation.[40]

Even the mail coach seemed in danger. When Palmer introduced the mail coach, it had been exempted from the tolls. In the meantime the number of coaches had gradually increased until by 1812 there were more than two hundred in use throughout Great Britain.

[38] Shelley's letters were frequently marked "single" on the outside. He occasionally franked letters with his father's name, for Sir Timothy Shelley was a member of Parliament. See *The Works of Percy Bysshe Shelley*, ed. Roger Ingpen and Walter E. Peck (10v., 1926), VIII, 202, 279, and *passim* for his practice in addressing letters.

[39] *Letters of Samuel Taylor Coleridge*, ed. Ernest H. Coleridge (2 vols., Boston, 1895) II, 459. See also for further examples of the use of the Speaker's franking privilege, *Life and Letters of John Rickman* by Orlo Williams (Boston, 1912), pp. 98-102.

[40] 52 Geo. III, c.88. Newspapers also suffered. The newspaper tax, raised to 2½d in 1798 and to 3½d in 1809, became 4d in 1815. Cobbett was not the only one who cursed this "tax on knowledge." A general relief from this burden, as well as the tax on letters, was not granted until twenty years later. See below, p. 246.

As they grew in number, the persons interested in tolls demanded some reward for this increased traffic. The turnpike trusts claimed that the exempted tolls for mail coaches amounted to £50,000 a year. This demand, if successful, would have meant, of course, still higher charges for letters. Nor would the stage coach proprietors have been averse to the toll charge for mail coaches, as they carried passengers. The government only avoided this additional tax on letters by deliberately lessening the number of coaches on the roads. Orders were given to the Post Office to withdraw coaches from a large number of routes, and permits for new coach-mail contracts were withdrawn. In 1815, the Post Office was operating only sixty-one mail coaches.[41]

The only financial result of the agitation to tax mail coaches was an act passed in 1813 requiring mail carriages in Scotland to pay toll, if they had more than two wheels.[42] To offset this charge on four-wheeled mail carriages, that is, the regular mail coaches, the Post Office made an additional charge of a halfpenny for each letter and packet carried by mail coach in Scotland.

Never before or since has the Post Office suffered such misuse as it endured in the decades we have been examining. The beginning of William Pitt's long rule saw the introduction of the stage coach and the beginning of higher postage rates. War brought increasing rates imposed by Pitt and his successors. Before the end of the war even the mail coach was endangered. To make the whole situation even more ironical, Parliament finally granted Palmer in 1813 his long-sought reward of £50,000 "in full satisfaction and Discharge for the Services performed by the said John Palmer, in the Accomodation afforded to the Public and the Benefit derived to the Post Office Revenue." This munificent grant came in the same year that mail coaches began to be charged turnpike tolls in Scotland and at a time when the Post Office was deliberately lessening their use in England.

[41] E. Halévy, *The English People in 1815* (1924), p. 32.
[42] 53 Geo. III, c.68.

Mail Overseas

THE insular position of Great Britain—its separation by water from Ireland as well as from the Continent—produced peculiar conditions for the Post Office as soon as the service began to expand beyond the post roads leading out of London. In addition, when the British planted colonies they had of necessity to be reached by water. By the end of the eighteenth century these oversea services had attained such importance that their place in the growth of the Post Office needs more consideration than has been necessary heretofore.

Postal communications overseas began in a very modest way, as we have found in examining the Post Office of the Tudors and the Stuarts. The chief communication with foreign lands was across the narrow Channel, especially at the Straits of Dover where Calais is only some twenty miles away. This service grew in the seventeenth century because of the increasing trade with the Continent and of the important foreign relations with France, Holland and Spain. The merchants, both foreigners and Englishmen, were allowed at first to develop their own mail service. But a change came in the reign of Charles I with the appointment by the government of a "Postmaster of England for Foreign Parts." The troubles arising for the De Questers, the first appointees, the efforts of the merchants to continue the older plan and the vicissitudes of Witherings have been treated earlier. Witherings organized the foreign service along lines used on the Continent and made connections with the Imperial post system of the Taxis family. The office that Witherings set up in London for his foreign post was distinct from the inland department, and was to remain a separate part of the postal establishment for two centuries.[1]

The carriage of mail to and from the Continent was then made in boats that would seem to the modern traveler altogether too frail, especially for dealing with the rough seas of the Channel. They were known as "post barks" in the early seventeenth century, although the name "packet boat" was coming into use about the time Witherings took over the foreign service. This name seemed natural, since the packet boats originally carried overseas the packet of state letters. An English packet boat, the *Speedy Post*, was used for crossing the Channel when John Evelyn, the diarist, had occasion to make the journey in 1641. Although he refers to the vessel as a "pretty frigate," it was but a bark of some fifty tons.[2]

The packet boat service was not only subjected to the vagaries of wind and weather. So dangerous was the crossing—no love was lost in those days between the English and the French and the Dutch—that the *Speedy Post*, for example, was armed with six brass guns. In 1635 the postmaster at Dover was robbed five times within seven weeks, four of those times by the French and once by a Flushinger. Another experience is thus described by the unfortunate captain: "They shot at him, and commanded him to strike, calling him and the rest 'English dogs'; and coming aboard, they used violence, beating them, stripping them of all their money, apparel and goods, and took from the post all his bundle of letters, among which was a packet from the king."[3]

By mid-century, the conditions of travel on the Channel were somewhat more secure. Weekly services were in use, according to the Post Office Act of 1654, and this Act included rates for letters sent abroad. They were largely re-enacted by the Act of 1660, which set up postal arrangements for the Restoration. The service was somewhat improved, for we learn that such places as Paris, the Hague, Brussels, Cologne, Hamburg and even Leghorn were receiving two mails a week.

Early in the Restoration, if not before, boats were plying between Harwich and Helvoetsluis in Holland. The vessels in use were called "hoys"—small sloops of about sixty tons, and very serviceable for this troublesome crossing. When Dutch William be-

---

[1] See above, pp. 27 ff.

[2] See the diary for Oct. 10 of that year. The word "packet boat" was soon transferred into French as *paquebot*, the name for French vessels on similar service.

[3] Hyde, *op. cit.*, pp. 31-32.

came King of England in 1689, the Harwich service was being carried on by three packet boats. The war that soon opened with France naturally led to an expansion of this service between allies, the only means of communication for England with the rest of the Continent.[4]

Between wars, the postal service with France was carried on under terms made with the French Postmaster-General. In 1698, for example, such a postal treaty provided for mails twice a week between London and Paris, the London mails leaving Mondays and Thursdays at midnight, and the Paris mails at 2 P.M. on Wednesdays and Saturdays. English boats carried English mails to Calais and French *paquebots* delivered the French mails at Dover. Letters beyond Paris for French towns and the letters for Spain, Portugal and Italy were carried at the French rates, the English government paying the French Postmaster-General 36,000 "French livers" [sic] for the service. The treaty required that the mail on its arrival at Calais or Dover was to be sent on without waiting for the "ordinary."[5]

The succession of French wars after 1689 led to other packet routes to the Continent, especially after the British capture of Gibraltar and Minorca, and the increase of commerical relations with Portugal following the Methuen Treaty of 1703.

An early service that did not go to France or Holland was the one that connected Falmouth with Corunna in northwestern Spain. Falmouth proved a very valuable port in the eighteenth century, not only for this service to the Iberian Peninsula, but for boats that sailed across the Atlantic to the colonies. Its extremely westerly position—fifty miles beyond Plymouth—gave it comparative immunity from the attacks of French privateers. Its harbor was well adapted for a packet station. Paterson in his *Road Book* of 1808 spoke of its harbor as "the second—if not the first—in Great Britain in point of safety and accommodation." Its anchorage was one of the safest in the country, not only because of headlands that broke the strength of the Atlantic rollers, but because of the castles of Pendennis and St. Mawes at the entrance.[6]

It was from here that two packet boats began, in 1688, the run

[4] Hyde, *op. cit.*, p. 329; A. H. Norway, *History of the Post-Office Packet Service,* p. 13; *Cal. S.P. Dom.*, 1671, 203; 1689-90, 301; 1702-3, 45-46; *Cal. Tr.B.*, XIV, 339; XIX, 108. At this time, the passenger fare between Harwich and Holland was 12s.

[5] *Cal. S.P. Dom.*, 1698, 29; *H.M.C. Rep.*, Bath III, 363.

[6] *Parl. Gazetteer of England and Wales* (1843), II, 74; Norway, *op. cit.*, pp. 16-18.

ATLANTIC

OCEAN

NORTH

SEA

Glasgow
Edinburgh
Ayr
Dumfries
Port
Patrick
Longtown
Carlisle
Belfast
Donaghadee
Whitehaven
Penrith
Barnard
Castle
Douglas
Boroughbridge
Irish Sea
Liverpool
Doncaster
Dublin
Howth
Parkgate
Manchester
Holyhead
Conway
Chester
Newark
Menai Sts.
Llanrwst
Corwen
Lichfield
Shrewsbury
Tamworth
Birmingham
Waterford
Wexford
Northampton
Huntingdon
Cork
Harwich
To
Holla
Milford
Carmarthen
St. Albans
Oxford
Swansea
Barnet
LONDON
Cardiff
Rochester
Bristol
Canterbury
Bath
Dover
Salisbury
To
Cala

VI   PACKET STATIONS AND THEIR
      CONNECTIONS IN THE
      EARLY NINETEENTH CENTURY

            Mail Coach
            Horse Post
            Water Route

      Scale of Miles
      0   50   100

Exeter
Weymouth
To the Channel
Islands

English Channel

Falmouth

To America
To Spain, Portugal and
the Mediterranean

to Corunna, or the Groyne, as it was often called at the time. A service was also in use early in the eighteenth century between Falmouth and Lisbon. We learn that the packet service to Lisbon was strengthened in 1739 when war—known as the War of Jenkins' Ear—began with Spain. More guns and men were put on the vessels, and two boats, in that year, were used between Lisbon and Gibraltar. One of these two boats was taken, naturally enough, from the Falmouth-Corunna service. Port Mahon on the Island of Minorca was also served by a packet at this time. Until war opened with France in 1740, it had brought the mail from Marseille. The *Carteret*, used in this service, was a vessel of 120 tons and was armed with ten guns.[7]

The mail service with foreign countries was not large in the seventeenth and eighteenth centuries. The Foreign Post Office, as it was called, had a staff of only four men in 1660. By 1688, this personnel was considerably increased; the office had its own Comptroller, two sorters, an alphabet man—he gave out letters at the window—and fourteen letters carriers and porters.[8] By 1750, little change had taken place in the size of the staff. Even as late as the end of the eighteenth century the Foreign Post Office had but ten letter carriers. Curious as it may seem, the mail that came to the Foreign Office was distributed in London by letter carriers who delivered foreign letters only, and this remained true down almost to the coming of penny postage in 1840. This office was a very distinctive part of the service with its own traditions. As late as the time of the Napoleonic wars, however, the Foreign Office business was not accounting for 10 per cent of the total net income of the Post Office.[9]

Foreign letters that came by other vessels than the packet boats were known as "ship letters." Such a service had to be recognized since the prevailing conditions and the slow growth of the packet service made it impossible to concentrate all mails on set routes and in specified vessels. Ship letters did not go to London even from Falmouth, but were delivered to the postmaster at any port

[7] Norway, *op. cit.*, p. 18; *Cal. S.P. Dom.*, 1702-3, 46; *Cal. Tr.B.*, XVIII, 394; *Cal. Tr.B & P.*, 1739-41, 39, 49, 50, 65. The packet service from Falmouth was not extensive for a long time after 1688. W. L. Clowes, *The Royal Navy* (1901), VI, 208, certainly gives a wrong impression in declaring that the Falmouth packet service was set up in 1688 "for conveyance of mails all over the world."

[8] *Cal. Tr.B.*, VIII, 1283-84; *H.M.C. Rep.*, XV, pt. 1, pp. 19-20.

[9] Chamberlayne, *Magnae Britanniae Notitia* (1755), General Lists, p. 70; *Rep. Com. on Palmer's Agreement*, p. 93.

where the vessel cast anchor. The Act of 1660 had required that incoming ships give their letters to the Post Office on arrival. There was no inducement for insuring their delivery, save a penalty for anyone who delivered letters contrary to regulations. About 1700, the practice grew up of paying the master of a vessel a penny for every letter he delivered.[10] The Act of 1711 charged an extra penny for ship letters going or coming, the penny belonging to the shipmaster who conveyed the letter overseas. But these requirements were "ineffectual," as the Act of 1765 pointed out. As a result, in that year, every ship was forbidden to break bulk until all letters and packets had been delivered by the master to the postmaster of the port his ship had entered.[11]

If it was hard for the Post Office to capture all the letters coming in on ships, there was even more trouble in routing letters outward to ships via the Post Office. Without question, many more letters left England without paying the penny than were caught in the meshes of the regulations. Shipmasters were accustomed to hang bags in coffee houses, or inns, or in the office of a ship's agent for the gathering-in of letters to be taken on the outward voyage. This practice doubtless arose from the permission allowed to carry letters that concerned the goods on the ship, that is, to carry them free of postage. The government hesitated to enforce the regulation that each of these outward letters pay a penny, since many of the letters, doubtless, concerned the goods on the ships, and also because the Post Office was not actually performing any service.

Just at the close of the eighteenth century, when the Post Office was seeking more and more ways of collecting profits for a grasping government, a Ship Letter Act was passed, requiring letters brought in or sent out by ships to pay 4d in addition to inland postage.[12] But the efforts to obtain more money from such letters was largely a failure. Another act making the charge 6d instead of 4d was also ineffective. The solution for this condition of things was to give private ships the carriage of letters under contract, paying a reasonable sum for the service. The enlargement of the restricted

[10] *Cal. Tr.B.*, XVI, 317.

[11] 12 Chas. II, c.35, sec. 7; 9 Anne, c.10, sec. 6; 5 Geo. III, c.25, sec. 3; *Hist. Sum.*, p. 47; Hyde, *op. cit.*, p. 324. Before 1700, a special effort was made to collect ship letters that had reached the Port of London, before they were disposed of by the masters in illegal fashion. A special boat was appointed for making this collection. It carried a curious flag: pictured on it was a man on horseback blowing a post horn!

[12] 39 Geo. III, c.76 (1799).

packet service, however, was not marked until after the Napoleonic wars.

Postal connections with the American colonies were very irregular before the eighteenth century. The government intended, seemingly, to extend the English service to the colonies as early as 1663, for a letter in the King's name to the Governor of Barbados in that year told of daily complaints of the lack of safe communication with the West Indies and the American continent. The English Post Office did not intend to start a packet service with the West Indies, but only to have a "constant correspondence as opportunity affords," whatever that may mean. Nothing came of the good intentions expressed in 1663.[13]

A much more ambitious scheme was that of Edmund Dummer. In 1702—war was on again with France—he proposed a regular packet service to the West Indies, boats to sail monthly from Falmouth and to serve the various islands on a definite schedule. Each of the four ships that Dummer agreed to furnish was to make three voyages a year, the voyage out and back to take no more than ninety-five days, not counting the time at harbors in the islands. His boats were not to carry goods out or back, so that "they shall be under no temptation on that score." Later, this prohibition was relaxed by allowing a limit of five tons to be taken out and ten brought back. They could carry passengers, the fare costing £12 each way.[14]

The Dummer sloops began their runs in October 1702, and for a time pretty well kept to the schedule. The *Bridgman* took three months and thirteen days in the winter of 1702-3, the *King William* made the run in 94 days, the *Mansbridge* in 91 days. The *Frankland* took one hundred days in 1705, the *Queen Anne* 105 days, though the latter lost her two topmasts and the foremast, and in the Soundings was chased all the way. The *Six Islands* made the return trip in 113 days, even though several French privateers were on her heels west of the Scilly Islands. Dummer took great pride in his "West Indian Packet Service," which was at first thought "impracticable by many of the best seamen in England." The "best seamen," however, proved right in the end, for the service was discontinued in 1711 after severe losses. During the course of the war

---

[13] *Cal. S.P. Am.& W.I.*, 1661-68, 463.

[14] *Ibid.*, 1702, 580, 628, 639, 854; 1702-3, 791, 1068; *Cal. Tr.P.*, 1708-14, 33; *Cal. Tr.B.*, XVIII, 170; XIX, 411.

Dummer had lost two ships at sea and ten to the enemy.[15] After 1711, communication with the West Indies was irregular until 1745, when the Treasury proposed to the Postmaster-General that four boats be put on this service, including two that were on the Lisbon-Gibraltar run at the time.[16]

Service with the American mainland seemed less imperative than a regular connection with Jamaica and Barbados. An official proposal of 1707 held that packets ought to sail every month for the islands, but only eight times a year to the mainland colonies.[17] No regular sailings, however, were tried for some time. Governor Cornbury of New York wrote in 1708, lamenting the situation: "I wish with all my heart that packet boats were established to some part of this Continent." He was sometimes many months without hearing from the homeland, in one instance fifteen months elapsing between the receipt of official letters. There were only two safe ways, in those warlike times, of sending information; one was by the Virginia fleet and the other by the mast fleet that went to and from New England. But use of the Virginia fleet was almost impossible since there was no post between New York and Virginia. Moreover, the Boston-New York service overland was infrequent. Cornbury wrote on one occasion of the post to Boston: "There is a post by which we can hear once a week in summer time and once a fortnight in winter."[18]

The usual way to send dispatches from England to America was by the use of a ship bound for America, especially set aside to carry express government packets, or one bound on merchandising activities. If a vessel was hired temporarily for the packet service, it was called a "bye-boat"; if it was sent express with official messages, it was known as an "advice boat." One reads of the *Hazard* sent express to America in 1714, unfortunately on its last journey. The *Hazard* was cast away upon the coast of Massachusetts, which lived up to its reputation, for the vessel was "broken to pieces on the rocks." No one lived to give any account of the wreck, the only record being "broken letters and pieces of packets, coming on

[15] *Cal. S.P. Am.& W.I.*, 1702-3, 323, 791, 1041; 1704-5, 1293, 1333, 1359, 1374; 1706-8, 17, 266, etc.; 1712-14, 10.

[16] *Cal. Tr.B.& P.*, 1742-45, 707.

[17] In 1703 Sir Jeffrey Jeffreys proposed to use a ship of 180 tons and fourteen guns for service to New York under the terms granted Dummer, but nothing seems to have come of it. *Cal. Tr.P.*, 1702-7, 532; *Cal. S.P. Am.& W.I.*, 1702-3, 388.

[18] *Cal. S.P. Am.& W.I.*, 1708-9, 10; William Smith, *History of the Post Office in British North America*, p. 5.

shore, found in the snow and sand." The *Hazard* was carrying packets for all the colonies north of Virginia.[19]

The germs of a postal service on the American mainland had already begun even before the Act of 1711 established rates to be used in the colonies. A brief postal connection was set up between New York and Boston by Governor Lovelace when the war with Holland began in 1672. Governor Dongan also provided service towards the end of the reign of Charles II. The charge was set at 3d for each one hundred miles, and the Duke of York was to have at least 10 per cent of the profits. When the Duke became King as James II, he even appointed a postmaster for the confederation of the New England colonies. But nothing came of his efforts, as the Revolution of 1688 soon brought his reign to a conclusion.[20]

Much more promising was the plan of Thomas Neale, Master of the Mint from 1679 to 1699, who was granted power by the government of William and Mary to erect posts in America. His patent, dated 1692, was to run for twenty-one years. He was required to report at the end of three years on his profits and expenses, and after that to make an annual report of the condition of the business. Thomas Neale had no intention, of course, of operating this monopoly personally, as he was mixed up in numerous projects in England. His deputy in America was a Scot named Andrew Hamilton. The interesting suggestion has been made that Hamilton, who had been made governor of East and West Jersey just at this time, may have become interested in postal matters because William Dockwra, of London Penny Post fame, had become an East Jersey proprietor.[21]

Andrew Hamilton, made Deputy Postmaster in 1692, soon began the work of starting his postal service for the colonists. He conferred with the various colonial governors as to uniform regulations and monetary assistance. Hamilton even drew up a draft bill for the consideration of the various colonial governments. There was to be a chief letter office and a deputy postmaster in each colony, to be appointed by Hamilton. The bill provided a

[19] *Cal. S.P. Am.& W.I.*, 1714-15, 88; *Cal. Tr.P.*, II, 289.

[20] Smith, *op. cit.*, pp. 6-8, and the same writer's "The Colonial Post-Office," *Amer. Hist. Rev.*, XXI, p. 259. An excellent account of the early post office in the American colonies is to be found in W. E. Rich, *The History of the United States Post Office to the Year 1829*, chap. I.

[21] *Cal. S.P. Am.& W.I.*, 1693-96, 2234; 1722-23, 30; *D.A.B.*, VIII, 180-81; Smith, *op. cit.*, p. 8.

monopoly of letter-carrying to the workers of the Neale contract. The rates were to be as follows: Letters from overseas were
to cost 2d if for addresses in Massachusetts, New Hampshire or
Pennsylvania, but 9d if for New York. The postage from Boston to Philadelphia was set at 15d for a single letter, and from
New York to Philadelphia at 4½d. The rate from New York
to Boston differed from the rate charged from Boston to New
York: it was 12d going north and only 9d coming south from
Boston. Letters on public business were carried free for an annual grant by each colony. Only in New Hampshire and Massachusetts were the governments sufficiently careful as to require
that the letters carried by Hamilton's couriers be marked with
the date of their receipt in the post offices, in order to insure
prompt and constant service. Massachusetts, Pennsylvania and
Connecticut granted free ferriage to the couriers, and New York
and New Hampshire freed the postmasters—generally innkeepers—from excise charges on ales and other liquors. Massachusetts included in its act provisions against a monopoly when it
granted Hamilton the right of carrying letters. When the acts
were sent to London, that of Massachusetts was the only one
disallowed. Despite that, Massachusetts used the Hamilton arrangements in much the same way as they were employed elsewhere.

The southern colonies were not much interested in the project.
Intercolonial communication appeared of so little value to Mary-
land that nothing was done about Hamilton's draft bill. Virginia
made independent plans directly with Neale, and they called
only for the carriage of letters within Virginia. Hamilton reported in 1699, in confirmation, as it were, of this disinterest,
that the interchange of letters between Virginia and the northern
colonies did not total more than one hundred letters a year.[22]

When the patent had run for half a dozen years, Andrew
Hamilton came to England to report. According to his own
statement, he had a regular post from "Piscataway [i.e., Portsmouth, N.H.] in New England to Philadelphia, in all, about
five hundred miles." The rates that he reported at the time of
his visit to England were somewhat different from those of the
original acts. Fourpence was being collected for letters from be-

[22] Smith, "The Colonial Post-Office," pp. 262-65.

yond the seas. One learns that a "single" between Rhode Island and Boston cost 6d, and that the charge from Connecticut to Boston "by the post road" was 9d.

But profits were not forthcoming. From 1693 to 1697 Hamilton had been able to collect only about £400 a year in postage, not enough to pay his salary, in addition to expenses. Neale and Hamilton, therefore, suggested to the government that it prevent the collection of letters at coffee houses, and that it grant the right of collecting higher rates of postage. The suggested charges included such outlandish rates as 1s 8d between Boston and Philadelphia for a single letter, and 3s 6d between Boston and Jamestown, Virginia. The Postmasters-General in England were opposed to these higher rates. Their judgment was put as follows: "It having been found by experience in the Office here that the easy and cheap correspondence doth encourage people to write letters, and that this revenue was but little in proportion to what it now is till the postage of letters was reduced from 6d to 3d." Sage advice that could have been conned profitably by such later officials as Pitt, Palmer, Freeling and Addington. The Post Office authorities in England expressed the hope that a few years of good management would make the American venture a success.[23]

At the time of Neale's death in 1699, his patent was taken over by his creditors, Robert West and Andrew Hamilton. When Hamilton died a few years later (1703), his widow and West continued the contract. They must have thought that the business would pay in time, for they sought an extension of the farm, and the right, as well, of setting up a packet service from England to New York. The authorities, however, were not in favor of continuing the farm of the American posts. Accordingly, the patent was bought out for the remainder of the term, in 1707, the Post Office paying the patentees £1664. Andrew Hamilton's son, John, was then appointed Deputy Postmaster-General in America at a salary of £200 a year.[24]

Shortly after the recall of the patent, the Act of 1711 regularized the rates to be charged in the colonies, at the same time

[23] *Cal. Tr.P.*, II, 289; Joyce, *op. cit.*, p. 113; Smith, *op. cit.*, pp. 1-16; Ruth L. Butler, *Doctor Franklin, Postmaster General*, pp. 14-17; Rich, *op. cit.*, chap. II.

[24] *Cal. S.P. Am.& W.I.*, 1717-18, 568; 1722-23, 30; Butler, *op. cit.*, pp. 18-19; Rich, *op. cit.*, p. 22.

that it systematized the rates in the British Isles. The charge in America for letters sent up to sixty miles from New York was 4d for a "single," and up to one hundred miles the rate was 6d. If the distance was greater than one hundred miles, the rate would be reckoned from New York to an important town like New London or Philadelphia, and the additional 4d and 6d rates would be charged from there. The charge to Philadelphia, for example, was 9d, instead of the former 4½d, and a letter from New York going beyond Philadelphia for another sixty miles would cost 9d plus 4d. The Boston-New York service was regularized: it became a shilling each way. The rate for a "single" from New York to Williamsburg, "the chief city in Virginia," was set at 1s 3d, and to Charleston, 1s 6d. The Act set up some thirteen postal centers in addition to New York.[25]

The higher rates did not make much improvement in the income: certainly they did not justify the purchase of the patent by the Post Office. John Hamilton complained some years later that the posts in America were not even paying his salary, that he was behind some £500. Not long after this complaint—it was made in 1722—the Postmasters-General believed, however, that the American Post Office was finally "upon such a foot that for the future, if it produce no profit to the revenue, it will no longer be a charge upon it." When John Hamilton ceased to be the Deputy Postmaster for America in 1730, there were due him arrears of some £350.[26]

The Post Office in America continued a small business with irregular service until the middle years of the eighteenth century. The line of deputies who had charge in America was quite undistinguished until 1753, when a rising Philadelphia printer by the name of Benjamin Franklin was made one of the joint deputies for the Post Office in America.[27] Since 1737 Franklin had been the postmaster of Philadelphia, a position that he found valuable, as it al-

[25] A single letter cost 6d from New York to Perth Amboy and Bridlington in New Jersey, 9d to New London, Conn., and Philadelphia, 1s to Newport, R.I., Boston, Portsmouth, N. H., and Annapolis, Md., 1s 3d to Salem, Ipswich, "the chief office in Piscataway" and Williamsburg, Va., and 1s 6d to Charleston in Carolina. For the general character of the act, see pp. 96 ff.

[26] Butler, op. cit., pp. 26, 29; Rich, op. cit., p. 26. The D.A.B., VIII, 180-81, also ends his tenure in 1730. But there has been confusion as to the date. Joyce, op. cit., p. 116, has him retiring in 1722, and this seems to be the statement made by Hamilton at the time. See Cal. S.P. Am.& W.I., 1722-23, 30. Smith, op. cit., p. 24, has him retiring in 1721.

[27] John Hamilton's successor, Alexander Spotswood, held the position from 1730 to 1739. Head Lynch was in charge from 1739 to 1743. He was succeeded by Elliott Benger, whose death in 1753 opened the way for Franklin and William Hunter of Virginia. On Hunter's death in 1761, John Foxcroft became Franklin's colleague.

lowed the free circulation of his *Gazette*. This earlier experience as a local postmaster was noteworthy for his introduction in Philadelphia of a town penny-post delivery for letters that were not called for at the office.

The administration of Franklin and Hunter proved a much-needed tonic. The American Post Office, which had been at a standstill for some years, was reinvigorated. The service between New York and Philadelphia, which had been weekly in summer and fortnightly in winter, was so quickened that the service was thrice weekly each way. It now took half the former time—six weeks—for a letter to go and an answer to return between Philadelphia and Boston. And the service, of course, became more frequent. The schedules were so improved that no longer could the printer at New London, for example, hold back the post from the west while he extracted the news from the papers that were en route.[28] The newspapers became so important a part of the load by the mid-century that the Postmasters-General in America decided to charge for their carriage. Franklin certainly instilled new life into the American service, for in 1761 a surplus of £494 was transmitted to London. The entry in the Treasury book contains the comment: "This is the first remittance ever made of its kind." It covered the eight years from 1753 to 1761. For 1761-64 the surplus was £2070.

Franklin, as one of the Deputy Postmasters when the Seven Years' War came to an end (1763), went to Canada in order to set up a postal service in that newly acquired possession. It was this addition to the Empire that largely stimulated the Act of 1765, with its more reasonable rates for longer distances.[29] The rates of the Act of 1711 had proved well-nigh prohibitive for letters from Quebec to New York: a single letter between the two places cost 3s. The Governor of Quebec insisted that the rates needed to be more moderate. The result was the recognition by the Act of 1765 of a widely felt need. Accordingly, a single letter went 200 miles for 8d, and every additional 100 miles for 2d. A letter from Quebec to New York, in consequence, cost less than half its former postage, 1s 4d instead of 3s.[30]

It is well known that Franklin remained a Deputy Postmaster in America until his dismissal occurred in 1774, shortly preceding the

---

[28] Butler, *op. cit.*, pp. 49, 57, 131; Smith, "The Colonial Post-Office," p. 270.
[29] See above, p. 111.
[30] 15 Geo. III, c.25; Smith, *op. cit.*, pp. 43-44.

opening of the American Revolution and the disruption of the postal arrangements as set up from London. It was the conclusion of a promising growth, for the Post Office in America showed surpluses from 1761 until the dismissal of Franklin. They were small, it is true—not averaging more than £600 a year—and certainly not justifying Franklin's claim that the American Post Office at the time was yielding a revenue three times that of Ireland. In 1772 a surveyor had been appointed. Hugh Finlay, who had been in charge of the Canadian section of the Post Office, began the survey of routes for better and more rapid service between Canada and New England. The usual route by way of Albany and north via Whitehall and Lake George was very roundabout for New England, and was not easy to use all the year, because of the large bodies of water traversed. Finlay explored a route from Quebec down the Kennebec, and also conferred with Governor Benning Wentworth of New Hampshire for a route along the Connecticut River.[31]

It was in 1775 that the revolting colonies resolved to appoint a postmaster of their own. Franklin was their natural choice, and thus became the founder of the Post Office of the later United States. The thirteen colonies selected the man who was best fitted by long experience for inaugurating the new postal service.

The British packet service to the American colonies was irregular during the early part of the century. Only with the approach of the Seven Years' War did the Post Office in England feel it necessary to set up a regular service to the American mainland. The Board of Trade had commented in 1765 on the "delays, miscarriages, and other accidents which have always attended the correspondence between this kingdom and his Majesty's colonies in America, from the very precarious and uncertain method in which it has usually been carried on in merchant ships." During the Seven Years' War, the service to New York proved very expensive, the cost for the period of the war being over £60,000.[32] By the end of the war, this service was using five packet boats on a monthly schedule. The service via New York for letters directed to the southern colonies was so slow that, after 1764, a separate packet service made its principal call at Charleston. At first, the letters were brought to Charleston on packets that went directly to the

---

[31] *D.A.B.*, VI, 389; Butler, *op. cit.*, pp. 137-41; Smith, "The Colonial Post-Office," p. 273; Rich, *op. cit.*, pp. 40-46.
[32] Smith, "The Colonial Post-Office," p. 272; Butler, *op. cit.*, pp. 61-62, 91.

West Indies, and then sailed on to the mainland, but this caused such a delay that a separate monthly packet soon plied between Falmouth and Charleston.

After the thirteen colonies broke away, Halifax became the American port, though there was an irregular service to New York and Philadelphia during the war. The monthly service to Halifax was irregular, as well, for it was likely to be icebound during the winter months. According to Paterson's *Road Book* of 1808, the packet from Falmouth "goes and returns by Halifax to and from New York every month, except November, December, January, and February, when it goes to New York direct."

During the American Revolution, the packets faced the danger not only of American privateers, but of the French, eager for revenge. Even before France entered the war on the colonial side, French vessels masquerading as American were capturing British shipping. After the spring of 1778, when France went openly to war, the packets were in even greater danger. In that year, several were lost to the enemy: of the five on the New York station in 1777, four were captured and the fifth put out of commission. Before the end of the war, nine packets used on the transatlantic service had been lost by capture and seven others disabled.[33]

Particularly worthy of note was the work of the packets during the long period of war from 1793 to 1815. The receipt of mail from the American continent and the West Indies was exceedingly important, and the sending of intelligence to the fleets absolutely essential. The service from Harwich as well as that from Falmouth was carried on under great difficulties. Occasionally during the first French war, Yarmouth was used as a packet station on the route to Helvoetsluis, and after the capture of Holland by the French recourse was had to Cuxhaven as the Continental station. Hamburg, also, was used as a postal station by the British, though it was unusable during a part of the winter. In 1794, a regular packet service was set up for the Channel Islands. It was essential that postal connection of a regular sort be maintained with Guernsey, Jersey and Alderney, lying, as they do, off the French coast. The English end of the service was at Weymouth.[34]

Packets on the high seas were under strict orders to safeguard

[33] Smith, *op. cit.*, p. 73.
[34] 34 Geo. III, c.18 (1794); *22nd Rep. Commrs. of Rev.*, p. 62; Joyce, *op. cit.*, p. 313.

the mails. A fight with the enemy was not to be sought, but, if necessary, battle must be given, and if there was danger of capture the mails were to be thrown overboard. The commander's duties were summed up in the terse formula: "You must run when you can, you must fight when you can no longer run, and when you can fight no more you must sink the mails before you strike."[35] Indeed, the usual preliminary to an unavoidable action with the enemy was to bring the mail on deck, weight it with pigs of iron, and place it near one of the portholes in charge of a sailor. It was his duty to throw it overboard if the enemy seemed likely to win the duel. There were many engagements between the British packet boats and the French and the American privateers in the wars that ended in 1815. Not infrequently, the packets, insufficiently armed and intended for fast service, fell victims in the duels that were seldom to their discredit.[36]

The losses of the packets during the wars with the revolting colonies and with France added greatly to the expense of this service, which, of course, was a charge on the Post Office. Before 1776 the annual cost of the whole service had been about £30,000. During the American Revolution, the expense increased four times, and even after the peace the charge did not drop to the pre-war levels. It was during these years, as we have found, that the packet service was a fruitful source of corrupt profits for the Post Office officials.[37]

During the Napoleonic wars, the expense again mounted to extravagant figures, despite considerable cleaning up of the corruption in the packet expense. In the year 1814, it reached a total of £160,-000, and again declined somewhat on the coming of peace.[38]

[35] Norway, *op. cit.*, pp. 30, 108-10.
[36] Norway, *op. cit.*, pp. 128, 204. Norway's volume deals at length with the fortunes and misfortunes of the packets, especially during these years.
[37] *Rep. Com. on Palmer's Agreement*, p. 79, furnishes the expense for these years. For the year ending April 5,

1775	£32,700	2s	9d	1780	99,534	14	3
1776	33,980	8	3	1781	104,233	14	1
1777	49,357	12	10	1782	122,292	17	0
1778	76,797	15	1	1783	85,876	19	2
1779	95,237	5	4				

[38] The totals, using every third year, will show the effects of war. They are taken from the *22nd Rep. Commrs. of Rev.*, pp. 376-77. For the year

1797	£63,760	11s	10d	1809	83,191	5	11
1800	72,962	1	3	1812	100,313	1	8
1803	73,580	5	4	1815	141,415	18	0
1806	78,708	5	10	1818	89,797	8	1

After the Congress of Vienna, the packet service was to enter on a long era unaffected by war. And as the Empire became more and more the home of emigrant Britishers, the service was to evolve into a valuable postal connection overseas and over all the seas. To this expansion of the postal service, we shall have occasion to turn in a later chapter.[39]

[39] Chapter 27.

The Irish Mails

THE separation of Ireland and Great Britain by water has had an unusually strong influence on their relations. The Irish, set apart by racial and institutional conditions, were definitely removed from the English influences that more easily affected Scotland and Wales. This produced an inevitable effect on Anglo-Irish postal relations. Unlike Scotland and Wales, Ireland needed a packet boat connection with the nearest ports in Wales some sixty miles away. Moreover, these sea connections with the Welsh ports of Milford Haven and Holyhead brought the Irish traveler and mails to roads through rough and sparsely settled country before they reached the better roads that led from Chester and Bristol to London. Despite these drawbacks, the postal connections of the two islands were very necessary, for the Irish population was sufficiently large to furnish considerable business, and the English government in Dublin as well as the plantations of Scots and English in other parts of Ireland required postal communication.

We have found that the postal connections between the two islands began in a very modest way in the days of the Tudors and Stuarts. Holyhead was chosen early as the port for the packets because it gave the shortest water crossing. But it had none too good a harbor, and the road between Holyhead and Chester seems to have been about as treacherous as the Irish Sea at its worst.

Mention has also been made of a service to southern Ireland by way of Milford Haven in Pembrokeshire. It was convenient for mail and traffic from southern England, since important towns like

Bristol, Cardiff and Carmarthen lay on the way. On the Irish side, the usual port for the Milford packets was Waterford. This southern route, however, was never so important as that via Holyhead, largely owing to the use of the Holyhead route for the mails to Dublin and northern Ireland. The harbor at Milford was regarded as safe and capacious in the days of sailing vessels, but its usefulness was impaired by "its remote situation," as a road book puts it. For these reasons, the modern development of the Milford route for continuous service only dates from the late eighteenth century— 1787, to be exact.[1]

Long before this time the Holyhead route had been receiving much attention. In 1768 three additional packet boats were added to the three already in use so that there could be a boat service both ways every weekday.[2] The mail for Ireland from the industrial towns of Lancashire and the north were so important by this time that they were brought directly to Chester by a cross post, where they were picked up by the postboys and later by the coaches that served the route from London to Holyhead. The Act of 1711 had set the postage for a single letter from London to Dublin at 6d: the cost of a letter to Waterford by way of Milford was the same.

The Scottish connection with Ireland was much easier, for the water parting was relatively narrow. From early times the two termini were Port Patrick and Donaghadee, the one in Wigtonshire and the other near Belfast. But the need for this postal bond was so slight for several centuries that it was not of much importance. Port Patrick was very remote from the centers of population. It was over four hundred miles from London, and was reached from Glasgow and Edinburgh by roads that were almost impassable. By 1711 this packet service was weekly, wind and weather permitting, a single letter crossing for 2d. Anthony Trollope is responsible for the statement that the mail was carried on this route before 1780 in an open boat.[3]

The political relations of Ireland and England changed in the eighties. The Irish Parliament, which had been strictly subordinated to the English government for centuries, was granted a greater measure of power as the result of a demand for "home rule." This concession was made just as the American colonies were

[1] Paterson's *Road Book* (1808), p. 90; *H.M.C. Rep.*, XIV, App. IX, 178; 27 Geo. III, c.9.
[2] *Ann. Reg.* (1768), p. 85.   [3] *3rd Rep. P.M.G.* (1857), p. 56.

winning their independence. Out of this grant of greater self-government grew a separated Irish Post Office, with a distinct service centered in Dublin.[4] It had its own Postmaster-General—like that office in England it was held jointly by two persons. The Irish office, of course, had its own Secretary, with a staff of clerks for the roads. A distinctive part of the Dublin arrangements was a British Office for oversea mail, not unlike the Foreign Office in London. In the year of the change, 1784, the Irish government appointed John Lees to the office of Secretary.[5] In 1801 John Lees associated his son with him, with the benefit of survivorship. The son, Edward Smith Lees, served the Irish Post Office as Secretary during the first three decades of the nineteenth century with much the same vigor as Francis Freeling, who held the corresponding position in London.

The Irish Post Office had the control of the postal rates in Ireland, on which and on other matters it made its own regulations. The postage on letters traveling in both countries was divided according to the distance traversed in each country. The rates in Ireland were very reasonable for some years after 1784, a single letter going as far as fifteen miles for 2d, up to thirty miles for 3d, and for greater distances the charge was 4d. The mile in this case was the Irish mile, of course. It was considerably longer than the one in use in England: 127 English miles equalled 100 Irish miles.[6]

The packet service between Great Britain and Ireland was kept under British control, with an allowance made to the Irish Post Office of £4000 a year as its share of the receipts. According to an act of the British Parliament at the time, this was to be effective "until the general post office in Ireland shall have established packet boats for the post and conveyance of letters and packets from Ireland to Great Britain."[7] In theory, at least, Ireland had as much right to carry its mails to England as France had to carry the French mails to Dover.

These terms led to some difficulty towards the close of the Na-

---

[4] The change was made by 23 & 24 Geo. III, c.17 (Irish Act).

[5] In fact, he was reappointed, as he had been Secretary in Dublin from 1774 to 1781. When Lees had taken the post originally, he had agreed to pay the previous Secretary, Walcot, the salary connected with the office, so long as Walcot lived, or, to put it more accurately, during the lifetime of the ex-packet agent at Dover, whose position Walcot had bargained for under the same terms. This was one of the irregularities that aroused the ire of Lord Tankerville. See above, p. 151; Joyce, *op. cit.*, p. 222; *19th Rep. Commrs. of Rev.*, p. 459.

[6] *19th Rep. Commrs. of Rev.*, pp. 361-62.   [7] 24 Geo. III, c.6.

poleonic wars, when the Secretary of the Irish Post Office decided that it was not receiving its due amount of the sea postage. Edward Lees took up the matter in 1813 with such determination that some wherries belonging to the Irish Post Office which were able to use the shallow port of Howth were put in service for carrying the Irish mails from Dublin to Holyhead. He informed Freeling that "until such time as regular packets should be stationed there [Howth], that the mails from Ireland should be dispatched in its own vessels." The wherries were so small that they carried but ten passengers each, but they took the mails and a greater share of the postage came to the Irish Office. The resulting inconvenience in London, both to the merchants whose letters were delayed and to the British Post Office whose packets came back without mail, led to so much concern that the Irish Post Office was bought off. The allowance to Ireland was doubled as the result of the temporary Irish counter packet service.[8]

This strain in Anglo-Irish postal relations is but one example of the differences that grew up. The Act of Union by which the two Parliaments were combined at the opening of the nineteenth century did not affect the Post Offices. That they remained separate was not, on the whole, for the good of the service. If corruption had to be stamped out in England during and following the days of Palmer, there was even greater need in Ireland, so much so that under the lead of Lord Clancarty, one of the joint Postmasters-General, a thorough overhauling took place in 1807. Both he and Lees made a personal examination of the office in London, and assimilated the Irish procedures to those in use in Great Britain. The possibility of plunder was much lessened by a system of checks. A distinct British Mail Office, to which reference has already been made, was set apart at the time to prevent confusion in deliveries by the uncertain arrival of these oversea mails.[9]

The franking privilege was very much more extensive in Ireland than in England. The list of privileged persons was large, and the practice even larger. The Postmasters-General, the Secretary, the Comptroller of the sorting office and the surveyors were given the legal right to frank letters, but the use of the frank went much beyond these offices. It was found in the twenties that privi-

[8] 55 Geo. III, c.145. See also Joyce, op. cit., p. 381. The Irish wherries were in use for some six weeks.
[9] 19th Rep. Commrs. of Rev., pp. 4, 113 ff.

leged persons in Ireland franked "by merely signing their names at the corner of the envelope and have been in the habit of receiving a much larger proportion of letters under cover than officers of the same rank in England." The investigators found, in addition, that "persons in the Post Office, who have no privilege of franking by any Act of Parliament, have certainly assumed the license." Nor did such persons think it necessary "to confine the privilege to their own letters." Letters were directed to the Post Office officials for other persons, various religious and charitable organizations sent their letters free and the clerks of the roads used the franking privilege for the circulation both of letters and periodicals.[10] What was even worse, the franking of all packages as if they were letters added literally a great burden to the Post Office.[11]

The four clerks of the roads connecting Dublin with Leinster, Ulster, Munster and Connaught seem to have arrogated to themselves all sorts of perquisites apart from franking. Originally, there were four clerks, each of whom presided over the sorting of letters for his road. By this time, these positions had become sinecures, with handsome profits accruing to the so-called clerks from the sending of newspapers and lottery slips express and postage free. These profits amounted in one case to nearly £900 a year, in addition to the regular salary. As these privileges were cut down, the clerks, as compensations for the loss of revenue from newspapers and other sources, obtained a lump sum in addition to their salaries. Moreover, these compensations adhered to the person after he ceased to be a clerk of the road.[12]

The case of the Secretary, Sir Edward Smith Lees, will serve as an

[10] This was an extension of the privilege of cheap postage granted to charitable institutions in 1819. They were allowed twelve notices or letters for a penny, unsealed, single sheets only, and strictly on the business of the institution. The privilege was abused in a number of ways. See Alcock & Holland, *op. cit.*, p. 201.

[11] *19th Rep. Commrs. of Rev.*, pp. 85, 86, 563, 722, 723. The *Report* in which these revelations are to be found was one of a series of inquiries made by the Commissioners to examine "the collection and management of the public revenue." A number of the *Reports* are not germane, but five, numbered 18 to 22, treat various aspects of the Post Office. The investigations were made in the twenties, and are voluminous. See Bibliography at end of volume. Thomas Moore, in his diary for Aug. 25, 1823, makes an interesting reference to the investigation of the Irish Post Office. "Skinner in whose packet we sail, . . told me of the havoc these English Commissioners are making in the Post Office. So much the better; it is the great seat of Orangeism; and Lord Wellesley says he knows that all the libels against him, during the late row, were circulated *gratuitously* through the medium of the Post Office." *Memoirs, Journals and Correspondence of Thomas Moore*, ed. Lord John Russell (1853), IV, 127.

[12] *19th Rep. Commrs. of Rev.*, pp. 79, 546.

illustration. It will be recalled that he was acting jointly with his father after 1801, until his father's death ten years later made him the sole Secretary. He was paid £400 a year as Secretary, but was receiving in the twenties £637 annually in addition as compensation for the newspaper profits he had enjoyed when clerk of the Leinster Road. Besides that, he was receiving £345 a year more as profits on the sale of English and Irish newspapers. Fees on appointments of postmasters brought in some £30 more, making the Secretary's annual income over £1400, in addition to furnished apartments.[13] The situation is still more extraordinary when we learn that his brother, Thomas Orde Lees, was chief clerk in the Secretary's office. Though the latter's salary was but £220, he actually received annually nearly £1300 in various ways.[14]

The holding of double offices and sinecures was also prevalent. One example will suffice. The offices of Resident Surveyor and Comptroller of By-letters, both of importance and distinct in themselves, had been united back in 1793 and granted to a Mr. Bushe. He still held them at the time of the investigation by the Commissioners in the twenties. The actual work was carried on by others. In regard to this curious situation, he declared that the offices were granted to him "as a total and absolute sinecure, in reward for the services of his father, and that it would be impossible for him to do any duty."[15]

The joint Postmasters-General is another illustration of needed reform. The salary of £1500 was a sinecure, even before 1822, when it was paid to one of them only, while the other enjoyed the patronage connected with the office. The work of administration was left to the Secretary. If one of the two Postmasters-General came to Dublin, he and the Secretary formed a board for transacting necessary business. Usually, on account of their places of residence, the joint Postmasters-General were 180 miles apart, so that it took the Secretary about a week to obtain the ruling of both on any important document—longer than if he had been required to communicate with London. Lees declared in 1824 that he had not seen the two Postmasters-General "in the same room together but once since the existence of their patent." And that once was not at the

[13] *Ibid.*, pp. 15, 459.
[14] Neither was so well fixed as the Secretary of the Post Office in London. For Sir Francis Freeling, see below, pp. 249 ff.
[15] *19th Rep. Commrs. of Rev.*, pp. 116, 134.

Post Office, but at a social gathering in Parsonstown, seventy miles from Dublin.[16]

Not only was the Irish Office run wastefully, but the cost of postage had grown greatly during the years of its separate existence. A slight rise had occurred in 1797 before the union of the two Parliaments. After 1800, the progressive advance in rates was not unlike that in the British Office across the Irish Sea. In 1803 the cost of a single letter traveling between fifteen and thirty miles was 3d, in 1805 it was raised to 4d, and in 1810 to 5d. Acts in 1813 and 1814 added charges for the longer distances, so that by the end of the Napoleonic wars, it is a wonder that the Irish did any corresponding, if postage had to be paid. Or to put it in the other way, one is not surprised to find the franking privilege so flexible and so widely used. A single letter going 100 miles in 1814 cost 10d, one traveling 175 miles cost a shilling. The single postage from Dublin to Belfast was 8d, to Cork 10d, to Derry or Galway 9d. A single letter from Belfast to Tipperary, via Dublin, cost 1s 5d, from Derry to Cork, 1s 7d. If someone in the west of Ireland, say in Limerick, wrote to London, the total cost of a single letter—Irish postage, packet charges and English inland postage—amounted to two shillings.[17]

Dublin was the overwhelming center of the postal business. The carriage of mails into the country was made by types of conveyances similar to those in use on the larger island. Mail coaches were employed, though their use, as in Scotland, was restricted by the tolls they had to pay turnpike trusts. Eight mail coaches left Dublin each evening. Otherwise, horse posts were in use. It was felt that horse posts would be inapplicable to the main roads and for carrying valuable mail traveling at night, "as there would be danger of robbery every night." In the twenties, Ireland had some 430 post towns, about four-fifths of the number in England. The gross revenue of the Irish Post Office, however, was one-tenth that of England, and about the same as that for Scotland. It had fallen off considerably since 1815.[18]

[16] Ibid., pp. 9, 12-14, 93.   [17] Ibid., pp. 361 ff.

[18] Ibid., 352, 446, 726. The gross revenue for selected years will furnish an idea of the amount of business.

1804	£118,435	8s	8d	1814	211,746	16	9
1805	139,362	18	9	1815	220,161	16	1
1809	182,136	12	3	1822	201,526	4	1
1810	195,694	10	4				

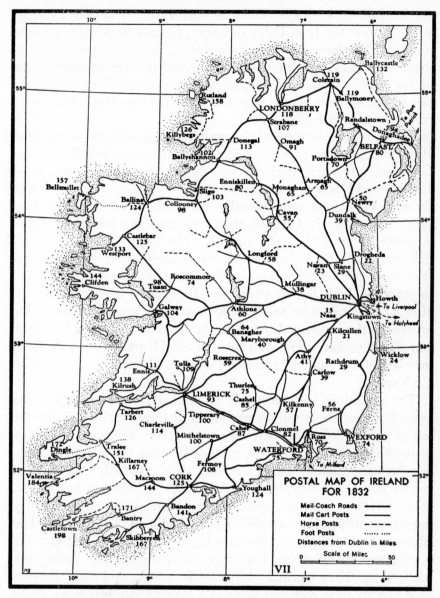

Ballycastle 132
Coleraine 119
119 Ballymoney
LONDONBERRY 118
Strabane 107
Randalstown
Rutland 158
Donaghadee
Killybegs 126
Donegal 113
Omagh 91
BELFAST 80
Ballyshannon 102
Portadown 70
157 Bellmullet
Enniskillen 80
Armagh 65
Sligo 103
Monaghan 65
50 Newry
Ballina 124
Collooney 98
Cavan 55
Dundalk 39
Castlebar 125
Longford 58
Drogheda 22
133 Westport
Roscommon 74
Navan 23
Slane 29
144 Clifden
98 Tuam
Mullingar 38
DUBLIN
Howth
Galway 104
Athlone 60
To Liverpool
64 Banagher
Maryborough 40
15 Naas
Kingstown
To Holyhead
Kilcullen 21
Wicklow 24
Roscrea 59
Athy 41
Rathdrum 29
111 Tulla 109
Carlow 39
138 Ennis Kilrush
Thurles 75
LIMERICK 93
Cashel 85
Kilkenny 57
56 Ferns
Tarbert 126
Tipperary 100
172 Dingle
Charleville 114
Mitchelstown 100
Cahir 87
Clonmel 82
Ross 70
WEXFORD 74
Tralee 151
Killarney 167
Cahel
WATERFORD 75
To Milford
Valentia 184
Macroom 144
CORK 125
Fermoy 108
Youghall 124
171 Bantry
Bandon 141

**POSTAL MAP OF IRELAND
FOR 1832**

Mail-Coach Roads ——
Mail Cart Posts ——
Horse Posts – – –
Foot Posts ·····
Distances from Dublin in Miles

Scale of Miles
0   50

Castletown 198
Skibbereen 167

VII

The differing practices in the two Post Offices, and the need of
a more complete check on expenditures led the Commissioners, in
their report of 1830, to recommend strongly the reuniting of the
Irish and British Post Offices. In 1827 the somewhat higher rates
in Ireland had been lowered to fit the charges made in Great Britain, and in 1831 the Postmaster-General of Great Britain became

the head of the Irish Post Office as well. In the next year a further act went over the Irish Office carefully, limited franking to prevent some of the abuses that we have found, permitted the establishment in Ireland of penny posts and checked the indiscriminate grant of low rates to charitable organizations by establishing a reduced rate in certain cases. These steps did much to bring about the needed reform of the Irish Post Office.[19]

Let us return, in concluding our view of conditions in the Irish Post Office, to the packet connections with Great Britain and the land routes through Wales. Even though these land routes from London to Holyhead and Milford and the packets thence to Dublin and Waterford were actually under the control of the Post Office authorities in London, they concerned the Irish Post Office as much or more than the English. The Irish seem to have acquiesced in the poor character of this connecting service so long as they had their own Parliament. But when the Irish members had to cross the Irish Sea to attend the Parliament in Westminster—after 1800—it became to them, at least, a different matter. Prime movers in the insistent demand for better road conditions in Wales and better packets were such men as Sir Henry Parnell, an Irish member of Parliament, and John Foster, Chancellor of the Irish Exchequer.

The conditions were certainly in need of amendment. The sea voyage was made in sailing packets until the twenties brought the use of steam. Before the twenties, the packets were usually vessels of less than one hundred tons, manned by some ten men. The journey between Dublin and Holyhead took, normally, eighteen to twenty hours each way, but this schedule was subject to much variation. Shelley, the poet, and his wife Harriet had a particularly unpleasant trip when crossing from Dublin in April 1812. The adverse winds lengthened the crossing to thirty-six hours, and the voyage was so boisterous that they could eat nothing during the whole time. They reached Holyhead at 2 A.M., and had "above a mile to walk over rock and stone in a pouring rain before we could get to the inn."[20]

The land routes through Wales to the packets were about as unpleasant as the sea crossing. It usually took some forty hours of

[19] 7 & 8 Geo. IV, c.21; 2 Wm. IV, c.15.
[20] *22nd Rep. Commrs. of Rev.*, p. 8; *The Works of Percy Bysshe Shelley*, ed. Roger Ingpen and Walter E. Peck (1926), VIII, 310.

travel from London to make either port of embarkation. The Welsh part of the journey was through very rough country, over roads notorious for their dangerous narrowness and steep grades. On reaching the Menai Straits, the mail and passengers were ferried across to Anglesey for another coach journey across the island to Holyhead.

The harbor at Holyhead was a "tide harbor," and the packets were occasionally damaged, in consequence, by the heavy swell. As the harbor master put it: "Their time of sailing was irregular and uncertain. . . . In fresh gales from the eastward—fair wind for Ireland—the packets could not warp out. The difficulties in entering the harbor in heavy gales from the westward was very great. . . . It was necessary in bad weather to keep out until daylight. The passengers in embarking and landing with their luggage experienced great inconvenience, and sometimes considerable personal risk, in small boats."[21]

In the eighteenth century, passengers for Ireland frequently took the boat at Parkgate to avoid the execrable Welsh roads. This "port" lies on the east side of the estuary of the Dee, some twelve miles lower down than Chester. Although the distance by water from Parkgate to Dublin was twice as far as from Holyhead—120 miles—the traveler felt that it was worth it. Jonathan Swift, for instance, usually went by way of Parkgate to his deanery in Dublin. An additional reason for the Parkgate variation was the unsavory reputation of Holyhead as a place to await the boat or the coach. Swift called it a "scurvy, unprovided, comfortless place." And Thomas Moore, who lived at the time which we are now considering, wrote of "that most disagreeable of all inns, Spencer's at Holyhead." In the early nineteenth century, Parkgate was still usable. Paterson's *Road Book* of 1808 spoke of it as a place where "passengers frequently take shipping to Dublin to save the land traveling through Wales." Its harbor facilities, however, were destroyed in the early nineteenth century, when the estuary of the Dee silted up. By 1843 Parkgate was described as "formerly an important station for vessels trading with Ireland, but at present the navigation is much impeded by a large sand bank, which prevents vessels of burthen from approaching the quay."[22]

[21] *Ibid.*, pp. 7, 189.
[22] *Memoirs of Thomas Moore*, IV, 100; *Correspondence of Jonathan Swift*, ed. Ball, II, 45; *Parliamentary Gazetteer* (1843), III, 605; Edward Watson, *The Royal Mail to Ireland*, p. 73.

The improvement of the roads in Wales and the harbors of Holyhead and Howth early in the nineteenth century made the use of Parkgate largely unnecessary. The harbor improvements were completed first. That of Holyhead was made much more useful and safe than ever before by the building of adequate piers and by the dredging of the harbor. The work was performed under the direction of the well-known engineer, John Rennie. At the Irish end of the sea journey, the packets had long used the Pigeon House, near the mouth of the Liffey in Dublin Bay. When it was decided that Howth would be preferable, Rennie undertook as well the elaborate and expensive improvements at Howth.[23]

The road through Wales to Holyhead had long been a concern of the Post Office. The surveyors had reported on the bad conditions; turnpike trusts and parish governments had been approached as to improvements, but little of real value was accomplished in this way. As we have already found, the Irish members of Parliament loudly complained after the Union of the condition of this main connection with their country. As a result, particularly of the incessant advocacy of Sir Henry Parnell, a continuous run of committee reports on the state of the Holyhead road appeared during the first quarter of the century. At first, the reports went at the problem in the old eighteenth century way, by discussing the width of wheels, the weight of the vehicles using the road, etc. Not until 1810 was a more thoroughgoing approach made. In that year Thomas Telford began a careful survey of the highway. Telford, who was the great successor of Metcalfe in the new art of road building, was at the time opening up the Highlands of Scotland by elaborate road construction and bridge building, and was well fitted for this new task. At last, in 1815, the Treasury granted £20,000 towards the Holyhead improvement, for it was out of the question to expect the residents of the area to support the construction any more than the Highlanders had been able to finance the road building there.

The difficulties in the way seemed almost insurmountable. The eighty-five miles of road in Wales crossed difficult terrain. It could not, at first, be handled as a unit, since the road was broken up into various trusts. Even after the re-creation of the highway was completed, turnpike trusts had to be influenced or coerced into allowing a single comprehensive system of survey and upkeep. But by

[23] Rennie died in 1821.

1830 the seemingly impossible had occurred. The Holyhead road, through Telford's engineering skill and Parnell's constant watchfulness, had been made a really national road. It was believed at the time to be the "most perfect road-making that has ever been attempted in any country." Telford not only made the road between Chester and Holyhead a comparative paradise for travelers, but also superintended similar improvements on the road between Chester and London. He took over, as well, the even worse road from London through Shrewsbury to Holyhead. The Welsh stretch of this road—it went through Corwen and Llanrwst to Conway—was so bad that mail carts rather than mail coaches were used on it into the nineteenth century.[24]

The crowning achievement of this remarkable engineer was the construction of the famous bridges over the estuary of the Conway and across the Menai Straits. The crossings had still to be made in open boats, with the mails and the passengers sometimes lost, as a result. The Menai Straits, in particular, were dangerous because of the strong current. The Menai Bridge was completed in the twenties, becoming one of the great suspension bridges of the world, as the total length of the bridge was a third of a mile. When the Menai Bridge was opened, January 30, 1826, the first vehicle to cross was the London and Holyhead mail coach.[25]

The expense of these vast improvements in harbors and roads was very great. Added to the mounting cost of the main route between London and Dublin was the actual outlay on the packet services in general during these years. They were a fruitful source of corruption and needless extravagance. This was felt so strongly by Lord Walsingham, as we have found, that investigations were made in the eighties as to fees and gratuities obtained by the Post Office staff. The Commissioners, in the year 1788, found that the packet services had caused an expenditure "so enormous as almost to surpass credulity": over a million pounds had been spent in seventeen years for the hire and upkeep of the packet boats, this applying, of course, to the packet stations in general, and not simply to the

[24] For this matter of the road-building, the works of Jackman and Smiles, already noted, are valuable. In addition, see Sidney and Beatrice Webb, *English Local Government, The King's Highway* (1913), pp. 167-70, and J. H. Clapham, *Economic History of Modern Britain*, I, 94 ff. Watson, *op. cit.*, has much of value on the Welsh roads. See esp. pp. 81-99.

[25] The Conway bridge was also a suspension bridge. See S. Smiles, *Lives of the Engineers* (1904), III, 252-77; Jackman, *op cit.*, 271-74.

Irish services. We have already noted the fat additions to his salary obtained by Anthony Todd, Secretary of the English Post Office, as a result of his 2.5 per cent "rake-off" from the packet establishment.[26] It was discovered, also, that members of the staff were "in" on the ownership of packet boats. One of the results of the inquiry of 1788 was an order prohibiting any person in the Post Office from having anything to do with packet ownership.[27]

The sailing packets, as a result, were hired until the close of the Napoleonic wars. For the Irish services, this included seven boats for the Holyhead route, six for Milford and four for Port Patrick. But in the twenties came a change. It was in 1818, apparently, that the use of steam engines for vessels making sea voyages first came into use. The *Rob Roy* of ninety tons, with an engine of thirty horsepower, began regular journeys from Glasgow to Belfast. Another, the *Robert Bruce*, started regular voyages between Liverpool and Greenock a year or so later.[28] This meant, inevitably, a revolution in the packet services. The Post Office made every effort to keep the older routes in use. This seemed the thing to do, since they had been used for centuries and because of the recent heavy expenditures for improving the roads and harbors for these traditional routes. But there were difficulties. Steam vessels began to take away the passenger traffic of the packet boats. At Holyhead, for example, the steam packets—not carrying mail—took away the majority of the passengers, as they made the journey from Holyhead to Dublin in eight to ten hours rather than the customary eighteen or twenty hours of the sailing vessels. This affected the mail packet owners, since their contracts with the government were based on the income from the passenger carriage. In 1819, the number of full-cabin passengers on the packets going from Holyhead to Howth was 5578. In 1820 the number dropped to 2862.[29]

At first, prejudice was strong against this new-fangled conveyance, just as it had been against the faster stage coach of 1784. But when a voyage by steam was found a more pleasant journey for the stomach, the old sailing packet was doomed. The new sensation of riding on a steam packet was discreetly described at the time as

[26] See above, p. 151.
[27] *Rep. Sel. Com. on Finance* (1797), p. 182; *22nd Rep. Commrs. of Rev.*, p. 3; *Hist. Sum.*, p. 48.
[28] *22nd Rep. Commrs. of Rev.*, pp. 4, 680.
[29] *Ibid.*, p. 8; Watson, *op. cit.*, pp. 114-15.

follows: "There is a tremulous vibration in the steam packet, occasioned by the action of the wheels, which, like the stroke of the oars in a boat, counteracts that smooth and gliding sensation in sailing which always affects the stomach." The narrator added: "I had a comfortable breakfast on board, and many of the passengers took luncheon."[30] It was not always thus, for Thomas Moore records an uncomfortable journey on the steam packet, *Ivanhoe*, in 1823: "Sailed on the *Ivanhoe*; took to my berth and peppermint lozenges, but felt deadly sick all the way."[31]

The Post Office met the competition from steam vessels by reverting to the older condemned policy of purchasing packets. The expense was heavy, and the purchases, at times, were very injudicious. The Commissioners who examined this phase of the Post Office expenditures in the late twenties found that Sir Francis Freeling did not insure public competition in the purchase of ships and materials. But the result, at any rate, was the transformation of the old sailing routes into faster services by steam, with much greater regularity and with greater comfort for the passengers. The first steam vessels were fitted with a mast and sail at the stern. The sail, in the early days, contributed much to safety, "if, in a heavy sea, any accident should happen to the machinery." Rowland Hill, the future postal reformer, crossed from Dublin to Holyhead on a steam packet—not a mail packet—in 1821. He reported that "the captain told them that his company intended to attempt running it throughout the next winter; and cautiously remarked that he thought in a storm a steamer might even have some advantages over a sailing vessel."[32]

Steam packets were put into the mail service at Holyhead in 1821, at Milford Haven in 1824 and at Port Patrick in 1825. The immediate effect was a great increase in the cost of the packet establishment.[33] But the public was not satisfied with the service. Liver-

[30] *22nd Rep. Commrs. of Rev.*, pp. 8, 115. The testimony of Richard Griffith, the agent at Holyhead, on a voyage to Howth in 1820.

[31] *Memoirs of Thomas Moore*, IV, 100. Moore records a crossing from Howth to Holyhead in August of 1823 that took "about seven hours."

[32] G. B. Hill, *The Life of Sir Rowland Hill*, I, 168. For criticism of the policy of purchase, see *22nd Rep. Commrs. of Rev.*, pp. 71, 448. Also *19th Rep.*, p. 137.

[33] The annual expense for the whole establishment during these years can be seen from the following sample figures. They are taken from the *22nd Rep. Commrs. of Rev.*, pp. 4, 7, 47, 57, 72, 377, 550.

For the year 1817	£78,857	1s	10d	For the year 1820	£85,349	5s	5d
1818	89,797	8	1	1821	134,868	11	4
1819	87,647	15	10	1822	115,429	15	0

pool and Dublin began to demand direct packet connection. The mails between the two places, as already explained, went by way of Chester and Holyhead, with the shortest possible time on this route about twenty-four hours. When steam vessels could make the journey between Dublin and Liverpool in less than fifteen hours, the roundabout course of the letters seemed a needless waste of time. The sea passage, though longer than via Holyhead, was certain, and even the mails from London to Dublin could be carried in about the same time as via Holyhead.[34] An additional argument for the Liverpool route was the increasing use of steam on railways. Liverpool naturally came into consideration, for it was just at this time that the first public railway was being constructed from Liverpool to Manchester. A packet establishment was set up at Liverpool in 1826. Not only were steam vessels used for the Dublin mails, but Liverpool became the terminus at this time for a steam packet service to the Isle of Man.[35]

All this proved very expensive. The profits of the Holyhead station disappeared. There was a loss also on the Liverpool station as well as a very heavy loss at Milford and Port Patrick. The condition was made worse by the use of Holyhead as a repair station for all the steam packets. It was certainly uneconomical to bring the packets boats working out of Dover, Harwich and Weymouth around to Holyhead for reconditioning. What made the policy of the ownership of the packets and their repair by the Post Office establishment even more calamitous was the inefficiency of this organization for the work they had taken on. Francis Freeling, the Secretary, naïvely admitted that nobody in the Post Office knew anything about running a dockyard.[36]

It was doubtless inevitable that the postal charges on the packet routes should increase during these years. In 1801 the packet postage to Irish ports from Holyhead and Milford was made 2d for single letters, and this in addition to land rates that were increased

[34] *Ibid.*, p. 27. The time bill for mail from London to Liverpool was about twenty-two hours at this time.

[35] *Ibid.*, pp. 27, 43, 60. A packet service between Whitehaven and the Isle of Man had been running since 1766. From 1822, steam vessels between Liverpool and Glasgow had delivered two mails a week in summer and one in winter. In 1828 mail deliveries were made three times a week from the beginning of April to the end of September, and once a week for the other six months, by a boat that plied between Liverpool and Douglas.

[36] *Ibid.*, pp. 472-75; *6th Rep. Commrs. P.O. Management*, p. 246.

at the same time.[37] Another penny was added in 1812 to the packet charges between Great Britain and Ireland, when the land rates were again increased by a penny. The climax to this policy of overcharging was reached in an act of 1827. By this measure, letters between Port Patrick and Donaghadee paid 4d for a "single," between Holyhead or Milford and Ireland 2d, and between Liverpool and Dublin, 8d.[38] The latter charge was established so as to make the postage the same whether a letter went to Ireland from Liverpool by way of Holyhead or directly across by water. And to add to the troubles of letter writers, this Act provided a cost of an additional penny for a letter crossing the Conway Bridge and another when it passed over the Menai Straits. Thus a single letter between London and Dublin by way of Holyhead cost 1s 4d, 2d for the packet, a penny each for the two bridges, and a shilling for the inland postage on the English side.

It is no wonder that the people were growing tired of the nuisance of the postal monopoly, and were taking more and more advantage of secret means of conveying letters, and were even beginning to look to a general reform of the Post Office. As a member of Parliament put it in the year of Waterloo: "It is highly unjust that the Post Office, which was originally intended for the purposes of public convenience, should be converted into a mere instrument of revenue."[39]

[37] 41 Geo. III, c.7. See above, p. 155.   [38] 7 & 8 Geo. IV, c.21.
[39] Cobbett, *Parl. Deb.*, XXX, 769.

How the Londoner
Got His Mail before 1840

FOR most of the eighteenth century—until 1773—London was the only urban center in Great Britain and Ireland where mail was delivered. Elsewhere those receiving or mailing letters had to go to the one post office of the town. But a great change came in the half-century before uniform postage was introduced in 1840. The influence of these town posts—most of them penny posts—was very great in preparing the public demand for a general uniform system throughout the country. Of these town posts, London's Penny Post was so influential, and itself so interesting an example of a well-developed town system, that it needs to be understood before we attempt to appraise other local penny posts, and before we can appreciate properly the influences back of the demand for a general penny post for the whole of the British Isles.

The beginnings of the London Penny Post have already been narrated. William Dockwra's unfortunate attempt to set up an independent postal service for London soon gave way to an official Post Office. It was patterned on Dockwra's Post and continued as a distinct division of postal activity. Queen Anne's Act of 1711 had given the penny charge legal sanction, and had limited the area of its service to a district within ten miles of the London Post Office. This restriction on its activities was made to prevent the Penny Post from conflicting with the area and charges of the Inland Letter Office on the roads leading up to London. Beyond the ten-mile area, the charge made by the General Post Office at that time for a single letter was 3d to a distance of eighty miles. It will be recalled as well that the local service in London was a parcel post: parcels up to a pound in weight were carried for the same charge as for a single letter.[1]

A further distinctive feature of the London Penny Post was the prepayment of letters and parcels, save for the collection by the messenger of an extra penny for the deliveries in the "country" area of the London Post. Early in the reign of George II difficulties arose over this second penny, some refusing to pay for delivery outside the urban districts. This was corrected in 1731 by an act that legalized the second penny. The postal Act of 1765 affected the Penny Post by lowering the limit for parcels from one pound to four ounces on the ground that "many heavy and bulky packets and parcels are now sent by such carriage, which greatly retard the speedy delivery thereof."[2]

The London Penny Post made little advance in the latter part of the eighteenth century, if receipts are any evidence. At the opening of the century the income had been nearly £5000 a year. Eighty years later, the annual receipts had only doubled, a rate of increase far behind that of the Post Office in general, and the income from the Penny Post was only about a fiftieth of the General Post Office receipts.

John Palmer was so well aware of this condition at the time he introduced the mail coach that he wished to reorganize the Penny Post, even offering to forgo the percentage that he claimed for his introduction of the mail coach, if he be allowed to farm the Penny Post at a rent equal to the highest net revenue it had as yet produced. He had definite plans for what he called a "New Penny Post."

But Palmer was dismissed, and the reorganization of the Penny Post was directed by an appointee of Palmer, a former letter carrier by the name of Edward Johnson. His plan, which may well have included features of Palmer's proposed New Penny Post, included the reduction of the principal offices from five to two, an increase in the number of daily deliveries and the doubling of the number of letter carriers—to eighty-one. But combined with Johnson's reforms were revenue-collecting provisions and other changes that made the London Penny Post less and less like the original plan of Dockwra. In 1794 a second penny was charged for a letter going from the sub-

[1] See above, pp. 69 ff., 98.   [2] 4 Geo. II, c.33; 5 Geo. III, c.25.

urbs into the urban district: the charge now became 2d in both directions. The same Act made a further change from the original design by allowing the charge for a letter to be paid by the sender *or* the receiver.[3]

But the end was not yet. The hunger for revenue swept the Penny Post more and more into the Treasury maw. In 1801 the lowest charge in London became 2d, and the Penny Post had ceased to be. The Twopenny Post, as it now became known, had an additional charge added four years later, when letters going beyond the General Post limits were charged an extra penny. The result of this legislation was to make the outer, that is, suburban sections of the Twopenny Post a threepenny post, so far as the cost went.[4]

Immediately following Johnson's reforms, the Penny Post expanded very rapidly: its gross revenue nearly doubled in a year. This was partly because of the higher charges.[5] The increase in revenue was remarkable during the next three decades. In the year following the end of the Napoleonic wars, the London District Post had a gross income of over £90,000, a fivefold increase since Johnson's changes, and ten times what the Twopenny Post was bringing in when Palmer wished to take it over. By the end of the twenties its gross receipts had reached £117,000, and the net income was £77,000. This is partly explained by the rapid expansion of the London region, not only in numbers, but in wealth.[6]

The heavy charges added during the wars with France were not removed after the victory at Waterloo, though many felt at the time that the charge was too high, so high that there was much smuggling of letters. Evidently the tax on letters was about as much as the public would stand, since the revenue of the Penny Post showed no cor-

---

[3] 34 Geo. III, c.17.

[4] The General Post limits in London were about the same as the old urban section of the Penny Post. See the map facing p. 198. The acts making these changes are 41 Geo. III, c.7; 45 Geo. III, c.11.

[5] During the years of the change, the revenue was as follows:

	GROSS REVENUE			NET INCOME		
April 5, 1793, to April 5, 1794	£11,768	0	8d	£6,085	3s	8d
The Act became effective March 28, 1794.						
April 5, 1794, to April 5, 1795	£22,099	14s	3d	£8,362	8s	4d
" " 1795, " " " 1796	27,128	5	3	5,947	16	9
" " 1796, " " " 1797	29,623	4	4	7,658	6	11

The figures are from *Rep. Com. on Palmer's Agreement*, p. 94.

[6] *21st Rep. Commrs. of Rev.*, p. 86.

responding advance between 1820 and 1840 when compared with the advance from 1800 to 1820.[7]

In turning next to the way in which the Londoner was served by the Post Office, it is necessary to realize that the Twopenny or District Post was only one of three overlapping services. The Inland Office, with its headquarters in London, had general charge of the whole postal system for the British Isles, including, of course, the carriage of mails by coach in and out of London. The staff of the Inland Office had its Superintending President, its clerk of the roads, numerous sorters and a staff of letter carriers for London. The Foreign Post Office gave a distinct service, caring for the mails going to and coming from foreign countries, and did so with a completely separate establishment.

The housing of these three departments had been very inadequate before 1829. The Lombard Street Post Office, which had been in use for over a century, had proved hopelessly unsuitable, though it had been enlarged from time to time by the addition of nearby buildings, until the whole was a cumbrous and inconvenient jumble. The change of site, projected in 1814, to a place just north of St. Paul's Cathedral, brought the center of the postal system somewhat closer to the large population of the West End. At last, in September 1829, the new Post Office at St. Martin's le Grand was ready for use. Much care had been given to the planning of the building, that it might not only be spacious but ornamental as well: Three Ionic porticoes decorated the front and above the eight columns forming the center portico was a pediment. The designers, as well as the Post Office authorities, thought it fitting to distinguish a "public building of this kind from the gloom of a prison, or the melancholy appearance of an hospital."[8] Of one thing there could be no doubt: the new Post Office satisfactorily housed all the various

---

[7] The official figures for every fifth year are as follows. They are to be found in the *9th Rep. Commrs. P.O. Management*, p. 92.

	GROSS REVENUE			NET INCOME		
April 5, 1800, to April 5, 1801	£38,422	11s	4d	£16,286	12s	3d
Jan. 5, 1804, to Jan. 5, 1805	62,256	4	4	37,478	11	8
" " 1809, " " " 1810	80,433	4	5	51,327	6	7
" " 1814, " " " 1815	94,247	18	4	57,128	5	11
" " 1819, " " " 1820	99,043	6	3	62,530	8	9
" " 1824, " " " 1825	111,511	7	5	73,647	1	2
" " 1829, " " " 1830	115,740	6	3	76,219	3	6
" " 1834, " " " 1835	109,148	13	11	63,722	16	0

[8] Cobbett, *Parl. Deb.* (1815), XXXI, 193. The original building stood until 1913.

activities centering in London, including the Foreign Office, the General or Inland Post and the Twopenny Post.

The Twopenny or District Post, whose working will be described first, served an area that was divided into a central region where letters were delivered for 2d, and an outer section where a 3d charge was made. The outer limits of the Threepenny Post, as we have found, were allowed, in 1794, to extend beyond a ten-mile radius from the General Post Office building in Lombard Street. By 1829 the distance was fifteen miles in some directions, with the average distance about twelve miles from St. Martin's le Grand. The outer limit, moreover, was very irregular. It included, on the east, such towns as Chigwell, Woolwich and Eltham, but not Epping, Romford or Dartford. To the south, Croydon was inside, but Bromley and Kingston were without the limits. Although Kingston on the Thames was not in the threepenny area, Sunbury, on the other side of the river and considerably farther up, was within. To the northwest and north, the Threepenny Post served Ealing, Finchley, Harrow and Enfield, but not Edgware though it was not so far away as Harrow.

The twopenny delivery was restricted to an area including the Cities of London and Westminster and the Borough of Southwark, comprising, on the whole, the thickly built-up area. The threepenny district beyond this area was spoken of in the Post Office as "off the stones," as its inner boundary doubtless coincided in an earlier day with the boundary between town and country. By 1829 the distinction between the two areas was having less meaning, as London grew to merge with many a district that in an earlier day had been a separate village. The difference, then and now, in London can be realized when one finds outside the twopenny area at the time of which we are writing such districts as Chelsea, Kensington, Paddington, St. Pancras, Hackney, Camberwell and Battersea. No wonder that the Commissioners of 1830 criticized the division as "irregular." When they asked the Comptroller why, in one instance, the circulation extended as far as fifteen miles, he replied: "How this anomaly crept in, I am not aware."[9]

Within the town area, the Twopenny Post no longer used the half-dozen offices of former times, but just two, one at the General Post Office in St. Martin's le Grand, the other to the west in Gerrard

[9] *21st Rep. Commrs. of Rev.*, pp. 50, 122; *18th Rep.*, p. 680.

St. The latter was usually referred to as the Westminster Office.[10] The two offices were fifteen minutes apart, and there were six interchanges of mail during the day. The transfer of mails between the two divisions was made on horseback. Each office had a window at which Twopenny Post letters were received, called the "paid-letter window." The unpaid letters, on which collection of postage was made at the time of delivery, were put in boxes conveniently located in the two main offices.[11]

Letters could also be mailed at numerous receiving houses scattered about the twopenny and threepenny districts—148 in the town and 202 in the country in 1830. Obviously, they were often not very far apart—some within a furlong of each other—but their purpose from the days of Dockwra had been to make the sending of letters an easy matter. These receiving houses, usually located in shops, were open until eight at night, for the receipt of both paid and unpaid letters. Letters could be mailed after 8 P.M. at the receiving houses through a hole cut in the shutter. Letters were taken to the chief offices from the receiving houses in town as frequently as six times a day, but only twice a day from those in the country. In the two main offices the letters were sorted, taxed and stamped as they came in, and then delivered by the carriers. Letters that came for the General Post Office and the Foreign Office were separated and turned over to those departments.[12]

Londoners received their letters through the District Post by means of carriers. There were 224 carriers in the twopenny region, and 165 more in the country or threepenny area. The carriers in town walked, but in some of the more remote country districts they rode. The "walks" and the "rides" were carefully laid out, though there was great inequality, in some cases, in their length and the time taken to deliver the mail. No general revision of the "walks" had taken place since 1794.[13] According to the directions of the Comptroller, "letter carriers are required to pass at a quick pace from house to house, to proceed in like manner throughout, and complete each delivery as early as possible." He "earnestly requested persons receiving letters not to detain the letter carriers at their doors, but dispatch them promptly." In the town or twopenny re-

[10] Gerrard Street is located near Leicester Square, and is officially in the City of Westminster, though everyday usage does not apply the name to that area. It served what was then the western part of the urban district. See *21st Rep. Commrs. of Rev.*, pp. 6, 122.

[11] *Ibid.*, p. 213.　　　　　　　　　[12] *Ibid.*, pp. 16, 17, 78, 198.

[13] *Ibid.*, pp. 12, 35-36, 136.

gion, the deliveries were made six times a day. The first was made
at eight o'clock, the others at ten, noon, two, four and seven in the
evening.[14] The letter carriers, on their return to the main office out
of which they worked, brought back bags of letters from the receiving houses on their routes.

The work was not easy. The carriers seem to have put in about
eleven hours a day. The delivery was necessarily slow, on account of
the need for collecting the postage on unpaid letters. It was estimated
that the carriers were able to deliver, on the average, only about
seventy letters in an hour and a half, the average length of a "walk."
Each carrier made three deliveries a day, and three collections on
his return. In the country districts, the mail service was not so frequent. Bags were taken out to the area three times a day for the three
deliveries that were made from house to house. One of these dispatches of mail from the central office was by convenient coaches,
which dropped bags on their way out of London at night.[15]

The Commissioners and others criticized the length of time
needed to receive an answer within the area of the District Post. In
the twopenny area, of course, the service would be fairly rapid. If a
letter were put into a town receiving house before 10 A.M., it would
be sent out for delivery on the twelve o'clock "walk." If answered
promptly, the reply might be received by the seven o'clock delivery
in the evening. On the other hand, at least twenty-four hours was
required for an answer from places in the "country" districts, even
if they were near the twopenny boundary. Thus, an interchange of
letters between Chelsea and Hackney would take over twenty-four
hours.[16]

A fertile cause for delay lay in the elaborate precautions taken for
taxing the letters and checking the accounts of bags received and
letters sent out. The mail was accumulated from receiving houses,
from the "paid window" and from consignments turned over by the
Inland Office, the Foreign Office and the Ship Letter Office. Mail
from the above offices came with "dockets": "They tell their own
letters and we check them in our office; those for town are then put
over to the charge-takers, and they check the amount in the same
manner as they do the twopenny-post letters, and they are put on
the same slip." There was a charge-taker, a check clerk and a slip

[14] *21st Rep. Commrs. of Rev.*, pp. 130; *9th Rep. Commrs. of P.O. Management*, p.
156.
[15] *21st Rep. Commrs. of Rev.*, pp. 36, 43, 130-31, 219, 224.
[16] *Ibid.*, pp. 43, 130, 141; *9th Rep. Commrs. P.O. Management*, p. 8.

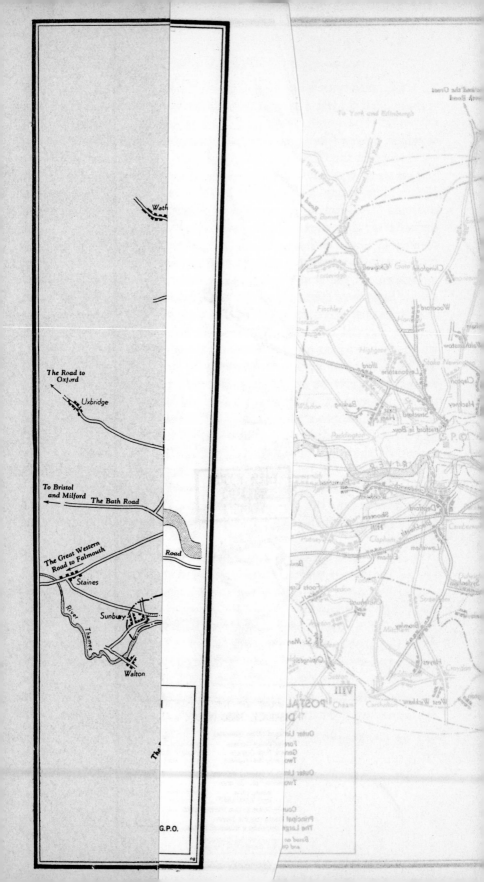

clerk, each doing his part to see that the telling of the number of letters and the charges were properly balanced. Before the final sorting in the letter carriers' office, the letters had to be taxed, if the postage was not prepaid, and most of it was not. General Post letters were taxed with a pen, the Twopenny Post letters with a stamp, for 2d or 3d as the case might be. After the sorting into walks, the bag of each letter carrier had to be checked for the charge against him of the postage due on his letters. Fortunately a settlement was not made at the end of each delivery: the letter carriers settled once a week for the letters they delivered. If one of the carriers brought back letters that were undeliverable, that is, dead or missent letters, or letters refused by the persons to whom they were directed, the carrier received credit against his account. The whole was a complicated procedure, since there were actually 985 collections a day from the town and country receiving houses.[17]

We are accustomed to receive letters bearing a stamp or cancellation by the sending office, and another, at times, for the receiving office. The London Penny Post used stamps of various kinds much more liberally. The two main offices, at Lombard Street and at Westminster, had stamps to indicate the time of delivery. Dockwra, it may be recalled, employed triangular date stamps, and the government continued their use after his post had been taken over.[18] After 1794, the triangular Dockwra stamps were discontinued. Instead, stamps more or less oval in form, but with indented frames, were used at the two offices. They were distinctive, as the stamp of the Chief Office had the month before the day, and the Westminster Office put the day before the month. After 1801 the stamps were oval in shape, the Lombard Street stamp having a double rim. Smaller types came into use in 1823 for both paid and unpaid letters. After 1834, when the Westminster Office was abolished, they became smaller yet and ceased to be oval.

It was only after 1794 that the receiving houses used official name stamps to replace the penned initials of the receivers. The simple stamp with just the name soon gave way to stamps indicating both paid and unpaid letters, since unpaid letters were permitted after 1794. There were no dates on these stamps.

All letters that were franked had a special stamp; a circle enclosing "To be delivered Free" was surmounted by a crown. If

[17] *21st Rep. Commrs. of Rev.*, pp. 198-99, 213; *18th Rep.*, p. 682.
[18] See above, pp. 73-75.

letters came in from the Inland Office or elsewhere too late for
sorting and delivery by the first post, they were marked by a stamp,
"Too Late for Morning Post." Another curious stamp was used
for letters to be delivered on Sunday. These were used on country

letters sent out on Saturday night, the letter to be delivered by ten
o'clock Sunday morning. This delivery was intended to take place
before church time, an accommodation that has long ceased.

Letters of the Twopenny Post were certainly bestamped in those
days. These elaborate arrangements were to prevent delays and to
provide checks. One of the regulations was as follows: "The date
stamp on letters, or if there be more than one, that having the latest hour, shows the day and time when they were dispatched for
delivery. . . . Persons having occasion to complain of the delay of

their letters, are requested to transmit to the Comptroller the covers, with a statement of the time of delivery, as the date stamp will assist materially in tracing their course." In order to prevent mistakes, persons who paid the postage on letters that they mailed at the window were advised "to see them stamped with the paid

THAMES S.T3

Two Py Post · Unpaid · Brompton

Aldgate 2py P·Paid

Penny Post Pd 2d. Grosvenor Squ

Kennington Unpaid Penny Post

stamp before they leave the office." One can only commend the care with which letters were treated. But delay was inevitable under a system which handed each letter in so individual a manner.[19]

The number of letters delivered was surprisingly large, if one considers the conditions of the time. In each of the town divisions, the number per day varied from three hundred to a thousand. The banking district, Grosvenor Square, St. James's Square, Portman Square and the Strand were among the divisions with the most letters. The total number of letters delivered during a given week in 1829—the first week in April—was almost 150,000, or an average of about 7,500,000 letters a year.[20]

As a result of the recommendations made by the investigating commissioners in 1830, a number of improvements occurred in the District Post in the next few years. The walks were remodeled. The

[19] *21st Rep. Commrs. of Rev.*, pp. 131-32. For additional illustrations, see Alcock & Holland, *op. cit.*
[20] *21st Rep. Commrs. of Rev.*, pp. 99-101.

country rides were made more useful by additional deliveries and extensions. Hampton, for example, was included in the Richmond ride. The outer limits of the Threepenny Post were also extended to include Kingston, Hounslow, Edgware, Barnet and Romford. The twelve-mile limit was made much more like a circle than ever before, and the boundary between the twopenny and threepenny

districts—three miles from the Chief Office—was also made more regular, so that such places as Chelsea came within the twopenny district. The Westminster Office was abolished in 1834. Letters were also dropped on their way into London by mail coach, at Hounslow, for example, if they were intended for the western part of the London District, so as to avoid the necessity of carrying a letter all the way into St. Martin's le Grand and sending it out again. Great improvements were made in the District Post just shortly before the greatest improvement of all, a general penny post for the whole country.[21]

---

[21] *9th Rep. Commrs. of P.O. Management*, pp. 4, 5, 15, 76-80. For these changes, see the map facing p. 198.

The system we have just described would seem sufficiently elaborate for serving the Londoners of a century ago. But in addition to the carriers for the Twopenny or District Post, London was served by two other completely distinct sets of carriers, for the Foreign Office and for the General or Inland Post Office.

The Foreign Office had had its own set-up from early days, as we have found, and the lapse of time had brought little change save to increase the staff.[22] The foreign letters had always been delivered in the heart of London by special letter carriers attached to the Foreign branch of the Post Office. The original walks were ten, one man being sufficient in the old days for each walk. They were still called, as late as 1830, by the name of the man who, sometime in the past, had been the letter carrier on that route. As one of the officers put it: "The names are from the letter carriers, perhaps a century or two ago." Sadler's Walk was in the Cheapside area, Peck's along the Strand, Pickering's from Oxford Street to St. James's Palace, and the Ambassador's "wherever the foreign ministers may reside in London." The ten carriers in use at the opening of the nineteenth century had increased to thirty-four carriers by 1830.[23]

The region served by the Foreign Letter carriers was smaller than those served by the twopenny region of the District Post. Their walks included the north shore of the Thames from the Houses of Parliament to the Tower, the countinghouse section of the City, and the region to the west as far as Hyde Park. In this area, the thirty-four letter carriers delivered twice a day, at ten o'clock and again at two, if any more foreign mails had arrived by that time. The carriers complained of their arduous duties: as one declared, "There are so many counting houses, and it is up and down stairs." Impatient merchants had recourse to the "alphabet" in the Foreign Office, that is, they obtained their foreign mail from the window of the Foreign Office.[24]

A third letter-carrying service was performed by the General or Inland Office, in an area somewhat larger than that served by the Foreign Office carriers, but smaller than that for the Twopenny Post. The General Post, like the Twopenny Post, had its own receiving houses, seventy-one in number: in some streets the receiving

[22] See above, pp. 27, 56, 110.   [23] *18th Rep. Commrs. of Rev.*, pp. 316, 667.
[24] *Ibid.*, pp. 655, 664, 667, 675. Letters and dispatches for the government and for the ambassadors were taken out first. The foreign staff, in general, was carefully trained and responsible. The last serious case of attempted fraud was in the nineties when an employer was detected secreting letters and not accounting for the postage. His surname was Angel!

offices of the General and of the Twopenny Post were side by side.

The Inland letter carriers did not make a delivery at eight o'clock in the morning, for the obvious reason that the mail coaches coming up to London usually arrived in the early morning. The latest of the mail coaches was generally at St. Martin's by ten minutes past seven. From then on, the sorters and letter carriers were busy preparing the mail for delivery. The letters were divided into fourteen main divisions, twelve for the letter carriers, one for those to be transferred to the Twopenny Post and one for the merchants.

That for the merchants needs some explanation. The merchants, who wanted an early delivery instead of waiting until late in the morning to receive their first mail, subscribed a fee for preferential treatment. They could get their letters, it is true, from the "alphabet," as was done in the Foreign Office, but an early delivery had distinct advantages. The letters were left at the subscribers' offices or lodgings, no attempt being made to collect postage at the time of the delivery. Though this greatly speeded the delivery, it compelled the carrier to return over the same route later in the day to make his collections. This preferential delivery was usually finished about two hours before the first regular carrying-out of letters on the same route. In the City—the countinghouse area—this early delivery was very large, often comprising three-fourths of the morning letters for that region.[26]

The Commissioners sharply criticized this preferential treatment: "No partial priority in the distribution of letters should be provided for." They made clear, however, the need for a speedier distribution of mail. The carriers on the regular delivery were much delayed by waiting for change, more so than the carriers of the Twopenny Post, since the letters from the General Post were of varying cost. One carrier was asked: "Have you ever made a calculation how long it takes you to deliver a letter and receive the postage?" He replied: "No, that depends on circumstances; sometimes a servant has to run up two or three pair of stairs, . . and sometimes they have to run out and borrow the money, and sometimes they want change for a sovereign." Another estimated that it took at least two minutes at every house, and at some houses he was detained "three, four or five minutes in giving change."[26]

[25] *Ibid.*, pp. 620, 622, 631.
[26] *Ibid.*, pp. 50, 622, 647. Interestingly enough, Rowland Hill seems to have received one of the principal suggestions for his reform from reading the evidence just quoted, for he used it in his *Post Office Reform*, 3rd ed., pp. 20-21.

To return to the sorting for the General Post divisions. When the bags were brought in from the mail coach to the tick clerk, he checked them in. After they were opened, the correct amount of paid letters was checked with the bill that came in each bag, and the unpaid and free letters were stamped. This latter task was a slow one. If the letters were franked, it was necessary to see that the sender or receiver had no more than the number allowed by law.[27] If unpaid, the letters had to be taxed, which included, of course, the necessity of examining the letters for double and treble postage. As one of the officers put it, "Every one is taken before a lamp."[28] It is true, in the matter of charging for letters, that the sending postmaster, say in Manchester or Leeds, had penned on the letter what the cost of postage would be, but this needed another check in London, and a stamp. After further examination by clerks, the letters came at last to the divisional boxes, where they were sorted. After that, each letter carrier obtained the letters from his divisional box for his own walk, arranged them in the order of delivery, reckoned up the charge against himself for the letters on which he collected postage, and had it checked and proved right. With 40,000 to 60,000 letters a day, and an early preferential delivery as well, it is a wonder the carriers got off by ten o'clock.

After the delivery was finished, the letter carrier returned to collect postage on the early delivery, and brought back bags from receiving houses on his route, if the mail cart did not pick them up. The receiving houses closed at five, and from then on until a quarter past six or half past at the latest, the letter carriers became bellmen. As one of them put it: "After we have made our collections, we have to ring the bell at five o'clock." Each bellman rang his bell on a set route. He carried what was called a "ringing bag." If letters were given to him prepaid, he made the settlement at the Post Office the next morning. The bellmen also called at countinghouses, coffee houses and club houses to pick up letters. For doing this, there was an extra fee paid, in addition to a "fee of one penny for each letter at night for ringing the bell." The bell ringing had to be over by six-thirty to allow time for all letters to be sorted, taxed and stamped for the general departure of the mail coaches at eight.[29]

The Commissioners who criticized so sharply the early preferential delivery and the overlapping sets of letter carriers recommended

[27] See above, p. 153.　　　　　[28] *18th Rep. Commrs. of Rev.*, p. 479.
[29] *Ibid.*, pp. 310, 484, 622, 644.

the unification of the three sets of carriers. Since foreign letters for Londoners who lived outside the area covered by the Foreign Office carriers were delivered by the District Post, little justification could be found for retaining the Foreign Office carriers: they were abolished in the early thirties. But the Post Office did not see fit to combine the Inland and Twopenny Post carriers, despite this recommendation by the Commissioners. These two sets of carriers remained distinct for some years even after the introduction of general penny postage.[30] The Commissioners also recommended the discontinuance of a double set of receiving houses, and that dead letters be handled in London as a unit rather than by three separate offices, and other suggestions for a simplified service. The reports of the Revenue Commissioners made clear the general need for a radical overhauling of the services within London both for the receipt and dispatch of mail. Their work was to prove of real value in the thorough reorganization soon to take place.

[30] *9th Rep. Commrs. P.O. Management*, pp. 10, 76; *Parl. Deb.*, 3rd s., LXXXV, 828.

Penny Posts
Outside London

NEARLY a century after Dockwra "invented" his Penny Post for London, town posts were extended to other urban districts in Great Britain and Ireland. The delay may be explained by the great difference in size between London and any other urban centers in the British Isles. In Dockwra's day, for example, London had over half a million population, and was some seventeen times larger than the places next in size. When Bristol and Norwich—the largest urban communities outside London in 1680—had only 30,000 inhabitants each, a single post office for each town served well enough.

The eighteenth century, however, brought great changes. Many industrial towns "boomed" into sprawling communities as factories gathered more and more workers from the country. What is more, places like Manchester and Glasgow and Leeds soon became centers for manufacturing activities in growing nearby villages. Not infrequently, these villages were away from the regular coach and horse-post roads. And yet they were linked industrially and commercially with their larger neighbor, for in the early stages of the industrial revolution and before the wide application of steam power the factories, or mills as they were often called, would be widely scattered over a region in order to utilize the available water power and labor supply.

The first step in satisfying the growing need for penny post systems was the Act of 1765: it legalized penny posts "for any city or town or the suburbs thereof," if the Post Office decided the service was "necessary and convenient."[1]

---

[1] 5 Geo. III, c.25, sect. 11.

The first community outside London to take advantage of the Act was Dublin where a penny post was set up in 1773. Although patterned after London, the Dublin Penny Post was on a much smaller scale. At the end of the eighteenth century only fourteen carriers were in use, and the gross receipts never exceeded £400 a year. But a change came in 1810 when the Dublin Penny Post was "new-modelled" by Lord Clancarty, one of the joint Postmasters-General of Ireland. As a result of the changes that he brought about, the number of carriers was increased to fifty-seven, and the number of daily deliveries from two to four. The efficiency of the service was increased in 1822 when six deliveries a day instead of four came into use, with no enlargement in the corps of carriers. The result was a sufficient increase in business to bring the Dublin Penny Post out of the "red" for the first time in 1823. In that year the receipts were over £4000.[2]

The Penny Post of Dublin, however, was not in a very healthy state, even though the income was satisfactory. Fifty-seven carriers were more than enough, as some were found by the Commissioners of Revenue to be habitual absentees, employing substitutes. Although the Commissioners were told by the carriers that eight of their number had died in the last nine months, "owing to excessive fatigue, cold, and fever, caught in the discharge of their arduous duties," this "melancholy" fact impressed the Commissioners so slightly that they recommended fewer carriers. The receiving houses, eighty-two in number, were also found to be too numerous, for in some cases receiving houses took in only a hundred letters in six months. And there was serious leakage through excessive free use of the Penny Post. The officers of the organization, including the sorters, sent their letters free, and helped their friends as well by taking letters out of the bags when they were opened, and not accounting for the letters so taken.[3]

The charge for delivery was a penny in the City proper, and 2d beyond the regular boundary that was marked by the circular road. Within the penny region the same sort of duplication existed as in London, for the General Post Office had sixty carriers working in that area, in addition to the carriers of the Penny Post. The General Post Office carriers were in two groups, making the comparison with

[2] *19th Rep. Commrs. of Rev.*, pp. 57, 73-74, 86, 144, 149, 186, 206, 518. Lord Clancarty was an Irish Postmaster-General who took his work so seriously that he did not leave the management and all the decisions to Sir Edward Lees.

[3] *Ibid.*, pp. 73, 187, 697, 913.

the London situation even more striking. Forty carriers distributed letters that came into Dublin from other parts of Ireland and twenty others distributed English letters and foreign letters that came to Ireland on the Holyhead packets. The General Post Office also had receiving houses in Dublin. The letters were put through a slot into a locked box located at a convenient place in the window of a receiving house, whence they were taken at five o'clock every afternoon by a messenger who kept the key of the box. The letters were not stamped and docketed as in the Penny Post. The Dublin Penny Post, like that of London, delivered General Post letters in the outer area, that is, beyond the circular road. The total letter delivery of the Dublin Penny Post amounted to some 12,000 a week. The Revenue Commissioners saw no reason why one set of carriers could not serve the Irish capital.

The only other town in Ireland that needs mention is Belfast. Although Belfast had no penny post at this time, its postmaster hired two carriers to deliver letters. Each letter that was delivered cost the receiver a penny, the receipts being pocketed by the postmaster. When John Baird, who described himself as "nothing but a letter carrier," was asked by the Commissioners if people in Belfast objected to paying the penny in addition to the postage, he replied: "Some odd people refuse. If they do, I merely tell them, 'If you do not wish to pay the penny, call at the office, and you shall receive it without the penny.'" The carriers took out what were called "particular letters" on the first delivery. This was somewhat like the early delivery in London, as it went almost exclusively to the merchants. The distinction seems to have been made on the ground that "persons who are not particular would not attend to them till their day's leisure, or the next day." There was also a late delivery for the "particular" group. As in London, delay was avoided for the "particulars" by their not paying for the letters on delivery.[4] Belfast serves as an example of a large commercial center without a penny post in the days before reform, and yet having facilities that looked in that direction.

The second place in Great Britain to set up a penny post was Edinburgh. It arose in somewhat the same way that London's Penny Post was started a century before. Edinburgh's service was the private venture of a certain Peter Williamson. His earlier life had been full of adventure. Williamson was taken by kidnapers in

---

[4] *Ibid.*, pp. 930, 941-42.

Aberdeen when a boy of ten, and sold in the regular course of business to a planter in America. After serving his time there, Williamson went to the frontier, was captured by the Indians, escaped, entered the British service and was finally discharged about 1757 as unfit. He then proceeded to earn his living by his wits, publishing accounts of his kidnaping and his life among the Indians, and finally setting up as a publisher and bookseller in Edinburgh.[5] He also ran a tavern there, called Indian Peter's Coffee Room. As he had published Edinburgh's first street directory in 1773, and as his coffee shop was situated in the hall of the Parliament House, Williamson was naturally employed by those frequenting the courts to forward letters to different parts of the City.[6]

Peter Williamson decided, about 1773 or 1774, to make his post of use to anybody who wished to send local letters or parcels.[7] In his second Edinburgh city directory, in 1774, Williamson inserted the following announcement: "The Publisher takes this opportunity to acquaint the Public that he will always make it his study to dispatch all letters and parcels, not exceeding three pounds in weight, to any place within an English mile to the east, south, and west of the Cross of Edinburgh, and as far as South and North Leith, every hour through the day for one Penny each letter or bundle." The central office was near St. Giles Cathedral, and there were other receiving houses as well. Williamson's carriers—also known as "caddies"—wore uniforms and had the words "Penny Post" on their hats. Each rang a bell as he went his rounds, so as to collect as many letters and bundles as possible while he was delivering those already in his possession. The "undertaker" warned the public that he was responsible only for letters marked before delivery "with a round stamp, Penny Post Not Paid, with black ink, and those paid, with red ink, Penny Post Paid."[8]

Williamson had no connection with the Post Office, nor was it

---

[5] It seems to have been a regular practice to decoy young boys, especially in the Highlands, and sell them as slaves to the planters in Virginia. Williamson's exposé of the system was largely responsible for its discontinuance. He was prosecuted by the Aberdeen authorities for libel, but won the case against them. See W. E. H. Lecky, *A History of England in the Eighteenth Century* (Cabinet ed.), II, 257, 274.

[6] *D.N.B.*, LXII, 7-8; *2nd Rep. P.M.G.* (1856), p. 80.

[7] The date of its founding as a town post is in doubt. Hendy, *op. cit.*, p. 127, has 1768; the *E.B.*, 6th ed., published in Edinburgh in 1823, makes his post begin in 1776, and is followed as to the date by the "Historical Summary" in the *2nd Rep. P.M.G.* (1856), p. 80. Joyce, *op. cit.*, p. 300, has 1777. The best evidence seems to point to 1774, as given in Alcock & Holland, *op. cit.*, p. 92.

[8] *2nd Rep. P.M.G.*, p. 80; Hendy, *op. cit.*, p. 127; Alcock & Holland, *op. cit.*, p. 92.

thought any infringement for his local delivery to serve Edinburgh in the absence of any government means of distribution. His service was so useful that it continued nearly a quarter of a century without interruption. Indian Peter was more fortunate than William Dockwra.

By the nineties the need for penny posts in other towns was becoming manifest. Francis Freeling, who was at that time a postal surveyor, made an official visit to Edinburgh in 1790. One of the results of this visit was the conviction that a penny post might be set up in Edinburgh by the Post Office "with some convenience to the

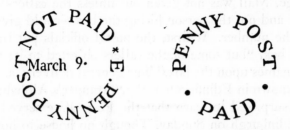

metropolis of Edinburgh and also with some advantage to the revenue." Accordingly, in July of 1793, Williamson's post ended, and the government took over. The former proprietor was granted a pension of £25 a year, "he having long had the profits of 1d a letter on certain letters forwarded through his receiving house at Edinburgh, which he will lose by our having established a penny post there." And the Postmaster-General added: "We have made it a rule always to propose that those who suffer in their income from services which are certainly beneficial to the public should receive compensation for the loss they sustain."[9]

The Post Office was both more and less ambitious than Williamson. The delivery system was enlarged to include the General Post letters, but only three deliveries were made each day instead of one every hour. Those in the morning and in the evening were the important deliveries, the noonday service only carrying out the mail that came in from the north. By 1797 Edinburgh had ten letter carriers; twenty years later, there were thirty. The Commissioners found that Edinburgh had nine receiving houses whence mail was collected five times a day. There was no real distinction between the General and the Penny Post, as in London. The Commissioners of

---

[9] *18th Rep. Commrs. of Rev.*, p. 351. Joyce, *op. cit.*, p. 301. One is tempted to invoke the shades of Witherings, Oxenbridge, Dockwra and Povey. Williamson died in 1799.

1829 were not slow to point out this divergence from the London practice. As they put it: "The general advantage of making the service of the whole body of letter carriers equally available for the distribution of both descriptions of correspondence appears to us to be so obvious that we should have thought it hardly necessary to draw attention to the adoption of this practice in Edinburgh, were it not for the objections that have been raised against it in London."[10]

The people of Edinburgh also received letters at the window of the main office. There were some eighty boxes in the Edinburgh office, each with the name and the number of the person who enjoyed this privilege. Mail was not given out unless the caller—if he was a messenger and not the person hiring the box—could give both the name and the number. At first, the postal officials put the number only on the box, "but some of the callers objected to it; they liked to see their names upon the box." The general delivery, as we would call it, was known in Edinburgh as the "Stranger's Alphabet." Readers may be surprised to learn that the Post Office served the good people of Edinburgh on Sunday. Though no house-to-house deliveries were made on that day, one could call at the Post Office and receive mail from eight to ten in the morning, and for an hour in the late afternoon. The letters were obtained on Sunday from the letter carriers at their windows.[11]

The Edinburgh Post Office maintained a frequent connection with Leith on the Firth of Forth, two miles away. In fact, Williamson had used messengers for Leith in his day. When the government took over Williamson's Penny Post, the Leith service was continued. It was the only penny-post town connected with Edinburgh for several years. By the twenties the two Leith foot messengers were carrying bags back and forth four times a day. The Leithites objected to the extra penny they had to pay. A letter from London to Leith should cost not more, so they felt, than a letter from London to Edinburgh. It was pointed out in reply that, if Leith were a post town, and paid a penny less, it would have just one delivery a day, instead of four.[12]

The Act of 1794, which allowed letters to be sent unpaid in the London Penny Post and allowed that service to extend beyond ten miles from the Post Office, also applied to other penny posts in Great

[10] *20th Rep. Commrs. of Rev.*, pp. 30-31.
[11] *Ibid.*, pp. 28-29, 142, 154, 286, 309-16.
[12] *Ibid.*, pp. 74-75, 130, 136, 234, 292. By this time Leith had a population of 25,000, about one-sixth the size of Edinburgh.

Britain.[13] This proved of very great importance to the penny posts just beginning to appear elsewhere than in London. It meant that a town like Edinburgh could have lines running out to nearby villages in all directions, and even beyond the distance of ten miles. In that way, it became possible for many villages that were not on the post roads to receive mail service for an additional penny through the large nearby community, of which they were natural satellites. These postally dependent villages were somewhat like the communities in the threepenny region of the London District Post. Despite their comparative smallness, the villages around such places as Edinburgh received the advantages of a penny service long before penny postage was applied to the entire kingdom.

The arrangements at Edinburgh will serve as an early example of the extension of this convenience to places outside London. Penny-post units in addition to Leith began to be added as early as 1796, when Lasswade was given the privilege. From time to time other villages were included in what were known as the outbounds, or the region beyond the tolls. In most cases, these "country" parts of the system were served but once or twice a day. The connection might even be by mail coach, if one went that way, and the village was too near or too small to be a post town. The coach would, in such cases, take up and leave mail as if the place were a receiving house. Others were served by horse posts, and to some of the nearer places—Leith is an example—the mail went on foot. By 1830 the spokes of Edinburgh's penny post radiated service to some twenty-one places. One of the farthest removed was Ford, thirteen miles away.[14]

Francis Freeling has already been quoted as saying that in 1790 a penny post might, with advantage, be set up in Edinburgh. At the same time he suggested to the Postmaster-General "that it would be desirable to try the experiment of opening posts in some of the great towns of the kingdom." In England, the extensions, according to Francis Freeling, "began at Manchester" and were then set up in Liverpool, Bristol and Birmingham.[15]

It was high time that something was done for Manchester. This thriving center of commerce and industry had, before 1793, an aged postmistress aided by her daughter and one carrier. When a penny post was opened in that year, the postmistress was pensioned and the

---

[13] See above, p. 194. The act did not apply to Ireland.
[14] *Ibid.*, pp. 234-35. The maps in the *Reports of the Commrs. of Rev.* include sketches of these town posts as they extended into the country.
[15] *18th Rep. Commrs. of Rev.*, p. 351.

THE PENNY POSTS OF EDINBURGH AND GLASGOW IN 1830

═══════	Mail Coach
───────	Horse Post
─ ─ ─ ─	Foot Post

The numbers on the roads indicate the mileage.
Further additions were made during the Thirties.

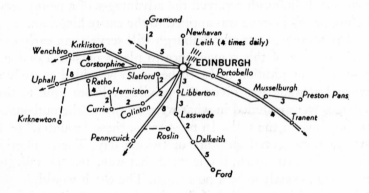

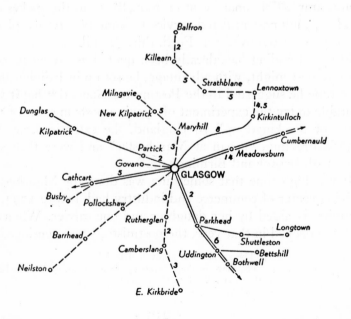

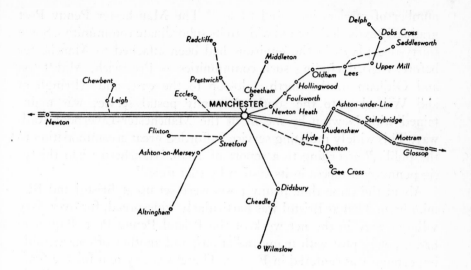

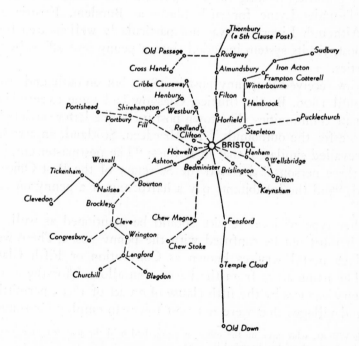

THE PENNY POSTS OF MANCHESTER AND BRISTOL IN THE THIRTIES

```
═══════  Railway
━━━━━━━  Mail Coach
─────────  Horse Post
─ ─ ─ ─ ─  Foot Post
```

number of carriers increased to six.[16] The Manchester Penny Post gradually extended far and wide to its subordinate communities. Some thirty-one places in the environs had been attached to Manchester before 1840, including such communities as Prestwich, Middleton and Oldham to the north, Glossop to the east, and Altringham and Wilmslow to the south. A penny postal service was maintained with Newton by means of the Manchester-Liverpool Railway. This widely radiating service "afforded great accommodation to the public," according to a report of 1836. Manchester had thirty-six penny-post offices in its system by that time.[17]

About the same time penny posts were set up at Bristol and Birmingham. That at Bristol was particularly widespread, for over sixty villages were in the net work of the Bristol Penny Post. Bath also had a penny post with many radiations, and another of considerable importance was centered in Exeter. There was a system for the Staffordshire potteries, making for a convenient interchange of mail via Newcastle-under-Lyme for such places as Burslem, Etruria and Stoke. Although Liverpool was not particularly well located for a penny post, yet its system included sixteen penny-post offices by the late thirties.

Glasgow received its penny post in 1800, but no outbounds were added until 1806. By the thirties, Glasgow had some twenty-eight subordinate communities. The town post used nine letter carriers besides those for the outbounds.[18] In Aberdeen, Scotland, an arrangement prevailed similar to that in Belfast: "The postmaster employs two or three persons," declared the Secretary of the Post Office in Scotland, "and the inhabitants pay a halfpenny or a penny on each letter."[19]

Another type of local service should be mentioned as well, although it must not be confused with the penny posts. These were the village postal services known as Convention or Fifth Clause Posts. The name arose from the permission allowed for these supplementary services by the fifth clause of an act of 1801, permitting towns and villages that were not post towns to employ messengers

16 Sarah Willatt, who gave up the office in 1793, had held the post for some twenty years—since the death of her husband in 1772.

17 4th Rep. Commrs. P.O. Management, p. 53.

18 20th Rep. Commrs. Rev., pp. 236, 292, 337-38; 3rd Rep. Sel. Com. on Postage, Abstract of Evidence, p. 15. The Exeter system had some thirty villages: one of them, Moreton Hampstead, was twelve miles away.

19 20th Rep. Commrs. of Rev., p. 292. As late as 1824, but seven towns in Scotland had any sort of delivery service.

"to carry and re-carry any letters or packets, to or from the post town." Under this permission towns and villages could set up a service, agreeing to pay a halfpenny or a penny, "whatever the convention may be." They differed from the penny posts in not being part of the official Post Office. If there was a deficiency, the inhabitants agreed by the convention to make it good.[20]

Fifth Clause Posts developed to some extent in the first decade of the nineteenth century. Bristol even had one such post in its environs, Thornbury by name. But when in 1807 the Postmaster-General decided that franked letters and newspapers were to be carried free by these posts, the result was to limit greatly the spread of Fifth Clause Posts. The surveyors were even instructed to arrange for a penny post, in case a village wanted service from some nearby town. "There may be places," declared the instruction to surveyors in 1811, "yet susceptible of arrangement under the fifth clause of the Act of the 41st of the King; but the penny post is always to be preferred." As a result, only fifty-two Fifth Clause Posts were in use at the coming of uniform penny postage. In most cases, one or two villages only would be attached by the Fifth Clause arrangement to a post town, though Newcastle in Staffordshire had twelve and Maidstone eight.[21]

Penny posts, on the contrary, flourished. The principal ones outside London were in Dublin, Edinburgh, Glasgow, Manchester, Bristol, Liverpool, Leeds and Birmingham. The Dublin Penny Post was the only one in Ireland before the thirties, since the Irish Post Office had been a separate establishment for the previous half-century, and no permission had been granted for penny posts on the island. After permission was granted by an act of 1832, they developed rapidly, for less than ten years later 295 towns and 248 villages in Ireland had penny posts. The same story of rapid growth applies to Scotland, where 81 towns and 199 villages were enjoying penny-post services in the thirties. The number in England and Wales was even larger, where 155 post towns had penny posts as early as 1820, and many of them were centers of systems that included subordinate villages. By the coming of uniform penny postage at the end of the

---

[20] *18th Rep. Commrs. of Rev.*, p. 351; *9th Rep. Commrs. P.O. Management*, p. 66.
[21] *20th Rep. Commrs. of Rev.*, p. 321; *1st Rep. Sel. Com. on Postage*, pp. 508-9; *42nd Rep. P.M.G.* (1896), p. 34. The act in which the Fifth Clause appeared is 41 Geo. III, c.7.

thirties, 356 towns in England and Wales had penny posts; they were serving 1475 villages.[22]

This surprising development—over 2500 places with penny postal service by 1840—was the consequence of a widespread desire for cheaper postage and better communications. The grasping Post Office had thought, for a time, that it had the power to make these penny posts into twopenny posts, and some few were established on that basis. But in 1837 it became clear to the Secretary and to the legal adviser of the Post Office that no more than a penny could be demanded. A general reduction to a penny was made, in consequence, in March 1837, save where a specific law allowed a greater charge, as in the arrangements for the London District Post. As a result of this decision, penny posts became very popular and were spreading rapidly at the time that uniform penny postage was introduced.[23]

The stamps of these local posts are of some interest, as preparing in a way for the later cancellation stamps used after adhesives came into use. For the Fifth Clause villages, the letters were stamped in the post town, and the name of the post town and not the village was used. They might appear with or without a frame and with no indication of the date. The only exception to using the name of the post town rather than that of the village that was served under the Fifth Clause arrangement was Thornbury. But as it was the only Convention Post in a crowd of penny-post villages surrounding Bristol, the practice of the group may have influenced Thornbury.

NEWCASTLE S 5" Clause Post

SHEPT? MALLET 5ᵗʰ Clause Post

In the stamps for the penny posts, the name of the central town was used at first. This would only be natural, since the penny post, in many instances, began as a town post, and, in some cases, remained so. In the earlier days, the villages and receiving houses in

[22] 3rd Rep. Sel. Com. on Postage, App., p. 168.
[23] 3rd Rep. Sel. Com. on Postage, Abstract, p. 11.

the town were indicated by a stamp with a number on it. This was done to assist in the tracing of a letter that might have gone astray. These number stamps were simple, and were impressed on a letter before it left the receiving house. In 1838 a change in practice be-

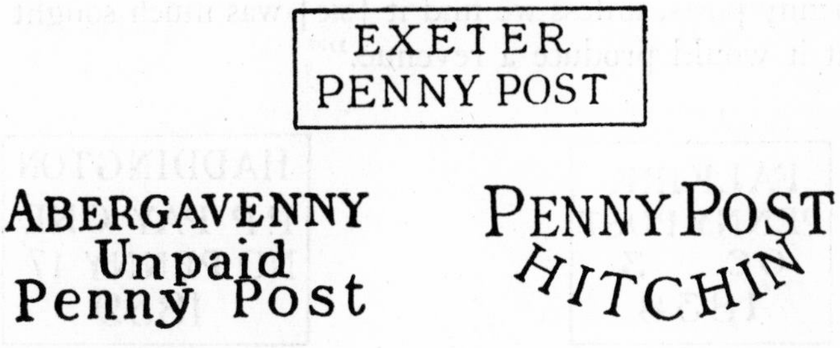

EXETER
PENNY POST

ABERGAVENNY
Unpaid
Penny Post

PENNY POST
HITCHIN

gan, the name of the village in a penny-post system as well as the number being used on the stamp. The stamps were simple, with the name framed or unframed, and occasionally the stamps were dated. As this practice of using the stamps with the name and the number was already in use when adhesive stamps were introduced in 1840, the stamps of the post towns came to be used as obliterating stamps, and were so employed, often for ten years or more after the use of adhesive stamps came in. Moreover, the number system

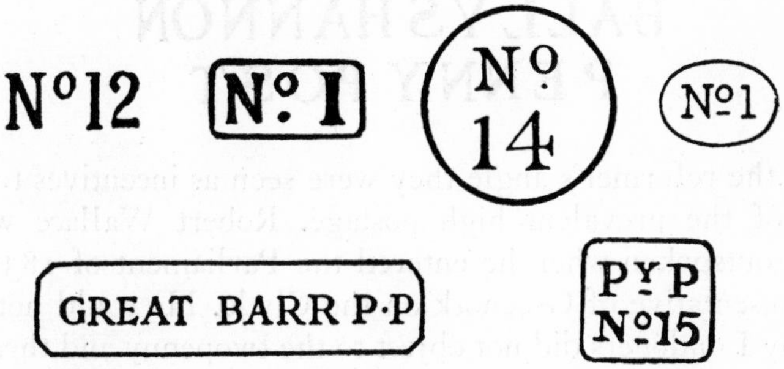

N°12   N° 1   N° 14   N°1

GREAT BARR P·P   P·P N°15

for offices and towns, which was practiced before 1840, found its successor in the numbering of the post offices as well as the districts in large post towns. For a time after 1840, the town number appeared only on the obliterating stamp, as every post town in the British Isles had its assigned number.[24]

This very surprising growth of penny posts is of chief interest, however, because it presages an even larger extension of penny

[24] For obliterating stamps, see below, p. 364.

postage to the kingdom as a whole. Everywhere, they were viewed as a great accommodation, even though as yet the service was local. The postal authorities saw them from the viewpoint of the revenue. Freeling felt that they "gave encouragement to persons to bring letters to the general post." And he added, "We have never established penny posts, unless we find it [sic] was much sought for, and also that it would produce a revenue."[25]

```
┌─────────────────┐        ┌──────────────────┐
│   FALKIRK       │        │ HADDINGTON       │
│ PENNY POST      │        │ P.P PAY ONE      │
│ O C    3        │        │ NO PENNY 17      │
│   1838          │        │   1839           │
└─────────────────┘        └──────────────────┘
```

Minehead
PennyPost

```
┌─────────────────┐
│ Penny Post      │
│ Kemp Town       │
└─────────────────┘
```

BALLYSHANNON
PENNY POST

From the reformer's angle they were seen as incentives to the reduction of the prevalent high postage. Robert Wallace was particularly outspoken when he entered the Parliament of 1832 as the first representative of Greenock on the Clyde. He could not understand why Londoners did not object to the twopenny and threepenny letter charges when in other parts of the country letters were carried even farther for a penny. He called attention to penny posts that went as far as twenty or more miles. From Manchester to Glossop, the post traveled fifteen miles, from Bristol to Harptree eighteen miles, from Edinburgh to Kirknewton by way of Kirkliston twenty miles, from Glasgow to Balfron via Lennoxtown it traveled twenty-four and one-half miles. Wallace pointed out quite rightly that in such places as Edinburgh and Manchester there were no distinctions

---

[25] *18th Rep. Commrs. of Rev.*, p. 351.

between penny, twopenny and threepenny post letters. There, he declared, the various duties are managed as a unit "with great satisfaction to the inhabitants and without any confusion."[26]

Such facts were working in the minds of reformers, and when Rowland Hill made the astonishing suggestion that a penny should carry a letter not fifteen miles or twenty-four and one-half miles, but from one end of the kingdom to the other, he found a multitude of persons who were ready to answer, "Why not?" It does not detract from the distinction accorded to those who fought for, and brought about, uniform penny postage that this penny rate had long been in use in the environs of great towns.

[26] *9th Rep. Commrs. P.O. Management,* pp. 57-58.

The Mail Coach Era

"IN sixty years the mail coach was born, attained perfection, and, alas, perished." This lament was written late in the nineteenth century by an Inspector-General in the Post Office, whose memories and acquaintances carried him back to the mail coach days.[1] Many, indeed, saw with regret the disappearance of the coaches when they were driven off the roads by the railways. A halo of romance has lingered from those old coaching days and coaching ways, resulting, often, in glowing and indiscriminate apostrophes to picturesque inns, gilded carriages and the well-horsed vehicles with their skillful drivers.

The era of the mail coach was, truly, very important in the record of postal transportation, so important in the early nineteenth century that it deserves description. The coach was, in its day, exceptionally well fitted for its task, and aroused constant interest at the time by the speed and punctuality with which it performed the work of carrying the mails. It is worth while, at this stage of our narrative, to inquire just what the mail coach was like, and what service it actually gave in the days of its glory.

About sixty years comprise the time when the mail coach was in its prime. Its work began with the introduction by John Palmer of this new method of transporting mails by which the horse posts were displaced on the main routes. Palmer's able young assistant in bringing about this change was Francis Freeling, who personally superintended their introduction on such routes as the Bristol-Portsmouth

[1] F. E. Baines, *On the Track of the Mail Coach*, p. 243.

run. Though Palmer himself was not long active in the Post Office, Freeling became more and more important. His connection with the Post Office, including his long service as Secretary, covered the whole era of the mail coach with which he had been so closely identified at the beginning. The use of the coach began in 1784, and it reached its zenith in the mid-thirties just as Victoria came to the throne and uniform penny postage was being broached with more and more insistence. It was at this time, too, that Francis Freeling, now Sir Francis, was giving way reluctantly to a successor. Freeling's death in 1836 was so clearly on the eve of great changes that the splendor of the mail coach may be said to have departed with his passing. By that time, the railway was already beginning its encroachments, and, in time, was to displace the horsed coach for all but the most remote routes.

In their day the coaches served a double purpose in much the same way that posting had done before Palmer's time, and that the railway was to do after Freeling's day. The older posting service will be recalled as a service for persons as well as for packets. One could go post by hiring, from the postmasters at the stages, horses and guides at so much per mile. When Palmer set up his mail coaches, it seemed only natural for the mail coach to serve as a passenger carrier as well as conveyer of the mails. Throughout its service, however, the mail coach was primarily the Royal Mail, taking a few passengers only, especially those who wanted a rapid journey at inconvenient times. The stage coaches—they did not carry mail—continued, of course, to serve as passenger vehicles during the whole of this period.

After the decline of the mail coach, the railway performed this double duty of carrying the mails and also passengers and their luggage. But with the railway there was more emphasis on the nonpostal part of its service than had been the case in the days when the mail coach carried the letters and newspapers. When the "coaches" were put on the rails, the greater usefulness to the public of the railways may well be regarded as a combination of the services of the stage coaches and the "mails." It has come to pass only in recent years that the automobile and the charabanc or bus have deprived the railway trains of many of their passengers. The railways, which had it pretty much their own way for a century, gave way, to a degree at least, to a revival of the mail and stage coach in a different form.[2]

[2] See below, p. 412.

The mail coach service regarded London as the hub of the Post Office. The Continental mails still went and came via London. Its population—over a tenth of the whole population of the British Isles—did much more than 10 per cent of the business of the Post Office. Even the services in Scotland were but extensions of those between London and the important towns of Glasgow and Edinburgh. As for the Irish services, they might be regarded in much the same way, though there was a greater distinction between the Irish and English mail service than between that of England and Scotland; Dublin was a somewhat more self-contained center for Ireland than Edinburgh was for Scotland. Yet, after all, the mail coach services out of Dublin were really an extension of the coach and packet route that ran via Holyhead.

In following the mail coach activities, it would seem well to treat this more distinctive Irish service first, and then return to the main island, where the Scottish coaches and routes can be examined before we finally return to England and London.

The postal services in Ireland were separately administered for most of the mail coach era, with consequent differences in many of the practices. When the mail coach was introduced by John Palmer, there was a desire for its extension to Ireland. Difficulties were faced, however, owing to the bad condition of the roads and because men of capital were unwilling to embark on so hazardous an undertaking as the finance of the mail coach. The needed leadership was at length undertaken by a Scot named John Anderson, who had removed to Ireland from Glasgow in 1780. He settled at Fermoy not far northeast of Cork on the main road to Dublin. His leadership in the improvement of roads and the institution of mail coaches provided the necessary stimulus. John Anderson may well be called the Palmer of Ireland.

The mail coach services developed somewhat differently from those of England. The Irish contractors for carrying the mails were fewer than in England, usually but one or two persons for a whole line of road, rather than numerous contractors for short stretches of road as in Great Britain. In Ireland, too, the contractors furnished their own coaches and cars as well as the horses. Possibly as the result of the comparative lack of competition in Ireland, mail coach costs were much heavier than in England. By the time of the Commissioners of Inquiry in the mid-twenties, mail coaches were traveling some 1450 miles daily in Ireland at an expense of £30,000 a year, about four times the cost of an equivalent service in England. This was considered to be partly the result of the lack of competition, partly because of the prevalence of jobbery. Another cause for the greater cost in Ireland was the charge for tolls exacted from the mail coaches; the tolls had been levied since 1789.

The Commissioners believed that the mail coach was used too extensively in Ireland. This may have been true, if one considers the amount of the mail that was carried. But there were reasons for what might appear an excessive coach mileage. The danger of robbery on the Irish roads was very great. Consequently, a coach with an armed mail guard was much more likely to reach its destination unscathed than a postboy on horseback. In fact, it was the practice for each coach to have not one guard as in England and Scotland, but two who sat together on the back seat. The coaches generally carried four outside passengers, one beside the coachman, and three in a seat just behind him at the front of the mail coach. The two armed guards were in a position to watch the passengers as well as the road.[3]

The actual mail-coach services worked out of Dublin, for the most part. In the twenties eight coaches left Dublin daily. At the height of their activity in the thirties, mail coaches departed at seven P.M. for Belfast, Londonderry, Galway, Enniskillen, Limerick, Sligo, Waterford, Wexford, and Cork via Clonmel and Fermoy. There were also three daytime mails out of Dublin, the one for Belfast leaving at 8 A.M., and covering the one hundred miles—English measure—in twelve hours. Kilkenny also received a day mail. A day coach left for Cork at noon, going via Cashel and Fermoy, and reaching its destination, 125 miles away, at eight the next morning. The average rate of speed for the Irish coaches was eight miles an hour, counting stops. Though the Irish high roads were excellent— by many thought superior to the English roads—the Irish mail coaches never attained the high speeds for which some of the British mail coaches were famed. Life went on more easily in Ireland, with less of the keen business competition that prevailed in England and Scotland.

The most distinguished Irish contractor by far, and a man of whom Ireland might well be proud, was Charles Bianconi. This remarkable man, born in Italy, was brought to Ireland in 1802, the bound servant of an Italian print seller. After his indenture ran out, Bianconi continued as an itinerant print seller for a time before

---

[3] *19 Rep. Commrs. of Rev.*, p. 908. For John Anderson, see *D.N.B.*, I, 384.

settling at Clonmel, in County Tipperary, as an engraver and gilder. Impressed in his travel as a seller of prints by the lack of cheap carriage for the poor, Charles Bianconi ventured in 1815 to become the proprietor of a line of cars that carried mails as well as passengers. His first car ran from Clonmel to Caher, eight miles away, a distance that could be cared for by one horse. He contracted with the Clonmel postmaster to carry the mails, and began in this modest way his later extensive business.[4]

This first vehicle used by Bianconi was not a coach, but a "car," the first use of a car for carrying cross mails in Ireland. It was two-wheeled, drawn by one horse, and carried six people besides the mail and the driver. The car was like the familiar family jaunting-car: three passengers on each side faced sideways and outwards. In the center behind the driver was the "well" for the luggage and mail. Though some people objected to "going sideways through the world," these Bians, as they were called, became very popular. They were gradually increased in size until Bianconi's four-wheeled cars, drawn by three or four horses, carried twenty people, ten on a side at a speed of eight or nine miles an hour.[5] The Bians spread all over Ireland. At the time of Victoria's accession to the throne (1837) Bianconi's cars and coaches were traveling over 3800 miles daily.[6]

Charles Bianconi intended his cars to serve as a boon to the poor. And they did, since the charges for passengers were as low as 1¼d a mile. If his cars were not filled with paying passengers, the vacancies were used for the poor, without charge. Bianconi believed so much in the "value of locomotion," as he put it, that his services gradually extended over much of southern Ireland. His mail coaches proper ran on some of the main routes in southern Ireland, on such roads as those from Clonmel to Waterford, Limerick to Tipperary, and out of Galway and Sligo. The service furnished by this public-spirited man was held in such high regard that the dangers of which the Commissioners had spoken never affected his services. "My conveyances," he declared in 1857, "many of them carrying very important mails, have been traveling all hours of the day and night, often in lonely and unfrequented places, and during the long period of forty-two years that my establishment is now in existence, the slightest injury has never been done by the people to my property or that intrusted to my care."[7] It is no wonder that Anthony Trol-

[4] Mrs. M. J. O'Connell, *Charles Bianconi. A Biography*, pp. 85, 116.
[5] *Ibid.*, p. 74.   [6] *Ibid.*, pp. 74, 95.   [7] *Ibid.*, pp. 83, 95.

lope, in his brief history of the Irish Post Office, wrote in extravagant terms of Bianconi, whom he knew well: "No living man has worked more than he has for the benefit of the sister kingdom."[8]

Bianconi did not retire from his car and coach business until 1865, so that his fifty years of service to the people and the Post Office is split about in half by the coming of the railway. He found it necessary to discontinue some of his coach lines as a result of railway building. But he was able to adapt himself surprisingly well to the new conditions. Even by 1865 his conveyances were traveling some 4000 miles daily in twenty-two counties.[9]

The service in Scotland, to which we turn next, labored under some disadvantages. The roads, as we have found, were improved rather late, so that the opening of northern Scotland, in particular, to the general use of horsed vehicles came only after the opening of the mail coach era. By the twenties, however, the public believed that they should have better communication on account of the "excellent state of the roads, from the Macadamized system." Another difficulty in Scotland was the toll on four-wheeled vehicles, imposed in 1813.[10] This hampered the mail coaches very greatly, especially as the stage coach operators made bargains with the turnpike trustees to allow their coaches to pass at lower rates than the mails. The result was a competition of which the mail coach contractors bitterly complained. At the same time that tolls became chargeable in Scotland, an additional charge of a halfpenny was made on every letter carried in Scotland by a vehicle with more than two wheels. This extra halfpenny was intended to compensate for the toll charges and to promote the improvement of the mail coach roads. Its effect was bad. The Superintendent of the Mail Coaches stated before the Commissioners in 1824: "It is highly probable that a much greater extension of the mail coaches would have taken place in Scotland but for their being subject to tolls."[11] It is surprising that the government of the day could not have realized the stifling character of such an arrangement, but public officials were beginning to learn only about this time

[8] *Ibid.*, p. 62; *3rd Rep. P.M.G.* (1857), p. 62.

[9] Bianconi died in 1865 in his ninety-first year. His daughter married Morgan John O'Connell, the nephew of the "Liberator," Daniel O'Connell. Shortly after her father's death she published his biography, to which reference has already been made. See also Baines, *Forty Years at the Post Office*, I, 87-91; the *D.N.B.*, IV, 461; Joyce, *op. cit.*, pp. 376-78. See above, p. 183, for a map of the Irish postal services.

[10] See above, p. 158.

[11] *20th Rep. Commrs. of Rev.*, pp. 39, 42, 266, 342. The cost of mileage, that is, for conveying the mails, was only about half that paid in tolls.

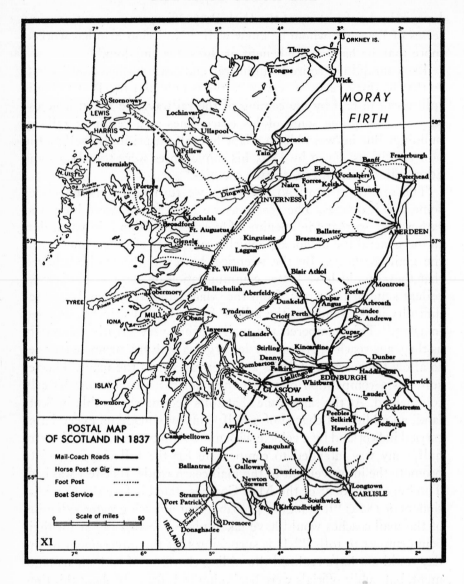

POSTAL MAP
OF SCOTLAND IN 1837

Mail-Coach Roads ———
Horse Post or Gig ⎯ ⎯ ⎯
Foot Post ···········
Boat Service ⎯ ⎯ ⎯

Scale of miles
0   50

XI

that lowered taxes and customs duties might so raise consumption
as to increase the revenue to the government.

Previous to 1800 there was but one mail coach running north of
the Firth of Forth: it went from Edinburgh to Aberdeen. When
the roads in northern Scotland were improved, the Aberdeen service was finally extended to Thurso, over 380 miles from Edinburgh, or nearly as far from Edinburgh as the Scottish capital was

from London. Services were also established from Aberdeen to Fochabers and Peterhead. Glasgow, as well, became the hub for a number of services in western Scotland. For most of the eighteenth century, Glasgow had received its London mail by way of Edinburgh. A direct mail-coach route was set up, however, between London and Glasgow in 1788. Arriving in Glasgow July 7, on its first run, the mail coach was escorted into town by a large body of welcoming horsemen, all of whom adjourned to the Saracen's Head for festive purposes after seeing the mail properly consigned to the Post Office.[12]

In the heyday of the coaches, there were some seventeen mail coach routes in Scotland, counting those that went from Edinburgh and Glasgow south to England. Glasgow, in addition to the coach to Carlisle and London, had mail coach connections with Perth, Greenock and Edinburgh. The Greenock mail coach had been taken off in 1813, as a result of the charge for tolls, but this service, through Paisley, was so important that it was running again in the twenties. Glasgow had only a horse port, however, to Port Patrick and the packet boat for Ireland. This was partly the result of the state of the road, and partly because direct steam communication with Ireland from the Clyde made the illicit carriage of letters faster and cheaper. Glasgow and Edinburgh were connected by two coach routes at this time, one by Whitburn and the other by Falkirk. Edinburgh had a mail connection with Carlisle, through which came the London-Glasgow coach. This connection of the Scottish capital with Carlisle was important, as coach service north from Falmouth through western England carried packet mail to Carlisle without its having to go by way of London.[13]

The rates of speed in Scotland were faster, on the whole, than those for Ireland. Two of the fastest runs in Great Britain were from Carlisle to Glasgow and from Edinburgh to Aberdeen. In the meridian days of the mail coach, the run from Carlisle to Glasgow, about ninety-five miles, was made in nine hours and thirty-three minutes. That from Edinburgh to Aberdeen, a distance of 134 miles, was covered in fourteen hours and twenty-two minutes.[14] The chief reason for the high speed on these routes was the severe com-

[12] Baines, *On the Track of the Mail Coach*, pp. 234-35; *20th Rep. Commrs. of Rev.*, p. 326.
[13] *Ibid.*, pp. 94, 353; Joyce, *op. cit.*, p. 360.
[14] These sample runs were made in the midwinter of 1830. See the *20th Rep. Commrs. of Rev.*, pp. 117, 126.

petition furnished by the stage coaches and the constant demand of a commercial center like Glasgow for quicker communication in the interests of business. The Aberdeen mail had as severe competition from the stage coaches as was to be found anywhere in the island. The famous stage coach, the *Defiance*, made the run in twelve hours and ten minutes, counting the crossing at Queensferry and thirty minutes for stops: it carried fifteen passengers, four "insides" and eleven "outsides," in addition to the coachman and guard.[15]

The mail coach service in Scotland was not separated from that in England; they were administered as one group by the Superintendent of the Mail Coaches, with his office in London. Indeed, it was in England and at the hub of the system, London, that the mail coach reached its prime. The finest services left London for the numerous English provincial towns, where a London post was by far the most important mail that they received. In London, too, the competition of the stage coaches was the keenest, as traveling to and from London was the chief concern of the moneyed interests and the upper social classes.

The British service differed from the Irish, as has been said, in having the coaches furnished by one contractor for all the routes. This had begun shortly after the introduction of the mail coach, as a means of having uniform and better constructed vehicles. A man named Besant had built a "patent coach" in 1787 that so appealed to Palmer that all Post Office coaches were soon supplied by Besant. As Palmer had speed in mind, the coaches were so constructed as not to carry the large number of passengers transported by stage coaches. He decided that the mail coaches should carry only four inside passengers and one "outside," in addition to the coachman and guard. It is true that the first run of the mail coach in 1784 provided for no "outsides," but when they were later allowed the number was severely restricted. In Palmer's day, the mail coaches seem to have traveled no more than seven or eight miles an hour.

The most important mail-coach contractor to succeed Besant was a well-known carriage builder by the name of Finch Vidler. When Besant received Palmer's favor because of the "patent coach," Besant entered into partnership with Vidler, whose Millbank coach works supplied the Post Office mail coaches for some forty years. After Besant's death in 1791, the supplying of the coaches became a monopoly of Vidler—until 1836. The contractors for the vari-

[15] Baines, *On the Track of the Mail Coach*, p. 251.

The *Quicksilver* ROYAL MAIL PASSING KEW BRIDGE, 1835, by Pollard

THE BRISTOL MAIL AT HYDE PARK CORNER, 1838, by Doyle

ous mail routes hired the coaches from Vidler at the rate of 2½d
the double mile. Vidler's men took over the coaches after they had
reached the Post Office in the morning, drove them to Millbank
where they were cleaned and greased, and then redelivered them to
the various coaching inns in the afternoon for the next night's run.
The early "patent" coaches were criticized on account of the discomfort, for they were hung so high on an arched spring that there
was little chance for the spring to work vertically, but every
tendency for a sidesway to develop. At least that was the judgment
of Matthew Boulton in 1798, after being made "very ill" from a
ride in one of them on the road to Exeter. The design improved in
time, and the roads also became better, but the traveling public continued critical, though the discomfort could be laid partly to the
speed of the "machines." By the mid-thirties, Vidler's monopoly
had become one ground of attack on the Post Office by its chief
critic, Robert Wallace of Greenock. He held that the lack of competition for the contract had led to a relative decline in the mail
coach. The Commissioners of 1835 felt this criticism to be so valid
that they recommended opening the coach contract to competition
and excluding Vidler from the bidding. As a result, one of Francis
Freeling's last important official acts was putting a whole new out-
fit of mail coaches on the roads early in 1836.[16]

The horses for the coaches were furnished in much the same way
as in the days of posting. Local contractors arranged with the Post
Office to furnish horses and run coaches on a certain route at a specified schedule, using Vidler's coaches. These contractors usually furnished horses and operated the mail coaches for a relatively few
stages of any given road. Likewise, the coachmen who drove on
specified routes handled the reins for a run of some thirty or forty
miles only, out and back.

Several outstanding contractors worked the London end of the
mail coach routes. This was not their only business, as they had, in
addition, numerous stage coaches having no connection with the Post
Office. Edward Sherman was one of the largest coach proprietors in
London, the center of his activity being the Bull and Mouth, St.
Martin's. This famous coaching house was the starting-point for the
Edinburgh and Carlisle mail coaches. Sherman had, as well, numer-
ous stage coaches running to important towns like Exeter, Bristol,
Shrewsbury and Manchester. Sherman was the pioneer for fast long-

---

[16] Harper, *op. cit.*, I, 178-79, and see below, p. 254.

distance stage coaches, many of them famous in coaching annals, such as the Shrewsbury *Wonder*, the Exeter *Telegraph* and the Manchester *Telegraph*. The last-named was traveling by 1833 the whole distance to Manchester in one day, 180 miles. The "day" was eighteen hours long, for the coach started at five in the morning and reached its destination at 11 P.M. Another important horse owner and coach proprietor was Robert Nelson of the Belle Sauvage, Piccadilly: he had some four hundred coach horses in the heyday of the business. A famous coaching firm was that of William Horne, continued by his son, Benjamin Worthy Horne, when the father died in 1828. His inns, such as the Cross Keys in Wood Street, the George and Blue Boar, Holborn, and the Golden Cross on the present site of Trafalgar Square were starting-points for both mails and stage coaches. This firm used seven hundred horses. Another well-known coach proprietor was Mrs. Ann Mountain of the Saracen's Head, Snow Hill, whose pride was the famous *Tally-Ho*: this fast coach ran between London and Birmingham.[17]

The most outstanding of the coach proprietors was William Chaplin. About 1825 the elder Chaplin acquired the Swan with the Two Necks, Lad Lane, located near the new Post Office at St. Martin's. At the Swan with the Two Necks, the Chaplin establishment housed some two hundred horses. In addition, this proprietor had large stables on all the important roads leading out of London, for Chaplin sent coaches in all directions to compete, in those very competitive days, with such rivals as have already been mentioned. Some of his best services went west from London by way of Hounslow, where at the Crown and Cushion Inn 150 Chaplin horses were always stabled for his various mail and stagecoach services. In 1838, when the business reached its height, Chaplin owned nearly seventy coaches, and some 1800 horses. Fourteen of the mails leaving London every night—half of the total—were horsed by Chaplin on their first stages out of town. He operated some of the fastest western mails, such as the New Holyhead, the Bristol mail and the famous Devonport *Quicksilver* Mail.[18] These western mails used Piccadilly as the London terminus, the mails and the passengers being conveyed in omnibuses from the inns and the Post Office farther east. This was done in order to save time on the western runs. The usual practice with mail coaches was for the passengers to be taken on at a specified inn, and then go to St. Martin's for the mail bags and the mail

[17] Harper, *op. cit.*, II, 210-15, 226-28.   [18] See illustrations, facing pp. 145 and 240.

guard. Famous stage coaches under the Chaplin control were the Manchester *Defiance,* which ran in competition with Sherman's *Telegraph,* the Birmingham *Greyhound,* the Liverpool *Red Rover* and the Southampton *Comet.*[19]

The number of horses required may seem excessive, but it must be borne in mind that the high speed attained by the coaches demanded frequent changes of horses. When the mail coach reached its greatest speed in the mid-thirties, the run for a change of coach horses averaged about ten miles only. The amount of horseflesh needed for such a system can be understood when one realizes that for a 400-mile run, say from London to Edinburgh or Glasgow, there were over forty changes each way. The horse contractors worked on the understanding that a horse a mile was needed for efficient services, that is, a ten-mile stage needed ten horses available for use. Thus the four hundred miles from London to Edinburgh required some four hundred horses for the mail coach service that went back and forth daily. So hard was this work on the horses, that the Chaplins found it necessary to change one-third of their horses every year.[20]

The change of the four horses, the two wheel horses and the two leaders, was made at the stages with all possible speed. Even the mail guard was required to give "his best assistance in changing whenever his official duties do not prevent it." A petition from Edinburgh in 1828 had suggested that if the "same expedition were used that is now exemplified on the Brighton and Bath roads," one and a half minutes could be saved at each change on the Great North Road, making it possible for the coach to reach Edinburgh an hour and a half earlier.[21]

As might be expected, the greatest speeds were reached during the thirties, when William IV was King, when Sir Francis Freeling was concluding his long service and when the great manufacturing towns were demanding more rapid mail communication. In attempting to meet the criticisms aimed at the Post Office, the authorities did what they could to tighten the schedules. In the early thirties the Post

---

[19] Gladstone's mail-coach trip from Exeter—see p. 235 below—ended at Piccadilly, as he rode on a Chaplin mail coach. Chaplin's stage coaches bore the familiar emblems recalling the names of his coaching houses, including a swan with two necks and two heads. For the coach proprietors, see Baines, *Forty Years at the Post Office,* I, 32, 56, and the interesting chapters in C. G. Harper, *Stage Coach and Mail in Days of Yore,* II, chaps. IX and X. For an amusing account of a stage coach ride, see chapter XXVIII of *Pickwick Papers;* Pickwick and his friends rode to a Christmas party at Dingley Dell on the "Muggleton Telegraph."

[20] *Ibid.,* I, 57; *20th Rep. Commrs. of Rev.,* p. 110.

[21] *20th Rep. Commrs. of Rev.,* pp. 126, 340.

Office attempted to answer the rising criticism of the institution by listing the principal improvements. This included the "general acceleration" of the mail coaches throughout the kingdom, "especially those to and from Liverpool, Manchester, Leeds, Glasgow, the principal commercial districts, and the main lines of cross roads." A writer of the time, who gloried in the progress of the nation, declared: "On all the principal roads communicating with London, the rate of travel is now nearly or quite ten miles an hour. . . . Notwithstanding the rapidity with which we are whirled along, the number of accidents is actually lessened, a result which is produced by the better construction of carriages, the greater perfection of the harness, the absence of such obstacles as were described by Arthur Young, and more than all, by the superior character of the drivers, a steady, well-conducted and sober class of persons."[22] The apogee of the mail coach can be realized by an examination of some of the services.

London, as has been said, was the great radiating center. In the early twenties some seventeen coaches left the central post office at the same or almost the same time in the evening. The schedules called for departures at 8:00 P.M. This had been the rule since the days of Palmer; previous to his reforms the departure of the mails took place about midnight or later. The departure of the coaches at 8:00 P.M. was regarded as one of the sights of London, as the gaily painted coaches, drawn by freshly groomed horses, waited in double line for the mails in the spacious yard of St. Martin's. By the time Victoria came to the throne in 1837, the sight must have been imposing indeed, for twenty-eight four-horse mail coaches were departing from St. Martin's every evening.

Some of the fastest runs went to the south and the southwest. We have had much occasion to note the services to Bath, Bristol, Falmouth and Milford. The run to Bath and Bristol was justly famed. It left at eight, and was in Bath at 6:32 the next morning, and at Bristol by 7:45 in ample time for breakfast. The distance from London to Bristol, 114 miles, was made, in consequence, at a speed of ten miles an hour. The route to Devonport was run by the famous *Quicksilver*, which did the journey of over two hundred miles at over ten miles an hour. Another mail via Exeter and Devonport continued on to the packet station at Falmouth, which was reached

---

[22] *Ann. Reg.* (1834), Chronicle, p. 337; G. R. Porter, *The Progress of the Nation* (1838), II, 17.

at five minutes past one of the second night—269 miles in 29 hours, counting stops for meals.[23]

The use of the Exeter road for a hurried journey is illustrated by an experience of William E. Gladstone in 1832. He was standing in the approaching election for Newark on the Great North Road. While staying at Torquay on the coast south of Exeter, Gladstone learned that "his presence was urgently needed at Newark." It was a Sunday. Despite his disapproval of Sunday traveling, Gladstone hastened to Exeter by chaise, in order to catch the mail coach that left at noon. His description of the journey follows. "Mail to London.

[23] The following list gives the mail coach routes out of London as they existed at the accession of Victoria in June 1837, just before they began to suffer from the opening of the first railway lines. The total mileage of the routes and the inns whence they started are also included. The data is to be found in the *Br. Almanac* (1837), pp. 75-78.

MILES	ROUTE	INN
55	Brighton	Blossom's Inn, Lawrence Lane
224	Carmarthen via Gloucester	Golden Crown, Charing Cross
243	Devonport via Bath & Exeter	Swan with Two Necks, Lad Lane
73	Dover	Golden Cross, Charing Cross and Swan with Two Necks
173	Exeter via Salisbury	Swan with Two Necks and Bell and Crown, Holborn
279	Falmouth via Exeter & Devonport	Spread Eagle, Gracechurch St., and Swan with Two Necks
396	Glasgow via Wetherby and Carlisle	Bull and Mouth, St. Martin's le Grand
196	Halifax via Nottingham	Swan with Two Necks and Golden Cross
261	Holyhead via Birmingham & Shrewsbury	Swan with Two Necks
177	Hull via Peterborough & Lincoln	Spread Eagle and Swan with Two Necks
197	Leeds via Nottingham & Sheffield	Bull and Mouth
203	Liverpool via Lichfield & Warrington	Swan with Two Necks
205	Liverpool via Chester and Woodside Ferry	Golden Cross
148	Louth via Boston	Bell and Crown, Holborn and Saracen's Head, Snow Hill
146	Ludlow via Worcester	Bull and Mouth
113	Norwich via Ipswich	Swan with Two Necks
118	Norwich via Newmarket	Belle Sauvage, Ludgate Hill
273	Pembroke via Bristol	Swan with Two Necks
296	Penzance via Exeter & Falmouth	Bull and Mouth
424	Port Patrick via Manchester & Carlisle	Swan with Two Necks
73	Portsmouth	White Horse, Fetter Lane & Bolt-in-Tun, Fleet Street
67	St. Leonard's via Hastings	Bolt-in-Tun & Golden Cross
116	Southampton & Poole	Swan with Two Necks
148	Stourport via Birmingham	King's Arms, Holborn Bridge
105	Stroud via Cirencester	Swan with Two Necks & Golden Cross
783	Thurso via Edinburgh	Bull and Mouth
133	Wells via Lynn & Cambridge	Bell and Crown & Swan with Two Necks
124	Yarmouth via Ipswich	White Horse, Fetter Lane

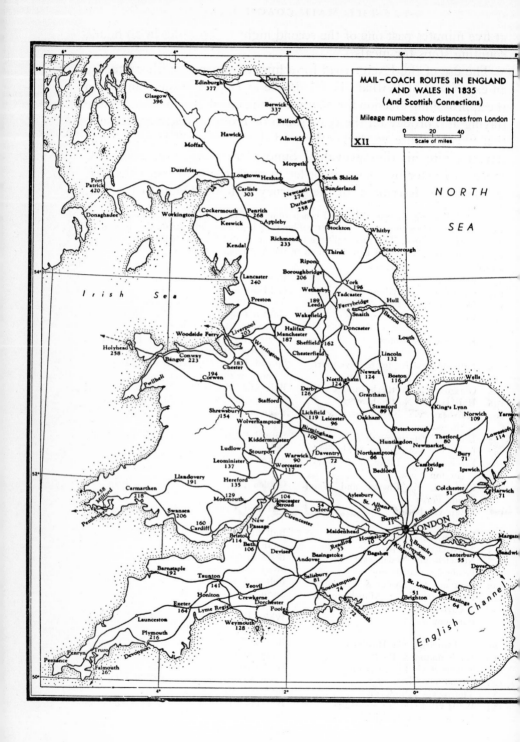

MAIL-COACH ROUTES IN ENGLAND
AND WALES IN 1835
(And Scottish Connections)

Mileage numbers show distances from London

XII

0   20   40
Scale of miles

NORTH SEA

Irish Sea

English Channel

Conversation with a tory countryman who got in for a few miles, on Sunday traveling, which we agreed in disapproving. Gave him some tracts. Excellent mail. Dined at Yeovil; read a little of the *Christian Year*. At 6½ A.M. arrived at Piccadilly, 18½ hours from Exeter. Went to Fetter Lane, washed and breakfasted, and came off at 8 o'clock by a High Flyer for Newark. . . . Tea at Stamford; arriving at Newark at midnight."[24] The mail coaches, it will be recalled, were timed so as to reach London in the early morning. Gladstone took a stage coach north to Newark, since the mails left London in the evening. The journey of 288 miles from Exeter to Newark lasted thirty-six hours. The mail coach section of the journey was traveled at nine miles an hour. The stage coach was slower, for the *High Flyer* took almost as much time to go 124 miles as the mail used for 164 miles.

The most famous and time-honored western route was the coach service to Holyhead. The fastest service in the thirties was by way of Shrewsbury and Corwen.[25] The *Wonder* did the journey of 154 miles to Shrewsbury in exactly sixteen hours. After a brief stop the mails continued on the road to Holyhead, the whole 261 miles from London being covered in less than 27 hours. The quickening of the mail coach speeds is well illustrated by this important run; it had been cut down by over two hours between 1830 and 1837.[26]

Manchester, Liverpool, Birmingham and Leeds had splendid services. The 203 miles to Liverpool was done in less than twenty-one hours. The *Telegraph* and the *Defiance*, whose rivalry has been noted, were famous coaches working between London and Manchester. The journey of 187 miles was being covered in 18 hours in 1837, an hour and fifteen minutes faster than the time taken in 1830.[27]

The two routes to Scotland seemed so important to the residents of Glasgow and Edinburgh that every effort was made to give these places the best possible service. Glasgow was 396 miles from London. The *Flying Cumbrian*, which took the Glasgow mails, was at Grantham for breakfast, at Wetherby for dinner where there was a stop from 4:36 to 5:11, and reached Carlisle, the border town 300 miles from London, before five of the second morning. There was a half-hour for breakfast at Carlisle before the Glasgow coach started

---

[24] John Morley, *The Life of William Ewart Gladstone* (1903), I, 90.
[25] See above, p. 187.
[26] Baines, *Forty Years at the Post Office*, II, 308; *Br. Almanac* (1837), p. 79.
[27] Baines, *Forty Years at the Post Office*, I, 55; II, 310.

over the Scottish part of the journey. If a passenger had sufficient endurance he could reach Glasgow with the mails at 2:00 P.M. of the second day—396 miles in 42 hours!

The most time-honored of the coaches went out the Great North Road for Edinburgh. It left the Bull and Mouth at eight, say on Monday, breakfasted forty minutes at Grantham, and reached York, 196 miles on, before 5:00 P.M. on Tuesday. After forty minutes for dinner at York, the coach continued by way of Newcastle, with breakfast the second morning at Belford. Edinburgh was reached at 2:23 of the second afternoon, that is, Wednesday of our sample journey. Its pace was nine miles an hour, including stops. This journey was being made in two hours' less time in 1837 than in 1830. The continuation of this route to Aberdeen, Inverness and Thurso made the run from London to Thurso 783 miles, the longest in the British Isles. The mails that left London on Monday and reached Edinburgh early Wednesday afternoon were at Inverness by Thursday evening. Thurso was reached Friday at 6:00 P.M.[28]

Such were some of the more important mail routes in 1837. Space does not permit noting others equally worthy of mention, nor considering the numerous effective cross-road coaches whose schedules meshed into the main runs to and from London. There were fifty-nine coach routes in all. So numerous were the mail and stage coaches when Victoria came to the throne that towns on the main routes out of London had a very busy time and a thriving trade. Famous inns on the main roads might have coaches stopping at every hour of the day and night, stopping at such coaching houses as the Pelican in Newbury, the Angel at Grantham, the Catherine Wheel in Andover —here the *Quicksilver* changed horses—and the Wheat Sheaf at Alconbury Hill on the Great North Road. Such inns as the Red Lion and the Green Man at Barnet must have been busy places in the thirties, for coaches were passing in one direction or another every fifteen minutes of the day and night.[29]

The actual structure of the mail coaches illustrates the advantages, and limitations, of travel and communication before the railway era. The coaches carried four "insides" on two seats facing each other, the seats being three and one-half feet wide. From the seat cushion

[28] Baines, *Forty Years at the Post Office*, I, 92, 97; II, 307.
[29] Baines, *On the Track of the Mail Coach*, p. 117, and his *Forty Years at the Post Office*, I, 7; *Br. Almanac* (1838), Companion, pp. 78-83; *18th Rep. Commrs. of Rev.*, pp. 110-11; *20th Rep.*, pp. 339-65; W. Outram Tristram, *Coaching Days and Coaching Ways* (1888), pp. 274, 338, and *passim*.

to the roof only three feet four inches were allowed. There was not much room in a mail coach, especially if one of the passengers was an unpleasant companion or of too generous physical proportions.[30] The "insides" were, at least, under cover. The outside passengers varied slightly in number at different times during the mail coach era. Three was the usual number on the outside, though on certain Scottish routes the liberty was granted of carrying four.[31] The "outsides" sat in front beside and behind the coachman. Back of them was a space on the roof for newspapers and luggage.

At the rear, facing forward and in solitary grandeur, sat the mail guard, a Post Office employee whose duty it was to watch over the mail. This was placed under his feet in a locked box that was built into the coach.[32] The guard was also given a locked timepiece to be delivered to his successor on the journey or to the postmaster at the end of the run, if the guard went the whole way. He also had a time bill, whose regulations had to be observed as far as was humanly possible. It bore the following injunction: "The time of working each stage is to be reckoned from the coach's arrival; and as any time lost is to be recovered in the course of the stage, it is the coachman's duty to be as expeditious as possible, and to report the horse keepers if they are not always ready, and active in getting it off."[33] So regular were the well-known coaches that people set their watches by the daily passing of the coaches. Their value is well brought out in the Introduction to George Eliot's *Felix Holt*, a novel of country life at the time of the Reform Bill of 1832. "The glory had not yet departed from the old coach roads. . . . The mail still announced itself by the merry notes of the horn; the hedge-cutter and the rick-thatcher might still know the exact hour by the unfailing yet otherwise meteoric apparition of the pea-green Tally-ho or the yellow Independent."

[30] The Irish mail coaches had an inch and a half greater inside height, as the Irishman averaged a greater stature. Baines, *Forty Years at the Post Office*, I, 76.

[31] *20th Rep. Commrs. of Rev.*, p. 94.

[32] One of the duties of the Post Office surveyors was to examine the mail coach box, to see if it was locked, or if anything besides mail was being carried in it. *18th Rep. Commrs. of Rev.*, p. 440; *20th Rep.*, pp. 103-8; Joyce, *op. cit.*, 287-88; Harper, *op cit.*, I, 258.

[33] *20th Rep. Commrs. of Rev.*, p. 113, e.g. One difficulty faced in a coach journey east or west was the difference in time. Standard time had not yet come into use, for the telegraph was only being introduced in the late thirties. Bristol's time, for example, was twenty minutes slower than London time. The timepiece on that route, consequently, had to be so regulated as to lose twenty minutes on the "down" run (west), and gain twenty minutes on the "up" run (east).

The mail guard's solitary position on the hind boot, or "dicky" as it was called, was intended for the better protection of the mail. Here he had an unobstructed range, and could actually defend the mails in case of need. In the sword case at his hand were always placed a cutlass, a brace of pistols and a blunderbuss. The case and the weapons were inspected by the Post Office armorer at the beginning of each journey. In the early days of the mail coach, the temptation for using the blunderbuss without need became too great, it would seem. A law of 1811 forbade indiscriminate shooting by the mail guards: any guard who fired off the blunderbuss save in defense was fined £5.[34] Another obligation of the mail guard was to see that the mail continued on its journey in case the coach broke down. He had the right and duty to commandeer one of the horses and ride with the mail bags to the next stage. In addition, the guard had a bugle by which he announced the approach of the mail coach so that others would give it the right of way and the toll keeper have the gates open. The long straight horn was occasionally replaced or supplemented towards the end of the period by a key bugle. The guard, sitting alone at the back, was sometimes thrown off by the roughness of the journey. In "thick" weather, he might not at first be missed—until his bugle calls became conspicuous by their absence.[35]

The guard's voluble bugle gave life to the journey, especially if he heralded some event of public importance with more than the usual gusto. The mail coach that brought the news of the passage of the Great Reform Bill, or of a notable victory on the sea or in Europe was received with more than ordinary attention. Frederic Hill, brother of the postal reformer, recorded in his *Autobiography* the arrival of the news of Waterloo in Birmingham. "Every one was aware that a great battle must be taking place, and while the result was yet unknown, we were all on the tiptoe of eager expectation. On the morning of the day when the decisive news was expected, many people stationed themselves far out on the London road to get the first view of the approaching mail coach. When at last it dashed into Birmingham, covered with waving boughs of laurel, there was a great shout."[36]

At times the urge to speed was stimulated not only by the locked timepiece, but by the rivalry of well-known drivers. One reads, for

[34] *18th Rep. Commrs. of Rev.*, p. 438; Harper, *op. cit.*, I, 251.
[35] Baines, *Forty Years at the Post Office*, I, 95; Joyce, *op. cit.*, p. 288.
[36] Page 36. For Frederic Hill, see below, p. 259.

example, of a resulting accident in the thirties. The Holyhead mail, via Shrewsbury, attempted to pass the Chester mail near St. Albans by galloping furiously on the wrong side of the road. The Chester coachman, resenting such an indignity, pulled his leaders across those of the Holyhead coach. The result can be imagined. One of the unfortunate passengers was killed, and the two coachmen were imprisoned for a year. Once again, the injunctions against racing were reinforced, but without too much effect.[37]

Such was the vehicle used for carrying the mails at the time that Robert Wallace and Rowland Hill were busying themselves with the reform of the Post Office. In truth, the death knell of the mail coach had been sounded before penny postage was won in 1840. The pioneer Manchester and Liverpool Railway had been carrying mail since 1830, to the great increase of communication between the two places. By the time of Victoria's accession there were four mails a day between these two centers. As the speed of the railway was twenty miles an hour at the time, the mails between the two were carried in half the time that could have been made by the best-horsed coach.[38]

By the midsummer of 1837, the Grand Junction Railway had already connected Birmingham with the Manchester-Liverpool line, and the Post Office was using it for carrying the mails. This meant, of course, that the Liverpool coach was taken off a large part of its former run.[39] The Grand Junction Railway did not confine its service to the needs of Liverpool and Manchester. A Dublin Express Day Mail left London at eight in the morning, went to Birmingham by coach, then on the railway for seventy miles, then by road again so as to reach Holyhead by 9:30 the next morning, where the packet awaited its arrival. There was no longer much point in sending the Holyhead mail through Shrewsbury, as the route via the Birmingham railway cut the former 27-hour journey to twenty-five and a half hours.[40]

The year 1838 was really the year of doom for the northern services. On September 20 the railway line connecting London with Birmingham was at last opened. As a contemporary put it—he was intoxicated by the prospect of traveling to Liverpool, 201 miles, in ten hours—the journey called to mind "the tales of fairies and genii by which we were amused in our youth, and contrasts forcibly with

[37] Tristram, op. cit., p. 346.   [38] Br. Almanac (1838), Companion, p. 82.
[39] This section of the Grand Junction was opened on July 4, 1837. Victoria had been a Queen for some two weeks.
[40] Ibid., p. 78.

the fact, attested on the personal experience of the writer of this notice, that about the commencement of the present century this same
journey occupied a space of sixty hours!" William Chaplin saw the
change from another angle. He declared as early as 1838 that it was
impossible for the coaches to compete with the railways. "The Grand
Junction," said Chaplin, "has put an end to all travelling upon the
road by which coaches went formerly." He added: "I am getting out
of my coaching."[41]

In the meantime other railways lines were removing coaches from
roads equally important. The glories of Barnet and the Great North
Road largely departed when a railway from Leeds to Derby and
Rugby made connection with the London-Birmingham line. The
southwestern coaches ceased their runs when the Great Western
Railway was completed to Bristol in June 1841. Thus the Bath road,
which has figured so prominently in our narrative, was shorn of its
splendor. And so the work went on. More and more the mail coach
was replaced on all important routes by "trains of coaches" running
on rails, and drawn by an iron horse. The last of the London coaches
—to Norwich and Newmarket—ceased its daily run in 1846.

Coaches continued to carry mails for some time in the more remote regions, in the west of England, in Scotland and in Ireland.
The last coach ran out of Manchester in 1858; in fact, it was the last
in the Midlands. The last coach left Newcastle-on-Tyne for Edinburgh in 1847, with the Union Jack at half-mast. One of the last
mail routes to be used was to Thurso in northern Scotland: when the
Highland Railway was finally completed in 1874, it was journey's
end for what had been the longest mail-coach route in Britain.[42]

To many the replacement of the coaches by the railway was no improvement. The belching engine did not add to the beauty of the
landscape and the encroaching industrialism seemed to spell doom to
much that was fine in the older tradition. One glorifier of the coaching days was sure that "railway ways, or rather the romance of them,
will not be written even when posterity has taken to balloons, for the
concern is fatal to romance." The true meaning of the change was
well put by one of the coachmen: "Them as 'ave seen coaches afore
rails came into fashion 'ave seen something worth rememberin'!
Them was 'appy days for old England, afore reform and rails turned

---

[41] *Ibid.*, p. 55; *Rep. Sel. Com. on Railroad Communication* (1838), pp. 89-93.
[42] Baines, *Forty Years at the Post Office*, I, 23, 30. The Mail Coach Office had become
so unimportant that it had been abolished in 1854.

everything upside down, and men rode, as nature intended they should, on 'pikes [turnpikes], with coaches and smart active cattle, and not by machinery like bags of cotton and hardware."[43]

[43] *Pickwick Papers* contains a realistic account of the nature of the old mail coaches in "The Story of the Bagman's Uncle" (chap. XLIX). There, in a dream, the old coaches, the decaying skeletons of departed mails, are refurbished and run again. " 'I wonder what these ghosts of mail coaches carry in their bags,' said the landlord, who had listened to the whole story with profound attention. 'The dead letters, of course,' said the bagman. 'Oh, ah—to be sure,' rejoined the landlord, 'I never thought of that.' "

The Rising Tide of Criticism—Robert Wallace

WE have now reached a point in the history of the Post Office when the demand for major changes became so insistent that the structure was remodeled. It culminated in 1840 with the introduction of uniform and prepaid penny postage. Though the basic novelties of the great reform in 1840 have often been presented as essentially new, it is clear that they were in limited use long before that time. Prepayment had been tried on a large scale in London for a century and a half, and was in limited use in the General Post Office as well. A penny charge was already widely employed for local posts. The success of Robert Wallace and Rowland Hill in bringing about such a surprising change as general uniform penny postage was owing in large part to an insistent demand for changes in the postal system. The coming of penny postage in 1840 has back of it nearly a decade of continuous criticism.

Nor was the move towards postal reform an isolated phenomenon. Among the numerous examples of humanitarianism that might be cited was the growing desire to spread education to the lower and working classes, an effort that was closely linked with the need for cheaper postage rates both for letters and printed matter. The schools of Lancaster and Bell were already having an effect among the working classes, and schools with new ideas on methods and the content of the curriculum were beginning to affect the education of the middle and upper classes.[1]

[1] Among these was the Bruce Castle School, in which Rowland Hill and his brothers were masters. See below, p. 260.

Publications intended for the newly educated groups were making their appearance, notably under the stimulus of the Society for the Diffusion of Useful Knowledge, established in 1826 by the publisher, Charles Knight. In the next year appeared the first volume of his "Library of Useful Knowledge"; in 1828 this enterprising publisher began to issue an annual *British Almanac* as an antidote to the trash still appearing under that mystic name; and in the early thirties Knight started his *Penny Magazine* and his immensely influential *Penny Cyclopedia*. About the same time an Edinburgh publisher, William Chambers, began the publication of his widely read *Journal*. The desire for a more general diffusion of education and the hope for cheaper communication were certainly widespread at the time—and they were naturally linked.[2]

The increase of the periodical and newspaper press was aided during these years not only by the broader education of the day, but by mechanical contrivances for more rapid printing. Cylindrical rollers were already in use, and the application of steam to the printing press was widespread. The *London Times*, which had used a steam press from about the time of Waterloo, was being printed by 1830 at the rate of two thousand copies an hour.[3] And just as large numbers of newspapers were being printed more rapidly than ever before, they were made more available to the public by the reduction of the stamp tax and the end of the system of franking newspapers. The farce of using a frank was finally ended by an Act of 1834. Henceforth, newspapers were sent free by post, if the stamp tax on the paper had been paid.[4]

The newspaper stamp tax had long been a heavy burden. Originally imposed in Queen Anne's time, it increased from a halfpenny per sheet until it stood at 4d by a law of 1815. Some discount, it should be said, was allowed from the 4d tax if the publishers paid promptly and made no higher charge than 7d for their papers. The leading newspapers of London, in fact, were sold at 7d during the time. The inconvenience of the tax to the publishers was very great, for each sheet of paper had to be stamped before it was put through the press. In the twenties and early thirties a vigorous campaign was

[2] For an account of the work of the Society, see Frederic Hill, *An Autobiography*, pp. 72-73. The *Penny Magazine*, started in 1832, soon reached a sale of over 200,000 copies for a single issue. The *Cyclopedia* appeared in 1834.

[3] Charles Babbage, *On the Economy of Machines and Manufactures* (1832), pp. 45, 218.

[4] See above, pp. 147-48; 4 Wm. IV, c.44, and 6 & 7 Wm. IV, c.54.

waged for the repeal of this "tax on knowledge," a campaign that reached its height in the very years when high postage—another tax on knowledge—was under fire. Largely through the efforts of Edward Bulwer-Lytton the newspaper stamp tax was vigorously attacked. As a result, it was lowered in 1836 to a penny "for every sheet or other piece of paper whereon any newspaper shall be printed." Along with the lowered tax came the regulation that each newspaper must have its own separate die or stamp, with the title or a part of it on the stamp."[5]

The newspaper stamp as used after 1835.

In a debate during 1834 on the stamp tax, Matthew Hill, the elder brother of Rowland Hill, had suggested that a stamped wrapper be prepared for the papers to be sent by post, and that the wrapper be stamped and sold for a penny by the distributor of stamps. This suggestion of replacing the stamp tax by a prepaid wrapper originated with Charles Knight, the publisher, in order, as he put it, "that unstamped papers pass through the Post Office by the use of a frank sold at a penny each." The proposal was to have considerable influence on Rowland Hill's plan for postal reform.[6]

The newspaper was becoming a major problem of the postal employees. The inspector of letter carriers testified in the mid-thirties that it took two hundred sorters in the London Office, with additional help from the letter carriers after they had finished ringing their bells, to get the newspapers off for the outgoing coaches in the evening. He declared that about 45,000 papers were sent out every evening, save on Saturday and Monday, when the total reached 60,000. The number of newspapers had of late greatly increased.

[5] The accompanying illustration of the stamp for the *Post Circular* serves as an example. See 6 & 7 Wm. IV, c.76; C. D. Collet, *History of the Taxes on Knowledge*, I, 50-62; and W. H. Wickwar, *The Struggle for the Freedom of the Press, 1819-1832* (1928). The tax was not entirely removed until 1855. See below, p. 355.

[6] See below, p. 268. *Mirror of Parliament* (1834), pp. 1838-39; Charles Knight, *Passages of a Working Life*, II, 249.

ROWLAND HILL

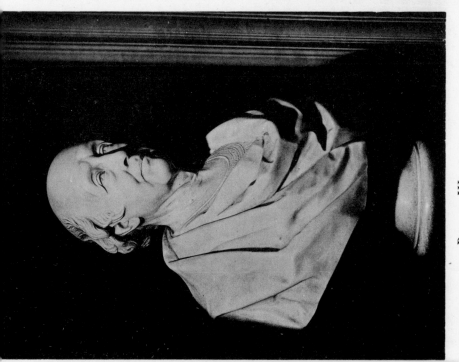

ROBERT WALLACE

This bust of Wallace is in the Council Chambers in Greenock, Scotland

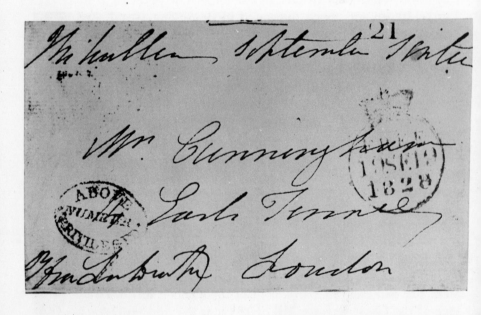

Two Franked Letters
Showing the franking signatures in the lower lefthand corner, and the frank stamp of the Post Office. The bottom letter was "above number privileged," apparently the twenty-first letter for that day. Both would appear to be on nonofficial business.

Sixty-one newspapers were published in the British Isles in 1782, 114 in 1790, 216 in 1821 and 369 in 1833. London had thirteen daily papers at this time, and Dublin possessed five.[7]

Not only was the desire for knowledge influencing postal reform, but also the wishes of the commercial classes were having the same effect. Business was becoming more and more restive under the various "shackles of trade." The effort to obtain complete free trade was organized in the early thirties. From the viewpoint of a Cobden the high taxes on letters were bad, not only because they hindered the increase of knowledge, but also because they hampered commerce. The distinguished economist, J. R. McCulloch, in a volume published in 1833 by the Society for the Diffusion of Useful Knowledge, expressed the view of the commercial world. McCulloch held that while it is reasonable that those who use the post should pay the expense of the conveyance, "no additions ought ever to be made to the postage of letters without mature consideration." And he added: "Nothing contributes more to facilitate commerce than the safe, speedy, and cheap conveyance of letters."[8]

Noteworthy among the reformers was Lord Althorp, who was Chancellor of the Exchequer in the important years 1830 to 1834. Lord Althorp was much interested in improving postal conditions, even suggesting changes that might add to the cost of the service. He saw to the correction and enlargement of the limits of the General Post and threepenny deliveries in London, and was responsible for ending the privilege enjoyed so long by the clerks of the roads in the matter of newspapers. Althorp's sympathy for postal reform was marked by a desire to reorganize the Post Office establishment so as to lessen the autocratic power of the Secretary, and to replace the large use of fees by fixed salaries as a means of paying the staff. A writer on the Post Office has well summed up Althorp's attitude on postal matters by observing that Althorp, while Chancellor of the Exchequer, was often "urging the Post Office to adopt some improvement, and the Post Office was attempting to frighten him with the bogey of cost."[9]

Robert Wallace, however, deserves the chief credit for initiating a criticism of the Post Office that was to have such far-reaching effects. He had entered Parliament in the election following the passage of the Great Reform Bill of 1832, as the first representative of

[7] *5th Rep. Commrs. P.O. Management*, p. 38; *Penny Magazine*, II (1833), 6, 71-72.
[8] *Of Commerce* (London, 1833), pp. 24, 25, 128.
[9] Joyce, *op. cit.*, p. 416; *Parl. Deb.*, 3rd s., XX, 376, 380.

the enfranchised town of Greenock. That his father had been a Glasgow merchant dealing with the West Indies, and that Greenock at the mouth of the Clyde was already a busy manufacturing and trading center, may have influenced his interest in packets and postage. His opening broadside came in August 1833, supporting a request for copies of instructions by which postmasters had the right to open letters. His speech proved to be a general attack on the institution, its personnel, its conservatism, the methods of distributing letters and its complicated and confusing mechanism. He declared that the "Post Office ought to be conducted on more liberal principles," that free trade ought to be applied "to the transmission of letters."[10]

In this and his subsequent criticisms he was abetted by such vigorous reformers as Lord Lowther, Joseph Hume, the representative for Middlesex, Labouchere, and, later, even members of the administration. Wallace threatened to move for a select committee if he did not have assurance that the government intended to do something. So constant were his attacks on the Post Office that one member of Parliament complained that "he never took up his papers in the morning that he did not find the name of the honourable member for Greenock there with some notice of motion for inquiry with respect to the Post Office."[11] The statement was not greatly exaggerated. For some time the efforts of this new member at calling attention to postal reform produced little result. "He called attention much more frequently than he got it."[12] In June 1834 Wallace raised another general debate on the Post Office, asking for the appointment of commissioners to inquire into its management. Not succeeding, he asked during the next summer for the appointment of a select committee to make an inquiry. Largely as a result of Wallace's incessant demands that something be done, the Treasury appointed Commissioners in 1835 "to inquire into the management of the Post Office Department."[13] He was not even satisfied by this concession, for he was busy in 1836 and 1837, again calling for a select committee, even though the Commissioners, appointed by the Treasury, were doing good work.

Wallace had carefully read the voluminous reports of the earlier

[10] *Ibid.*, XX, 371-72.　　　　　　　　[11] *Ibid.*, XXIII, 743.
[12] *Fraser's Magazine*, LXVI, 329.
[13] *Parl. Deb.*, 3rd s., XXIII, 743; XXIV, 866; XXIX, 372. The appointment resulted from a Treasury minute of May 9, 1835, and the First Report is dated June 12, 1835. Joyce, *op. cit.*, p. 423, would seem to make the date 1834. For the work of the Commissioners, see the concluding pages of this chapter.

body of Commissioners, reports that had appeared in 1829 and 1830, and which we have had frequent occasion to use for illustrating the condition of the unreformed Post Office. In his first attack in 1833 Wallace brought to Parliament one of the folio reports of the Commissioners of 1829, and read from it. He averred that "so far as he could learn, they had not been attended with any effect; neither had the previous recommendations made in the reports of 1788 and 1797, though very wise and salutary." He read extracts to Parliament again in 1834 and insisted two years later that all these commissions from 1787 to the one now meeting had found difficulties put in their way by the Post Office. The various commissions had all arrived at more or less the same conclusions, but there had been little noticeable effect on the Post Office in the last fifty years.[14]

The constitution of the Post Office came in for especial attack. It was still under an autocratic Secretary, Sir Francis Freeling, who had held the office for over thirty years. The nominal head of the Post Office was a Postmaster-General, who was always a "noble lord." This seems to have aroused the ire of the critics in the House of Commons, and it fitted well into the current dislike of the Lords because of their stubborn resistance to the Reform Bill of 1832. Such critics as Wallace and Lowther, and even the Chancellor of the Exchequer, felt that the Post Office, as a great spending organization, should be in a position to face questions in the House of Commons. Sir Francis Freeling was attacked as one who managed the Post Office with "meanness and parsimony." Any merit in the arrangements of the Post Office, in Wallace's view, "was not Sir F. Freeling's, . . and now was the time when a change had become necessary, in consequence of his great age." Wallace felt that no more favorable opportunity "was likely to offer itself."[15]

The Secretary's office was also criticized for its expense, as revealed in the Report of 1829. Like others, Freeling's salary had grown up from special emoluments for former privileges that no longer existed. Though his salary was nominally £500 a year, he was receiving over £4500. Nearly £3000 of this total was in compensation for the privilege, abolished in 1825, of sending news-

---

[14] *Parl. Deb.*, 3rd s., XX, 369; XXIX, 372, 540; XXXIV, 866; XXXV, 418-19. The Post Office was so conscious of the need for defense that it circulated a statement of recent improvements among the members of the House, and it even appeared in the *Annual Register* in 1834, pp. 336-38 of the Chronicle.

[15] *Parl. Deb.*, 3rd s., XX, 370; XXV, 1002; XXVI, 1240; XXIX, 375. See also *18th Rep. Commrs. of Rev.*, p. 16, where Freeling admitted that the "Secretary's office is the controlling office of the whole Department of the Post Office."

papers to the colonies and collecting the postage. Another £700 had been granted him early in his career as Secretary "as a mark of distinction and a reward for services which at the time were fully recognized and understood," to use his own words. But the Commissioners were unable to find "the grounds for this special allowance," to which the Secretary made such vague allusions. A third part of his total salary was in lieu of a residence in the Post Office, for Sir Francis lived in Bryanston Square. The Commissioners of 1829 had recommended that the Secretary receive only £1000 a year.[16]

What made it worse was that the son of Sir Francis was Assistant Secretary. This position had been created for George H. Freeling in 1810, with an original salary of £320 per annum, but it had since been raised to £800. In addition, George Freeling occupied the quarters in the Post Office intended for the Secretary. Here was a case of nepotism not unlike that found in the Irish Post Office.[17] Wallace contended that Sir Francis Freeling kept his town house and his country house and loved his ease, and that he "humbugged them all."[18] Lord Lowther referred to Freeling as the immovable force in the establishment, who "had not adapted his notions to the altered circumstances of the times."[19]

[16] His emoluments totaled £4565. See *18th Rep. Commrs. of Rev.*, pp. 24-27, 90. The Commissioners could have found the source of the £700 that the Secretary was unwilling to explain if they had examined the *Report of the Select Committee on Finance* of 1797. Sir Francis Freeling had received £700 as Resident Surveyor. When this office was abolished, and he became joint Secretary with the aged Anthony Todd, the salary of £700 was continued. See above, p. 152. Francis Freeling became Sir Francis in 1828 when a baronetcy was conferred on him in recognition of his public services.

[17] See above, pp. 178, 180-81.

[18] *Parl. Deb.*, 3rd s., XXIV, 862.

[19] *Ibid.*, XXIX, 386. Sir Francis Freeling had been recognized so long as the real head of the Post Office, that it seemed only natural for Thomas Hood to dedicate the first issue of his *Comic Annual* (1830) to the seemingly permanent Secretary of the Post Office.

TO SIR FRANCIS FREELING, BART.

the Great Patron of Letters, Foreign, General and Two-penny; distinguished alike for his fostering care of the

BELL LETTERS;

and his antiquarian care for the

DEAD LETTERS;

whose increasing efforts to forward the spread of intelligence as Corresponding Member of All Societies (and no man fills his POST better) have

SINGLY, DOUBLY, AND TREBLY

endeared him to every class; this first volume of *The Comic Annual* is with FRANK permission, gratefully inscribed by

Thomas Hood.

Nor did the critics have any respect for the lordly Postmasters-General. Wallace held that a postmaster ought to be one accustomed to the routine of business. The inference, of course, was that the lord at the nominal head of the Post Office was not. "Now if a Duke resigned, they must look out for an Earl or a Marquess to fill his place. He did not wish to discourage noblemen from holding office, but regard ought to be had to their being in every respect fully qualified."[20] The rapid succession of Postmasters-General at this time was an additional cause for pointing out the political aspects of the position. The Duke of Richmond was succeeded in 1834 by the Marquess of Conyngham. After four months he was followed by Lord Maryborough, who was succeeded by Conyngham again for a month. At the end of May 1835, Lord Lichfield became Postmaster-General, and held the office for the remainder of the decade. Maryborough, who had been appointed at the age of seventy-two, was ironically referred to by Wallace as the "apprentice of Sir Francis Freeling," though Wallace had some doubt as to "what his lordship was likely to learn." Wallace stated bluntly that the office ought to be in the hands of men "bred up to business."[21]

A few days later, in July 1835, replies to Wallace were made in the House of Lords, including speeches by Richmond, Lichfield and Maryborough in defense of the institution and of Sir Francis Freeling. On the next day there was a reply in the House of Commons to what Lord Lowther facetiously called a "field day of Postmasters-General." Wallace took an active part in the retort to the Postmasters-General, "who from their remarks showed that they were ignorant of the office they administered." He concluded his speech by saying that "he was ready to meet the five Postmasters-General in the largest hall in London, .. and let the public be the umpire." Not long after it looked as though the controversy between Wallace and the Earl of Lichfield might result in a duel with weapons. Lichfield attacked Wallace so severely in the House of Lords that Wallace sent him a message tantamount to a challenge, but the quarrel did not reach the dueling stage.[22]

[20] *Ibid.*, XXIV, 868, from a speech of Edward Bulwer-Lytton in the House of Commons. This is the well-known novelist—a member of the Commons during the thirties on the reforming side.
[21] *Ibid.*, XXIX, 374; *Mirror of Parliament* (1835), pp. 1801, 1803. For the succession of the Postmasters-General during these years, see the Appendix.
[22] *Ibid.*, pp. 1842-46, 1888; *Parl. Deb.*, 3rd s., XXIX, 435-48, 538-43. For the

All this sparring was to aid the course of a bill to replace the Post-masters-General by a board—the uniform conclusion of all the commissions from 1787 to 1835. In the next year, 1836, a bill was brought before the House of Commons to effect the change. It was hoped that a board would prevent all the power going into the control of a single subordinate officer, since the responsible chief of the board would be a member of the House of Commons. The Chancellor of the Exchequer was in favor of the change, arguing that the present constitution of the Post Office was indefensible. The measure passed the House of Commons, but was defeated in the House of Lords.[23]

Robert Wallace found fault with much else in the Post Office besides the Secretary and the Postmasters-General. He objected to the opening of letters in order to find out the nature of a letter's contents. To him, the whole matter of charging single, double and treble postage according to the number of sheets was a wrong principle because it encouraged this prying into letters. He had much to say on deliveries, especially the early preferential delivery, which has been found to exist in London and elsewhere. The poor, he believed, should be placed on the same footing with the rich. The latter should not get an early delivery by paying 5s a quarter, "especially when the aristocracy of this country were born to have their letters passed free." Wallace would have the four-ounce limit for mail matter in the London Twopenny Post made general, that is, as a basic weight, presumably, for the lowest rate of postage. He criticized, also, the limited means of sending out mails from London. As no mails left on Sundays, letters were held over after 7 P.M. Saturday night until 7 P.M. Monday night. The coaches went out on Sunday, it is true, but they were not carriers of mail until they were outside London. If a person wished to send a letter or a newspaper by a Sunday mail coach, he had to take it to the outskirts. Nor could Wallace see why mail coaches should leave London at only one time of the day. He would have two mails leaving the General Post Office, one at ten in the morning and one at ten or twelve at night.[24]

Nor was he silent as to the charges for letters. In suggesting

<hr>

possible duel, see *The Greville Memoirs, 1814-1860*, ed. Lytton Strachey & Roger Fulford (1938), III, 402.

[23] *Parl. Deb.*, 3rd s., XXXV, 426-27, 906, 1270; *Mirror of Parliament* (1836), pp. 1956-57, 2874; *4th Rep. Commrs. P.O. Management*, dated July 1835.

[24] *Parl. Deb.*, 3rd s., XX, 371-72, 381; XXIV, 858, 861; XXV, 422, 918; XXVI, 1239-41; XXIX, 544; XXXV, 419.

changes in rates, he seems to have been considerably influenced by the practices of the French Post Office where he found much more liberality and an example "well worthy of imitation." He had especial reference, in making these invidious comparisons, to the French practice of charging by weight rather than by the number of sheets. Wallace pointed to the contrast between the practice in Great Britain and that in use on the Continent. All over Europe, he said, letters were charged by weight, but "here every scrap of paper is held to be a letter." He concluded a long speech in 1835 with twenty-four resolutions, number fifteen being that "Letters shall be charged by weight, and that the charge on letters having envelopes, or on double and such-like letters, shall be discontinued." He would also have the rates lowered, suggesting at one time that a letter should go at least fifty miles for 3d, 100 miles for 4d, 200 miles for 6d, and that there should be no higher charge than 9d. He believed that a general reduction of rates would increase the revenue as well as give a more liberal and more extensive postal communication. As he succinctly put it in 1835: if the "Post-Office system were placed on a more liberal footing, the revenue collected by it would be much greater, and all the complaints which now were so generally made throughout the country respecting it would cease." It is evident that Robert Wallace had made a thorough study of the Post Office and that he had definite ideas of reform in many departments of the service.[25]

In the meantime the Commission appointed in 1835 had been actively at work. The three Commissioners—Lord Duncannon, Henry Labouchere and Lord Seymour—issued ten reports in the next three years. They are of great interest in the history of the Post Office, despite the similarity of many of their recommendations to those of the Commissioners of the twenties, particularly because they resulted in positive action at a time when the Post Office was very heavily beleaguered by its critics.[26]

In the matter of mail coach contracts, the Commissioners held that

[25] *Ibid.*, XXIV, 856, 858, 861; XXIX, 375, 381; XXXV, 422-24; *Mirror of Parliament* (1835), p. 1808. The quotations on charges by weight and on low rates are taken from the twenty-four resolutions presented to the Commons in 1835: a year later he suggested nineteen more.

[26] The ten *Reports on the Management of the Post Office Department* are not so extensive as those of 1829 and 1830. See the Bibliography for the subjects treated by each Report, and for the dates of their appearance. On February 8, 1838, Mr. Wallace asked for a return in abstract of the recommendations. The abstract is in the *Accounts and Papers* for that year.

the mileage rate was too high, and that it was high because the contracts were not open to competitive bidding. They recommended that the contractor, Finch Vidler, who had held the contract for some forty years, be given an extension of his current contract for six months only, and that models and drawings for improved mail coaches be invited. When Vidler declined to accept such an extension of his contract, the Third Report of the Commissioners recommended that the Post Office ask for bids, and that Vidler be forbidden from tendering a bid. This change was effected, as we have found, in July 1835.

As to the packet services, the report of the Commissioners of 1835 proved to be a thoroughgoing condemnation of their operation. They found losses during the previous four years on every station, the heaviest losses being in the Milford and Holyhead services. At Holyhead where the greatest actual loss had occurred, the expense was more than double the receipts. The use of Holyhead as a general repair station was strongly condemned: it seemed foolish to take a Weymouth packet, for example, around to Holyhead for repair. George H. Freeling, who was in charge of the packet establishment, admitted that he had never visited Holyhead, nor did anyone else inspect the place. He also admitted that nobody at the Post Office possessed a practical knowledge of how to manage a dockyard. It need be no surprise that the Commissioners' recommendation that the packets be turned over to the Admiralty was effected by an Act of Parliament in the spring of 1837. The Post Office continued to have something to say as to the times of departure of the packets and the nature of the routes for the carriage of letters.[27]

The Commissioners were concerned also over the Money Order Office and the means of registering letters. No change had taken place in the arrangements since a semi-private Money Order Office had been organized in 1792.[28] Earlier commissioners had been critical, for the registration of letters was very limited. And for a good reason. George H. Freeling stated to the Commissioners that the fee that had to be paid for registration was purposely heavy in order to check the practice! The Commissioners found the French system much more intelligent and useful, for there one registered a letter by paying double postage, and paying it at the time of putting the letter into the Post Office. As a result of recommendations made in 1835, this "smug private property concern," as Wallace called it,

[27] *4th Rep.*, Recommendations, and *6th Rep.*, especially pp. 3-7, 246. The act that brought the change was 7 Wm. IV & 1 Vict., c.3.
[28] See above, p. 149.

was taken over by the Post Office. The Act allowing the Postmaster-General to register letters and packets required that the cost of registration be prepaid.[29]

The merchants were much interested in the easy transmission of prices current, or price lists as they would now be called. Here again, the Commissioners found Britain niggardly and France liberal. If the advance of trade and commerce were in mind, surely the Post Office should allow prices current to go through the mails at low rates, instead of charging double postage if lists were enclosed with a letter. The Commissioners accordingly recommended that the charge be no more than a halfpenny up to half an ounce in weight, and that the charge or tax be a stamp tax rather than a postal charge, "as this tax would be collected with much greater facility and certainty than a postage." In other words, price lists would be treated in the same way as newspapers. This would also avoid the difficulty of paying double postage if the price list went in a wrapper. One merchant told the Commissioners that the French merchants could not understand the British practice: "If we tell them that, if they put a small piece of paper into a letter—coming to England—it is double, they will not believe it." Again, the recommendations of the Commissioners proved effective.[30]

Throughout the reports made by the Commissioners of 1835 runs the idea of lessening the cost for postage, and a belief that the cheapening of rates would actually increase the revenue. Wallace expressed this conviction to the Commissioners in the following words: "I am convinced of two things—that the cheapening of postage rates would increase the revenue . . . and the expense [from more correspondence] ought not with good management to be increased at all." Lord Lowther, before the same body of Commissioners, declared that "the rate of postage was pitched so high that it deterred correspondence." He added: "I should look to England as being in a great degree the post-office of the world if facilities were offered."[31]

Sir Francis Freeling had lent a deaf ear to such ideas for so many decades that it was probably as well for his comfort of mind that death took him from the secretaryship of the Post Office in June of 1836, just as this rising tide of criticism was reaching a crest. He had outlived his usefulness. No better proof could be given than his own words. In the last month of his life, Sir Francis Freeling put down his views on all this turmoil and dissatisfaction in the following way:

[29] 4th Rep. Commrs. P.O. Management, pp. 54, 59, 63; 42nd Rep. P.M.G. (1896), p. 27; 5 & 6 Wm. IV, c.25, sec. 5.
[30] 5th Rep., no. 2, p. 34; 7 Wm. IV & 1 Vict., c.34. [31] 6th Rep., pp. 256, 272-73.

"Cheap postage! What is this men are talking about? Can it be that all my life I have been in error? If I, then others—others whose behests I have been bound to obey. . . . Is it not within the last six months that the present Chancellor of the Exchequer has charged me not to let the revenue go down? What! You, Freeling, brought up and educated as you have been, are you going to lend yourself to these extravagant schemes? You with your four-horse mail coaches, too!"[32]

The climax to the mounting charges against the confusion within the Post Office came a year after the death of Sir Francis Freeling, in a series of parliamentary acts. On July 12, 1837, five statutes brought something like order into the vast organization. The first repealed the numerous acts, some one hundred and twenty-five, that related to the Post Office, and the other four, all passed on the same, day, summarized the constitution of the Post Office.[33]

One of the statutes regulated the duties of postage. This collected and re-enacted the various rates with which the reader should now be familiar. The packet charges were continued, 4d by way of Port Patrick, 8d from Liverpool to Dublin, and 2d via Holyhead or Milford, as well as the penny charges for the Menai and Conway bridges. The 2d and 3d rates in London remained as before. The general charges for inland postage were not lowered, but simply re-enacted in convenient form. The high rates of 1812 remained, with 4d as the lowest rate for a single letter, and that for a distance of only fifteen miles. The halfpenny charge was continued in Scotland for a letter traveling in a carriage having more than two wheels. The Irish rates began at 2d for seven Irish miles, with the rates working out about the same as in Great Britain: a single letter going between 95 and 120 miles in Ireland cost 10d.[34]

[32] Joyce, *op. cit.*, 427-28.

[33] 7 Wm. IV & 1 Vict., chaps. 31-35. The first one repealing the former statutes since 1711 occupies some 25 pages in the *Statutes at Large*. Mark B. Peacock, the Solicitor of the Post Office, prepared the measures.

[34] The inland postage rates for Great Britain are subjoined for purposes of reference, in view of the successful fight made for lower postage during the late thirties.

For a single letter not exceeding			15 miles	4d
"	"	"	20 "	5d
"	"	"	30 "	6d
"	"	"	50 "	7d
"	"	"	80 "	8d
"	"	"	120 "	9d
"	"	"	170 "	10d
"	"	"	230 "	11d
"	"	"	300 "	12d

For every additional 100 miles or fraction 1d

Another of the statutes summarized the existing practices regarding franking. Members of Parliament, it will be remembered, could frank during a session of Parliament and for forty days before and after. This entitled them to send, within the country, ten letters a day and to receive fifteen, none to exceed an ounce in weight. A member could send or receive as well printed votes and proceedings in Parliament, and could receive petitions free, each not to be over six ounces in weight.

These Acts of 1837 did not bring about a reform in the Post Office: they simply brought order into the regulations and revealed more clearly than ever just what needed to be done to modernize the institution. Some of the recommendations of the Commissioners were heeded, though the Acts were passed before the Commissioners had completed their investigations. They were examining the London District Post at the time the Post Office Acts were going through Parliament.[35]

But a matter of much greater importance had occurred while they were studying the London Post Office earlier in that year. In January a hitherto unknown person by the name of Rowland Hill published an arresting pamphlet entitled *Post Office Reform: Its Importance and Practicability*. Its surprising suggestions came as a climax to the demands of Robert Wallace and other parliamentary critics. Wallace was to win his fight after all, and the victory was to be more sweeping than he, in all probability, thought possible.

[35] The *9th Rep.*, on the London District Post, was dated July 7, 1837.

Rowland Hill and
Post Office Reform

WHEN Rowland Hill published *Post Office Reform: Its Importance and Practicability* early in 1837, he was not connected with the Post Office, nor had he a firsthand knowledge of the workings of the department: to use his own words, "I had never been inside the walls of a post office."[1] The environment in which Rowland Hill matured was of the sort that led him to take a consuming interest in the desire for economic and humanitarian progress that was so strong in the decades following the Napoleonic wars. That he should have chosen postal reform as a cause was more or less accidental, but a brief account of his family background and earlier labors will show that a concern for postal changes was a congenial outlet for his "improving" mind.

Rowland Hill was born in 1795 in Kidderminster, a thriving manufacturing town some twenty miles south and west of Birmingham. His family was of the middle class, but had come down in the world. The father was an unusual man of inventive interests, so un-

---

[1] When Pearson Hill republished his father's famous pamphlet fifty years after the introduction of penny postage, he noted that all the great reforms effected in the postal service originated with persons "wholly unconnected with that department." Pearson Hill then linked his father's name with "Mr. Dockwra, who in the time of the Commonwealth instituted the town and local penny posts, Mr. Allen, who about the year 1750 established cross posts, and Mr. Palmer, who in 1784 effected the substitution of mail coaches for horse and foot posts." See *The Post Office of Fifty Years Ago* (1887), p. 14. Though Rowland Hill is rightly linked with Dockwra, Allen and Palmer, Pearson Hill's reference to the other reformers is surprisingly inaccurate: Dockwra did not do his work in the time of the Commonwealth nor had he anything to do with local penny posts apart from London, Allen was connected with the Post Office from the beginning, and cross posts were established long before 1750, and not by Allen.

conventional and idealistic that it was said of Thomas Wright Hill that he had every sense but common sense. He was an ardent free trader, a born reformer, a man with a speculative turn of mind. Fortunately his wife had a large measure of practical wisdom—and needed it to rear successfully a family of six boys and two girls. While Rowland Hill was yet a child, his mother persuaded her idealistic husband to quit his work as a journeyman brassworker and start a school in the outskirts of Birmingham. In this environment the sons grew up, obtaining a better education than their father's scanty resources could otherwise have provided. "From their father's inability to pay for sufficient assistance, the boys became teachers at a very early age, and had to begin their task by teaching themselves." Hazlewood was in many ways a pioneer school. It was even commended by Jeremy Bentham, to whose attention it was first called by a volume entitled *Public Education*, the work of Matthew and Rowland Hill.[2] By the mid-twenties, their reforms were attracting so much attention, and their ambitions for a larger school were so strong that a more pretentious offshoot was established in the London district—the Bruce Castle School at Tottenham.[3]

Several of the boys grew up to be well-known figures in Victorian England. Matthew, the eldest, became a lawyer and a reformer of the law, sat in the first reformed Parliament for Hull, and ended a distinguished career as the Recorder of Birmingham. Matthew's love of literature and bent for writing made him a useful assistant to Rowland Hill when Rowland wished to give effective written expression to his views on the Post Office. Another brother, Frederic, also attained distinction. He was the author of a work on *National Education, Its Present State and Prospects* (1836). On the passage of an act in 1835 for the appointment of inspectors of prisons, Frederic was made the first inspector for Scotland, a position that he resigned in 1851 to become Assistant Secretary of the Post Office under his brother Rowland. Edwin Hill, who was of an inventive turn of

[2] The volume, published in 1822, had for its subtitle, "Plans for the Government and Liberal Instruction of Boys in large numbers; drawn from experience." A second edition (1827) had further material added by Arthur Hill. See *Memoir of Matthew Davenport Hill*, p. 6; E. Edwards, *Sir Rowland Hill*, pp. 10-11, 33.

[3] Bruce Castle continued as a school until 1891, when it was purchased by the District Council, and the surrounding park opened to the public. In 1906 a small museum was housed in Bruce Castle; since 1928 it has included a postal history collection of interest and value.

mind, also worked in the Post Office under his brother: he is best known as the inventor of the machine for folding envelopes.[4]

The will to succeed was dominant in this remarkable brood of an unworldly dreamer. They worked in close union for some years in their father's school, establishing a "Family Fund" for furnishing aid to any of the group who might be in need of assistance. For over a quarter of a century, long after their paths had diverged, it continued as a source of family assistance. This "league of brothers" was much more than financial, for they pooled their experience, knowledge and judgment. This close bond of the Hill brothers had its part in making several members of this mid-Victorian family so well known.[5]

The removal of the brothers to the Bruce Castle School near London in 1827 opened wider opportunities for work and friendship. They became ardent advocates of popular education, both Matthew and Rowland being original members of Charles Knight's Society for the Diffusion of Useful Knowledge. The environment of the capital furnished opportunities that led several of the brothers away from the schoolmastering in order to satisfy a strong ambition to "get on" in the world.[6]

Rowland Hill tried several other schemes before settling down to postal reform. He attempted, for one thing, to interest Lord Brougham in a project for the education of pauper colonists, and the gradual extinction thereby of pauperism. Though Rowland Hill published a small volume on the subject in 1832, entitled *Home Colonies*, nothing came of this venture. While in France in 1833 for the benefit of his health, he was asked by Edward Gibbon Wakefield to become Secretary in England for the projected colonization of South Australia, a position he accepted in 1835. In the meantime he was working at a more effective printing machine that was intended

[4] For Matthew's life, see *A Memoir of Matthew Davenport Hill* by his daughters. Frederic's *Autobiography of Fifty Years in Times of Reform* was published, with additions, by his daughter, Constance Hill. Not the least important of the brothers, Arthur, continued as a schoolmaster at Bruce Castle.

[5] For the Family Fund, see Frederic's *Autobiography*, pp. 110-11. The cohesiveness of the family resulted in an unusual number of family productions. Matthew's life was written by his daughters, Frederic's *Autobiography* was edited by his daughter, Rowland's life, largely autobiographical, was edited by his nephew, George Birkebeck Hill, the son of Arthur, and another life of Rowland Hill was written by his daughter, Mrs. Eleanor C. Smyth. See the third section of the Bibliography. The *D.N.B.* includes sketches of Thomas Wright Hill, the father, of three of his sons, Matthew, Edwin and Rowland, of Rosamond Davenport Hill, the daughter of Matthew, and of George Birkbeck Hill, the son of Arthur.

[6] See G. B. Hill, *The Life of Sir Rowland Hill and the History of Penny Postage*, I, 203-5, to which frequent reference will be made.

to operate at a higher speed than had been attained heretofore, and to make possible the use of paper in large rolls. The only difficulty was the stamp tax, which had to be impressed on each sheet *before* it was used in a press. "This necessity for cutting the paper into sheets before printing was absolutely inconsistent with printing the newspaper from a continuous scroll."[7] To overcome this difficulty, Rowland Hill memorialized the Treasury, asking that the stamp be affixed by machinery as the "scroll passed through the press." He showed how greatly this would improve the printing of newspapers, but Lords of the Treasury turned down the suggestion.

Just about this time he became interested in postal reform, possibly led to seek a new task by the difficulties facing the South Australian Commissioners, for they were finding serious trouble in the actual settlement of Adelaide.[8] His interest in postal reform need not surprise the reader. By 1836 Rowland Hill's long connection with education and his interest in the Society for the Diffusion of Useful Knowledge would have led to a desire for better postal arrangements. He also took an active part in the effort to repeal the newspaper stamp tax. The movement for postal reform was already well on its way. Robert Wallace had begun his continual attacks on the postal system as early as 1833. A new body of inquiring Commissioners had been sitting since 1835, and some six of their reports had been printed by the summer of 1836. The time was ripe, as well, for suggesting schemes to reduce taxation. These were prosperous years for the government, the surplus being a million and a quarter pounds in 1835, and more than two millions in 1836.[9] Rowland

[7] See above, p. 245; G. B. Hill, *op. cit.*, I, 226.

[8] Rowland Hill did not resign as Secretary, however, until he received an appointment to the Post Office in 1839. *Ibid.*, I, 223.

[9] See *Br. Almanac* (1837), Companion, p. 152, and the Companion for 1838, p. 169. A sharp change came with the Panic of 1837, and led to deficits for some five years. The total government expenditure in the thirties was between fifty and sixty million pounds a year. The surpluses or deficits for these years are appended for reference, since the state of the exchequer had much to do with the arguments for and against postal reform, as had the possibility of a drop in the revenue that might result thereby.

For the year ending Jan.	5, 1834	a surplus of	£1,440,151
" " " " " "	1835	"	1,410,429
" " " " " "	1836	"	1,707,093
" " " " " "	1837	"	2,075,993
" " " " " "	1838	a deficit of	655,760
" " " " " "	1839	"	441,818
" " " " " "	1840	"	1,381,938
" " " " " "	1841	"	1,593,970
" " " " " "	1842	"	2,149,885
" " " " " "	1843	"	4,075,121
" " " " " "	1844	a surplus of	1,433,281

Hill's reaction to the comfortable surplus was a scheme for postal reform that would release the public from a heavy tax, that on postage. He talked over the project with his brothers: "After long and careful consideration, they concurred in advising that the Post Office should be preferred to the printing machine, and as this recommendation seconded my own opinion, I decided to act upon it."[10] The result was the appearance of his famous pamphlet on *Post Office Reform* in January 1837.

Rowland Hill's serious study of the revenue and of the shortcomings of the Post Office was made possible by the kindness of Robert Wallace. They became acquainted in 1836, Frederic Hill, then Inspector of Prisons in Scotland, serving as the intermediary.[11] Rowland requested of Wallace the loan of any books he might possess relating to the Post Office. In reply, Wallace sent Hill a cabful of books, "those heavy blue books," as Rowland Hill called them, "in which invaluable matter too often lies hidden amidst heaps of rubbish." Largely as a result of these parliamentary reports, Hill was able to marshal effective evidence in favor of his proposals. When the pamphlet was ready at the beginning of 1837, he sent Wallace a copy, in the hope of receiving encouragement and assistance. He obtained both. As Rowland Hill later said, in a speech commemorating Robert Wallace, as the "pioneer of postage reform": "So far from evincing any jealousy, Mr. Wallace at once gave me all the advantages of his position, and before the public had declared in favor of my plan, he had adopted it with all his accustomed heartiness."[12]

The plan was first printed early in the month of January 1837, in a small edition marked, "Private and Confidential," and was circulated only among friends and public officials. A second edition appeared late in February, intended for general distribution. A third was issued in November, and a fourth printing seems to have occurred in 1838. There were some additions and changes made in the second and third editions. The title, *Post Office Reform: Its Importance and Practicability*, was chosen in preference to "Uniform Penny Postage," as less likely to scare away prospective readers.[13]

---

[10] G. B. Hill, *op. cit.*, I, 230. [11] *Ibid.*, I, 258, 531.

[12] *Ibid.*, I, 246, 531-32; Eleanor C. Smyth, *Sir Rowland Hill*, p. 100. Internal evidence indicates that Rowland Hill was working on the pamphlet in the last months of 1836. His calculation of the number of letters was based on data "at the present time, Nov., 1836."

[13] See Pearson Hill, *The Post Office of Fifty Years Ago*, p. 17. The first edition has no preface: those of the second and third editions bear the dates of Feb. 22 and Nov. 15

Rowland Hill

Private and confidential.

POST OFFICE REFORM;

ITS IMPORTANCE

AND

PRACTICABILITY.

___

BY ROWLAND HILL.

___

PRIVATELY PRINTED,
BY W. CLOWES AND SONS, STAMFORD STREET.

1837.

Title page of the first edition of *Post Office Reform*, with the author's signature.

Hill began his work by expressing a hope that the reduction of taxation "may shortly take place," because "the present revenue of the country greatly exceeds the expenditure." He then examined the revenue from the Post Office for its relation to the total receipts of

A memorandum in Rowland Hill's handwriting as to the editions of *Post Office Reform*.

the Treasury. An analysis of the Post Office receipts, based on the high rates then in use, showed that since the postal charges had reached their maximum in 1812, the Post Office had been "remarkable for its non-increasing productiveness." The net revenue had not grown since 1812: actually the Post Office turned over to the Exchequer in 1835 less than in 1815. He pointed out, next, that if the increase in population were taken into account as well as the spread of

respectively. The pamphlets are octavo in size, and the number of pages are 73, 104 and 97, respectively. The printer of all three editions was William Clowes, though the second and third editions bore the name of Charles Knight and Co. as the publisher. The authority for a fourth edition in 1838 is a memorandum in Rowland Hill's handwriting in a volume containing the three editions bound together, and now in the possession of Harvard University. Mr. Hill's memory may have failed him in making this statement. I have found no other evidence for an edition in 1838. And see below, p. 281, where W. H. Ashurst seems to imply that there was none.

education and the increasing trade and prosperity of the country, there would be a great comparative loss.[14]

This comparative loss was contrasted by Rowland Hill with the actual gain in a comparable tax, that on stage coaches. Since the stage coach revenue had more than doubled between 1815 and 1835, he concluded that there had been in reality a loss in the Post Office revenue of £2,000,000 a year, since the demand for the conveyance of letters should have been as great as that for the conveyance of persons and parcels. He supported this contention by citing the French postal increase of 54 per cent between 1821 and 1835, "where the rates of postage are less exorbitant than with us." Sir Henry Parnell was quoted to fortify this judgment: "The revenue of the Post Office has been stationary . . . since 1818. This can be accounted for only by the great duty charged on letters; for with a lower duty the correspondence of the country through the Post Office would have increased in proportion to the increase in population and national wealth."[15] Moreover, the decrease in the price of an article in general demand always increased its use. The price of tea, for example, since the opening of the China trade had fallen off by a sixth and consumption had increased by a half. Coffee was cheaper by a fourth since 1823 when the duties were lowered, and consumption had tripled. Why not assume that the same thing would happen with letters? If the reduction of postage were considerable, the tendency to smuggle letters—so general at the time—would be lessened. For these two reasons, Rowland Hill confidently expected a much greater use of the Post Office.

How much of a reduction could be made? Hill first endeavored to find the "natural cost of distribution," that is, the cost relieved of taxation. This was difficult, as the postal authorities had no record of the number of letters transmitted. Hill arrived by sampling at an

[14] His table was as follows:

YEAR	POPULATION	NET REV.	REV. IF IT KEPT PACE WITH POP.	COMP. LOSS.
1815	19,552,000	£1,557,291	£1,557,291	
1820	20,982,000	1,479,547	1,674,000	£194,453
1825	22,362,000	1,670,219	1,789,000	118,781
1830	23,961,000	1,517,952	1,917,000	399,048
1835	25,605,000	1,540,300	2,048,000	507,700

2nd ed., p. 3. It should be added that the Postmaster-General objected to the use of net revenue as a basis for calculation.

[15] 2nd ed., pp. 5-6. References are to the second edition, though any important differences in the editions will be noted. The second edition was reprinted by Pearson Hill in *The Post Office of Fifty Years Ago*.

estimate of about 88,000,000 letters a year, 7,400,000 additional franked letters and 30,000,000 newspapers. If this total of about 125,000,000 pieces of mail was divided into the actual annual expenses of the Post Office, the distribution of a letter or a newspaper, including the collecting of the tax, "is, under the present arrangements, about 1 1/3d." But this calculation of the cost of sending a letter was felt to be unfair, since the letters that paid their way were compelled to carry the financial loss on franked letters and free newspapers.[16]

The actual cost was also worked out by finding the cost of a load of mail from London to Edinburgh on a particular day. The result of this sample mail was surprising. A letter weighing a quarter of an ounce—the average weight of a single letter—if charged for its share of the whole journey from London to Edinburgh should be taxed but one thirty-sixth of a penny. Hill felt that it was manifestly unfair for a letter weighing a quarter of an ounce to be charged over a shilling for making the journey between London and Edinburgh. He concluded, therefore, that the charge for letters sent anywhere in the British Isles should not only be low, but that the tax should be uniform, since the distance from London to Edinburgh was more than the average distance that letters traveled in Great Britain. Not only should it be uniform, but precisely the same for every packet of moderate weight "without reference to the number of enclosures." In this way Rowland Hill arrived at two of the principal features of his reform—the uniform charge and the charge by weight, rather than by the number of enclosures.[17]

After computing the actual expense of conveying a letter and finding it so small a fraction of the whole cost, Rowland Hill next examined the cost of collecting and delivering letters. Here he found conditions with which the reader is familiar. The clerks had to adjust accounts for postpaid letters, tax the unpaid letters according to the distance each traveled, stamp them all and charge each the correct amount. This included, of course, checking each letter "with a candle to see whether it was double or single." He concluded, logically, that a great saving in time and expense would result if the postage were collected *before* the letters started their travels. The work of the London carriers was examined at some length and found to be "tedious, inconvenient and expensive." If the collection of postage

---

[16] *Ibid.*, pp. 11-12.
[17] *Ibid.*, p. 19. Weight was already the basis of the charge in France and in London.

could be avoided, the work of the letter carriers would be greatly speeded since they would not have to stop to collect the postage, "and probably it would soon be unnecessary to await the opening of the door, as every house might be provided with a box into which the letter carrier could drop the letter and, having knocked, he would pass on as fast as he could walk." Hence a third essential feature of his plan, the prepayment of letters.

If the tax were uniform and prepaid, how much should it be? Manifestly, one could not collect one thirty-sixth of a penny for each letter. Rowland Hill believed that the cost of each letter and newspaper would be much less than a penny even if all the costs connected with distribution were included. Various practices already in use fortified his belief in the sufficiency of a penny charge. The penny posts, then in use, were known to be profitable, and the Twopenny Post of London, where four ounces was permitted and where the establishment was conducted in an expensive manner, distributed the letters at a cost of about two-thirds of a penny. He also cited the example of the *Penny Magazine*, with which he was familiar as a member of the Society for the Diffusion of Useful Knowledge. This publication was delivered to every part of the kingdom and in large towns was even carried to the houses of subscribers, "yet it is well known," he declared, "that the undertaking is a profitable investment." Moreover, the penny charged for the magazine included not only the cost of distribution but the cost of eight large pages of letterpress and woodcuts.[18]

Rowland Hill proposed, as a result of his investigation, that a penny be made the basic charge "on all letters received in a post-town and delivered in the same or any other post-town of the British Isles." This uniform rate was to carry letters of not more than half an ounce: "All letters and other papers, whether single or multiple, and not weighing more than half an ounce, being charged one penny, and heavier packets charged an additional penny for each additional half ounce."[19]

One more feature of his plan remains. How to collect this prepayment most efficiently, and thereby help to make the low and uni-

---

[18] *Ibid.*, pp. 34, 96-102.

[19] *Ibid.*, p. 36. In the first "confidential" edition, Hill had suggested an ounce as the limit for a penny, but it was lowered to half an ounce in the second edition at the suggestion of the Chancellor of the Exchequer, Thomas Spring-Rice. As the public might not take to prepayment easily, he proposed that letters not prepaid be sent for twice the charge to offset the cost of collecting the postage when they were delivered.

form rate more certain of success? In the first edition, Hill proposed
what he later called the first mode of collection. Receiving houses
would still have slits for putting in letters, but they would be used
only for franked letters and newspapers. Prepaid letters would be
brought to the counter, the letter weighed if necessary in the presence of the bearer, and the postage paid, as is the case today when
there is doubt about the weight and cost of a letter. The letter would
then be stamped with the date and address of the receiving house by
means of a "tell-tale stamp" that would also count the letters "as
they were impressed."[20]

By the time of the second edition—February 1837—Rowland
Hill had worked out a second mode of collection. This proposal
added one of the most distinctive features of the reform. It was an
outgrowth of a suggestion of Charles Knight, by which he had proposed that the newspaper stamp tax be abolished; Knight would have
had a newspaper sent free through the post on being enclosed in a
stamped wrapper for which the penny had already been paid. To
quote Hill: "Availing myself of this suggestion, I propose the following arrangement: let stamped covers and sheets of paper be supplied to the public from the Stamp Office or the Post Office or both,
and sold at such a price as to include the postage. Letters so stamped
would be treated in all respects as franks, be put into the letter box
as at present, instead of being delivered to the Receiver."[21]

Covers of various values would be needed, but each would have
the weight it would be allowed to carry "legibly printed with the
stamp." Hill would have not only wrappers such as were used for
newspapers, but the stamp would be impressed on sheets of letter
paper and on covers made of cheap paper. If a stamped sheet of letter paper were used, the stamp would have to be "in the part used
for the address," that is, would have to show when the sheet was
folded and sealed ready for mailing. When these stamped sheets
and wrappers and covers (envelopes) were mailed, the "stamp of
the receiving house should be stuck upon the frank-stamp to prevent the letter being used a second time."[22] This means that a stamp
impressed on the paper and indicating prepayment would be canceled

[20] *Ibid.*, p. 38.
[21] For Knight's suggestions, see above, p. 246. For Hill's reference to Knight, *ibid.*,
p. 42.
[22] *Ibid.*, p. 43. In using the term "frank-stamp," Mr. Hill had in mind the sort of
stamp that appears today upon the stamped envelopes and wrappers purchasable at the
Post Office.

by the rubber stamp of the receiving house. Such a rubber stamp was already in use, as we have found, but not for cancellation purposes: it indicated the source of a letter and the time of its receipt by the Post Office.

The obvious advance of his second mode of collection over the first lay in the speed with which letters could be posted. They would not have to be paid for as they were brought to the Post Office, but could be put in the box for prepaid and franked letters.[23]

One difficulty might occur in the general adoption of this plan. Through ignorance or carelessness persons might write a letter and take it to the Post Office without having used stamped paper. In that case, the letter would have to go to the window for payment, as in the suggested first mode. The bearer could purchase an envelope or wrapper, of course, and redirect the letter. But this would often be impossible, as letters were frequently mailed by messengers or servants whose illiteracy would make it impossible for them to redirect a letter. This led to Rowland Hill's proposal of what we know today as the adhesive postage stamp. His description of the adhesive is quaint, to say the least: "The bringer would sometimes be unable to write. Perhaps this difficulty might be obviated by using a bit of paper just large enough to bear the stamp, and covered at the back with a glutinous wash, which the bringer might, by applying a little moisture, attach to the back of the letter, so as to avoid the necessity for redirecting it." The adhesive was not intended originally for envelopes, but for folded unstamped sheets, and the suggestion was made originally for the sale of adhesives *in* the Post Office, in case unstamped letters were brought to the window. We shall find later how this tentative proposal became so fundamental a part of the reform. The use of adhesive stamps was not one of Mr. Hill's original proposals, but an afterthought, in the second edition of *Post Office Reform*, to facilitate prepayment.

Mr. Hill was keenly aware of the cost of delivery in country districts, and had no desire to burden his proposals with such expenses. He proposed, therefore, to separate such places from the general or primary delivery, and to make the secondary delivery pay its own way. He seems to have had in mind arrangements not unlike those used in the Fifth Clause posts. But the place at which to draw the

---

[23] The second edition of *Post Office Reform* included both "modes," but in the third edition the first mode of collection was omitted. "In former editions, two modes of collection were submitted for consideration, but the public having evinced a decided preference for one, the other is here, for the sake of brevity, omitted." 3rd ed., p. 27.

line distinguishing primary from secondary distribution was so difficult to locate that no attempt was made to follow this recommendation.

Nor did the proposal fit well into the methods of handling foreign and colonial letters. A uniform rate would depend, manifestly, on intergovernmental agreements. Hill's solution was ingenious, if utterly impracticable. Charge all letters that were intended for a foreign country double, that is, 2d, he advised, and make no charge for foreign letters coming in. But this again would require intergovernmental agreements, since any charge required by a foreign country would be paid there whether the letter were going or coming. He would include colonial letters in this category, on the ground that "in many minds, the distinction between a foreign country and one of our colonies is not clearly defined."[24]

The point of most importance to the success of the plan was its effect on the revenue. Unless the Lords of the Treasury found it satisfactory from this point of view, the plan had little chance of adoption. The average cost of a letter, according to the current income, was about 6d. If the postal charge was lowered to one penny, six times as many letters would be needed to maintain the present revenue. What was the probability that his scheme of a prepaid, low and uniform postage would bring about this increase? He counted on various sources of supply for the postal business. For one thing, a large undetermined amount of correspondence was carried on outside the Post Office: this he felt would naturally be drawn in by the low charge. Smuggling would no longer pay. Then, also, much mail that went under the franking privilege to members of Parliament might pay the small charge voluntarily. Rowland Hill's friends, particularly Charles Knight, felt sure that a very large increase of letters would come from using the cheap postal rate for printed circulars, catalogues and price lists. In addition, the Post Office would be open to new classes, very numerous ones, who were unable to write letters before. "When we consider that from increased and increasing facility of travelling, growing knowledge, and rising spirit of adventure, this locomotive disposition is rapidly advancing; and, again, that the very facility of communication here recommended would greatly stimulate its progress, it will be difficult to fix a limit to the amount of correspondence that may be looked for in this quarter."[25]

[24] *Ibid.*, p. 61.
[25] *Ibid.*, p. 92. The sentence illustrates Mr. Hill's difficulties with the language.

Rowland Hill was very sanguine as to a sixfold increase at least in the number of letters, though he was careful not to state a time when this increase would come into effect. But the inference is clear that he expected the introduction of his plan to be without any serious effect on the revenue. As he put it: "It is very possible the revenue may not suffer at all, and it is highly probable that it will not suffer much."[26] In order to make the transition doubly safe, he suggested that the plan be applied first to some particular area. He recommended that the Twopenny Post in London be the place for the initial trial. This seemed appropriate as the Twopenny Post was already a distinctive department, under the direct eye of the government, and would simply lower the London rates to those of the penny posts throughout the country. A successful trial in the London district, where one-twelfth of the population of the British Isles lived, would prove the worth of the plan sufficiently well, so he said, to justify its extension throughout the United Kingdom. If faults were found in the plan as applied to the London District Post, changes could be made before the plan was extended.[27]

Such were Hill's reflections on postal reform. He would have a uniform rate for all distances in the United Kingdom with the charge at a penny for a half-ounce, with an additional penny for each additional half-ounce. Letters would be prepaid by means of stamped letter sheets, wrappers and covers, with the addition, "perhaps," of a small adhesive stamp. The advance in business resulting from the increase of chargeable letters would entail little, if any, increase over the present postal establishment, and the revenue would not suffer much, possibly not suffer at all.

The "private and confidential" edition was placed in the hands of the government early in January 1837, "in the hope that no publication would be necessary."[28] The Chancellor of the Exchequer gave Hill a sympathetic hearing and suggested some changes. The author offered to allow the government to have entire credit for the scheme if they would introduce it, though one may feel sure that Mr. Hill's

[26] *Ibid.*, p. 95. In another part of the pamphlet (p. 63), he prophesied that the number of chargeable letters would increase $5\frac{1}{4}$-fold, and that the probable net revenue would be £1,278,000. The actual net revenue for 1836 was £1,486,000. Rowland Hill's ingenious calculations proved to be at variance with the actual results. But there were explanations, as we shall find.

[27] *Ibid.*, p. 104. It should be said that Rowland Hill showed his wisdom in making this suggestion, as the plan would have its most favorable application in such a region as London.

[28] G. B. Hill, *op. cit.*, I, 262 n.

disinterestedness did not include his voluntary retirement from an active share in the application of the plan.

The whole tone of his *Post Office Reform* is such as to indicate that the author hoped to influence the government to adopt the plan rather than force the government to submit to outside pressure. The Duke of Richmond, a former Postmaster-General, was praised. The recently appointed successor to Sir Francis Freeling was also lauded for his "known talent and energy." Rowland Hill pointed out, as well, that postal reform was not a party question, since some of the "leading men of each political party" have expressed themselves as favorable to great changes. Because action on the proposals would necessarily require legislation, the author was also careful not to alienate the members of Parliament by suggesting an end of franking: all his suppositions were based on the continuance of franking.

His hope that the government would sponsor the scheme proved vain. The "deep-rooted prejudice of routine," as Hill put it, was too much for so striking a departure from current practices. Nor was the government deterred by the veiled threat of an appeal to the public. "Judging from the rapid growth of public opinion which we have recently witnessed with regard to other institutions, we may expect that in a few years, or even months, if the 'still small voice' which, at present, gives scarcely audible expression to half-formed desires, be neglected, it will swell into a loud, distinct and irresistible demand."[29] As a result of the unwillingness of the government to father the plan, and because Post Office legislation was coming up in 1837, Hill determined to appeal to the larger public.[30] Thus the confidential printing of January was succeeded by the so-called second edition late in February. This was followed by the third edition in November, with a new and longer preface: it was a vitriolic and sarcastic presentation of the obscurantist opposition of the Post Office half a century earlier to the reforms of John Palmer. By November Rowland Hill no longer desired to placate the postal authorities.[31]

During 1837 the demand for a reform of the Post Office became loud and insistent—and ultimately irresistible.

---

[29] *Ibid.*, pp. 65-66. Another of his less felicitous sentences.

[30] The Post Office Acts treated at the end of the previous chapter were passed on July 12, 1837.

[31] See above, pp. 134 ff.

The Agitation for
Uniform Penny Postage

WHEN Rowland Hill's pamphlet appeared in February 1837, the demand for postal reform was given an immense stimulus. It served in a splendid way to support the previous efforts of Robert Wallace, and to concentrate attention on what was certainly a remarkable proposal. To the postal authorities, Robert Wallace had seemed a public bore. When Rowland Hill injected his novel suggestions into the agitation for reform, he seemed to them not only a public bore, but a crazy enthusiast.

Post Office Reform made a widespread appeal because it combined shrewd common sense and humanitarian feeling. The suggestion for so great a drop in postage seemed to forecast another great reform, not unlike the recent revision of parliamentary representation or the abolition of slavery. Richard Cobden, for example, was a whole-souled enthusiast for the plan: he even offered to bear part of the expense of a low-priced edition, already thinking, doubtless, of its value to the lower classes, and to the anti-Corn Law agitation. Daniel O'Connell saw its possibilities for Ireland and the repeal movement: he was willing to move in Parliament for a committee on the plan. The conversion of the well-known labor leader, Francis Place, is an amusing instance of the effectiveness of the pamphlet. At first he thought it but another eccentric proposal. For a time he delayed the reading, and when he began, it was with misgiving, for he expected to find the "hitch." As he read on, so goes the story, he still looked for the "hitch," but finished the book with the remark, "I'll be damned if there is a hitch!"[1] Some of Rowland Hill's calculations were wrong, and some of his ideas never proved practicable, but his deductions were much more dependable than the criticisms of the official opposition. Let us now trace the running battle of words that was finally won in 1839 by Wallace, Hill and their supporters.

The Commissioners who had been inquiring into the organization of the Post Office since 1835 were still at work in 1837. They were examining the London Twopenny Post on the first appearance of *Post Office Reform*. Since Rowland Hill had made sharp criticisms of the London postal service, and had suggested that his plan might well be tried first in London, the Commissioners summoned him to give evidence. He asserted that the Twopenny Post was open to great improvement, especially in the distribution of mail. He would have a dispatch in town—the twopenny district—every half-hour instead of six times a day, proposed the use of mail coaches to bring up the threepenny letters in the morning, and the use of stage coaches for more remote regions where a regular service then existed for passengers but not for mail. Hill made the interesting suggestion that London be divided into ten districts, with each district a distinct postal unit, so that mail could be interchanged between districts rather than go to the central office to be sent out again. He suggested a uniform charge for the whole of the District Post. Even if the expense doubled as a result of this change, he prophesied that only a threefold increase would be needed to maintain the revenue.[2]

They also interrogated Robert Smith, Superintendent of the Twopenny Post. He was able to point out a number of reforms already effected. One of the most useful was the correction of the boundaries of the 2d and 3d deliveries. In 1831 the delivery of twopenny letters had been extended to a circle three miles from St. Martin's le Grand, and in 1834 the external limit of the 3d delivery was made a circle twelve miles from the Post Office.[3] Robert Smith could report as well six daily deliveries in town and three in the country. In reply to Hill, Smith asserted positively that the districting of London would be a great expense. When asked whether there would be a loss if the twopenny rate was reduced to a penny, he replied: "There cannot be a doubt of that." It was his "firm conviction that any attempt to fetter the post by compelling payment of letters when

[1] G. B. Hill, *op. cit.*, I, 276-78.
[2] He also repeated the proposal for house letter boxes in order to speed delivery. For his evidence, see *9th Rep. Commrs. P.O. Management*, pp. 26-34.
[3] See map, p. 198.

put in, would check correspondence, cause much dissatisfaction, and be considered a very oppressive measure." He was also opposed to the union of the two sets of carriers, those of the Twopenny Post and those of the General Post.[4]

The Commissioners seem to have been more impressed by Hill than by Smith. When they presented their report to the Treasury— it was dated July 7, 1837—their recommendations for the Two- penny Post included the use of stamped covers, and the reduction of prepaid letters to a penny for the whole of the District Post. They suggested no change in the postage if the letters were not prepaid. They recommended, also, the possible extension of the District Post to a fifteen-mile radius, the increase of deliveries from six a day to seven, and the already familiar proposal for combining the two sets of letter carriers.[5]

The recommendations produced no immediate effect. Commis- sioners of the Treasury appointed to inquire into the Post Office probably expected no better result than an addition to the collection of blue books. Robert Wallace certainly thought as much, for in May he irritated the government, then busy putting through an Irish Poor Law Bill, by moving for a select committee "to report on the present rates of postage, and especially to examine the improvements recom- mended, and the mode of charging postage proposed, in a pamphlet by Mr. Rowland Hill, with a view to the general reduction of post- age duties." He withdrew his motion when the government in- formed the House that the plan was under consideration. Later in the month Lord Ashburton raised the matter in the House of Lords in presenting a petition for postal reform signed by bankers of the metropolis, solicitors and attorneys, and many men of science. He used the opportunity to emphasize the neglect of the Post Office, the present high charges and the value of a pamphlet "written by a gentleman named Rowland Hill." Viscount Duncannon, chairman of the Commissioners issuing the report just reviewed, took part in the discussion. He declared that the plan was recommended in part, though not practicable in its complete form, particularly with regard to foreign letters.[6]

When the second reading of the Post Office bills occurred in June 1837, Lord Ashburton regretted that the bills proposed no reduc-

---

[4] *9th Rep. Commrs. P.O. Management*, pp. 16, 22, 35, 40.
[5] *Ibid.*, pp. 7-9.
[6] *Parl. Deb.*, 3rd s., XXXVIII, 755-60, 1098-99; G. B. Hill, *op. cit.*, I, 278-79.

tion, but thought them useful as a preparation for further changes. This provoked the Earl of Lichfield into statements that were unfortunate as coming from the Postmaster-General. He insisted that the revenue had been considerably increased, that the number of letters annually circulated was 170,000,000 a year, and that the reduction of the duty would require the enormous number of 416,000,-000 letters annually to produce an equivalent amount of revenue. Lord Lichfield then gave his judgment of the pamphlet in the following words: "With respect to the plan set forth by Mr. Hill, of all the wild and visionary schemes which he had ever heard or read of, it was the most extraordinary."[7]

Five days after this debate, King William IV died, and was succeeded by his young niece, Victoria. As the death of the ruler still required the dissolution of Parliament, the session of 1837 was brought rapidly to a close. The resulting general election returned the Whigs in triumph in August, and Parliament resumed its work in November. During this time the interest in postal reform had grown stronger and stronger. The Commissioners' Report on the Twopenny Post appeared in the summer, and a third edition of *Post Office Reform* followed in November.

Shortly after Parliament opened Robert Wallace renewed his motion for a select committee, "on the present rates and modes of charging postage, with a view to such a reduction thereof as may be made without injury to the revenue: and for this purpose to examine especially . . . a pamphlet published by Mr. Rowland Hill." The Select Committee was finally granted, after efforts that had extended over four years and two parliaments. What was even more gratifying to the reformers was the announcement of its membership. Robert Wallace was made chairman of a committee of fifteen that included a number of friends of postal reform, notably Lord Lowther and Henry Warburton. This Select Committee—it might well be called the Wallace Committee on Mr. Hill's Plan—held hearings from November 1837 to August 1838. The Wallace Committee served as an excellent sounding board for the expression of public interest in postal reform, and the fullness of the evidence in its three reports had much to do with the success of the movement.

Just before Christmas 1837 Lord Brougham spoke on the subject when presenting a petition from the Lord Mayor and aldermen

---

[7] *Ibid.*, XXXVIII, 1464. Hill's estimate of 88,000,000 letters proved much more accurate.

of the City of London in favor of Hill's plan. He emphasized its practicability and recalled in sarcastic tones how their predecessors had thought Palmer's proposal for mail coaches utterly absurd. At the same time and in the same debate the Postmaster-General made statements even more wild and curious than those he had uttered in the same place a year before. He now believed that the total number of letters carried annually by the Post Office was but 42,000,000, that the expected increase would mean twelve times as much mail, and "therefore the charge for transmission, instead of £100,000 as now, must be twelve times that amount." He concluded that the "walls of the Post Office would burst—the whole area in which the building stands would not be large enough to receive the clerks and the letters, if the circulation were increased to anything like that amount." Nor was the Duke of Wellington deterred by Brougham's sarcasm from asserting that "no experiment could be more fatal than a great and sudden diminution of the rate of postage, and consequently, of revenue."[8]

Petitions to Parliament were becoming numerous as the agitation increased. Six of them, with over nine hundred signatures, had appeared in 1837. In the session of 1837-38 the number greatly increased—320 petitions bore over 9000 signatures. Among the petitions were several from Aberdeen, four from Edinburgh, five from Glasgow, eight from Liverpool, as well as numerous individual appeals, including one from the well-known publisher, Samuel Bagster.

Rowland Hill, aided by his brother Arthur, wrote a series of letters in reply to Lord Lichfield's criticisms: they appeared in the London papers early in 1838. In one he answered Lord Lichfield's statement about the increase in the amount of correspondence. The Postmaster-General had said that the increase required to prevent a loss in revenue would be so great that the "whole area on which the Post Office stands would not be large enough to receive the clerks and the letters." Hill replied that the size of the Post Office should be regulated by the correspondence, not the correspondence by the size of the Post Office. But in general Rowland Hill left to others the agitation for his plan.[9]

A very powerful organ for what we would now call propaganda was a group formed in February 1838, known as the Mercantile

---

[8] *Ibid.*, XXXIX, 1201-6, 1210. Lord Lichfield's statement about the bursting walls of the Post Office is not in the *Parliamentary Debates*. For it, and the debate as a whole, see *Mirror of Parliament* (session of 1837-38), pp. 829-34.

[9] G. B. Hill, *op. cit.*, I, 293-94.

Committee. It collected witnesses and evidence for examination by Wallace's Committee, furnished forms of petition with which to bombard Parliament and published very effective appeals to public opinion. George Moffat, a wealthy London tea dealer, had become greatly interested in the question of postal reform. Largely through him, this influential committee of bankers and merchants gave time and money for the cause of cheap postage. Joshua Bates of the banking house of Baring Brothers became chairman. Moffat served as treasurer. The solicitor was W. H. Ashurst, an enthusiastic radical who was liberal of funds and labor in procuring evidence for the parliamentary committee. The secretary was that indefatigable worker, Henry Cole.[10]

Henry Cole devised various ways of demonstrating the inequalities of postage. The principal medium for influencing the public was the *Post Circular*, issued from time to time as a newspaper. If documents consisting of addresses, petitions and other material had gone through the mail in the ordinary way, the postal cost would have been too high. Henry Cole, therefore, planned to print his material in the form of a newspaper so that the tax would be but a penny for each copy of the *Post Circular*.[11] As he explained: "If a small sheet of paper, partially filled with addresses, petitions, or documents relating to the discussion of the postage, together with the news of the day . . . be entered at the Stamp Office, it would be carried by the post freely." The news was the legal basis for the newspaper. The device seemed all the more apt to Henry Cole, since by this means the Post Office would become the chief instrument for reforming itself. The first number appeared in March.[12]

This widely distributed "newspaper" was sent to members of Parliament through the mails, as one way of showing the curiosities of the postal charges. If delivered to them by hand, it would have cost at least thirty shillings; if sent by the Twopenny Post, there would have been a total charge of several pounds, since newspapers

[10] For its membership, see Cole's autobiography, *Fifty Years of Public Work*, II, 101. Joshua Bates was born in Massachusetts in 1788, had gone to Europe in 1816, and became associated in the twenties with John Baring. At the time of which we are writing he was a partner in the house of Baring Brothers, and was building up a large fortune. See *D.A.B.*, II, 52. John Baring, with whom he was at first associated, was a brother-in-law of Henry Labouchere. Lord Ashburton, also interested in postal reform and well known for his part in negotiating the Webster-Ashburton Treaty, was a brother of John Baring.

[11] See above, p. 246, for the newspaper tax stamp used on the *Post Circular*.

[12] Cole, *op. cit.*, I, 381. Charles Whiting was the printer.

paid postage in the local posts. They were taken, therefore, to Gravesend or Watford, the first post towns out of London, and there posted, with the result that there was no postal charge over and above the stamp duty that had already been paid. One example of the effect of charging by the number of sheets of paper rather than by weight was shown up by the dispatch of two letters to the various members of Parliament, one so small as to require a forceps to handle it, and yet charged double postage because it had an enclosure, and another, weighing nearly an ounce, eight inches broad and a foot wide, charged but single postage because it was but one sheet of paper. J. W. Croker mentions receiving from some Post Office reformers such a circular letter on a single sheet of paper "as large as a tablecloth."[13]

The *Post Circular* was also the vehicle for window bills, petitions,

GREAT WEIGHT AND NO PRICE! LITTLE WEIGHT AND ALL PRICE!!

Henry Cole's caricature of a loaded Edinburgh mail coach.

various kinds of placards and calls for public meetings in provincial towns. One of the most interesting issued was a drawing by Thackeray for a valentine, showing a postman struggling with letters that

[13] *Quarterly Review*, LXIV (Oct. 1839), p. 296 n.

nearly smothered him. An effective argument for cheaper postage was a caricature of the actual load carried by the Edinburgh mail coach on March 2, 1838. The coach was shown with its inside and outside passengers, its driver and guard. On the top were several sacks of newspapers weighing 273 pounds, a sack of 484 franks weighing 47 pounds, as well as a parcel of revenue stamps. In front of the guard was a small sack containing 1565 letters, weighing 34 pounds, and marked as paying £93 postage. The Postmaster-General was asked "to study our sketch, in which we have placed the letters on the top of the mail, the better to contrast them with newspapers, their [the letters'] usual place being in the hind boot." A further point was made by calling attention to the load of the coach: it was only 531 pounds, though a coach was able to carry over 1600 pounds of mail. Thus the load, even if enlarged several times, could still be paid for by charging only a penny for each letter carried.[14]

One of the most influential issues of the *Post Circular* was an imaginary scene at Windsor Castle. It opens with Queen Victoria "sitting at a large table, on which are lying the Parliamentary and Commissioners' Reports on Postage, copies of the *Post Circular*, and annual reports of the French and American Post Offices." The Queen is "in deep study over *Post Office Reform* by Rowland Hill. Lord Melbourne at the Queen's right hand is watching her Majesty's countenance." The scene begins with the Queen exclaiming, "Mothers pawning their clothes to pay the postage of a child's letter! Every subject studying to evade postage without caring for the law! Even Messrs. Baring Brothers sending letters illegally every week to save postage! Such things must not last!" She then turns to Lord Melbourne and asks if he is "able to say anything about this postage plan, which all the country seems talking about." At this point, the Postmaster-General and Mr. Rowland Hill are ushered into Her Majesty's presence. Hill explains his plan briefly, Lord Lichfield interrupting by saying it is "the most wild and visionary scheme that I have ever heard or read of." After Lichfield finds his arguments of no avail with the Queen, Lord Melbourne says aside to the Postmaster-General: "My dear Lichfield, I fear the Queen has found you in a scrape."

The matter of increased weight is also taken up in the imaginary interview. Lord Lichfield repeats his statement that twelve times as much weight would make the cost of transmission twelve times as

[14] Cole, *op. cit.*, II, 102-3. 531 lbs. was the weight of the mail *and* the bags.

great. The Queen replies by finding in the Report of the Select Committee that the Leeds mail on April 20 weighed only 158 pounds, of which the letters weighed but 38 pounds, "so that this mail might have carried at least twenty-four times the weight of the letters without overloading the mail." Lord Lichfield thereupon accepts "your Majesty's compassionate corrections," and remarks as he bows out, "With your Majesty's leave I will retire." The Queen, after his departure, says, "It is clear to me that his Lordship had better retire from the Post Office."

After further statements by the Queen showing the general benefit of penny postage, Victoria rises "and in a most emphatic manner" says, "My Lord Melbourne, you will be pleased to bear in mind that the Queen agrees . . . in recommending a uniform penny postage. . . . Mr. Hill, the nation will owe you a large debt of gratitude, which I am sure it will not be unwilling to repay. I wish you good morning, gentlemen."[15]

In the meantime Wallace's Select Committee, which we started on its labors several pages back, was busily taking evidence. It sat for sixty-three days, and published three elaborate reports. The Committee had gathered its evidence during the spring and summer of 1838, but the third and final report did not appear until March 1839. Despite this delay, the evidence was made available to the public during 1838 in various ways. The *Post Circular* printed the more striking testimony. W. H. Ashurst published a pamphlet in the summer of 1838 that included much of the evidence, as well as data on postal inequalities that he had obtained in other ways.[16]

Wallace's Committee, by the terms of its appointment, was concerned chiefly with the rates of postage and the plan proposed by Rowland Hill. Its work was confined, therefore, to the domestic Post

[15] Cole, *op. cit.*, II, 95-101, 105. This was probably the most widely spread production of the Mercantile Committee. Nearly 100,000 were printed for circulation, and 40,000 more were stitched into one of the parts of *Nicholas Nickleby*. Part XIII, which appeared in April 1839, carried the "advertisement leaf" headed "Queen Victoria and the Uniform Penny Postage." It was not inappropriate that *Nicholas Nickleby* was used for the purpose, as it portrayed the need for improved educational conditions, and illustrates traveling conditions interestingly when Nicholas and Mr. Squeers take the coach for Dotheboys Hall. For the bibliographical data, see John C. Eckel, *First Editions of the Writings of Charles Dickens* (1932), p. 65.

[16] The third and final Report was prepared for publication by Henry Warburton. Ashurst's pamphlet was entitled *Facts and Figures in Support of Mr. Rowland Hill's Plan for a Universal Penny Postage*. The preface is dated June 1838, and the reason given for its publication was Hill's inability to issue a new edition of his pamphlet because of "public engagements." The Ashurst pamphlet consists of nearly 100 closely printed pages.

Office, to the tendency of high rates to curb postage, and to the amount of correspondence that went through legal and illegal channels. The Twopenny Post in London had been considered so fully by the Commissioners of 1835 in their recent Ninth Report that this branch of the Post Office was not gone over again in any detail.[17]

The number of letters in circulation was a main point at issue between Mr. Hill and the Post Office. He had set the number at 88,-000,000 a year. Two different estimates by the Postmaster-General have already been quoted. Before the Committee, Lord Lichfield declared the number of chargeable letters at 67,000,000, thus making three different figures furnished by the Postmaster-General. Col. Maberly, the successor of Freeling, put the chargeable letters at 70,000,000, or 12,000,000 more than he had stated originally. Mr. Hill's evidence before the Committee reduced his earlier estimate from 88,000,000 to 78,000,000. The Committee, after pointing out that the Post Office had no accurate record, concluded that Mr. Hill was probably much nearer the truth, and the Committee made its calculations of possible reductions in the rates on the figures of Rowland Hill rather than those of the Post Office.[18]

The Committee went at great length into the losses of postage by the use of illegal methods for sending letters. The Committee found this loss enormous, and, of course, a very strong argument against postage rates that tempted evasion. The evidence taken by the Committee reveals an amount of shiftiness that shows the people of the British Isles were anything but law-abiding in the matter of postage. Smuggling of goods had largely disappeared because of the lowering of tariffs, but the smuggling of letters went on more merrily than ever. Various were the ways used for avoiding high postage. Franks had been found a useful device for sending letters free by persons who had no right to use the privilege. This abuse still continued. Dr. Lardner, who managed publications and required a large correspondence, used franks for his six to seven thousand letters a year. His facility for using franks was so great, he declared, that the "Post Office is almost free to me." Before he had come from Ireland to

---

[17] The three folio Reports of the Select Committee are not sharply defined. The first contains evidence taken by the end of April 1838. The second, dated August 1, 1838, continues with 400 more pages of evidence, an appendix of statistical data and 153 pages of index. The third Report, dated Aug. 13, 1838, contains the actual report of the findings of the Committee, in 69 pages, followed by more statistical data, an abstract of the evidence and a supplementary abstract, as well as several large folding maps.

[18] 3rd Rep. Sel. Com. on Postage, pp. 7-9, and 1st Abstract, pp. 4, 9, 16.

England his letters had gone free "under the frank of the late Post-master-General, Lord Rosse."[19] John W. Parker, publisher to the University of Cambridge, admitted evading postage in various ways, including the use of franks "volunteered by public officials." Mr. L. F. de Porquet, a publisher and scholastic agent, declared that a very large number of his letters from schoolmasters and teachers were "franked by parties who have nothing to do with this inquiry."[20]

Evasion was widely practiced by the use of newspapers. Rowland Hill had told in his pamphlet of a "friend of mine" who when in Scotland in 1823 had kept his family informed of the state of his health by the use of old newspapers, each franked, as was then necessary, with the name of a member of Parliament. If the traveler used the name of Sir Francis Burdett, for example, it meant vigorous health. If Lord Eldon's name had been used, it would have been enough warning to hurry help to a very sick traveler. Rowland Hill later admitted that "this friend of mine" was himself.[21] Advertisements in newspapers were marked in order to give information. Sympathetic ink was employed, printed letters were pricked on a pre-arranged plan, and "even the dashes and ornaments of penmanship might carry a meaning." A "bygone" (old) newspaper was used by some as a "preconcerted signal of the occurrence of a certain event!" A device for sending trade information was the variation in the address on the newspaper sent to a regular correspondent. Thus, if Brown of London wanted to let Smith of Edinburgh know about the state of the market in tea and sugar, he would vary the name and address. "Mr. Smith" meant Monday, "Mr. John Smith" Tuesday, "Mr. J. Smith" Wednesday, etc. Differences in the writing of his business as "Grocer" and "Tea Dealer" would indicate whether the price of tea was rising or falling, whether the market was dull, what was the state of the sugar trade, etc. Thus, in an example given, "Mr. Smith, Tea Dealer" would indicate that the price of tea was rising on Monday.[22]

Another way of evading postage was by sending a letter for which the receiver would decline payment. A well-known example

---

[19] This was not unlike the experience of Sir Walter Scott, though he was not available for the Committee, having died in 1832. In 1828 Scott wrote from Edinburgh to a Miss Wagner in Liverpool: "Any parcel will reach me safely addressed under cover to Francis Freeling, Esq., General Post Office." See *Nineteenth Century* XXXVII (Feb. 1895), 272.

[20] *3rd Rep.*, 1st Abstract, pp. 35, 37, 46.

[21] *Post Office Reform*, pp. 91-92; G.B. Hill, *op. cit.*, I, 240.

[22] Ashurst, *op. cit.*, pp. 29-30.

occurred in the experience of Samuel Taylor Coleridge. One day, when passing a cottage near Keswick in the Lake District where a letter carrier was demanding a shilling for a letter, which the woman of the house declined to pay, Coleridge obligingly paid the postage, although he admitted that he had not a shilling that he could spare. When the carrier was out of sight, the woman said the letter was from her son, who took this means of letting her know that he was well. The letter, which was not meant to be paid for, was found when opened to be blank. The anecdote was used by Rowland Hill in his *Post Office Reform*, and the Committee refers to the practice as being widespread among the lower classes.[23] The Coleridge story has had an extensive history. Harriet Martineau in her *History of England* ascribed the experience to Rowland Hill, and even when this was corrected in the later editions, she appears to consider Coleridge's little misadventure the chief cause for the awakening of Hill's interest in postal reform! The story has been used by many other writers, often in hardly recognizable form.[24]

The law was extensively evaded by the illegal carriage of letters, especially in the neighborhood of large towns. Women and children were often used as collectors. The stage coach was also a letter carrier, large quantities of letters going in parcels. Booksellers' shipments were also used for letters: they were commonly left at any of the large booksellers along with 2d each, and were sent to all parts of the country for this sum. It was found that weavers' bags were letter bags as well, in the neighborhood of Glasgow. "Family boxes" of provisions sent from a farmer once or twice a week to a son in the University—Glasgow again—was the carrier, as well, of all the letters of the farm neighborhood. One witness asserted that the thriving town of Walsall, in the neighborhood of Birmingham, did not send one-fiftieth of its letters to nearby towns through the post. Glasgow

[23] *Letters, Conversations, and Recollections of Samuel Taylor Coleridge* (1836), II, 114; *Post Office Reform*, p. 102; *3rd Rep. Sel. Com. on Postage*, p. 12.

[24] In *La Grande Encyclopédie*, Rowland Hill, at a modest inn in *Ireland* in 1836, was served by a *jeune fille fort bavarde*: she told of writing every week to her fiancé in London, sending only an envelope (!) with marks traced on it. The *Grand Dictionnaire* of Larousse has Hill pay for a letter in the north of England—a letter that came from the maid's brother. The incident led him, according to the account, to think of means of preventing such frauds. Rothschild's *Histoire de la Poste*, II, 49-51, has Hill in Scotland this time, paying for a letter refused by a young lady who got news in this way from her fiancé in London. The Spanish *Enciclopedia universal illustrada* (1927) LV, 61, ascribes the experience to Rowland Hill. In *Her Majesty's Mails* (p. 120), William Lewins has the woman, who refused the letter for which Coleridge paid, not a cottager, but a barmaid hearing from her brother, and there were "hieroglyphics" on the back of the letter.

letters, it was declared, went by illegal conveyance ten times as frequently as by post. Richard Cobden testified that five-sixths of the letters that were sent to London from Manchester did not pass through the Post Office.[25]

One of the most surprising admissions was made by John Reid, a former bookseller and publisher in Glasgow, who was able to be particularly frank about his previous practices. He had carried on evasion as a system for the past eight years. His firm scarcely ever sent their letters by post, "having other ways of transmission that were equally certain." He declared that he still practiced evasion, saying that he had a letter in his pocket—it cost him 2d—"which he had received from Glasgow this morning, an hour and a half sooner than he would have received it by the Post Office." Reid was equally frank in saying that he saw no need for acquiescing in a bad law, even if his conscience would not allow him to make use of the Post Office illegally![26]

The evidence for evasion was so abundant that the Post Office officials admitted a fact at which everybody had more or less winked in the past. Secretary Maberly held that it was likely to grow worse with the increase of transportation facilities. Steam navigation between Ireland and England had deflected letters from the regular routes. Now that there were twelve trains a day each way between Manchester and Liverpool, the railway was largely used for parcels that might carry as many as five hundred letters at the cost of a shilling. There was every reason to believe that high postage was defeating its own object.[27]

A large body of possible correspondence was suppressed by the high postage. Businessmen's remittances were not acknowledged because of the cost, printer's proof was inadequately checked since the expense often prevented its going out of town to the author. The Society for the Diffusion of Useful Knowledge believed its correspondence would greatly increase with low postage. The Religious Tract Society assured the Committee that it was greatly hampered in its correspondence. Trading firms were very sure of the advantages of cheap postage. One Manchester house expressed itself in the following fashion: "We should consider the general reduction of the rate to one penny as one of the greatest boons that could possibly be conferred on the trading interest: indeed, if we

[25] *3rd Rep. Sel. Com. on Postage*, pp. 13-16. [26] *Ibid.*, 1st Abstract, p. 42.
[27] *3rd Rep.*, p. 15; Ashurst, *op. cit.*, p. 71.

were asked what favor as mercantile men we should desire from government, we should not hesitate a moment to desire the change proposed as one of almost equal importance but of greater safety than even the repeal of the Corn Laws."[28]

The relief that it would bring to the poor was certainly an important argument to the advocates of low postage. With education spreading more and more generally among the poorer classes, the possibility of correspondence was great, provided the expense did not smother the desire. A working hosier of Nottingham declared to the Committee that he had given his wife instructions not to take letters in unless they came from particular persons. He held that the number of letters written by the working classes did not average more than one letter a person in a year.[29] Cobden told the Committee that "we have 50,000 Irish in Manchester who are almost as precluded as though they lived in New South Wales, from all correspondence with their relatives in Ireland." A postmaster in western England told of a laboring man who received a letter from his daughter upon which the charge was eightpence. He at first hesitated to receive it, saying "it would take a loaf of bread from his other children." This "pinching of the affections" as well as the weakening of the ties of blood was brought out by the instance of a person being unaware of the death of his relative for six or eight months, because the postage could not be afforded.[30] It was believed also that high postage was "not only a bar to the education of the poor, but to their keeping up that amount of education which they had already attained."

Much discussion and testimony occurred over the extent of the reduction needed to free this correspondence or bring it into legal channels, and estimates varied as to the amount of increase that might be expected. Hill had stated in his pamphlet that a sixfold increase would take care of the drop in postage rates, and he had expected little, if any, loss to the revenue.[31] Before the Committee, he held that the introduction of the penny rate might mean a temporary loss of about one-eighth of the income of the Post Office. But he was sure that "there is no reason for believing that the proposed reduction in postage will at all diminish the revenue of the country."[32]

---

[28] Ashurst, *op. cit.*, p. 59.
[30] *Ibid.*, p. 24.
[32] *Ibid.*, p. 56, and First Abstract, pp. 7-8, and also his "Facts and Figures as to the

[29] *3rd Rep. Sel. Com. on Postage*, pp. 21-23.
[31] See above, p. 271.

The heads of the Post Office departments were sharply at variance with Rowland Hill as to the effect on the revenue from any extensive reduction of postage. Lord Lichfield said before the Select Committee that a penny letter would require an increase of correspondence to 550,000,000 letters, and to him this was "impossible." Col. Maberly believed any reduction in rates, however trifling, "would in the first instance be attended with a considerable loss." He paid his respects to Hill's suggestions as follows: "He considers the whole scheme of Mr. Hill as utterly fallacious, and thought so from the first moment he read the pamphlet. . . . The plan appeared to him a most preposterous one, utterly unsupported by facts and resting entirely on assumption." Maberly's considered judgment on the effect of reducing the rates to a penny was that "the revenue would not recover itself for forty or fifty years." Robert Smith, in charge of the Twopenny Post Office in London, held that a reduction there from 2d to 1d would so affect the revenue that it would not recover for two or three years. And it was in his jurisdiction that Hill wanted his plan first tried.[33]

The recommendations of the Wallace Committee did not constitute a complete acceptance of the Hill plan. They agreed to the idea of a uniform rate: "The Committee are of opinion that the nearest approach to a fair system would be to charge a uniform rate of postage between one post-town and another, whatever may be the distance." They held this to be highly desirable, "not only on account of its abstract fairness, but because it would tend in a great degree to simplify and economize the business of the Post Office.[34] They also favored payment in advance at a lower rate by the use of "stamped paper," but did not recommend prepayment as compulsory. They felt, however, that the use of stamps or stamped paper should be made compulsory "as soon as warranted by experience." They also agreed that a charge by weight would be fairer than the present system, that it would be more acceptable to the public, and would tend to prevent fraud and error.[35]

The Committee found agreement difficult as to the rate to recom-

Increase of Letters," which was printed as a number of the *Post Circular*, and reprinted in G. B. Hill, *op. cit.*, I, 534-38.

[33] *3rd Rep. Sel. Com. on Postage*, 1st Abstract, pp. 11, 18, 26; 2nd Abstract, pp. 11, 18.

[34] *Ibid.*, p. 31; *Br. Almanac* (1839), Companion, p. 109.

[35] The motion for the establishment of a uniform rate was passed only by the casting vote of the chairman, Mr. Wallace. G. B. Hill, *op. cit.*, I, 327.

mend. Warburton's motion for a penny per half-ounce was lost, as well as the proposal for 1½d. The Committee finally agreed on 2d as the uniform rate, with a penny for each additional half-ounce. The recommendations included the hope that "as soon as the state of the revenue will admit of the risking of a large temporary reduction, it will be expedient to charge all inland letters at one penny per half ounce." They agreed that a penny charge be made for prepaid letters going no farther than fifteen miles, influenced in making this recommendation by the strong evidence of "evasion of postage between neighboring towns." The hesitation of the Committee and especially of the members who were in the government can be understood if the state of the revenue is recalled. Although there had been a large surplus the year before the appearance of *Post Office Reform*, the government faced deficits in 1838 and 1839.[36]

Apart from the recommendations already noted, the most important one was the proposal for the abolition of franking. The Select Committee believed this to be only fair, since it was enjoyed by those better able to pay, and was liable to much abuse. As some five million franks were used annually by members of the two houses of Parliament, the ending of the privilege would greatly assist in keeping up the revenue.[37]

[36] See above, p. 261n.
[37] *3rd Rep. Sel. Com. on Postage*, p. 62.

It Only Costs a Penny

UNIFORM penny postage resulted from varied influences. Robert Wallace had begun his incessant efforts as early as 1833. The ten reports of the Commissioners on Post Office Management came out during the years 1835 to 1838. The three reports of the Wallace Committee were issued in 1837 and 1838. The appearance of Rowland Hill's *Post Office Reform* in 1837 gave a great stimulus to the popular demand for reform by presenting a definite set of striking suggestions. The Mercantile Committee carefully fostered the public interest under the guidance of its vigorous Secretary, Henry Cole: more efficient and cheaper postal arrangements naturally appealed to the business world.

Humanitarians, especially educators of the common man, gave the movement enthusiastic support. Charles Knight, through the Society for the Diffusion of Useful Knowledge, had given penny postage hearty allegiance. His suggestion of the use of prepaid envelopes for newspapers, it will be recalled, had prompted Rowland Hill's plan for the prepayment of letters. The "Year Book of General Information" that accompanied Knight's *British Almanac* for 1838 had a full report on the "New System of the Twopenny Post," and the Companion for 1839 noticed very favorably "The Uniform Penny Postage" in an article that reinforced the recommendations of the Wallace Committee. In summarizing the work of the Committee, the article stated the outlook for postal reform: "The progress this question has made in the public mind gives great hope of its success. Scarcely two years have passed since its projector modestly sent the scheme in a small pamphlet to make its way in the world. Its novelty startled everyone, and it seemed a thing too good to be feasible. It has been talked over by the whole country, and the result is a conviction that it is no idle dream."[1]

The chorus of approval was becoming very widespread. At the first appearance of *Post Office Reform*, the proposal of prepayment seemed very "bold" to *Chambers' Edinburgh Journal*. By the spring of 1839, however, this periodical was giving the plan its complete support.[2] One of the most valuable advocates of the reform was the *Spectator*, edited by Rintoul. *Fraser's Magazine* cordially backed the plan, declaring in August 1838 that the interest in the scheme "is intense in all classes and pervades the length and breadth of the land." It even poured ridicule on Lord Lichfield, "nominally the head of the Post Office, but really the tail of the jockeys of Newmarket."[3] The *Athenaeum* gave its assistance in several leaders during the height of the agitation.[4]

The newspaper press was nearly unanimous in giving aid. The "provincial" papers, especially, saw the value of uniform postage to their constituents. One number of the *Post Circular* listed eighty-seven country newspapers favoring penny postage. The London papers were not so single-minded at first, but the leading newspapers in the capital came to the aid of the movement long before its acceptance. The *Times* asserted that uniform penny postage "may well be termed the cause of the whole people against the small coterie of place holders in St. Martins-le-Grand and its dependencies." The *Morning Post* believed the reform "justified by common sense," and the *Standard* was sure of its value to popular education.[5]

When the final report of the Wallace Committee appeared, its welcome almost took the form of an assault on one of the remaining strongholds of the old regime. The situation was not unlike that before the passage of the Reform Bill of 1832, though, of course, on a smaller scale.

On March 23, 1839, a remarkable scene occurred in the House of Commons. The member for Birmingham desired to present a petition for penny postage. Thereupon, the Speaker desired members who had other petitions on the same subject to bring them forward.

[1] Page 107.
[2] VI (May 20, 1837), 131; VIII (April 27, 1839), 108-9.
[3] XVIII, 250, 252.
[4] See, e.g., April 21 and 28, 1838.
[5] Quoted in *Edinburgh Review*, LXX, 289. See also G. B. Hill, *op. cit.*, I, 341.

As a result, a large number of the members "advanced in a crowd to present them, amidst cheering on all sides."[6] Both Houses of Parliament were "overwhelmed with petitions" during the session of 1839, in the words of Henry Warburton.[7] We have found that in the previous session, 1837-38, Parliament had received 320 petitions signed by nearly 9000 persons. During 1839 the flow became torrential. The total reached the amazing figure of over 2000 petitions, and they carried the signatures of over a quarter of a million people.[8] One of the most remarkable petitions was presented by the Duke of Richmond, a former Postmaster-General. It was from the City of London, and bore the signatures of the Lord Mayor and 12,500 of the merchants of the City. What made it outstanding was the speed with which it had been prepared: the Duke told the House of Lords that he understood it had been signed in twelve hours. This petition asked for "no delay in the introduction of so important a measure as a uniform penny postage."[9]

The government was hesitant and with some reason. Lord Melbourne's Whig administration was finding the going pretty rough. The deficit in the budget, the troubles in Ireland, the Durham report on Canada, the deadlock in Jamaica over the abolition of slavery, all culminated during this spring. In fact, Melbourne resigned early in May 1839, and Peel was asked to form a government, but declined to do so when the young Queen refused to dismiss the Whig ladies of the bedchamber. Whereupon Melbourne returned and carried on until August of 1841.

It was just as these troubles were causing the ministry so much worry that a deputation in behalf of penny postage waited on the Prime Minister. Some 150 members of Parliament, chiefly his supporters, urged adoption of the reform as a measure "which a Liberal party had a just right to expect from a Liberal administration."[10] Daniel O'Connell added a word for Ireland. "My countrymen do not smuggle [letters]," he said, "for the high postage works a total prohibition to them. They are too poor to find out secondary conveyances, and if you shut the Post Office to them, which you do now, you shut out warm hearts and generous affections from home, kindred,

[6] *Post Circular*, no. 12, as quoted in G. B. Hill, *op. cit.*, I, 339.
[7] *Parl. Deb.*, 3rd s., XLIX, 302.
[8] *Br. Almanac* (1840), Companion, p. 220.
[9] *Parl. Deb.*, 3rd s., XLIX, 687; *Mirror of Parliament* (1839), p. 3678.
[10] The words of Henry Warburton, who was the leader of the deputation in the absence of Robert Wallace. Cole, *op. cit.*, I, 48.

and friends." Attorney-General Sir John Campbell said that his constituents in Edinburgh were in favor of it, that the feeling was "general and intense," and not limited to a political party. Mr. Moffatt of the Mercantile Committee, a leading London merchant, declared that if the government felt any doubt as to the safety of the revenue and would be willing to farm out the Post Office "there would be no difficulty in finding a body of high mercantile character to carry out the plan proposed and secure to the government the full amount of the revenue which is now obtained from the Post Office."[11]

The government was not so sure as Mr. Moffatt of the financial outcome. Lord John Russell, the leader in the House of Commons, tells in his *Recollections* that the Cabinet was unanimous for the measure, as conferring great benefits on the public. At the same time he felt sure that it would mean a temporary deficit.[12] The government, however, really had little choice: public opinion was too strong, and the ministry's fortunes at such an ebb that penny postage, despite all its dangers, might well help to strengthen the government.

Finally the Chancellor of the Exchequer, Thomas Spring-Rice, moved in July 1839 that the report of the committee be received. The recommendation of the Wallace Committee that twopence be the uniform rate was by that time outdated, in view of the widespread demand for penny postage. The Chancellor, therefore, proposed to the House of Commons a resolution: "To reduce the postage charged on letters to one uniform rate of one penny, . . . Parliamentary privilege of franking to be abolished and official franking strictly regulated; this House pledging itself at the same time to make good any deficiency of the revenue which may be occasioned by such alteration of the rates of the existing duties." A long debate ensued. When the Conservatives led by Peel criticized the pledge, fearing a possible deficiency in the revenue, the Chancellor stressed the great benefit that would be felt "at once," especially among the lower classes. He believed that the loss would be very considerable at the outset. "Mr. Hill supposes," added the Chancellor, "that the loss will be about £400,000: I wish I could believe that it would be so little." Robert Wallace thought there might be a loss of £500,000 or £600,000 the first year, but believed that "the revenue in the

[11] *Ibid.*, I, 51-52; *Br. Almanac* (1839), Companion, p. 107.
[12] *Recollections and Suggestions* (1875), p. 268; *Mirror of Parliament* (1839), p. 2578.

course of another year would be equal to its present amount." And he prophesied that the loss of the first year would be made up in three years. Henry Warburton objected to looking at the proposal as a mere financial measure, for the public rightly viewed the Post Office as an institution whose "primary object was to contribute to their convenience." On a division, the advocates of penny postage were victorious two to one.[13]

Shortly afterwards a penny postage bill began its course through the two houses. It was introduced in the House of Commons by the Chancellor of the Exchequer on July 18, 1839. On the second reading, the Conservatives again opposed the measure, but their opposition was so perfunctory that there was no division: the bill was ready for the House of Lords before the end of the month. Would the Lords dare to scuttle this measure, or would they retreat when faced by the demand of public opinion, as they had done on the Great Reform Bill seven years before?[14] The Mercantile Committee endeavored to see the Duke of Wellington on the matter, but he declined to be interviewed. Thereupon they induced Rowland Hill to write the Duke in behalf of the measure and to send a copy of "Facts and Estimates as to the Increase of Letters." Rowland Hill stated in his communication to the Duke that "if the postage were reduced to one penny the revenue would be more likely to gain than to suffer."[15]

When the bill came up for the fateful second reading in August, Lord Melbourne was cautious about the financial arrangements, but justified the government's course on the "very general feeling and general concurrence of all parties in favour of the plan." The Conservative opposition was chiefly represented by the Postmaster-General and the Duke of Wellington. Lichfield, though sure of a considerable loss, supported the measure because of the universal demand. The victor of Waterloo also retreated gracefully before the public insistence, though he said that he "never felt more reluctant that he did to give the vote which he should give on this question." He doubted whether there would be a great increase in correspond-

---

[13] *Parl. Deb.*, 3rd s., XLVIII, 1384; XLIX, 277-307; *Mirror of Parliament* (1839), p. 3679.

[14] *Parl. Deb.*, 3rd s., XLIX, 494, 623-41. Only a year before a second effort had been made to replace the Postmaster-General by a board of commissioners. But, like the earlier attempt, the bill passed the Commons but was defeated in the House of Lords. See *ibid.*, XLIV, 586, 1112, and above, p. 252.

[15] G. B. Hill, *op. cit.*, I, 354. He had been much more cautious, as we have found, in his public statements.

ence: a poor man would not go ten or fifteen miles to post a letter "merely because the Post Office only charged a penny." His rambling speech was concluded with the words: "I shall, though with great reluctance and pain, vote for the bill, and earnestly recommend you to do likewise." There was no division on the bill, and on the third reading no debate. The royal assent made the bill law on August 17.[16]

The general satisfaction is well reflected in an American publication. *Niles National Register* for September 14 noted the victory in its "correspondence of the New York Express." "The passage of the penny postal bill to a law has given great satisfaction; and people here [that is, in London] seem to know little of what has been done during the session, excepting that the penny postal bill has passed. This is the most important act of the session, and will naturally attract great attention to the postal tax in the United States. . . . In a mercantile point of view it is most important, and we anticipate a considerable increase of trade and commerce in consequence."[17]

The Postage Act was a provisional measure, allowing the Treasury to regulate the postal duties. According to the Act the charges were to be reduced to a uniform rate of one penny for a given weight. The Treasury was authorized, as well, to abolish franking and to provide stamped paper and covers and adhesive stamps.[18] The measure was tentative because the resulting state of the revenue might require a modification of the scheme. In addition, careful study and much preparation was needed before the plan could be put into force. No provision, for example, had yet been made for stamped covers and adhesives.

One criticism causing some stir at the time of the victory came from the stationers. They feared that the regulations regarding stamped paper and stamped covers might mean a government contract for a favored few, thereby affecting the sales of letter paper. This objection to the plan was met by providing for a wider use of the prepaying stamp. It was to be "struck" not only on official paper

---

[16] *Parl. Deb.*, 3rd s., XLIX, 1207-38; *Mirror of Parliament* (1839), pp. 4667-73.

[17] LVII, 38. In June of the next year (1840) Daniel Webster presented a resolution in Congress regarding "the use of stamps or stamped covers" together "with a large reduction of the rates of postage." See below, p. 379.

[18] 2 & 3 Vict., c.52. The arrangements were to be effective until Oct. 5, 1840. It was a year later that a thirty-page act replaced the provisional one, with full details as to rates, weight, prepayment, etc. 3 & 4 Vict., c.96 (August 10, 1840).

and envelopes and adhesives, but "on paper of any description which the public may send to the Stamp Office for that purpose."[19]

As a matter of fact, stamped envelopes were thought much more likely to receive public favor than the adhesive label. Rowland Hill had suggested the latter in his *Post Office Reform* as an alternative where stamped envelopes or stamped paper were not easily available. Before the Select Committee on Postage, John Wood had not been favorable to the adhesive on the ground that it would be very likely to rub off. He thought an adhesive, like a medicine label, might be printed on Dickinson paper, that is, paper with silk threads running through it. Dickinson himself was of the opinion that an adhesive might be of value where a cover was not a "sufficient envelope," but did not think that a great many labels would be used because of the trouble of pasting them on letters: "If the public had to affix labels, they would rather have a cover than a label."[20]

Controversy on the subject of postage reform was not yet over. It was greatly enlivened in October by a bitter attack on penny postage in the *Quarterly Review*. This belated consideration of Hill's book and of the reports of the Select Committee was written by J. W. Croker.[21] He accused Wallace of seeking notoriety by his constant "hammering" for six or seven years. Hill was credited with a "bold novelty," which had even dazzled Croker at first. But sounder reflection had convinced the reviewer that "Mr. Hill's plan has broken down on almost every point." Croker denied that only good moral influences would work through the enlarged postal service, asserted that it was intended originally as a convenience to trade, and affirmed the fairness of charging more for a letter to Edinburgh than one to Barnet. "The gods must annihilate time and space," wrote Croker, "before a uniform rate of postage can be reasonable or just." When he came to treat Hill's calculations of the increase in correspondence, Croker declared that "our feeble mind has no capacity to follow them." He denied the value of the analogy of the increased use of coffee, tea and silk as a result of lowered duties. It would not apply to a "matter in itself

[19] *Parl. Deb.*, 3rd s., XLIX, 279; *Br. Almanac* (1840), Companion, p. 220; *Gentleman's Magazine*, n.s., XIII (Feb. 1840), p. 197.
[20] *1st Rep. Sel. Com. on Postage*, questions 2215 and 2455.
[21] Croker is too well known to need identification. As one of the founders of the *Quarterly*, and a brilliant Tory both with tongue and pen, no one was better able to pick flaws in the scheme.

troublesome, if not distasteful, like letter writing." And he asked whether, if the tax were taken off drugs, one would swallow any more physic than one could help. A long and severe indictment was concluded by the wish "that the results of this extraordinary affair may not prove a gigantic exemplification of the old proverb—penny wise and pound foolish."[22]

Sidney Smith, prominent clergyman and essayist, spoke of the "nonsense of this penny postage." Another opponent of importance was the economist, J. R. McCulloch, who has already been quoted as a believer in speedy postal communication. But he came out against Hill's plan, believing that a change from a relatively high rate of postage to one penny was "to rush from one extreme to another, and to endanger a considerable amount of revenue without an equivalent advantage." A moderate drop, with circulars going at a penny or twopence, would have done away, to his mind, with all this clamor for a uniform penny rate.[23]

The worry uppermost in the mind of Rowland Hill, after the successful passage of the bill, was not the opposition of Croker or the hostility of McCulloch. The projector of penny postage was concerned with the way in which the plan would be received by, and tried out in, the Post Office. Colonel Maberly and Lord Lichfield were so sure of its failure that they might well assist the wreckage of the plan by a half-hearted support of the changes. Moreover, Hill had hoped from the start that its adoption would result in a better government position than the one he now held as Secretary of the South Australia Commissioners. He was not disappointed. Early in September he received the offer of a two-year appointment from the Chancellor of the Exchequer, Sir Francis Baring.[24] But the salary offer of £500—the same as he was then receiving—was so unsatisfactory that, with the aid of his brother Matthew, he wrote a strong letter to the Chancellor. As a result, the salary was raised to £1500 a year, though the term of service remained for two years only. Nor was Hill to be attached to the Post Office but to the Treasury, and he

---

[22] LXIV (October 1839), 513-74. So well-written and biting attack needed a refutation. It appeared in the *Edinburgh Review* (LXX, 286-300) for January 1840, from the pen of Matthew Hill. Another reply to the "Tory Croaker" was written by Henry Cole, and was published in the *London and Westminster Review* (XXXIII, 263-71). See Cole, *Fifty Years of Public Work*, I, 65.

[23] Baines, *On the Track of the Mail Coach*, pp. 307-8. Rowland Hill attributed McCulloch's opposition to his recent appointment in the Stationery Department. See G. B. Hill, *op. cit.*, I, 338.

[24] Sir Francis Baring had just replaced Thomas Spring-Rice as Chancellor.

could not give orders to the Post Office but only make recommendations to the Treasury.[25]

After making a visit to France at the Chancellor's suggestion, Hill set to work on the gradual introduction of penny postage. He proposed the prepaid penny rate at once for the London District, but a maximum charge of 4d for the rest of the country. This transitional rate was defended as preparing the Post Office officials for the later reduction to a penny. This first step was taken on December 5; the maximum charge for domestic letters not over half an ounce in weight became 4d.[26]

The public was greatly dissatisfied, believing that the 4d rate was evidence of the government's desire to cheat them of the complete reform. Even Rowland Hill came in for criticism through this halfhearted proceeding. On account of the clamor, the Treasury and Mr. Hill decided on the general introduction of penny postage early in January 1840, even though the arrangements for stamps were not far enough along to make their use possible by so early a date. January 10 was chosen as the time when "a letter not exceeding half an ounce may be sent from any part of the United Kingdom, to any other part, for one penny, if paid when posted."

Franking for members of Parliament was to cease at the same time. Henceforth members of Parliament and of the government could make free use of the mails for official purposes only. The older "free" cancellations were replaced by post-paid envelopes and wrappers for the use of members of Parliament. The Queen, who had been represented by Henry Cole's famous circular as deeply interested in the reform of the Post Office, gave up her privilege of franking at the same time. It proved a popular act for the young Queen to set a voluntary example to those deprived of the privilege. Henceforth she paid the normal charge for her letters.[27]

[25] He entered on his new duties September 16, 1839. Henry Cole, at Hill's request, was made his assistant. Rowland Hill's relation to the Post Office was strikingly like that of Palmer, when he was allowed to introduce the mail coach. Palmer's salary was the same, and he was attached to the Treasury. Palmer found friction inevitable, and Hill's experience was similar. See G. B. Hill, op. cit., I, 370.

[26] The minute is given in full in the Br. Almanac (1840), Companion, pp. 261-63. It is dated Nov. 12. Ten days later a Treasury warrant appeared in the London Gazette: it is reprinted in part in the Bulletin of the Postal History Society, no. 13 (1940).

[27] The "franking world" that died in January 1840 is well depicted in Disraeli's novel, Endymion, chap. XII. About the time of the Reform Bill of 1832 Lord Ferrars had been compelled to retire to the country. But the high cost of letters hardly applied to the Ferrars. "They had never paid postage. They were born and had always lived in the franking world, and although Mr. Ferrars had now himself lost the privilege, still

POST OFFICE REGULATIONS.

On and after the 10th January,
a Letter not exceeding **half an ounce in weight,** may be sent from any part of the United Kingdom, to any other part, for **One Penny,** if paid when posted, or for **Twopence** if paid when delivered.

THE SCALE OF RATES,

If paid when posted, is as follows, for all Letters, whether sent by the General or by any Local Post,

Not exceeding ½ Ounce ....**One Penny.**

Exceeding ½ Ounce, but not exceeding 1 Ounce. . **Twopence.**

Ditto 1 Ounce.................2 Ounces **Fourpence.**

Ditto 2 Ounces ....3 Ounces **Sixpence.**

and so on; an additional Two-pence for every additional Ounce. With but few exceptions, the WEIGHT is limited to Sixteen Ounces.

If not paid when posted, double the above Rates are charged on Inland Letters.

COLONIAL LETTERS.

If sent by Packet Twelve Times, if by Private Ship Eight Times, the above Rates.

FOREIGN LETTERS.

The Packet Rates which vary, will be seen at the Post Office. The Ship Rates are the same as the Ship Rates for Colonial Letters.

As regards Foreign and Colonial Letters, there is no limitation as to weight. All sent outwards, with a few exceptions, which may be learnt at the Post Office, must be paid when posted as heretofore.

Letters intended to go by Private Ship must be marked "*Ship Letter.*"

Some arrangements of minor importance, which are omitted in this Notice, may be seen in that placarded at the Post Office.

No Articles should be transmitted by Post, which are liable to *injury,* by being stamped, or by being crushed in the Bags.

It is particularly requested that all Letters may be *fully* and *legibly* *addressed,* and *posted as early* as convenient.

January 7th, 1840.

By Authority:—J. Hartnell, London.

A poster announcing the introduction of penny postage, 1840.

When penny postage was introduced on January 10, 1840, the increase in the number of letters was greater than had occurred under the transitional arrangements, but still not as much as the friends of penny postage wished. In the London District Post, the increase had been 30 per cent for a week in December over a similar period in November before any change had taken place. The increase in February, as compared with November, was 70 per cent. For the General Post, the record was more encouraging. During the week in February, the number of letters rose from a 25 per cent increase in December to a 120 per cent increase in February over the number carried before any change had been made.[28]

The beginning of penny postage was without the benefit of stamps. It was not until early in May that the stamps were ready, a Treasury minute of April 22 announcing May 6 as the day when prepayment by stamps should begin. Thus the anniversary of the adhesive postage stamp and the stamped envelope is almost four months later than that for penny postage. But it was some time before prepayment was made compulsory, though unpaid letters continued to be charged double. By the middle of 1840 the unpaid letters had dropped to 10 per cent of those that were prepaid. Nor was the use of the stamp for prepayment made compulsory at the outset, for the very good reason that stamps and stamped paper could not be supplied at once to all the offices. As a matter of fact, the number of letters prepaid without stamps largely exceeded those prepaid with stamps, as it took some time for the public to accustom itself to the new device.[29]

Besides the novelty for the letter writer of 1840 of sending his letter for a penny and having that penny prepaid by a small piece of paper "with a glutinous wash at the back," an even greater change in habit was the use of an envelope to enclose the actual letter, in place of the centuries-old custom of folding the letter and writing an address on the outer face of the folded sheet. Previous to 1839 the use of an envelope would have meant a charge for it as an extra piece

---

all their correspondents were frankers, and they addressed their letters without compunction to those who were free."

It might be added that the sovereign's right of franking was revived on the death of Queen Victoria in 1901, and has been continued by the successors of Edward VII. Royal letters are not autographed, but a monogram is impressed by a private hand-stamp.

For the official paid stamps used after the abolition of franking, see Alcock & Holland, *op. cit.*, pp. 220, 342-46.

[28] *Br. Almanac* (1841), Companion, p. 100, where elaborate comparisons are to be found.

[29] For a fuller account of the origin and introduction of stamps, see the next chapter.

of paper. The "bon ton" were using them before 1840 to some extent. Dickinson, the paper maker, referred to them before the Select Committee in 1838 as the "new fashioned envelopes, with the four corners of the paper meeting under the seal."[30]

At first the envelopes were closed by the use of the time-honored sealing wax, or an adhesive wafer, which bound the flap over the opening at the back. But before the end of the year someone had suggested that "if a small lick of gum which is used for the stamp were put at the angle where the wafer or wax is put" it would save the use of a wafer. Stamped envelopes issued by the government were not provided with a gummed flap until 1850. It was a long time, of course, before the use of sealing wax was largely discontinued: it still is in some use. Basil Hall, the writer who has just been quoted as to the new way to seal envelopes, wrote in December 1840: "Every one now uses envelopes."[31]

Another novel experience was the way in which letters were now received. Instead of answering the knock at the front door, and hearing some such greeting as "Two letters, two shillings sevenpence halfpenny," the householder or servant simply took the letters from the house letter box. Rowland Hill had suggested in his pamphlet, as we have found, that every house might be provided with a box in which the carrier would drop his letters. Harriet Martineau wrote amusingly of the effect of this system, combined with prepayment. "We are all," she wrote, "putting up our letter boxes on our hall doors with great glee, anticipating the hearing from brothers and sisters—a line or two almost every day. The slips in the door are to save the postmen time, the great point being how many letters may be delivered within a given time, the postage being paid in the price of the envelope or paper. So all who wish well to the plan are having slips in their doors." Not all acquiesced in the suggestion of letter boxes. One noble lord, the Marquis of Londonderry, wrote indignantly to the Postmaster-General, asking him if the Post Office actually expected him "to cut a slit in his mahogany door."[32]

The introduction of penny postage brought about a social change

[30] *1st Rep. Sel. Com. on Postage,* ques. 2413; C. F. D. Marshall, *The British Post Office,* p. 188.

[31] Letter to Rowland Hill, in G. B. Hill, *op. cit.,* I, 418. He was exaggerating. In a cartoon of Sir James Graham prying into letters at the Post Office—it appeared in *Punch* in 1844—he is shown peeking into a letter that had been folded. See below, p. 342.

[32] G. B. Hill, *op. cit.,* I, 390; II, 91. The letter box was on the *inside* of the hall door, a practice still almost universal in Great Britain.

that can hardly be overestimated. Disraeli pictured well the contrast between the old and the new: "It is difficult for us who live in an age of railroads, telegraphs, penny posts, and penny newspapers, to realize how uneventful, how limited in thought and feeling, as well as in incident, was the life of an English family of retired habits and limited means only forty years ago."[33] A revolution had taken place. Elizabeth Barrett Browning wrote to an American friend at the time, "Why will you not as a nation embrace our penny post scheme, and hold our envelopes in all acceptation? You do not know—cannot guess—what a wonderful liberty our Rowland Hill has given to British spirits, and how we 'flash a thought' instead of 'wafting' it from our extreme south to our extreme north, paying a penny for our thought, and for the electricity included. I recommend you our penny postage as the most successful revolution since the 'glorious three days' of Paris."[34]

Mrs. Browning and Harriet Martineau seem to have enjoyed the additional letters that came as a result of cheap postage, but there was another view of the matter. Croker had written in his vitriolic attack in the *Quarterly* that "we must write seventy-nine letters a week" to make the scheme a success. And he added that he had neither the time nor the patience, nor seventy-nine possible subjects for letters, nor seventy-nine persons "on the face of the whole earth from whom a letter would be welcome once a year, much less once every week in the year." Others, doubtless, felt the same way, though they may have been less disgruntled. We know that William Wordsworth, for example, disliked the disturbance of his quiet peace in the Lake District. He wrote in February 1841, "The multitude of communications which reach me, especially since the reduction of postage to a trifle, is so great that I have neither time nor eyesight to acknowledge the greatest part of them." He repeated the complaint a month later: "I am so pestered in consequence of the deluge of letters and small pamphlets in prose and verse, that if I were to attend to one half of them I should really have no time for myself."[35]

The grant of penny postage was one of the signal benefactions of the time, in a country where social democracy was, as yet, far from attainment. Harriet Martineau, in the letter already quoted, saw its

[33] *Endymion*, chap. XII. The novel appeared in 1880, though some of the earlier chapters were written in 1872.
[34] *Letters* (1897), I, 135. She had the Revolution of 1830 in mind.
[35] *The Letters of William and Dorothy Wordsworth. The Later Years* (1939), pp. 1066, 1070.

value for the poor, "who can at last write to one another as if they were all M.P.'s." After the plan was established, Richard Cobden wrote Rowland Hill: "It is a terrible engine for upsetting monopoly and corruption; witness our [Anti Corn-Law] League operations, the spawn of your penny postage." He is said to have remarked, on hearing of the passage of the postage bill in 1839, "There go the Corn Laws."[36]

When the servant class, hitherto largely illiterate, began their awkward attempts to write letters, the results were sometimes disconcerting. It took an expert "blindman" at the Dead Letter Office to unravel some of the attempts made by the unlettered in addressing their missives. Rowland Hill, for example, received a letter from a grateful admirer—doubtless an Hibernian—who addressed it to "Mr. Owl Oneill." The change was, in truth, a revolution, not a political one such as that of 1830 in France, but a social change that fittingly followed the British political revolution wrought by the Great Reform Bill.

> Hail joyous day! The Postage Bill
>   Brings blessings great and many:
> And best of all, say what we will,
>   It only costs a penny.

> From John o' Groats to England's End,
>   From Norfolk to Kilkenny,
> A letter now may reach a friend,
>   And only costs a penny.

[36] Cole, *op. cit.*, I, 57; Smyth, *op. cit.*, p. 143.

The Birth of
the Postage Stamp

PENNY postage had a low, uniform rate, along with prepayment, as two of its most important features. They came into effect on January 10, 1840. By that time a third change was already planned—the prepayment by means of stamps of various sorts. Their use, it was believed, would aid greatly in the success of penny postage, for stamped paper could be bought in quantity, and prepaid letters would be handled with greater ease and speed by the Post Office. Any advantages to be gained by the use of stamped paper were held off for some time. The birth-date of the postage stamp proved to be May 6, 1840, although more time was to elapse before stamped paper was generally distributed to the offices throughout the country. Despite these delays attending the introduction of stamps—now so familiar a feature of our daily lives—their use spread rapidly. Their value to the British Post Office was so obvious that they were soon adopted by other countries as a necessary part of their postal services.

The origin of the postage stamp has additional interest because the collecting of postage stamps, or philately, has attained very widespread popularity. The attractiveness of the early stamps soon led persons with a collecting instinct and a feeling for beauty and color to preserve specimens of the various issues, to distinguish varieties and errors, and to arrange their possessions to show the changes in form and design. It is estimated that some fifteen million persons are philatelists. They range from presidents and kings and other men of wealth to the schoolboy attracted by pictures of ships or trains or the portraits of famous men and women.[1] Philately even takes on scientific aspects when men of the keenest intelligence examine the peculiarities and difficulties of the issues of a particular country or even of a single issue. The world's number one stamp, the Penny Black, has been carefully studied.[2]

Stamps of various kinds had been used long before 1840 for paying diverse duties, just as today we have revenue stamps on cigarette packets, on baggage after it has gone through the customs, on legal documents, and even on automobiles to register the payment of the use tax. The similarity of adhesive postage stamps to other revenue stamps was brought out in Richard Cobden's evidence before the Select Committee of 1838, where he refers to the suggested adhesive as a "vignette stamp," and added: "I should be partial to the use of small vignettes, something similar to the stamp on patent medicines."[3]

The stamp tax against which the American colonists made so much objection in the reign of George III was indicated by an attached revenue stamp on vellum, parchment and paper. As the stamp was not easily impressed on parchment, it was embossed on a small piece of paper, which was attached to the sheet of parchment. It might be held in place by gum, which was not very efficient, or by having a strip of tinfoil put through two slits of the document and fastened at the back to hold the stamp in place. To make the attachment doubly secure, a second adhesive piece of paper called a "ticket" covered the ends of the tinfoil clip. Present-day British postage stamps are also general revenue stamps, and so named on the stamp, as the reader will find if he takes the trouble to examine the current issue.

The prepayment of postage had been indicated before 1840 by a stamped "Paid" on the folded letter, and this "Paid" mark is sometimes regarded as an example of a postage stamp before 1840.[4] An early example, possibly the earliest, was a post-paid local service in

[1] The late President Franklin D. Roosevelt, King George V of Great Britain and King Fuad of Egypt were well-known collectors.

[2] See the Bibliography (II, D) for titles of works by Melville, Philbrick & Westoby, E. D. Bacon, Nissen & McGowan. Wright and Creeke's *A History of the Adhesive Stamps of the British Isles* is now regarded as the authoritative treatment of British issues: it was compiled for the Philatelic Society of Great Britain. A useful volume is C. F. Dendy Marshall's *The British Post Office*, in which the historic aspects are treated from a stamp collector's viewpoint.

[3] *2nd Rep. Sel. Com. on Postage*, questions 6733 & 6738, and index, p. 59.

[4] Present-day stamp collectors usually distinguish "paid" marks from postage stamps, and generally collect adhesives and stamps issued since 1840. The well-known British catalogue of Gibbons does not even list stamped envelopes.

Paris, established by François Velayer in 1653. He issued bands of paper bearing his personal stamp and carrying the words *Port-payé*.[5] Dockwra's Penny Post of 1680 may have been inspired by Velayer's short-lived attempt to give Paris a prepaid local post twenty-five years earlier. Dockwra's triangular stamp showing that the penny had been paid is a postmark or stamp indicating prepayment. The penny posts established in other parts of the British Isles after 1765 had a uniform rate, but, in general, the penny was paid on delivery, so that the markings are more truly postmarks than stamps showing prepayment. But the local posts, especially the penny posts of large urban centers like Edinburgh, stamped letters "Paid" as well as "Unpaid."

Letters in the General Post were usually paid for when delivered, though the writer, if he wished, could pay for the letter when it was sent. London paid stamps were in use from the early eighteenth century, but they are not found in the General Post letters from provincial towns until after 1800. Prepayment, however, was not common before 1840. It was so little used that Rowland Hill did not dare impose compulsory prepayment when uniform penny postage was introduced.[6] Yet it is well to know that the principles of the reform were already in existence to some degree: there were penny posts, though local in extent; prepayment was in use; and uniformity of rate was practiced in certain areas. Postmarkings on letters of the franking system can hardly be regarded as early examples of stamps, since such letters were sent free and so marked. The confusion in this whole matter is illustrated by the practice, not uncommon about 1840, of speaking of letters prepaid by adhesive stamps as being "franked," that is, they were sent to their destinations free of any charge after mailing.

Charles Knight had suggested in 1834 that the stamp tax on newspapers be paid by the use of a prepaid wrapper, or, to use his own words, "that unstamped papers pass through the Post Office by the use of franks sold at a penny each." As the reader has already found, the stamp tax on newspapers was lowered in 1836 to a penny a sheet, though Charles Knight's suggestion of the prepaid wrapper was not

---

[5] They bore the date of issue, cost a sou each, could be purchased in quantity, and one could even be enclosed for a reply. These *billets* were dropped in convenient receiving boxes and delivered three times a day. Velayer's arrangements were of short duration. See *La Grande Encyclopédie*, "Timbre-poste," and Rothschild, *op. cit.*, I, 173-75.

[6] G. B. Hill, *op. cit.*, I, 396; *Post Office Reform*, p. 96.

adopted. The tax, however, did amount to a prepaid penny postal charge on newspapers *irrespective* of the distance that they traveled. This proposal by Charles Knight is of some interest, as Rowland Hill declared that the suggestion for stamped covers, which he put forth in the second edition of *Post Office Reform*, grew out of his knowledge of Knight's plan of stamped covers for newspapers.[7]

It was also in the second edition of *Post Office Reform*, appearing in February 1837, that Rowland Hill first mentioned adhesive stamps. They were intended to serve where bearers of letters to the post office were unable to write, and therefore could not redirect the letters they brought, by using a prepaid stamped cover or envelope. To repeat his suggestion: "Perhaps this difficulty might be obviated by using a bit of paper just large enough to bear the stamp, and covered at the back with a glutinous wash, which the bearer might, by applying a little moisture, attach to the back of the letter, so as to avoid the necessity of re-directing it."[8] Out of this tentative proposal to meet a situation where it would not be easy to use stamped covers came the adhesive postage stamp, as *one* of the forms of prepayment.

The Treasury decided to make stamps available in four forms. Owing to the uproar by the stationers, they were to be "struck" on paper furnished by private individuals: when folded for mailing, such paper would have the stamp showing on the outside.[9] A second form was the stamped official cover—a sheet used for writing that would show the stamp when folded and sealed. A third form, the stamped envelope, was thus described: "the stamp being struck on pieces of paper of a lozenge form, of which the stationers and others may manufacture envelopes." The fourth form was the adhesive stamp "on small pieces of paper with a glutinous wash at the back."[10]

The Treasury decided to ask for suggestions on the best form for these varied stamps. It announced, accordingly, a public competition with a prize of £200 for the best proposal and £100 for the second prize. The Treasury wanted ideas on convenience as regards public

[7] See above, pp. 246 ff., 268; Knight, *op. cit.*, II, 249-50; G. B. Hill, *op. cit.*, I, 218, 265.

[8] 2nd ed., p. 45. Rowland Hill takes pains in his autobiography to state that Charles Knight, when he made his suggestion of stamped covers for newspapers, was under no obligation to M. Velayer. He added that "adhesive stamps were as yet undreamed of." Rowland Hill was carefully protecting his right to be called the originator of postage stamps, in view of the claims of others, to which attention will presently be given. See G. B. Hill, *op. cit.*, I, 218, 377.

[9] See above, p. 294.

[10] G. B. Hill, *op. cit.*, I, 383; Wright & Creeke, *op. cit.*, p. xviii, where the warrant is reprinted.

use, security against forgery, ease in checking the stamps in the Post Office and reasonableness in the cost and distribution of the stamps. The public response to the request for suggestions exceeded all expectations, for some 2600 proposals of one kind or another were sent to the Treasury. Many of them were of little value, but others came from expert printers, engravers and men of science, and displayed "much ingenuity," as the official announcement put it. The government did not decide to adopt any one plan "without modification and combination with other arrangements." As a result, four awards instead of two were granted, the four to be for £100 each. The successful competitors were Bogardus and Coffin, acting together, Cheverton, Whiting and Cole.[11]

Bogardus and Coffin would have stamped or engraved labels attached to the letter by means of a seal or wafer, thus avoiding the use of an adhesive stamp. The label or stamp with a hole in the center was to be placed at the back where the letter was sealed, and partly covered by the wafer or wax. One wonders why this award was granted, for it differed widely from the adopted form.[12]

Charles Whiting was a London printer, long interested in postal matters. In 1830, even before Charles Knight's suggestion already mentioned, Whiting had made experimental stamped wrappers for newspapers and printed matter, under the name of "go-frees." They were "stamped envelopes" to carry printed matter, though not intended for printed matter only. He told the Select Committee on Postage: "I made the proposal with reference to printed matter, though I thought written matter would follow as a matter of course." Some of Whiting's essays for stamps were in two colors and were printed on bands to be put around the letters. They were to be canceled by the words "Post Office—Go Free." The cancellation device had a series of fine points around the outside of the circular design for pricking the paper.[13]

Henry Cole, who was one of the winners in the competition, was the editor of the *Post Circular*, which was printed by Charles Whit-

---

[11] Marshall, *op. cit.*, pp. 22-23; Cole, *op. cit.*, I, 62, where he is in error as to one of the winners; Bacon, *The Line-Engraved Stamps of Great Britain*, I, 4; *Rep. Sel. Com. on Postage Label Stamps* (1852), p. 162.

[12] The wafer, or gummed sticker, was often used in place of wax to seal a letter. The lovesick Sam Weller, when writing to Mary the housemaid in Ipswich, prepared his letter as follows: "Having folded the letter in a very intricate manner . . . he put it into his pocket, wafered and ready for the General Post." *Pickwick Papers*, chap. XXXIII.

[13] For his evidence, see *2nd Rep. Sel. Com. on Postage*, p. 391.

ing. His proposed adhesive—also printed by Whiting—was about an inch square, the design engraved with complicated machine patterns, and printed in two colors, blue and red. He believed that the stamp would, in consequence, be hard to imitate. As a further safeguard, the paper on which the stamp was printed had a watermark. The stamped cover or envelope proposed by Cole was engine-turned to prevent imitation, with a rather elaborate design on the face of the envelope, the center being left blank, so as not to conceal the watermark and in order to give a space for the address.[14]

Another successful competitor, Benjamin Cheverton, preferred adhesive stamps as less liable to forgery than stamps that were struck on any and every kind of paper brought to the Stamp Office. Adhesive stamps could be affixed at the time of posting—even the London bellmen might be required to carry them. Cheverton suggested that the design should be a head, possibly that of Mercury, or better a female head of the greatest beauty "executed by Mr. Wyon." As Cheverton put it: "The eye being educated to the perception of differences in the features of the face, the detection of any deviation in the forgery would be more easy—the difference in effect would strike an observer more readily than in the case of letters, or any mere mechanical or ornamental device." The Treasury agreed with Cheverton in distrusting the use of private paper and in preferring a female head for the central design of the stamp.

Cheverton's essay was embossed on narrow bands of watermarked paper—the paper the exact width of the stamp. The narrow band was first made in mile lengths, wound on spindles and then coated with "the jujubes or gum." It would then pass between embossing rollers. The final process was cutting the mile of stamps into fifteen-foot lengths—each length a pound's worth of stamps—to be rewound in the same way as a roll of ribbon. The form in which the stamps were to be sold to the public is not unlike that used today in postage stamp slot-machines. Cheverton declared that he had tried out his proposal with such success that he had produced 220 impressions per minute "at a very moderate velocity." He estimated that one machine could produce twenty-five miles of stamps in a working day of ten hours, or more than two million stamps. Only one machine would be

[14] Cole's plan is reprinted in full in his autobiography, I, 109 ff. It was submitted October 8, five days before he entered the Treasury to assist Rowland Hill inaugurate penny postage. An award to Cole had the look of favoritism. See also an anonymous article by Cole, entitled "The Postage Stamp" in the *London and Westminster Review*, XXXIII, 267, and Bacon, *op. cit.*, II, 19-20.

needed, and the cost per stamp would be 1/260th of a penny. He clearly deserved a part of the reward.[15]

Some of the unsuccessful competitors submitted ingenious but impracticable plans. John Henry Clive proposed a double stamp to be placed on the back where the folded sheet was joined. When the letter was opened the design would be divided. Samuel Forrester of Falkirk suggested a stamp not unlike a circular cancellation stamp. Across the circle in the center was the charge, along the top the place of use, and at the bottom whether the sheet of letter paper used was folio, octavo or quarto. The date was also indicated, and the stamp, made in color, was to have the color changed every quarter. Joseph Hanson proposed a design consisting entirely of a carefully executed engraving of an ancient work of art, the design to be changed every year, apparently as an aid in art education. R. Prosser of Birmingham had the idea of using two stamps on each letter, one end of each stamped slip stuck on the letter with the blank portion projecting. The address was to be written on each projecting slip, one to be given to the sender as a receipt when the letter was taken up, and the other detached by the postman when he delivered the letter. It is easy to see why so cumbersome a plan would not have appealed to the postal authorities.

The firm of Rowe, Kentish & Company submitted an elaborate scheme. On a paper chemically treated, they printed stamps made distinctive by the use of three designs of a geometrical character, one each for the day, month and year. A triangle indicated an odd day, month or year: a square an even number. The largest figure was the year, the next the month, and the inner square or triangle represented the day. Thus a square and two triangles meant an even year and an odd month and an odd day—for example, January 1, 1840; a triangle, square and triangle could stand for February 3, 1841, etc. Robert Sievier, the engraver and sculptor, offered a design with an embossed subject in the center, "such subject to be the head of Her Majesty, the Royal Arms, or any other device, the stamp surrounding the embossment being printed in two or more colors."[16]

Many of the proposals were much under the ones that have been noticed, often of type-set designs that would have been easy to forge.

---

[15] The text of his proposal was only found as late as 1910, in the possession of one of Cheverton's descendants. See *London Philatelist*, XIX (Dec. 1910), 283-99; *London and Westminster Review*, XXXIII, 268; *Penny Postage Centenary*, p. 81.

[16] The fullest account of the various proposals of 1839 is Robson Lowe's "The Birth of the Adhesive Postage Stamp" in *Penny Postage Centenary*, pp. 75-127. It is lavishly illustrated.

One of the unsuccessful competitors, James Chalmers of Dundee, requires a somewhat fuller notice, not so much because of his proposed stamp, but on account of the strenuous efforts made by his son, Patrick Chalmers, to prove that James Chalmers was the inventor of the postage stamp. The father was a bookseller and printer in Dundee, Scotland. He had long been interested in postal improvements. The shortening by a day for the time of the mails between London and Edinburgh—it had occurred in the mid-twenties—was credited to his initiative.

When Henry Cole was busy furthering the cause of penny postage by the use of the *Post Circular*, Chalmers wrote Cole proposing the use of adhesive stamps, the letter being published in the *Post Circular* for April 5, 1838. His idea was to use a stamped slip with a device resembling that on newspaper stamps and "rubbed over the back with a strong solution of gum." They could be sold in sheets or singly and affixed to letters as needed, "with as much facility as applying a wafer, for which, in many cases, the slip might answer." To prevent their re-use, postmasters would "put the post-office town stamp across the slip."[17]

When the Treasury announced the competition, James Chalmers submitted a plan, "which so far back as December, 1837, I announced to Mr. Wallace, .. which was published in the *Post Circular*, .. and which I have now more fully matured." The chief difference between his early proposal and the one "now more fully matured" was the size of the slip and its method of attachment to the letter. The slip, two inches long, was partly blank, the unused part of the slip "for the purpose of inserting under the fold of the letter—the *stamp* to be left wholly exposed." This would mean that the slip would be on the other side of the letter from the address, thus saving the use of an extra wafer—"one wafer will be sufficient both for letter and stamp." This larger slip like the small one suggested earlier was to be canceled by the town mark. His idea of having the end of the slip loose was to give the postmaster the chance to examine the watermark. He believed there was little likelihood of the stamp being torn off: in any case, it could not be used again. The design Chalmers submitted was a type-set circle. There is no reference to gumming

[17] This letter is reprinted in full in Leah Chalmers, *How the Adhesive Postage Stamp Was Born*, pp. 7-10, and a facsimile extract from the letter appears in H. W. Hill, *Rowland Hill and the Fight for Penny Post*, p. 135. It will be recalled that Mr. Hill had made a tentative suggestion for the use of adhesive stamps in his *Post Office Reform* of February 1837.

the sheets. He would have the slip affixed with "wax, wafer, gum, or paste." As this proposal was a considerable variation from the postage stamp as finally adopted, James Chalmers received no part of the award for his suggestion of a slip ungummed and which was to be attached to the back of the folded letter. It should be added that the suggestion of a slip or stamp on the back of a letter seems more odd today than it did a century ago. At the time, the town mark, which Chalmers would have used for canceling the slip, was generally stamped on what we would call the back of the folded letter, on the side that did not contain the address.[18] Chalmer's entry in the Treasury competition was in no way unique. Some fifty competitors had advocated various sorts of adhesive stamps, "many of them recommending that the stamp should be inserted in the seal of the letter, leaving one end loose. This utterly impracticable plan was also favored by Mr. James Chalmers, whose suggestions were laid aside as useless."[19]

The space granted the unsuccessful efforts of James Chalmers is necessary because of a persistent controversy resulting from efforts to prove that Chalmers was the inventor of the postage stamp. The Dundee bookseller was himself interested in obtaining credit for the "invention." He wrote Mr. Hill at the time of the Treasury competition: "If slips are to be used, I flatter myself that I have a claim to priority . . . it being now nearly two years since I first made it public in a communication to Mr. Wallace, M.P."[20]

James Chalmers died in 1853, but controversy over who invented the postage stamp did not expire. At the time of Rowland Hill's death in 1879, when he was receiving praise on every hand for his postal reforms, Patrick Chalmers powerfully revived the claim for his father. In the ten years before his own death in 1891, Patrick Chalmers issued dozens of pamphlets and single sheets, and even paid for advertisements to broadcast his father's claim. An advertisement appearing in the *Athenaeum* in 1881 asserted that Rowland Hill had deliberately avoided reference to "pre-existing documents"

[18] For Chalmers, see Leah Chalmers, *op. cit.*, pp. 15-19, where the sample stamp is also reproduced. According to his granddaughter, James Chalmers wrote the Treasury on Oct. 7, expressing his preference for gummed labels, that is, his earlier proposal. He also sent the Treasury his earlier contribution to the *Post Circular*.

[19] From a letter published in 1890 by F. A. Philbrick, president of the Philatelic Society of London, and co-author of a standard work on the stamps of Great Britain.

[20] Leah Chalmers, *op. cit.*, p. 19. Note that the date James Chalmers suggested was 1837, which does not antedate Rowland Hill's tentative proposal of February of that same year.

and that the "principles of the penny postage scheme of 1837 were not the invention of Sir Rowland Hill." After printing a reply by Rowland Hill's son, Pearson, and a counter reply by Patrick Chalmers, the editor refused to insert further correspondence, declaring that "no one who knew the late Sir Rowland Hill can suppose that he would claim credit for ideas which were not his own."[21]

The contention of Patrick Chalmers received some contemporary recognition. The article on the "Post Office" in the Ninth Edition of the *Encyclopaedia Britannica*, published in 1886, granted James Chalmers the credit of priority of invention, on the ground that Chalmers had made postage stamps experimentally in 1834. This date was announced by Patrick Chalmers as the time his father first made postage stamps, though the father seems to have made no such assertion. The date, 1834—it would give priority—was supported by evidence of workmen in his printing shop who remembered having gummed and cut the stamps. This claim is also supported by the *Dictionary of National Biography* in the article on James Chalmers, where it is said that he drew off a sample of an adhesive stamp, had it set up in type, of which a few copies printed and gummed were exhibited to several merchants in Dundee in August 1834.[22] To make the cause of James Chalmers more secure, a tombstone was erected, reading "Originator of the adhesive postage stamp . . . which has since been adopted throughout the postal systems of the world." Some years later (1912) a plaque was affixed to the wall of his former bookstore, which reads, "Book-shop of James Chalmers, 1822-1853, the originator of the Adhesive Postage Stamp."[23]

[21] *Athenaeum*, April 30, 1881, pp. 578, 690. Some forty pamphlets, not counting second editions, were issued by Patrick Chalmers between 1880 and his death in 1891. See the Bibliography for a selection of the more important titles. Equally vigorous in defense of Rowland Hill was his son, Pearson Hill, whose letters and articles were vitriolic. Pearson Hill seems to have invited an action for libel, but it was not forthcoming. His principal contribution to the controversy was entitled *The Origin of Postage Stamps . . . The Chalmers' Craze Investigated*. In his *The Post Office of Fifty Years Ago*, he refers to numerous claimants, "generally insane," who have asserted from time to time that someone other than Rowland Hill was the originator of the plan or of some of its essential features (p. 36).

[22] *D.N.B.*, IX, 447. The volume appeared in 1887. The 11th ed. of the *E.B.* did not continue to credit James Chalmers with the invention. No mention is made of him in the article "Philately."

[23] See article by N. J. K. Strachan, "First Adhesive Postage Stamp," in the *Post Office Magazine*, Jan. 1939. This article, written by a native of Dundee, is pro-Chalmers. When the centenary of the postage stamp occurred in 1940, the Hill-Chalmers controversy revived. Patrick Chalmers' daughter, Leah, issued a pamphlet on *How the Adhesive Postage Stamp Was Born*. It has been answered by Col. H. W. Hill in *Rowland Hill and the Fight for Penny Post*. The latter is a medley of postal items. Chapter XI, "A

If James Chalmers made adhesive postage stamps in 1834, he anticipated the idea of uniform prepaid letters by several years. In that same year, Charles Knight had suggested stamped wrappers for newspapers, but Knight's proposal was a feasible one, as it would have meant a transfer to the wrapper of a uniform tax already in use. There seems little relation between the proposal of Knight and that of Chalmers, if it was made that early.[24] His stamps, if made in 1834, were not practicable, since prepayment was in little use, and uniformity of rate was not yet suggested by Rowland Hill. If a Chalmers slip of 1834 had been applied to a letter at that time, additional postage would have had to be paid for the slip. James Chalmers could, of course, have advocated an idea impracticable at the time.

The interesting problem remains, where did Rowland Hill get the idea of the small adhesive stamp mentioned in the second edition of *Post Office Reform?* Mr. Hill credits Charles Knight's proposal regarding newspapers, while making clear, at the same time, that Charles Knight did not have in mind any application of stamped covers to letters. As the proposal of stamped covers and of adhesives did not appear in the first edition of *Post Office Reform*, Hill must have formed the idea in the month before the second edition of February 1837. Whence came the notion? If from outside his own reflections, Mr. Hill never vouchsafed publicly any other source than Charles Knight's proposal for stamped covers on newspapers.[25]

Curiosity in Claims" (pp. 129-70), takes up the controversy with the accustomed rancor. See also R. Quarendon, "He Invented the Postage Stamp," in *Scotland* (Spring 1939), supporting the Chalmers claim.

[24] Miss Chalmers thinks there is: "But the failure of the proposals in Parliament in 1834 with respect to penny postage on newspapers in place of the impressed fourpenny stamp having failed, Chalmers made no effort to bring forward his invention, which was intended for letters" (pp. 2-3). In 1834, the franking of newspapers ended, and in 1836 the 4d tax was lowered to a penny. See above, pp. 245-46.

[25] See G. B. Hill, *op. cit.*, I, 218, 265, and above, p. 268. The article in the 9th ed. of the *E.B.* (1885) would have it that Hill's hesitant suggestion of adhesives came from outside his own mind: "It is a quite fair inference that this alternative had been suggested from without," (XIX, 585). Part of the acrimony attending this relatively unimportant matter has arisen from the unwillingness of Rowland Hill and his family to grant any appreciable credit for the penny postage scheme to anyone else. This attitude appears again and again in the autobiography. His daughter, Eleanor C. Smyth, in *Sir Rowland Hill, The Story of a Great Reform*, pp. 186-96, goes out of her way to ridicule other contenders for the credit of inventing the stamp, and even belittles Velayer and Charles Whiting. She asserts that "some days" after suggesting stamped covers only, "the convenience of making the stamp separate, and therefore adhesive, occurred to him, and he at once proposed its use." She concludes, "that priority of suggestion as well as of publication belong to Sir Rowland Hill." See also Pearson Hill, *The Post Office of Fifty Years Ago*, p. 35, where even Robert Wallace is carefully deprived of any credit for the idea of uniformity of rate; and G. B. Hill, *op. cit.*, I, 528, where Rowland Hill

It is high time to return to the main course of our narrative, in order to see what the stamps were like and how they were received by the public. After the four most ingenious proposals had been selected, the Treasury announced in December 1839 that it was fully decided "on the use of stamps," and that they would be in the four forms already described. The Treasury went on to say that the necessary experiments were "already far advanced," but they expressed fear that a "considerable time will be required for completing the preparation of the dies, plates and machinery (much of which is unavoidably of a novel construction) necessary for the manufacturing of stamps." The public was promised them "with the least possible delay, and when ready due notice will be given of their introduction."[26]

Rowland Hill, with the help of his brother, Edwin Hill, and Henry Cole, set about preparing the stamps in their various forms. For the stamped covers and envelopes, William Mulready of the Royal Academy prepared an elaborate design.[27] In fact, it was) complicated that the engraving could not be started until April 1840. The design for the stamped covers and envelopes was the same. It filled the top and sides of an envelope about the size and shape of an envelope of today. Not much more than half of the space was left for the address. The design was, as Henry Cole put it, "highly poetic," and was intended to be symbolic of the advantages of cheap postage. The conception was imperial in its scope, although cheap and uniform postage was not to become imperial for many years. In the center Britannia and the British lion are seated on a rocky islet. Winged messengers fly to the right and left where there are rather complicated collections of figures. On the left are found Chinese, East Indians and elephants, Arabs with laden camels, and merchant ships at anchor in the distance. On the right American Indians are apparently concluding a treaty with the Quakers. There are also Negroes packing casks of sugar, with a reindeer and sled in the distance. In the

himself, in praising Mr. Wallace, makes careful reservations. Rowland Hill was chiefly responsible for the startling suggestion put into force in 1840, but "my plan" might have had less emphasis, and men like Wallace, Chalmers, Knight, Hume, Whiting, and Cole might have been treated more generously.

[26] Wright & Creeke, *op. cit.*, p. xviii. Stamps were actually issued at the time in but three forms, stamped envelopes, official stamped covers and adhesive stamps. Stamps for letter paper brought to the Stamp Office were distrusted. This kind of stamp was not in use until 1855. See *Parl. Deb.*, 3rd s., LXXIII, 1056-58.

[27] Lewins, *op. cit.*, p. 257, gives the erroneous impression that Mulready received an award in the competition.

left foreground, a young person is reading a letter to a sick or aged woman, and at the right another is eagerly perusing a letter with her two children. It is certainly an inclusive and crowded design.

The face of the Mulready envelope was elaborate in order to prevent forgery, an artistic production in the hope of elevating the public taste, and a confused collection of imperial interests and emotions of gratitude to portray the blessings of cheap postal communication. One of the flying angels was drawn without a second leg, possibly to entrap the unwary forger, but it was soon noticed by the public. As early as May 8 Sir Robert Peel asked in Parliament "whether the multiplication of figures was any security against forgery." If not, he added, "the engraving should be curtailed so as to afford more space for the address." As it was, he very much doubted its utility.[28]

The general public was so critical that the Mulready envelope proved a dismal failure. The public laughed it to scorn. Thomas Hood, writing in 1840, refers to

> That hieroglyphical call
> To a geographical Fancy Ball
> On the present Post-Office covers.

In *The Ingoldsby Legends*, published at this time, there is a humorous description of this envelope—

> And with him he brings
> A set of those odd-looking envelope things,
> Where Britannia (who seems to be crucified) flings
> To her right and her left funny people with wings
> Amongst Elephants, Quakers, and Catabaw Kings;
> And a taper and wax,
> And small Queen's heads, in packs,
> Which, when notes are too big, you're to stick on their backs.

A versified description appearing in a contemporary newspaper ran, in part, as follows:

> Britannia is sending her messengers forth
> To the east, to the west, to the south, to the north.
> At her feet is a lion wot's taking a nap,
> And a dish-cover rests on her legs and her lap.
> To the left is a Mussulman writing a letter,
> His knees form a desk for the want of a better. . . .
>
> To the right is the king of the Cannibal Islands,
> In the same pantaloons that they wear in the Highlands;

---

[28] *Parl. Deb.*, 3rd s., LIII, 1317.

Some squaws by his side with their infantine varmints,
And a friend in the front whose forgotten his garments. . . .

Below to the left as designed by Mulready,
Is sorrow's effect on a very fat lady;
While joy at good news may be plainly descried,
In the trio engaged on the opposite side.[29]

Henry Cole admitted the design was unsuitable "for a dry commercial use in which sentiment has no part." Rowland Hill was aware by May 12, less than a week after its appearance, that the Mulready was a failure: "I fear we shall have to substitute some other stamp for that designed by Mulready, which is abused and ridiculed on all sides. . . . I now think it would have been wiser to follow established custom." Numerous caricatures of the design appeared, for one of which Thackeray was responsible. So decisive was the rejection of this ornate envelope that a large stock had to be destroyed.[30]

These first stamped covers and envelopes were printed in sheets of twelve. The covers were rectangular, about eight by nine inches in size: they were folded and sealed by the writer. The envelopes were diamond-shaped, and also were to be folded and sealed by the user. When ready for the mail they were the same size as the letter sheets. The covers and envelopes designed by Mulready were canceled by having the Post Office stamp impressed on the figure of Britannia. The directions on the side of the sheet indicated that the envelopes were sold in sheets only, "and consequently not made up." The public was advised that "for weights exceeding one ounce, use the proper number of labels, either alone, or in combination with the stamps of the covers or envelopes."

Though the Mulready was ridiculed out of use, the envelope soon became popular. New stamped envelopes appeared in 1841, the Mulready design being replaced by an embossed circular reproduction of the Queen's head, similar in size to that on the adhesive stamp.

The adhesive stamps or "labels," as they were then commonly called, were prepared with the greatest care. The fear of forgery,

[29] The verses from Thomas Hood are to be found in "Miss Kilmansegg and Her Precious Leg," and those from *The Ingoldsby Legends* in "A Row in an Omnibus (Box)."
[30] Cole, *Fifty Years of Public Work*, I, 64; G. B. Hill, *op. cit.*, I, 394-95. For a full treatment of the Mulready envelope, see Maj. E. B. Evans, *A Description of the Mulready Envelope and of the Various Imitations and Caricatures of Its Designs*, and T. Martin Wears, *The History of the Mulready Envelope*.

which was almost an obsession of the Treasury, led to such painstaking production of the world's number one stamp that it remains today one of the finest specimens ever produced. The design chosen was the portrait of young Queen Victoria. It was based on the medal struck for the occasion of the Queen's first official entrance into the City of London in 1837. The medal, which had been executed by William Wyon, was re-engraved in the proper size by Perkins, Bacon & Petch, who were given the contract for furnishing the adhesive stamps. The drawing from the medal was made by Henry Corbould, the engraving on the steel die by Frederick Heath. Perkins, Bacon & Petch received the contract, as they were highly expert printers of bank notes from engraved steel plates. Jacob Perkins, founder of the firm, was an American, who had gone to England in 1819, hoping to secure the contract for printing notes for the Bank of England. The firm agreed to engrave a steel die, transfer it to any number of plates wanted and print as many stamps as would be needed. "You are probably aware that having prepared the original die, we could insure perfect facsimiles of it for a century."[31]

A brief explanation of the process for making the first stamps will reveal the care with which the Queen's head was reproduced. After the drawing had been made from the medal of 1837, the engraver transferred the design to a piece of softened steel, which had already received by machinery a background of fine net work. The engraver also added the words "Postage One Penny," and star-shaped ornaments in the upper corners, but left the squares of the lower corners blank. This die or matrix was then hardened for use. It, of course, was not employed for actually printing the stamps, but was used to impress the design on a transfer roll of softened steel, large enough in circumference to hold eight impressions of the die end to end. This transfer roll was hardened in its turn, and then used for impressing the design of the original die on steel plates. As a rule, but one impression on the transfer roll was used to make the 240 impressions on a plate. The plates were then used for printing the stamps. When new plates were necessary, they were in turn derived from the original die.[32]

[31] There is an interesting article on "The Queen's Head" in *Household Words*, IV (1852), 510 ff: it was written by Charles Dickens. See also G. B. Hill, *op. cit.*, II, 192; *Rep. Sel. Com. on Postage Label Stamps* (1852), p. 162.

[32] Bacon, *op. cit.*, I, 55; Melville, *op. cit.*, pp. 23-27. The impressions were rolled into a plate from top to bottom. It took about a day to make a plate. Stamp collectors, it might be added, distinguish between this first die, and another *almost* identical, which was made in 1854.

The plates used for printing were oblong pieces of steel, large enough to take 240 impressions from the transfer roll, that is, twelve across and twenty down. Thus each sheet of stamps printed from a plate would be exactly one pound's worth of penny stamps, since twenty shillings of twelve pence each make a pound. Before the plates were hardened, the so-called check letters were inserted in the lower corners by means of steel punches. The arrangement is curious. The first stamp of the first row had A in the lefthand corner, and A in the other corner as well, the next stamp A and B, the third A and C, and so on to A and L. The second row started with B and A, to be followed by B and B, B and C, and so on. The lowest row would, therefore, be marked T and A, T and B and so on to T and L. The purpose of this series of letters was to make the forger's job even harder. He might make a steel engraving but hardly 240, and if he tried to issue forged stamps with but one combination of letters in the lower corners, the counterfeit was more likely to be noticed.[33]

Each plate was numbered, and an inscription for the use of postal clerks and purchasers was engraved on each side of a sheet of stamps. This rather curious piece of advice is worth quoting: "Price 1d per Label, 1s per Row of 12, £1 per Sheet. Place the Labels *above* the Address and towards the *Right Hand Side* of the Letter. In wetting the Back be careful not to remove the Cement." This advice was by no means superfluous, as the seal or wafer was put on the back side of the letter; at first labels were used occasionally to seal the letter, and sometimes they are put on the backs of letters even now. The change to the adhesive meant cancellation on the side where the address was found. Formerly it had been more common to put postmarkings on the back.

If a plate became worn in time, it would be discarded. They were remarkably long lived. Eleven plates were used to print penny blacks in the first year, and they produced over sixty-eight million stamps.[34]

[33] See *Gibbons' Stamp Monthly*, VII, (March 1934), 113. I might add that letters were put in all four corners of the stamps in 1858, the upper letters being the reverse of the lower. This was done to prevent industrious penny savers putting together unused parts of two stamps. See below, p. 361.

[34] Specialists in the stamp collecting fraternity often collect stamps by plates, and cherish stamps with the marginal plate numbers attached. The differences between stamps from different plates are often minute. The penny black has been the subject of careful study in Nissen & McGowan, *The Plating of the Penny Black Postage Stamps of Great Britain, 1840.* I might add that the chief reliance in plating penny blacks is on variations in the check letters. They were punched by hand.

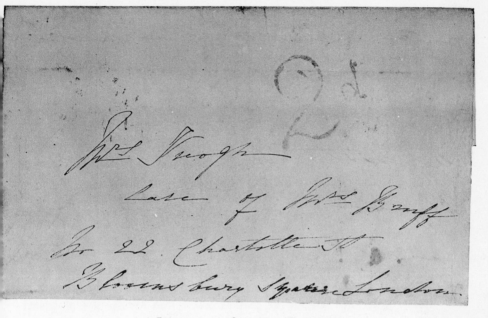

A LETTER OF 1840, NOT PREPAID

The address on a folded letter sent from Halifax to London, April 30, 1840, before adhesive stamps were in use. As the letter was not prepaid, it was charged twopence, that is, double postage, and is so marked. The postmarks of the receiving and sending offices were stamped on the back of the letter. Adhesive postage-due stamps were not used in Great Britain until 1914.

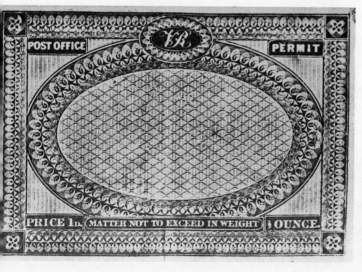

PROPOSALS BY CHARLES WHITING FOR AN ENVELOPE AND FOR THE ADHESIVE STAMP, 1839

The "slip" of 1839.

The suggestion of James Chalmers in 1838

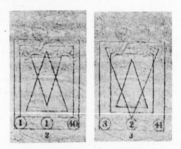

Examples of the proposal of
Rowe, Kentish & Company.

Two essays submitted by Robert W. Sievier.

The stamped delivery slip of R. Prosser, somewhat reduced from the actual size. The other side bore the following directions: "A letter not exceeding One Ounce weight, bearing this Stamp firmly attached with the Post Town and the date and the address legibly copied on the back of this Stamp, will be conveyed free to all parts of the United Kingdom."

FURTHER PROPOSALS FOR A STAMP MADE TO THE TREASURY IN 1839

A USED MULREADY WRAPPER, SHOWING THE MALTESE CROSS CANCELLATION
(Actual Size)

AN UNUSED AND UNFOLDED MULREADY ENVELOPE, AS IT WAS SOLD TO THE PUBLIC

To use, the side triangles were first folded under, and then the bottom and top. The 2d envelope was printed in blue. (Reduced in reproduction.)

WYON'S MEDAL OF 1837
Used as the basis for the Queen's head on the Penny Black,
the first British postage stamp.

A PENNY BLACK, USED ON A LETTER IN FEBRUARY 1841
The postmarks of the sending and receiving offices are shown, on a piece of the original letter.
They were stamped on the back of the letter, which was folded just above the stamp. (Actual
size.)

One of the causes for delay in issuing the stamps was the need for choosing a satisfactory paper for the stamp. It had to be of good quality, capable of taking gum easily, and of the right thickness to adhere well. The paper was watermarked as an additional precaution against forgery. After the sheets were printed they were backed with an adhesive. There was a groundless fear at first that the licking of the stamp would cause harm to the mouth because the materials were poisonous. "Diseases were said to be engendered in the systems of rash letter writers who used their tongues to moisten the labels," wrote Charles Dickens in 1852. And he continued: "Even the cholera was traced to that pernicious practice. The dreadful ingredients of the diabolical manufacture were said to be a mystery. That dark secret we have succeeded in penetrating, and now reveal it for the benefit of our readers, in two words—Potato Starch!"[35] Joshua Bacon stated in 1852 that there was a "good deal of nonsense" about the injury to health of the gum used on the stamps. It was composed, he said, of potato starch, wheat starch and gum.

The stamps were finally ready for the public early in May. The penny stamps were printed in black, as a result of the recommendation of Perkins, Bacon & Petch that black ink was superior to any other for steel plate engraving.[36] Instructions had to be dispatched to the postmasters as to the way they should treat these new stamps and covers. Samples of the new stamped covers and adhesives were sent out, along with a cancellation stamp and the directions for making the ink to be used with it. The canceling stamp was of a Maltese Cross design, and a red ink was used to deface the stamps. As one of Col. Maberly's instructions put it: "You will carefully Stamp with the Cancelling Stamp that has been forwarded to you, the Stamped Cover and Envelope, as well as the adhesive Stamps, the two former must be struck on the figure of Britannia; and in case of more than one adhesive Stamp being attached to a letter, each stamp must be separately obliterated. The use of the Cancelling Stamp, however, will not dispense with the use of the ordinary dated Stamp, which will be struck on the letter as usual."[37]

---

[35] *Household Words*, IV, 512. Early in the use of postage stamps arose the story with which many readers, doubtless, are familiar. "A postage stamp is a new coin of the realm, expressly devised for the prepayment of letters, and said an Irishman in describing it to his mate, the only difference I can see between it and a donkey is that one you lick with a stick and the other you stick with a lick." From Sir Francis Head's article on "The Mechanism of the Post Office" in the *Quarterly Review*, LXXXVII (1850), 61; *Rep. Sel. Com. on Postage Label Stamps* (1852), p. 165.

[36] Bacon, *op. cit.*, I, 27.

[37] Alcock & Holland, *op. cit.*, pp. 222 ff.; Philbrick & Westoby, *op. cit.*, p. 45;

Red ink was used as red ink had been employed in the Post Office to indicate prepayment. But the red ink seemed ineffectual: it could be washed off and the stamp design remained, since it was printed in fast colors. Black canceling ink was tried next—with little success. Finally Rowland Hill hit upon the idea of using an oleaginous or fugitive ink for printing the stamp and making the cancellation. As red was a fugitive color, the color of the penny stamp was soon changed to red; it appeared in that color after February 10, 1841. The twopenny stamps and covers were printed in blue. At last, even the ingenious troublemaker was conquered.[38]

The adhesive stamp proved a remarkable success. The public took to the licking of stamps as though it were a suddenly released instinct. Over sixty-eight million penny blacks were moistened during the first year of penny postage. As the usefulness of the stamp increased the number of stamps rose to astronomical figures. Yet, in spite of changes in the appearance of the stamp and in the manner of its printing, the engraved penny black remains one of the most attractive ever issued. The young Queen became increasingly endeared to her subjects by the ever-present attractive portrait. Queen Victoria herself liked it so much that she refused to allow any other portrait of herself to be used on British stamps during her entire reign. To the end of her long rule of over sixty years, therefore, the stamps of Great Britain never carried any other portrait than that of the young Queen in her eighteenth year.[39]

Thus began a feature of the modern postal system which is now taken for granted—the use of adhesive stamps and of stamped envelopes for prepaying a uniform rate. Rowland Hill deserves great credit for the successful launching of the new arrangements.

Melville, op. cit., p. 42; T. Todd, A History of British Postage Stamps, pp. 272-73. For a sample of the cancellation, see the reproduction of the Mulready stamped cover.

[38] Cancellations with the Maltese cross were frequently heavy. For a discussion of the trouble over ink, see G. B. Hill, op. cit., 1, 399-404. So much care was taken in the matter of engraving, in the choice of paper and in canceling that forgery of British stamps has been rare. A few attempts were made in the early days.

[39] One peculiarity of British stamps that may have escaped the reader is the lack of the name of the country. When first issued, the stamps did not need identification, since there was no other postal system using stamps. Then, too, their use was largely domestic. Even after other countries adopted stamps and put on them the name of the issuing country, Great Britain continued the original practice. The stamps always picture the head of the reigning sovereign, in line with the precedent set in 1840. Commemoratives, with which so many countries—including the United States—have been deluged, are rarely issued in Great Britain. The commemorative of the penny postage centenary, issued on May 6, 1940, was a stamp with the original Queen's head reproduced, along with that of the reigning king, George VI. See below, p. 443.

The Post Office and
Its Leadership.—1840-1854

PENNY postage began in January 1840, and stamps of various kinds were first used by the public in May. Although Rowland Hill was employed by the Treasury to aid in making the fundamental changes of that year, the Post Office remained under the control of Lord Lichfield and Col. Maberly. As they and many of the Post Office staff looked with great doubt on the novelty of a uniform penny rate, the effects of the reform, therefore, were watched with much interest. Which would prove more accurate, the confident estimates of the reformers or the pessimistic prophecies of the postal officials?

The forecasts of officials and reformers had diverged widely. Robert Smith, the Superintendent of the Twopenny Post Office, had declared that the reduction in the London rate from 2d to 1d would result in no proportionate increase in correspondence, that the revenue would not recover for two or three years. Col. Maberly held that "considerable loss" would result, and that the revenue would not recover for forty or fifty years. Lord Lichfield regarded the necessary increase to keep up the present revenue as "impossible." The Duke of Wellington was sure that a sudden drop in postage would be "fatal."[1]

Rowland Hill had been equally positive as to the success of his plan. He had made elaborate calculations in *Post Office Reform*, concluding that "it is very probable that the revenue may not suffer at all, and it is highly probable that it will not suffer much." In his evidence before the Wallace Committee, he had forecast a temporary

[1] See above, pp. 276-77, 287.

loss of one-eighth of the postal income. Later, in a summary for the *Post Circular*, he asserted that there "was no rational ground for fear that the gross revenue of the Post Office will be diminished." "On the contrary," he added, "its increase may be safely predicted, even if no other change was contemplated than the proposed reduction." In the hope of influencing the Duke of Wellington's vote on the postage bill in July 1839, Rowland Hill had written the Duke even more confidently: "If the postage were reduced to one penny, the revenue would be more likely to gain than to suffer." Robert Wallace had been somewhat more cautious: he felt that any loss would be made up in three years' time. Both the officials and the reformers had placed themselves far out on the proverbial limb.[2]

Was the reform penny wise or penny foolish? The number of letters mounted rapidly. For a week in November 1839—before any changes—they amounted to 1,586,000; for a week in December when the uniform but transitional fourpenny rate was in force, the letters numbered more than 2,000,000; for a week in February 1840, with the penny rate but no stamps, 3,200,000 letters went through the Post Office; and for a week in June after the stamps were available the number was 3,221,000.[3] These figures would seem to indicate that the number of letters would double, but this was far from the fivefold increase that Rowland Hill had estimated as necessary to offset the lower cost of postage. The revenue declined alarmingly. The gross revenue of the Post Office for 1839 was nearly £2,400,000, but in the year 1840 it fell off nearly a half, to £1,340,000. The drop in the net income was even greater, from £1,633,000 for 1839 to less than half a million pounds for 1840—a 70 per cent loss. Hill admitted in his autobiography that "like most projectors I was over-sanguine," and that "many circumstances which could not possibly have been foreseen" tended to delay the financial success of his postal reform. Lord John Russell was nearer the truth than either Hill or his critics in declaring that the change to penny postage was sure to bring a "temporary deficit."[4]

The *British Almanac*, a stout supporter of the reform, had an article in the volume for 1841 on the "Effects of the New Post-Office

---

[2] G. B. Hill, *op. cit.*, I, 354, 536; *Post Office Reform*, p. 95; and above, pp. 271, 286, 293.

[3] *Br. Almanac* (1841), Companion, pp. 100, 103.

[4] G. B. Hill, *op. cit.*, I, 347; above, p. 292. See also Rowland Hill's paper before the Statistical Society in 1841, "Results of the New Postal Arrangements"; it was reprinted in the *Journal of Statistics* (July 1841), pp. 85-99.

Arrangements upon the Number of Letters." There the hope was expressed that the loss would be but temporary. In the next year another article treating the "Effect of the Penny Postage . . . on the Revenue of the Post Office" stated that "if the present rate of increase is maintained, the five-fold increase predicted will be realized in less than five years from the reduction of the rates, or during the year 1844."[5]

The "temporary" loss continued, however, throughout the forties: the gross revenue did not reach the total for the last year of the old system (1839) until 1851. Even by that time the net revenue was as yet but two-thirds of that for 1839. Not until 1854 did the total of letters reach the fivefold increase needed to offset the lowered uniform charge of a penny.[6]

Rowland Hill was not slow in defending his plan, and explaining its seeming financial failure. He asserted in addressing the Statistical Society in 1841 that the plan would succeed if fully applied. He emphasized, in addition to the low uniform rate and the use of stamps, the need for "greater facilities"—a rather vague phrase—in the sending and delivery of letters. According to Hill, they were scarcely inferior to the lowered postage as a means of increasing correspondence. He believed, for one thing, that an increase in rural distribution would greatly help: "This I conceive to have been a main cause

[5] *Br. Almanac* (1841), Companion, p. 105; (1842) Companion, p. 95. In Hill's article in the *Journal of Statistics* (p. 92), the same time is given for making up the loss in the gross revenue.

[6] *1st Rep. P.M.G.* (1855), p. 65; Joshua Leavitt, "The Finance of Penny Postage" in *Merchants' Magazine and Commercial Review*, XXI, 410-14. Hemmeon, *op. cit.*, 241 ff, has useful expenditure and revenue tables. The following tabulation shows the gradual advance.

	GROSS REVENUE	NET REVENUE	TOTAL OF LETTERS
1839	£2,390,764	£1,633,764	82,470,596, including 6,563,024 franks
1840	1,342,604	465,927	168,768,344
1841	1,495,540	561,249	195,500,191
1842	1,578,145	600,614	208,434,451
1843	1,635,215	640,217	220,450,306
1844	1,705,067	719,957	242,091,684
1845	1,887,576	761,982	271,410,789
1846	1,963,857	825,112	299,568,762
1847	2,181,017	984,491	322,146,243
1848	2,143,679	740,429	328,830,184
1849	2,165,349	840,789	337,399,199
1850	2,264,684	803,898	347,069,071
1851	2,422,168	1,118,004	360,647,187
1852	2,434,326	1,090,419	379,501,499
1853	2,574,407	1,400,679	410,817,489

of delay in the recovery of the gross revenue." More important in his mind was the need for simplifying the workings of the Department where expense seemed to be mounting out of proportion to the needs for handling the increased amount of mail.[7]

The presumed lack of reform in the Post Office was blamed by Rowland Hill on the Secretary and the Postmaster-General, since they were opposed to the scheme from the first. As he put it: "I found, with great concern, that augmentation was rapidly proceeding; and, indeed, the addition during the first year of penny postage amounted to something more than £100,000, . . an amount sufficient to produce a very serious injury to fiscal results, the whole of which I knew would be attributed by many to my reform."[8]

An important cause for the growing cost of the postal service was the greater use of the railways for carrying the mails. Yet this could hardly be blamed on the officials. The high cost of mail carriage by the railways was the result of strong railway interests. The Duke of Richmond, in 1838, when presenting a petition in behalf of penny postage, had used the increasing cost of railway mail service as a reason for not lowering the postage. Letters going from London to Birmingham, for example, cost much more by railway than by mail coach. When a Select Committee had examined the relation of the railways to the mail service in 1838, Col. Maberly asserted that the railways had an entire monopoly as against the Post Office, and could charge just what they pleased. The Committee reiterated much the same charge in its report, even proposing as a partial relief that the Post Office should be given power to run its own trains on any railway. In one instance—in 1843—mail that weighed about eighty pounds was charged for space equal to that occupied by sixteen passengers, though it weighed no more than the luggage of one passenger. The desire for a rapid service was natural, as speed was one of the "facilities" Hill so much desired. Yet it was accompanied by an increasing cost that was arousing much concern. Apparently, the reformer had not realized that railway expense would rise so rapidly.[9]

---

[7] *Parl. Deb.*, 3rd s., LXX, 426; G. B. Hill, *op. cit.*, I, 347; Lewins, *op. cit.*, p. 139. The Chancellor of the Exchequer was sure that extending the rural service to places receiving few letters would greatly increase the expense. Hill's argument that the increasing cost of the Department was at fault hardly applied to his calculations of increased income, as that was based on the gross and not on the net revenue.

[8] G. B. Hill, *op. cit.*, I, 411.

[9] *Rep. Sel. Com. on Railroad Communication* (1838), p. 1; *Rep. Sel. Com. on Conveyance of Mails by Railways* (1854), pp. iii, xiv; *Parl. Deb.*, 3rd s., XLIX, 687;

Rowland Hill's position in the Treasury had its drawbacks. His recommendations could not be made to the Post Office, but only to the Chancellor of the Exchequer. The responsibility for the success of "my plan" was divided and ineffectual. In 1841 he even proposed to the Treasury that Col. Maberly be transferred to another post so that he might direct the arrangements: "It is highly important to the success of the measure that I should henceforth take a position in the Post Office." He even believed that the transfer of Col. Maberly to some other scene of action would be "agreeable to him: it would relieve him from the unpleasant task of working out a measure which he dislikes, and which he has repeatedly affirmed cannot succeed."[10]

The Chancellor did not accept Hill's suggestion, or even make his position with the Treasury more secure. This arose partly from the difficulties being faced by the Melbourne government. Since the Bedchamber crisis of 1839 it had continued in office more or less on sufferance—until the summer of 1841. Nor was the change to a Conservative government under Sir Robert Peel of any benefit to Rowland Hill. Although the new Postmaster-General, Lord Lowther, had been favorable to postal reform, it was largely a Whig measure. The Treasury discontinued the services of Henry Cole in November and less than a year later Rowland Hill was informed that his "assistance" would be needed no longer. The reformer was bitter. As he put it: "My right to complete my own plan was denied, .. and the measure was to be handed over to men who had opposed it stage by stage, whose reputation was pledged to its failure, and who had unquestionably been caballing to obtain my expulsion from office."[11]

For the next three years Rowland Hill had no government post, but his interest in the Post Office and his efforts to return to government service were unflagging. In his behalf, Lord Brougham approached the Home Secretary, Sir James Graham; the Merchants Committee interviewed the Prime Minister; Mr. Ashurst of the Committee circularized mayors of towns urging that petitions be sent

LXX, 413; Hill, "The Results of the New Postal Arrangements," *op. cit.,* pp. 86-87; Lewins, *op. cit.,* p. 141. The cost of conveyance for these years of transition was

FOR THE YEAR ENDING	MAIL COACHES	RAILWAYS	TOTAL
Jan. 5, 1839	£105,107	£9,883	£114,996
1840	109,246	39,724	148,971
1841	130,352	51,125	181,477

[10] This rather naïve and revealing letter of June 1841 is reprinted in G. B. Hill, *op. cit.,* I, 542-43.

[11] *Ibid.,* I, 459, 469-72, 476.

up in behalf of the full execution of the reform; Hill's friends in Parliament interested themselves in his cause; and in April 1843 a petition prepared by Rowland Hill was presented by Sir Francis Baring to the House of Commons. It asserted that scarcely any progress had been made since August 1841—when the Tories replaced the Whigs—"toward the completion of your Petitioner's plan."[12]

In June 1843 a long debate resulted from a motion for a select committee on "Rowland Hill's recommendations for Post-Office improvement." His dismissal was characterized as the "death knell of the plan." The government replied through the Chancellor, Mr. Goulburn. He objected to the imputation that no one but Mr. Hill was solicitous for the public interest, and showed how far off had been the reformer's calculations as to the effect on the revenue. Goulburn highly praised Lord Lowther, the current Postmaster-General, as favorable to penny postage, and as one who in earlier days had received unstinted praise from Rowland Hill himself. The Prime Minister emphasized the social advantages of the lower rate and the government's determination "to ensure full justice to the system." The motion for a select committee was accepted by the government.[13]

The work of the Select Committee of 1844 does not need much attention, as it served to air grievances and viewpoints already familiar. The Committee gave so full a hearing to Hill that his evidence occupied over 130 pages of the folio report. The evidence and the report appeared in August 1843, the report being brief and without any positive recommendations. Rowland Hill took advantage of the opportunity by preparing a pamphlet based on the evidence before the Committee—under the title *The State and Prospects of Penny Postage*.

Rowland Hill justified the publication of his very biased interpre-

[12] *Ibid.*, I, 476, 486. The petition is in *The State and Prospects of Penny Postage*, pp. 81-84.

[13] *Parl. Deb.*, 3rd s., LXX, where the debate occupies 47 columns. Rowland Hill and his brother Arthur were present below the gallery on the opposition side of the House for furnishing any needed information. Lord Lowther was credited by Goulburn with being the "first person to suggest the adoption of a penny postage for a certain class of letters, and now Mr. Hill got the credit for being the originator of the system." He referred to prices current. The Chancellor made the surprising statement in the debate that the Post Office did not now pay its way. This was so stated in a return that had charged the packet service to the Post Office. G. B. Hill, *op. cit.*, I, 488, records Rowland Hill's indignant denial of the "absurd attribution to Lord Lowther of the origination of penny postage."

tation of the evidence on the ground that he had been unable to counter the statements of the postal officials at the hearings. He emphasized the need for greater security of correspondence, a reduced registration fee and the enlargement of the rural services. Further financial guesses appeared in the pamphlet. He concluded: "It would surely not be too much to hope that with revived trade and with renewed resources, a few years would suffice to raise the net revenue to that amount on which I had calculated as the ultimate result, namely £1,300,000 per annum." The few years were to include another decade.[14]

An indirect, if not direct, result of the airing of his grievances was a public testimonial. Two months after the appearance of *The State and Prospects of Penny Postage*, the Mercantile Committee invited subscriptions. The result must have been gratifying to the reformer, for the total reached £13,000. At the testimonial dinner, his return to public office was strongly urged. The treatment of Hill by the government even aroused the ire of "Mr. Punch." The first volume of *Punch*—for 1844—included a "Penny Post Medal and Its Obverse": one showed Rowland Hill's triumphant entry into St. Martin's le Grand, the other "Britannia presenting Rowland Hill with the Sack."[15]

A week after the testimonial dinner in June 1846, the Conservative government was defeated and resigned. With the return of the Whigs under Lord John Russell, Rowland Hill's friends were again in office. The result was his return to government service. The new Postmaster-General, Lord Clanricarde, wished the reformer to be adviser to the Postmaster-General, rather than a direct assistant to the Treasury as he had formerly been. Hill himself demurred, as such an appointment would again mean an end of his services with a change of government. Once more he proposed the removal of Col. Maberly to make way for himself as Secretary, or that he be made Surveyor-General, after the analogy of Palmer. He was finally made Secretary to the Postmaster-General, entering on his duties in December 1846.

During the next eight years a sort of dual secretaryship existed, with Hill making constant efforts to displace Col. Maberly. The relation of the two men was no more amicable than in the days when

---

[14] The pamphlet appeared in 1844, the publisher being Charles Knight. Some correspondence was included that had been withheld or garbled, according to Rowland Hill.
[15] VI, 192-93.

Hill was in the Treasury, though his position made possible some division of the duties, and gave the reformer a chance to show what he could do.

The Post Office had taken over the money-order business in 1838, and its rates had been lowered at the suggestion of Rowland Hill.[16] When he returned in 1846, the Postmaster-General placed in his hands the care of the Money Order Department, with a view to its further extension. By various devices the business increased rapidly. During 1850 the number of orders granted was nearly five million, for a total of over eight million pounds. Four years later, when Rowland Hill succeeded Maberly, the annual number of orders was five and a half million, and the amount transmitted nearly ten and a half million pounds.[17]

Another innovation of these years was the Book Post. Henry Cole had proposed a uniform parcel post at the time of the competition of 1839, but the railway companies objected strongly to a general parcel post. Though they were opposed to the Book Post as well, the government was induced by Rowland Hill to consent to its creation, because no other system of delivery could so effectually serve the rural districts, and other regions not yet reached by the railways. The government was influenced also by the moral and political importance of a book post. As set up in 1848, the cost was 6d a pound. At first a package could contain but one book, and no writing whatever was allowed inside the wrapper. This meant that a secondhand book or one containing any indication of ownership was forbidden, but such restrictions were soon relaxed. This use of the postal service proved a great boon, especially to those who received books from lending libraries. In 1855 the Book Post was made of even greater use when the rate was lowered to a penny for four ounces.[18]

[16] Before 1838 the rates had been 6d for sending £2, and 1s 6d for sending up to £5. The total amount sent by money orders in 1838 was £2623, in 1839 it was £5854. In November 1840, the rates were reduced to 3d for amounts up to £2, and from 1s 6d to 6d for amounts up to £5. For 1841, the amount sent by money order was five times that of the previous year. See *42nd Rep. P.M.G.* (1896), p. 27; *Parl. Deb.*, 3rd s., LXX, 428.

[17] G. B. Hill, *op. cit.*, II, 254; *1st Rep. P.M.G.* (1855), pp. 23-24; *42nd Rep. P.M.G.* (1896), pp. 26 ff. For a diverting account of the Money Order Office in 1852, see *Household Words*, V, the first article. Rowland Hill was greatly assisted at this time by the appointment of his brother Frederic as Assistant Secretary. Rowland seems to have wanted someone in whom he had absolute confidence. Frederic remained in the postal service for the rest of his active life, proving a useful administrator. Frederick Hill, *An Autobiography* (1893), pp. 288 ff., 310, though the volume has little on the Post Office.

[18] Lewins, *op. cit.*, p. 166; G. B. Hill, *op. cit.*, II, 65, 87-88; *42nd Rep. P.M.G.*

Another of Hill's efforts to speed up the postal services and thus add to the revenue was his effort to make greater postal use of Sunday. This led, as he put it, to "one of the most painful passages of my whole life." Sunday had always been a "blank post-day" in London. An American visitor in 1839 reported that the London office was not open on Sunday: "This is, however, the only office in the United Kingdom where Sunday is so strictly observed."[19] No Sunday deliveries were made by postmen and there was very little attendance of employees at St. Martin's. It occurred to Rowland Hill, however, that "facilities" would be increased and therefore the business of the Post Office, if the so-called "forward letters" could be dispatched from London on Sunday, since the trains, of course, ran on that day. A "forward letter" was one that was sent from one provincial town to another via London. Under the practice in use, such letters, if coming on Saturday afternoon, were not sent on from London until Monday. If such letters could be forwarded on Sunday, the letters would be received a day earlier, business would be increased by a larger exchange of letters and the postal profits would rise.

The plan proved acceptable to the Postmaster-General and to Col. Maberly. The need of additional labor was slight, and the few men needed would work voluntarily. The plan—it began in November 1849—was kept secret in order not to arouse the public conscience, but when the practice leaked out a tremendous uproar was the result. The Lord's Day Society felt sure it was an opening wedge for the general desecration of the London Sunday by the Post Office—a desecration of the Lord's Day at the center of the kingdom. It brought such bitter criticism that the sabbatarians demanded the total abolition of Sunday postal work everywhere. A deputation of the Lord's Day Society visited Rowland Hill to urge that *all* mails be stopped throughout the kingdom for the twenty-four hours of Sunday. But their efforts were unsuccessful, as Lord Ashley, the well-known reformer, records in his journal for Sunday, November 20, 1849: "On this day will begin the new ministerial scheme of Sabbath labour at the Post Office. Should it succeed, should it increase rev-

---

(1896), p. 2. Charles E. Mudie, the founder of Mudie's Lending Library, London, began lending books in 1842.

[19] George Plitt was a special agent of the Post Office of the United States. See his *Report* (1841), p. 2. Both Wallace and Hill had criticized this "blank post-day." See above, p. 252, and *Post Office Reform*, p. 51.

enue, and gratify moneyed men, alas, humanly speaking, for the Sunday altogether! But we pray and trust that God will bring to confusion the vile attempt. The true remedy lies in closing every post office, metropolitan and provincial, from twelve o'clock on Saturday night till 2 o'clock on Monday morning."[20]

Lord Ashley took to action in the House of Commons in May 1850, by moving an address to Her Majesty praying that the collection and delivery of letters on Sunday be discontinued throughout the kingdom. He based the address on the very general desire to relieve postmen of Sunday labor. The Chancellor of the Exchequer opposed the motion, but the government was caught napping, and others who voted for it to please constituents, in the belief it would not pass, were surprised by the victory of Lord Ashley. The government bowed to the decision: Sunday, June 23, 1850, the collection and delivery of mails was stopped throughout the country, no exception being made even in favor of foreign correspondence.[21]

The sabbatarian victory, however, was short-lived. The isolation of the rural districts was so complete that the order was in force for a few weeks only. Lord Brougham and numerous others stressed the inconvenience to those who had to send or receive important information or materials. It must be remembered, of course, that the telephone was not yet dreamed of, and the telegraph was in its infancy and largely unavailable to the general public. Lord Campbell believed that, even in Scotland—the land of his birth—it would not promote better Sunday observance. All sorts of objections were raised by those in the provinces who would not receive their London Sunday newspapers by post. Numerous news agents found it necessary to employ boys to distribute the papers, thereby actually increasing Sunday labor. J. A. Roebuck declared that the effect of the measure was to multiply labor fivefold. Another opponent, who did not pretend to be better than his neighbors, declared that the saints had stolen a march on the "philosophers and the utilitarians."

The advocates of Sunday observance pointed out the practice in London, and asked the opposition why they did not suggest opening the London Post Office on Sunday. What was good enough for a

---

[20] Edwin Hodder, *Life and Work of the Seventh Earl of Shaftesbury*, (1887), II, 305. Lord Ashley, later Lord Shaftesbury, had previously brought about the discontinuance of the sale of money orders in the provincial offices on Sunday. It was first tried in Bath, and during 1849 extended to all the post offices in England, Wales and Scotland.

[21] *Parl. Deb.*, 3rd s., CXI, 467, 470, 484. The vote was 93 to 68 in a small House. See also Hodder, *op. cit.*, II, 305.

metropolis of over two million souls was surely good enough for lesser towns. They denied that this was an attempt to make people religious by act of Parliament, but was rather a step towards granting a day of rest to overworked men. Ashley pointed out that on the first day of Sunday relief, the postmen in various provincial towns had marched in groups to the church services. A motion citing the "great inconvenience which has arisen from the total cessation of any delivery or collection of letters on Sunday" was supported by the government and passed. A few weeks later the Sunday services in the provinces began again with deliveries somewhat less numerous than before. The Report of the Commissioners appointed as a result of the motion recommended that practices in London continue as formerly—without deliveries—and that in the provinces there be no more than one delivery and one collection. The labor of the postmen was to be at such a time that it would not interfere with "divine service." Rural letter carriers were to have every other Sunday free if their walks prevented them from attending church. Any householder could order his mail to be undelivered on Sunday, but that meant he was to receive no mail whatever, no matter how important. The matter of Sunday work in the Post Office had cost Rowland Hill trouble and anxiety for more than sixteen months.[22]

The resulting practice is described by Lewins, writing in the early sixties. "The London office has remained closed ever since on the first day of the week. In Scotland, and in one or two English towns, no letter delivery takes place from house to house, a short time only being allowed for the public to apply for their letters at the post-office windows. In the majority of English towns, the early morning delivery only is made. The day-mails, as a rule, do not run on Sundays. The post offices in the major part of our English and Scotch villages are entirely closed on Sundays."[23]

[22] *Rep. Commrs. on Sunday Labour in the Post Office* (1850), pp. 5-6. The vote on the motion was 195 to 212. See Hodder, *op. cit.*, II, 307; *Parl. Deb.*, 3rd s., CXII, 326, 1055, 1057, 1191-217.

[23] *op. cit.*, p. 168. The question of Sunday labor in the Post Office was not raised in Parliament again until 1870. It was then suggested, by a unanimous resolution, that such labor be reduced as much as seemed prudent. In 1887, a committee reported on conditions. At that time, 1534 employees out of 22,000 in the London District worked on Sunday, and it was voluntary. Deliveries to the government departments and the foreign embassies were made on Sunday—a regular practice for centuries. Letters from abroad were delivered to the editors of the London newspapers at 10:30 Sunday evenings, enclosed in red envelopes. Of the rural carriers throughout the two islands, only about a third were working on Sunday in 1887. England and Wales had house-to-house de-

Several other devices for speeding the services began at this time. The greater speed of railway trains as compared with mail coaches and their larger accommodation aided greatly in the usefulness of the Post Office. Mail had been carried by railway since 1830, when it began between Manchester and Liverpool, though the regulation of this service was first arranged by an act of Parliament in 1838. It provided that mails should be carried by ordinary "trains of carriages," or by special trains. The Post Office could make use of the "whole of the inside of any carriage if necessary." Even more interesting was the provision that a railway could be required to furnish a separate carriage for sorting letters.[24]

The first journey by a railway post office was made in 1838 on the Grand Junction, connecting Birmingham with the Manchester and Liverpool Railway. As soon as the line was completed from Birmingham south to London in the next year, the traveling post office went the entire length. This sorting of mails during the journey was not possible, of course, in the days of the mail coach. The Post Office, in order to expedite the mails in the days of the horsed coaches, had used forward offices along the main lines of travel. By this earlier system, all letters going north for post offices between Birmingham and Lancaster, for example, were sent to Birmingham and there sorted, all letters for towns between Lancaster and Carlisle were sorted in the forward office at Lancaster, etc. The immediate result of the introduction of traveling post offices on the railways, naturally, was the speeding up of the movement of mail, and less sorting for the local postmasters. Previously, each had made up a large number of bags for the mail coach, whereas only one was necessary for the railway post office, when the sorting into bags could be performed en route.[25]

By the fifties, railway services had greatly improved. Railway trains almost wholly devoted to carrying mail were in use. It was at this time that Rowland Hill hit upon a more effective use for the railway post office. Letters from towns near London that were in-

liveries in over 600 post towns, and only eight had no deliveries, even at the window. Scotland had 20 towns with house-to-house delivery, 122 with window delivery and 15 with no delivery. In Ireland, 120 towns had letters brought to the houses, nine where they could be obtained at the window and none, apparently, without some sort of delivery. See *Rep. Com. on Sunday Postal Labour* (1887), pp. iii-iv, 5.

[24] 1 & 2 Vict., c.98.

[25] *Hist. Sum.*, p. 44; *1st Rep. P.M.G.* (1855), p. 18; Lewins, *op. cit.*, pp. 177, 214-16; Plitt, *Report* (1841), p. 4; *Rep. Sel. Com. on Postage* (1843), p. 181.

tended for London were not given time enough for sorting on the railway, if sent direct. But if these letters for London were taken *away* from London on one night train and then transferred to another night train bound for London, the required time for sorting the letters was obtained, with no actual delay in their delivery. This method of increasing the use of the railway post office was a boon to the overtaxed facilities at St. Martin's le Grand.

Another improvement connected with the railways was the surprising device by which mail was put off and received while the trains were in rapid motion. A primitive form of this machine had been used with the mail coach: the guard took on the local mails of small villages by grasping a projecting handle or strap while the coach was passing the post office.[26] The problem of doing this from a moving train was more difficult to solve, but the use of a projecting mechanical arm and a receiving net made possible the putting off and receiving of mail while the train was in rapid motion. It had been used as early as 1838 on the Grand Junction Railway. A coachman on that railway line, John Ramsey, had taken out a patent for an invention that "will take the bags up and down without slackening at all." George Plitt, an American visitor to England in 1839, saw this "ingenious machine" working successfully when the train was going thirty miles an hour. It has been in use ever since.[27]

In order to make the mailing of letters easier, street letter boxes, or pillar boxes, as they came to be known in Great Britain, were introduced at this time. The collection of letters by bellmen—an ancient practice in London—had been discontinued in 1846, and was being given up during these years in other towns as well. George Plitt reported that, in 1839, there were 95 bellmen in London, "who call at every house in their walk for letters to go by the evening dispatch." Each carried a locked bag, with a slit for inserting the letters, and persons dropping in the letters paid the bellmen one penny for each letter. He was, therefore, a sort of traveling letter box.[28]

Both Rowland Hill and Anthony Trollope have claimed to be the originator of the British pillar box. The former asserted that in 1840 he proposed "my plan for having letter boxes put up through-

[26] See illustration of the Bath mail taking up the mail bags, above, p. 241.
[27] *Rep. Sel. Com. on Railway Communication* (1838), p. 56; *Hist. Sum.*, p. 44; G. B. Hill, *op. cit.*, II, 137, 236; Plitt, *Report* (1841), p. 4; Lewins, *op. cit.*, p. 220. The machine was improved in 1848 by John Dicker, an inspector of mail coaches. He was, in consequence, awarded the office of Supervisor of Mail-Bag Apparatus.
[28] *Report* (1841), p. 5.

out London and other towns." If Rowland Hill did have the idea in 1840, it was not acted upon for over a decade. In January 1852 he reported that the Postmaster-General was agreeable to a trial of them in the London thoroughfares. They actually appeared in London in March 1855, the first one being erected at the corner of Fleet and Farringdon Streets.[29] An official circular issued by Rowland Hill on October 11, 1854, announced their use. They were to be placed at intervals of half a mile along the leading streets: "It is proposed to fix the boxes on the side of the footway, in such a position as not to obstruct traffic of any kind." Pillar boxes were an immediate success. By 1857, they were being placed beside roads as well as streets.[30]

That Anthony Trollope, the novelist, should have a claim to their introduction may seem strange, unless the reader is aware that Trollope spent much of his life as a Post Office surveyor; in fact, he wrote many of his novels while doing the work of inspection. According to a biographer, he had for some time reported their usefulness on the roadsides of France and advised their being tried in England. "On his suggestion of the exact spot for the purpose, the first pillar box was erected at St. Heliers, Jersey, in 1853." In his *Autobiography* Trollope asserts his desire for pillar letter boxes "of which accommodation in the streets and ways of England, I was the originator, having, however, got the authority for the erection of the first at St. Heliers in Jersey."[31] It was an old maid, Miss Jemima Stanbury of Exeter, in Trollope's *He Knew He Was Right*, who so disliked "the iron pillar boxes which had been erected of late for the receipt of letters. . . . She had not the faintest belief that any letter put into one of them would ever reach its destination. She could not understand why people should not walk with their letters to a respectable post office instead of chucking them into an iron stump— as she called it—out in the middle of the street with nobody to look after it. Positive orders were given that no letters from her house should ever be put into the iron post."[32]

[29] According to Mount Brown, one of Great Britain's first stamp dealers. The statement is in the preface to the *Catalogue of British, Colonial, and Foreign Postage Stamps* (1862).

[30] G. B. Hill, *op. cit.*, I, 417; II, 259; *Athenaeum* (Oct. 21, 1854), p. 1280; *2nd Rep. P.M.G.* (1856), p. 7.

[31] T. H. S. Escott, *Anthony Trollope* (1913), p. 114; *Autobiography* (1923), p. 258. Hill does not notice the Trollope claim. Trollope's district included the Channel Islands.

[32] Chapter 8.

Whoever deserves the credit for their introduction, they proved a great convenience. The number of receiving houses was much reduced, and the public soon came to appreciate their value, and to entrust their letters without fear to these new pillar boxes. It might be added that the first letter boxes in America were set up in Boston in 1858.

Such were some of the increasing facilities with which Rowland Hill's name was connected. They serve as examples of what he meant by the "completion of my plan." But it is difficult to believe that he expected such devices to bring any sudden increase in revenue, and it is equally difficult to know just what arrangements would have completed his plan. The phrase was indefinite, and cloaked as well an ambition to serve in the Post Office.

His eagerness to become the manager of the Post Office did not abate during these years. He was conscious of various "cabals" to drive him from office.[33] His position still seemed to him "anomalous," so much so that he approached the Postmaster-General in his own interest again and again. Hill suggested a co-equal secretariat with Col. Maberly, and even the retirement of Col. Maberly on full pay, so that he, Hill, might succeed to the coveted position. Such a suggestion seemed unduly pertinacious to the Chancellor of the Exchequer, who pointed out that Col. Maberly was not an old man and "cannot with decency be shelved."[34]

This was certainly true, for Col. Maberly was three years younger than his would-be supplanter. Maberly had been opposed to reform in the first instance, but the Post Office had made remarkable progress even under his direction. That he and Hill were antipathetic goes without saying. Col. Maberly is said to have alluded commonly to Hill as "that man from Birmingham." Hill was no more liked by Anthony Trollope, who had entered the postal service back in 1834, even before the appointment of Maberly. Writing of Rowland Hill, Trollope declared, "With him, I never had any sympathy, nor he with me. In facts and figures, he was most accurate, but I never came across anyone who so little understood the ways of men—unless it was his brother Frederic." Trollope believed Hill "entirely unfit to

[33] He attributed to one the difficulties he encountered in the forwarding of letters on Sunday from St. Martin's.

[34] G. B. Hill, *op. cit.*, II, 143, 166, 194. Chapters XIX and XX of his autobiography show Hill's views clearly. They are entitled respectively "Partial Improvement in Position" and "Efforts for Further Improvement in Position."

manage men or arrange labor."[35] And this was the judgment of other postal employees. Trollope's viewpoint at least helps to explain the attitude of the civil servant, who thought the financial success of the experiment was not the only norm for making decisions regarding "advances" in the Post Office.

Rowland Hill's fortunes seemed at low ebb when the Liberal administration fell in 1852. The succeeding Conservative government of Lord Derby insisted on recognizing Col. Maberly as the chief Secretary, much to Rowland Hill's disgust. But the Derby ministry lasted for less than a year. When the Aberdeen coalition of Whigs and Peelites succeeded in December 1852, the aspiring inventor of penny postage came into his own. In 1854, Hill was at last made Secretary of the Post Office in place of Col. Maberly, who was transferred to the Audit Office. If Rowland Hill had seemed unduly persistent, his final good fortune was to make possible the handling of a department he had done so much to reform fifteen years before. At least he was not to be another William Dockwra or a second John Palmer. The "inventor" was to supervise the workings of the reformed Post Office. And it was high time, for Rowland Hill was nearly sixty when his ambition was realized.

[35] For Maberly, see *D.N.B.*, XXXIV, 394-95. Trollope, *Autobiography*, pp. 122, 259. "I was always an anti-Hillite. . . . It was a pleasure to me to differ from him on all occasions;—and looking back now, I think that in all such differences I was right." Col. Maberly died in 1885, six yeaers after the death of his supplanter.

The Sanctity
of Correspondence

DURING the years when Rowland Hill was trying to displace Col.
Maberly, the Post Office was under bitter criticism for faults entirely
unconnected with the introduction of penny postage. In 1844 the
public learned with general surprise that letters sent through the
Post Office were liable to be detained, opened and read by government officials, that the hated Secret or Inner Office—in existence in
the days of Thurloe and Samuel Morland—was still active. The
horror and disgust at this well-nigh forgotten spy system aroused
much concern and general condemnation. The revelations of 1844
aired a situation not unlike that of 1735 when Robert Walpole was
faced with accusations of letter-opening for political purposes. The
general public indignation in the mid-forties at the continuing practice serves to reveal the relation of the Post Office to the government,
and the limitations of the freedom that correspondence was supposed
to enjoy in Great Britain.

Thomas S. Duncombe presented a petition to the House of Commons on June 14, 1844, from Joseph Mazzini and several others in
Queen's Square, London. The petitioners claimed that several of
their letters had been detained by the Post Office, their seals broken,
and that they had been opened and read. They declared that the
letters were sent "for no political purpose, and contained no libellous
matter or treasonable comments upon the Government of the country." As this practice of opening and reading private correspondence
seemed to them repugnant to the British constitution and an introduction of the spy system of foreign states, they prayed for a com-

mittee of inquiry and for redress, and that the recurrence of so unconstitutional and infamous a practice be prevented.[1]

When presenting the petition Mr. Duncombe addressed his question to the Home Secretary, Sir James Graham—was he aware that this had been done, and if so, had the opening been by authority of a principal Secretary of State? Sir James Graham replied in an irritating manner. The letters of one of the petitioners had been detained and read—it proved to be Mazzini, though it was not admitted by the Home Secretary at the time. He added that it had been done by a warrant from him, but that the warrant was no longer in force. Graham refused to discuss the matter further and expressed the hope that they would make no other inquiries: "It was not consistent with his duty to give any more explicit explanation." When Mr. Hume asked how long the warrant had been in force, Sir James "firmly declined to say anything further on the matter."[2]

The reader will recall a somewhat similar situation nearly a hundred years before when Robert Walpole's government was sharply questioned as to the opening of letters.[3] At that time the Post Office Act of Queen Anne's reign (1711) had allowed letters to be detained and opened by the express warrant of one of the Secretaries of State. When the consolidation of the various Post Office acts had occurred in 1837, this power was retained: it could be used "in obedience to an express warrant in writing under the hand of one of the principal Secretaries of State." The practice that was so sharply criticized in 1735 was in use during the century following, though it was exercised more carefully after 1815 than in the war-filled eighteenth century. When the Post Office acts were consolidated in 1837, this right of opening letters by warrant was continued.

If Sir James Graham thought he could stifle inquiry by his rather disdainful refusal to give information, he was sadly mistaken. It would have been much better for him to have made a fuller and franker statement of the practice and the justification for it, but that would have led to more embarrassing questions. The knowledge that this sort of "spy system" was in use in a "free country" aroused storms of wrath within and without the doors of Parliament. Even the House of Commons was unaware that this right existed and was being used. Mr. Duncombe admitted that the Act of 1837 gave the

[1] For Mazzini's statement on the matter, see *Mazzini's Letters*, tr. Alice de Rosen Jervis (1930), pp. 89-92, a letter to his mother, dated June 21.

[2] *Parl. Deb.*, 3rd s., LXXV, 892-93.

[3] See above, pp. 121 ff.

power to the Secretaries of State, but he "did not believe that one man in twenty thousand knew of the lines that had been smuggled into the Act, placing their correspondence at the mercy of the Secretary of State." It was a power that ought to be taken away, he continued, particularly when exercised in such an unscrupulous manner as it had been within the last two years. Mr. Duncombe then asked if the "right honorable Baronet" would say which of the four petitioners had suffered this indignity. Sir James Graham replied, "Certainly not." Robert Wallace supported the petition with his usual vigor. The right had been "insidiously inserted" into the Consolidation Act of 1837: "It was without the knowledge of the House that this more extended power was introduced, and the Act was passed without the words being discovered." Wallace declared that he had frequently drawn the attention of the House to this evil, "one of the accusations which he had been in the habit of bringing forward year after year, while he was agitating the question of Post-Office reform." He asserted that there was regular machinery at the Post Office for opening letters, in a room set apart for the purpose, and that persons had been sent abroad to study in the school of Fouché how to open, fold and reseal letters.[4]

Mr. Hume, already well known as a postal reformer, flew to the attack on this "outrage against public liberty." Slaves who touched British soil were free—"and were freemen to be made slaves by such a power?" Now, he declared, that "we are in a state of perfect tranquillity," nothing could interfere with the public peace. Under the circumstances, therefore, the opening of Mazzini's letters "was one of the most disgraceful transactions ever avowed in the House of Commons since he came into Parliament—it was degrading and disgraceful and discreditable" for the Secretary of State to allow himself to be made the tool of other sovereigns.

Three days later the House of Lords took up the matter. The Earl of Radnor could imagine "nothing more unconstitutional" and "utterly at variance with the principles of the British constitution and the feelings of the British people." Lord Campbell believed that the right should be used most cautiously, and "not to satisfy the curiosity,

---

[4] *Ibid.*, 896, 900-1. Fouché, who died in 1820, was an adroit French politician, who, like Talleyrand, survived the French Revolution and the Napoleonic regime. He was an adept at intrigue, and at various times Minister of Police. Wallace knew, or should have known, that the Post Office Acts of 1837 were not, as we have found, new measures, but acts that consolidated the numerous Post Office laws. They naturally included the right of detaining and opening letters on the warrant of one of the Secretaries of State.

much less malignity, of any foreign state." Lord Denman, the Chief Justice, was against the right, since it meant opening not only one letter but all the letters of a suspected person: "How is such a state of things to be tolerated in a civilized country?" It ought not, he declared, to be borne with for a moment. The Duke of Wellington, as one might expect, upheld the practice.[5]

A week after presenting the Mazzini petition, Mr. Duncombe presented another from a Polish refugee. In doing so, he emphasized again that Great Britain had "nothing to do with foreign powers or their squabbles with their subjects so long as those subjects conducted themselves peaceably . . . in this country." He then read a letter from Mazzini asserting that "since the beginning of March sixty or seventy letters addressed to me have been opened, . . every care being taken to avert suspicion, impressions of the seals taken, the cut sometimes so delicate that it almost required a magnifying glass to follow its trace." Mazzini believed that the practice could have been continued only for the sake of a foreign power, and in support of his belief quoted a Milan paper to the effect that "the English Cabinet had addressed to that of Vienna promises extremely satisfactory concerning the agitation prevailing in Italy, and especially in the territory of the Pope." Mr. Duncombe then recalled the earlier case of 1735 when Robert Walpole had at first opposed the request for inquiry, and then agreed, provided that there should be no inquiry into the secrets of the government. Mr. Duncombe disclaimed any wish to know the secrets of the government—"he doubted if they were worth knowing." He thereupon asked that a select committee be appointed to look into the practice and decide on any possible alteration of the law allowing the secret opening of post letters.[6]

An interesting debate followed. Sir James Graham again insisted this was no place to answer such queries, that his conscience was "pure," that he objected to a public inquiry of this kind. He would neither affirm nor deny that he had issued a warrant in the case of the Polish refugee. Macaulay, the historian, took part in this discussion. He could see no difference between having a letter taken from him in the Post Office and a letter taken from his desk. He cited Wilkes' successful case when his letters were seized. Macaulay pointed out that their ancestors had given up the spy system long

[5] *Ibid.*, LXXV, 973-85. Sir Joseph Arnould, *Memoir of Thomas, First Lord Denman* (1873), II, 162-63.
[6] *Parl. Deb.*, 3rd s., LXXV, 1264-70.

ago, and, therefore, he objected to this form of its use. There was no difference to him "between the government breaking the seal of his letter in the Post Office, and the government employing a spy to poke his ear to the keyhole, and listen to the conversations he carried on." He thought the law should be repealed altogether. One member—R. L. Sheil of Dungarvon—had examined Mazzini's letters and insisted that the letters had been opened "and the postmarks had been altered by another stamp having been impressed upon them." Some very harsh accusations were made, among others, that the Pope was "in all probability under the care of the Home Department," that no minister of the Crown should be entrusted with opening the letters of foreigners to oblige a foreign minister. The efforts of Mr. Duncombe to obtain a select committee were unavailing, the government refusing the committee by a majority of 44 in a House of 368.[7]

But the matter was not at an end. What the opponents of Peel's government could not obtain in the House was at last forced by the feeling in the country. A general storm of indignation came down upon the Cabinet, and particularly on Sir James Graham, such a storm that they found retreat necessary and further explanation wise. Mr. Hume declared that "even to the extremity of Scotland no question had ever occupied the public mind more thoroughly." One of the reasons given by the government against a public committee was the effect on the witnesses of the general excitement over the matter. The public anger was directed almost exclusively at Sir James Graham, when, in fairness, it should have included the ministry as a whole. It happened that the Home Secretary had asked for the opening of Mazzini's letters, which were transmitted, unread by him, to the Secretary of State for Foreign Affairs.[8]

The public excitement was fed by the press. Newspapers were unusually free in their comments, with all kinds of stories about the Post Office going the rounds. There was hardly a public print, a public speaker or perhaps a private family that did not heap insults and expressions of disgust upon the name of Sir James Graham. Advertisements appeared of envelopes that could not be opened, and "anti-

[7] *Ibid.*, LXXV, 1273, 1275, 1279, 1291, 1303.

[8] Sir Robert Peel, the Prime Minister, came to his defense, but others, who should have spoken, remained silent, particularly the Foreign Secretary, Lord Aberdeen. Palmerston, who had used the right in an earlier administration, absented himself from the debates. See Charles Stuart Parker, *Life and Letters of Sir James Graham* (1907), I, 433, 443, 445. *Parl. Deb.*, 3rd s., LXXV, 1343; LXXVII, 718.

PAUL PRY AT THE POST OFFICE.

A *Punch* cartoon of 1844.

Graham wafers" were advertised, wafers that would so effectively seal the envelopes that they would be safe from the prying activities of a Home Secretary. Thomas Carlyle voiced the public anger in a letter to the *Times* at this "opening of men's letters, a practice near of kin to picking men's pockets." Loyal citizens offered themselves as media for the foreign correspondence of exiles who wished to hear from their loved ones at home.[9]

Mr. Punch, still in his youth, took an active part in condemning and picturing the indignity of letter-opening. The volume for the second half of 1844 had "Punch's Complete Letter Writer" as a regular feature. The author dedicated the series in the first letter to Sir James Graham, on the ground that he had "the whole run of the Post Office, as he has the unquestioned fingering of all the letters of the Queen's subjects." The author was sure that he would never think of St. Martin's le Grand "without seeing you in imagination working away with a crow-bar, smashing red and black wax—or, by the more subtle agency of steam, softening wafers, that the letter may open its lips, and yield up the contents of its very heart to the Secretary of the Home Department." The appeal to the natural desire for privacy in domestic matters was the basis for an extension of the letter-opening incident: "I felt assured that my letters had all of them been defiled by the eyes of a spy; that all my most domestic secrets had been rumpled and touzled, and pinched here and pinched there—searched by an English Minister as shuddering modesty is searched at a French customs-house." Another article on "The Graham Letters—Private and Confidential" purports to give some letters from the Emperor of Morocco to the "great Graham." They had fallen into the hands of *Punch*, "who profiting by the example of the Home Secretary, immediately opened them." In one, the Emperor sent the "mighty Graham" the Order of the Umbrella.

Several biting cartoons decorated *Punch's* attack on letter-opening, one depicting Sir James Graham as "Paul Pry at the Post Office," another a Post Office Peep-Show—with the Duke of Wellington in the audience—and a third pictures the Home Secretary holding a "Grand Review of the London Postmen." *Punch* also announced "Anti-Graham Wafers" that were backed with such extraordinarily

---

[9] Lewins, *op. cit.*, p. 512; Harriet Martineau, *A History of the Thirty Years' Peace* (1878), IV, 330; Punch, VII, political summary.

GRAND REVIEW OF THE LONDON POSTMEN.

YESTERDAY, at the Home Office, Sir James Graham reviewed that very efficient body of men, the London Postmen, general and petty. Indeed, from the peculiar interest taken in them by Sir James, they may be called the Graham's Own. The men were on the ground as early as nine, and presented a very imposing appearance. Nothing could be more satisfactory than the way in which they went through their evolutions, opening and reading the letters with a despatch that called forth the admiration of Sir James and all his clerks. The men being ranged in treble line, the review began. The word of command was given as follows, by Sir James:—

"Present letters!" | "Thumb on seal!" | "Read letters!" | "Re-seal letters!"
Feel for seal! | Open letters! | Re-fold letters! | Pocket letters!"

Sir James gave the word in a fine sonorous voice; and was admirably responded to. Nothing could be more dexterous than the manner in which the postmen, by means of lucifer and wax, resealed the various missives. When wafers were to be used, the word of command was thus:—

"Wet wafer! | "Insert wafer! | "Stamp!"

The review over, Sir James emphatically complimented the body on their efficiency; and they were then dismissed for their several walks.

adhesive gum that they would stick to Sir James "Fouché" Graham for life.[10]

The "tumult of disapprobation" created in the country had its effect. When Mr. Duncombe, two weeks after the failure of his first effort, moved for a select committee to examine the so-called Secret or Inner Office of the Post Office, he referred to the disgust and apprehension of the public mind "which was much increased by the tone in which the right honorable Baronet [Sir James Graham] had discussed this subject in the first instance." The Home Secretary countered by showing an eagerness now for investigation: "I agree that the time has arrived when I must say more. . . . I can now indulge my private feelings consistently with my public duty, . . and I will be a party to the most searching inquiry." But Sir James Graham, nevertheless, did not second Duncombe's motion for a select committee, but proposed instead that a secret committee make the inquiry. The reason for his preference for a secret committee was that the evidence presented to such a committee was not printed. Graham named a committee of nine, excluding himself and Mr. Duncombe, and any member who had held or was holding office. After the failure of efforts to add Mr. Duncombe's name, the Secret Committee was appointed. Two days later a similar committee was appointed by the House of Lords.[11]

The reports of the two committees appeared in August, that for the Lords running to three pages only, that for the Commons somewhat longer, with appendices of nearly one hundred pages of information on the history of official letter-opening. Despite the withholding of much information by these Secret Committees, their reports furnish considerable material on a practice that, by its very nature, receives almost no publicity.

The reports found that Mazzini's letters had been opened under warrant from the Home Secretary, who transmitted the letters unread to the Foreign Secretary. The action was justified by the belief that Mazzini was plotting to incite an insurrection in Italy that would disturb the peace of Europe. The warrant was not issued at the suggestion of a foreign power and the information furnished was not such as "to compromise any individual within reach of that foreign power, nor did that power know how the information was obtained."

[10] *Punch*, VII, 2, 10, 15, 34, 118. The cartoons are of interest not so much for their attack on Sir James Graham, but because they illustrate the feeling of the time, and furnish examples of letters without envelopes, and closed with seals or wafers.

[11] *Parl. Deb.*, 3rd s., LXXVI, 213, 223-25, 227, 258.

The Lords' Committee declared that Mazzini's letters had been opened for about four months; the Commons' Committee asserted that the warrant ran only from March 1 to June 3.[12]

The earlier use of warrants was fully examined. From 1712 to 1798 there were 101 warrants: since 1798 the number had been 372. In the nineteenth century they had been issued uniformly from the Home Office, and only since 1822 had the original warrants been preserved at the Post Office. The Lords' Committee admitted that it had long been the practice to forward to the Foreign Office the correspondence of foreign ministers passing through the Post Office before it was sent on to the persons or office for which it was intended. The Lords' Committee reported that this practice had been discontinued since June, as there was no sufficient authority for it. Of the 372 warrants in the nineteenth century, over half were in connection with murder, theft, fraud and treason, twenty were for "foreign correspondence," a few originated with the Bank of England and some thirteen concerned prisoners of war. But over 100 of the 372 warrants were unclassified and their character was undisclosed by the Committees, though the reports agreed in declaring that no letters were detained where civil rights alone were concerned, and that the practice had never been used for personal or party motives. Admittedly, the letters were resealed and sent on "with no indication that they have been detained and opened." No denial was made in the reports or in Parliament as to the existence of the Secret or Inner Office at St. Martin's. It was held that the power should not be abolished, "though it is more requisite in time of war than in our present state of peace."[13]

[12] Though the Italian side of this issue is not germane to British postal matters, it might be added that a number of Italian exiles who were living on Corfu—then a British possession—had written Mazzini of their intention of making a descent upon papal and Neapolitan territory in the hope of arousing a revolt. Mazzini had tried to dissuade them, but 22 misguided individuals went unarmed from Corfu to Calabria. One of their party, a Corsican, betrayed them, and all save the Corsican were condemned to be shot, though eight were finally sent to the galleys. On July 23, 1844, the rest were executed, including two sons of the Austrian Rear-Admiral Bandiera. They believed that they died in the cause of liberty and of an independent and united Italy. Peel asserted that the Austrian government had complained to the British government that Austrian refugees were organizing attempts "hostile to the tranquillity of Italy, particularly the Papal States," and doing so from British territories in the Mediterranean. The Prime Minister stretched the incident into one that endangered the "public tranquillity," and justified a warning in general terms to the Austrian government. He denied that the men who left Corfu were trapped by the information furnished by the British government. *Parl. Deb.*, 3rd s., LXXVII, 678-79, 746-51.

[13] *Ibid.*, H.C., pp. 9-11, 15, 16; H.L., pp. 2-3.

The following letters are highly interesting examples of warrants used about this

But the end was not yet. Mr. Duncombe refused to give the names of witnesses who could prove his charges unless he were present and in a position to elicit the evidence by cross-questioning them. An appeal to the House of Commons that he be allowed to attend the sessions of the Secret Committee failed of success. The report of the Committee was sharply criticized as exhibiting a great deal of historical and antiquarian research, the Committee giving extremely minute attention to what happened two or three hundred years ago, "but we find all this ardour for research as we approach the nineteenth century, evaporate, and then grow suddenly and most interestingly reserved." Mr. Duncombe declared that Mazzini's letters had been opened since Christmas, both before and after the admitted time of the warrant's existence. One disillusioned member of the

time. They concern Irish agitators of the early thirties. These letters, among others, were sold a few years ago in an auction of the letters of Sir Francis Freeling. Needless to say, such material seldom comes to light. Lord Melbourne was the Home Secretary at the time, his brother, G. Lamb, was the Under Secretary, and G. H. Freeling was the assistant to his father, Sir Francis. They have been reprinted in the *Bulletin* of the Postal History Society, no. 21 (1942).

PRIVATE

My dear Sir,—   Home Office, Nov. 8th, 1831.

Lord Melbourne approves of your having opened and copied Curran's letter—and authorizes you to do the same with any other letters of the same description where it is an object that no delay should take place in forwarding the original. Lord Melbourne relies on the greatest caution being used to keep as secret as possible the contents of the letters to which his Warrants relate.

Believe me,
My dear Sir,
faithfully yours,
G. LAMB   Approved Richmond

G. H. Freeling, Esq.

PRIVATE AND CONFIDENTIAL

                                                     H. Office—Monday
Sir,—   Septr. 10th, 1832.

By direction of Visct. Melbourne I transmit a warrant to detain the letters directed to John Lawless. As it is of the greatest importance that no such interference with his correspondence should be at all suspected by him, it will be better if (as was done once before) the letters should be opened at the Post Office and copies taken of any parts of them that seem important. This of course should be done only by the most confidential person, and as it was before done by Mr. Freeling it should be adviseable that the same hand should do it again.

It is important that the least possible delay should take place in the delivery as he will probably be suspicious.

I am, Sir,
Yrs., &c., &c.,   G. LAMB

Sir Francis Freeling, Brt.,
    Post Office.

Commons sincerely hoped they might never appoint another secret committee: "It appeared to him that they were nothing but white-washing machines for Government."[14]

What the Committees had said as to the practice in the forties was not very comforting. During the outbreaks in the manufacturing and mining districts during 1842 a clerk had been sent from London to open letters of six persons taking a prominent part in the disturbances. And in the next year two clerks were sent to south Wales to examine the letters of persons in two different towns. Some forty-four warrants had been issued in the years 1842 to 1844, more even than those issued by the hated Lord Sidmouth in the years 1812 to 1814. "The right honorable Baronet [Sir James Graham] beats Lord Sidmouth by five."[15]

Obviously much important and interesting data on letter-opening had been suppressed. Gradually the public realized that Mr. Duncombe's absence from the Committee of the House of Commons, nominated as it was by the government, was because of the great embarrassment his presence would have caused. Not only would he have questioned his witnesses, but he would have learned whether his own letters had been opened. Of this he seems to have become aware only as he went to the aid of Mazzini. "When I presented to this House Mr. Mazzini's petition, I certainly knew nothing at all of my letters having been opened. . . . I never would have suspected that the government could have committed so base and mean an act as that of opening my letters." He became conscious of this extension of warrants when Mazzini informed Duncombe that he—Mazzini—had heard that the opening of Mr. Duncombe's letters was a matter of general conversation at the Post Office among the clerks, the sorters and the subsorters. They had said to Mazzini, "What is the use of Mr. Duncombe bothering himself about opening the letters of foreigners; he had much better look after the villainy that has been perpetrated towards his own."[16]

This was a horse of another color. Duncombe was a member of Parliament when his letters were opened during the Chartist troubles of 1841 and 1842. Here was a matter of privilege such as had exercised parliamentarians in 1735. Duncombe was rightly aroused: "On my making the statement that I had reason to believe my letters were opened, a great number of gentlemen said to me, 'We

[14] *Parl. Deb.*, 3rd s., LXXVI, 1014, 1024; LXXVII, 672, 675, 740.
[15] *Ibid.*, LXXVII, 674.   [16] *Ibid.*, LXXVIII, 140-41.

cannot suppose your letters have been opened; government cannot be so base and mean and shabby as to issue a warrant to open your letters, or those of any other member of Parliament.' " To this, Mr. Duncombe replied, "Give me a Committee and I will prove that my letters were daily opened by order of the right honorable Baronet." The result was one of the most bitter debates that had taken place in years. On February 18, 1845, Mr. Duncombe began it with a long speech asking for a select committee to inquire as to the mode of detaining, opening and resealing letters, and of "the circumstances under which every warrant for that purpose has been issued by any Secretary of State from the 1st day of January, 1840, to the present time." He declared with feeling: "I cannot conceive a greater personal insult, a greater insult to the constituency I represent, for I am not the representative of a rotten borough or the nominee of a Peer. . . . If my correspondence is not free, I am not a fit representative of the people."[17] This was to be no mere antiquarian research.

He was strongly supported. Viscount Sandon, representing Liverpool, declared that they were not guilty of "prurient curiosity," as Sir James Graham had assumed: the investigation should be full and ample. Peel in a speech on the "high trust" of government office had not a word to say about Duncombe's letters. Warburton defended the Committee on the ground that it was not for the public good to give all names where warrants had been issued. The debate was adjourned at a quarter to one in the morning.

The heated discussion of letter-opening was renewed two days later at 4 P.M. R. M. Milnes held that Duncombe's letters might have been opened two or three years ago when he ventured to present a petition from the Chartists, and that Duncombe had a right to an answer. Macaulay affirmed strongly the need for the sanctity of correspondence: "A letter directed to me, and put into the mail-bag, is my property in the same sense as a letter which has been delivered to me. . . . And the exposure of my secrets is the same whether the information be obtained from a letter delivered to me this morning or from a letter which is to be delivered to me tomorrow morning." He believed that Mr. Duncombe's letters had been opened—"the right honorable gentlemen opposite do not deny it"—and that he was entitled to an answer. To Macaulay, the issue was very clearly a "question of privilege." Charles Buller spoke to the same effect:

17 *Ibid.*, LXXVII, 690-91. Duncombe represented Finsbury in London.

"We are the representatives of the people and therefore our correspondence may turn on matters of great public interest."[18]

Disraeli brightened the debate by an attack on Peel and the Secret Committee. He held that there should not have been so much antiquarian research in "musty" records, but more "attention to something nearer their noses." Disraeli affirmed the privilege of the letters of members of Parliament. "A member of Parliament is a sort of political confessor," he said, "and even if one of his constituents were to consult him about a conspiracy, it is better that he should be dissuaded from the step by his representative than have his letters opened by a Secretary of State." And he added, "The government may open and read all my letters, provided they will answer them."[19]

J. A. Roebuck denied that anyone had the right to "impute to us or the public a prurient curiosity." He even made the assertion that in 1837 and the commencement of 1838, "I believe that letters of mine were opened." After the bitter debate had gone on for hours, Sir Robert Peel expressed the wish for an end of the discussion that evening. He opposed adjournment—and further debate—on the ground that it was holding up other business. Others justified adjournment, despite a debate that had lasted since four o'clock, for at least twenty persons had been trying to get the Speaker's eye for seven hours. Adjournment finally came at 1:15 A.M. The third night of the debate, February 21, 1845, was one of the "most disagreeable and painful he had ever heard," according to the Solicitor-General. He gave it as his opinion that the legal right of opening letters existed at common law, and that members of Parliament possessed no greater privileges with regard to the power of the Secretary of State over their letters than anyone else. Lord John Russell commented on the "great degree of public indignation," on the cry that was raised from one end of the kingdom to the other. He believed the Mazzini case was not a legitimate use of the power, and that the government should have given information on Mr. Duncombe's case. "If you wish to do justice," he said "you ought not to refuse in-

18 *Ibid.*, LXXVII, 838, 841-44, 882.
19 *Ibid.*, LXXVII, 904-8. Disraeli ridiculed Peel's explanation of the Italian affair. "The letter sent—the solitary colony in the Mediterranean in commotion—the invasion of Calabria by an expedition of twenty men without arms—Italy in insurrection—the Austrians crossing the Apennines and the French crossing the Alps—England arming and in motion—and all prevented by intercepting the letters of Mr. Mazzini. Certainly since the celebrated narrative of *The House That Jack Built*, never was detail so consecutively precise."

quiry." But the efforts of the opposition were unavailing in view of the Conservative party strength. The motion on the select committee was defeated at 1 A.M. by 240 to 145.[20]

Mr. Duncombe made several other attempts in the spring of 1845 to put through resolutions, but they all failed. In April, he asked for leave to bring in a bill to secure the inviolability of letters in the Post Office. He argued that letters were inviolate in the United States, in Canada and even in France, where M. Guizot had recently affirmed the safety of letters in that country. But Duncombe failed again, and there the matter rested—and rests. The law remains unchanged, for by the Consolidation Act of 1908 permission was given for "opening or detaining or delaying a postal packet . . . in obedience to an express warrant in writing under the hand of a Secretary of State."[21]

Presumably, the Secret Office continued. Yet the anger aroused by the issue was not without some effect. For one thing, the excessive use of the power by Sir James Graham made his name famous for having opened letters at the Post Office, an unjust loading of the responsibility on one member of the Cabinet. The debates and disclosures had the further effect that henceforth the letters of foreign ministers resident in England were no longer detained and examined. In addition, greater care was used in the exercise of the power. From 1845 to 1853 warrants were used only six times for opening letters, and in each case the warrant applied to one person only; the letters concerned embezzlement, murder and fraudulent bankruptcy. So careful was the government after the disagreeable experience of 1844 that no warrant was issued until November 1848.[22]

It is going too far, however, to say, as does Lewins, that the "law is virtually a dead letter." Rowland Hill, after he became Secretary of the Post Office, declared that during his time they were issued only in a very few instances, "relating, so far as I can recollect, exclusively to burglars, and others of that stamp." Spencer Walpole, the historian, was not so reassuring, and he should have known for he had been private secretary to his father when the latter was Home Secretary in the fifties. Spencer Walpole declared that the "practice is more usual than is generally supposed."[23]

[20] *Ibid.*, LXXVII, 914, 977, 986, 991, 995, 1022.   [21] 8 Ed. VII, c.48, sec. 56.
[22] See *Accounts and Papers* (1852-53) in Vol. XCV of *Parl. Papers* for the session.
[23] Lewins, *op. cit.*, pp. 160-64; Charles Stuart Parker, *Life and Letters of Sir James Graham* (2 vols., 1907), II, 446-47; May, *Const. Hist. of England* (1866), II, 280-81; Spencer Walpole, *A History of England from the Conclusion of the Great War in 1815* (1890), V, 378-79. Walpole was Secretary of the Post Office from 1893 to 1899.

The use of warrants was again questioned in 1881 when Irish matters were at tension. The Secretary then said the power was a grave responsibility, and that it was used only upon urgent necessity, but he refused to say whether it had been used at the time against the letters of a member of Parliament. Later in the same decade the government was questioned again as "to what extent 'Grahamizing' is now exercised," as it had been alleged that letters were opened in the Dublin Post Office. Again the answer was inconclusive. The commotion aroused by Mr. Duncombe in 1844 and 1845 seems at least to have restricted the range of the warrants, if it did not abolish the practice. And to that extent Mr. Mazzini and Mr. Duncombe had not suffered in vain.[24]

[24] *Parl. Deb.*, 3rd s., CCLVIII, 766; CCLX, 564; *Chambers's Edinburgh Journal*, LXXXIII, 29-30. Mr. Duncombe referred in his efforts of 1845 to the inviolability of letters in the United States. The *Postal Laws and Regulations* of the United States (sec. 600) are strict regarding letter-opening by postal employees. Though obscure and disloyal matter is immailable, "no person other than an employee of the Dead Letter Office, duly authorized thereto, or other person upon a search warrant authorized by law, shall be authorized to open any letter not addressed to himself."

Mid-Victorian Growth

THE record of the reformed postal services has been carried to 1854, the year that Rowland Hill became Secretary. For the next ten years he was the guiding force in the organization, deeply concerned with making it a success, both financially and in the popular estimation. After 1864—the year of his retirement—the Post Office continued to make new records in the amount of its business. A natural break in the account seems to appear in the seventies, when the Post Office took on some startlingly novel duties, and assumed the more complex character that it has borne ever since. The two decades that begin with Rowland Hill's secretaryship form a natural unit, and will be treated together.

A number of his long-cherished ideas were made effective when he had the power to put them in force. One was the union of the London District and the General Post. They had been separate organizations from the days of William Dockwra, with overlapping services and, for long, different rates. Two sets of carriers traversing the same ground seemed anomalous, especially after the rates became uniform in 1840. One cause for the delay in making the two bodies of postmen one was the difference in status, one receiving much higher rates of pay than the other.[1]

Another change made at this time in the London postal service was the division of the metropolis into postal districts. Rowland Hill had suggested this as early as 1837, but he was opposed by the Su-

[1] *1st Rep. P.M.G.* (1855), pp. 33-35; Lewins, *op. cit.*, p. 170; Plitt, *Report* (1841), p. 4; G. B. Hill, *op. cit.*, II, 247.

perintendent of the Twopenny Post. The change was at last begun in 1856. Each of the ten postal districts was named from its geographical position, and the initials for the region were used in the address on letters and in the postmarks. Thus the east-central section in which St. Martin's was located became E.C., the Westminster area in the southwest was S.W., etc. The initials are still in use, and have been further elaborated by the addition of numbers to indicate the various parts of a district.[2]

The districting of London brought many advantages. London's postal business was much greater than even its proportional population when compared with the country as a whole; its population was about a tenth of the whole, but its mail business about a fourth. The Post Office receipts for London were ten times that of the next urban center, Liverpool. By means of the railway post office the bags were prepared for the districts as the mail was brought up to London. The bags would then go directly to the districts from the railway stations rather than to St. Martin's. Another advantage was the more rapid delivery of local letters. If a letter was to go from one district to another, or remain in the same district, it would not need to travel to the central office. The change began in 1856. For this and other reasons a great advance occurred in the number of local London letters, a jump in the annual increase from less than 4 per cent before 1856 to 8 per cent by 1860. By that time nearly eleven million letters were being delivered annually in the same districts in which they were mailed.[3]

An innovation of this time was the issuance of annual reports, and the appearance of the quarterly *Postal Guide*, both intended to make the Post Office more usable and more appreciated by the general public. The first of the series of annual reports by the Postmaster-General appeared in 1855, when Lord Canning held that office. It was, officially, a presentation of information to the Lords of the Treasury, the purpose being to show the "general scope and extent of the progress made by the Department." The reports were intended, however, to be read rather than filed. The volumes contain

---

[2] The initials of the original ten districts were E., E.C., N., N.E., N.W., S., S.E., S.W., W. and W.C. The N.E. and S. districts were short-lived: they were absorbed by neighboring areas in the late sixties. See Alcock & Holland, *op. cit.*, pp. 251-52. A somewhat similar arrangement for large American cities was put into use during the Second World War, though the areas indicated by numbers are not geographically self-evident. Times Square in New York, for example, is New York 18.

[3] *2nd Rep. P.M.G.* (1856), pp. 9-10; *7th Rep.* (1861), p. 10; *Fraser's Mag.*, LXII (1862), 332; *Br. Almanac* (1857), Companion, p. 20.

interesting historical summaries, data as to the increase of letters, new practices, recommendations and even amusing instances of difficulties encountered with the public. The first *Report* had an historical summary of some ten pages, the second a brief account of the rise of the Post Office in Scotland, the third a similar treatment of Ireland (written by Anthony Trollope); and additional matter on the history of the Money Order Office and other departments appeared in later issues. The idea of an annual report seems to have originated with Frederic Hill. The *Postal Guide* made its appearance for the first time in 1856.[4]

The handling of newspapers was also improved at this time. The newspaper stamp tax had been lowered, as the reader may recall, to a penny a sheet in 1836. This tax was an impressed stamp on the newspaper that gave it free carriage in the mails, and greatly added to their bulk, without any addition to the postal receipts. The burden became heavier in the forties, as the weight of newspapers increased with the improvement of the printing machine. It was stated in Parliament in 1846 that the number of newspapers sent out from London by the morning mails "is now 729,000 per week."[5]

The newspapers were asking for greater liberty in circulating a form of reading that was becoming more and more popular. They were supported by the growing belief that news itself was not a desirable subject of taxation. The result was the discontinuance of the stamp tax in 1855, though free transmission of newspapers through the post might continue if a newspaper preferred to retain the stamp tax. The proper crediting of the service to the Post Office was, therefore, not immediate: in 1858, according to the *Report* of the Postmaster-General, three-fourths of the 71,000,000 newspapers using the mails bore the impressed newspaper stamp, and in some cases it was used until 1870. Newspapers that paid their way were handled by the Book Post that had been set up in 1848. The rates of the Book Post, which had been 6d per pound, were lowered to four ounces for a penny, eight ounces for 2d and a pound for 4d. The general result

---

[4] Frederic Hill, *Autobiography*, p. 310; G. B. Hill, *op. cit.*, II, 267, 310. The Historical Summary in the *First Report* was written by Alfred Hill, the son of Matthew, according to Smyth, *op. cit.*, p. 250. The Hills did not originate annual Post Office reports. The *Post Circular* (No. 9) reprinted the *Report* of the Postmaster-General of the United States for that year. The accompanying comment expressed the hope that the American *Report* would stir sufficient improvement in the British Post Office so that it could produce a statement "equally satisfactory." The Postmaster-General of the United States had been issuing an annual report since 1823.

[5] *Parl. Deb.*, 3rd s., LXXXV, 1290; *Rep. Sel. Com. on Newspaper Stamps* (1851), p. 288.

of the change was to provide for a freer circulation of newspapers. Henceforth, those that went via the Post Office paid postage, if unstamped, and were delivered along with the other mail.[6]

The burden soon increased. Before the end of Rowland Hill's secretaryship in 1864, about 72,000,000 newspapers were passing through the mails every year. This caused concern to the Secretary, as he wished the newspaper to pay its way, and to pay the carriage to the Post Office. As he put it: "The sole purpose for which the [newspaper] stamp is now resorted to is to obtain for the newspaper the advantage of postal transmission." And the rate appeared to Hill as too low. It worked out at about one-seventh of the charge made for a letter, if the weight of the two was compared. Here was a case where "facilities" were carried too far, according to Rowland Hill. His desire, naturally, was to put the Post Office in a better financial light. The newspaper press did not take kindly to his efforts at restricting their privileges. Some unpleasant publicity appeared, and attacks on him were found even in the *Times*. When the newspaper stamp tax was abolished in 1870, there were over 80,000,000 newspapers a year going via the mails—and they were bigger than ever.[7]

The extension of deliveries to the rural districts had been urged by Rowland Hill for increasing both the usefulness and the revenue of the Post Office: the lack of this extension he held "to have been a main cause of delay in the recovery of the gross revenue."[8] This was said in 1843, when Rowland Hill seems to have assumed that there would be a great increase in the use of the Post Office by rural districts if delivery were granted. The Post Office authorities at the time questioned his proposal on the ground of expense. The government of Peel decided in that year that rural posts should be established only where more than one hundred letters a week were received. A considerable increase in rural free delivery followed. In the next two years—Rowland Hill was not in the Post Office during this time—nearly seven hundred new posts were set up for delivering more than 7,500,000 letters a year. In 1850 a new principle was

[6] See above, p. 328. Alcock & Holland, *op. cit.*, p. 385; *Hist. Sum.*, pp. 13, 16–17; Joshua Leavitt, *Cheap Postage*, p. 43; *4th Rep. P.M.G.* (1858), p. 17; *Sel. Rep. Com. on Newspaper Stamps* (1851), p. xii. The tax on advertisements, which had begun in the same year (1712) as the tax on newspapers, had been discontinued two years earlier, in 1853.

[7] *7th Rep. P.M.G.* (1861), p. 12; Hill, *op. cit.*, II, 467–68. A copy of the London *Times*, for example, then weighed about three ounces.

[8] See above, p. 323. Rowland Hill may have been influenced by the French use of rural delivery. See below, p. 373.

adopted for determining whether a delivery should be started: if a post paid its way on the basis of a halfpenny for each letter received, a delivery was set up. It was assumed that the establishment of a post would double the number of letters.

The surveyors were busy long before Rowland Hill became Secretary at the work of finding how letters were delivered in the country, and where changes should be made. One of the surveyors most concerned in this was Anthony Trollope. "Early in 1851," he wrote in his *Autobiography*, "a plan was formed for extending the rural delivery of letters, . . which up to that time had been done in a very irregular manner." He noted how a letter carrier might be sent in one direction where there were few letters to be delivered but where some influential person lived, whereas another route with no letter carrier might be in greater need. Another evil was the letter carriers' practice of charging for letters delivered on the excuse that a house was off the route. Trollope did the investigation for the Irish district to which he was attached, and then made a careful survey, on horseback, of the needs of all western England from Wiltshire and Oxfordshire to Cornwall and as far north as Herefordshire and the southern Welsh counties. His district included the Channel Islands. "The object was to create a postal network which should catch all recipients of letters," though "we were not allowed to establish any messenger's walk on which a sufficient number of letters would not be delivered to pay the man's wages, counted at a halfpenny a letter." Trollope was so eager to enlarge the mail service that somewhat oversanguine reports often resulted, for his great ambition was to cover the country with rural letter carriers: "I should have liked to ride over the whole country, and to have sent a rural post letter-carrier to every parish, every village, every hamlet, and every grange in England."[9]

Letters were delivered free by the mid-fifties to increasing areas around the large towns, to the number of over 4000 a week around such towns as Norwich and Halifax, to take examples cited by the Post Office. The general revision, begun in 1851, was pretty well completed by 1858, when there was even some thought of delivering every letter to every house no matter how remote. But this was not found practical, especially as the rural posts did not increase the rev-

[9] *Autobiography*, pp. 80-85, 88. One reason for Trollope's enthusiasm was the opportunity riding around the country gave him to indulge in his passion for hunting. It was while in Salisbury, in the course of his work, that he conceived the story of *The Warden*, the first of the delightful Barchester novels.

enue with the expected rapidity. Yet the results are remarkably impressive. During the fifties and early sixties over ten thousand places were receiving a free delivery for the first time: by 1864, over 94 per cent of the letters were delivered at the houses to which they were addressed. As Rowland Hill well put it: "At the present day the work [of extending free delivery] is so far advanced that to many readers the term 'free delivery' must have lost its significance."[10]

This early development of rural free delivery should strike the American reader as nothing short of amazing. Free delivery was a long time in coming to the United States. When Anthony Trollope visited America in 1863 to examine the working of the Post Office, he remarked on the difference. There was no free delivery at all in the United States before 1863: in the large cities, there was a delivery but it was paid for by the receivers of the letters. In that year, however, free delivery began in some American cities, though it was to be thirty years before it was extended to the rural districts. Britain's geographical compactness accounts, in part, for the remarkable extensions of postal service made so early in the history of the reformed Post Office of Great Britain.[11]

Rowland Hill was rebuffed by the public in 1859 when he attempted another pet reform, the compulsory prepayment of letters. By the fifties, about 95 per cent of the letters were prepaid, though this was not entirely by means of the adhesive stamp. Many letters were prepaid in the forties without the stamp, the postmaster simply marking in red the penny paid, or using the handstruck paid stamp, inked in red. This had been the practice before the adhesive appeared, and so conservative were many of the letter-sending public that as late as 1850 about one-third of the letters were still prepaid without the use of the stamp. But this holdover from earlier days ended shortly afterwards. No letters could be prepaid without the use of stamps in the provincial offices of the United Kingdom after November 1, 1851, and during 1852 it was discontinued as well in Edinburgh, Dublin and London, save that the older practice was not dis-

[10] See *44th Rep. P.M.G.* (1898), pp. 32-39, the basis for an excellent account of rural posts in *Hist. Sum.*, pp. 36-44. See G. B. Hill, *op. cit.*, II, 270. Free delivery to every house, even the most remote, was made in 1897 as a part of the Diamond Jubilee concessions. See below, p. 422.

[11] Trollope, *North America*, II, 276; Clyde Kelly, *United States Postal Policy* (1931), pp. 70, 107 ff.

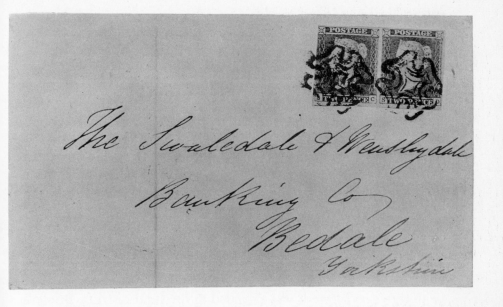

A FOLDED LETTER OF 1842

The front and back of the letter, showing the Maltese Cross obliteration, and, on the back, the sealing wax (red) and the dated stamps of Bedall, the sending office, and Newcastle, the receiving office.

A Folded Letter of 1843 Without the Adhesive Stamp
It was sent from Woodstock to London. The sender marked it "pd."

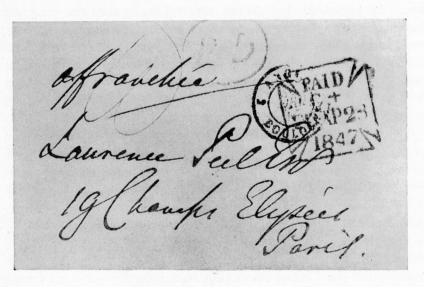

A Prepaid Letter Sent to Paris in 1847 by Sir Robert Peel. (Actual size.)
Sir Robert inscribed it "affranchie" so that no additional charge would be made for delivery when it reached his cousin. The "C+" indicates that it was mailed at Charing Cross.

continued at the head office in London until 1855.[12] Thus a desirable uniformity was brought about for the great bulk of the letters.

By the fifties, only 5 per cent of the letters were unpaid, and less than half of these were domestic letters. It is no wonder that Rowland Hill hoped that the further step could be taken, in 1859, of enforcing prepayment in stamps for all domestic letters. With the approval of the Postmaster-General, an announcement was made that, beginning on February 10, 1859, letters partly paid would be sent on to the addressees, charged with the additional postage and a penalty of a penny, and that letters wholly unpaid would be returned to the senders.[13] Violent objection resulted. The change was likely to cause considerable inconvenience to some people, and it seemed to press heavily on certain interests. Even though but 2 per cent of the letters were unpaid, the number amounted to some 2,500,000 a year. The newspapers objected strongly. Adverse opinion was expressed in both houses of Parliament. The Post Office was accused of being an engine of taxation, though the Chancellor declared that the Treasury had no ulterior interest in the proposed change. One member of the Commons declared that the "convenience of the Post Office was quite secondary to the interests of the public; in fact, the Post Office was made for the public, not the public for the Post Office." An argument that proved very telling against the proposed compulsion arose from the need of opening unpaid letters to find out the address of the senders to whom they were to be returned. The sanctity of correspondence came up again for wordy defense, on the ground that "an important check over the sanctity of letters would be destroyed altogether." This was a tender point with the public, as the government had found in the forties.[14]

Those upholding compulsory prepayment argued that it was part of the original postage plan, that it would put a stop to insulting and offensive letters and valentines, as well as the many advertisements sent by mail—above all, that it would speed the postal services. The delay in delivering unpaid letters was caused by separate handling, marking them with ink of a different color, and the need for collecting double postage when delivered. The Postmaster-General pointed out that compulsory prepayment existed in the Australian colonies and the United States. But such precedents did not count.

[12] *Quarterly Review*, LXXXVII (1850), 60; Alcock & Holland, *op. cit.*, pp. 152 ff.
[13] *Athenaeum* (Feb. 5, 1859), p. 194.
[14] *Parl. Deb.*, 3rd s., CLII, 251-58, 675-78, 1476.

The British were determined to send letters unpaid if they wanted to do so. The objection to the obnoxious order was so vociferous that it was withdrawn after a few weeks, much to the chagrin of Rowland Hill. As he wrote at the time to a sister in Australia: "You will learn by the newspapers that we have been in hot water with the public . . . in an attempt to make the prepayment of inland letters compulsory. . . . This is the first time I have had to retrace a step, and, to confess the truth, I don't like it." Nor have his successors succeeded where he failed. Letters may still be sent unpaid, and are still charged double postage.[15]

A number of changes had been made in the postage stamps, which were by now in well-nigh universal use. The original penny black and twopenny blue stamps, engraved by Perkins, Bacon & Company, had been supplemented by other values and other types of stamps. A brief notice of these changes will illustrate the process of experiment by which the stamp received its final and accepted form.

The envelopes that replaced the ridiculed Mulreadys in 1841 had an embossed oval stamp about the size of an adhesive label, showing the Queen's head. These envelopes were made of "Dickinson paper," that is, paper having colored silk threads running through it. Like the Mulreadys, they were unfolded and without gum until 1850, when machines for folding envelopes came into use. They appeared gummed at the same time, and bore on the flap an embossed circular device not unlike a seal. This, it was thought, might take the place of a seal, since it was no longer necessary to close the letter in the old way with wafer or wax. By the mid-century, therefore, a fundamental change had occurred in letter-sending habits, though the use of sealing wax and the practice of sending a folded letter without an envelope died very slowly. It was estimated that 93 per cent of the domestic letters were sent in envelopes by 1855.[16]

Until 1847 the only adhesive stamps were the original line-engraved penny and twopenny issues. But in that year a shilling stamp was provided for use on foreign mail and to pay the registration fee on letters. The new stamp was embossed on Dickinson paper. In

[15] G. B. Hill, *op. cit.*, II, 335-36; *3rd Rep. P.M.G.* (1857), p. 15; *5th Rep.* (1859), pp. 43 ff., where Rowland Hill answers fully the objections to compulsory prepayment.
[16] *2nd Rep. P.M.G.* (1856), p. 19. Edwin Hill, who had an important position in the Stamp Office, perfected the machine for folding envelopes. See Edwards, *Sir Rowland Hill*, pp. 49-50. Official envelopes did not bear the imitation seal after 1878. In 1855 the right was finally granted, after a persistent demand that began in 1839, of having the postage stamp "struck" on private paper. Provision was made by 18 & 19 Victoria, c.78. The paper had to be taken to the Stamp Office for the purpose.

1848 an embossed 10d stamp was issued, and one of the value of 6d in 1854. These three stamps were the only embossed ones issued by the British Post Office save for the envelope stamps and the little-used stamps on private paper: other forms proved more economical to produce.

When the postage to France was lowered from 10d to 4d in 1855 a stamp of this value was needed. It was neither line-engraved nor embossed, but surface-printed. This process, used in printing postage stamps for France, was adopted by the British Post Office because it was less expensive than engraving or embossing. In surface printing, the die was first engraved on steel, from which molds were made in sufficient number to form a plate, and then an electrotype cast was made. Surface-printed stamps of other values soon appeared, although it was not until 1880 that De La Rue and Company issued a full series beginning with the ½d. By that time line engraving had been discarded—to the regret of many who preferred the fine linear execution of the first stamps.[17]

Changes also occurred in the stamp design during these years, though the use of the Queen's head remained. Letters that had been used in the bottom corners to prevent forgery were also put in the upper corners beginning with 1858. The letters in the upper corners were the reverse of those in the lower. Robert Smith, head of the London District Post, made the suggestion to prevent the combination of unused parts of stamps that had already been carelessly canceled. As the directions to the postmasters put it: "If any postage label passing through your office should appear to have been formed by pieces cut from separate stamps, you will be careful to ascertain whether the letters at the corners are arranged in the manner above described; and whether the number on each side of the label is the same." This last injunction referred to the plate numbers.[18]

The perforating of stamps did not come into use until 1854. Previously the labels had to be separated from each other by a knife or scissors. To meet the need for single stamps, it was customary for all the stationers' shops to have small boxes of postage stamps ready for use; they were sold for a trifle beyond the usual shilling a dozen.

[17] A 1/2d line-engraved stamp issued, in 1870, was the only stamp in that form apart from the 1d and 2d Queen's heads.

[18] Bacon, *op. cit.*, I, 136, 157-58; Wright & Creeke, *op. cit.*, p. 3. Corner letters were discontinued in 1887. Plate numbers on the line-engraved stamps are often difficult to decipher, save with a magnifying glass, but they have proved of much interest to stamp collectors. For a plate number on a surface-printed stamp, see illustration on p. 366.

Henry Archer first approached the government in 1847 with regard to the use of his perforating machine. He held that the stamps could be easily detached "without the operation of cutting," that sheets of stamps might be folded more conveniently and regularly, and that the stamps would stick better to the letters—"the rough or dental edges which it will give the stamps will render them less liable to be removed by hand or otherwise." This last value of perforation should have appealed to workers in the Post Office, as many stamps were found loose in the mail bags.[19]

The first machine submitted by Archer did not perforate the stamps in the current use of that term, but rather rouletted them by piercing a series of slits in the spaces between the stamps. He had a true perforating machine ready, however, by the end of 1848; by little discs of paper were removed. Though some of the postal officials were much interested in the device, there was considerable delay in the adoption of the perforating machine. In 1851 an inquiry was made in the House of Commons as to why this "operation of great mechanical ingenuity" had not been put into service. A year later—matters being still at a standstill—a motion for a select committee on postage label stamps was the result. Stamps first appeared with perforations in 1854.[20]

The perforation of stamps was a very important step in making the penny postal scheme capable of still further advances, but it did not appeal to Rowland Hill. Strangely enough, he makes no reference to the Archer improvement in his autobiographical account of postal developments. His silence and lukewarmness may have resulted from the added expense to the Post Office, or because this invention was not a part of his original plan. "My opinion is," he testified, "that it would be useful and acceptable to the public to a certain extent."[21]

---

[19] *Rep. Sel. Com. on Postage Label Stamps* (1852), pp. 1-3; correspondence regarding the Archer machine in *Accounts & Papers* (1851); Bacon, *op. cit.*, I, 121; II, 311-14.

[20] Wright & Creeke, *op. cit.*, p. 8; *Parl. Deb.*, 3rd s., CXVII, 1081-82; CXIX, 1157-59; CXLII, 1284-96; *Rep. Sel. Com. on Postage Label Stamps* (1852), pp. 16-19. Archer had first been offered £500 for his machine, then £600, and later £2000, all of which seemed to him inadequate. After the hearings of the Select Committee he was offered and accepted £4000.

[21] *Rep. Sel. Com. on Postage Label Stamps* (1852), p. 93. Edmund Yates, long in the Post Office and a friend of Rowland Hill, declared that Rowland Hill never believed a suggestion about postal affairs was of any use unless it was to be found in what he called "my pamphlet." *Recollections and Experiences*, II, 227.

During these years the handling of letters by the Post Office was greatly improved, especially by new and more efficient ways of cancellation. When postage stamps first came in, a Maltese Cross obliterator was added to the name-and-date stamps used by the sending and receiving offices.[22] In 1844 a change was made to numeral cancellation stamps. This suggestion, made by Francis Abbott of the General Post Office, was intended to aid in tracing a letter. The obliterator had a number in the center, each office being assigned one. There were several series of numbers, distributed, apart from the London District, in general alphabetical order. The English and Welsh list had the number surrounded by horizontal bars forming a circle, the Scottish list by bars forming a square or oblong, and in the Irish list the bars were in a diamond shape. In this way, three towns would have the same number. Thirteen, for example, belonged to Ambleside in the English and Welsh list, to Arbroath in Scotland and to Ashbourne in Ireland. Numbers of frequent appearance were those of Liverpool (466), Manchester (498), Glasgow (159) and Dublin (186).[23]

Double canceling stamps, with the name and date and also the numbered obliterator, appeared in the late forties—an obvious saving of time and labor. By the end of the fifties, these double stamps were being struck by machines. In the eighties, the familiar dated circle stamp with horizontal bars for canceling the postage label came into use. The hour at which a letter was posted was not added to the date until 1895. By this addition, the Post Office finally returned to the practice of William Dockwra of two centuries earlier.[24]

Rowland Hill was not responsible for all the improvements that the Post Office adopted while he was the Secretary, but he gave to the Department a vigorous leadership and showed deep concern in its greater efficiency. Col. Maberly, who had retired in 1854, was a clear-headed man of business, but inclined to let matters run in their

---

[22] For examples of Maltese Cross cancellations, see above, pp. 314, 320.

[23] See the *British Postal Guide*—especially that for 1856—where they were listed from time to time. The use of these numbered obliterators continued into the twentieth century, an amended list appearing in 1924. They were generally discarded, however, by that time. A full list is given in Marshall, *The British Post Office*.

[24] For the addition of the hour, see *40th Rep. P.M.G.* (1894), p. 7. Though Great Britain preceded other countries in adopting the practices we have been describing, she was not the first in the precise dating of the cancellation. J. Henniker Heaton had urged its adoption in Great Britain as early as 1891. See *Parl. Deb.*, 3rd s., CCCLII, 878.

OBLITERATING STAMPS.

It sometimes occurs that the Stamps on letters used to denote the places at which such have been posted are not sufficiently plain. In such cases the *stamp used to obliterate the postage label* may supply the information. The shape of the stamp and its number will prove the office in which it has been used. The following are *fac similes* of the obliterating stamps:—

Used in London District Office and in places within its delivery.

Used in the London Office for letters passing by the *General* Post.

Used in all places in England and Wales except London and the London District.

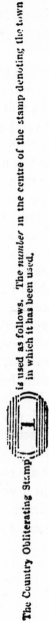

Used in Scotland.

Used in Ireland.

The London District Obliterating Stamp is used at the following places. The *number* on the stamp indicates the particular Office.

Higbgate,

Finchley, and so on. The *number* in the centre of the stamp denoting the particular office in which it has been used.

The Country Obliterating Stamp

is used as follows. The *number* in the centre of the stamp denoting the town in which it has been used.

1 Abergavenny	38 Aylesbury	73 Bilstone	111 Bingley	147 Bungay
2 Aberystwith	39 Aylsham	74 Birkenhead	112 Braintree	148 Buntingford
3 Abingdon	40 Bagshot	75 Birmingham	113 Brampton	149 Burford
4 Wantage	41 Bakewell	76 Campden	114 Brandon	150 Burnley

Part of the official statement on obliterating stamps, 1856.

ordinary grooves. He detested all projects of reform, and had an abiding dislike of Rowland Hill.[25] Col. Maberly had chosen excellent men for the chief executive positions, including John Tilley, who became the first Assistant Secretary when Rowland Hill took over in 1854. The other Assistant Secretary under Rowland Hill was his brother Frederic. In parceling out the departments over which the two assistants had charge, he gave to John Tilley those in which but "moderate change" was likely, and to Frederic Hill those most likely to show improvement. It could hardly have been otherwise, since he was determined to make the greatest possible advance in postal business, in order to prove that his "plan" was a success.[26]

He incurred the ill will of the employees of the great organization in the fifties on the grounds that the men were overworked and underpaid. There was much unrest, and even threats against his life —part of what he called a "cabal." The accusations came to a head in 1862 when a request was made in the House of Commons for a select committee to inquire into the grievances alleged to exist in the Post Office Department. The select committee was not appointed.[27]

Rowland Hill's relations with the Treasury had been, on the whole, satisfactory. He got on well with a number of the Postmasters-General, though there was likely to be difficulty when the Postmaster-General was determined to be the real head of the Department. Such were the Earl of Hardwicke (1852-53) and Lord Stanley of Alderley, Postmaster-General from 1860 to 1866. Difficulties between Lord Stanley and the energetic and reforming Secretary led to Hill's resignation in 1864. The two men simply did not get on. Rowland Hill's daughter refers to the trouble as "a quarrel that lasted for four years" between her father and "the man who was probably the most unpopular Postmaster-General of his century." Hill found the opposition against him so determined, in what he chose to call a "fourth cabal," that there seemed no option but resignation. His health, none too good at the time, was made worse by departmental difficulties. Hill resigned the Secretaryship in the spring of 1864.[28]

[25] The judgment of Edmund Yates, *op. cit.*, I, 98. See also above, p. 335.
[26] G. B. Hill, *op. cit.*, II, 264-65; Smyth, *op. cit.*, p. 248.
[27] G. B. Hill, *op. cit.*, II, 321-28; *Parl. Deb.*, 3rd s., CLIX, 212; CLXVIII, 672-82.
[28] G. B. Hill, *op. cit.*, II, 362, 384 ff.; Smyth, *op. cit.*, pp. 284-85. The 9th ed. of the *E.B.* (1885) praises Hill's "conspicuous energy," but thought it not sufficiently supplemented by "suavity of manner, tact in dealing with large bodies of inferiors, and reverence for the good things of past times" (XIX, 570). Edmund Yates, a friend of Rowland Hill and a worker in the Post Office, credited Hill with a "peculiarly effective

Thus ended the relations of Rowland Hill with the Post Office he had done so much to remake. When Lord Stanley was confronted in the House of Lords with the "strongly expressed desire of the public to know the truth" about the resignation, he attributed it to the state of Rowland Hill's health and its lack of improvement after six months' leave of absence: "Those were the whole circumstances connected with Sir Rowland Hill's resignation, as far as he was acquainted with them." The Postmaster-General thereupon praised Hill for "one of the greatest improvements of the present age," and expressed "the regret which would be felt by the public [!] at his retirement." Rewards of honors and pecuniary benefits were also heaped upon the retired Secretary. His salary was continued as a pension for life, and Parliament made a special grant of £20,000. The discussion of the grant in the Commons brought out high praise from Lord Palmerston and Sir Francis Baring. There was some dissent on the part of a few members, the member for Lambeth pointing out that Rowland Hill was not the only person who was concerned with carrying out the change. "The late Mr. Wallace . . . urged the subject upon the attention of the House, and did more to introduce the plan to the country than Sir Rowland Hill." In general, however, the praise was without qualification.[29]

The retirement of Rowland Hill in 1864 did not affect the remarkable expansion of the postal services. The new Secretary, Sir John Tilley, held the office until 1880, with Frederic Hill as the first Assistant Secretary and Frank I. Scudamore as the second assistant. The number of letters—slightly over 400,000,000 a year in 1853—had risen to 675,000,000 in 1864. By 1870 the total was well over 800,000,000; ten years after the retirement of Rowland Hill

way of saying a caustic and unpleasant thing." As he thought Lord Stanley "insolent and overbearing," there could hardly have been peace in the postal household. *Op. cit.*, I, 103, 106; II, 225.

[29] *Parl. Deb.*, 3rd s., CLXXIII, 1626; CLXXV, 1595-601, 1705. Several years before, he had been made a Knight Commander of the Bath. At the time of his resignation, he was granted a D.C.L. by the University of Oxford. Sir Rowland Hill lived on for fifteen years. Much of this time was given over to the preparation of an elaborate autobiography—the apologia of his efforts and of his place in postal reform. As his daughter put it: " 'My plan' was often on his lips and ever in his thoughts." It appeared in 1880, the year following his death, edited by his nephew, George Birkbeck Hill. A few months before his death in 1879 Rowland Hill was granted the freedom of the City of London. He had hoped that his burial might take place in Westminster Abbey, nor was he disappointed, as there was general agreement that he deserved a place in the national shrine. G. B. Hill, *op. cit.*, II, 430.

the figure was 900,000,000. To this should be added some 80,000,-
000 post cards, and an annual total of 125,000,000 newspapers.[30]

The increase in the gross and net revenue for these two decades
reflects the constantly growing use of the organization. The gross
revenue, £2,700,000 in 1854, increased to £4,231,000 in 1864 and
to £5,751,000 in 1874. The net revenue, £1,195,000 in 1854, was
only £1,153,000 in 1864, and still below the net revenue of 1839.
By 1874, the net revenue was £1,836,000 when it finally topped for
the first time the net income for 1839. Various causes had delayed
for thirty-five years the recovery of the net revenue—the carrying
of stamped newspapers free of charge, the placing of the cost of the
packet service against the Post Office after 1860, and the greatly increased packet charges after 1868.[31]

England and Wales were responsible for the largest share, by far,
of the postal income. In 1874, for example, 7 per cent of the revenue
came from Ireland, 9 per cent from Scotland, and 84 per cent from
England and Wales. The overwhelming importance of the postal
service in England arose partly from its greater population, but even
more from the industrial and commercial activity centered in such
places as London, Liverpool, Manchester and Birmingham. London
was far in the lead, its postal revenue in the sixties being about ten
times that of Liverpool or Manchester. Behind these three centers,
but not in close competition even with Liverpool and Manchester,
came Glasgow, Edinburgh, Dublin, Birmingham, Bristol, Leeds
and Newcastle, in that order.[32]

[30] *20th Rep. P.M.G.* (1875), p. 7. The record of inland letters and postcards is taken
from the official *Reports of the P.M.G.*

	CHARGEABLE LETTERS	POSTCARDS		CHARGEABLE LETTERS	POSTCARDS
1854	443,650,000		1865	720,467,000	
1855	456,216,000		1866	750,000,000	
1856	478,393,000		1867	774,831,000	
1857	504,421,000		1868	808,118,000	
1858	522,874,000		1869	831,914,000	
1859	544,796,000		1870	862,722,000	
1860	564,002,000		1871	867,000,000	75,000,000
1861	593,240,000		1872	885,000,000	76,000,000
1862	605,471,000		1873	907,000,000	72,000,000
1863	642,324,000		1874	967,000,000	79,000,000
1864	679,084,000		1875	1,008,392,000	87,116,000

[31] See the annual *Reports of the P.M.G.*, esp. the *20th*, p. 45.
[32] *5th Rep. P.M.G.* (1859), p. 34; *6th Rep.* (1860).

The greater population of England does not altogether explain its overwhelming postal importance. In 1854 the average number of letters per person in England and Wales was nineteen, with fifteen for each person in Scotland, and seven in Ireland. Ten years later, in 1863, the ratio had increased to twenty-six for England and Wales, twenty for Scotland, and nine for Ireland, and by the early seventies, the annual number per person in England and Wales was thirty-three, twenty-five for Scotland and thirteen for Ireland.[33]

The usefulness of the Post Office was greatly increased by several changes that came in the early seventies. Wrappers bearing half-penny stamps were first issued in 1870, with a charge of a halfpenny above the postage for ten wrappers. A much more welcome addition to postal stationery was the post card. It had been suggested first by Dr. von Stephan to the German Postal Union in 1865. But his proposal was not welcomed there, and Austria first put them to use in 1869. Their immense popularity led to their introduction in Great Britain during 1870. The postage was a halfpenny, and at first no charge was made for a post card above the value of the stamp. They "took" immediately, as the average number used per week in 1871 shows: it was over one and a half million, or 75,000,000 for the year.[34]

In 1870 the newspaper rate was lowered as well, at the same time that the newspaper stamp tax was finally abolished. The rate was set at a halfpenny for each newspaper passing by post, irrespective of its weight. The same act that provided post cards and allowed newspapers at the lowered rate also lessened the rate on books: it became a halfpenny for every two ounces. It is not surprising to learn that the total for book packets and newspapers jumped from 130,000,000 in 1870 to over 200,000,000 for 1871.[35]

[33] *9th Rep. P.M.G.* (1863), p. 114; *17th Rep.* (1871), p. 24; *21st Rep.* (1875), p. 18. The reader may be interested in the letters per person in the leading English towns, postally speaking. The date is 1863.

London	48	Liverpool	31
Birmingham	28	Malvern	103
Bradford	26	Manchester	21
Brighton	48	Oxford	36
Bristol	29	Sheffield	16
Cardiff	20	Southport	52
Leamington	57	Windsor	40

[34] A. D. Smith, *The Development of Rates of Postage*, pp. 241 ff.; *17th Rep. P.M.G.* (1871), pp. 3-4.

[35] *Hist. Sum*, p. 14; 33 & 34 Vict., c.79. A newspaper was defined by the act as "any

One of the lucrative sources of postal revenue in those days was the valentine—the day of picture post cards had not yet come. The valentines at the time numbered annually a million and a third for London only. They had caused some discussion when compulsory prepayment was attempted, on the ground that humorous and unpleasant valentines would be less numerous if prepaid. The Post Office Act of 1870 forbade sending through the mails "indecent or obscene prints, paintings, lithographs, engravings, books, or cards." The regulations had long forbidden sending in letters sharp instruments, knives, scissors, or glass, leeches, game, or fish, gunpowder, lucifer matches "or anything which is explosive."[36] Yet the post was still used for strange purposes. The *Report* for 1872 noted that a live snake had been mailed the year before. The Post Office objected at first to accepting the animal, but took it finally lest the feelings of the "eccentric gentleman" who sent it be wounded. It seems the animal was a "pet who had been out on a visit." And what was perhaps worse, over 15,000 letters were posted in the previous year without any address! Moreover, 60,000 postage stamps were found separate in the mails, as the result of carelessness in attaching them to the mail matter they were supposed to prepay.[37]

One other important change, and the record for these two decades can be concluded. A new scale of letter postage was established in 1871. The rate had been one penny for the first half-ounce since 1840. In 1847 the upper limit of sixteen ounces was abolished, in 1865 the progression of weight above the ounce was made a penny for each half-ounce. In 1871 the rate was further reduced, the first ounce going for a penny, the second ounce for a halfpenny, and every succeeding two ounces up to twelve ounces costing a halfpenny each. Thus a letter weighing just under twelve ounces cost 4d. If over that weight, the cost was a penny per ounce, beginning with the first ounce. At last the original proposal of Rowland Hill, that an ounce letter should go for a penny, came into force. This had been his proposal in the first edition of *Post Office Reform*, but the second edition

---

publication consisting wholly or in great part of political or other news, or of articles relating thereto, or to other current topics, with or without advertisements." It had to appear once a week and to be printed on unstitched paper.

[36] *Br. Postal Guide* (Oct. 1, 1872), p. 13.

[37] *18th Rep. P.M.G.* (1872), pp. 8, 10; *19th Rep.* (1873), p. 8, etc.

had changed the ounce to a half-ounce as the result of advice from the Chancellor of the Exchequer.[38]

[38] *Br. Postal Guide* (Oct. 1, 1872), p. 9; A. D. Smith, *op. cit.*, pp. 31-32. A tabulation may make the changes between 1840 and 1871 clearer.

Weight not exceeding	1840	1865	1871
½ oz.	1d	1d	} 1d
2nd ½ oz.	1d	1d	
3rd ½ oz.	} 2d	1d	} ½d
4th ½ oz.		1d	
5th ½ oz.	} 2d	1d	
6th ½ oz.		1d	} ½d
7th ½ oz.	} 2d	1d	
8th ½ oz.		1d	

and so on up to 16 oz. limit   etc.   etc. to 12 oz. 1d per oz. if more than 12 oz.

26

The Flattery
of Imitation

WHEN Robert Wallace was pushing the adoption of uniform penny postage and the use of stamps in 1839, he urged the early adoption of this "magnificent plan," as giving "this country an opportunity of taking the lead in bestowing one of the greatest boons that could be conferred on the human race before any other country."[1] The change was so revolutionary and was done by virtue of so much public discussion that the people of other countries could hardly help passing judgment on the novel plan. Great Britain was a particularly effective place in which to make the change, as England was the most important commercial and financial center of the day. Since British oversea interests were spread to every continent and all the oceans, the device of stamps, in particular, could hardly fail to impress the rest of the world.

Within a decade the more wide-awake nations in Europe and America began to introduce the recent British innovations associated with the adhesive stamp. Nor were the colonies backward in following the lead of the mother country. By the end of the fifties, stamps were well-nigh universal, and many other features of the British system had served to bring fundamental changes in other national post offices. An examination of some of these early influences will bring out in even clearer relief the sweeping nature of the British reform; and the partial acceptance, here and there, of the principles advocated in *Post Office Reform* will furnish another appraisal of penny postage.

[1] *Parl. Deb.*, 3rd s., XLVIII, 1384.

The first European government to adopt postage stamps was the Swiss canton of Zurich. In August 1842, the postal department laid before the Council of State a report for simplifying the system. It was frankly based on the changes in England. Uniformity was not adopted, however, as there were two sets of rates, one for local letters in Zurich, and another for the canton as a whole. The first stamps used in Zurich were issued in 1843, lithographed and printed in black. In the same year the canton of Geneva issued stamps. M. de Candolle of Geneva urged some features of the plan that he had seen in its beginnings in London in 1839. He believed the benefits of penny postage "somewhat doubtful for England," but held that certain of the features could be used to advantage in Geneva. Prepayment, the use of stamps and one rate for the canton were advocated, but no emphasis was put on the lowering of the rate. The third canton to issue stamps was Basel, in 1845. When the Confederation claimed the right of postal control, beginning in 1850, stamps were issued for the whole of Switzerland. Still there was not one rate, but four zones and four rates. The directions issued for applying the stamps directed their attachment on the address side in the upper *left*-hand corner.[2]

Belgium became so interested in the British reforms that the government applied to Rowland Hill for a statement of the results of penny postage. Stamps were actually adopted at the end of 1847, although not issued until July 1, 1849. There were two rates, one for a letter going no more than thirty kilometers, and another for greater distances within the kingdom. The stamps were made *à notre effigie*, as King Leopold announced in 1849. They are commonly called "epaulettes," since the profile of the King shows the shoulder decoration prominently. The stamps were designed in Belgium but engraved by H. Robinson of the firm of Perkins, Bacon & Company. Like the penny black, the first Belgian stamp did not bear the name of the country.[3]

The Post Office in France was naturally affected by the changes taking place in Great Britain. The two postal systems had been in close relation for centuries by means of the Dover packets, and much of Britain's continental mail was routed through France. The British, too, were more familiar with the French postal system than any

[2] P. Mirabaud and A. de Reuterskiöld, *The Postage Stamps of Switzerland, 1848-1862*, pp. 3, 14-18, 41, 73, 81-82.

[3] J. B. Moëns, *Les timbres de Belgique depuis leur origine jusqu'à nos jours*, I, 27-42; Willy Balassa, *Grand Catalogue des Timbres de Belgique* (1940), pp. 32, 52.

other foreign service. Robert Wallace had referred to the charge by weight, already in use in France, when he was attacking the backward British system in the early thirties. In the third report of the Select Committee of 1838, the steady progress of the French Post Office was noticed in contrast to the lethargy of the British.[4] The Post Office in France may have influenced Rowland Hill's thinking more than he admitted. He had visited France shortly before writing *Post Office Reform*, and had inspected the French postal system in 1839, previous to entering on his duties at the Treasury.

The postal charges of France were reckoned by weight, and had been since the French Revolution, but the cost of a letter depended on the distance it traveled. The last tariff before 1840, that of 1827, charged letters weighing no more than seven and a half grammes two décimes (twopence) if not going more than forty kilometers, three décimes up to eighty kilometers, etc., the distance being reckoned as the crow flies. The highest charge for letters was twelve décimes, or a shilling—less than the highest charge in Great Britain.[5] A feature of the French system that received much praise was the rural post set up in 1829, with a charge of a décime for letters weighing fifteen grammes. M. Piron of the French Post Office credited this rural service with much of the steady progress made by the French Post Office in the thirties.[6] Another feature that may have influenced British thinking was the required prepayment of newspapers and printed matter, and their enclosure in wrappers. The increase in French postal income in the twenties and thirties was over 50 per cent, a fact that the British critics of their own Post Office were not slow to point out.[7]

After the appearance of Rowland Hill's pamphlet, the sub-director of the French Post Office, M. A. Piron, published proposals for reform in France, proposals that seem to have been responsible for the remark of Robert Wallace quoted at the beginning of this chapter. He advocated the single charge of a décime for letters of seven and a half grammes in weight, if they did not go outside the department where posted, and a charge of two décimes or twopence for anywhere else in France. He also proposed stamps, with or without

[4] *3rd Rep. Sel. Com. on Postage*, p. 11.
[5] A décime equaled ten centimes, and was equivalent to an English penny or two cents in American money.
[6] *Athenaeum* (1843), p. 458.
[7] Ernest Guy, *La conception moderne du paiement des transports postaux et le timbre-poste*, p. 40; Plitt, *op. cit.*, pp. 8-20; *3rd Rep. Sel. Com. on Postage*, p. 11; A. D. Smith, *op. cit.*, pp. 78 ff.; Rothschild, *Histoire de la poste aux lettres*, I, 264-68.

envelopes, for the different weights and distances.[8] The matter was first raised in the French Chamber in July 1839, where M. Lherbette asked the Minister of Finance if the postal tax was to be reduced. The reply indicated that they were awaiting the results of the English experiment. When the matter was brought up again in 1841, the Minister of Finance pointed out the miscalculations resulting from the change in Great Britain.[9]

During the forties there was a growing demand in the press and in the Chamber of Deputies for postal reform. M. Saint-Priest suggested in 1844 a minimum weight of ten grammes, which would be carried forty kilometers for two décimes. But the plan, opposed by the government, was defeated by the narrowest of margins. Again in 1846, the reformers, Saint-Priest and Emile de Girardin, made another attempt that failed, though the government took off the rural décime. In 1847 M. Glais-Bizoin proposed a uniform rate of twenty centimes (two décimes) for all of France for a seven and a half gramme letter if paid in advance, and double that charge if not prepaid. Girardin strongly supported this measure—much like the actual British practice—but it failed of passage.

When the Revolution of 1848 replaced Louis Philippe's government by a republic, the way was open for a change. In August 1848, the Assembly voted a rate of twenty centimes (twopence) as uniform throughout France for letters of seven and a half grammes weight or less, with prepayment obligatory. There was so much objection to this compulsory feature of the reform that unpaid letters were later allowed. The new rates went into effect on the first day of 1849. The change included the use of adhesive stamps. After the offer of Perkins, Bacon & Company to manufacture the new stamps was rejected as too high, the production of the stamps was granted to M. Hulot, an engraver of money in Paris. The surface-printed stamps had the female head of Liberty as its central design. When Louis Napoleon captured the Republic, the head of Liberty on the stamps was replaced by that of the Napoleonic aspirant, and when he took the final step of transforming the Republic into the Second Empire, the country's name at the top of the stamps was changed as well.

[8] *Du service des postes et de la taxation des lettres au moyen d'un timbre* (1838). See also Guy, *op. cit.*, p. 71; Arthur Maury, *Histoire des timbres-poste français*, p. 13; *Quarterly Rev.* (London, Oct. 1839), LXIV, 289; *Chambers' Edinburgh Journal*, VIII (1839), 292.

[9] Georges Brunel, *Le timbre-poste français*, p. 47; Guy, *op. cit.*, p. 85.

A Letter of 1868 Sent from Glasgow to New York

howing the double canceling stamp with numeral. The postage stamp, surface-printed, has
orner letters and a plate number (just above the lower letters).

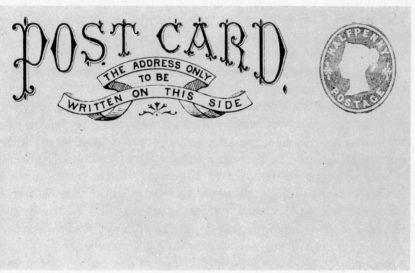

An Early Embossed Post Card, 1872

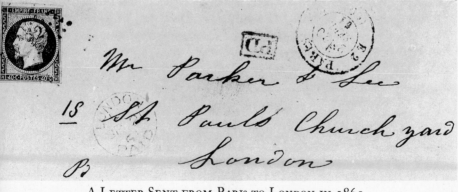

A Letter Sent from Paris to London in 1861

ctual size. The imperforate stamp bears the portrait of the Emperor. The letter was fully
aid, as indicated by the sender, by the French Post Office (PD), and by the London paid
amp.

A Letter Sent from the United States to England in 1855
Perforated stamps were not yet in use.

An Envelope on Behalf of Ocean Penny Postage
Issued in Great Britain to further Burritt's efforts. A space was provided for the insertion the official postage stamp.

The results of the reform were not so striking as in Great Britain. The public did not take to prepayment very rapidly, nor was the stamp popular at the start. Even by 1854 less than half the letters were prepaid. But the number of letters nearly doubled by the mid-fifties, and the gross revenue, in contrast with that of Great Britain, recovered within six years. The French, in this instance, were less impulsive than the British. An acute observer, M. Bronne, writing in 1858 of the postal reform in England, believed the slower advance in France and Belgium to have been justified. He doubted, too, whether *penny* postage was so much responsible for the increase in the British Post Office as the progress of commerce and the spread of education. He also pointed out the errors in prophecy made by the British reformers, and believed that if twopence instead of a penny had been made the basic rate, the revenue would not have suffered.[10]

Rowland Hill wrote in 1843 that the first countries to adopt the British improvements were Russia and Spain, two unlikely regions for liberal advances.[11] In the Czarist Empire, stamped envelopes appeared as early as 1845, when they were first used in Finland. Three years later they were employed in the Empire as a whole. But adhesive stamps were long in coming: not until 1858 did they appear for all Russia, though they had been used in Finland two years before. The Spanish government seems to have made inquiries in 1843 as to the British postal reforms, but it was not until 1850 that a lowered tariff and postage stamps came into use. And then it was the recent introduction of stamps in France that was as much of a stimulus as the British practice. The stamps bore the diademed head of Queen Isabella II. Portugal adopted stamps in 1853, showing the embossed head of Queen Maria.[12]

In the Italian peninsula, as yet decidedly disunited, adhesive stamps began to appear in the fifties. Several decades before that time a stamped sheet or wrapper had been used in the Kingdom of Sardinia. But the money obtained in this way was not so much postage, as a permit for correspondence to circulate outside the government post office. This stamped paper was used from 1818 to 1836.[13] The first adhesive stamps for Sardinia appeared in 1851, showing an

---

[10] Louis Bronne, *La réforme postale en Angleterre*, pp. 40-43. For the introduction of stamps in France, see Brunel, *op. cit.*, pp. 50-58; Guy, *op. cit.*, pp. 98-100.

[11] G. B. Hill, *op. cit.*, II, 13.

[12] Hugo Griebert, *The Stamps of Spain* (London, 1919), pp. 1-3, 17.

[13] Rothschild, *op. cit.*, I, 281-88; William H. Tower, "Sardinia Correspondence Paper," *Collectors' Club Philatelist*, XXII, 287-93.

effigy of Victor Emmanuel II. In the next year adhesive stamps were introduced in Modena, Parma and the Papal States. Stamps were put into use about the same time in northern Europe—in Denmark in 1851, in Holland and Luxemburg the next year, and in Norway and Sweden by 1855.

Central Europe was at this time a complicated political mosaic of confederated states, among which Austria and Prussia were the largest and most influential. There had been for centuries a sort of international post in central Europe under the control of the family of Thurn and Taxis. This family, originally Italian, had, as we have seen, acquired the mastership of the posts from the Emperor in the fifteenth century. In the year 1616 it became an hereditary fief of the family, and was still a widespread service in the nineteenth century, though it was no longer so far-reaching as in the days of Charles V, when the service included Italy, Spain and the Low Countries. There was considerable jealousy of this Imperial Post among the various German states, so much so that rival domestic systems were also in use. But the Taxis posts gave central Europe a sort of postal union at a time when the region was shot through with localism. The Taxis posts only ceased when they were bought out by Prussia in 1867, at a time when Prussia had brought much of Germany under her control.[14]

Prussia may serve as an example of the effects of British influences in central Europe. A messenger service had begun there in the days of Witherings, but it was very restricted. The rates were high throughout the growth of Prussia, as the constant demand for funds, in its effort to survive and expand, made the Prussian government use the Post Office as a revenue-gathering organization. As late as 1824 the rates were so high that a letter weighing only three-eighths of an ounce was carried but two miles for one groschen (about 1¼d), four miles for one and half groschen, seven miles for two groschen, etc.[15] Changes were made in 1844 that only slightly relieved the situation, since the Prussian King was not willing to sacrifice revenue in the English manner. Not until 1850 was there any great change: in that year the table of distances was simplified, a half-ounce letter

[14] Louis Rolland, *De la correspondance postale et télégraphique dans les relations internationales* (Paris, 1901), pp. 50-60; A. D. Smith, *op. cit.*, pp. 349-55. For this early post, see also Fritz Ohmann, *Die Anfänge des Postwesens und die Taxis* (Leipzig, 1909), and Joseph Rübsam, *François de Taxis, le fondateur de la poste moderne* (Berne, 1891). See above, pp. 4, 27, 159.

[15] A groschen or ten pfennigs (one-tenth of a mark) was worth about 2½ cents or 1¼d.

going ten miles for a groschen, twenty miles for two groschen, and all other distances for three. But the changes, even then, were far short of the British or the French reforms.[16] When the North German Confederation was formed in 1867, the various independent postal systems disappeared along with that of Thurn and Taxis, and charges were made irrespective of distance for the first time. A half-ounce letter went anywhere in the Confederation for a groschen or ten pfennigs, a letter of greater weight for two groschen.

Stamps had appeared some years earlier. The first German state to issue them was Bavaria: they were issued in 1849. Prussia, Austria, Hanover and Saxony followed in 1850, Baden and Wurtemberg in 1851, and the Thurn and Taxis service in 1852.

Such were the changes wrought in Europe by the influence of the British postal reforms of 1840. Rowland Hill could say with pardonable pride in 1854 that "my plan has been adopted more or less completely by every considerable state in Europe."[17]

Britain's postal reforms brought quick response from two of the states of the Western Hemisphere. Brazil was far in the lead in South America: in fact, it was the second state in the world to adopt postage stamps. The Brazilian consul in London wrote home as to the value of the change in Great Britain, with the result that a decree soon followed announcing the compulsory use of stamps, uniformity of rate and the establishment of town deliveries. The basic rate of 60 reis for a letter carried by land anywhere within the country was some two and a half times higher than the penny rate in Great Britain—and with reason if we consider the size of Dom Pedro's dominions. The stamps began to appear on letters in August 1843. They were engraved, and had as the central feature of the design the amount of the postage—the so-called "Bull's eyes." The portrait of the Emperor did not appear on the first stamps, partly because it was thought irreverent to place the portrait where it could be defaced, and partly owing to the difficulty of producing a satisfactory engraving in Brazil at that time. Such scruples and difficulties were overcome by 1866, when stamps appeared with the engraved head of Dom Pedro.[18]

[16] A. D. Smith, *op. cit.*, pp. 97 ff. See also H. von Stephan, *Geschichte der preussischen Post* (Berlin, 1859).

[17] G. B. Hill, *op. cit.*, II, 252.

[18] C. Ottoni Vieira, *Catalogue historique des timbres-postes et entiers du Brésil*, pp. 11, 17. See also *Collectors' Club Philatelist*, XIX (July 1940), 217-18; XXII (July 1943), 129-32. Lewins, *op. cit.*, p. 261, made an egregious error in declaring that "for eight long years the British people may be said to have enjoyed a complete monopoly of postage stamps."

In the United States the postal arrangements before 1840 were not unlike those of the unreformed British Post Office—in some regards they were worse. Letters were charged by the number of sheets and according to the distance they traveled. At the opening of the nineteenth century a single letter going forty miles cost 8¢, going ninety miles 10¢, etc. A single going over three hundred but no farther than five hundred miles cost 20¢, and greater distances brought a charge of 25¢. During the War of 1812 these rates were increased 50 per cent for the purpose of obtaining revenue. The prewar rates were simplified and lowered after the close of the war. In 1816 a single letter going thirty miles cost 6¢, if more than thirty and not more than eighty miles 10¢, if between 80 and 150 miles 12½¢, if between 150 and 400 miles 18½¢, and 25¢ for a "single" traveling more than 400 miles. Newspapers were carried anywhere within a state for one cent, otherwise one cent was charged for one hundred miles, and 1½¢ if going farther than that beyond a state line. These were the rates, save for slight changes, when the reforms in Great Britain began to affect American opinion.[19]

Other backward features were a complete lack of free delivery in the cities and the absence of arrangements for the safe transmission of money. Correspondence by the official postal routes was so difficult that private carrier systems for letters and packages had grown up. A New Haven clergyman declared in the forties that half the letters between New Haven and Hartford were not carried by the Post Office. About the same time, George Plitt, a Post Office official, asserted that half the correspondence between New York and Boston never went by the recognized route. Franking was an even greater abuse than in Great Britain, as there was no limit in the United States to the number of letters franked. Not only did huge shipments of government documents burden the mail without paying their way, but other objectionable practices occurred as well. It was stated in 1843 that a "member from one of our western states regularly sent his linen home during the session to be washed, under the title 'public

---

[19] The changing rates are given in the official *Postage Rates, 1789-1930*. See also Pliny Miles, "History of the Post Office," *Bankers' Magazine and Statistical Register*, n.s., VII (1857), 361 ff. The odd 18½¢ rate was made even odder in 1825, when it became 18¾¢. During that time the Postmaster-General was Return Jonathan Meigs: he proposed that the lowest rate be 4¢, but Congress was unwilling. These odd rates, including fractions of a cent, resulted from the use of small foreign coins such as the Spanish real and the threepenny bit. Their use became illegal about the middle of the century. See A. D. Smith, *op. cit.*, p. 71; Rich, *op. cit.*, pp. 139-40.

documents.' "[20] Nor was the financial condition as healthy as that of the British unreformed Post Office. During these years the American Post Office was always in the "red." The total number of letters was some forty million, or about half the number that were circulating in Great Britain.[21]

The coming of penny postage in Great Britain had immediate effects in the United States. In June 1840, Daniel Webster introduced a resolution in Congress for "connecting the use of stamps or stamped covers with a large reduction of the present rates of postage." The printed resolution included a likeness of the British penny black. Barnabas Bates argued powerfully for "cheap postage" in that same spring. The surprising change in Great Britain caused criticism of the American Post Office to take the form of petitions to Congress and of public meetings agitating a like change in America. Even before penny postage had begun in Britain, the American Postmaster-General sent a special investigator to observe the workings of the post office systems of Europe. George Plitt, the official agent, left in June 1839, returning in August the following year. The result of his observations was an interesting report and some strong recommendations. They included abolition of franking, charge for letters by weight and prepayment of newspapers and printed matter, also to be charged by weight. He proposed that there be only two rates of postage on letters "for the whole Union," a half-ounce letter to go as far as five hundred miles for 5¢, and beyond for 10¢. As a convenience to the public, he suggested adhesive stamps—"small cards of an adhesive nature to be affixed upon the face of the letter mailed."[22]

No immediate change resulted. Amos Kendall, who had sent Plitt to Europe, was out of office in 1840. After two brief administrations, the Post Office was headed by Charles A. Wickliffe, from 1841 to 1845. He was no friend of reduction. During the next administration, when Cave Johnson was Postmaster-General under President Polk (1845-49), more liberal steps were taken. In March 1845, the rates were modified so that a half-ounce letter was carried three hundred miles for 5¢, and beyond that distance for 10¢. In his *Report* for 1847, Johnson was able to note a surplus of over $200,000: "It is gratifying to find that, within so short a period after the great reduction of the rates of postage, the revenues of the Department have in-

---

[20] *Merchants' Magazine*, IX, 538, 540; Plitt, *Report* (1841), p. 37.

[21] Miles, *Postal Reform*, pp. 26-27; *Bankers' Mag. and Statistical Register*, n.s., VII (1857), 436.

[22] Plitt, *Report* (1841); *Merchants' Magazine* (March 1840).

creased much beyond the expectations of the friends of the cheap postage system." He believed that postage should be reduced to the lowest point that would enable the Department to sustain itself.

The change of 1845 did not include the use of stamps. Local postmasters had issued stamps at various offices in 1845, those of the New York office bearing a head of George Washington as it appeared on the current bank notes. The postmaster stamps of St. Louis, also appearing in 1845, had two bears upholding the Missouri coat-of-arms. Finally, in 1847, the first general issue appeared. It consisted of two stamps, engraved and printed in New York, the five-cent stamp of an orange color bearing Franklin's portrait, the ten-cent black that of George Washington.[23] In 1851 the rates were again lowered, a half-ounce letter going three thousand miles for 3¢ if prepaid, and for 5¢ if not prepaid. Beyond three thousand miles the charges were doubled. Four years later the rates were raised to 10¢ for a half-ounce letter going more than three thousand miles, prepayment was made compulsory and a system of registration was provided. Stamps appeared with perforations in 1857. Money orders were put into use towards the end of the Civil War, proving of great value to the soldiers.[24]

That the influence of the British reform was great in the United States can be judged from the analogous changes that have been listed. But the friends of cheap postage were not satisfied. They argued that penny postage, that is, a 2¢ rate, should be allowed in the United States. The most active proponent in the late forties for this further reduction was Joshua Leavitt. He published numerous pamphlets, and organized branches of the Cheap Postage Association, of which he was the corresponding secretary. Leavitt's principal pamphlet, *Cheap Postage*, was a careful examination of the British experiment, and its probable success if fully set up in the United States. He,

[23] John K. Tiffany, *The History of the Postage Stamps of the United States of America* (St. Louis, 1887), p. 19; John N. Luff, *The Postage Stamps of the United States* (N.Y., 1902), pp. 7-8, 45. The centenary of the first official postage stamps of the United States was celebrated in elaborate fashion by an International Philatelic Exhibition in New York during May 1947. The first official stamps were actually issued July 1, 1847.

[24] There was less precaution against forgery in the United States than in Great Britain. Early United States stamps were unwatermarked, and did not bear any elaborate arrangement of corner letters and plate numbers. The letters "U" and "S" appeared in the lower corners of a new series of stamps issued in 1861, but this was to distinguish them from the earlier issues, some of which were still in the hands of Confederate postmasters. Also, in the sixties a grill was impressed on the stamps to make their reuse more difficult.

at least, felt that his main arguments were unanswerable "until men disprove arithmetic." Another ardent advocate of the British reform *in toto* was Pliny Miles. Writing in *The Bankers' Magazine* for 1857, he contrasted the United States with the "monarchist system of Great Britain," the former being without a free delivery, a low rate or a money order system. Moreover, the population of Great Britain, of whom "one half can scarcely read and write," numbered about the same as that in the United States, of whom "nearly all are able to read and write"! And yet this supposedly half-literate British nation sent almost 500,000,000 letters a year, and the Americans only 131,000,-000. To Pliny Miles the difference was explained by cheap postage and a uniform rate in Great Britain.[25]

But the government in America remained unconvinced. Not until 1863 was a single rate, irrespective of distance, put into effect, and it was 3¢ for half an ounce. The Americans had to wait until 1883 before a letter could be sent anywhere in the United States for 2¢.[26]

Postage stamps naturally penetrated the outlying parts of the British Empire during the years of their adoption in foreign countries. But any impulse for the extension of the reforms of 1840 came from the colonies themselves, since Rowland Hill had perfected his plan for Great Britain only. Colonial conditions were not as favorable to the scheme as even those in the United States, since the populations were small and widely scattered. Yet it might have seemed natural for the home government to attempt the improvement of the colonial postal systems during the forties. Though the British Postmaster-General was at the head of them all, neither he nor the Secretary of the British Post Office had much interest in the betterment of colonial postal regulations.

In Canada, the most mature of the colonies of settlement, the general dissatisfaction with misrule led to the Rebellion of 1837 and finally at the end of the forties to the grant of internal self-government. The postal administration was one of the causes of ill-feeling. The mother country had been unwilling to risk losses in the Post Office administration of the British North American colonies, where it was necessary for the general welfare to run some risk in order that

---

[25] *Op. cit.*, n.s., VII, 348-49.

[26] See Leavitt, *Cheap Postage*, and his articles in *The Merchants' Magazine* on "The Moral and Social Benefits of Cheap Postage" and "The Practical Working of Cheap Postage," XXI, 601-10; XXII, 44-53. The articles appeared in 1849 and 1850. It is clear that the merchants in America had an interest in cheap postage not unlike that of the Mercantile Association in Great Britain.

remote settlers might be kept in touch with the government of the colony. For some time before 1850 the colonial legislatures had even appropriated grants for postal purposes, though they had no control over the expenditure. This was finally ended in 1849 by an act that conceded to the colonial legislatures the complete control of their own inland posts.[27]

In the next year Canada took over its own posts, and established a rate of 3d per half-ounce for letters anywhere within the colony. The other colonies, Prince Edward Island, New Brunswick and Nova Scotia—as yet they were not united—did the same. Stamps were soon introduced. In the first half of 1851, 3d, 6d and 1s stamps were issued by Canada, the first depicting the beaver in red, the second Prince Albert in purple and the third the Queen in black. They were engraved in New York. Nova Scotia and New Brunswick issued stamps in September 1851, the engraving being the work of Perkins, Bacon & Company of London. The first stamps of the two colonies were very similar save for the name of the colony—a royal crown in the center and the heraldic flowers of the United Kingdom on the four sides. Stamps were first issued by Newfoundland in 1857, and by Prince Edward Island four years later. Stamps for British Columbia were manufactured by De La Rue & Company: they appeared in 1860.[28]

In the southern hemisphere stamps were early introduced in the various colonies where settlement was taking place so rapidly following the discovery of gold. In New South Wales, the oldest of the Australasian colonies, embossed letter sheets and envelopes had been issued as early as 1838, even before their appearance in Great Britain. This was the result of reading the *Reports* of the Committee on Postage of 1837 and Rowland Hill's pamphlet. The letter sheets and envelopes were to be used for a town delivery in Sydney. But this early arrangement for prepayment was not popular. The first adhesives in Australia were also issued by New South Wales. The so-called "Sydney Views" appeared in January 1850. The engraving, made in Sydney, showed the town in the background, a convict suppliant in front and Britannia seated on what appears to be a bale of wool. In

---

[27] 12 & 13 Vict., c.66. This was the result of an intercolonial conference in Canada, suggested by Lord Clanricarde, the British Postmaster-General. He was willing to hand over the power to the colonies, but wished to be sure that no friction would result in their relations with each other.

[28] A. D. Smith, *op. cit.*, pp. 37 ff; C. A. Howes, *Canada, Its Stamps and Postal Stationery*, pp. 17-30; W. S. Boggs, *The Postage Stamps and Postal History of Newfoundland* (1942), pp. 20-26.

the same year the colony of Victoria issued its first stamp, appropriately enough an engraving of the Queen enthroned. Western Australia's first stamps appeared in 1854, to be followed in the next year by South Australia and Van Diemen's Land (Tasmania). New Zealand's stamps also appeared for the first time in 1855.[29]

India was still under the control of the East India Company when postage stamps were introduced. This enormous possession had a complicated postal system, with widely varying local differences. An Act of 1837 had attempted to unify the Post Office for British India, but there was so much variation that an Indian Commission was appointed by Lord Dalhousie in 1850 to report on the workings of the Post Office. It recommended uniform rates and the introduction of stamps. The result was the establishment of a simple rate for all of India in 1854. A letter weighing no more than a quarter of a tola was carried for a half-anna.[30] The stamps carried the portrait of Queen Victoria. Newspapers were transported for an anna (three halfpence) irrespective of distance. A reviewer rightly declared in 1856: "It is not easy to realize the extent of these postal reforms. Rowland Hill has been eclipsed in India."[31]

This rather cursory listing of the changes in other post offices during the two decades following the British reform will serve to show some of the effects of penny postage. The impulse to a modern postal system in almost every other country in the world stemmed from the introduction of penny postage in Great Britain. Some improvements were in train, particularly in France, before 1840, but in general it was the stimulus afforded by the British innovations that remade postal arrangements far and wide. In many instances, the British ex-

[29] A. Houison, *History of the Post Office . . . in New South Wales*, pp. 25-29; *The Postage Stamps . . . of Australia and the British Colonies of Oceania* (Philatelic Society, London, 1887), pp. 1, 41-44, 77; R. J. G. Collins and H. T. M. Fathers, *The Postage Stamps of New Zealand*, p. 21. Stamps were issued by the Cape of Good Hope in 1853 —the well-known "triangles"—and by Natal in 1857. Stamps were used in these years by colonies of lesser importance. The penny and twopenny stamps of Mauritius, issued in 1847, are now among the most valuable of all postage stamps. The first postage stamps of British Guiana, initialed by the postmasters, appeared in 1850. They are also of great value to collectors. St. Helena had its own stamps in 1856 and Ceylon in the next year.

[30] A half-anna was equal to three-fourths of a penny, a lower rate than used in England, but a quarter of a tola was but one-tenth of an ounce, or a fifth the weight allowed for a penny in England. The reason for so small a weight was the prevalence of "clubbing."

[31] Geoffrey Clarke, *The Post Office of India and Its Story* (London, 1921), pp. 17-25; I. J. G. Hamilton, *An Outline of Postal History and Practice with a History of the Post Office in India* (Calcutta, 1910), pp. 151-72; *Blackwood's Magazine*, LXXX (1856), 656.

perience made possible more cautious steps elsewhere, though the source of the inspiration is clear enough. Postage stamps were accepted everywhere, and rates were lowered, but there was a general disinclination to adopt penny postage. The features of most value in the plan of Rowland Hill were the charge by weight and the making of that charge irrespective of distance. The changes made in the postal systems of the more advanced countries during these two decades were an indispensable preliminary to a larger postal union that was to take form in the seventies.[32]

The vogue for postage stamps soon led to an interest in stamp collecting. The hobby was well started by the sixties. William Lewins, in his volume on *Her Majesty's Mails*, published in 1864, devoted a chapter to postage stamps, with some concluding observations on collecting, or as he called it *"timbromanie."* Though he was not a collector, he conceded that the "gathering of a complete set of postage stamps, and a proper arrangement of them, is at least a harmless and innocent amusement."

The idea of collecting arose much earlier than 1864. *Punch* noted in 1842 that "a new mania had bitten the industriously idle ladies of England. . . . They betray more anxiety to treasure up Queen's heads than Harry the Eighth did to get rid of them." The observation was prompted by such whimsical interests as appeared in an advertisement in the *Times* for October 29, 1842, in which "a young lady" expressed the desire of "covering her dressing room with cancelled postage stamps." There was not much point in collecting stamps in a more serious mood until there were varieties to collect. By the mid-fifties, however, the interest in stamps had grown, especially among boys who were attracted by the foreign stamps that were appearing in greater numbers every year. E. Stanley Gibbons, founder of the great London stamp firm of that name, began collecting in 1854 when he was a boy at school. Two years later he was dealing in stamps, using a window of his father's chemist shop in Plymouth to show his wares. Early collectors on the Continent included Oscar Berger-Levrault of Alsace, and J. B. Moëns of Belgium: the latter claimed to have started as a boy in 1848. Dr. J. A. Legrand was one of the earliest in France.[33]

[32] *Br. Almanac* (1857), Companion, pp. 36-37, lists the chief improvements in foreign postal systems since 1840. See below, pp. 397 ff, for the Postal Union.

[33] Charles Phillips, *Stamp Collecting*, pp. 33-35, 219; Fred J. Melville, *Chats on Postage Stamps* (n.d.), Chap. III; P. J. Anderson and B. T. K. Smith, *Early English Philatelic Literature*, pp. 1-4.

It was in Paris that serious collectors first began a systematic study of watermarks, minute differences in design, the changes in perforation, etc. At least three catalogues had appeared in Paris in 1861, as noted in Dr. J. E. Gray's *Hand Catalogue of Postage Stamps* of 1862. J. B. Moëns of Brussels issued a manual for collectors in 1862. In 1864 Moëns published his elaborate *Les timbres-poste illustrés,* "containing the general nomenclature of all stamps and the reproduction of all types." Manuals and catalogues and magazines for the collectors of stamps began to appear in England in the early sixties. The first stamp catalogue was issued by Mount Brown of Cheapside, London, in 1862. In the same year appeared Frederick Booty's *Aids to Stamp Collectors,* in which he emphasized the tasteful arrangement of stamps so that the collection might become a "handsome appendage to the drawing room table." Bellars & Davie, in their *Standard Guide to Postage Stamp Collecting,* issued in 1864, attempted to justify the pastime. They reply to persons "who, having no taste for collecting themselves, cannot understand why others should find both instruction and rational amusement in the gathering of postage stamps." They call attention to the collection of odd things by people high in society, such things as "walking sticks, snuff-boxes, shop-bells, old keys, old shoes worn by eminent people." "Surely," they add, "seeking after the paper coins of the civilized world, bearing the effigies of the monarchs, or the national badge, and with scraps of the language on the borders, is as instructive and proper a pursuit as any of these."

Dr. J. E. Gray's *Hand Catalogue* appeared towards the end of 1862. It is of especial interest because of a rather long introduction by this distinguished scientist of the British Museum. He admitted that the fashion for stamp collecting had been ridiculed, but held that it was quite as instructive as "the collection of birds, butterflies, shells, books, engravings, coins or other objects." Stamps were an "epitome of the history of Europe and America for the last quarter of a century." Then followed a statement which aroused much controversy: "I began to collect postage stamps shortly after the system was established, .. and I believe I was the first who proposed the system of a small uniform rate of postage to be prepaid by stamps. . . . It was, in fact, the mere application of the system used with regard to newspapers to letters in general." Dr. Gray then went on to state that he had not time to give to the plan, owing to his duties at the British Museum, but that Rowland Hill put the plan through because "he had leisure at his command by the dissolution of the South Australia Company." Rowland Hill replied to the claim in a letter to the *Athenaeum* in December 1862, flatly contradicting Gray's claim: "If this strange story is not intended as a joke, it amounts to one of the most extraordinary hallucinations on record." Charles Knight also answered Gray in the same magazine in January of 1863, with regard to the relation of newspaper stamps and those for letters. Knight asked the alleged appropriator of his ideas why they had remained unnoticed until 1862.[34] Gray's preposterous claims were continued in later issues of his catalogue. It was only in 1875 that all reference to his claim to priority was omitted. It is curious to what lengths the pride of paternity will carry individuals. Dr. Gray is not the only example of this weakness to be found in the narrative of British postal history.

The first stamp magazine ever published appeared in Liverpool in 1862, *The Stamp Collectors' Review and Monthly Advertiser*. In the next year began the much more important *Stamp Collectors' Magazine*. As Lewins put it a year later: "About a year ago we witnessed the establishment of a monthly organ for the trade. . . . At this present moment there are no less than ten such publications in the United Kingdom." In 1869 the Philatelic Society of London was started, becoming the Royal Philatelic Society in 1906. This most distinguished of stamp collectors' organizations has had as president such well-known collectors as Judge Philbrick, King George V and the Earl of Crawford.[35]

Thus began the most widespread of all hobbies, aptly named by the late Charles J. Phillips, "the king of hobbies and the hobby of kings."

[34] Volume for 1862, p. 806; for 1863, p. 18.
[35] One of the earliest collectors in the United States was John Walter Scott. Born in England, he came to the United States in 1863, and four years later started the famous business now known as the Scott Stamp and Coin Company.

27

The Movement for Cheaper Ocean Postage

THE reformers of 1840 were concerned almost wholly with lowering domestic postage and speeding the mails within the United Kingdom. In time, however, an equally serious problem faced reformers —the need for organizing and simplifying the oversea postal connections with the colonies and foreign lands.

This need grew as the distant colonies were peopled year after year by immigrants who left the British Isles in ever-increasing thousands. The older British North American settlements were spreading westward both before and after the Canadian Confederation of 1867. New Zealand was the home of British settlers and an organized government from 1840. Australia, where settlement had begun a half-century earlier than in New Zealand, became of great value after the gold discoveries in the mid-century. British India had enlarged in the first half of the century to include two-thirds of that enormous subcontinent with its countless resources. Postal relations with the United States—the other great English-speaking nation—grew in importance as cultural bonds, migration, economic relations and faster steamships linked Britain and America more and more closely. Indeed, the matter of oversea postal communication assumed during the latter part of the nineteenth century an importance equal to the domestic problem that had been faced in the thirties and forties.

The older packet arrangements, as we have found, had become inadequate by the time of penny postage. The Post Office Department seemed incapable of handling efficiently the contracts for the vessels or the stations where they were based. Nor was the carriage of letters by private ships properly controlled, despite the creation of a separate Ship Letter Office just at the end of the eighteenth century. The mismanagement of the packet stations was so much criticized by Robert Wallace and others that the packets were turned over to the Admiralty in 1837. There they remained until 1860.

A motive back of this change was the feeling of the commercial community and the government that the building-up of a merchant marine was desirable and that vessels used for carrying mail could also serve other purposes. Not only should the packets minister to the Post Office, but they should be used to "promote the convenience and wealth of the country in time of peace, and assist in defending its shores against hostile aggression."[1]

Back of the desire for a superior class of vessels was also the need of making effective use of the new application of steam to ships. A revolution was occurring in ocean transportation. This came out in startling fashion just before the transfer of the packets to the Admiralty. A group of merchants in Bristol put on the transatlantic route in 1838 a steamship named the *Great Western*. Its first crossing took but fourteen and a half days, to the stupefaction of the commercial world. The *Great Western* proved the harbinger of a new era, for it made regular crossings from 1838 to 1844, averaging about fifteen days to the trip.[2]

The owners of the *Great Western* were unwilling, however, to carry mails on the basis of the ship-letter rates: they demanded half the postage received by the Post Office on the ground that the venture was costly and the risks great. In the meantime Samuel Cunard —he had come from Halifax, Nova Scotia, to England in 1838—arranged in the next year to set up a regular service between Liverpool on the one side and Halifax and Boston on the other. The original subsidy of £55,000 a year, shortly increased to £60,000, ran for seven years. When the contract was renewed in 1845 it included a trip every week, alternating between Halifax and Boston one week and New York the next, with a subsidy of £145,000 a year until 1858. Clearly much more than mere mail service was in the Admiralty mind.

One motive, in addition to furnishing better vessels for use in time of war, was the competition already rising for the blue ribbon of the Atlantic. The American Congress, not to be outdone, gave the Postmaster-General permission in 1846 to make contracts on a basis

[1] *Hist. Sum.*, p. 53, and *Report Com. on P.O. Management*. See above, p. 254.
[2] *Br. Almanac* (1851), Companion, p. 62.

similar to that of the British Admiralty. As a result, the Ocean Steam Navigation Company, commonly called the Collins Line, received a ten-year contract in 1848 for carrying American mails and building up the national trade and marine.[3] The *Atlantic* and *Pacific* of the Collins Line were "luxurious" liners of some three thousand tons— by far the largest of the time—but were soon countered by Cunard's *Asia* and *Africa*. The race was on.

The Collins Line gave Cunard a good run for it for a few years, until in the late fifties a series of disasters to their ships made it impossible to continue. The contract was not renewed in 1858 for the additional reason that the United States Post Office had decided to turn from expensive subsidies to hiring vessels on the basis of the actual amount of mail they carried. The British Admiralty, however, continued expensive subsidies even though it seemed to many too great a drain on the Exchequer. The transatlantic business was so competitive that many felt no such high subsidies were needed. Such at least was the judgment of a committee appointed in 1853, of which Lord Canning, the Postmaster-General, was the head. When the Cunard contract came up for renewal in 1858 the Admiralty was for and the Post Office against renewal. The Admiralty won out and the Cunard subsidy was continued to 1867 at an even higher figure, £176,000 a year.

Canada, it should be added, disliked very much the subsidizing of a British line to the United States, and proceeded to set up its own subsidized vessels. The resultant confusion led to a Select Committee Report of 1860 on Packet Contracts. It recommended abandonment of the idea of mail packets for possible use in time of war, lessening of the subsidies and return of the packet control to the Post Office. The result of the Report was the return of the packets to the Post Office in 1860.[4]

Expensive subsidies were used on other routes as well. The West Indian mails had been carried by sailing vessels on a twice-a-month schedule until a new company contracted for a fleet of steam vessels that would more effectively bind the scattered West Indian possessions to the mother country. The Royal Mail Steam Packet Company

[3] Collins was not so well paid as Cunard, the American line receiving $100,000 a year, though increased to twice that amount before the end of the ten-year contract. T. L. James, "The Ocean Postal Service," *Century Mag.*, n.s., XXI (1892), 946.

[4] *1st Rep. Sel. Com. on Packet and Telegraphic Contracts* (1860), pp. iii–xiv. 23 Vict., c.26 returned the packet control to the Post Office. This did not mean an end of subsidies, though they were sharply cut down on the renewal of the contract with Cunard in 1868.

—it had been chartered in 1839—built new ships for this service and even purchased the *Great Western*, and well it might for the subsidy was £240,000 annually. Rowland Hill was much opposed to this West Indian contract, regarding it as one primarily for political and not postal purposes. So true was this that when it was renewed in 1857 it was without the knowledge of the Post Office Department. A Pacific mail contract for vessels plying from Panama along the South American coast was made in 1845 for £25,000 a year. Another for the west coast of Africa, entered into about the same time, added another £21,500 to the annual expenditure, nominally for carrying the mails.[5]

Another route of great importance led to Britain's Far Eastern holdings—to India, China, the East Indies and Australasia. Here the problem of expense was a serious one because of the long distances to be traversed. The old route around the Cape, in use for sailing vessels, often took six months or more. It was a cheap, if slow, way of transporting mails and goods, since the ship-letter rate to India was but 2d for three ounces. Nor did the competition of non-British lines ever enter seriously into the arrangements for mail and commercial traffic with the Far East. Though some attention was given to steam service on this ancient route of trade, the short road to India and the East via the Mediterranean seemed more promising. Subsidies were used very liberally as this Mediterranean short cut became more and more important.

Two possible courses could be followed in crossing from the Mediterranean to the Indian Ocean, one by way of Syria and the Euphrates, the other across Egypt to the Red Sea. Capt. F. R. Chesney was sure that the route through Syria was preferable. In the thirties he was able to prove the Euphrates River to be navigable. Two iron steamers, sent out in parts to Antioch and across Syria to the river, and then set up, were used for this venture. One was able to reach the mouth of the river in 1836, but conditions were such that Capt. Chesney had the mortification of being unable to return with the Indian mails.[6] Lieut. Thomas Waghorn, formerly with the East India Company, urged the alternate route by way of Alexandria and the Red Sea. His persistent efforts led to an arrangement for the transportation of the Indian mails under his care across Egypt. This was in

[5] *Br. Almanac* (1851), Companion, pp. 67-72; Thomas Rainey, *Ocean Steam Navigation and the Ocean Post*, pp. 160-63; G. B. Hill, *op. cit.*, II, 288-89.
[6] H. L. Hoskins, *British Routes to India* (1920), pp. 160 ff.

1837, following an exhaustive report by a committee of the House of Commons.

The Waghorn service in Egypt needed water connections at each end. The East India Company cared for the mails from the Red Sea eastward. The transportation of the mails to Alexandria from Great Britain was made by vessels that used the long-established packet station at Falmouth. Soon a contract not unlike that with Cunard was made with a company for the Mediterranean route. From 1837 to 1840, the Peninsular Steam Navigation Company was carrying mails to Gibraltar, whence they were transported by Admiralty packets to Malta and Alexandria. As the Admiralty vessels were inadequate for the service and the route overland via France was still a slow and un-developed service, the government agreed with the Peninsular Line to carry the mails to Alexandria, and also to furnish vessels for the service east of Suez. It was in 1840 that the Peninsular Company be-came the Peninsular and Oriental Steam Navigation Company. The P & O steamers only gradually displaced the vessels of the East India Company east of Suez. In time, the P & O extended its operations to Singapore and China: early in the fifties P & O liners were going to Australasia from Singapore.[7]

A variation of this Mediterranean route has proved of importance in postal history. In the course of time the all-sea carriage of mails to Alexandria became much slower than by a route from Dover to Calais, thence overland via Paris to Marseilles, where vessels received the mails for the next stage of the journey—to Malta. This alternative route was in use as early as 1839: it was more expeditious despite the lack at that time of through railway connections from Calais to Marseilles. The Franco-Prussian War of 1870 disrupted the course of the mails via Paris. After that year the fast overland mail service went to Brindisi, near the heel of the Italian boot, whence the mails were taken directly to Alexandria. This partly overland service proved expensive. The British Post Office was paying the French and Italian governments £100,000 a year by the end of the century, or a rate of about a penny a letter. The effect on the postage to the Far East will be noted presently.[8]

[7] *Br. Almanac, loc. cit.*, pp. 52-56; *1st Rep. P.M.G.* (1855), p. 18; Hamilton, *op. cit.*, pp. 147-55; Baines, *Forty Years at the Post Office*, II, 222 ff.; Hoskins, *op. cit.*, pp. 236 ff.

[8] The French and Italian post offices made a handsome profit from this transit service, as the railways companies were paid less than half the amount received from the British government. See *Hist. Sum.*, p. 61; Hoskins, *op. cit.*, pp. 407-11; *Nineteenth Century,*

The other overland section of the route—through Egypt—was without the benefit of a railway until a line was completed in 1858 from Alexandria via Cairo to Suez. A further shortening of this route occurred when the Suez Canal was at last opened in 1869. At first the steamers could only use the Canal in daylight at the rate of five miles an hour. After 1888 night travel was permitted, and the railway ceased to be the quickest form of transport across Egypt. All mails for the Far East via Egypt were not transmitted through the Canal until that year.[9]

The network of lines created by the P & O proved of great value, colonially speaking, for their services fanned out to all parts of the British Empire east of Suez. The expenses for this widely ramified service were even greater than those of the lines traversing the Atlantic. The subsidies for the India and China mails during this time were over four shillings a mile. This occasioned, of course, a large deficit despite the high cost of postage, the deficit being credited to the political and colonial advantages obtained by an excellent service. The grave situation created by the Indian Mutiny of 1857 did not lessen the political value of the P & O subsidy. Moreover the Crimean War of the same decade seemed to justify a system that made available the steam vessels of this route: they were taken off the services for the purpose of transporting men and supplies to the battle front in southern Russia. All through the nineteenth century the subsidy of mails to the East was high: it was nearly £600,000 a year as late as 1870, and by the end of the century it was still more than £300,000 a year. The amount obtained by the actual postage was a mere fraction of this sum.[10]

Falmouth had been for centuries the recognized port of departure for packets bound to the Mediterranean, the south Atlantic, the West Indies and North America. The P & O proposed in 1837 that their ships start from Southampton instead, as this would result in the saving of a day. An investigating committee of the Admiralty at first favored Dartmouth, and the Post Office preferred Plymouth. In 1843, however, Southampton was finally chosen for the East and West Indian mails. Dover and London served the nearby Continent, the one for mails to France and central Europe, the other for mail

XXVII (1890), 911. For a chronology of this development, see *Bulletin* of the Postal History Society, no. 15 (1940).

[9] Sir Evelyn Murray, *The Post Office*, p. 63; Hoskins, *op. cit.*, pp. 367, 407, 418.

[10] *55th Rep. P.M.G.* (1909), p. 52.

packets bound to Rotterdam and Hamburg. Harwich as a packet station had declined in importance from the lack of a through railway service with London.[11]

At the time that the packets were returned to the Post Office in 1860, a total of nearly £900,000 a year was being paid in subsidies to the various steamship lines. The Post Office endeavored to lower the high cost of the mail services, but the improvement was only gradual. Little change resulted in the cost of the subsidy for the Far East, since the P & O had a virtual monopoly on a route that seemed of great imperial value. There was more success in the Atlantic.

When the Cunard contract came up for renewal in 1868, the Post Office sought tenders on the basis of the actual mail carried, "a system which the United States had for some years adopted." The new contracts, though not on the basis of sea postage, were at least cut to £115,000. By 1886 the British mails were being carried at the rate of 4s a pound for letters and 4d a pound for printed matter, still too high from the viewpoint of the Post Office. The Postmaster-General, Mr. Raikes, endeavored at that time to bring the companies to agree on a 25 per cent cut. The shipowners refused, and were only brought to the Post Office terms when mail was actually sent from Southampton by the North German Lloyd on the basis of actual letter postage. A patriotic cry was raised at the use of this "foreign line," though the vessels were British-built and largely British-manned. Mr. Raikes succeeded in lowering the cost of the service by £25,000 annually. A legal decision in 1889 completed the transaction by requiring the shipowners to accept mails at the sea-postage rates when tendered to them by the Post Office. By the end of the century the transatlantic subsidies were down to £37,000 a year. The contracts with the Royal Mail—to the West Indies—were also reduced from a high of £240,-000 to some £90,000 by the end of the century.[12]

The effect of such payments on the actual rates for letters going overseas can be imagined, since the lowering of any sea postage only increased the deficit. Not only were the rates slow in coming down, but they showed little tendency toward uniformity. Separate postal treaties were made with each country, rates differing even for mails

[11] *Br. Almanac, loc. cit.*, pp. 72-75.
[12] For the troubles of the Post Office with the so-called "Liverpool Shipping Ring," see H. S. Raikes, *Life and Letters of Henry Cecil Raikes*, pp. 257-65; *Hist. Sum.*, pp. 55-56; *Parl. Papers, Returns* (1878), xlvi, no. 92; *Fortnightly Review*, LXX (1898), 909. By 1900 the annual subsidies to the so-called "mail lines" still reached a high figure, £640,000 annually, of which the greater part went to the P & O.

traveling by different routes between the same countries. The British Post Office had nine different rates for the nearby European countries, each country naturally driving the best bargain possible. There was much disagreement between the United States and Great Britain over the cost of mail. The minimum cost of a letter exchanged with the United States was 1s or 24¢ in the fifties. The American Postmaster-General had suggested a rate of 12¢ or 6d in 1859, but the two post offices could not agree on the proper division of the sea postage and the land carriage.[13]

Nor were the rates of postage to the colonies uniform or reasonable. Here, too, separate negotiations were necessary since the colonies, in postal matters, were much like foreign countries. Before 1855 the cost of colonial letters had been a shilling or more, but in that year it was lowered to an average of about 6d. But uniformity in rates was conspicuously lacking. Letters to Newfoundland cost 6d, those to British Columbia 1s, those for three eastern mainland colonies in North America 3d if sent direct, and 4d if by way of the United States. Those to the West Indies, St. Helena and the Cape cost 1s, to Mauritius 10d. Postage to the Australasian area was 6d by the Cape, but to the four eastern Australian colonies and New Zealand letters cost 9d if they went by way of Brindisi and Suez. The lowest rate to India was 9d, but 1s if by way of Brindisi. If Singapore letters took the Brindisi route, they cost 1s 3d. Could confusion be carried further? To make the anomalies more startling, the rates to many foreign countries were lower—to France, Austria, Switzerland, Holland, Belgium, Germany, and the United States 3d, to Denmark 4d, to Sweden and Russia 5d, and to Greece 8d.

This utter lack of uniformity seemed in strange contrast to the low, uniform domestic rate within the United Kingdom. Agitation began even in the forties for the extension of low and uniform postage to oversea mail. The leader of the movement for ocean penny postage was not an Englishman but Connecticut's learned blacksmith, Elihu Burritt. He was a pronounced humanitarian, so strong a believer in the possibilities of a common world citizenship that he spent many years advocating a League of Universal Brotherhood. Out of such thinking grew his project for ocean penny postage as a means of bringing the world more closely together. In 1846 Burritt came to

[13] *6th Rep. P.M.G.* (1860), pp. 57 ff. Not until 1868 was an agreement reached for a 6d rate on Anglo-American mail. For a letter sent at this rate, see p. 366.

Great Britain and there began his agitation for the extension of uniform rates to oversea mail.

Burritt's proposal for an ocean penny postage was just that, a penny or two cents for the sea postage of a letter from port to port: the domestic charges of the countries at each end of the voyage were to be added in reckoning the total cost of sending mail. Burritt believed that Great Britain was the ideal country to make this advance, for he held that England's domestic penny post was one of the greatest of "God's gifts to man." He believed the penny rate reasonable, since newspapers weighing three ounces were being sent overseas at the time for a penny. If Great Britain recognized the integrity of her Empire in the matter of newspapers, why not for letters as well? He pointed out that Paris was nearer to London than Edinburgh, but the charge for a half-ounce letter sent from London to Paris was 10d, of which 6½d was charged for an ocean passage taking but two hours. At the same time letters traveled for a penny from Jersey to the Shetlands, a distance of nearly a thousand miles, including two ocean trips. His arguments were decidedly convincing if one could but forget the high subsidies then being paid the steamship companies.[14]

Elihu Burritt held that ocean penny postage was much needed for the benefit of the poor emigrant who found it so difficult to keep in touch with relatives at home. For this reason he believed that the United States should cooperate with Great Britain in furthering the movement, so that the 400,000 who came to the United States every year might be able to use the mails.[15] But his deepest desire was to bring about by this reform a close bond between the "sea-divided communities of mankind." This, he felt, was particularly important for the Anglo-Saxon race. "In 145 years, unless some physical revolution supervene, the English race will number 880 million, outnumbering the present population of the globe. Will she be the center then?" He urged England to "apprehend her destiny and duty now." When appealing to American opinion, he also stressed the growth of Anglo-Saxondom wherein the "United States must constitute the

[14] *Ocean Penny Postage, Its Necessity,* pp. 1-2, 11; *Ocean Penny Postage. Will It Pay?,* p. 2. The rate to France was lowered from 10d to 4d in 1855.

[15] The emigrants themselves hailed this possibility. See, e.g., *Atlantis,* a German-American monthly, n.s., 1 (1854), 210-12, where an article on "Ozean-Penny-Porto" by one of the German 48'ers argued for the change. It would result in the free circulation of ideas, would bring American concepts of political and social freedom to the reactionary governments of the European Continent and help weld the family of nations into a "league of peace and friendship."

grand family center of this mighty race." And he added, "Now is the juncture!"[16]

Burritt held the plan to be entirely feasible. He realized that the current heavy subsidies were in the way. In America, the two great obstacles to overcome were the franking system and the Collins Line. In Great Britain, it was the high subsidy paid to Cunard. He believed that the British government could save half the high subsidy of £145,000 paid to Cunard in 1851, if she would take advantage of the competing service on this route. Screw steamships, he said, were ready to convey letters across the Atlantic for a penny each. His arguments remind one of those made by Rowland Hill in *Post Office Reform*. The reduced rate between Great Britain and the United States, counting the inland rates, would work out as 3½d or 7¢—about a quarter of the current shilling rate. To offset this reduction, the number of letters, therefore, must increase four times. How would this needed increase come? Present writers, he believed, would send twice as many letters at a quarter of the rate. The 400,000 emigrants going to the United States would write on the average at least two letters per person annually, and receive two in return. As these were all new correspondents, the accumulation of letters from this source would be 5,000,000 in three years. To support this guess, Burritt pointed out that in 1852 the Irish sent across the sea about five million dollars in some 250,000 letters.[17]

Burritt found much support for his ideas when he was in England for a number of years following his journey there in 1846. He was aided by the free trade and internationalist school of thought of Cobden and Bright; Lord Ashburton headed a committee on the matter and some eighty members of Parliament, led by Milner Gibson, visited the Prime Minister in 1853 to urge penny postage. Speeches by Burritt, posters in the railway stations, and propaganda envelopes aided the cause. In 1851 he wrote Charles Sumner: "I will enclose a few of our envelopes. . . . More than a million of them have been put into circulation." The envelopes bore marine scenes and appropriate mottoes, such as "Britain! from thee the world expects an ocean penny postage—to make her children one fraternity." Another made the appeal to self-interest: "Britain! bestow this boon, and be in

---

[16] *Ocean Penny Postage, Its Necessity*, pp. 28-29; *Ocean Penny Postage*, another pamphlet of four pages (n.d.).

[17] *Ocean Penny Postage*, pp. 1-4; *Will It Pay?*, p. 3; *The Proposition of a Universal Penny Post*, pp. 3-4; M. Curti, *The Learned Blacksmith*, p. 116.

blessing blest—Ocean Penny Postage will link all lands with thee in trade and peace."[18]

Many found his argument convincing, but legislation was not forthcoming, and the one person who might have helped more than any other, Rowland Hill, was no friend of the movement. He did nothing to second the warm-hearted impulses of Elihu Burritt, possibly because at that time he was awaiting the departure of Col. Maberley. Rowland Hill wrote, on hearing of the deputation to Lord Aberdeen, that the demand for ocean penny postage was based on a false analogy. Strangely enough, he now held that the multiplication of letters was but moderately affected by the lowering of the rate, and that it had been found at home that a penny charge was more than sufficient to defray all expenses, "while no such proof was given with regard to expenses abroad." To Hill, it might become a practical question when contractors would undertake to carry letters to India or Australia for the same charge as to Glasgow and Aberdeen."[19] Rowland Hill was too much concerned with the fulfillment of his financial prophecies of 1837, and too closely allied to the Treasury whose good will he did not wish to alienate. Yet Rowland Hill and Elihu Burritt lived to see the winning of ocean penny postage. Before they died—in the same year, 1879—the Universal Postal Union had been formed with a uniform rate that made sea postage what Burritt had hoped it would be, and Hill had held to be hardly possible.

The origins of the Universal Postal Union, which began in 1875, go back at least to the early sixties. In 1862 the Postmaster-General of the United States, Montgomery Blair, addressed a letter on the matter to all countries with which the United States had postal relations. He wrote of the "many embarrassments to foreign correspondence," and noted the bewildering differences in rates even between the same places, "in some cases as many as six different rates, according to the route of transit." He suggested that an international conference be held in Paris in the next year to discuss common postal problems. Fifteen states responded. The series of resolutions adopted at Paris resulted in recommendations that transit charges should be no more than half the postage of the country through which letters

---

[18] Evans, *op. cit.*, pp. 191-201; Curti, *op. cit.*, p. 93. For illustrations of other penny postage envelopes, see "Ocean Penny Postage" by Samuel Graveson in *Bulletin* of Postal History Society, no. 19 (1941).

[19] G. B. Hill, *op. cit.*, II, 241-42.

were passing, and that sea transit be no more than the actual cost to the agency carrying the mails.[20]

The real inception of the Postal Union was largely the work of a German postal reformer, Heinrich von Stephan. He published in 1868 a project for a postal union, to be arranged by a congress that would have power to make regulations. Owing to the Franco-Prussian War and other causes for delay, the proposed congress did not come into being until 1874, when it was held in Berne on the invitation of the Swiss government. Twenty-two states, mostly European, but including Egypt and the United States, sent their representatives. The Postal Union went into effect on July 1, 1875.

The results were revolutionary. A single postal territory was formed embracing the great majority of the world's correspondence. Uniformity of rate and weight was reached with twenty-five centimes (2½d or 5¢) for letters of the basic weight of fifteen grammes (½ ounce), as the general union rate, though the countries were permitted a minimum and a maximum as a means of transition, if any state felt it necessary to vary from the standard rate. As most countries had adopted the penny rate, there was sufficient margin for the international transmission. Transit charges came up for considerable discussion. Complete liberty of transit by land and sea was guaranteed to every country by every other. Closed mails had to be forwarded by the most rapid routes. Transit charges based on weight and distance were agreed upon, especially where a country like Belgium, for example, was so located as to be much used. Where the sea transit was over three hundred nautical miles, additional charges were allowed to the carrying country.[21]

The difficulties facing an international postal union were greatly simplified by the use of stamps and the prepayment of mail matter. All letters had to be prepaid by means of stamps or stamped envelopes of the country where the journey was started. Post cards could be carried if prepaid, and registration, likewise, had to be prepaid, as

[20] Rolland, op. cit., p. 76; Raoul Blayac, Origine, évolution et organisation de l'Union Postale Universelle, pp. 49, 66; John F. Sly, The Genesis of the Universal Postal Union, p. 11; A. D. Smith, op. cit., p. 265. Montgomery Blair, the Postmaster-General in Lincoln's cabinet, has a number of postal advances to his credit—the establishment of a postal system for the army, of compulsory prepayment, of free deliveries in the cities, and of the railway post office. See D.A.B., II, 339-40.

[21] France was particularly opposed to free transit. Great Britain, too, in the matter of ocean carriage, stood out for compensation, and no wonder, with the subsidies what they were. Later Congresses were able to lower considerably the original high charges, but the movement for free transit has not succeeded.

well as the postage on newspapers and printed matter. Free re-addressing of mail was provided as a necessary part of the arrangements, even though a country like Great Britain did not readdress its domestic mail at that time without an additional charge. Each national post office kept its own receipts, on the belief that the exchange of mail between countries would be approximately equal. In this way, the Union avoided the need for a complicated system of financial reckonings, or the creation of some form of international postage stamp.[22] Lastly, an international office was provided at Berne for the collection and distribution of information, with a central organization that has been kept at a minimum. It is largely a clearinghouse for information. Disputes were to be settled by arbitration, and further congresses were to be held periodically. The delegates showed an unusual amount of common sense and a praiseworthy forbearance from petty national aims.[23]

The British Post Office soon communicated with the various colonial offices and India, stressing this "very important event in postal history." The colonies were invited to join the Union, as Great Britain's entry, of course, had not involved any of the colonies. When the Indian Post Office applied for admission in November 1875, a special conference was called at Berne to consider the request because India's application raised the whole question of the extension of the Union to distant countries. When India joined in 1876, the only change in the regulations was a larger transit charge for distances beyond three hundred nautical miles. The charge was made equal to the general Union rate. Thus Great Britain could make the charge to India 5d, by adding the transit charge to the basic rate.[24] It was not long before most of the colonies joined the Postal Union, with the standard 2½d or 5¢ rate applying to an increasing number as time went on. Yet even ten years after the creation of the Union the charge on letters between Great Britain and many of her colonies was still higher than the approved Union rate. J. Henniker Heaton declared in 1887 before Parliament that nine-tenths of the British colonies in

[22] An international postage stamp has been discussed from time to time, but its creation would seem to imply a single monetary system. The reply coupon provides a means of prepaying the reply to a letter from a foreign country. The idea of the reply coupon, originating with the British Post Office, was adopted by the Congress of 1906. It is exchangeable in any country for a postage stamp at the standard Union rate.

[23] Sly, *op. cit.*, pp. 20 ff.; A. D. Smith, *op. cit.*, pp. 266-70. It is refreshing to find that even as late as 1929 this office had not succumbed to the bureaucrat. The total staff at that time was made up of nine persons, of whom one was a typist.

[24] *Parl. Deb.*, 3rd s., CCCIV (1885), 282.

the Postal Union received letters from Great Britain at charges in excess of the Union rate, whereas letters over the same routes were carried from France and Germany, for example, at the rate of 2½d. It was not uncommon for Londoners to send letters, intended for India, to France by friends crossing the Channel, whence they went for half the rate charged on the British side of the Channel. Henniker Heaton was loud in his protests at a practice that allowed commercial rivals in France and Germany to send letters to the British colonies by British vessels at a cheaper rate than the British themselves could. It certainly did not make sense.[25]

Several references have been made to John Henniker Heaton. This vigorous and untiring postal reformer played a part in the late nineteenth century not unlike that performed by Robert Wallace fifty years before. Born in England in 1848, he had gone to Australia in early life, and spent many years there, at first on the great sheep stations in the bush, and later as a newspaper editor and public servant in the colony of New South Wales. He returned to England in 1884, and was soon in Parliament as the member for Canterbury, a constituency that he represented for the next twenty-six years. It would be more correct, however, to say that he represented the cause of postal reform. As he was keenly aware of the vast distances that separated people in the colonies from their friends in the mother country and of the effects on correspondence of the high postage still charged, Heaton gave most of his time to an ardent advocacy of imperial penny postage.[26] He did not confine his attention to improvements in oversea mail, but attacked the Post Office all along the line with much the breadth and range and persistence—and ultimate success—of Robert Wallace. The *Parliamentary Debates* are strewn with tormenting questions that he addressed to the Postmaster-General. Almost every day for almost every week in every session, he would enliven question-time with queries as to small or large points in postal administration. His favorite form of sport seemed to be the baiting of postmasters-general, no matter to which party they belonged. He was the victim of hostility and ridicule, the subject of severe reproofs and official snubbings, but he was no more inclined to

[25] *Fortnightly Rev.*, n.s., XL (1886), 537; *Parl. Deb.*, 3rd s., CCCXII (1887), 1329.

[26] Heaton had married, while in Australia, the daughter of an influential Sydney journalist, Samuel Bennett. Though Henniker Heaton was in comfortable circumstances, he had keenly realized the need for a low and uniform rate of oversea postage. See his daughter's biography, Mrs. Adrian Porter, *The Life and Letters of Sir John Henniker Heaton*, pp. 3-12.

heed them than was Wallace a half-century before. Not only through his parliamentary activity, but by numerous articles in the reviews, by several volumes and many speeches he "went to the country" in the cause of postal reform.[27]

No serious attempts to lower the British postal rates to the colonies so that they might accord with the general Union rate was made until Heaton opened his campaign in 1886. The government replied to a question in that year on the lowering of such rates by saying that the government had no intention of doing it, and that there was no intimation the colonies desired it.[28] In the same year, Heaton was able to arouse a considerable debate on a resolution for international penny postage. He was supported by G. H. Reid, who saw in the doubts cast on the proposal by officialdom the old story of departmental obstruction to reform. Henniker Heaton wrote an article for the *Fortnightly* in the same year, stressing the analogy of 1840 with his own day. Apparently, he declared, the woeful prophecies of Rowland Hill's time were to be repeated, and any advantages that came from penny postage were to be "bounded by the seas that wash our coasts." Heaton expressed a view, so often found in British postal controversy, that the government had no right to make a "thumping profit" out of the Post Office, for mail-carrying should be regarded as having as its one end the improvement of the "inter-communication of citizens." He urged the Post Office to be alive to the "teachings of postal history," and complete the beneficent work of Rowland Hill by making world communication "as easy as speech, as free as air."[29]

Largely as a result of his incessant pounding away, the Post Office announced in 1890 that on and after the 1st of October, 1891, postage on letters addressed to places abroad "will be reduced to 2½d in all cases in which it is now higher." Heaton held this to be the first fruits of his reform agitation, in view of the announcement four years before that the government had no intention of lowering the rates. The government announced, as a sign of its self-sacrifice, that the lowering of the rates would add £100,000 a year to the loss already incurred. Heaton retorted with truth that the stupendous subsidies for mail steamers were unfairly reckoned in the loss, since an insignificant amount of space in each vessel was required for the mails.[30]

Though a uniform oversea rate of 2½d had been obtained by

[27] See Mrs. Adrian Porter, *op. cit.*, pp. 132, 175, and elsewhere.
[28] *Parl. Deb.*, 3rd s., CCCII, 879.
[29] "Universal Penny Postage," *Fortnightly Rev.*, XLVI (1883), 533-41.
[30] *37th Rep. P.M.G.* (1891), p. 6; *Nineteenth Century*, XXVII (1890), 909.

1891, Henniker Heaton continued during the nineties to agitate for ocean penny postage—a cause that was not completely won until 1911. It will be traced in a later chapter. Before continuing the account of the winning of ocean penny postage, it would be well to see how the British Post Office was enlarging its usefulness during the latter half of the nineteenth century by taking on activities that had little to do with the carriage of mail.

An Expanding Post Office
Takes on New Services

THUS far we have been concerned largely with what might be called the essential work of the Post Office—the carrying of the correspondence of the country. The Money Order Department, it is true, has needed attention. But for long it was not an integral part of the Post Office, coming into the organization rather late after having been for years a side interest of the clerks of the road. Despite the long, if loose, attachment of the Money Order Department to the Post Office, the older men considered this department as a sort of stepchild. Anthony Trollope, in his downright way, held that the Money Order Department could not be "regarded as part of the Post Office."[1]

In the later years of the nineteenth century a number of other services, not strictly of postal character, were taken on by the Post Office. They were added because the numerous local post offices scattered over the land were convenient centers for various activities, and also because some of these services, such as those performed by the telegraph and the telephone, seemed but extensions of postal communication. At any rate, they served to add enormously to the size of the growing department in the last quarter of the nineteenth century. It became more than ever the chief department of the government for serving the public.

In 1861 the Post Office became a banker, with the creation of the Savings Bank. A chief reason for the step was the inadequate distribution of private savings banks. Though they numbered over six hundred in 1861, as many as fifteen counties had no savings banks at all.

[1] *North America*, p. 273.

Of the banks in existence, only twenty were opened daily, and none of them was to be found in some hundred towns with populations of ten to thirty thousand.[2]

The greater security of small deposits and the encouragement of thrift by the use of the Post Office Savings Bank appealed very much to Mr. Gladstone, the Chancellor of the Exchequer, and to Lord Stanley of Alderley, the Postmaster-General from 1860 to 1866. The original suggestion had come from C. W. Sykes of Huddersfield, who was connected with the savings bank of that town. The proposal was worked out as a postal measure by George Chetwynd, the Bookkeeper of the Money Order Department, and Frank I. Scudamore, the Receiver and Accountant-General. The measure became law in 1861.[3] The first banks were opened in September of that year. The arrangements provided that deposits could be made at any post office, and could be withdrawn wherever desired—at first, on ten days' notice. Interest of 2½ per cent was paid on complete pounds for complete months. The best feature, of course, was the absolute security of deposits, backed as they were by the government itself. The interest was kept low so as not to compete with commercial banks, though the Post Office Savings Bank did bring about the discontinuance of numbers of the older private savings banks.[4]

The Post Office Savings Bank proved an immediate success, and has ever since remained one of the most profitable and useful features of the British Post Office. When Henry Fawcett was Postmaster-General in the eighties and Gladstone again Chancellor of the Exchequer, the system was made more adaptable for small savings by the use of the "stamp slip deposit": a slip when filled with twelve penny stamps was received as a shilling deposit. This led to thousands of new accounts, particularly among children. This device appealed so largely that by the end of the century, the Post Office Savings Bank had over eight million accounts, totaling about £125,000,000.[5]

[2] *Parl. Deb.*, 3rd s., CLXII, 880; Lewins, *op. cit.*, pp. 268 ff.

[3] 24 Vict., c.14.

[4] An additional precaution against competition with other banking institutions was the limitation of deposits by one person in one year to £30. This was later (1893) extended to £50, and in 1915 the limit was entirely removed. In 1893, also, withdrawal without notice and by telegram was made possible.

[5] L. Stephen, *Life of Henry Fawcett*, pp. 431-32; *Hist. Sum.*, pp. 113 ff.; E. T. Crutchley, *G.P.O.*, pp. 187 ff. Crutchley recounts the amusing request of a depositor who wrote as his reason for a withdrawal: "I require the money urgently as I am always falling into areas with my landlord."

During this time the Money Order Department was made more useful. In 1862 the limit of a money order, which had been five pounds, was raised to ten. The number of orders greatly increased as a result. When further reductions in their cost were made in 1871, it became possible to send any amount less than ten shillings for a penny, and ten pounds for a shilling. By the end of the seventies, eighteen million orders were being written yearly.

The system was further simplified when the Postmaster-General, Henry Fawcett, introduced postal notes in 1881. The sending of small remittances was relatively expensive. To meet the problem, postal notes, or postal orders as they came to be called, were put into use. These were for set amounts from one shilling to twenty shillings, and cost from a halfpence to twopence. At first it was proposed not to have even the name of the payee on the order, but his name was added on the ground that the danger of theft would be lessened. The postal orders could be cashed, of course, at any money order office. In 1884 it became possible to send them for odd sums by adding the necessary amount of postage stamps to the face of the order. Before the end of the century postal orders could be purchased at offices that did not issue the regular money orders. They proved so generally useful that nearly ninety million postal orders were circulated annually by 1900.

The sending of money orders from abroad began as the result of the need of some such convenience for those who were at the front during the Crimean War. The Army Post Office sent money home from the soldiers, but civilians attached to the army had to be cared for in some other way. For some months, the versatile Florence Nightingale met the need, until it was decided to issue orders through the Army Post Office at inland rates. After the war, the system was extended to Malta and Gibraltar, though orders could only be sent one way, homeward. At the end of the fifties, the Canadian government suggested that such orders might be sent both ways between Canada and Great Britain. From this beginning in 1859, the money order system gradually spread to the other colonies. The first foreign countries with which money orders were exchanged were Switzerland and Belgium, in 1868 and 1869. By the end of the century, the exchange was world-wide and the rates had been lowered. The widespread use of money orders was a part of the work of the Postal Union.[6]

[6] *Hist. Sum.*, pp. 110-12; Stephen, *op. cit.*, pp. 427-29; *42nd Rep. P.M.G.* (1896),

Somewhat more akin to the job of communications than banking was the assumption by the British Post Office of the telegraph business of the country, another attack on "private enterprise" resented by business interests. As a result of the growing knowledge of the power of electricity, the idea of using it for transmitting information was developed on both sides of the Atlantic at the same time. About 1837, Cooke and Wheatstone in Great Britain and Morse in America perfected usable apparatus, Morse's instrument printing the dots and dashes on a paper ribbon, and Cooke and Wheatstone's needle form of telegraph recording the message by a pointer that made the necessary indications of the letters on a panel. Morse's sounding instrument proved more effective and superseded the other forms in time.

By the mid-fifties a number of private telegraph companies catered to this new form of communication, but the service they gave was far short of the need. The telegraph was still confined largely to railroad stations, which were often distant from the business centers of the towns. Some railways did not even use the telegraph. Towns of five or six thousand were not infrequently without any telegraph facilities. The rates were very high in the early fifties: it cost, for example, eight or nine shillings to send twenty words from London to Manchester or Liverpool, and fourteen shillings for a message to Glasgow. Although these rates were lowered before the telegraph was taken over by the British Post Office in 1870, they were still based on distance, with additional charges for each additional hundred miles. The use of the telegraph was confined, of course, to a small section of the population.[7]

It was only natural that the Post Office should be thought a good medium for improving the telegraphic service by putting it within everybody's reach. In 1855, Thomas Allan had published a proposal that would "annex an electric telegraph system to the Post Office." F. E. Baines, later a prominent Post Office official, proposed in 1856 that the telegraphs go under the Post Office, his idea being a monop-

pp. 26-32. Another service performed by the British Post Office, and not having the remotest connection with communications, is the granting of life-insurance annuities. This was started in 1864, and later linked with the Post Office Savings Bank. When old age pensions came early in the present century, payments were made through the Post Office. At this convenient government office purchases are made, as well, of various licenses, including those for dogs and guns. At the Post Office, also, one renews his motor vehicle license. These, of course, are not Post Office functions, in any strict sense.

[7] Baines, *Forty Years at the Post Office*, I, 327; *39th Rep. P.M.G.* (1893), pp. 33-38; "Report by Mr. Scudamore on the reorganization of the telegraph system of the United Kingdom," pp. 1-3, in *Parl. Papers* (1871, C. 304).

oly by government, with every post office as a telegraph station, and with a uniform charge—on the analogy of penny postage—of 6d irrespective of distance. J. L. Ricardo, a member of Parliament and chairman of one of the telegraph companies, made a similar suggestion in 1861.[8] In the sixties, the determination grew to take over the private companies, because of delays and inaccuracies in transmission, and the feeling that much more could be made of the telegraph than was being done at the time. Various chambers of commerce, particularly that of Edinburgh, worked actively for a change of ownership and a system that would charge for telegrams irrespective of distance. The privately owned United Kingdom Company had tried the plan of payment without regard to distance, but rivals had forced it to abandon a uniform shilling rate.

The result of the general feeling was the passage of two telegraph acts in 1868 and 1869.[9] The first gave the Post Office the right to purchase the private systems, including the few cables belonging to the telegraph companies, though the Post Office was not to have the exclusive right of operating telegraphs. But when it appeared that the private companies might attempt to retain the most profitable business in large cities and leave to the Post Office the expensive extension of the telegraphs in new and sparsely populated areas, a second act gave the Postmaster-General the exclusive privilege of transmitting telegrams within the United Kingdom.

The new official charges were at the rate of twenty words for a shilling, the names and addresses of senders and receivers going free. This included delivery within a mile of any post office. At first, of course, the services did not reach all parts of the country, but under the vigorous lead of Frank I. Scudamore the telegraph was rapidly extended—a tremendous task, as the companies had done little to improve their services during the time the question of purchase was being debated, that is, from 1860. Trunk lines had to be run, branch offices within large towns connected with the main office by means of pneumatic tubes, and new transmitting instruments and other up-to-date equipment provided.[10]

The purchase of the telegraphs proved a very expensive venture

[8] Baines, *op. cit.*, I, 299-300; J. H. Clapham, *An Economic History of Modern Britain*, II, 207 ff.

[9] 31 & 32 Vict., c.110, and 32 & 33 Vict., c.73.

[10] There were over three hundred stations opened in London, with double tubes connecting them, and forming a sort of pneumatic railway system. See the Scudamore *Report* (1871), pp. 21-24, 71.

on the part of the government. The capital sunk in the telegraphs amounted to over £10,000,000. Every effort was made by extending the business to bring a favorable financial return. Within four years the number of telegrams doubled, and between 1873 and 1885, the number doubled again, to about 33,000,000 messages a year. In 1885 the rate was lowered, through the urgency of the Postmaster-General, Henry Fawcett, to 6d for twelve words, including the address. By the end of the century over 90,000,000 telegrams were being sent annually. After 1889 money orders were sent by telegraph. The great vogue of the telegram in the last quarter of the nineteenth century is explained by the lack of other rapid forms of communication, such as is now offered by the telephone. But such facilities had been purchased at too high a price. The cost of the original transfer was excessive, the capital invested proving a continuous and only slowly diminishing burden. During the last decades of the century the telegraph operation faced continuous deficits, not counting the charge on the capital investment. To make the outlook even darker, the use of the telegraph began gradually to decline. The Postmaster-General, in summarizing the situation in his *Report* for 1893, concluded, however, that the loss "is offset by the benefits which the system confers on the community." Unfortunately, it furnished an additional drain on the profits coming from letters.

By that time the newer system of communication by telephone was seriously affecting the income from the telegraph system. The telephone first appeared in the United Kingdom in 1876 when Graham Bell's device was exhibited at a meeting of the British Association in Glasgow. The Post Office became interested in the telephone early, at first as an assistant in the working of its telegraph monopoly. In the meantime, private companies were starting—the Telephone Company, Ltd., in 1878 and the Edison Telephone Company of London in 1879. With the latter company, I might add, G. B. Shaw undertook for a brief time what he describes as his last attempt to earn an honest living.[11] The two companies united in 1880. The government became alarmed, so alarmed that it declared the telephone an infringement of its telegraph monopoly. The High Court to which the matter was taken in 1880 pronounced a telephone conversation to be a telegram within the meaning of the Acts of 1868 and 1869.[12]

[11] Crutchley, *op. cit.*, p. 104.
[12] This occurred also in Henry Fawcett's regime. See Stephen, *op. cit.*, p. 424; Murray, *op. cit.*, pp. 119 ff.; Clapham, *op. cit.*, III, 390. For a detailed treatment, see F. C. G. Baldwin, *The History of the Telephone in the United Kingdom* (1925).

As a result of this decision, the Post Office set up its own lines, and licensed others, though by 1890 the amalgamated companies had many times the mileage of the Post Office. Finally, in 1896, just as the telegraph was facing calamitous deficits as a result of telephonic competition, the Post Office was authorized to purchase the trunk lines of the company. As in the case of the telegraph, the lack of adequate service over wide areas was the reason given for the governmental action. It was held that exorbitant rates were charged for inferior service. The purchase of the trunk lines was not so expensive as the taking-over of the telegraph companies thirty years before. Nor did it result in a government monopoly. For a time the National Telephone Company worked its independent system, though there were agreements to prevent unnecessary duplication. Finally, in 1912, the Post Office took over the National Telephone Company. It might be added that the telephone has paid its way.[13]

A natural outgrowth of the telegraph monopoly was the extension, in part, of postal control over the cables. Foreign cables were excluded from the authority granted the Post Office by the Telegraph Act of 1869. There was no question, on the other hand, of the supervision by the Post Office of cables used for sending telegrams to various parts of the British Isles. Even the service to the Channel Islands was included. By 1889 some cables to the nearby Continent came under government control—to be included in the multifarious workings of the Post Office. More distant cables of a particularly imperial character did not develop until after 1900. The first link, connecting Canada with Australasia, was the joint property of Great Britain and the connected Dominions. The British Post Office was not used as a medium for its operation. But when two imperial cables connecting Great Britain and Canada were acquired at the time of the First World War, they were under the supervision of the British Post Office. In 1928, these two cables were transferred to a company known as the Cable and Wireless, Ltd. The Post Office continued to accept messages for this transmission, and the cable company, with offices in the larger towns, made use of wires leased from the Post Office.[14]

A long-sought addition to the postal service was the Parcel Post. It had been in use in London after 1680 when Dockwra's Penny Post

[13] *Rep. P.M.G.* (1911-12), p. 39; *Rep. Sel. Com. on the Post Office (Telephone Agreement)* (1905), pp. iii, iv. See below, p. 429.
[14] Murray, *op. cit.*, pp. 87-90; Crutchley, *op. cit.*, pp. 152-54.

included the carriage of parcels weighing up to a pound. But it was dropped in the mid-eighteenth century, owing to a belief that the post should not be encumbered with heavy parcels. When the Book Post was started in 1847, a step was made toward a re-established general parcel post. After Rowland Hill had inherited the undivided enjoyment of the Post Office, he found so many other difficulties to face that the parcel post remained unrealized. The work of carrying parcels was left to other agencies.[15]

One advocate of the Parcel Post, writing in 1861, asked "whether it is not possible to have a penny parcel post." And he added: "Tens of thousands of small parcels which no one now thinks of sending by the expensive agencies in existence would, if the Post Office could be used for such a purpose, freely circulate."[16] A Royal Commission on Railways proposed a plan for such a postal service in 1867—with no result. Meanwhile, other national post offices had begun the carrying of parcels, and in 1880 an international parcel post was discussed and adopted at the Postal Union Conference in Paris. British delegates attended despite the lack of such a service in Great Britain. This stimulus brought about new negotiations with the railways by that tireless Postmaster-General, Henry Fawcett. He was especially eager to set up an inland parcel post that would make possible Britain's participation in the international exchange of parcels. The railway companies held out for better terms, so that it was not until 1882 that the agreement could be embodied in an act.[17] By it, the railway companies received 55 per cent of the postage collected on parcels, as their part of the work of distribution. They drove a hard bargain, for the governmental work of collecting, sorting and delivering the parcels, as well as taking them to and from the trains, was more nearly two-thirds than one-half of the expense.[18]

The government's Parcel Post began in August 1883. As in the other extensions already described, the Post Office was actuated by a genuine effort to give better service at a more reasonable price. Certainly this was the motive of Henry Fawcett, the blind Postmaster-General, whose chief accomplishment among a number of vigorous measures was the Parcel Post.[19] At first, seven pounds was the limit for a parcel, the charge being 3d for a pound and so on up to a shilling for seven pounds. In 1886 the maximum weight was increased

---

[15] G. B. Hill, *op. cit.*, II, 336. [16] Owen Howell, *The Post Office*, pp. 22-24.
[17] 45 & 46 Vict., c.74. [18] Stephen, *op. cit.*, p. 421.
[19] See the eloquent tribute paid by *Punch*.

PARCELS POST
OFFICE

REPLY
POSTCARDS

SWAIN Sc.

THE MAN FOR THE POST.

A *Punch* cartoon by Sir John Tenniel, showing Henry Fawcett, the blind
Postmaster-General, as an overloaded postman.

to eleven pounds, and by 1900 a parcel of that weight could be sent for 11d. The increase in the traffic was marked: over 67,000,000 parcels were being carried annually by the end of the century.[20]

This enlargement of the Post Office service proved an aggravation to the already overworked letter carriers. Plans were made for a delivery of parcels in the towns by a separate set of carriers, and the use of hand-carts. The extortionate charge obtained by the railway companies for their part of the carriage of parcels so affected the success of the new venture that the Post Office faced a serious loss. As a mode of economy, the Parcel Post delivery was saddled on to the ordinary letter carriers and that without any extra pay. The letter carriers, consequently, were more heavily burdened than ever, and their walks were made slower by the need of delivering parcels. The nature of these loads, as given in the evidence of the carriers before the Tweedmouth Committee in the nineties, make *Punch's* caricature seem much like reality. One carrier complained that the bags might include, in addition to letters, "bandboxes, or umbrellas, or fishing rods, or other parcels which are awkward to carry. There may be eggs and all that kind of thing." Another emphasized the danger to letters of carrying such a miscellany as "tin, wooden, and cardboard boxes, butter, Devonshire cream, fruit and flowers. And I have instances of game, partridges, rabbits, fish, and the whole of these have to be carried in the same bag with the letters." One witness declared that he had seen carriers come out of the post office with their bags full and parcels tied around their bodies. In order to prevent the carriers from having grounds on which to object to this additional work, the class designation was officially changed from "letter carrier" to "postman" in October 1883, with about as much effect as renaming black, white.[21]

The grant to the railways of more than half the postage on the parcels they carried naturally led the Post Office to think of a reintroduction of the road service. Not only would it save in revenue, but a parcel put into a van at the post office and not rehandled save at the office for which it was destined would cause less risk to the contents. In addition, the vans could leave at times not set by the railway

---

[20] *Hist. Sum.*, pp. 17-20; A. D. Smith, *op. cit.*, pp. 183 ff. The United States was even slower than Great Britain in this form of service. Despite efforts made in the nineties to start a parcel post in the United States, it did not come until 1912. The express companies vigorously opposed such a government service.

[21] *The Postmen's Case for Enquiry,* "as submitted to the Interdepartmental Committee on Post Office Establishments" (Glasgow, 1896), pp. 97, 317-18.

schedules, and could carry other postal material as well for the routes that were followed. The return to something like the horsed coaches of an earlier day began in 1887 when Henry Raikes was the Post-master-General. The first service was a night coach to Brighton, after an experimental daytime run with all the accouterments of the bygone mail coach. The constantly improved highways made the plan so useful that other night mail parcel vans were running out of London —to Liverpool, Manchester, Oxford and other towns. Schedules were set that called for a speed of eight miles an hour. There were, of course, changes of horses along the road and armed guards to safe-guard the mails. Indeed, the day of the mail coach seemed to have returned. The revival of the horsed coach was not for long. Just as the century came to a close, motor vans were tried on these routes, and soon superseded horses on the services out of London to pro-vincial towns: the motor made possible even faster service over longer routes.[22]

The work of the Post Office was bettered in a number of other ways during these years. The use of pillar boxes had been greatly extended since their introduction at the mid-century. They were soon to be found along roads as well as streets. They even made possible the closing of some sub-offices, since the postmen not only collected and delivered mail, but were empowered to sell stamps and enve-lopes, and do a general postal business. Before the end of the century it looked as though the Post Office would attach letter boxes to any-thing. They were multiplied in railway stations, attached to the rail-way sorting carriages, hung on lamp posts, and even attached to tram cars. This latter resting-place for the letter box was first used in Hud-dersfield. The days were long past when the Post Office had made it difficult to mail a letter.[23]

The post card underwent some changes after its enthusiastic recep-tion in 1870. Its sale at face value so aroused the watchful stationers that they induced the Post Office to make an additional charge of a halfpenny a dozen in 1871; it was raised to a penny in 1875. The first thin cards were supplemented by stouter ones in the mid-seventies, at a slightly higher cost. The only cards allowed at first were those issued by the Post Office, and bearing the impressed stamp. The de-mand for private cards, that is, cards that could be sent to the Stamp

---

[22] *Hist. Sum.*, p. 19; Baines, *Forty Years at the Post Office*, II, pp. 128 ff.
[23] *39th Rep. P.M.G.* (1893), p. 7; *40th Rep.*, p. 6; *44th Rep.*, p. 25; Stephen, *op. cit.*, p. 438.

Office for receiving the stamp, was met in 1872, but they never proved widely popular. Henry Raikes, the Postmaster-General in the late eighties, found that De La Rue and Company were making a profit of some 55 per cent on the manufacture of the official post cards. The reduction of this profit through a new contract led to a lower price for cards, though they still cost more than the postage charge.[24] Not until 1911 were they again sold at face value.

The vogue of the post card was much increased in the nineties when private cards were sanctioned. Private cards, that is, cards to which one attached a halfpenny adhesive stamp, had been used in other countries for some time, and in the Postal Union by countries permitting them, since the Postal Union Congress at Lisbon in 1885. Henniker Heaton had sent one from Austria to the Postmaster-General, asking for their introduction in Great Britain. Although he received the reply that there was little likelihood of their adoption, they came, nevertheless, in 1894. The private card was capable of all sorts of uses. One that appealed particularly was the picture post card, which grew in favor with the expansion of the tourist business. In the first year of their use, the number of post cards jumped by 25 per cent. By the end of the century over 400,000,000 post cards were sent annually, with more than half of them picture post cards.

Henniker Heaton had long and vainly urged the Post Office to issue larger and stouter cards and to sell them at face value, "as in other civilized countries." As late as 1894 he called the British post card one of the "meanest, smallest, and dearest" used anywhere. The cards did improve in size, but were not sold at face value until some years later (1911). He also urged on a laggard Post Office the use of the letter card, that is, a card of double size that could be folded and closed by means of its gummed edges. They were first issued in Great Britain in 1892, were sold at face value after 1911, and are still in general use.

Another inconvenience was removed at this time, the charge for redirecting a letter. After 1840 a letter had been subject to a second postage if redirected. This fee had been removed in 1855, if the change of address was in the same town, and in 1864 for letters within the same delivery. Ten years later the International Postal Union provided for the free readdressing of foreign mail, a rule that applied, of course, to Great Britain as well as the other members. But

<hr>

[24] Raikes, *op. cit.*, pp. 298-99; *19th Rep. P.M.G.* (1873), pp. 298-99; *42nd Rep.* (1896), p. 3.

the British Post Office was reluctant to give up the charge for redirecting domestic letters. It was finally surrendered by a hesitant Treasury in 1892, both Postmaster-General Raikes and Henniker Heaton agreeing for once on the change.[25]

The sixty years following the beginning of penny postage have been years of uninterrupted progress in these notable additions to the postal services. The Post Office became the very core of British national life. What a British writer described as its activities during the recent war were already becoming true by 1900: "The young take their earliest savings to the Post Office, the old go to it for their pensions. The Post Office is our banker, it deals with our short and long distance talks . . . our war payments, our billeting allowances, our health insurance, our unemployment, entertainment duty and income tax stamps, our licenses, our investments and our national savings."[26]

[25] Raikes, *op. cit.*, pp. 288, 366-67; *41st Rep. P.M.G.* (1895), p. 4; *Parl. Deb.*, 3rd s., CCCLII, 878.
[26] Ivor Halstead, *Post Haste*, pp. 1-2.

Years of Jubilation—
1887-1914

THE closing decades of the century brought several opportunities for celebrating jubilees. By 1887 the Queen had reigned for fifty years of unexampled peace and prosperity, and the reform of the Post Office had taken place when the young Queen was but just seated on the throne. The Department naturally desired to stress its half-century of penny postage as well by making further advances in its services and by contributing to the chorus of praise for the Queen.

A new issue of postage stamps appeared on the opening day of 1887, the Golden Jubilee year. It included some novel differences in appearance, with several of the stamps in two colors and others on tinted paper. The series of values began with the halfpenny, but, strangely enough, a penny stamp was not part of the series. The central design of all the stamps, of course, was the Queen's head—as it had looked in 1840.[1]

Henniker Heaton had hoped that the Golden Jubilee might be celebrated by the introduction of imperial penny postage. He advocated this advance both in Parliament and in print, but to no effect. As the desire for a federated empire was already finding support, he had hoped that penny postage might be granted as a means of increasing the "cousinly feeling" between Great Britain and the self-governing colonies. Heaton even addressed the Royal Colonial Institute on the matter, an address that was heard by a number of postal offi-

---

[1] One reason for the combination of colors and for the tinted paper was the belief that they furnished greater security. *33rd Rep. P.M.G.* (1887), p. 2. The penny stamp of 1881—the one then in use—was not changed.

cials. Among those who strongly condemned his Utopian ideas and answered his proposals with denunciatory speeches was Pearson Hill. The latter's participation in the discussion and his strong opposition to imperial penny postage drew from Henniker Heaton the retort that such an utterance coming from Pearson Hill was likely to make his father turn in his grave.[2]

The Colonial Conference that met in the Jubilee year discussed the matter and even listened to Henniker Heaton urge its adoption. Mr. Raikes, the Postmaster-General, countered his arguments, and asserted, among other things, that imperial postage was not practical: "At present," added the prophetic Mr. Raikes, "it is a very distant prospect."[3] But the prospect was to become decidedly nearer and more pleasing to the reformer during the next decade, for public sentiment was growing in favor of a cheaper and more rapid communication with the colonies. As colonial rivalries became keener among the imperial-minded nations, the idea of empire-wide penny postage found more and more support in a world growing suspicious and selfish; there seemed a greater need than ever within the British family of "kind cleaving to kind."

In 1890, three years after the Golden Jubilee, domestic penny postage reached its fiftieth anniversary, with much congratulation of the Post Office over the half-century's record. The work of Rowland Hill was recalled again and again as the amazing changes and marvelous growth since 1840 were reviewed and appreciated. The Chairman of the Committee of Management was F. E. Baines, the Inspector-General of the Mails, to whose entertaining volumes we have had occasion to refer. None looked back with more nostalgic yearning to the older days, for he had been active in the Post Office for many years. In January a postmasters' dinner was held at the Holborn Restaurant, attended by some two hundred and fifty officers and ex-officers of the Post Office. Facsimiles of the Mulready envelope indicated each guest's place at table. The group included Henry Cecil Raikes, the Postmaster-General, Sir Arthur Blackwood, the Secretary, and Sir John Tilley, whom Blackwood had succeeded in 1880. Pearson Hill, the only son of Rowland Hill, was there, as well as Herbert Joyce, the Third Secretary, whose readable *History of the Post Office* was to appear in 1893. The occasion was enlivened by the presence of Edmund Yates and several former Postmasters-General.

[2] *Parl. Deb.*, 3rd s., CCCIV, 261-70; *Nineteenth Century*, LXIV (1908), 592.
[3] *Proceedings*, Col. Conf. of 1887, pp. 164-86; *Fortnightly Rev.*, LXI (1894), 340.

Mr. Yates recalled that it was eighteen years since he had "gracefully retired from the Post Office." His memories went back to the days of Col. Maberly, his "first chief," who used to impress upon him the necessity of not overworking himself. Mr. Yates assured the group that he had given the Colonel the pledge that he would not, and he had solemnly adhered to that sacred obligation.

Sir Lyon Playfair, a former Postmaster-General, referred to Rowland Hill as one "who grasped an idea and made it his own, who grappled with prejudice and monopoly, who awakened public conviction." The Post Office was complimented for its perfect freedom from political interference. "I believe," he said, "that the only survival of politics in it is the appointment of rural messengers by members of Parliament for the district. This miserable remnant of patronage ought to be swept away." He contrasted the situation with that in America: "The present President has been in office only a few months but when I left America in November 17,000 postmasters had been dismissed because they were Democrats, .. and party newspapers were urging increased activity in the process of disorganization."[4]

Mr. Shaw-Lefevre, another former Postmaster-General, made remarks that seemed to have particular significance. He recalled Rowland Hill's statement that no improvement had ever been devised within the Department, and then attemped to show that a demonstrable change had occurred in this respect. He cited the work of the late Mr. Fawcett, "whose name is imperishably connected with Post Office improvements, and than whom no one since Sir Rowland Hill has more adequately grasped the needs of the people." Mr. Shaw-Lefevre seemed, however, to sense the "disposition of the Press to complain of the tardiness of the Post Office to adopt improvements." There was no denying the delay in meeting "public desires," but this was laid to the Exchequer, which hesitated to forgo the increasing net revenue of the Post Office. He called attention to the fact that "no other country in the world drew a revenue from its Post Office." Mr. Shaw-Lefevre pointed out that the net revenue was twice what it had been before the introduction of penny postage, and proposed

[4] *Account of the Celebration of the Jubilee of Uniform Inland Penny Postage* (1891), pp. 74-75. This was over a fourth of the total number of American postmasters. Ever since the days of President Jackson, when the Postmaster-General became a Cabinet member, he had been the principal patronage broker of each new administration. See Dorothy G. Fowler, *The Cabinet Politician, The Postmaster-General, 1829-1909* (N.Y., 1943).

that the best way of celebrating the Jubilee was by applying this increase "to improvements in simplicity, uniformity, universality, cheapness, and there are many directions in which these great principles may be carried further."[5]

Mr. Raikes referred in happy vein to the scheme of penny postage as "one of the greatest peaceful revolutions of the century." The enormous enlargement of the service gave him special cause for satisfaction. He cited the Savings Bank and the telegraphs and the parcel post, "of the convenience of which we are all sensible," and the reduction of the price of postal cards, and the establishment of parcel coaches during his administration. He described the parcel coach as a "picturesque and telling manner of bringing home to the attention of the nation the fact that in existing circumstances the contract between the railways and the Department is one which is not beneficial to the public service." "Talk of armies," continued Mr. Raikes, "the number of officers of whom I may say I am for the time being Commander-in-Chief are more numerous than any regular forces which the Secretary of State for War can show within the compass of Her Majesty's dominions." He recalled for his hearers that there were 18,000 post offices in the United Kingdom and 20,000 additional receptacles for receiving letters, that the force of the Post Office consisted of 58,000 established officers and 50,000 other persons employed in the service of the Post Office, that the increase in letters during the last two years, 172,000,000 was more than twice the whole number of letters which were posted in the year 1840. "I think this will justify me in saying that the Department had become the most important administrative Department of the State."[6]

The Postmaster-General could not refrain from making allusions before this friendly gathering to the current accusations against the dilatoriness of the Post Office. "We are always making new departures," he averred. He undoubtedly had Mr. Henniker Heaton in mind, though his name was unmentioned, in referring to those "who sometimes wish to pose as postal reformers." And Mr. Raikes then proceeded to illustrate by referring to the question of international penny postage "of which we hear a great deal in the newspapers, and something occasionally in the House of Commons." He pointed out the hollowness of the agitation, the false analogy with domestic penny postage. The high cost of transportation to such distant possessions

[5] *Account of the Celebration of the Jubilee*, pp. 67-70.
[6] *Ibid.*, pp. 52-55.

as India, China and Australia was cited, a cost "three times the total sum which the reformer proposes to levy by way of postage." Raikes, who died in 1891, did not live long enough by seven years to see the success of the agitation. To him it was a "bubble which is blown before our eyes," and which he believed that "merciless logic" had burst.

The official Post Office celebrations were held at the Guildhall and the South Kensington Museum in May and July. A Post Office was established at the Guildhall for actual business. Coaches in the yard

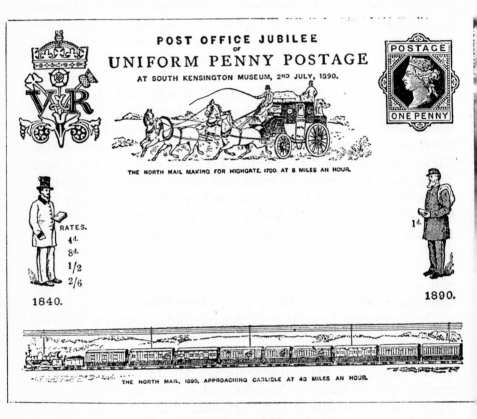

The South Kensington Jubilee envelope.

were dispatched to the Post Office with the mail made up in the Guildhall, a pageantry that gave the impression to some that the old coaching services were to begin again. Though there were no commemorative stamps for the Jubilee, special post cards and letter cards were sold, and obliterated by a special stamp. The card had on it a portrait of Rowland Hill, and the envelope pictured the changes since 1840, by showing the postmen, the rates and the conveyances of 1840 and 1890. The contrast offered a striking lesson in postal history, even if the envelope can hardly be regarded as an artistic production. A roaring trade in Jubilee envelopes and other postal business was also carried on at the South Kensington Museum in July. Parcels were received at the Post Office set up in the Museum, whence mail coaches dashed away with their loads. The climax of the celebration was the telegraphing of announcements at ten o'clock to all parts of the United Kingdom for simultaneous cheers in honor of a reformed Post Office, fifty years old.[7]

In 1892 Henniker Heaton, still eager to obtain imperial penny postage, made an offer to the Chancellor of the Exchequer: he and two friends, an Australian millionaire and an English capitalist, were willing to guarantee the British government against loss if penny postage were established between the English-speaking peoples within the British Empire and with the United States. Mr. Goschen, the Chancellor, did not see fit to accept the offer. Two years later, Heaton pointed out that a penny rate to the colonies did not necessarily mean a penny rate from the colonies. He showed as well, contrary to the general belief, that the International Postal Union allowed "more restricted unions." Heaton cited the case of Canada and the United States where there was a restricted union and unequal rates, each country charging its domestic rate for letters going across the border, 2¢ for a letter from the United States and 3¢ for a letter mailed in Canada. He stressed the desire of the Australian colonies and New Zealand for a penny rate to them, even if they felt unable to reciprocate at the time. The indefatigable reformer even visited Australasia in 1896, and found the seven colonial governments unanimous for penny postage from Great Britain.[8]

In 1897, the Queen being still on the throne, an even more enthusiastic Jubilee occurred, in view of the continuance of what promised to be the longest reign in Britain's history. Henniker Heaton contributed an article to the *Fortnightly* in 1897 on "Postal and Tele-

---

[7] See the illustration of the Jubilee envelope. The money derived from the envelopes was used to increase a benevolent fund for aiding postal employees, a fund established in honor of Rowland Hill at the time of his death. Collections of postage stamps were on exhibit, including specimens from the collections of the Duke of Edinburgh and the Prince of Wales. See *ibid., passim*; Baines, *op. cit.*, II, 281 ff.; *The Penny Postage Jubilee and Philatelic History* by Phil (A. D. Blackburn).

[8] *Fortnightly Rev.*, LXI (1894), 340; LXVII (1897), 844; *Century Mag.*, n.s., XXI (1892), 950.

graph Progress under Queen Victoria." He paid tribute to the advances of sixty years, and urged various additional steps that would honor the jubilee year. He hoped, of course, that imperial penny postage might be one of them, and was encouraged in the hope by Joseph Chamberlain's speech in its favor before the meeting of the colonial premiers held in London in that year. Chamberlain had said: "I think that one of the very first things to bind together the sister nations is to have the readiest and easiest possible communication between their several units, and as far as this country is concerned I believe we should be quite ready to make any sacrifice of revenue that may be required in order to secure a uniform penny post throughout the Empire."[9]

A number of changes occurred in the service, beginning, as far as possible, on Jubilee Day, June 22, 1897. The cost of inland parcels was lowered, free delivery of telegrams was extended to three miles and rural delivery was henceforth to include every house in the United Kingdom, no matter how remote. Inland letter rates were also reduced. Since 1871 a penny had paid for an ounce letter; by the new rate a penny paid for the first four ounces, with each additional two ounces an additional halfpenny.[10] But imperial penny postage was conspicuous by its absence.

Henniker Heaton was not satisfied with the postal reforms of 1897 and continued to prod what he called the "mandarins of St. Martin's," hoping to speed up some of the changes he felt to be so necessary. In a sweeping summary made in 1898, called "A Postal Utopia," he listed no less than fifty changes that should occur in the postal and telegraphic departments. He frequently enlivened his attacks in the House of Commons by calling attention to various anomalies in the service.[11]

At the Washington Congress of the Postal Union in 1897 general transit rates were further reduced, and there was some discussion of a twopenny rate for a restricted union within the British Empire, the British Post Office expressing favor for the twopenny charge. Canada, on the other hand, advocated a rate of 1½d (3¢), the domestic rate

---

[9] Mrs. Adrian Porter, *op. cit.*, p. 178.

[10] *44th Rep. P.M.G.* (1898), p. 1; *46th Rep.*, p. 4. Two years were required to extend rural delivery to every house in the Kingdom. 55,000,000 letters were brought into the official delivery as a result.

[11] *Nineteenth Century*, XLIII (1898), 764-79. On one occasion he inquired of the Postmaster-General if he was aware that in a telegram "Charing Cross" counted as two words, but "St. Pancras" as but one, that "father in law" counted as three words in a telegram but "mother-in-law" went as one. See Mrs. Adrian Porter, *op. cit.*, p. 211.

SIR JOHN HENNIKER HEATON

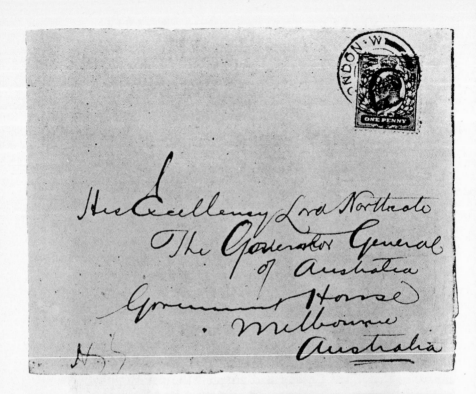

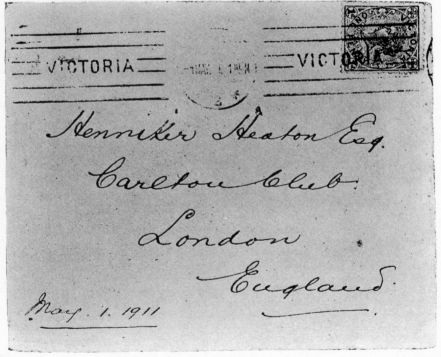

THE FIRST PENNY LETTERS TO AND FROM AUSTRALIA
From Sir John Henniker Heaton to the Governor General of Australia, in 1905.
To Sir John Henniker Heaton from the Australian Postmaster-General, on May 1, 1911.

in Canada at the time and the one for letters to the United States. The Dominion announced that on January 1, 1898, the rate of 1½d would extend to every part of the Empire. The British Post Office protested and suggested a conference, still hoping to obtain a general imperial twopenny rate. As a result, a meeting of representatives of the more important colonial post offices occurred in London at the Westminster Palace Hotel in June and July of 1898. The British postal authorities did everything possible to induce Canada to withdraw its suggestion. At this juncture, Henniker Heaton approached Joseph Chamberlain on the matter. As a result, pressure was brought to bear on the British postal authorities to abandon their twopenny proposal. When Sir William Mulock, the Postmaster-General of Canada, moved that a rate of one penny be established, the resolution passed seven to five, with Britain's vote in its favor.

The new rate became effective on Christmas Day of 1898.[12] Where the rate came into force it was to be reciprocal. The old rate of 2½d remained for letters to and from the Australian colonies and the Cape, as those parts of the Empire were not ready for the lower rate. The *Report* of the British Post Office for 1900 was able, however, to announce that Cape Colony had adopted the penny postal scheme, "which now only requires the adhesion of Australia to make it practically coterminous with the British Empire."

New Zealand went even further by introducing universal penny postage on January 1, 1901, "as a befitting commemoration of the new century." Penny postage from Great Britain to Australia was begun in 1905, though the rate from Australia to Great Britain remained 2d. The government of the Commonwealth, with its tremendous distances and small population, feared a probable loss annually of £250,000 with a penny domestic rate, and this would be necessary if oversea penny postage were introduced. Not until May 1, 1911, were letters sent from Australia to Great Britain for a penny. This was an especial satisfaction to Henniker Heaton, who always kept on his writing table the first letter he sent to Australia for a penny, and the first letter sent from Australia at the penny rate: it

---

[12] According to Mrs. Porter's biography of Henniker Heaton (p. 180), the day was chosen on the spur of the moment. When the Postmaster-General, the Duke of Norfolk, conveyed to the Queen the news of the introduction of penny postage, she inquired as to when it was to come into force. "We thought of the Prince's birthday," replied the Duke, referring to the Prince of Wales, who was born on Nov. 9. "And what Prince?" she inquired, in her most icy tones. But the Duke was equal to the occasion: "The Prince of Peace—on Christmas Day," he replied. "Thus it came about that penny postage was established on Christmas Day, 1898."

was addressed to him by the Australian Postmaster-General. Henniker Heaton's work in these years has been happily characterized as an effort "to stick the Empire together with a penny stamp."[13]

Penny postage between Great Britain and the United States began in 1908, and again Henniker Heaton was the leading spirit. He had visited the United States in 1890 to confer with the Postmaster-General, John Wanamaker, on the possibility. Mr. Wanamaker greatly favored the project, even after he had ceased to be Postmaster-General. In 1904 Henniker Heaton formed a league to work for this extension of penny postage, and two years later a strong delegation visited the Chancellor of the Exchequer to urge American penny postage. When the government held back on the ground of probable loss of revenue, Henniker Heaton, with the support of Andrew Carnegie, Lord Blyth, John Wanamaker and others, offered to underwrite any loss of revenue for the first five years. Though the government demurred at the time on the ground that it was opposed to the acceptance of private donations, it finally conceded penny postage in 1908—and Henniker Heaton had another victory to his credit.[14]

Queen Victoria, who died in 1901, was succeeded by Edward VII. What is sometimes called the post-Victorian age began the new century. Yet many of the traditions of the nineteenth century were carried forward with little interruption—until the World War of 1914 wrote finis to the long period of peace. Until that year postal progress was along lines already sketched, but the coming of the First World War so sharply set off the years ahead that 1914 serves almost better than 1900 as the closing year of the century. At least, it is a point at which postal advances can be appraised before they were modified profoundly by the war years.

[13] See Heaton's "Fight for Universal Penny Postage" in *Nineteenth Century*, LXIV (1908), 595—an excellent summary of the long fight. For the changes, see the *Reports of the P.M.G.*, 45th (1899), p. 7; 46th (1900), p. 47; 51st (1905), p. 6; 55th (1909), p. 3; *Rep.* for 1911-12, p. 3.

[14] See *Nineteenth Century*, LXIV (1908), 588-602. Heaton was accorded many honors: like Rowland Hill, he received the freedom of the City of London. He was offered the K.C.M.G. several times, and in 1912 became a baronet when absent in Australia. On his return, at a formal welcome by the British Empire League, Lord Curzon said: "In my opinion, the work of Sir John Henniker Heaton has done more to draw the Empire together than all the speeches of all the statesmen on both sides of the ocean." The Postmaster-General, Herbert Samuel, was equally cordial: "As the latest of the long line of Postmasters-General whom he has harassed so efficiently . . . I should like to pay my tribute of thanks for his many suggestions." And he added that Henniker Heaton, on his 62nd birthday, had sent the Postmaster-General a list of 62 desirable postal reforms! See Mrs. Adrian Porter, *op. cit.*, pp. 242-47.

By 1914 the actual size of the Post Office staff had increased almost beyond recognition, if it is compared with that of seventy-five years earlier. Henry Raikes became eloquent at the time of the postal jubilee in 1890 over his army of some 100,000 Post Office officers and employees. By 1914—a quarter of a century—the "army" had grown to more than 200,000. The Post Office had become the most imposing business organization in Great Britain.

The proper handling of this army of workers had not been easy. For seventy-five years—from the time when Rowland Hill began his reforms—the employees had wanted better conditions of work. We have found how much trouble the matter of Sunday postal labor caused Mr. Hill. A Select Committee faced the same issue in 1887.[15] By that time the laborers in Britain were organizing more effectively than ever before to demand higher pay, shorter working hours and better conditions for work.

The Post Office "servants" were helpless for a long time in making any progress towards collective action, as a regulation had been passed in 1866 forbidding meetings of postal workers outside the Post Office for the discussion of official questions. Not until the early eighties did the disaffection in the ranks of the letter carriers find effective vent through petitions. The result was what was known as the Fawcett Revision, by which wages were somewhat improved, and some provision made for annual holidays.

The Fawcett regime, however, only augmented trouble. With the introduction of the Parcel Post the carriers were burdened more heavily than ever. In order to protect their own interests, a Postmen's Association was formed in the eighties, to be followed in 1889 by a Postmen's Union. The success of the great Dock Strike at that time emboldened the postmen to attempt the strike as their ultimate argument.

Henry Raikes, the Postmaster-General in 1890, was facing serious labor trouble in the Department at the very time that the fiftieth anniversary of penny postage was being so loudly acclaimed. At the time of the Guildhall banquet to celebrate the Jubilee, a procession of postmen had to be broken up by the police. Over four hundred men were dismissed for this and other offenses. The trouble led, however, to a departmental committee of inquiry, with Herbert Joyce as chairman. This was followed in 1896 by the Tweedmouth Committee on Post

---

[15] See above, pp. 329-31, 365 and 331n, for the 1887 *Report*.

Office Establishments: it resulted in some improvement in conditions. By that time a Postmen's Federation was becoming effective.[16]

Several other investigations took place before 1914. The Bradford Committee on Post Office Servants reported in 1904, in the hope of quieting the almost continuous unrest of the postal employees. But the management was unwilling as yet to recognize trade unionism in the Post Office. When the Liberals, allied with the rising Labor Party, came into power in 1905, the relations with the postal employees improved greatly. Sidney Buxton, Postmaster-General from 1905 to 1910, took a friendly view of the problem, receiving deputations from the trade unions of the staff, thus giving official recognition to the various associations. Another report was made in 1907 by the Hobhouse Committee. Herbert Samuel, Postmaster-General from 1910 to 1914, was much concerned with this matter, as the trade union movement in Great Britain had reached a high development just before the First World War. The report of the Holt Committee of 1913 on wages and conditions of employment resulted in a general revision of the inadequate rates of pay for a body of men and women so large that it contained more than half the entire civil service. During the Samuel regime, the lot of the boys who served as telegraph messengers was improved. Previous to 1914, the three main organizations of the staff were the Postmen's Federation, the Postal and Telegraph Clerk's Association and an organization of the London sorters known as the Fawcett Association. Only after the First World War—in 1920—did the various sectional organizations unite to form the U.P.W., the Union of Post Office Workers.[17]

The advance in revenue by 1914 was just as amazing as the growth in personnel. In the year 1840 the gross revenue had been about £1,-360,000 and the net some £500,000. Fifty years later, in 1890, the gross income was £9,847,000, and the surplus had increased to £3,245,000—the gross income enlarging seven times and the surplus six times. By 1914 the income had reached £21,935,000 and the surplus £6,640,000, an increase in total income of fifteen times in the seventy-five years since 1840.[18]

[16] See *Rep. of the Interdepartmental Committee on Post Office Establishments*, in *Reports, Committees*, XLIV (1897), pp. 9, 19, 33. The evidence was also reprinted by the Postmen's Federation. The reprinted evidence was prefaced by a "Chapter in Post History from the Postmen's Point of View."

[17] Viscount Samuel, *Memoirs* (1945), pp. 77-79.

[18] These figures do not include the telegraph, telephone or savings bank accounts. See below, p. 431, for the figures and above, p. 323, where the revenue for 1840 is stated as somewhat smaller.

The increase in correspondence was nothing short of spectacular. Post cards, used first in 1870, had reached a total of 900,000,000 annually by the First World War. Letters by 1900 had reached the figure of 2000 million, more than double the number for 1870, and some thirty times greater than those sent in 1839. By 1914 the number had nearly doubled again to 3500 million letters. To put it another way, in 1839 the British had exchanged but three letters per person each year. Just before the First World War the number of letters per person was sixty-six for England and Wales, fifty for Scotland and thirty-five for Ireland.

For other classes of mail matter there is much the same record of advance, with less growth in the number of newspapers carried than in the amount of books, circulars and parcels. By 1914 the number of letters, post cards, newspapers and printed papers carried by the Post Office had reached the grand total of 5,784,000,000. About two-thirds of this number consisted of letters.[19]

Henniker Heaton had asserted in 1897 that the true test of the degree of civilization attained by a given country was to be found in the number of its letters, though he was quick to qualify his statement by denying that the British were barbarians at the opening of the Queen's reign just because they exchanged but three letters per person annually. The wider use of the Post Office by 1914 at least showed a greater appreciation of its varied facilities than ever before.

[19] For the figures, see *The Statistical Abstracts, The Statesman's Year Book,* and the *Annual Reports* of the Postmaster-General.

The Post Office during
War and Peace—1914-1939

FOR almost exactly a century—from 1815 to 1914—Great Britain took part in no major world conflict. Colonial wars occurred during the long peace, and the Crimean War, fought against Russia in the Black Sea area, only confirmed the average Britisher's conviction of the virtue of nonintervention. During this century of relative peace, the British Post Office grew and prospered, reaching its greatest size by 1914 and giving the best service in its long history.

The years of war from 1914 to 1918 and the unstable decades of peace that prefaced a second world-shaking conflict in 1939 brought a new era in postal history. Two major wars—not unlike the two against Napoleon that had just preceded the century of peaceful progress—have dislocated the international postal services more severely than ever before. The financial strain of the wars as well as the boom and the depression that separated them have not contributed to a stabilized, peaceful evolution of such institutions as the Post Office. There have been backward steps, postally speaking, in obedience to the national strain, steps not unlike those that seemed necessary in the days of Napoleon. Yet even in the troubled decades since 1914 the British Post Office has shown some notable advances and a number of striking changes. These years afford an opportunity, as well, for appraising British postal administration under conditions it had not faced since the days of Robert Wallace and Rowland Hill.

After 1914 the amount of mail fell off, so that it did not reach the 1914 high again until 1925. Increased rates—to be considered presently—account in part for this decline. Between 1925 and 1940 the business of the Post Office continued to expand until well over 8000 million pieces of mail matter were being carried annually as the Second World War began.

The revenue shows much the same effects. The gross revenue, nearly £22,000,000 in 1914, continued to advance rather slowly until 1925, and then moved upward rapidly to the highest point in its history in 1939: it was over £50,000,000 in that year. The net revenue was more seriously affected, dropping badly during the war period and the years immediately following the peace: by 1925 it was still below the figure set in 1914. The net revenue for 1939 was less than £11,000,000. During the quarter-century following 1914 the gross revenue had increased two and a half times but the net had not doubled.[1]

These figures do not include the telegraph and telephone receipts and expenditures, for they have been handled, necessarily, in a separate way. The telegraphs have not paid, even if the capital investment is left out of the reckoning: the deficits have been continuous for many years. In 1940, for example, the income was only four-fifths of the expenditure. The record of the telephone service is in sharp contrast. The purchase of the trunk lines in 1896 and the local system of the National Company in 1912 led to a large increase in business. For a while deficits were the result, but surpluses had become regular in the telephone account by 1914. The telephone account showed deficits from 1918 to 1922, but since that time it has not been in the "red." By 1940 the income was about £35,000,000, nearly ten times that being realized by the telegraphs. The latter, like the horse and buggy in the face of motor cars, has found the competition of the telephone much too powerful. The telegraph income of 1940 was only about half what it had been twenty years before. It is the "white elephant" of the Post Office Department.[2]

The First World War made greater demands than ever before on the public for taxes both direct and indirect. The Treasury naturally looked to the Post Office as one of the sources for much needed funds. A government Committee on Retrenchment, accordingly, recommended among other things that a halfpenny tax be levied on all in-

---

[1] See below, p. 431, for the revenue figures.

[2] The characterization of Lord Wolmer in his *Post Office Reform, Its Importance and Practicability* (1932), p. 156. The volume is a sharp criticism of the Post Office by a former Assistant Postmaster-General. The title, exactly like that of Rowland Hill's famous pamphlet of 1837, includes an account of the work of Rowland Hill, and recalls his strictures on the postal organization at that time.

land postal packets. This use of the Post Office for taxing communication seemed like a return to the days of William Pitt, and the misuse of the Post Office for obtaining income during the Napoleonic Wars. This tax would have meant the abandonment of the penny post, which had enjoyed an uninterrupted life of seventy-five years. Owing to a natural reluctance to give up the penny rate, the tax on letters was not immediately added, despite the Committee's suggestion. But other changes in rates began a new epoch of high postal charges. Even if the penny charge for letters remained, it no longer paid for four ounces, but only for one ounce. The Book Post which had merged with the Letter Post at the time of the Diamond Jubilee was set up again for the purpose of gathering more returns. The newspaper rate, which had been a halfpenny for five pounds, became a halfpenny for six ounces, and a halfpenny for each additional ounce, with the limit at two pounds. The 6d telegram disappeared, the minimum becoming 9d. Such were some of the increased charges that affected the whole of the postal services.

The war ended with a presumed victory in 1918, but it did not mean an end of high taxation through the Post Office. The government finally, and no doubt reluctantly, abandoned the penny post in June of that year for a basic charge of 1½d on letters and of a penny for post cards. The oversea rate to the United States and the British Empire was also increased to a like figure. When the postwar slump of the early twenties made conditions even more difficult, more was exacted from the public through the Post Office. Letters became 2d in June 1920, and post cards 1½d in 1921. The minimum charge on a telegram was raised to a shilling. Fortunately, these high rates were soon removed. In May 1922, the basic letter rate returned to 1½d for the first two ounces, and penny post cards reappeared. The rate to the British Empire and the United States was likewise 1½d, but only for an ounce letter, and each additional ounce cost a penny. And there the rates remained during the rest of the twenties and the depressing thirties.[3]

The pressure for funds since 1914 has brought a return to the idea of using the Post Office frankly as a taxing machine. During the seventy-five years of penny postage, the general conception became firmly fixed, seemingly, that the Post Office was to give its service at approximate cost, but even then there were occasional dissenters in the Post Office. Lord Stanley of Alderley wrote in the Postmaster-

---

[3] The basic rate for letters to foreign countries, apart from the United States, of 2½d was untouched until June 1921, when it became 3d. In May 1923 the 2½d rate reappeared.

General's *Report* for 1866: "So long as it [the net revenue] continued to be a little less or a little more than half a million, the statement so frequently made that the Post Office ought not to be a source of revenue did not demand examination." But when the net revenue of the Post Office reached a million and a half, Lord Stanley thought otherwise. He pointed out that there was no revenue less burdensome or more equitable in its operation than the postal revenue, "which exacts no payment without giving a service in return and which is not open to the appellation of a tax." The various administrations since 1914 seem to have acquired Lord Stanley's viewpoint. Despite much talk of restoring penny postage, the advance of 1918 has persisted. Sentimentally, a return to penny postage would make a strong appeal.[4] Its advocates argue, too, in the style of the days of old, that a reduction in the rate would so increase the use of the Post Office as to offset any possible losses. The Treasury has held, on the contrary, that five to seven million pounds a year would be sacrificed by the restoration of penny postage. The postal net profit was about £10,-000,000 annually during the decade preceding the Second World War, even though this was a time of economic stagnation. A harried Chancellor of the Exchequer, however, sees Post Office finance as part of the total budgetary plan. He would of necessity have to find that £5,000,000 elsewhere, were penny postage restored.[5] Lord Wolmer,

[4] In 1924, J. Saxon Mills, writing on *The Press and Communications of the Empire*, declared that penny postage "was extended to the whole Empire in 1898, by that great reformer, Sir John Henniker Heaton. The European War interfered with this as with most other good things, but the object must be to get back to that cheap, uniform rate" (p. 101).

[5] The revenue and the surplus for the century will show the growth of the postal taxing power. The figures for the postal business do not include the telegraph, telephone or savings bank accounts. The data is taken from the Postmaster-General's *Reports*, the *Statesman's Year Book*, and Hemmeon, *op. cit.*, App. Occasionally, different totals are found for the same year, as a result of different methods of reckoning the revenue. After 1861, the cost of the packet services was included in the gross revenue of the Post Office, causing a sharp drop in the net that did not recover for over ten years. This was another misuse of postal funds, as we have found.

	GROSS REVENUE	NET REVENUE		GROSS REVENUE	NET REVENUE
1839	£2,390,763	£1,633,764	1890	9,847,778	3,244,561
1840	1,359,466	500,789	1895	10,734,885	2,975,173
1850	2,264,684	803,898	1900	13,394,335	3,710,336
1860	3,531,165	1,577,931	1905	16,274,978	4,828,699
1870	4,664,512	1,493,610	1910	18,710,027	4,910,794
			1914	21,935,326	6,642,067
Year ending March 31			1920	36,234,661	3,469,828
			1925	38,457,226	6,612,113
1875	5,818,032	1,894,141	1930	44,865,882	9,658,770
1880	6,558,445	2,497,687	1935	45,499,743	10,910,819
1885	7,906,406	2,589,193	1939	52,846,493	10,808,259

who has so severely criticized the present-day Post Office, has bluntly called the Post Office "the milch cow of the treasury."[6]

It is bad enough for the Post Office to be an appendage to the Treasury. But what has seemed as unfortunate to its critics has been the misuse of the charge on letters to support other parts of the service that are run at a loss. Lord Wolmer sharply censured the Post Office in the early thirties on this ground as well. The actual cost of distributing a letter, he held, was about three-fourths of a penny. And yet the letter by a heavier charge becomes the broad back on which are piled other kinds of mail matter. This dead weight includes the Parcel Post, the newspapers, printed matter and even post cards, to say nothing of the telegraph system. Other forms of mail cost the Post Office as much to handle per piece as letters, and yet they are distributed at rates two and three times cheaper than the cost of letters. It is the situation of 1837 over again, in less aggravated form— the days of the Edinburgh coach of Cole's famous caricature in a modern guise. The surplus from letters is not a profit so much as a tax. The history of the postal revenue illustrates only too well how easy it is for a surplus to become a permanent tax. The very success of penny postage has made the Post Office, for all practical purposes, a revenue department.[7]

The troubles faced by the Post Office have been emphasized, so say its critics, by faulty executive organization. The Postmaster-General is subject, of course, to parliamentary criticism. In addition, he is responsible to the Treasury, which can veto postal proposals on the ground of their financial effects. The Postmaster-General has been occasionally, though not commonly, a member of the Cabinet, where, again, there is an overriding authority. As the headship of the Post Office is a political position, it is subject to change—too frequently in the opinion of critics. A Postmaster-General's average term of office in the present century has been about two years. One is reminded again of the conditions that Wallace attacked with so much zest a century earlier.[8] Under the political head is the permanent staff, headed by the Secretary. Here again there has been faultfinding with the arrangements, for the Secretary and his immediate assistants tend to become a body of autocrats. An Assistant Postmaster-General was

[6] *Op. cit.*, pp. 64-65.

[7] Wolmer, *op. cit.*, pp. 64-67; Murray, *op. cit.*, p. 30; Crutchley, *op. cit.*, p. 222.

[8] Wolmer, *op. cit.*, p. 236. Between 1914 and 1940 but three of the Postmasters-General were of Cabinet rank. See Appendix.

first appointed in 1909 to serve as a sort of parliamentary representative. Under the Secretary is a Second Secretary.

Some have desired to sever the Post Office from politics, so that an office such as that of the Postmaster-General would no longer be regarded as a steppingstone in a political career. After all, the widely ramified Post Office is really a collection of large business organizations that should be operated on business principles, and not as a branch of the political power centered in the Cabinet. The excessive centralization of the Post Office executive has also been questioned, since such diverse matters as telephone exchanges, the Post Office Savings Bank, the Parcel Post and the telegraph system cannot be effectively promoted as one.[9] A beginning of reform was made shortly after the First World War by the appointment of a Post Office Advisory Council, composed of men with business experience outside the Department. Their assistance could be, and was, sought by the Postmaster-General.[10]

The climax of the attacks on the organization of the Post Office was a memorial signed by over three hundred members of Parliament: it was addressed to the Prime Minister in December 1931. The lead was taken by Viscount Wolmer, whose concern over *Post Office Reform* has already been noticed. It asked for an inquiry on the efficiency of the Post Office. The request was soon followed by the appointment of a committee to report on "whether any change in the constitutional status and system of organization of the Post Office would be in the public interest." The committee, headed by Viscount Bridgeman, reported in the same year.[11]

The Postmaster-General, Sir Kingsley Wood, received a report from the Committee that combined criticism, commendation and suggestion. Although the sharp attacks of faultfinders like Lord Wolmer seemed extreme, the Bridgeman Committee recognized the need for changes. The Committee was not prepared to remove the Post Office from government control, or to separate the telegraph and telephone branches from the Post Office. The connection of the telegraph with the postal service had grown so intimate and interlocking that

[9] The Lever Committee, for example, made a thorough examination of the telegraph division in 1927.

[10] Wallace had tried much earlier to make the headship of the Post Office a body of commissioners. Henniker Heaton suggested a plan similar to the change that occurred with the Advisory Council in his "A Postal Utopia" of 1898. See *Nineteenth Century*, XLIII, 765.

[11] The other members were Lord Plender and Sir John Cadman. The *Report* is to be found in the *Parl. Papers* for 1931-32, Cmd.4149.

the Committee believed a separation would only increase costs. The telephone and the telegraph had become so closely linked that the Committee suggested that they be closely allied within the Post Office under the name of Telecommunications. The rest of the varied business of the great organization was to be combined under two main departments, to be known as Postal Services and Personnel.[12]

The Bridgeman Committee also advised a thorough recasting of the executive. The Postmaster-General was to become the head of a board for forming policy, the board to include a Director-General, who was to act as deputy chairman and the chief permanent officer of the Post Office. This meant the disappearance of the officer whom we have come to know as the Secretary. Other suggested members of this central board were the Assistant Postmaster-General, a deputy Director-General, the Director of Telecommunications, a Public Relations Officer and others to the total of twelve. This functional board was soon set up by the government. The last of the Secretaries, Sir Evelyn Murray, was succeeded in 1934 by the first Director-General, Col. Donald Banks.[13]

As a further means of decentralizing Post Office control, the Committee advised the division of the Post Office into geographical divisions, each with its regional board. Previously, all telephone questions, or postal matters, or personnel difficulties needing executive attention came to the central organization in London. In order to prevent this excessive concentration, more or less autonomous regions were created. In fact, this decentralization was the chief innovation proposed by the Bridgeman Committee. By the mid-thirties, a region consisting of the whole of Scotland and centered in Edinburgh was in working order, soon followed by a region including northeast England with its head office in Leeds, and a third for the London area. Others centering in Manchester, Birmingham, Cardiff, and Bristol were in process of formation as the decade came to a close. One interesting result of this change to regional boards was the abolition of the group of surveyors, who have become about as familiar to the reader as the Secretary.[14]

The Bridgeman Committee also dealt with the financial difficulties.

[12] The word "Telecommunications" might well have aroused A. P. Herbert, that archenemy of cumbersome English and hybrid neologisms. The word received its official baptism in the Madrid Communication Conference of 1932.

[13] When Col. Banks went to the Air Ministry in 1936, his deputy, Thomas Gardiner, succeeded as Director-General.

[14] See *Report*, esp. pp. 28-36; Crutchley, *op. cit.*, pp. 220-35.

They asserted that the close connection of the Post Office and the Treasury tended towards inertia in the Post Office. They favored a system of self-imposed finance, similar to that already enjoyed within the Post Office by the Savings Bank. A yearly grant to the Treasury was proposed as a means of attaining this financial self-control. The Post Office was to make a fixed "contribution" to the Treasury of £11,500,000, plus 50 per cent of any annual excess over that amount. The rest of the revenue was to be kept by the Post Office for approved uses. This arrangement for financial self-control would appear to be decidedly limited. It perpetuates, of course, the tax-collecting function built up in the last seventy-five years. The Post Office remains as a revenue-gathering Department, with a pittance for its own unconditional use. As the suggested "contribution" was actually higher than the net revenue at the time, the amount was set at £10,750,000. Needless to say, this tender treatment of the Exchequer came in the midst of a severe depression. It made less likely, naturally, the possible restoration of penny postage, a matter which the Committee did not feel called upon to consider.[15]

The successful introduction of the Bridgeman recommendations was due in no small part to the cooperation of the Postmaster-General, Sir Kingsley Wood: he held office from 1931 to 1935. His vigorous and effective administration brought new life to the Post Office. Not only was the reorganization of the great Department effected, but much else was done. A "brighter Post Office campaign" made the services more pleasant to use. Sir Kingsley Wood also instituted a Public Relations Office for winning good will and "selling" the often misunderstood functions of the Post Office to the public. Major Tryon, the successor of Sir Kingsley Wood, also gave much attention to promoting a better understanding of the numerous Post Office services.[16]

The twentieth century history of the Post Office includes something more than demands for reform. A number of new and effective services were introduced. To them, we shall turn in conclusion.

For one thing, the Post Office had to face a world at war. Never before 1914 had it met such conditions on a scale so large. The Cri-

[15] The net revenue from 1931 until 1939 was about £11,000,000 annually. In the fiscal year 1937-38, the Post Office Fund had accumulated some £3,000,000. But the net revenue dropped below £7,000,000 with the approach of war.

[16] The first Public Relations Officer was Sir Stephen Tallents, whose powers of persuasion had been matured in the Empire Marketing Board. See Crutchley, op. cit., pp. 246-49.

mean War of the fifties created some trouble for the organization, and brought some changes. The carrying of mail to the war areas proved no easy matter, since for the first time in the history of the British Post Office thousands of soldiers' and sailors' letters had to be taken to and from the seats of war. The old penny rate, begun back in 1795, was used for such servicemen's letters when carried by British ships. This means of conveying mail not proving adequate, French ships also became letter carriers, but the charge was 3d a quarter-ounce, and the French vessels did not go beyond Constantinople. As a result, the Post Office set up a service in the Black Sea, establishing an Army Post Office for the first time.

The next time that an Army Post Office functioned in a fully organized way was in the summer of 1882 when an expeditionary force was sent to Egypt. The Boer War at the close of the century presented greater difficulties, because of the great distances in South Africa and the widely separated fronts. The main office was at Cape Town, with a number of base and field offices and even traveling post offices.[17]

The British Post Office was strained as never before in the years from 1914 to 1918 to meet the demands of a world-wide war. The regular oversea postal services were disrupted, of course, by the demands on ships for military service and by the battle with the submarine. The Brindisi route to India had to be abandoned for a service from Marseilles. During the latter part of the war, mails for Mesopotamia and India were sent from England by the all-sea route around the Cape of Good Hope, and Australian mails during the latter part of the war were often dispatched by way of Vancouver and San Francisco.

The Army Post Office, with a staff of only three hundred men when war broke out in 1914, had to be enlarged almost overnight to meet the needs of a war fought over all continents and on all oceans. By 1918 the Army Post Office, serving overseas, numbered 4000 men. Field offices reappeared, with the addition of cross posts for mail passing between different fronts or separated units of the same front. The mail for the soldiers and sailors was sent "c/o G.P.O., London." At first, it was forwarded unsorted to the base post office of the area where it was to be delivered. This was soon found to be less effective than the so-called "unit" sorting, by which

[17] *46th Rep. P.M.G.* (1900), p. 8; Alcock & Holland, *op. cit.*, pp. 524 ff.; *Br. Postal Guide* (May 1st, 1856), p. 35.

mail was made up at home for the units abroad. At first, this sorting was done in London, but towards the end of the war the large provincial offices were used for sorting purposes. The size of the army mail was so great as to try all the resources of the Post Office. Outward mails often totaled 12,000,000 letters and 1,000,000 parcels a week, and the Christmas mails were much larger. Letters from the Army Post Office did not bear stamps, for the old custom of charging a penny for the letters of soldiers and sailors ended at the start of the war. The letters from the front were sent free, and postmarked with the number of the Army Post Office (A.P.O.).[18]

So much for the Post Office in the First World War. A number of subsequent peace-time advances deserve attention if the varied activities of the Post Office are to be fully appreciated. One has been the amazing development of long-distance communication by cable and wireless. These natural extensions of the telegraph and telephone monopoly by the Post Office began in the nineteenth century with the postal operation of the cables within the British Isles and to the nearby Continent.[19]

The wireless, however, is a distinctive growth of the twentieth century. The Wireless Telegraph Act of 1904 gave the Postmaster-General the power to license wireless sending and receiving apparatus, and to collect the fees for this new method of communication. Its first important use was to connect shore stations and ships at sea. The Post Office issues licenses to British seagoing vessels, makes inspections and examines operators. More powerful long-distance stations, when they came into being, were placed under government ownership, and are operated by the Post Office. Short-waved transmission was in use by the mid-twenties. One of the most powerful stations in the world is that at Rugby, which is connected by means of underground lines with the Central Telegraph Office in London. The sending of telephone conversations over long distances without wires also began in the twenties, the public service with America opening in 1927.

During this time, as well, the use of radio and broadcasting began.

---

[18] Murray, *op. cit.*, pp. 200 ff. Letters to and from prisoners of war were also sent free of postage, according to the action of the Postal Congress held at Rome in 1906, and based on a recommendation of the Hague Peace Conference. Such mails were received from and sent through Switzerland, Holland and Sweden. They were subject, of course, to censorship. And it goes almost without saying that the sanctity of correspondence, as it existed in the comparatively peaceful reign of Queen Victoria, gave way before the needs of war.

[19] See above, p. 409.

Here, too, the Post Office has been in close relation to the extensive use of the broadcasting apparatus. The service in Great Britain has been a government monopoly from the first, with the British Broadcasting Corporation as the operating agent. Though separate from the Post Office, the two are related in a number of ways. The Postmaster-General approves the location, power and wave length of each station. He is also responsible for the issuance of all licenses, and has the painful duty of seeing that owners of all receiving sets have paid the government fee. The postal technical staff are supposed, as well, to detect by means of locators any interference with a satisfactory service. The relation of the Post Office to broadcasting is largely regulative.[20]

A more purely postal service is furnished by the London Post Office Railway, the only one of its kind in the world. Though this

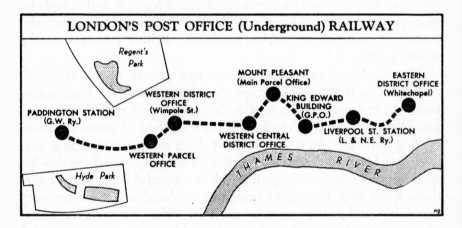

underground (or "subway") was authorized in 1913, the delays caused by the First World War and by the expensiveness of the equipment prevented its completion before 1927. The railway is some seventy feet below the busiest streets in the heart of London, for it runs from the Eastern District Office in Whitechapel to the Paddington Station of the Great Western Railway. It passes under two important railway stations and six sorting offices, with a total length of six and a half miles. The chief stations are beneath the so-called King Edward Building, that is, the G. P. O., just west of St.

[20] The most recent extension of wireless has been the introduction of television, Great Britain being the first country to provide regular television programs. They began in 1936. The original stimulus to this advance came from the report of a committee appointed by the Postmaster-General. See the volumes by Murray and Crutchley.

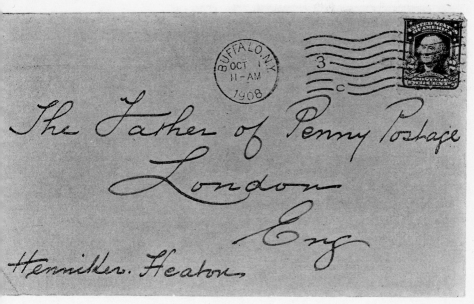

THE FIRST PENNY LETTER FROM THE UNITED STATES TO ENGLAND

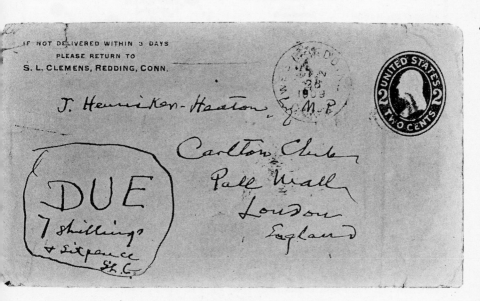

A LETTER FROM MARK TWAIN TO SIR JOHN HENNIKER HEATON
The note on the envelope acknowledges Twain's indebtedness for money saved in postage.

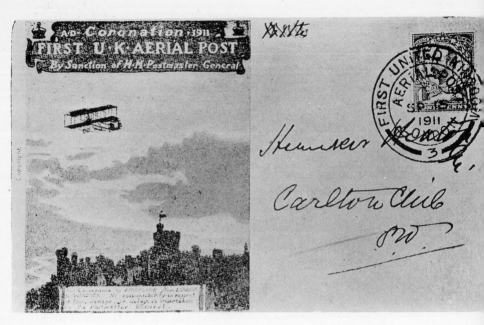

THE FIRST AIRMAIL LETTER POSTED IN LONDON
Appropriately, it was addressed to Sir John Henniker Heaton.

A BLOCK OF FOUR HALFPENNY STAMPS COMMEMORATING THE CENTENARY OF
PENNY POSTAGE
The letter was posted on the exact centenary of the first use of stamps.

Martin's le Grand, and Mount Pleasant, the main parcel office, located in Finsbury to the east of Gray's Inn Road. This double-track railway is operated by electricity; the cars have neither passengers nor drivers. At the various underground stations, conveyor belts make connections with the above-ground offices. The advantages of this unique postal railway are obvious: letters and parcels are transferred by a four-minute train service at the rate of forty miles an hour in a part of London where surface traffic is notoriously congested, and where delays are likely to result from road repairs and from adverse weather conditions. The well-known boast, originally penned by Herodotus, seems peculiarly appropriate to this effective service: "Nor snow nor rain nor heat nor gloom of night stays these couriers from the swift completion of their appointed rounds."[21]

And lastly the Post Office, during these years, began to send mail by air. Feeble beginnings, it is true, had been made before 1914. Balloon and pigeon posts were employed in the nineteenth century under stress of circumstances. Even before 1914 the airplane had been used for carrying mail. In 1911, at the time of King George V's coronation, they went back and forth from Hendon to Windsor. Letters carried in this way during September 1911 were postmarked "First United Kingdom Aerial Post." In 1919 a plane piloted by Sir Ross Smith carried mail between Great Britain and Australia. But this was, of course, a highly experimental journey: a regular service between Great Britain and Australia had to wait for another fifteen years. In 1909 Hawker's flight from Newfoundland to the British Isles also carried mail that was ultimately delivered in Great Britain by the Post Office. The letters were postmarked "First Transatlantic Air Post," but this did not inaugurate a regular transatlantic service.

The most promising region for the early growth of the British air mail was the nearby Continent. A London-Paris service was opened in 1919. In the next year the Netherlands and England were linked by air. By the mid-twenties numerous routes went to European points and even to North Africa. These early services were not regular, even though they would now seem rather short runs. Night flying had not become feasible during the twenties, long mail journeys being a combination of flights by day and a train journey by night. An additional handicap was the necessity for discontinuing flights during the winter when weather conditions were unfavorable.

[21] Murray, *op. cit.*, pp. 50-52; Halstead, *op. cit.*, pp. 120-27; Ian Hay, *The Post Office Went to War*, pp. 27-30.

A Secretary of State for Air had been appointed first in 1917 as a part of the war-time administration of Lloyd George. After peace came, a Department of Civil Aviation in this Ministry took much interest in furthering air communication within the Empire. Much the same encouragement was given this new form of communication as that which backed the early steamship ventures of Cunard and the P & O, because it was believed that air travel would serve much the same purpose as the steam packet nearly a century before: it would aid political and commercial communication, and might even serve the Empire in case of war. At the Imperial Conference of 1921 the use of airships was given more attention than the employment of airplanes. In the next few years, however, the heavier-than-air machines were proving of more promise than the dirigibles. By 1924 Imperial Airways was being subsidized rather liberally, while the government was spending considerable money in the building of enormous and relatively cumbersome airships. At the Imperial Conference of 1926, air communication received much emphasis. The new method of transport, though it had been organized but seven years, was seen to be full of great promise for shortening the distances for travel and mail within the Empire. Already Canada and Australia had domestic air services, but interimperial communication had not yet been set up. It is true that military machines had been carrying mails for five years between Egypt and Baghdad, but as yet there was no air connection between Britain and Egypt, or Egypt and India.

The earliest imperial extension of the air mail was certain to be along the route to India via Egypt, where Waghorn and the P & O had pioneered a century before for a faster steamer transport. In 1926 an air service from Egypt to Karachi was begun. The first machine from England for India left in March 1929. By the end of the year, the service had been extended to Delhi. Two years later the first link in the air-mail route between Cairo and Cape Town was opened: it went as far as Kisumu in northwest Kenya. In the next year mail was being carried the whole length of the African Continent. In the meantime the route to India was extended—to Rangoon in 1933, to Singapore in 1934, and thence to Australia and New Zealand. The air ship had pretty well given way to the airplane by this time, despite determined efforts to use the former for long non-stop flights. The loss of the *R 101* at Beauvais, France, in October 1930, with the death of forty-eight passengers including the Secretary of State for Air, strengthened the growing preference for the airplane.

The only imperial line yet unrealized by the mid-thirties was the link with Canada. The north Atlantic proved a stubborn barrier. Not until 1939 just before the Second World War was a regular trans-atlantic service opened: in August of that year the *Caribou* of Imperial Airways carried 960 pounds of mail to New York. These, in brief, were some of the main events that had brought a revolution in postal communication within two decades. In 1925 some 200,000 letters were sent by air: ten years later, the number was over 19,000,000. Before the airways were again disorganized by war in 1939, the amount of air mail on the routes within the Empire had risen so rapidly that it is better to think of it in terms of weight than of number of letters. South Africa was receiving some five tons a week, and nearly twice that amount was carried on the Indian route. It was a revolution indeed.[22]

The charges for air mail had a history not unlike that in the earlier days for letters going by the first steamship packets. Letters by air were, at first, subjected to a surcharge, that is, the ordinary rate was levied, plus an additional charge for this express service. An air letter of the minimum weight to a Continental country cost 2½d, which was the ordinary postage, plus an extra charge, amounting to 2d for the nearby European countries, 3d for Austria, Czechoslovakia, Poland and Scandinavia, and 4d for Greece. These rates were simplified in 1930 by making one inclusive rate of 4d for the first ounce to any European country, irrespective of distance. But in 1936 an important change occurred. Letters were sent to all the countries in Europe, with few exceptions, at the ordinary rate of 2½d for the first ounce. The airplane had ceased to be an express vehicle for carrying mail at a premium.[23]

Rates to the other parts of the Empire were, at first, variable, a surcharge being added to the basic rate of 1½d, totaling 3½d for air mail to Palestine and Egypt, and 7½d for mail to India. In 1931 an inclusive rate was used for this longer route, with a letter to East Africa, for example, costing 7d, and to Karachi in India 6d. Further reductions were made in 1934, 6d being charged for longer distances, and 3d for letters going to such "nearby" places as Egypt and Pales-

[22] Crutchley, *op. cit.*, p. 95.
[23] *The Times* (London), May 31, 1930. Post cards were first accepted for air mail by the British Post Office in 1932. Crutchley, *op. cit.*, p. 94.

tine. The climax in this trend towards reduction and uniformity was reached in the late thirties when the airplane became the normal rather than the exceptional means of transportation within the Empire. In 1937 letters were sent for the first time to South Africa at the rate of 1½d the half-ounce. During the next year this low and uniform rate by air was extended to India, Burma and Malaya, and on to Australia and New Zealand as well. Empire mails had become empire air mails.

Air-mail letters were distinguished, almost from the beginnings, by a special sticker. The Post Office furnished without charge a blue label to be attached to the upper lefthand corner of a letter. At first the public did not appreciate the advantages of the air-mail service, despite campaigns by the Post Office to popularize the new, and as yet, expensive service. The public became somewhat more "airminded" when special blue air-mail pillar boxes first appeared in 1930. They had a short life, however, being removed in 1938 when mail was being sent by air at ordinary rates.

Not until 1934 was there any general effort to carry mail by air within the British Isles. The domestic services by railway had been so highly developed by "night mail" that all parts of the British Isles were but a day's journey from each other. The first air-mail service on a domestic route was between Inverness and the Orkney Islands: it began in May 1934. Other inland routes were soon added, a number of large towns being linked by air with London in the autumn of that year. Glasgow and Belfast were included as well as towns in England like Manchester and Birmingham. The service was by day, a letter that left Manchester at noon, for example, being delivered in London about four o'clock. From the first, domestic air mail was not distinguished in any way from ordinary first-class letters. It soon became the practice of the Post Office to send first-class domestic mail by air wherever air routes were available and there was a saving of time. Letters that were sent by air were simply ordinary letters forwarded by the speediest route available.[24] The rapid approach of a Second World War boded ill for the various air services that had matured between the wars. Yet sufficient advance had been made by 1939 to assure even greater use of the air for mail carriage when peace again would make ordered growth possible.

Great Britain is one of the few countries that has not seen fit to issue special stamps for air mail, though most other countries have

[24] *Ibid.*, May 24, 1934, p. 9; Nov. 15, 1934, p. 14.

been prodigal in this form of postal stationery. One reason is the conservatism of the British Post Office in the matter of special stamp
issues. Then, too, the late development of domestic air mail, at a time
when air service was regarded as another way of sending an ordinary
letter, made a distinctive stamp superfluous. The Dominions and
India have issued air-mail stamps, the dates of their appearance giving a fair idea of the beginning of local air transportation for letters.
They appeared in Canada in 1928, in Australia, India and South
Africa in 1929, and were issued by New Zealand for the first time in
1931. Newfoundland, which has much overdone the business of
stamp issues, provided air-mail stamps for special flights and attempted flights as early as 1919.[25]

The appearance of such a variety of air-mail stamps following the
First World War is explained partly by the favor with which many
national post offices looked upon commemorative stamps. Great Britain has been chary as well in printing stamps for special occasions. The
first British issue of this kind commemorated the British Empire
Exhibition in 1924. The two special stamps put on sale at the Exhibition showed the portrait of the King accompanied by the British lion.
An issue of three stamps appeared in 1929 to record the meeting of
the Postal Union in London. In 1935 a series honored the Silver
Jubilee of George V. A solitary commemorative appeared at the time
of the coronation of King George VI and Queen Elizabeth, including
the portraits of both the King and Queen.[26]

And, lastly, came those commemorating the centenary of Penny
Postage. The war-time conditions of 1940 made any elaborate jubilee
impossible. A special set of stamps, nevertheless, was issued to recall
the day when Penny Postage was won, despite the fact that the basic
postal rate for the last quarter of the century since 1840 had been

---

[25] Non-British countries notable for early issues of air-mail stamps include Italy, which
printed stamps for an experimental air post between Rome and Turin in 1917, and the
United States where the first issue appeared in 1918. Air-mail stamps were issued by
Switzerland in 1919, by Czechoslovakia in 1920, by China in 1921 and by Russia and
Germany in 1922. Some fifteen countries in Central and South America have issued air-
mail stamps, many being intended, one suspects, for the albums of collectors.

[26] British stamps, as has been said earlier, have never borne the name of the country,
nor had any other central design than that of the reigning monarch. The portrait of
Rowland Hill appeared on a number of penny postage commemoratives issued in 1940
by other countries eager for any excuse to issue new stamps, examples being Portugal,
Cuba and Dominica. The United States, which has been particularly prolific in putting
forth commemoratives since the First World War, saw no reason for honoring the centenary of British penny postage. The year 1947 has proved more appropriate: the portraits of Washington and Jefferson, as used in 1847, reappeared together on a 3-cent centenary stamp. Souvenir sheets with replicas of the original stamps were also issued.

higher than a penny. The issue consisted of six stamps, and were beautiful examples of the postage stamp at its best: the dates 1840 and 1940 were below the familiar Queen's head of a century ago and the portrait of the reigning King. It served to recall a remarkable step in postal annals, and to bring to a close this record of British postal history.

Though the Second World War is too recent to make possible a careful valuation of the Post Office during the years 1939 to 1945, it should be said that the postal services showed a resourcefulness greater than ever before. The bombing of Britain caused much disruption. An Army Home Postal Center was established in the Midlands for the safer and more effective distribution of mail to and from the fighting services. Mobile post offices, already in use before 1939 for country shows and sport meetings, were greatly increased in numbers in order to keep up service in areas subject to heavy air attacks. An innovation for military mail was the use for the first time of airgraph letters—photographs of correspondence conveyed on microfilm.

The Second World War increased the gigantic part that the British Post Office of today takes in the life of the people. It is the largest group of employees in the country, with a staff of indoor and outdoor workers numbering well over a quarter of a million. These workers are now well organized into a trade union, the Union of Post Office Workers. Not only because of its size does the Post Office greatly affect British life, but on account of the multifarious services it furnishes, and the many points at which it touches every human being. Even in its more strictly postal activities, the Department performs a task immensely larger than in the far-off days when the postage stamp was first put to use, for by 1939 the Post Office was finding it necessary to print an average of 23,000,000 stamps every day.

APPENDIX

The Headship of the British Post Office since 1830

* An asterisk indicates membership in the Cabinet. A peerage granted after holding office is within parentheses.

Postmasters-General		*Secretaries*	
Duke of Manchester	1827-1830	Sir Francis Freeling	1797-1836
*Duke of Richmond	1830-1834		
Marquis of Conyngham	1834		
Lord Maryborough	1834-1835		
Marquis of Conyngham	1835		
Earl of Lichfield	1835-1841	Col. W. L. Maberly	1836-1854
Lord Lowther (Earl of Lonsdale)	1841-1846		
Earl of St. German's	1846		
*Marquis of Clanricarde	1846-1852		
*Earl of Hardwicke	1852-1853		
Viscount Canning, in Cab. from Feb. 1855	1853-1855	Sir Rowland Hill	1854-1864
*Duke of Argyle	1855-1858		
Lord Colchester	1858-1859		
*Earl of Elgin	1859-1860		
Duke of Argyle	1860		
*Lord Stanley of Alderley	1860-1866	Sir John Tilley	1864-1880
Duke of Montrose	1866-1868		
*Marquis of Hartington	1868-1871		
William Monsell (Lord Emley)	1871-1873		
Lyon Playfair (Lord Playfair)	1873-1874		
*Lord John Manners	1874-1880	Sir Arthur Blackwood	1880-1893
Henry Fawcett	1880-1884		
*George J. Shaw-Lefevre (Lord Eversley)	1884-1885		
*Lord John Manners	1885-1886		
Lord Wolverton	1886		
Henry Cecil Raikes	1886-1891		
Sir James Fergusson	1891-1892		
*Arnold Morley	1892-1895	Sir Spencer Walpole	1893-1899
Duke of Norfolk	1895-1900		
*Marquis of Londonderry	1900-1902	Sir George H. Murray	1899-1903
*J. Austen Chamberlain	1902-1903		
*Lord Stanley	1903-1905	Sir H. Babington Smith	1903-1909
*Sydney Buxton	1905-1910		

*Herbert Samuel (Visc. Samuel)	1910-1914	Sir Matthew Nathan	1910-1911
*C. E. H. Hobhouse	1914-1915	Sir Alexander F. King	1911-1914
Herbert Samuel (Visc. Samuel)	1915-1916	Sir Evelyn Murray	1914-1934
J. A. Pease (Lord Gainford)	1916		
A. H. Illingworth (Lord Illingworth)	1916-1921		
Frederick G. Kellaway	1921-1922		
Neville Chamberlain	1922-1923		
Sir William Joynson Hicks, (Visc. Brentford)	1923		
Sir Laming Worthington Evans	1923		
*Vernon Hartshorn	1924		
Sir William Mitchell-Thomson (Lord Selsdon)	1924-1929		
H. B. Lees-Smith	1929-1931	*Directors-General*	
C. R. Atlee	1931		
W. G. A. Ormsby-Gore (Lord Harlech)	1931		
*Sir Kingsley Wood	1931-1935	Sir Donald Banks	1934-1936
George C. Tryon (Lord Tryon)	1935-1940	Sir Thomas Gardiner	1936-

BIBLIOGRAPHY

THE following lists include the principal materials of use in preparing this account of the British Post Office. Unless otherwise indicated, London is the place of publication. Where the citation in the footnotes has been much abbreviated, the form of abbreviation is given within brackets following the title. The Bibliography does not include all works used or appearing in the footnotes. Titles of well-known periodicals as well as biographies, books of travel, and collections of letters from which have been taken illustrative materials on changing habits in letter-writing are not repeated here: sufficient identification has been made, it is believed, in the footnotes.

The titles are divided into the following groups:

I Source Materials
II Books, Pamphlets, Articles and Serials
   A Of General Scope
   B On the Unreformed Post Office (before 1830)
   C On the Reformed Post Office (since 1830)
   D Primarily Philatelic

I. SOURCE MATERIALS

Acts and Ordinances of the Interregnum, ed. by C. H. Firth and R. S. Rait. 3v., 1911. [Firth & Rait]

Acts of the Parliaments of Scotland, 1124-1707, ed. by T. Thomson and Cosmo Innes. 11v., Edinburgh, 1814-44.

Acts of the Privy Council of England, ed. by Sir John R. Dasent and Sir H. C. Maxwell-Lyte. n.s., 1890- . [*Acts of P.C.*]

British Postal Guide, 1856- .

Calendar of Letters and Papers, Foreign and Domestic, of the Reign of Henry VIII. 21v., 1852-1910. [*Letters & Papers*, Henry VIII]

Calendar of State Papers, 1856- [*Cal. S.P.*]. The following series have been used:
America and West Indies [*Am. & W.I.*]
Domestic [*Dom.*]
Home
Treasury Books [*Tr.B.*]
Treasury Books and Papers [*Tr.B. & P.*]
Treasury Papers [*Tr.P.*]

A Collection of State Papers of John Thurloe, ed. by T. Birch. 7v., 1742.

Ireland under the Commonwealth, "being a collection of documents," ed. by Robert Dunlop. 2v., Manchester, 1913.

Journals of the House of Commons. 1742f. [*Journal H.C.*]

Journals of the House of Lords. 1767f. [*Journal H.L.*]

The Mirror of Parliament. 1828-41. Somewhat fuller than *Parl. Deb.* for the years covered.

Parliamentary Debates, 1803- . The first series, 1803-20, cited as Cobbett, *Parl. Deb.,* and later series as, e.g., *Parl. Deb.,* 3rd s., XLIX (1839), 1207.

Parliamentary History of England, 1066-1803, ed. by William Cobbett and J. Wright. 36v., 1806-20. [*Parl. Hist.*]

The Postmen's Case for Enquiry, "as submitted to the Inter-Departmental Committee on the Post Office Establishments. Published by authority of the Postmen's Federation." Glasgow & London, n.d. (1896).

Proceedings and Ordinances of the Privy Council, 1386-1542. 7v., 1834-37. [*Proc. & Ord. of P.C.*]

Proceedings of the Colonial Conference of 1887 (C.5091 & 5091.1). 1887.

Report of George Plitt, Special Agent to the Post Office Department (U.S.). Senate Docs., 26th Cong., 2nd Session, v.4, no. 156. Washington, 1841.

Report of the Postmaster-General on the Post Office. Issued annually from 1855 (for the year 1854, etc.). Numbered through the 57th Report (1911), thereafter dated, 1911-12, etc. There are no Reports in this form after 1915-16. [Cited as, e.g., *1st Rep. P.M.G.*]

Reports of the Royal Commission on Historical Manuscripts. 1870f. The earlier Reports are numbered. The later ones are cited by title of the manuscript collection, as, e.g., *H.M.C. Rep.,* Salisbury, IX, 97.

State Papers during the Reign of Henry VIII. 11v., 1830-52. [*State Papers, Henry VIII*]

The *Statutes at Large* are cited by the year of the reign, the session, if necessary, and the number of the act, as, e.g., 9 Anne, c.10 (1711).

Parliamentary Papers. The chief groups of materials of value are the *Accounts and Papers,* and *Reports* of Select Committees and of Commissioners. The *Accounts and Papers* are referred to by the year and volume, and also, occasionally, by the command number. The principal *Reports* of value in compiling this volume follow in chronological order.

Report of the Commissioners appointed by an Act of Parliament to enquire into the Fees, Gratuities, Perquisites, and Emoluments which are or have been lately received in the several Public Offices therein mentioned. The Tenth Report was on the Post Office. 1788, ordered printed, 1793. See p. 151n.

Report from the Committee who were appointed to consider the Agreement made with Mr. Palmer, etc. 1797, reprinted, 1807. [*Rep. Com. on Palmer's Agreement*]

Report from the Select Committee on Finance. The 7th Report was on the Post Office. 1797, reprinted 1803. [*7th Rep. Sel. Com. on Finance.*]

Report from the Committee appointed to inquire into certain Abuses in the Post Office Department. 1797.

Reports of the Commissioners of Inquiry into the Collection and Management of the Revenues arising in Ireland and Great Britain. Cited as, e.g., *18th Rep. Commrs. of Rev.* Reports 18-22—bulky folios —are on the Post Office.

18th on Post Office revenue, United Kingdom, 697 pp., 1829.

19th on Ireland, 951 pp., 1829.

20th on Scotland, 365 pp., 1830.

21st on England, Twopenny Post Office, 234 pp., 1830.

22nd on packet establishments and home stations, 781 pp., 1830.

Report from the Select Committee on Post Communications with Ireland. 1832.

X Reports of the Commissioners appointed to inquire into the Management of the Post Office Department. 1835-38. There were ten Reports, cited as, e.g., *9th Rep. Commrs. P.O. Management.*

1st, 2nd and 3rd on mail-coach contracts, June and July, 1835.

4th on clerks' salaries and accounts, July 1835.

5th, no. 1, on mail-coach contracts, Aug. 1835.

5th, no. 2, on prices current, April 1836.

6th on packet stations, April 1836.

7th on contracts for horsing mail coaches, etc., Febr. 1837.

8th on the Secretary's office, April 1837.

9th on the Twopenny Post, July 1837.

10th on registration, Jan. 1838.

X Reports from the Select Committee on Postage. Robert Wallace was the Chairman. There were three Reports issued in April, Aug., and Aug., 1838. See p. 282n. [*Rep. Sel. Com. on Postage*]

Report from the Select Committee on Railroad Communication. 1838.

Report from the Select Committee on Post Office Communication with Ireland. 1841. A brief Report.

Report from the Select Committee on Post Office Communication with Ireland. 1842. A full Report, pp. i-xii, 1-344, 1-60.

X Report from the Select Committee on Postage. 1843.

X Report from the Secret Committee on the Post Office (of the House of Commons), together with the Appendix. 1844. [*Rep. Secret Com. on P.O.*, H.C. (1844)]

Report from the Secret Committee of the House of Lords Relative to the Post Office. 1844. [*Rep. Secret Com. on P.O.*, H.L. (1844)]

Report of the Commissioners Appointed to Investigate the Question of Sunday Labour in the Post Office. 1850.

Report from the Select Committee on Newspaper Stamps. 1851.

Report from the Select Committee on Postage Label Stamps. 1852.

Report from the Select Committee on Communication between London and Dublin. 1853.

Report from the Select Committee on Conveyance of Mails by Railways. 1854.

Report from the Select Committee on Packet and Telegraphic Contracts. 1859.

Report from the Select Committee on Packet and Telegraphic Contracts. 1860. There were three parts to this Report, issued in May, June and July, and a full index.

Report from the Select Committee on Mail Contracts . . . with Messrs. Cunard & Company and with Mr. William Inman for the Conveyance of Mails from This Country to the United States. 1869.

Report from Mr. Scudamore on the Reorganization of the Telegraph System of the United Kingdom. In *Accts. & Papers*, 1871 (C.304).

Report from the Select Committee on the Post Office (Telegraph Department). 1876.

Report from the Select Committee on Sunday Postal Labour. 1887.

Report from the Inter-Departmental Committee on Post Office Establishments. 1897.

Report of the Committee Appointed to Inquire into Post Office Wages. 1903.

Report from the Select Committee on the Post Office (Telephone Agreement). 1905.

Report from the Select Committee on Post Office Servants, 2v. of evidence, 1906, and Report, 1907.

Report from the Select Committee on Post Office Servants (Wages and Conditions of Employment). 1913.

Report of the Committee on Retrenchment in the Public Expenditures (Cd. 8067). 1915.

Report from the Committee of Enquiry on the Post Office (Cmd. 4149). 1932.

II. BOOKS, PAMPHLETS, ARTICLES, AND SERIALS

A. Of General Scope

The Annual Register. 1758-   [*Ann. Reg.*]

Bennett, Edward, *The Post Office and Its Story.* 1912.

The British Almanac. The Companion to the Almanac; or Year-Book of General Information. 1828-1914. [*Br. Almanac*]

Brunel, Georges, *La poste à Paris depuis sa création jusqu'à nos jours.* Amiens, 1920.

Clarke, Geoffrey, *The Post Office of India and Its Story.* 1921.

Collett, C. D., *History of the Taxes on Knowledge, Their Origin and Repeal.* 2v., 1899.

The Dictionary of National Biography and *The Dictionary of American Biography.* [*D.N.B.* and *D.A.B.*, respectively]

Encyclopaedia Britannica. Articles on the Post Office in the 3rd, 6th, 8th and 9th editions. [*E.B.*]

Halstead, Ivor, *Post Haste, The Story of the Post Office in Peace and War.* 1944.

Hamilton, Ivie G. J., *An Outline of Postal History and Practice, with A History of the Post Office in India.* Calcutta, 1910.

Harlow, A. F., *Old Post Bags.* N.Y., 1928.

Harper, C. G., *Stage-Coach and Mail in Days of Yore.* 2v., 1903.

Hartmann, Eugen, *Entwickelungs-geschichte der Posten, von der ältesten Zeiten bis zur Gegenwart, mit besonderer Beziehung auf Deutschland.* Leipzig, 1868.

Hemmeon, J. C., *The History of the British Post Office.* Cambridge, Mass., 1912.

(Hill, Matthew D.), "The Post Office," *Fraser's Magazine*, LXVI, 319-36 (1862).

Hoskins, H. L., *British Routes to India.* N.Y., 1928.

Hyde, J. W., *The Royal Mail, Its Curiosities and Romance.* 1885, 3rd ed., 1889.

————, *A Hundred Years by Post. A Jubilee Retrospect.* 1891.

Jackman, W. T., *The Development of Transportation in Modern England.* 2v., Cambridge, 1916.

Joyce, Herbert, *The History of the Post Office from Its Establishment down to 1836.* 1893.

Lang, T. B., *Historical Summary of the Post Office in Scotland.* Edinburgh, 1856.

Lewins, William, *Her Majesty's Mails: An Historical and Descriptive Account of the British Post Office.* 1864. 2nd ed., 1865, has as the subtitle "A History of the Post Office and an Industrial Account of Its Present Condition." The 2nd ed. is somewhat more accurate, and has much of the descriptive material omitted. Unless otherwise indicated, reference is to the 1st ed.

————, *History of Banks for Savings.* 1866.

Murch, Jerome, *Ralph Allen, John Palmer and the English Post Office with Notice on the Bath Post Office.* 1880.

Murray, Sir Evelyn, *The Post Office.* 1927.

O'Connell, Mrs. Morgan John, *Charles Bianconi, 1786-1875. A Biography.* 1878.

The Penny Cyclopedia of the Society for the Diffusion of Useful Knowledge. 27v., 1833-43.

Postal History Society, *Bulletin* of the. Quarterly, 1936f.

The Post Office. An Historical Summary. Published by order of the Postmaster-General. 1911. [*Hist. Sum.*]

Pratt, Edwin A., *A History of Inland Transport and Communication in England.* 1912.

Rolland, Louis, *De la correspondance postale et télégraphique dans les relations internationales.* Paris, 1901.

Rothschild, Arthur de, *Histoire de la poste aux lettres depuis ses origines les plus anciennes jusqu'à nos jours.* 3rd ed., 2v., Paris, 1876.

Smith, A. D., *The Development of Rates of Postage.* 1917.

Smith, William, *The History of the Post Office in British North America, 1639-1870*. Cambridge, 1920.

Smyth, T. S., *Postal History. A Story of Progress*. Dublin, 1941. Largely on Irish postal history.

Stephan, Heinrich von, *Geschichte der preussischen Post*. Berlin, 1859.

Tombs, R. C., *The Bristol Royal Mail, Post, Telegraph and Telephone*. Bristol, 1899.

———, *The King's Post*. Bristol, 1905.

Tristram, W. Outram, *Coaching Days and Coaching Ways*. 1888.

Walker, George, *Haste, Post, Haste! Postmen and Post-Roads through the Ages*. 1938.

Watson, Edward, *The Royal Mail to Ireland*. 1917.

Webb, Sidney and Beatrice, *The Story of the King's Highway*. 1913.

Wheatley, H. B., "Post-Office Reform," *The Academy*, XVI, 463-65 (1870).

B. On the Unreformed Post Office (before 1830)

Burgess, Henry, *A Plan for Obtaining a More Speedy Postal Communication between London and the Distant Parts of the Kingdom*. 1819.

Butler, Ruth Lapham, *Doctor Franklin, Postmaster General*. N.Y., 1928.

Chalmers, George, *An Historical View of the Domestic Economy of Great Britain and Ireland*. Edinburgh, 1812.

Chamberlayne, Edward, *Angliae Notitia, or the Present State of England*. 1669f. Continued by John Chamberlayne *et al.* as *Magnae Britanniae Notitia*. 1708-1755.

Clapham, J. H., *An Economic History of Modern Britain*. 3v., Cambridge, 1930-38.

Clear, C. R., *The Birth of the Postal Service*. 1935. Reprinted in *Penny Postage Centenary*, pp. 21-30.

Coke, Dorothea, *The Last Elizabethan, Sir John Coke, 1563-1644*. 1937.

De-Laune, Thos., Gent., *Angliae Metropolis, or the Present State of London*. 1681, reprinted in 1690.

Entick, John, and others, *The Present State of the British Empire*. 4v., 1774-75.

Firth, C. H., "Thurloe and the Post Office," *Eng. Hist. Rev.*, XIII, 527-33 (1898).

Graveson, Samuel, "The Posts of the 17th Century," *Bulletin* of the Postal History Society, No. 20f.

Hill, John, *A Penny Post or a Vindication of the Liberty and Birthright of Every Englishman in Carrying Merchants and Other Man's Letters, against any Restraint of Farmers of Such Employments*. 1659.

Housden, J. A. J., "Early Posts in England," *Eng. Hist. Rev.*, XVIII, 713-18 (1903).

———, "The Merchant Strangers' Post in the Sixteenth Century," *Eng. Hist. Rev.*, XXI, 739-42 (1906).

Hyde, J. W., *The Early History of the Post in Grant and Farm*. 1894.

Jordan, W. K., *Men of Substance. A Study of the Thought of . . . Henry Parker and Henry Robinson.* Chicago, 1942.

Konwiser, H. N., *Colonial and Revolutionary Posts.* Richmond, Va., 1931.

A New and Accurate Description of the Present Great Roads of England and Wales. 1756.

Norway, A. H., *History of the Post-Office Packet Service between the Years 1793-1815.* 1895.

Ogilvie, A. M., *Ralph Allen's Bye, Way, and Cross-Road Posts.* 1897.

———, "The Rise of the English Post Office," *Econ. Journal,* III, 443-57 (1893).

Ohmann, Fritz, *Die Anfänge des Postwesens und die Taxis.* Leipzig, 1909.

Parkes, Joan, *Travel in England in the Seventeenth Century.* Oxford, 1925.

Paterson, Daniel, *A New and Accurate Description of All the Direct and Principal Roads in England and Wales . . . with Correct Routes of the Mail Coaches.* 14th ed., 1808.

Rich, Wesley E., *The History of the United States Post Office to the Year 1829.* Cambridge, Mass., 1924.

Rocque, J., *Rocque's Traveller's Assistant; Being the Most General and Compleat Director Extant, to all the Post, Principal and Cross Roads in England, Wales, Scotland and Ireland; .. by J. Rocque, Topographer to His Majesty.* London, 1763.

Rübsam, Joseph, *François de Taxis, le fondateur de la poste moderne et son neveu Jean-Baptiste.* Berne, 1891.

Smiles, Samuel, *The Life of Thomas Telford, with an Introductory History of Roads and Travelling in Great Britain.* 1867.

Smith, William, "The Colonial Post-Office," *Am. Hist. Rev.,* XXI, 258-75 (1916).

Turner, E. R., "The Secrecy of the Post," *Eng. Hist. Rev.,* XXXIII, 320-27 (1918).

C.   On the Reformed Post Office (since 1830)

Account of the Celebration of the Jubilee of Uniform Inland Penny Postage. 1891.

The Administration of the Post Office from the Introduction of Mr. Rowland Hill's Plan of Penny Postage up to the Present Time. 1844.

Ashurst, W. H., *Facts and Reasons in Support of Mr. Rowland Hill's Plan for a Universal Penny Postage.* 1838, 2nd ed. enlarged, same year.

Baines, F. E., *Forty Years at the Post Office. A Personal Narrative.* 2v., 1895.

———, *On the Track of the Mail Coach.* 1895.

———, *Posts, Telegraphs, and Telephones, and Their Relation to. Trade.* 1896.

The Bankers' Magazine and Statistical Register. N.Y., 1846f.

Bates, Barnabas, "Post-Office Reform—Cheap Postage," *Merchants' Magazine and Commercial Rev.,* II, 261-66 (1840).

Beadon, Robert J., *Uniform Imperial Postage, an Enquiry and a Proposal.* 1891.

Blayac, Raoul, *Origine, évolution et organisation de l'Union Postale Universelle*. Montpellier, 1932.

Bronne, Louis, *La réforme postale en Angleterre; examen de ses résultats depuis son origine jusqu'à ce jour*. Bruxelles, 1858.

Bruce, Sir Robert, *Postal Organization, with Special Reference to the London Postal Service*. 1912.

Burritt, Elihu, *Ocean Penny Postage; Its Necessity Shown and Its Practicability Demonstrated*. n.d. (1849).

————, *Ocean Penny Postage*. n.d. (1851).

————, *An Ocean Penny Postage. Will It Pay?* n.d. (1851).

————, *The Proposition of a Universal Penny Postage*. n.d.

Chalmers, Leah, *How the Adhesive Postage Stamp Was Born*. 1939.

Chalmers, Patrick, *The Adhesive Postage Stamp of 1837. Was It an Invention or a Copy?* 1881. And see p. 312n.

————, *The Adhesive Postage Stamp. A Fresh Chapter in the History of Post Office Reform*. 1881.

————, *The Position of Rowland Hill Made Plain*. 1882.

————, *James Chalmers the Inventor of the "Adhesive Postage Stamp," Not Sir Rowland Hill*. 1884.

————, *The Adhesive Postage Stamp. Decision of the "Encyclopaedia Britannica."* 1886.

————, *Concealment Unveiled*. 1886.

————, *The Adhesive Postage Stamp. Submission of the Sir Rowland Hill Committee*. 1886, 1887.

————, *How James Chalmers Saved the Penny Postal Scheme*. 1890.

Chambers's Edinburgh Journal. 1832f.

Chesmore, Stuart, *Behind the Letter Box*. 1936.

Cole, Sir Henry, *Fifty Years of Public Work*. 2v., 1884.

(Cole, Henry), "The Postage Stamp," *London and Westminster Rev.*, XXXIII, 263-71 (1840).

(Croker, J. W.), "Post Office Reform," *Quarterly Rev.*, LXIV, 513-74 (1839).

Crutchley, E. T., *G. P. O.* Cambridge, 1938.

Curti, Merle, *The Learned Blacksmith*. N.Y., 1937.

Davenport-Hill, Rosamond and Florence, *A Memoir of Matthew Davenport Hill*. 1878.

A Descant on the Penny Postage. 1841.

Edwards, Eliezer, *Sir Rowland Hill, K.C.B.; A Biographical and Historical Sketch*. 1879.

Evans, Major E. B., *A Description of the Mulready Envelope and of the Various Imitations and Caricatures of Its Designs*. 1891.

Field, F. J., and C. W. Baldwin, *The Coronation Aërial Post, 1911*. Sutton Coldfield, 1934.

Guy, Ernest, *La conception moderne du paiement des transports postaux et le timbre-poste*. Paris, 1938.

Hay, Ian, *The Post Office Went to War*. 1946.

Head, Sir Francis, "The Mechanism of the Post Office," *Quarterly Rev.*, LXXXVII, 37-62 (1850).

Heaton, J. Henniker, "Universal Penny Postage," *Fortnightly*, XLVI, 533-41 (1886).

——, "A Penny Post for the Empire," *Nineteenth Century*, XXVII, 906-20 (1890).

——, "Postal and Telegraphic Reforms," *Contemp.*, LIX, 327-42 (1891).

——, "Post Office 'Plundering and Blundering,'" *Nineteenth Century*, XXXIII, 994-1008 (1893).

——, "Imperial Five-Farthing Postage," *Fortnightly*, LXI, 338-46 (1894).

——, "Ten Years Postal Progress," *Contemp.*, LXVIII, 1-14 (1895).

——, "Postal and Telegraphic Progress under Queen Victoria," *Fortnightly*, LXVII, 839-49 (1897).

——, "A Postal Utopia," *Nineteenth Century*, XLIII, 764-79 (1898).

——, "Imperial Penny Postage at Last," *Fortnightly*, LXX, 385-95 (1898).

——, "An Agricultural Parcel Post," *Nineteenth Century*, LIII, 253-63 (1903).

——, "The Postal Savings-Banks of Great Britain," *The Arena*, XXXIII, 31-38 (1905).

——, "Fight for Universal Penny Postage," *Nineteenth Century*, LXIV, 588-602 (1908).

——, "The Imperial Conference and Our Imperial Communications," *Nineteenth Century*, LXX, 265-78 (1911).

Hill, Frederic, *An Autobiography of Fifty Years in Times of Reform.* 1893.

Hill, Col. H. W., *Rowland Hill and the Fight for Penny Post.* 1940.

(Hill, Matthew D.), "Post-Office Reform," *Edinburgh Rev.*, LXX, 286-300 (1840).

Hill, Pearson, *The Origin of Postage Stamps . . . The Chalmers' Craze Investigated.* 2 eds., 1888 and Supplement, 1889.

(Hill, Pearson), *The Post Office of Fifty Years Ago*, "containing a Reprint of Sir Rowland Hill's famous Pamphlet dated Feb. 22, 1837." n.d. (1887).

Hill, Rowland, *Post Office Reform; Its Importance and Practicability.* Three eds., 1837. See p. 262n.

——, *Uniform Penny Postage. Facts and Estimates as to the Increase of Letters.* 1839.

——, "The Results of the New Postal Arrangements," *Journal of Statistics*, IV, 85-99 (1841).

——, *The State and Prospects of Penny Postage as Developed in the Evidence Taken before the Postage Committee of 1843.* 1844.

Hill, Sir Rowland, and George Birkbeck Hill, *The Life of Sir Rowland Hill and the History of Penny Postage.* 2v., 1880. [Cited as *G. B. Hill*, etc.]

Horne, L. T., "Postal Communications of the Empire," *British Empire Series*, V, 313-31. 1902.

Household Words, conducted by Charles Dickens. 1850-59.

Howell, Owen, *The Post Office*. 1861.

James, Thomas L., "The Ocean Postal Service," *Century Mag.*, n.s., XXI, 944-50 (1892).

Jevons, W. Stanley, "State Parcel Post," *Contemp.*, XXXIV, 209-29 (1879).

Jürgensohn, Arved, *Weltporto-reform, das nahende Welt-pennyporto in neuer Beleuchtung*. Berlin, 1909-10.

Knight, Charles, *Passages of a Working Life*. 3v., 1864.

Leavitt, Joshua, *Cheap Postage*. Boston, 1848.

——, "The Finance of Cheap Postage," *Merchants' Mag. & Com. Rev.*, XXI, 410-14 (1849).

——, "The Moral and Social Benefits of Cheap Postage," *Merchants' Mag. & Com. Rev.*, XXI, 601-10 (1849).

——, "The Practical Workings of Cheap Postage," *Merchants' Mag. & Com. Rev.*, XXII, 44-53 (1850).

London and Westminster Review. 1836-40, continuing *London Rev.*, 1824f.

Maclay, William B., "Post-Office Reform," *Merchants' Mag. & Com. Rev.*, X, 250-67 (1844).

Melville, Fred J., *A Penny All the Way. The Story of Penny Postage*. 1898.

The Merchants' Magazine and Commercial Review, conducted by Freeman Hunt. N.Y., 1839-70.

Miles, Pliny, *Postal Reform: Its Urgent Necessity and Practicability*. N.Y., 1855.

——, "History of the Post Office," *The Bankers' Mag. & Statistical Register*, XII, 337-65, 433-48 (1857).

——, "Our Postal System. Its Advantages, Requirements, and Shortcomings," *Bankers' Mag. & Statistical Register*, XVI, 577-88 (1862).

——, "Advantages of Uniform Postage," *Merchants' Mag. & Com. Rev.*, XLVI, 443-48, 527-34 (1862).

The Parliamentary Gazetteer of England and Wales, . . "compiled with a special Reference to the Lines of Railroad and Canal Communication, as existing in 1840-43." 4v., 1843.

Penny Magazine of the Society for the Diffusion of Useful Knowledge. 1832-46.

Penny Postage Centenary, ed. by Samuel Graveson. 1940.

Piron, A., *Du service des postes et de la taxation des lettres au moyen d'un timbre*. Paris, 1838.

Platt, J. C., "The Post Office," *London*, ed. by Charles Knight, III, 273-88 (6v., 1841-44).

Porter, Mrs. Adrian, *The Life and Letters of Sir John Henniker Heaton*. 1916.

Porter, G. R., *The Progress of the Nation*. 3v., 1836-43.

The Post Circular, or Advocate for a Cheap, Swift, and Sure Post, ed. by Henry Cole. 1838-39.

"The Post Office," *Fraser's Mag.*, XLI, 224-32 (1850).

The Post Office Magazine, 1934-39, continuing *The Blackfriar's Magazine*, 1885-1890, and *St. Martin's-le-Grand Magazine*, 1890-1933.

"Post-Office Reform and the British System of Postage," *New Englander*, VI, 111-120, 153-165 (New Haven, 1848).

Raikes, Henry St. John, *The Life and Letters of Henry Cecil Raikes, Late Her Majesty's Postmaster-General.* 1898.

Rainey, Thomas, *Ocean Steam Navigation and the Ocean Post.* N.Y., 1858.

Rothschild, Arthur de, *La poste à un penny.* Bruxelles, 1872.

————, *Notice sur l'origine du prix uniforme de la taxe des lettres, et sur la création des timbres-poste en Angleterre.* Paris, 1872.

Scudamore, Frank (son of Frank I. Scudamore), *A Sheaf of Memories.* 1925.

Sly, John F., *The Genesis of the Universal Postal Union.* N.Y., 1927.

Smyth, Eleanor C., *Sir Rowland Hill, The Story of a Great Reform Told by His Daughter.* 1907.

Stephen, Leslie, *Life of Henry Fawcett.* 1886.

Swift, H. G., *A History of Postal Agitation from Eighty Years Ago Till the Present Day.* Rev. ed., Manchester, 1930.

Tegg, William, *Posts and Telegraphs, Past and Present.* 1878.

Trollope, Anthony, *Autobiography.* 1883. I have used ed. of 1923.

————, *North America.* 2v., Philadelphia, 1863.

Wears, T. Martin, *The History of the Mulready Envelope.* Bury St. Edmonds, 1886.

Whiton, James M., "Post-Office Reform and Uniform Postage," *Merchants' Mag. & Com. Rev.*, x, 27-38 (1844).

Wolmer, Viscount, *Post Office Reform, Its Importance and Practicability.* 1932.

Yates, Edmund, *His Recollections and Experiences.* 2v., 1884.

D. PRIMARILY PHILATELIC

Alcock, R. C., and F. C. Holland, *The Postmarks of Great Britain and Ireland.* Cheltenham, 1940.

Anderson, P. J., and B. T. K. Smith, *Early English Philatelic Literature, 1862-1865.* 1912.

Armstrong, D. B., *British and Colonial Postage Stamps: A Guide.* 1920.

Bacon, E. D., *The Line-Engraved Stamps of Great Britain, Printed by Perkins, Bacon & Company.* 2v., 1920, and Supplement, 1929.

————, *Catalogue of the Philatelic Library of the Earl of Crawford, K.T.* 1911.

Brown, Mount, *Catalogue of British, Colonial, and Foreign Postage Stamps.* 1862.

Brumell, George, *The Local Posts of London, 1680-1840, with a Description of the Postmarks Used Therein.* Cheltenham, 1939.

————, *A Short Account of the Franking System in the Post Office, 1652-1840.* Bournemouth, 1936.

Brunel, Georges, *Le timbre-poste français.* Paris, 1896.

The Collector's Club Philatelist. N.Y., 1922f.

Collins, R. J. G., and H. T. M. Fathers, *The Postage Stamps of New Zealand.* Wellington, 1938.

Daniels, J. H., *A History of British Postmarks.* 1898.

Ewen, C. L., *The Earliest Postal Stamps, Introducing Some Recent Discoveries,* 1939.

Foster, G. A., *Pre-Victorian Postage Stamps and Franks.* 1910.

Gibbons' Stamp Monthly, 1923f., continuing *Stanley Gibbons' Monthly Journal,* 1890-   .

Gladstone, E. S., *Great Britain's First Postage Stamp.* Liverpool, 1924.

Gray, J. E., *Hand Catalogue of Postage Stamps for the Use of Collectors.* 1st ed., 1862; 6th ed., "much enlarged," 1875.

Guy, Ernest, *Histoire du timbre-poste en France, 1849-1937; les tarifs postaux depuis l'origine des postes.* Paris, 1938.

Hendy, J. G., *The History of the Early Postmarks of the British Isles.* 1905.

———, *The History of the Postmarks of the British Isles from 1840 to 1876.* 1909.

Houison, Andrew, *History of the Post Office, Together with an Historical Account of the Issues of Postage Stamps in New South Wales.* Sydney, 1890.

Howes, C. A., *Canada, Its Stamps and Postal Stationery.* Boston, 1911.

Leroy, Louis, *Histoire du timbre-poste français.* Paris, 1892.

The London Philatelist. 1892f.

Lowe, Robson, *Handstruck Postage Stamps of the Empire, 1680-1900.* 3rd ed., 1940-41.

———, *The Postage Stamps of Great Britain, 1661-1942.* 2nd ed., 1943.

Marshall, C. F. D., *The British Post Office from Its Beginnings to the End of 1925.* Oxford, 1926.

Maury, Arthur, *Histoire des timbres-poste français.* 2v., Paris, 1907.

Melville, Fred J., *Great Britain: Line Engraved Stamps.* 1910.

———, *Great Britain: Embossed Adhesive Stamps.* 1910.

Mirabaud, P., and A. de Reuterskiöld, *The Postage Stamps of Switzerland, 1848-1862.* Paris, 1899.

Moëns, J. B., *Les timbres de Belgique depuis leur origine jusqu'à nos jours.* Bruxelles, 1880.

Nissen, Charles, and B. McGowan, *The Plating of the Penny Black Postage Stamps of Great Britain, 1840.* 1922.

Phil (A. D. Blackburn), *The Penny Postage Jubilee and Philatelic History.* 1891.

The Philatelic Adviser. Cheltenham,   .

Philbrick, A., and A. S. Westoby, *The Postage and Telegraph Stamps of Great Britain.* 1881.

Phillips, Charles J., *Stamp Collecting, The King of Hobbies and the Hobby of Kings.* N.Y., 1936.

Seymour, J. B., *The Stamps of Great Britain. Part I. The Line Engraved Issues.* 1934.

Todd, T., *A History of British Postage Stamps.* 1941.

Vieira, C. Ottoni, *Catalogue historique des timbres-poste et entiers du Brésil.* Paris, 1894.

Wright, Hastings, and A. B. Creeke, Jr., *The History of the Adhesive Stamps of the British Isles for Postal and Telegraphic Purposes.* 1899.

INDEX

Aberdeen, postal connection with Edinburgh, 93; postal service in, 216; mail coaches to, 228

additional halfpenny, 158, 227, 256

adhesive stamps, proposed by R. Hill, 269; penny black of 1840, 303, 306, 317, 319; labels for prepayment, 307; priority of invention of, 312, 386; commemorative, 320 n., 443; perforated (1854), 361-62; provision against re-use, 361; surface printed, 361; Jubilee issue (1887), 416; for air mail, 442-43; number (1939), 444

   adoption of, in Australia, 382-83; Belgium, 372; Brazil, 377; British North America, 382; France, 374; Germany, 377; India, 383; Italy, 375; New Zealand, 383; Russia, 375; South Africa, 383 n.; Spain, 375; Switzerland, 372; United States, 380

air mail, beginnings, 439; development of imperial, 440-42; across Atlantic, 441; rates, 441-42; stamps, 443

Allen, Ralph, early career of, 101-2; contracts of, with Post Office, 102-3, 105-6; postal profits of, 109; importance of, 111-12; and mail coaches, 126; work of, belittled by Palmer, 142

alphabet (window delivery), 55, 56, 110, 163; Strangers', in Edinburgh, 212

Althorp, Viscount, 247

American colonies, rates in, 97, 168, 170; postal connection with, 165; early service in, 167, 172; deputy postmasters of, 170 n. See also United States.

Anderson, John, the Palmer of Ireland, 224

annual reports of the Post Office, begun, 354-55

Archer, Henry, perforating machine of, 361-62

Arlington, Lord, Postmaster-General, 52-53

Army Post Office, before 1900, 405, 436; in First World War, 436; in Second World War, 444

Ashburton, Lord, 275, 278 n., 396

Ashley, Lord (Earl of Shaftesbury), against Sunday postal service, 330

Ashurst, W. H., 281, 287

Australia, postal reforms in, 382-83; rates to (1855), 394; rates to (1898), 423; penny postage (1911), 423; air mail, 440

Austria, post cards first used in, 368. See also Germany; Thurn and Taxis posts.

Baines, F. E., postal official, 406, 417

bank notes, cut in half for mailing, 132, 149

Barnet, 20, 57

Barnstaple, footpost to, 31

Bath, 19, 20; early coach service to (1667), 68; Ralph Allen of, 100-2; John Palmer of, 131; mail coaches to, 143, 233-34, 242. See also Bristol Road.

Belfast, early delivery in, 209

Belgium, influence of British reforms, 372; early philatelists in, 384

bellmen, London, of Povey, 88-89; of government, 88-89, 205; discontinued (1846), 333. See also letter carriers.

Bennet, Sir John, 53-54

Berwick, early postal objective, 8, 10, 13-16, 20 n., 49, 91. See also North Road.

Bianconi, Charles, career of, 225-27

Bigg, Stephen and Richard, farmers of byposts, 82

Billingsley, Henry, 25-26

Birmingham, stage-coach service to (1731), 128; penny post of, 216-17; mail-coach service, 232, 233

Bishop, Henry, Postmaster-General, 49; postmarks of, 58

Blair, Montgomery, Postmaster-General (U.S.), 397

Bonnor, Charles, deputy of John Palmer, 144 n.

book post, begun (1848), 328, 410; newspapers by, 355; lowered rates, 368; merged with letter post, 430

branch posts, see byposts

Brazil, postal reforms in, 377

Brewster, William, postmaster of Scrooby, 18

Bridgeman Committee, 433-35

Brighton, mail coaches to, 233

Bristol, 19, 51, 60, 64, 103; cross post from, to Exeter (1696), 81; stage-coach service to (1750), 130; mail-coach service with London, 138, 234; penny post of, 215-16, 217; and oversea service, 388

Bristol Road, 55, 59-60, 130, 143; stages on, 19; mail coaches off, 234, 242

broadcasting, see Wireless, Act of 1904

Brougham, Lord, 330; attack on postal service by, 276-77